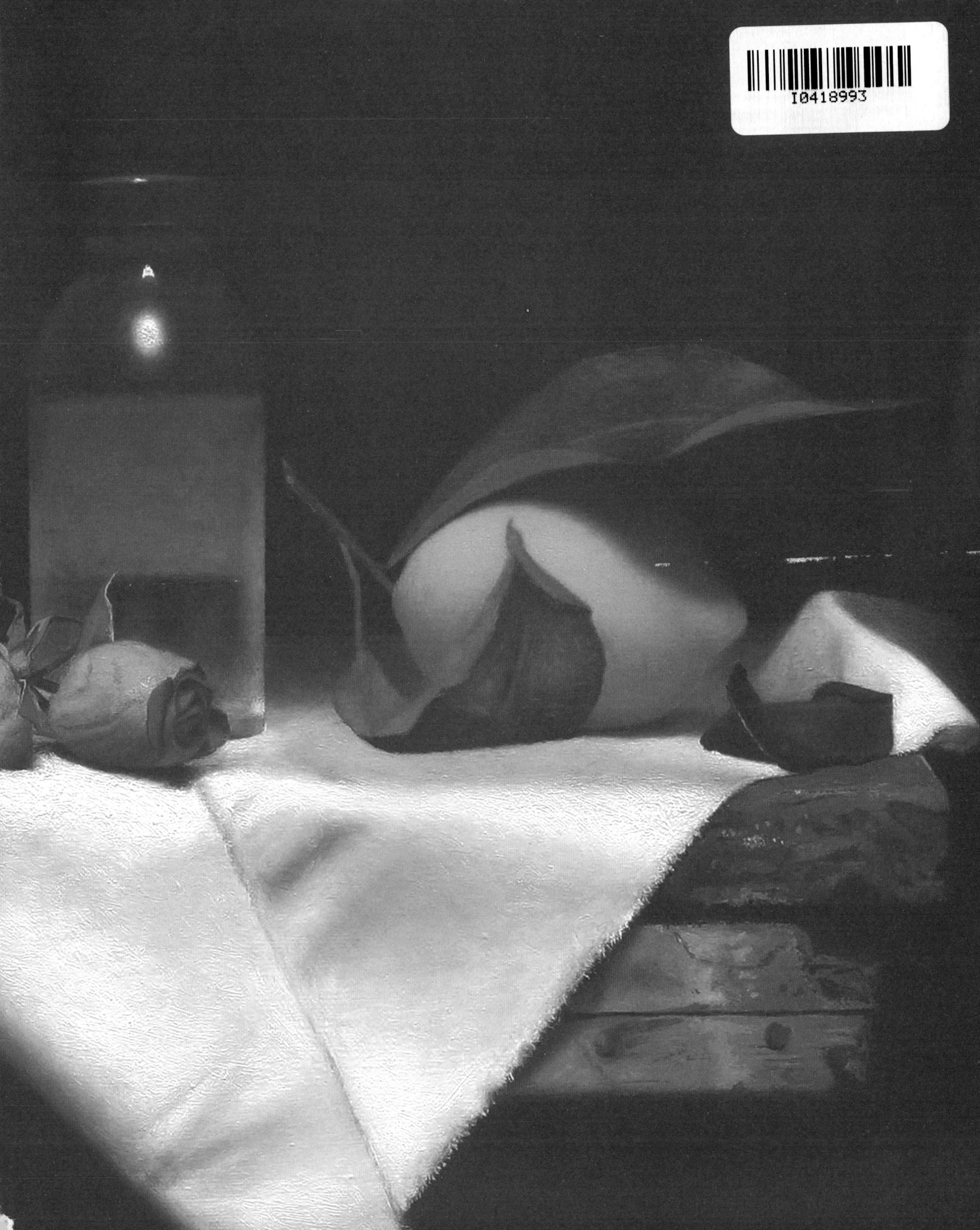

THE
ART OF
STILL LIFE

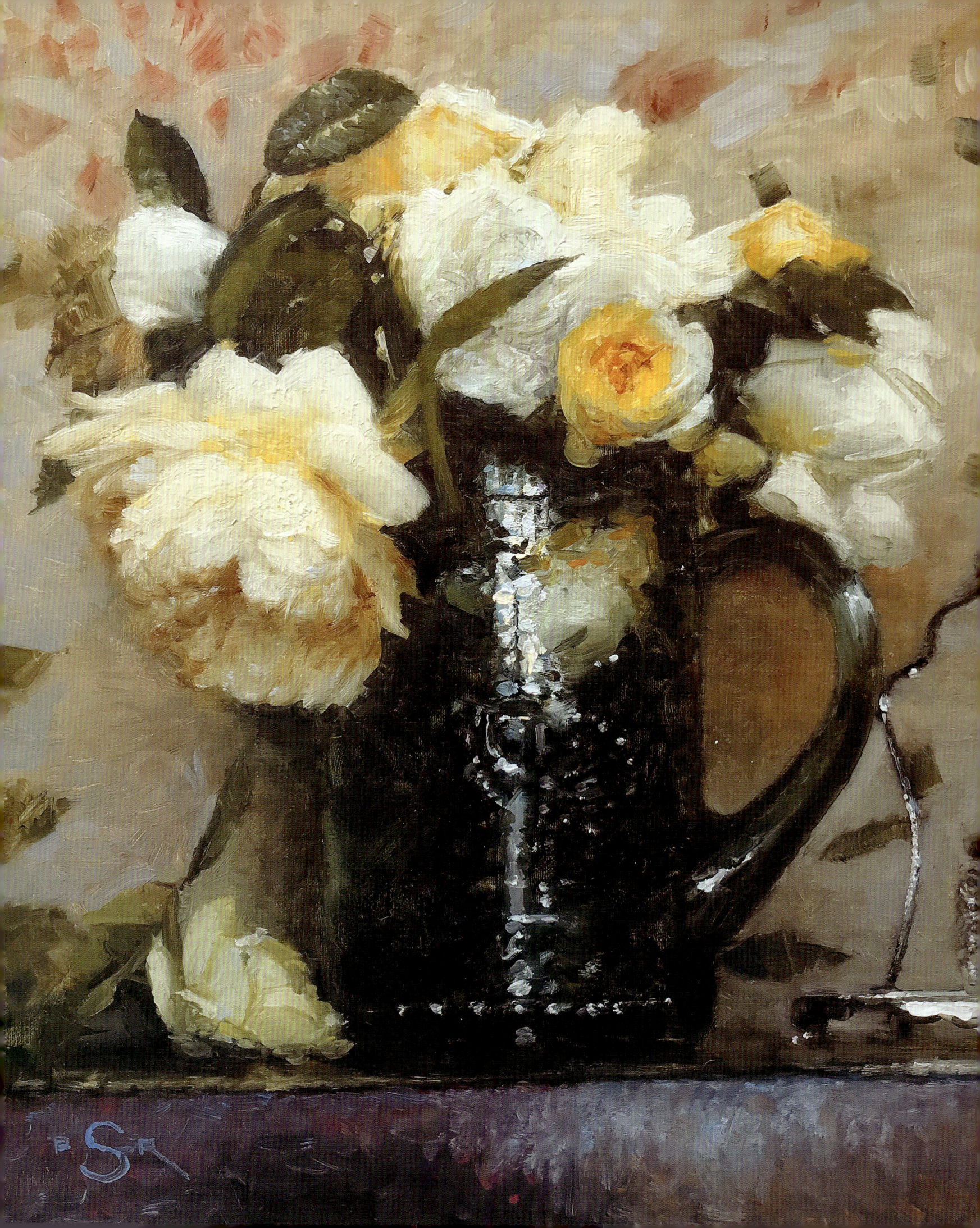

THE ART OF STILL LIFE

A Contemporary Guide to Classical Techniques, Composition, and Painting in Oil

TODD M. CASEY

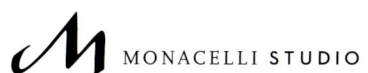
MONACELLI STUDIO

Library of Congress Control Number: 2019946225

ISBN: 978-1-58093-548-7
Printed in China

Design by Jennifer K. Beal Davis
Cover design by Jennifer K. Beal Davis
Cover illustrations by Todd M. Casey and Paul Seaton

Monacelli
A Phaidon Company
111 Broadway
New York, New York 10006

www.phaidon.com/monacelli

Phaidon SARL
55, rue Traversière
75012 Paris

PAGE 2:

Paul Seaton, *Yellow Roses*, 2018, oil on canvas, 14 × 12 inches (35.56 × 30.48 cm). Courtesy of the artist.

PAGE 5:

Nicolai Fechin (Russian, 1881–1955), *Still Life with Cherries, Pitcher, and Bouquet*, n.d., oil on canvas, 24 × 20 inches (61.0 × 50.8 cm). Photo courtesy of Heritage Auctions, HA.com.

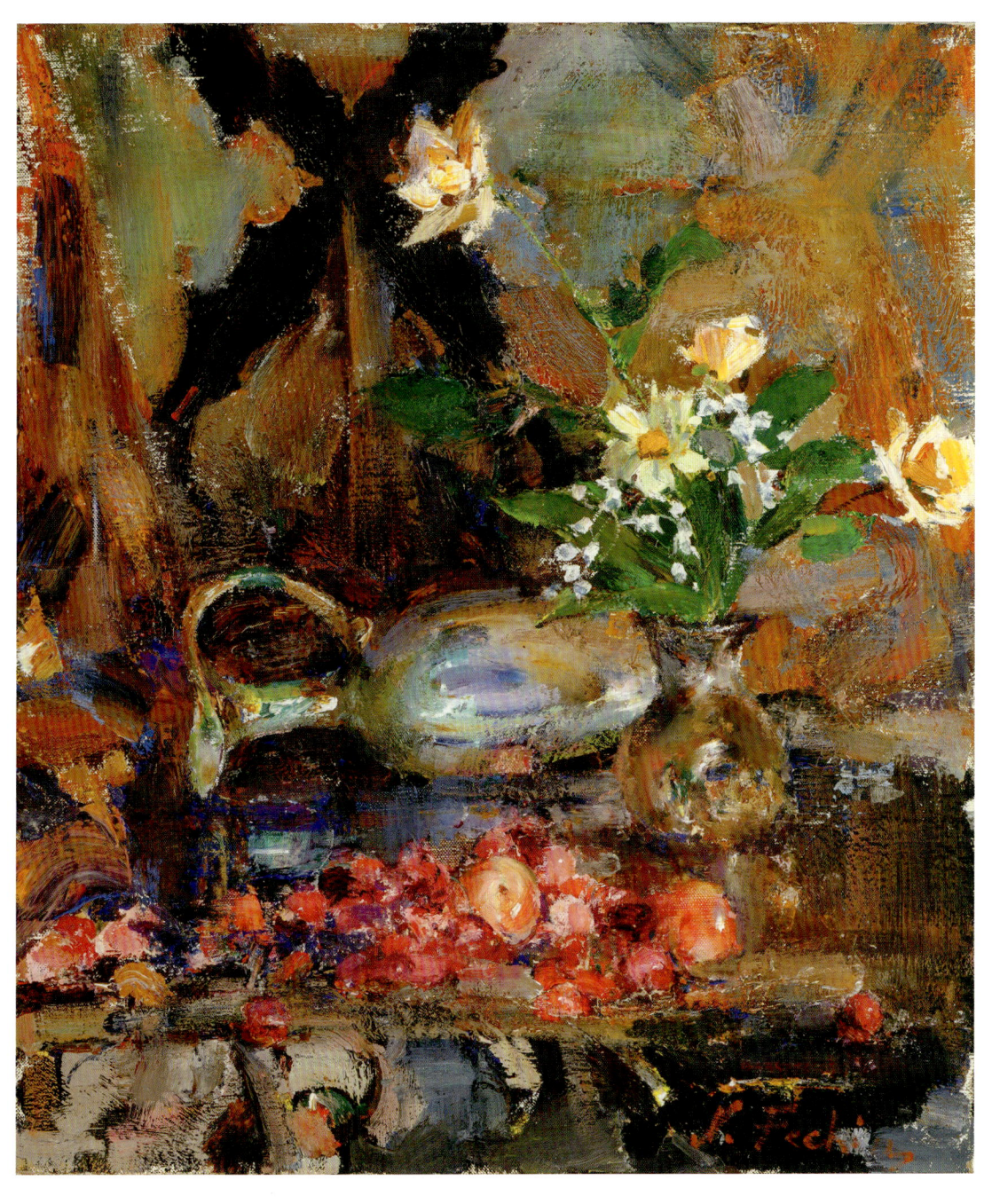

THIS BOOK IS DEDICATED TO MY WIFE, GINA,
MY DAUGHTER, SCARLET, MY MOM, LESLIE A. CASEY,
AND MY DAD, ALBERT F. CASEY.

CONTENTS

ACKNOWLEDGMENTS

If I have seen further than others, it is by standing
upon the shoulders of giants.

ISAAC NEWTON

It is with my warmest gratitude that I acknowledge and thank the people who have helped me in my art career and supported me in all my endeavors. I will start with my wife, Gina, and our lovely daughter, Scarlet. Gina, you have stood by me from the beginning of our relationship and supported everything I do. Scarlet, I cannot wait to show you art as a way of seeing the world. As Robert Henri once noted, "I am interested in art as a means of living a life; not as a means of making a living."

Thank you to all of my teachers. Warren Chang, you acted as the herald at the beginning of my journey. Jacob Collins, you were the threshold guardian who really tested me to make sure I wanted to do this. Max Ginsburg, you have taught me so much as a teacher, a painter, and just as a caring individual. Camie Salaz, you are my ally—I learned so much from you as a person and also from your teachings. You are in my ear, always reminding me to paint from my heart. Doug Flynt, you clarified so much in the short time I worked with you. You also helped me out so much with this book, which would be a shell of what it is without your input. Also, a special thank you to Carlos Madrid, Travis Schlaht, Tony Ryder, and Celeste Ryder for patiently working with me. Each one of you has left your mark on my thoughts.

My deepest appreciation goes out to my parents, Leslie A. Casey and Albert F. Casey, for all that you have done.

When I was a kid I wanted to play professional basketball for the Boston Celtics. I was inspired by my mom, who was an incredible athlete and taught me how to play. Dad, I was able to work with you as a mailman, and I saw your work ethic firsthand. You were a highly respected mailman, and you may be one of the hardest workers I know. I certainly didn't make it to the NBA, but the work ethic I learned from my parents is the reason I am who I am today. You've both supported me in everything I've done and always made me believe I could fly.

My story of how I got into art always starts with my brother, Christopher. I grew up sharing a room with him. I remember Auntie Brenda coming into our room to award you with some art supplies, and from then on I wanted to do art so I could be just like you. Chris, you and I have gone on this journey together, and I'm so happy to have done all this with you. We both went to college together, worked at Ralph Lauren together, and now live in the same city. I'm happy to share the life of an artist with you. You inspire me.

To my sister Charliene: you set the bar high for academics and sports, and I followed in your footsteps in school (although you are a far better athlete). Without the two of you, I would not be me. I've learned so much from you both over the years and still continue to learn.

Thank you to my extended family—to Janet and Roland, my godparents, who have always supported me in all that I've done, and to Ronnie, Paula, Antoinette, Joanie, Christa, Cliff, Jon Paul, Emily, Sharon, Lois, Xander, Mae, and Jake. Your support is unrelenting and always appreciated.

Thank you to my art family, the Rehs: Howard, Amy, Lance, and Alyssa. You believed in me and continue to make me feel special. I don't know what kind of career I would have without you. I consider you family and always will. A special thank you to Gabriel and Yvonne Weisberg for all their help with this book.

What amazes and inspires me is the dream team of talented friends and family who were willing to help me with this book. I was able to call on all of their skills to make this book into something special. Thank you to Alex Archimbaud for your film and photography work—you are a true artist in every sense. And thanks to James Leocadi for helping out with photography and for always challenging, inspiring, and supporting me. Kevin Wueste, you have always supported me and I learn so much just from talking with you. Thank you to Rodney Davis for always lending an ear and for your support. A big, hearty thank you goes out to Ken Salaz, who performed the ultimate magic trick by making this book happen. Thanks to James Decker for your help with the conceptual illustrations for this book, and to Jose Canon for always talking art, science, and philosophy with me.

Thank you to my students, who continue to make me a better teacher and artist. I gain as much from you as you do from me. It's the thrill of teaching. This book is a culmination of all the things that I say to my students on a regular basis. A humongous thank you to Dorothy Lorenze, Linda Lutzai, and Lori Ganz for all your feedback. Also, thank you to Barbara, Dede, and Claire for encouraging me to write this book and for reading the early drafts. Your feedback helped make this book much clearer.

Lastly, thank you to Monacelli Press and especially Victoria Craven for giving me the chance to write a book. I also want to thank James Waller for the wonderful job he did editing this book. It's a difficult thing to try to acknowledge all of those who have helped me without missing someone, so thank you, too, to anyone I have missed.

TODD M. CASEY
CORTLANDT MANOR, NEW YORK
SUMMER 2019

FOREWORD
ON THE IMPORTANCE OF STILL LIFE PAINTING

BY GABRIEL P. WEISBERG

PROFESSOR EMERITUS, UNIVERSITY OF MINNESOTA

From the moment in the 1860s that the French art critic Jules-Antoine Castagnary wrote about how still life painters were undermining the well-established hierarchies of themes in order to paint still lifes, the study of inanimate objects took on a new relevance and life.[1] Still life painting was no longer seen as a refuge for artists who had little imagination or who were recognized only as copyists, and still life painters were multiplying like rodents. Their increasing numbers were undermining the well-established traditions of portraiture, landscape painting, and narrative imagery. Even in the twenty-first century, still life painters have had to continue fighting for recognition, maintaining the battles of earlier historical moments into their own era. Why is this? Why are these issues from the past haunting us today?

In examining still life painters from the past, certain aspects of their works have established a continuum that must be recognized: painting inanimate objects, no matter how skillfully done, has a number of built-in challenges that must be continually confronted by contemporary artists. The reasons for this are worth noting here.

Still life painters frequently selected objects that were most meaningful to them— objects from their immediate world that signaled quiet, reflective moments in their lives. The objects were also selected because they referenced moments known to the artist but unknown to a viewer. Once these items were selected they were arranged in a pattern that allowed the painter to display awareness of the importance of the chosen pieces by painting them with care, skill, and reverence. But the intrinsic meaning of these things did not always carry over to collectors.

The eighteenth-century artist Jean-Baptiste-Siméon Chardin became the godfather of still life painters by demonstrating an awareness of the simple organization

OPPOSITE, TOP: Jean-Baptiste-Siméon Chardin (French, 1699–1779), *Still Life with Eggs, Cheese, and a Pitcher*, 18th century, oil on canvas, 14 7/8 × 17 15/16 inches (37.8 × 45.6 cm). Philadelphia Museum of Art. John G. Johnson Collection, Cat. 786.

OPPOSITE, BOTTOM: François Bonvin (French, 1817–1887), *Still Life with Asparagus,* dated 1881, oil on canvas, 24 1/4 × 19 4/5 inches (61.6 × 50.3 cm). National Galleries of Scotland. Purchased 1990.

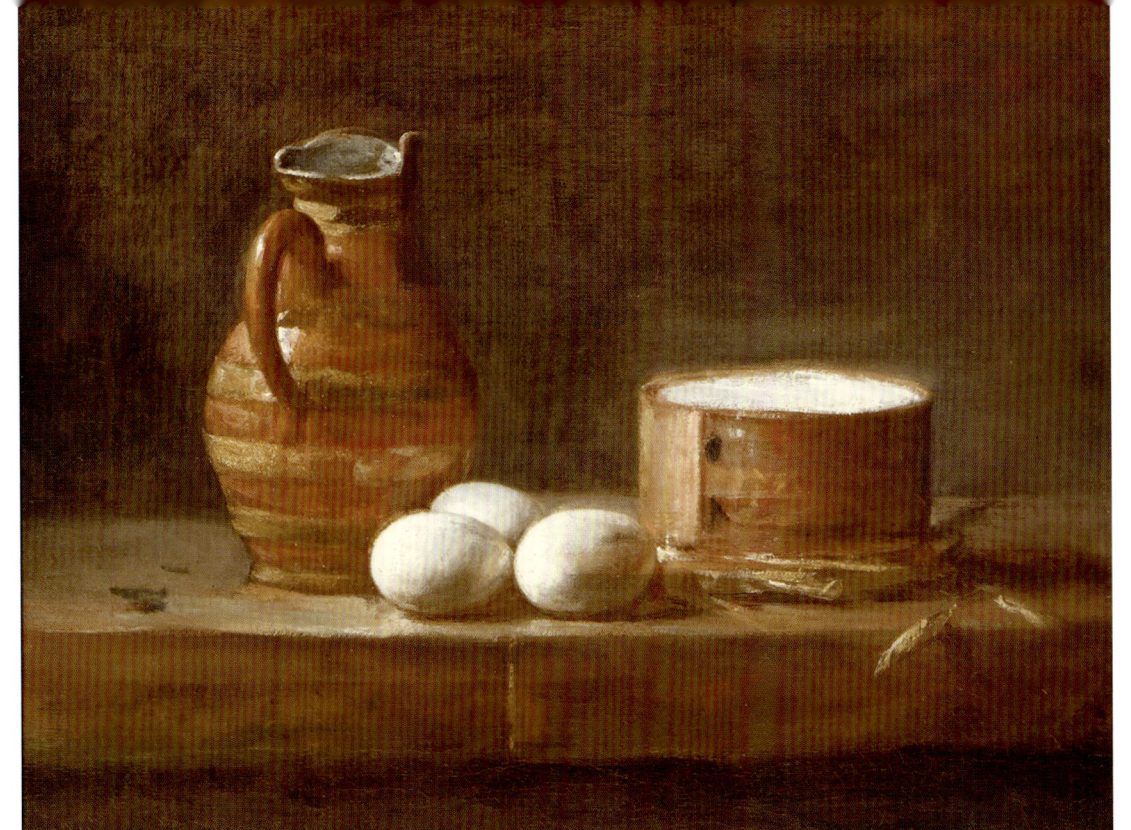

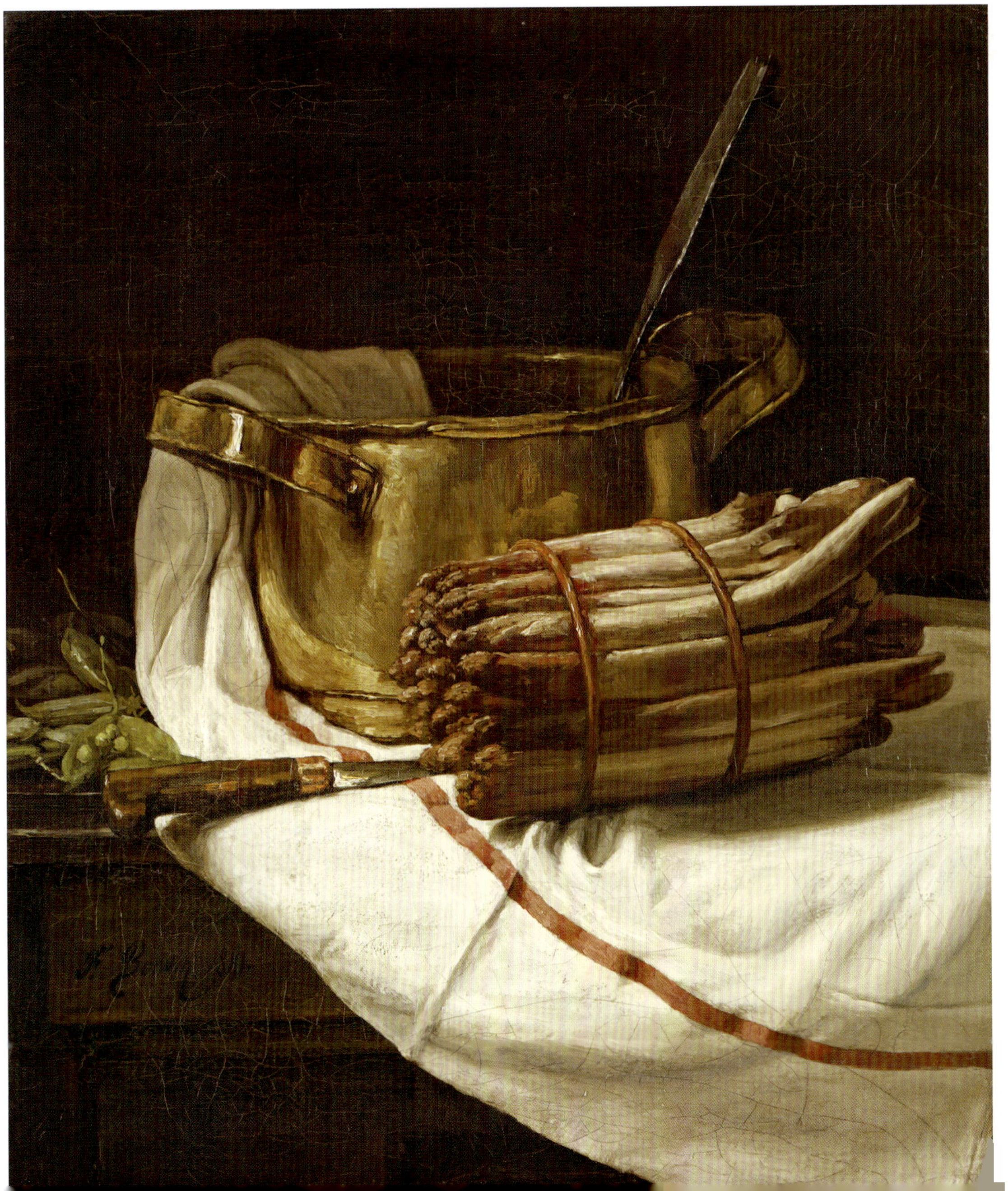

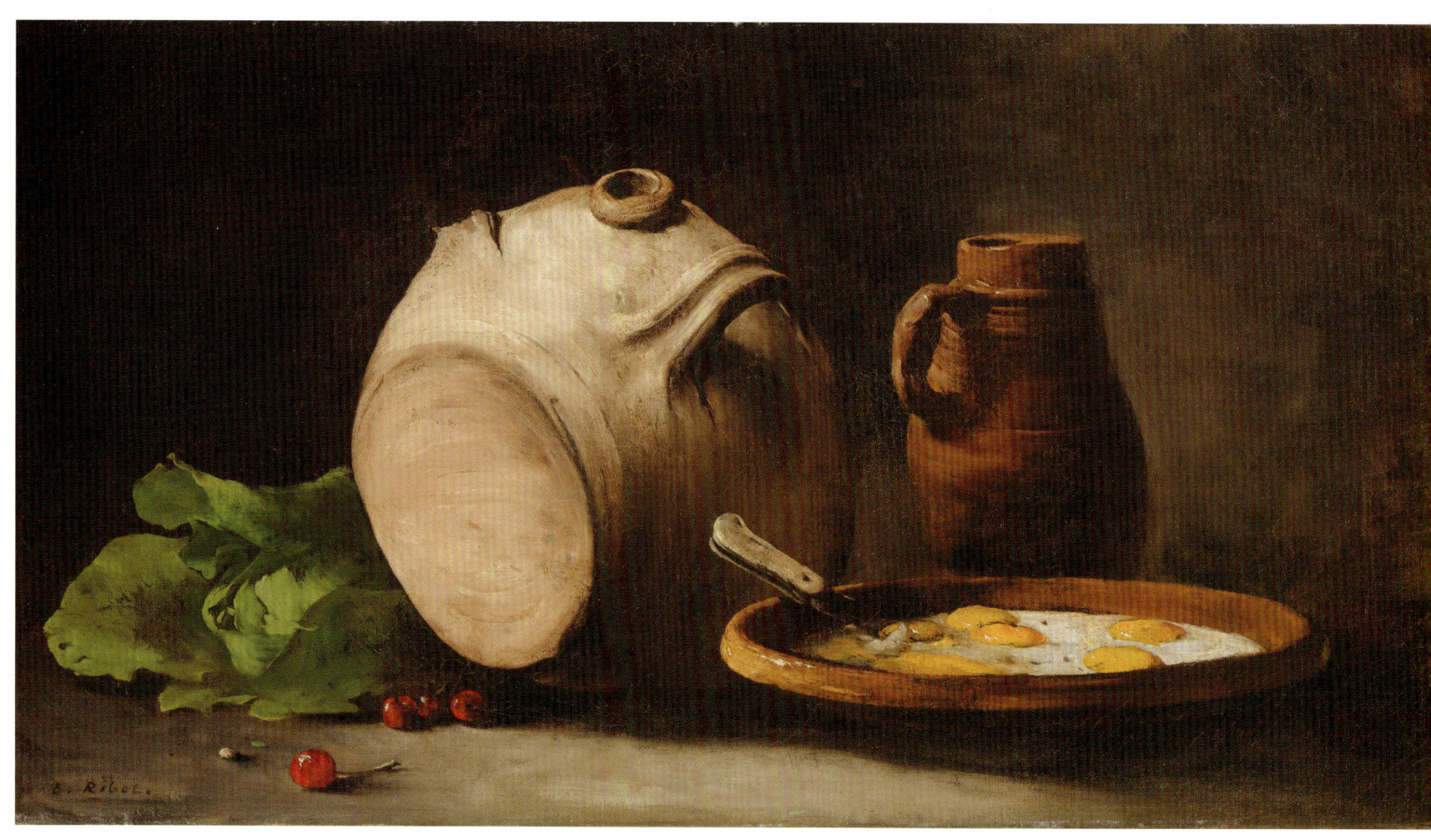

of daily useful objects that were studied carefully and illuminated with the utmost clarity. Even when Chardin completed paintings that emphasized symbolic attributes of creativity, such as writing, painting, or music, the compositions that he created remained simple, direct studies of the chosen items. In less symbolic circumstances Chardin's works were characterized by the elimination of all unnecessary qualities. He concentrated on objects from his home life so that he could bring a humanizing quality to his paintings. Often positioning things on a spare tabletop, without elaborate accessories, he provided models for painters to follow in the nineteenth century.

II

In the nineteenth century, as still life emerged as a legitimate subject for painters to depict, artists appreciated Chardin for what he could teach them. As part of a Chardin revival in France, painters such as François Bonvin dedicated a good part of their life to creating still life arrangements.[2] Bonvin's uncomplicated compositions of bunches of asparagus or glasses of wine emphasize only the preparation of a modest meal rather than anything elaborate. He studied his forms as if they were simple

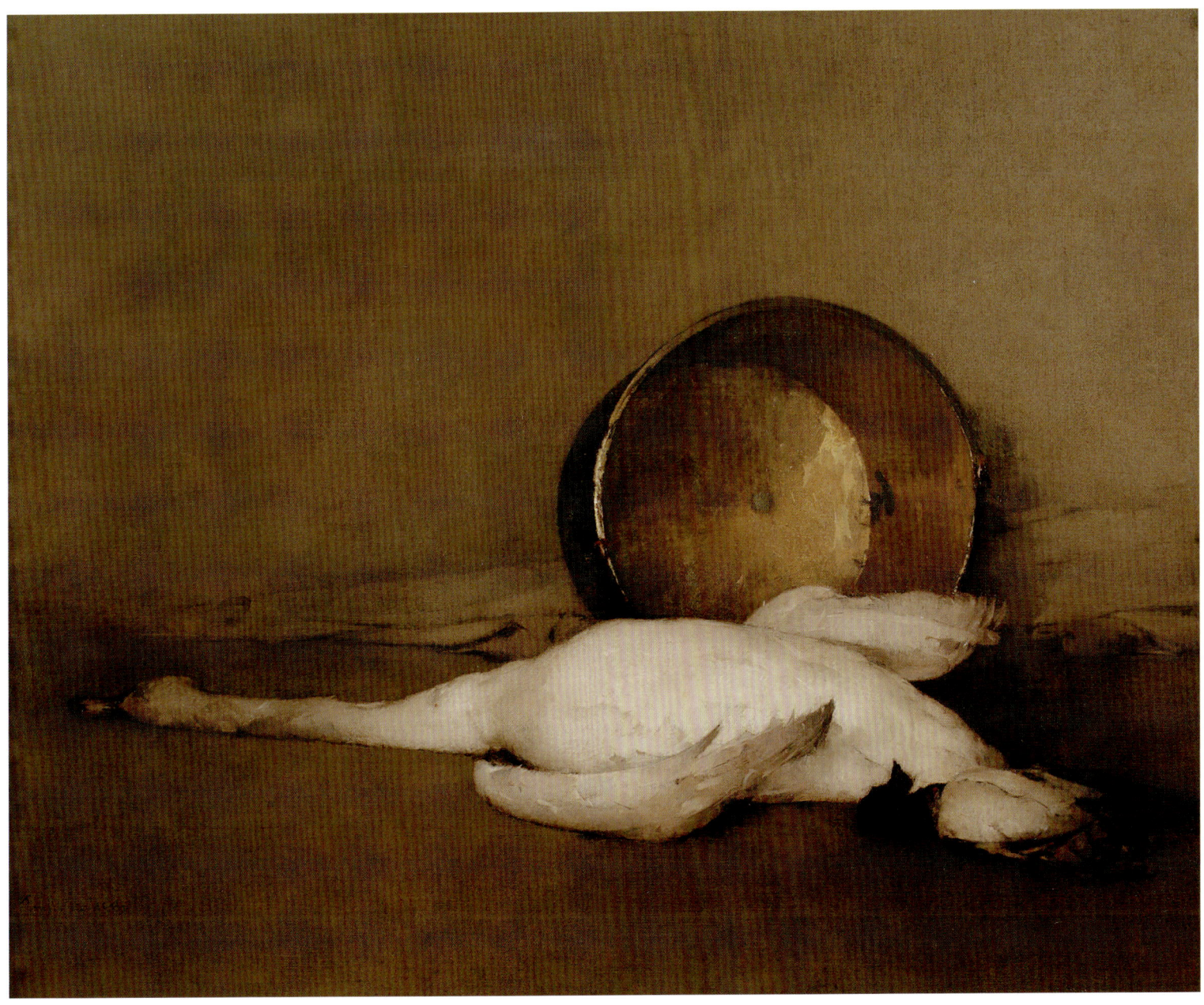

ABOVE: Emil Carlsen (American, 1848–1932), *The Wild Swan,* 1902, oil on canvas, 48 ¼ × 58 inches (122.55 × 147.32 cm). Courtesy of Emil Carlsen Archives (emilcarlsen.org).

abstract shapes, all the while providing images for an increasingly lively trade in these canvases, becoming in the process, as critics noted, the "new Chardin." Collectors wanted these works. And some in the twentieth century continued to acquire still lifes for their own collections.[3] Whether Bonvin's still lifes influenced contemporary painters remains a moot point, although many artists followed the same direction as the pioneering French painter.

With another nineteenth-century still life painter, Théodule Ribot, an interest in removing anything extraneous became even more conspicuous. The objects he selected were often coarse ceramics, and the space in which these forms were situated was pared down further. Seen as a reincarnation of the seventeenth-century Spanish master Jusepe de Ribera, Ribot was also recognized as a follower of Chardin. There is nothing mysterious about his works. Everything in them is direct, with great care given to reveal the power of uncomplicated forms. They do not belong to the environments found in rich people's homes but speak of a simple and straightforward life. They reinforce the idea of simplicity we have about the artist. His work was also collected in the twentieth century, often by those who appreciated Bonvin.[4]

As the still life revival flourished, American painters with a European orientation, such as Emil Carlson, also completed compositions with few objects positioned in direct lighting, in a spare setting. A devotee of French painting, Carlson reiterated the significance of Chardin in his work. He encouraged the Chardin revival in the United States, creating many compositions that owed a direct allegiance to French artists and the inspiration from Chardin.

III

The use of only a few objects in a composition has become a hallmark in the still life paintings of Todd Casey, as can be seen in his *Bottles with a Book and Letters,* completed in 2011. In this composition, the utilization of a spare support, at eye level, helps to bring sheaves of paper, an overturned bottle, and an open book into an uneasy harmony. By pushing the forms very close to a viewer, Casey makes sure that a viewer has to confront the forms; there can be no averting the eyes from the shapes themselves. Perhaps closest to Chardin, this work also suggests that the artist is trying to do the same thing that nineteenth-century painters did—simplify shapes and force a viewer to understand the relationship with objects that mean a lot to the artist. The result is almost an abstract relationship between the items. This is an astounding effect for a painting that uses so few objects but maintains a stillness that is haunting, similar in effect to the qualities found in certain canvases of Bonvin or Ribot.

Whether contemporary still life painters know the artists from the past is often irrelevant. They may have seen some of their works in museum exhibitions; this is certainly the case with Chardin. But if they have seen these compositions by earlier still life painters, they would intuitively recognize that what they are doing has echoes from the past. What they achieve follows in the same direction, making the still life movement one of the most significant ways to paint while using the traditions of the past to inform the present.

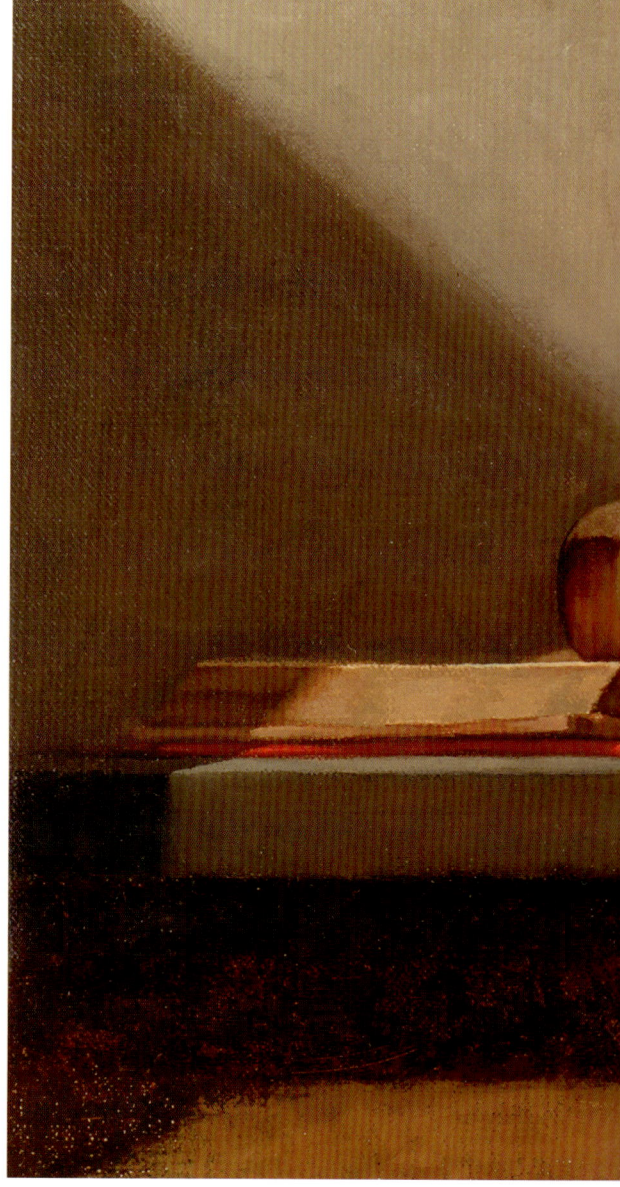

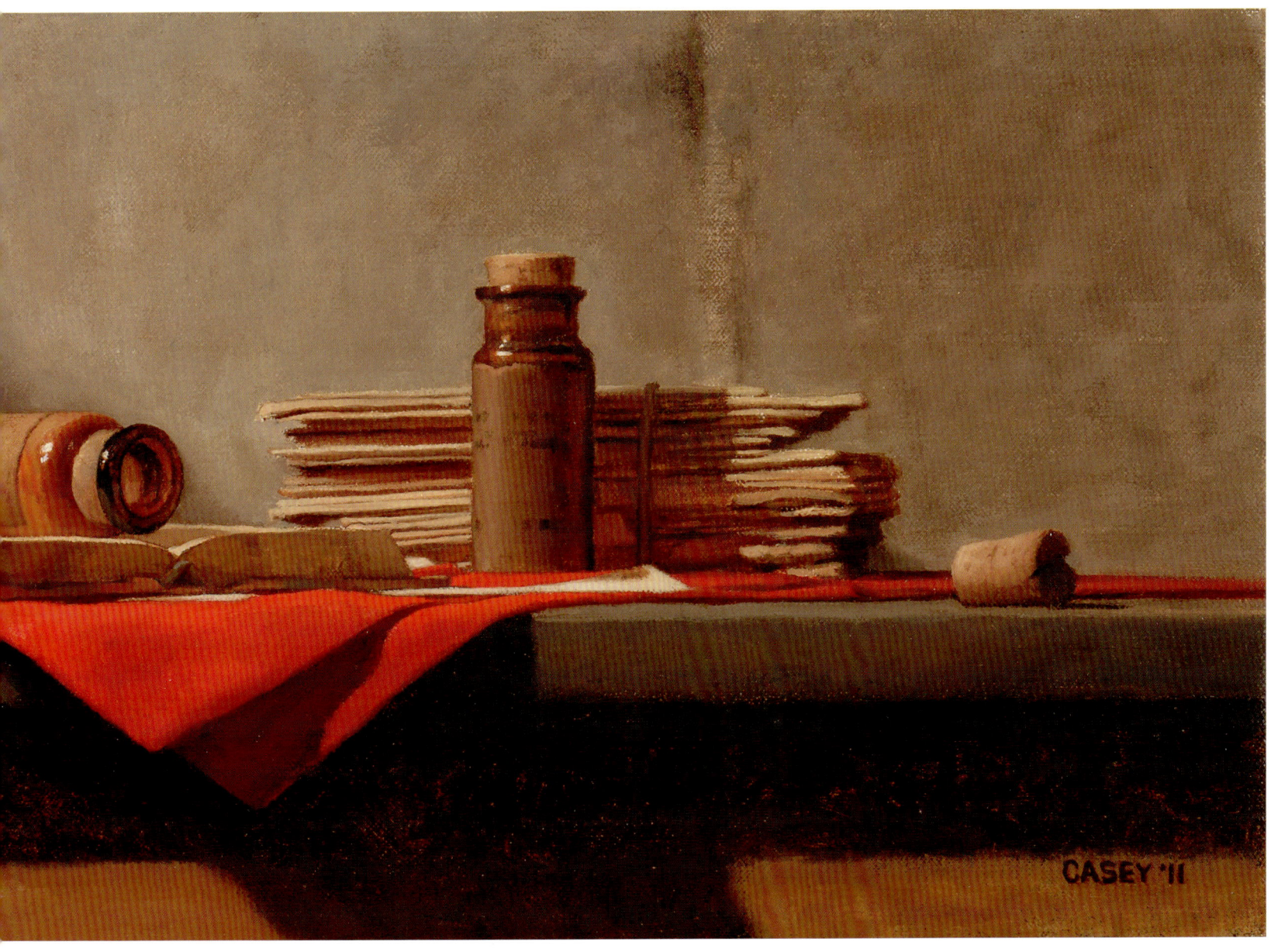

ABOVE: Todd M. Casey, *Bottles with a Book and Letters,* 2011, oil on canvas, 9 × 17 inches (22.86 × 43.18 cm). Collection of Lucia and Brad Ginesin.

1 Gabriel P. Weisberg with William S. Talbot, *Chardin and the Still-Life Tradition in France* (Cleveland: The Cleveland Museum of Art, 1979).

2 Gabriel P. Weisberg, *Bonvin: La Vie et l'oeuvre* (Paris: Geoffroy-Dechaume, 1979).

3 These include museum directors such as Sherman E. Lee of the Cleveland Museum, who at one time hung this painting in his dining room.

4 The painting *Still Life with Eggs,* now in the Van Gogh Museum, also hung in the dining room of Sherman E. Lee, director of the Cleveland Museum of Art. Also see Gabriel P. Weisberg, "Théodule Ribot's *Still Life with Eggs* and the Practice of Still-life Painting in the Late 19th century," *Van Gogh Museum Journal* (1997–98): 76–87.

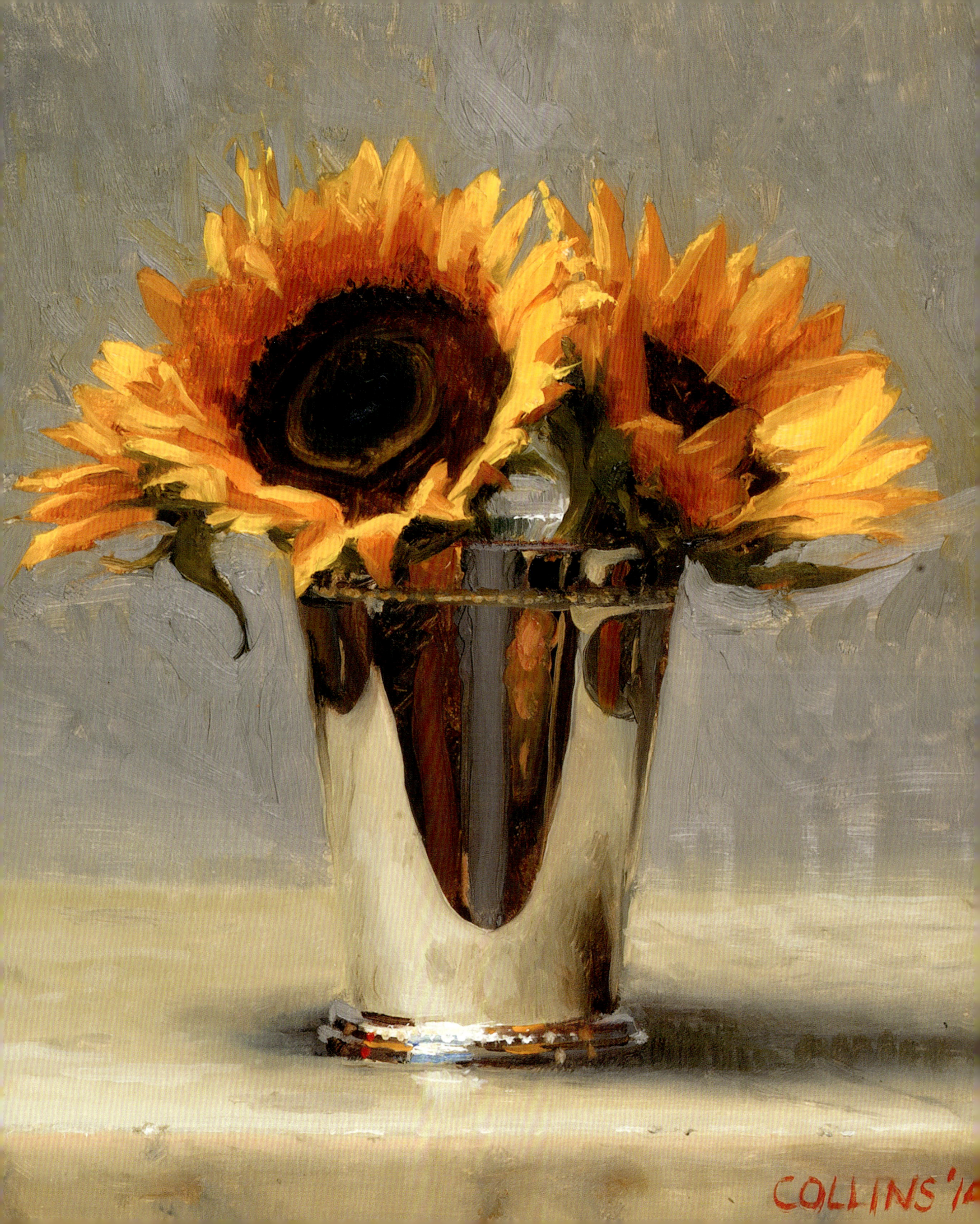

COLLINS '1

PREFACE
EMBRACING THE JOURNEY

*I saw that my life was a vast glowing empty page
and I could do anything I wanted.*

JACK KEROUAC

Here is the story of my artistic journey. I took a very roundabout way to becoming a professional fine art painter. In a lot of ways I followed my heart and let it take me where it needed to go.

I was born and raised in Lowell, Massachusetts, which I found out years later was also the birthplace of painter James Abbott McNeill Whistler and Beat writer Jack Kerouac. Like many American families, we had Norman Rockwell prints hanging in our home. I was captivated by these images and by how Rockwell could tell a story through them. I knew from a young age that I wanted to be a storyteller, too.

In the fall of 1997 my brother and I both enrolled as freshmen at the Massachusetts College of Art and Design (MassArt) in Boston, commuting from Lowell by train. While at MassArt, I would frequently go to the Museum of Fine Arts, because it was right next to MassArt and free for art students. I was always drawn to a picture by the artist Jean-Léon Gérôme entitled *L'Éminence grise*, which you can see on page 19. For the life of me, I could not figure out how this picture was painted, since the training I was receiving at the time didn't give me an idea how someone could make a picture like this. What intrigued me about the painting was the narrative quality of the scene, the well-thought-out composition, and the masterful technique.

OPPOSITE: Jacob Collins, *Sunflowers*, 2014, oil on canvas, 12 × 10 inches (30.48 × 25.4 cm). Courtesy of Adelson Galleries.

After a little over four years, I got my BFA in illustration. Then I moved back home with my parents to figure out the next chapter in my life. I had no idea where to go with my degree in illustration, so I took time off from art. During that year, I worked alongside my dad as a mailman, and a part of me considered walking away from being an artist and becoming a mailman like my dad.

I also worked a construction job, and I remember talking to one of the guys on the site and asking him how he had gotten into construction. He told me that he'd never intended to but that he'd found himself in a situation where he had to support his family. When I asked him what he'd really wanted to do, he said . . . to be an artist. That sounded too familiar, so I quit construction shortly thereafter.

Not too long after that, I moved out of my parents' home and back to Boston, where I worked as a waiter. I rented a small room at a friend's apartment and slept on the floor because I couldn't afford a bed. I did this for three months before moving in with my brother in Boston's Mission Hill neighborhood.

Then an opportunity arose for me to move to New York City. A friend of mine was working as a waitress at the Plaza Hotel, and she got me a job there. After a little over a year as a waiter, I finally got an art-related job, working as a computer artist for Ralph Lauren.

I knew nothing about fashion. I was grateful for the job, but eventually I found it to be very uncreative and not the direction I wanted to go with my career. I knew that corporate life was not for me, and I began looking into going to graduate school to broaden my skill set.

At the time, the movie *The Incredibles* had just come out, and I was fascinated by how good the animation was. I started thinking that this could be the way to make a career for myself as an artist, and so in 2005 I moved to San Francisco and enrolled in an MFA program in 3-D animation at the Academy of Art University.

But I changed my major a number of times, trying to find where I fit in. At one point, I found myself back in the illustration department, in a class of Warren Chang's called "Heads and Hands." That's where everything changed for me.

Warren and I shared a love for illustration, and we often spent time before class talking about artists we admired. In class we did some long drawings—about three hours long, which I found to be a very long time. I remember Warren mentioning the artist Tony Ryder, who might spend close to sixty hours on a single drawing. This concept just blew me away, as three hours felt like an eternity to me.

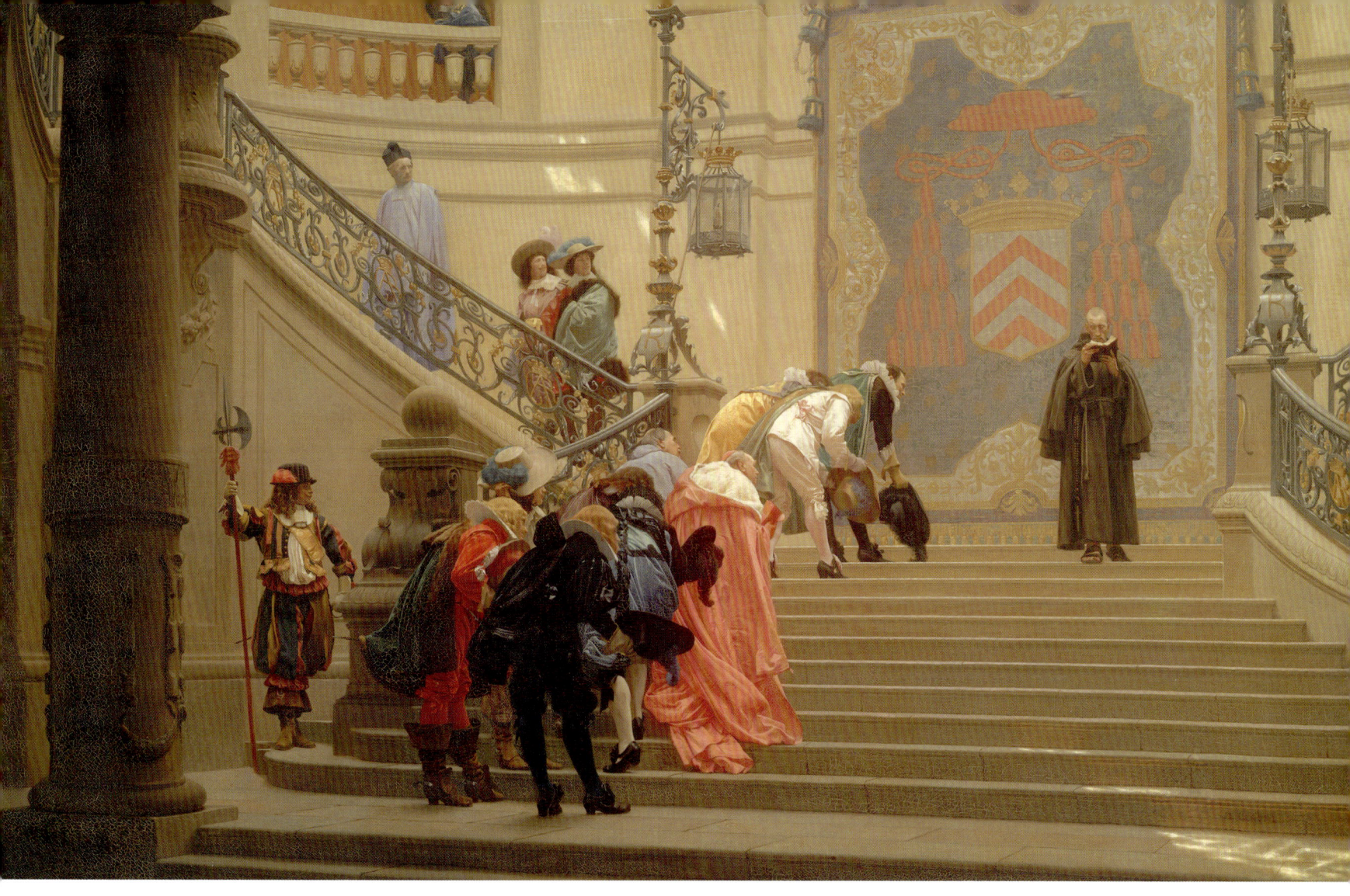

That conversation opened the door for me to start looking around. Warren was the first to bring up the names Jacob Collins and Max Ginsburg, mentioning that if I made it back to New York I should try to study with them. Being a good student, I wrote the names down in my sketchbook and looked them up later. I was definitely fascinated by their work.

In the summer of 2006, I attended the Illustration Academy's summer program in Florida, living there for two months. The program was intense, and I felt inspired by what I had learned, but I questioned whether animation/illustration was the right path for me. I didn't return to San Francisco, instead going back to NYC and freelancing for the Ralph Lauren art department for a few months. By that time, I'd decided not to go back to graduate school. But I needed to get the stuff I'd left behind in San Francisco, so a friend and I planned a big cross-country road trip to pick it up. Our plan was to drive from New York to San Francisco and back again—and to visit as many artists and their studios as possible along the way.

ABOVE: Jean-Léon Gérôme (French, 1824-1904) *L'Éminence grise,* 1873, oil on canvas, 27 × 39 ¾ inches (68.6 × 101 cm). Courtesy of the Museum of Fine Arts, Boston. Bequest of Susan Cornelia Warren. Photo © 2019.

Gérôme's work, a masterpiece of nineteenth-century academic painting, depicts French courtiers bowing to François Leclerc du Tremblay, a Capuchin monk known as L'Éminence grise (the Gray Cardinal), who was the adviser to Cardinal Richelieu, chief minister to French king Louis XIII.

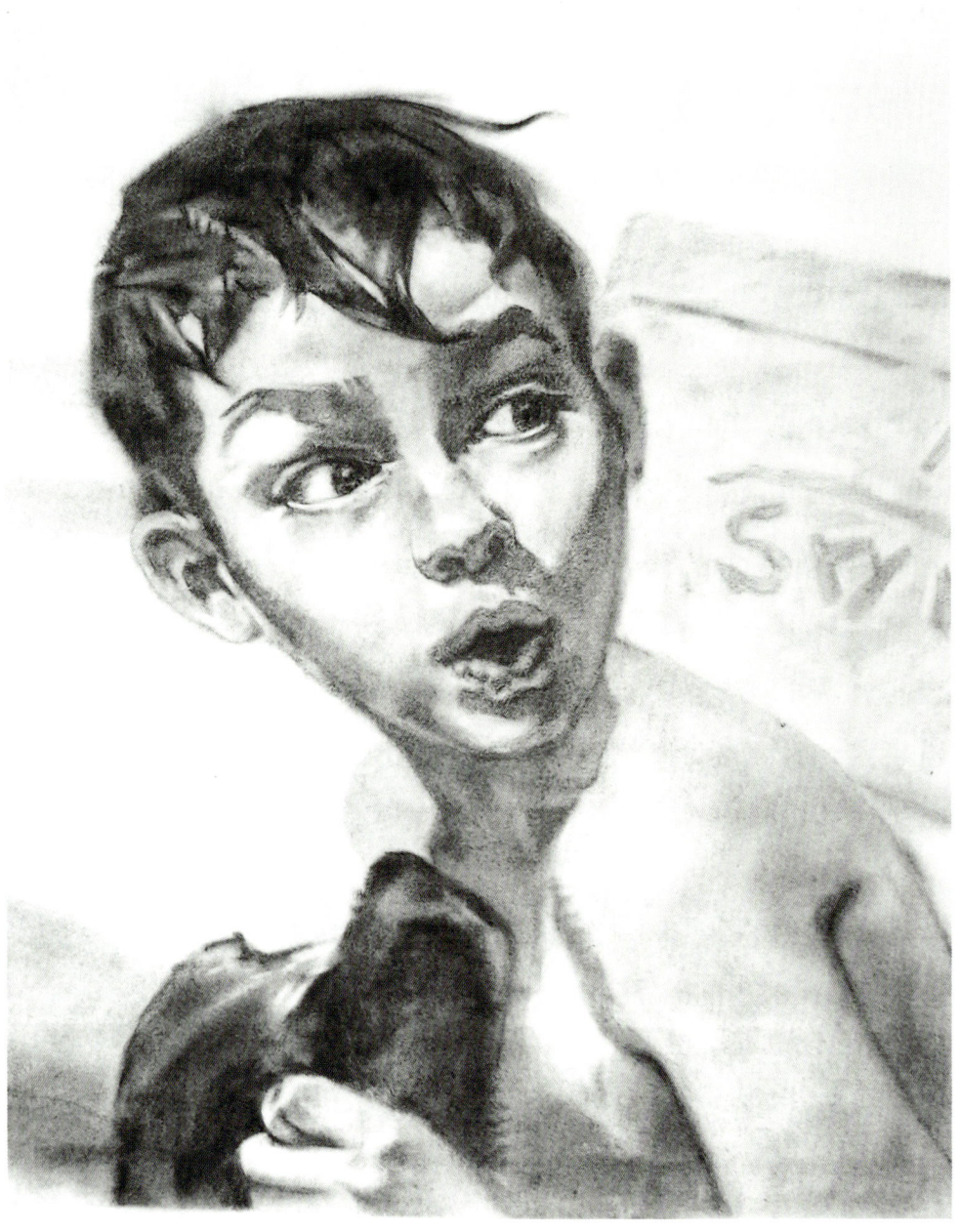

The trip was an enlightening experience. We visited illustrators, painters, conceptual artists, and industrial designers—all in their studios. One of the first artists we visited was the illustrator Thomas Fluharty, at his place in Minnesota. I remember telling him that I wanted to continue to learn how to paint and asking him what he thought I should do. He said that to really learn how to paint, I should study classical techniques, as illustration could only take me so far. We also visited the studios of Gary Kelley, Syd Mead, C. F. Payne, Eric Tiemens, Scott Robertson, Mark English, John English, Brent Watkinson, and my Academy of Art teacher Warren Chang. Each artist offered some words of wisdom and shared their career stories with us. A few mentioned Jacob's and Max's names, so I wrote them down again, but this time

ABOVE: Todd M. Casey, master copy after Norman Rockwell's *No Swimming*, 2005, charcoal on paper, 24 × 18 inches (60.96 × 45.72 cm).

I did this master copy in graduate school because I'd wanted to emulate the work of Norman Rockwell ever since I was a child. Master copying is an important part of an artist's training. This was done in Warren Chang's class—the turning point for me in deciding to pursue painting as a career.

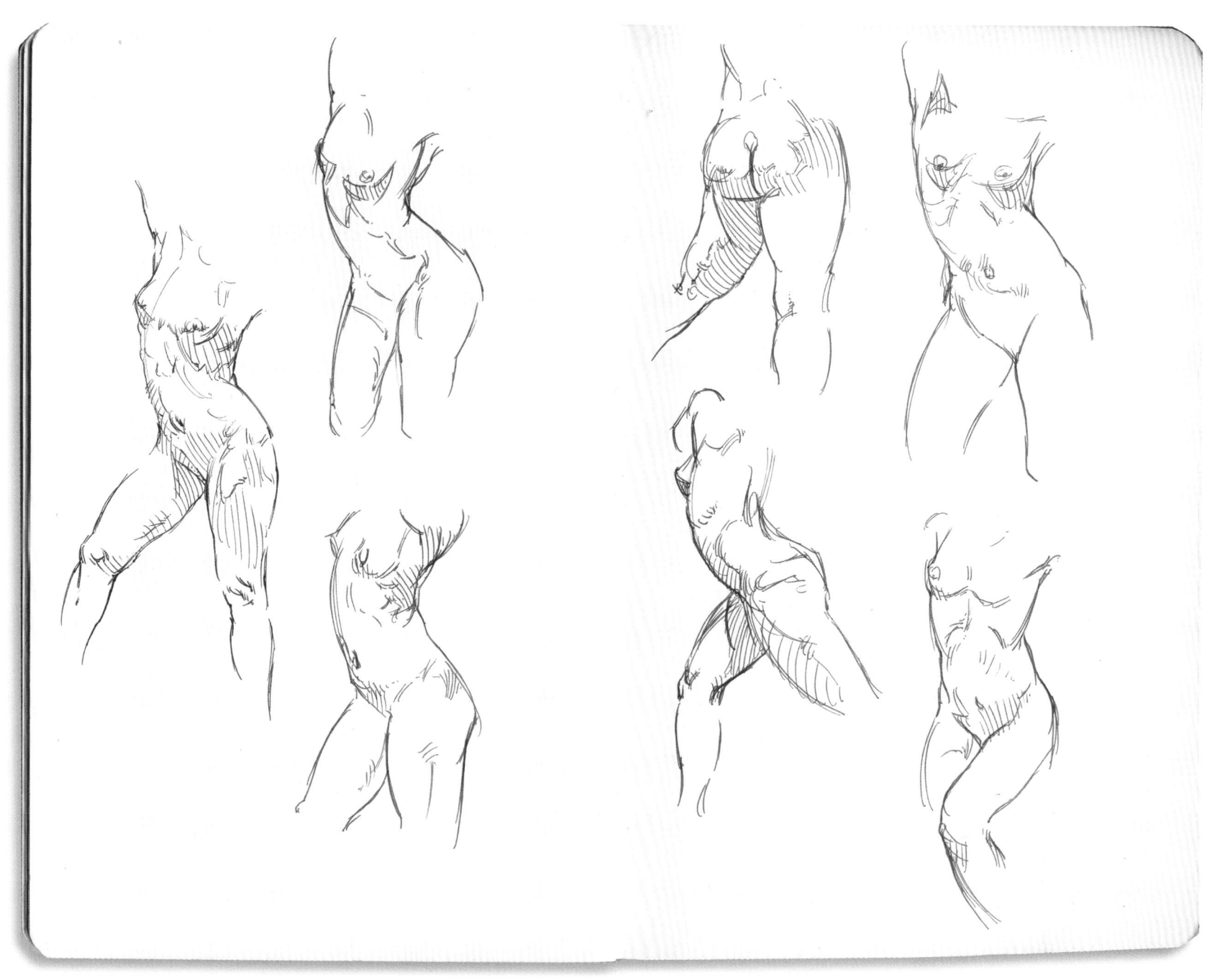

ABOVE: Todd M. Casey, sketchbook studies, 2005.

I knew I had to look them up. When I finally got back to NYC and settled in, I emailed them. Jacob emailed me back quickly, and we made plans for him to interview me for admission into his Water Street Atelier.

When I arrived at Jacob's studio for the interview, a man greeted me at the door. I assumed he was a student because he looked so young, and I said, "Is Jacob here?" He said, "Yep, follow me." As I followed him, I realized that he was Jacob.

Jake's studio was in the back of the school, which was in the garage of his carriage house on the East Side of Manhattan. As we walked through the atelier, I saw about a dozen students standing around a model, painting the figure. Each painting was so incredibly good that I knew in that moment that I wanted be there.

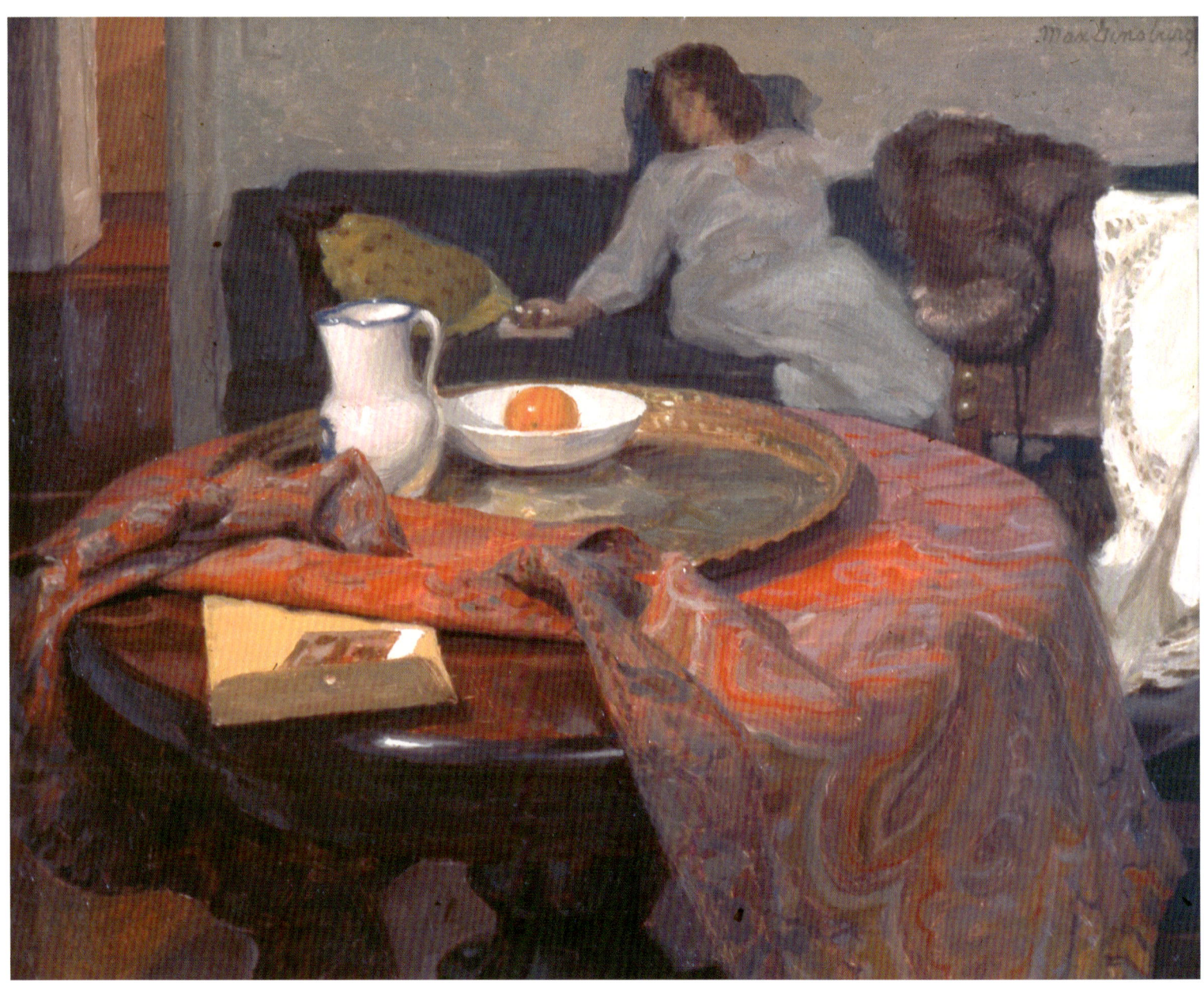

ABOVE: Max Ginsburg, *Repose,* 1977, oil on canvas, 10 × 12 inches (25.4 × 30.48 cm). Courtesy of the artist.

When we sat down in his studio, he asked me a lot of questions—whom I'd studied with and why I wanted to do this. I showed him my portfolio, but he didn't seem very impressed. He sent me on a mission: He said I should take the cast-drawing class taught by his former student Camie Davis (now Camie Salaz) at the Grand Central Atelier. He said I should do a cast drawing and bring it back to him when I finished. I called the GCA that night and enrolled. But part of me was thinking, Who is this guy to ask me to take a class and show him what I do in the class—and also, what is a cast drawing, anyway?

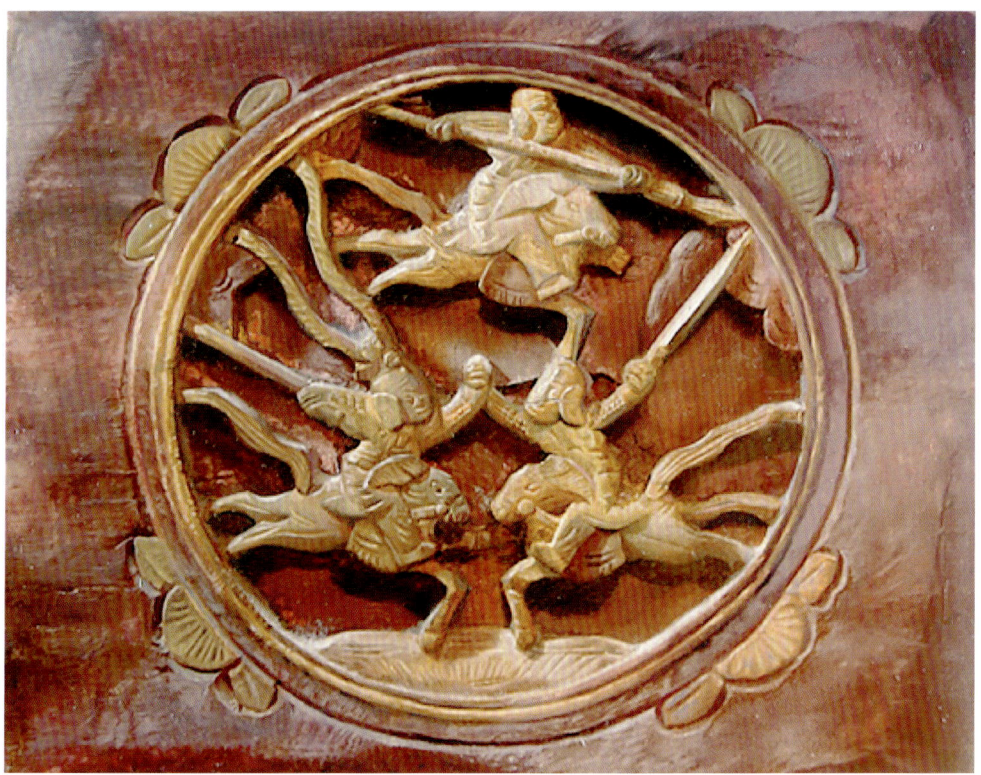

In classical training, cast drawing is where aspiring artists begin. A cast drawing is a drawing of a plaster cast of a sculpture—typically a Greek or Roman figure, a portrait bust, or an anatomical sculpture. The cast-drawing class met every weeknight, Monday through Friday, from 6:30 to 9:30 pm. I remember walking into a full room of students (of all ages) and looking at their drawings. I asked them a ton of questions: How long did the drawings take them to do? What materials were they using? It blew my mind that they were all working on one drawing for about three months and using just one pencil, an HB. Frankly, I thought this wasn't for me—there was no way in the world I could draw that slowly! What were they doing with all that time? But then I figured, Why not give it a shot?

As it turned out, Camie was a fantastic teacher and really got me to slow down. As the sessions went by and I worked on the drawing, I started to see how this could be the foundation I had always been looking for. This was the link to the Gérôme painting *L'Éminence grise* that had fascinated me at the MFA Boston when I was an undergrad. In fact, the lineage of the training I was doing with Camie could be traced back to the French Academy, where Gérôme himself taught. I took my time and did the drawing at the pace Camie suggested. When I completed the drawing,

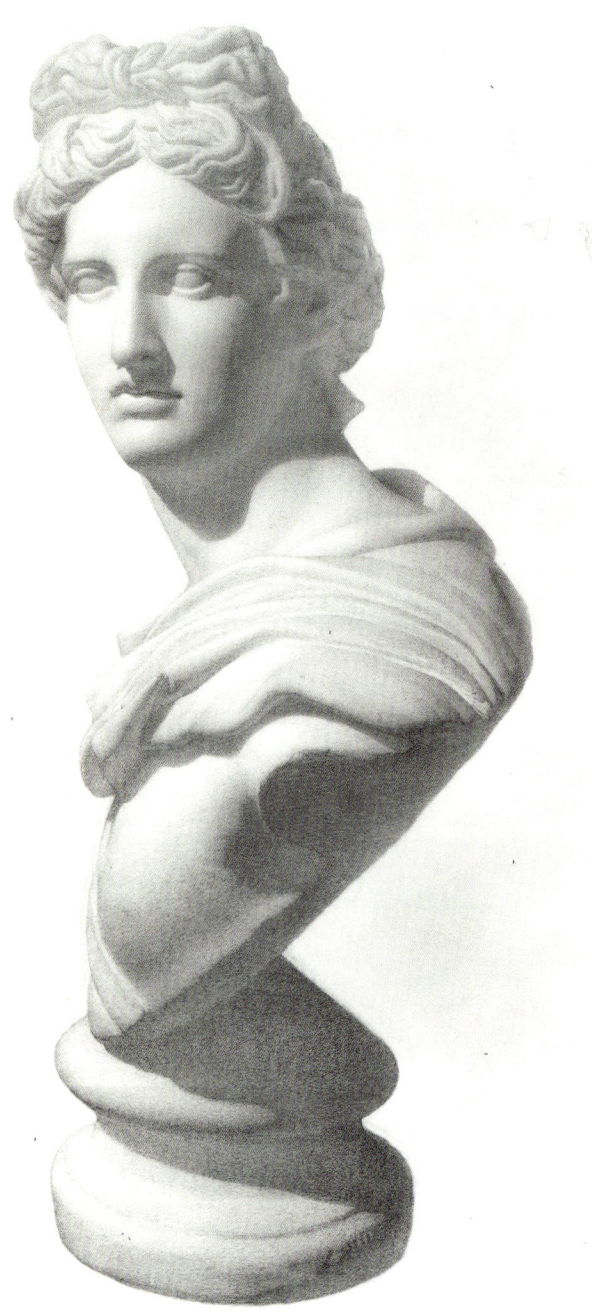

I was pretty happy with it. I let Camie know that I intended to show it to Jacob in hopes that I would get into his atelier.

When I showed up for that second meeting with Jacob, I felt confident. I showed Jacob my drawing with pride. He wasn't overly impressed with it, however. All I kept thinking was, What is he seeing that I'm not? And how can I learn to see like him?

This second interview didn't seem to be going as planned, as he kept asking why I wanted to do this. He strongly challenged me to make sure I really wanted to do this intensive program of study. After about an hour, I remember him finally saying, "Show up on Monday with a pencil and paper." I remember saying, "Wait. What? Am I in?" "Yes," he said, and that's how my classical training began.

The training consisted of coming to the atelier Monday through Friday from 8:30 to 5:00. The program was similar to those developed at the Académie Julian and the École des Beaux-Arts in Paris. The day was broken into morning and afternoon sessions, with a thirty-minute lunch break. Curriculum varied by year: First-year students did cast drawing in the morning and figure drawing in the afternoon. Second-year students did cast painting in the morning and figure drawing or monochromatic painting in the afternoon.

Third-year students worked on monochrome (grisaille) figure paintings in the mornings and figure paintings with a limited palette in the afternoons. It wasn't until the fourth and last year of training that you could paint the figure in color in the morning and afternoon. On Wednesday afternoons, the whole atelier would do portrait painting in the afternoon. This went on from September until May. In addition to the training at the atelier, there were landscape-painting trips.

Almost all the students stayed late at the atelier, painting as much as possible. They hired models and did still life paintings in their workspaces. That's where I started doing still life paintings.

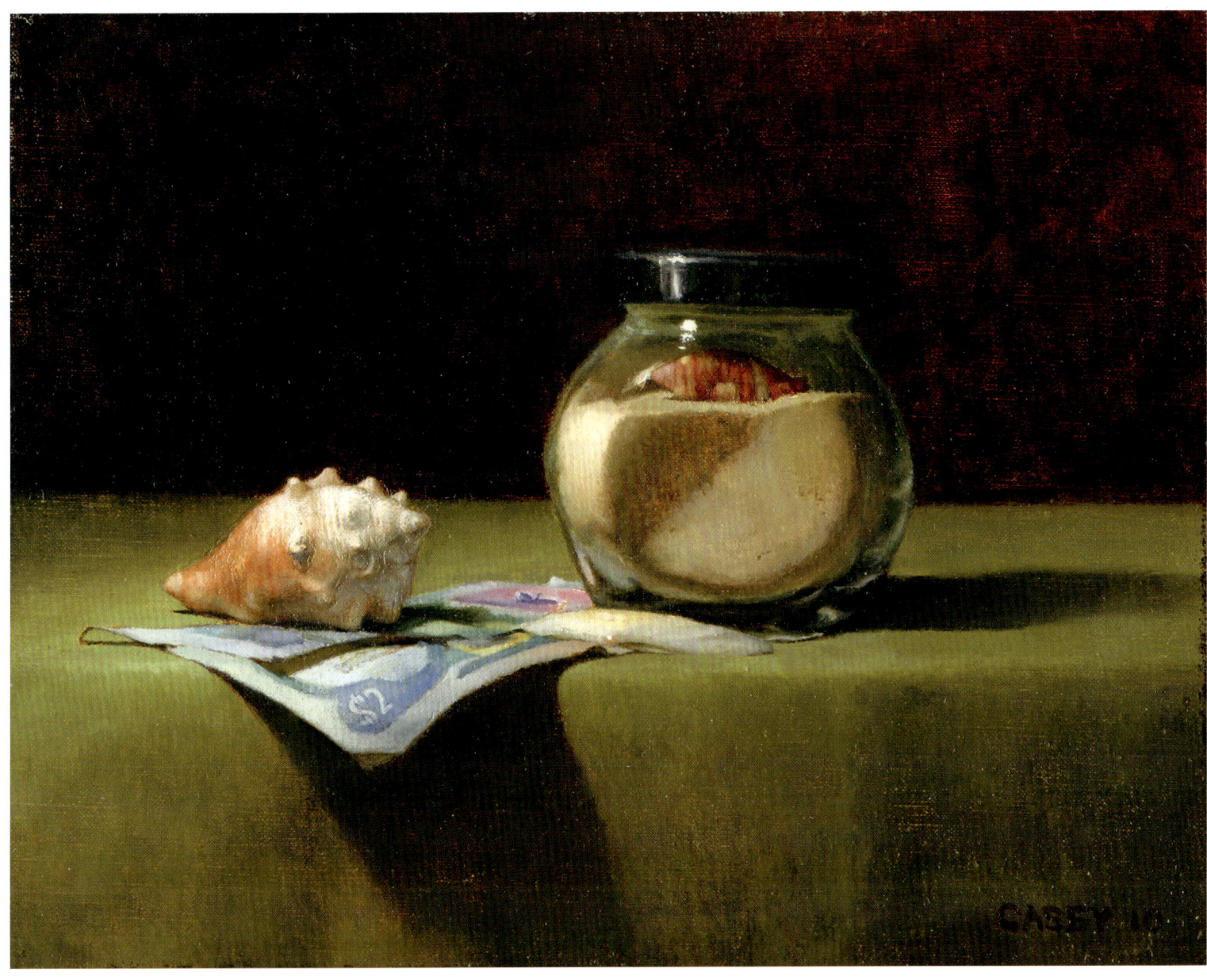

I finished my studies at the Water Street Atelier in 2010. After graduating, I studied *alla prima* painting with Max Ginsburg and Travis Schlaht over the next few summers, learning slightly different approaches to painting using the same basic concepts. When I left Water Street in 2010, I had a great sense of drawing, color, and form, and it was clear how I could apply this skill to making paintings. I had not had this kind of confidence after graduating from my undergrad program.

After my studies concluded, I began to paint objects in my home, as they were accessible. I fell in love with still life and continue to paint still life professionally. I am a storyteller at heart, and still life painting has afforded me the opportunity to tell my stories through objects. Yes, I found my way into still life painting inadvertently, but I love it!

ABOVE: Todd M. Casey, *Chaplin Bay*, 2011, oil on canvas, 8 × 10 inches (20.32 × 25.4 cm).

This is the second still life painting I ever did. The title refers to Chaplin Bay Beach in Bermuda—the spot where I proposed to my wife. It was with this painting that I really started to dig into objects that had a deep meaning to me.

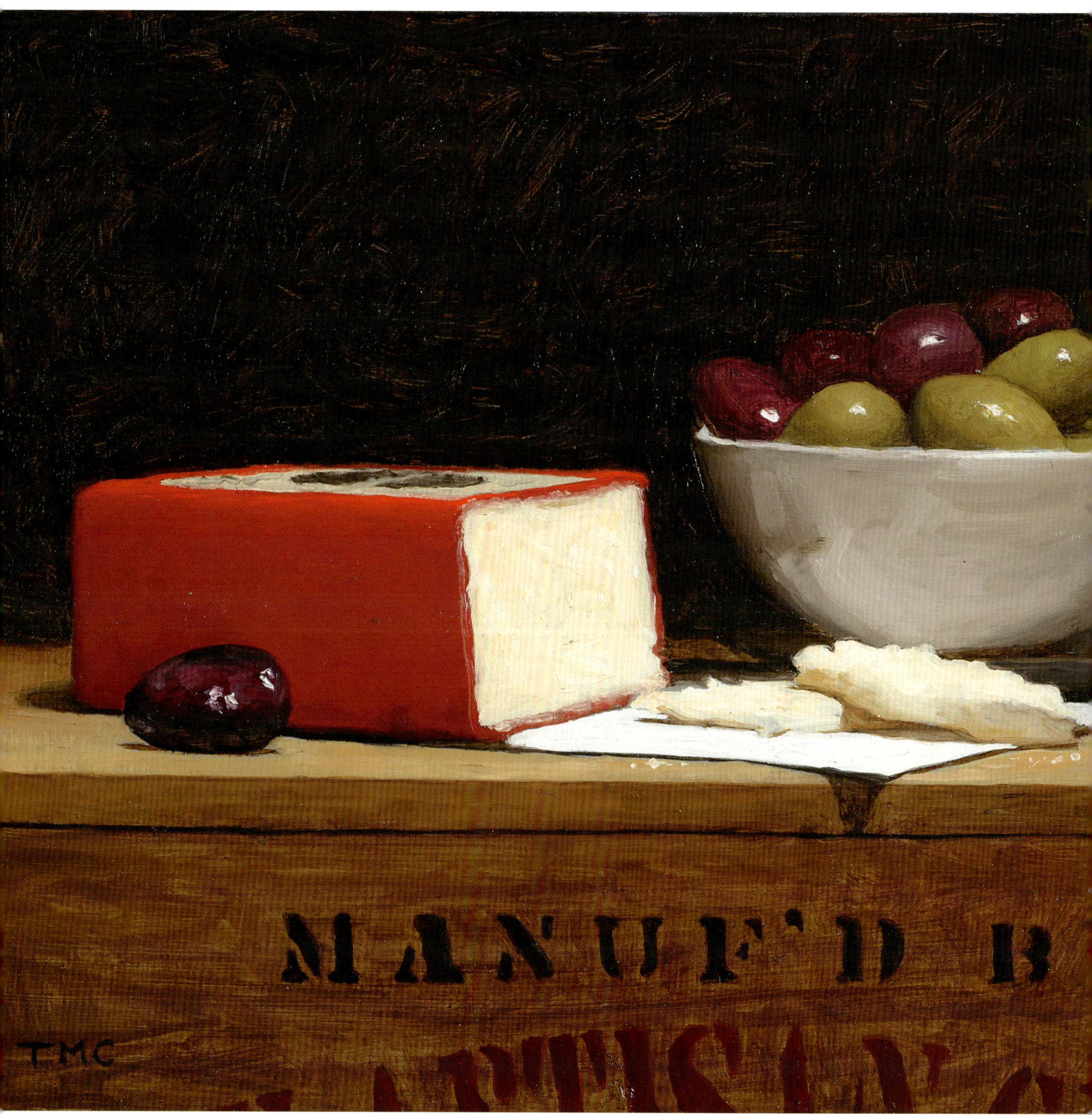

TMC

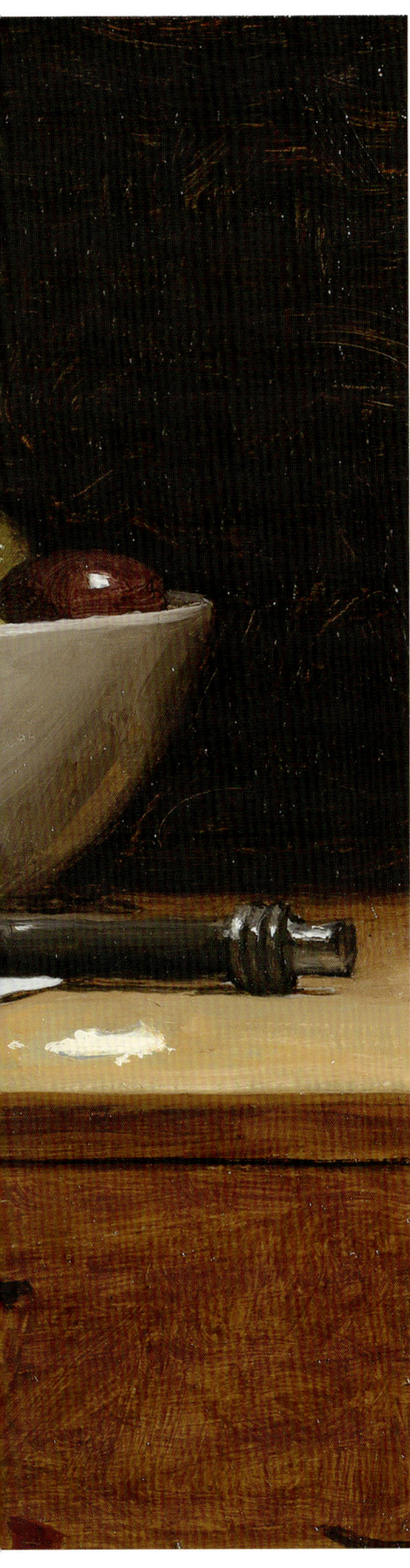

INTRODUCTION

Nature contains the elements, in colour and form, of all pictures, as the keyboard contains the notes of all music. But the artist is born to pick, and choose, and group with science, these elements, that the result may be beautiful—as the musician gathers his notes, and forms his chords, until he brings forth from chaos glorious harmony.

JAMES ABBOTT MCNEILL WHISTLER

When training as an artist, you must master the many concepts that go into making a great painting. All training begins with a deep understanding of the concepts of drawing, light, shadow, color, value, form, and composition. In addition, you must understand your materials, become an excellent draftsman, and learn the techniques you'll need to convey the message you desire.

Still life painting is a great place to start. In an essay on the topic of still life painting, American painter Emil Carlsen wrote, "Still life painting is considered of small importance in the art schools, both here and abroad, the usual course being drawn from the antique, the nude, and painting the draped figure and from the nude. . . . Then why should the earnest student overlook the simplest and most thorough way of acquiring all the knowledge of the craft of painting and drawing, the study of inanimate objects, still life painting, the very surest road to absolute mastery over all technical difficulties."

Still life lets you work out all the concepts of painting in a controlled environment. You can start with a simple setup and then build much more complex ideas as you progress from painting to painting. In a sense, you become the director of the world you create in your studio. As you begin still life, I encourage you to paint objects that are meaningful to you, because this will keep you interested in the painting. When you paint meaningful things, a love of the genre begins to emerge.

LEFT: Todd M. Casey, *Plymouth Artisan Cheese,* 2015, oil on panel, 6 × 8 inches (15.24 × 20.32 cm). Collection of Howard and Amy Rehs.

Painting is not throwing paint on a canvas and hoping it falls in the right place. It is, in fact, just the opposite—ordered and intentional, with each stroke articulated to convey a message. The ultimate goal is to apply paint in a way that will provide an understanding of the forms we see in front of us. Each concept is therefore taken into consideration with each brushstroke.

ABOUT THIS BOOK

I never could have done what I have done without the habits of punctuality, order, and diligence, without the determination to concentrate myself on one subject at a time.
—CHARLES DICKENS

In my training as an artist, I found it very difficult to tackle the many challenges that go into creating a painting. I was constantly trying to juggle everything all at once but had very little success doing it that way. It wasn't until I began my atelier training that I started focusing on one concept at a time and on mastering each individually. After compartmentalizing the concepts, I was able to put them all back together to create cohesive images.

The six concepts that I find most important in making a painting are these:

1. Idea or vision
2. Light and shadow
3. Composition
4. Drawing
5. Color
6. Value and form

All these concepts serve the final painting just as each instrument serves a piece of music. But just as the final musical performance is more important than the instruments, so the final work of art is more important than the individual concepts.

This book presents the concepts in the same order: An artist usually starts with a spark of inspiration, or the *idea/vision* for the painting. The idea or vision is then worked out by putting the objects together in a *composition*. Then *lighting* is introduced, as a tool for composing. With the composition worked out, a *drawing* is created to guide the final painting. After the drawing is transferred to a canvas, *color* is considered. Lastly, *value and form* are applied. Of course, you'll be keeping all the

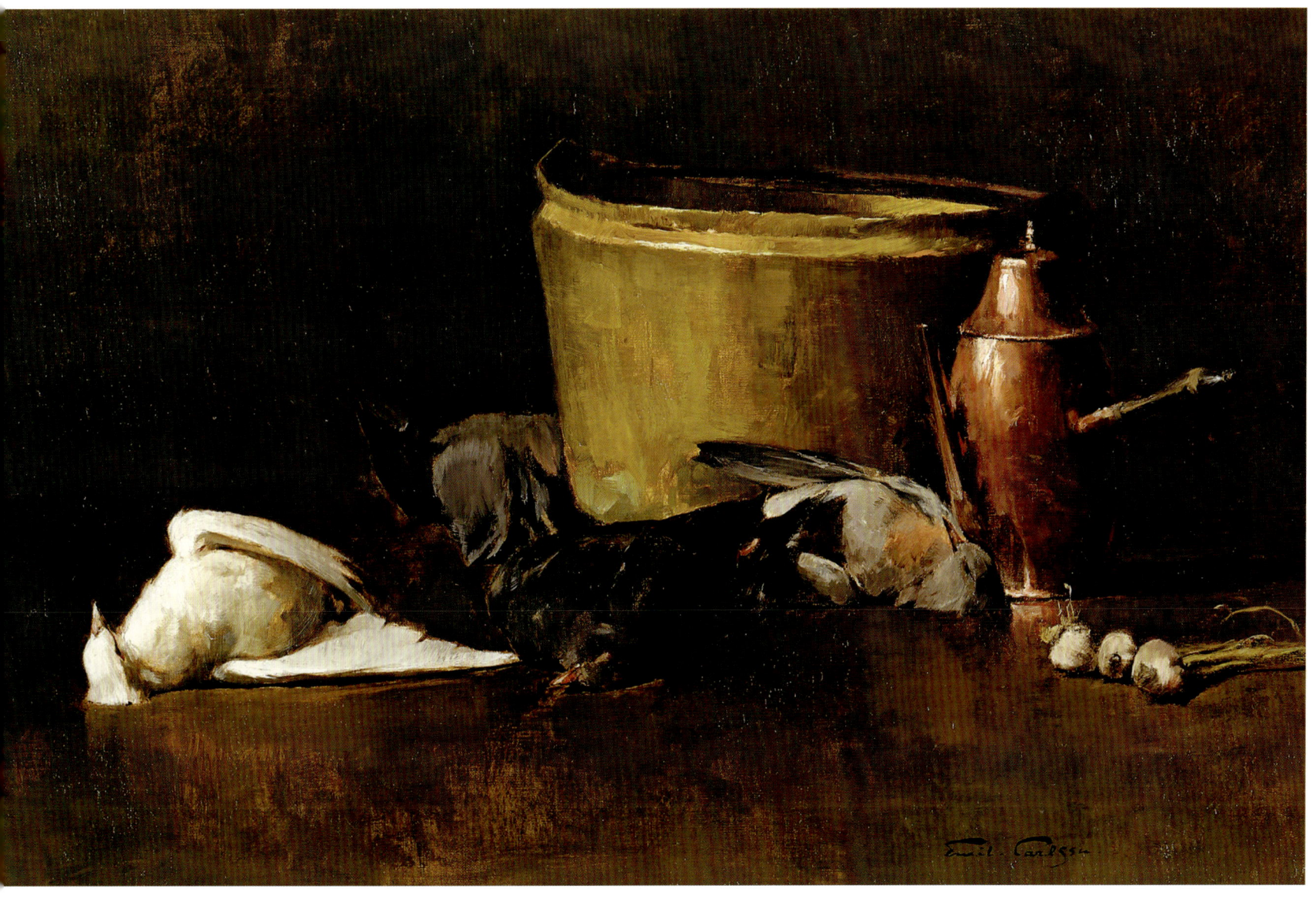

ABOVE: Emil Carlsen, *Still Life—Brass Bowl, Copper Coffee Pot and Pigeons*, c. 1894, oil on canvas, 22 × 33 inches (55.88 × 83.82 cm). Courtesy of Emil Carlsen Archives (emilcarlsen.org).

concepts in mind as the final painting is constructed, but I've found that breaking down the process into these separate, compartmentalized concepts helps you focus. I conclude the book with a thorough step-by-step description of how I made a single painting so that you can see how I tackled each of the concepts and combined them in my creative process.

Along the way, I also bring in a touch of psychology to help you see what you're up against. Artists want to be able to paint what we see. However, our judgment often fails us, and we paint what we *think* we see instead. Throughout the book, I'll note some of the obstacles to seeing. Being aware of the obstacles will help you work around them.

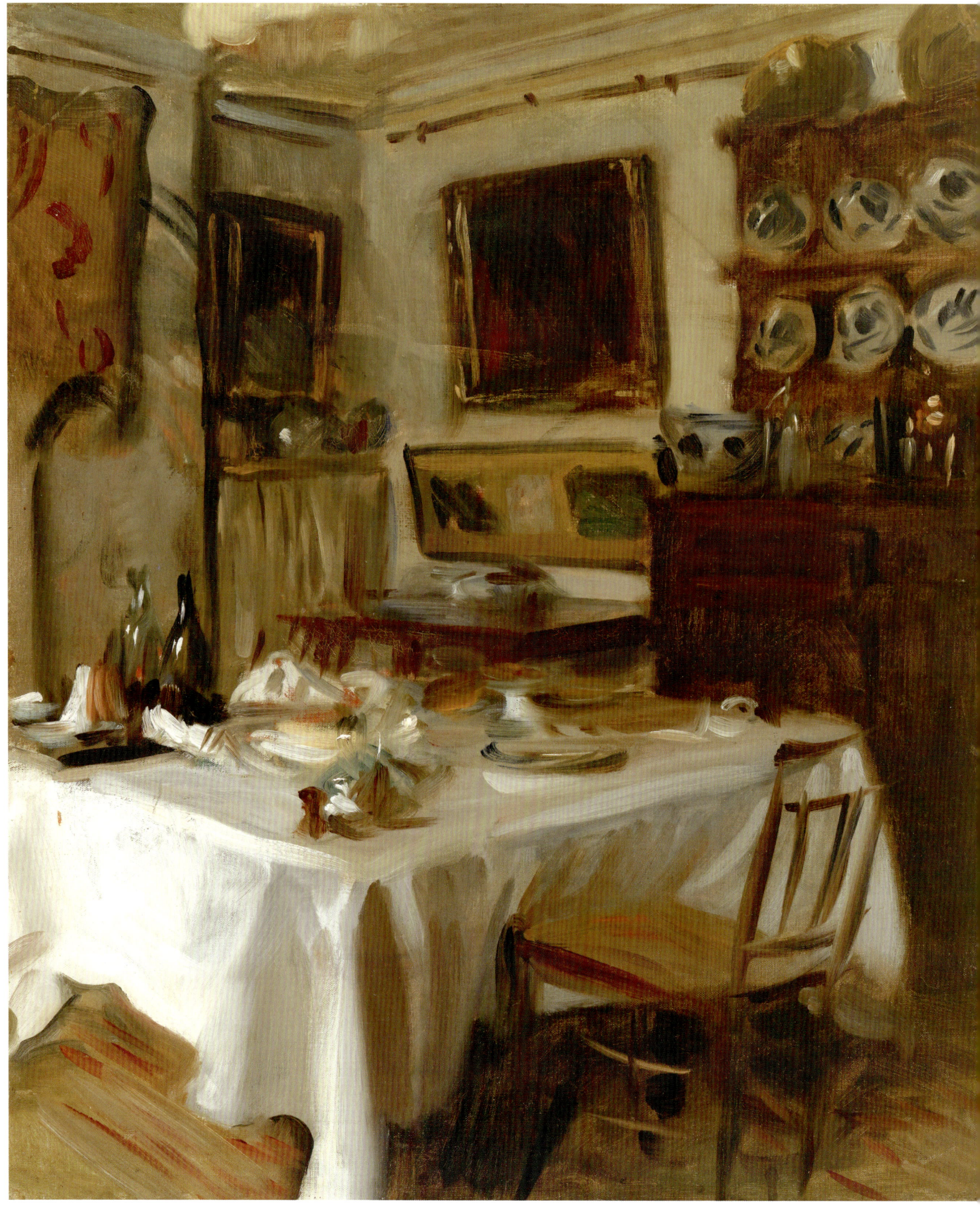

MY GOAL

Develop your senses—especially learn how to see. Realize that everything connects to everything else.
—LEONARDO DA VINCI

When I set out to write this book, I had one major goal: to create the book I wish I'd had when I was studying painting. I learned so much on my journey, and I want to share it with you.

This book discusses both the scientific and the expressive aspects of still life painting. On the scientific side are the concepts of light, color, and form. The expressive side includes the idea or vision, the composition, and the language you create with your mark-making. Each artist has their own language. I cannot teach you the expressive side—what to paint or what your paintings should look like—but I can teach you the principles that each painter must consider, no matter what style you work in.

This book encourages you to heighten your senses and to use that heightened awareness when painting. Just as someone training to become a sommelier must heighten their senses of smell and taste, you'll want to train your senses to be so keen that you operate on a very high level of sensory awareness. Also, throughout the book I balance the practical information I present with a lot of advice from the heart. Painting should be made from the head and the heart, never just one or the other.

OPTICAL VERSUS CONCEPTUAL

In this book I talk about two different ways to approach a painting: the optical and the conceptual. In a nutshell, the optical is what we see and the conceptual is what we know. The optical is directly copying what we see in front of us. That means looking at values in relation to one another and translating them to the painting surface. This tends to be a very two-dimensional way of thinking, as you are always making something lighter or darker in relation to something else. The conceptual approach articulates the direction of the planes in relation to light. This develops a deep sense of the object in space, which translates into a three-dimensional, sculptural way of thinking.

Different movements in art have focused on one concept or the other. For instance, the Impressionists were almost purely optical, copying what they saw in front of them. Oppositely, comic book artists must be able to construct a believable world out of their imagination, which requires a deep understanding of structure, perspective, and so on.

In the French academic tradition, the optical and the conceptual are intertwined. That's the manner in which I was taught to paint—and the method presented in this book. When a painter considers both these ideas, the painting will be more than just a copy of what the painter sees. Combining observation with knowledge will make your paintings much stronger. It's like building a bridge from two sides and having them meet in the middle.

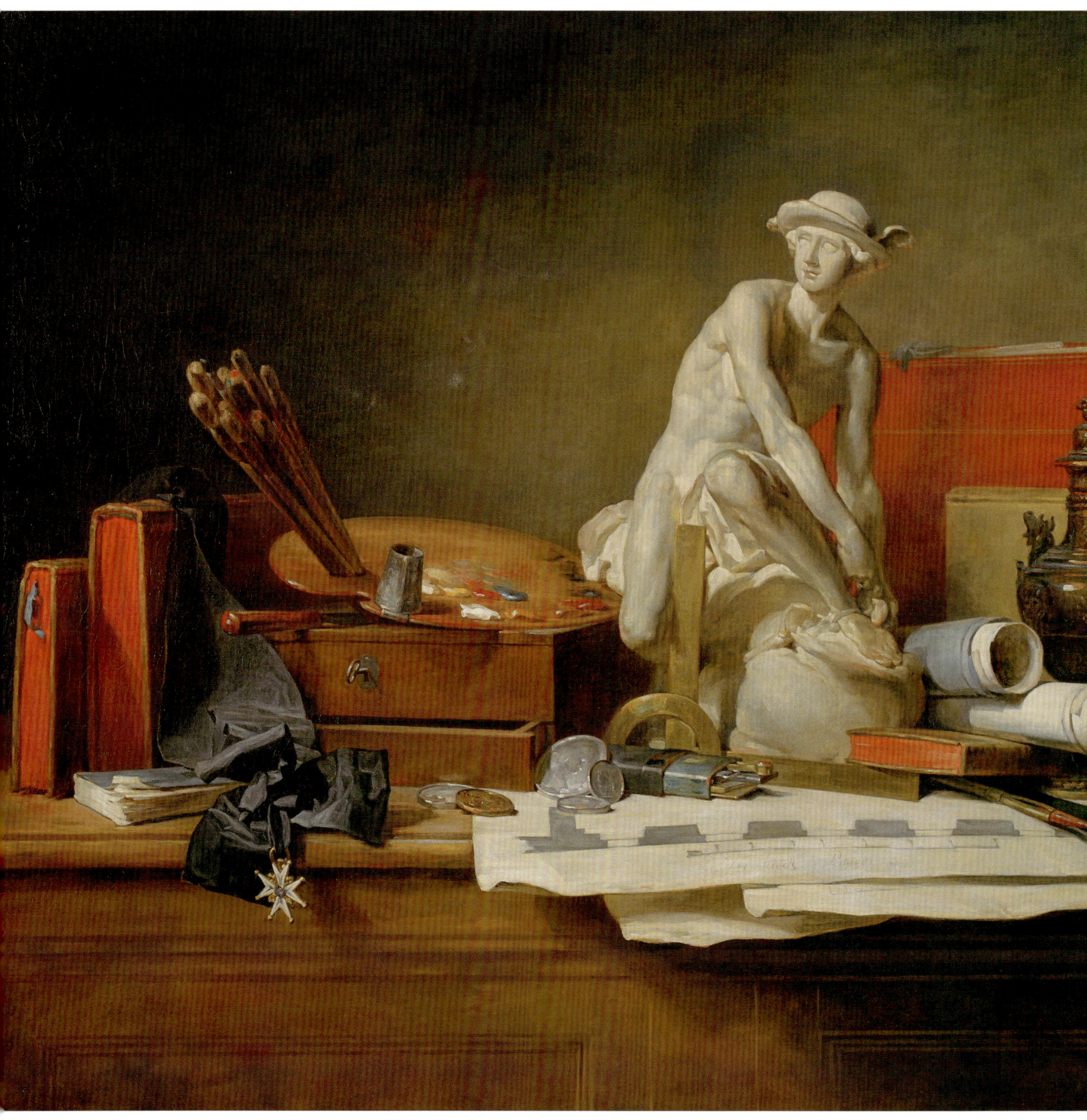

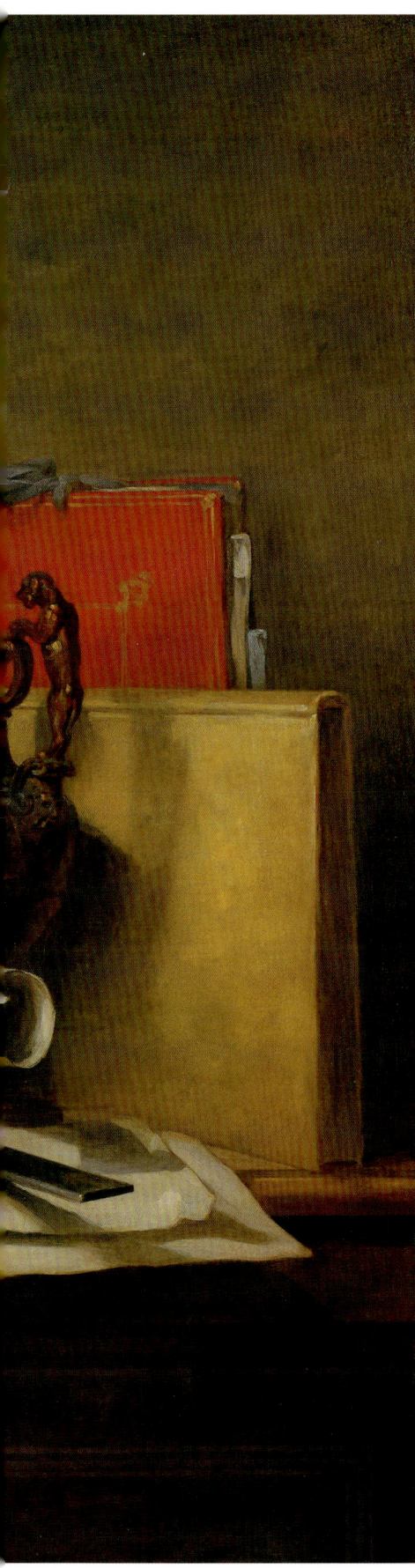

CHAPTER 1

SETTING UP: MATERIALS, TOOLS, AND THE STUDIO SPACE

Genius is not a possession of the limited few, but exists in some degree in everyone. Where there is natural growth, a full and free play of faculties, genius will manifest itself.

ROBERT HENRI

O il painting is a wonderful, versatile medium that's been around for centuries. But the process of oil painting can sometimes be frustrating because you are continually solving problems. You don't want to have to struggle with tools and materials that don't yield good results.

LEFT: Jean-Baptiste-Siméon Chardin, *The Attributes of the Arts and the Rewards Which Are Accorded Them,* 1766, oil on canvas, 44 ½ × 57 ¼ inches (113.03 × 145.42 cm). Minneapolis Institute of Art, the William Hood Dunwoody Fund 52.15.

Having good tools and materials will help you achieve your artistic goals, so I encourage everyone to buy the best art supplies possible. Stay away from student-grade paints and poor-quality brushes. Of course, buying the best supplies does not guarantee that you will make great art! But at least your tools and materials won't be getting in your way.

In this chapter, I introduce you to some of the tools that I use for my own visual language—and, at the end, I offer some tips on setting up your studio space. Use my suggestions as a basic reference, but feel very free to explore other materials as you learn how to draw and paint. Every artist has their own favorite tools and materials, and you will compile your own set of favorites as you build your own mark-making language.

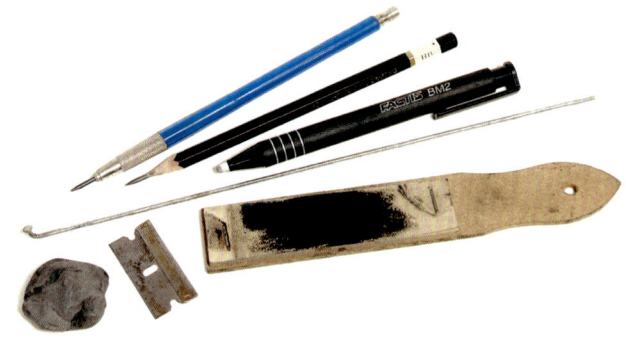

DRAWING TOOLS AND MATERIALS

Drawing is a prelude to painting, so let's look at drawing tools first. Good tools will help you do good drawings. These tools will eventually feel like an extension of your hand, and the more you use them, the more you will master them.

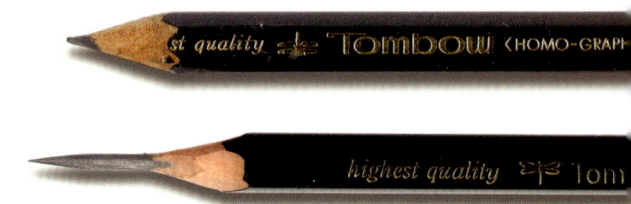

Pencils, Sharpeners, and Erasers

The most essential drawing tool is a pencil. Artist's pencils come in a very wide range of hardnesses, from 8H (the hardest) to 8B (the softest). H pencils tend to score the paper, while B pencils can be difficult to erase. I do almost all my drawing with an HB pencil—which is right in the middle of the range (see image bottom right). You can get a nice range of values from an HB, without the disadvantages of harder or softer pencils. I recommend using a high-quality brand like Staedtler or Tombow.

Besides choosing a degree of hardness, you'll want to decide whether to use a traditional pencil with a wood casing or a mechanical pencil. Mechanical pencils don't need to be sharpened, but traditional pencils do, of course. To sharpen a traditional pencil, you can use a standard sharpener, but many artists prefer to use a single-edged straight razor blade to carve the wood away, exposing the lead.

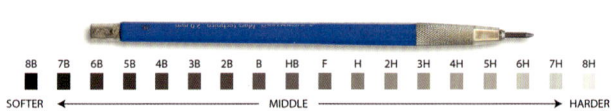

TOP: Tools for drawing include, clockwise from the top: a mechanical pencil, a wooden pencil, a mechanical eraser, a measuring tool (in this case a spoke from a bicycle wheel), a sanding pad, a razor blade, and a kneaded eraser.

CENTER: When cutting the wood back, expose about half an inch of lead.

BOTTOM: Mechanical pencils like the one shown above the value scale can hold leads of a full range of hardnesses.

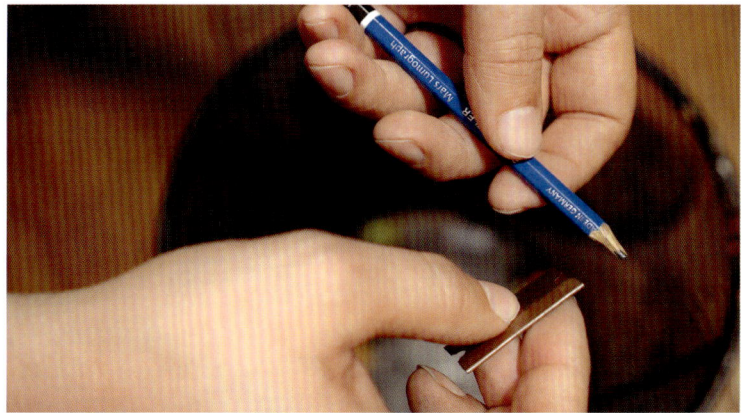

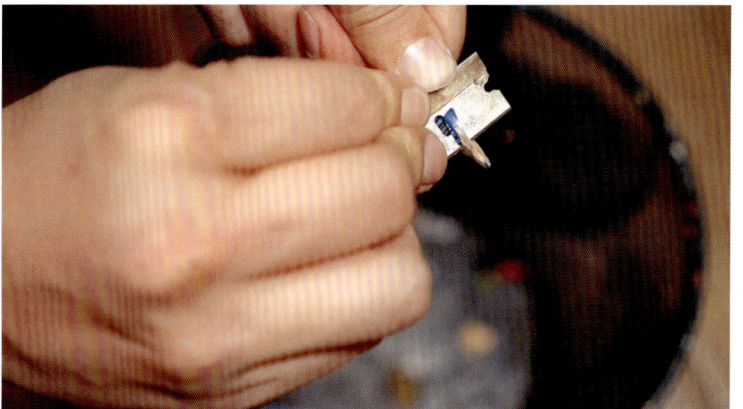

ABOVE: When sharpening a pencil with a razor blade, carve the wood back very slowly to expose the lead. Try not to score the lead, as that will weaken it. This method takes a lot of practice, so be patient. And please don't cut yourself—remember that you're using a very sharp blade!

BELOW, RIGHT: Rotate the pencil as you sand so that the point is symmetrical. When you're finished, the lead shaft should resemble a spear.

Photos by Alex Archimbaud.

Once the lead is exposed, use a sanding pad to rub the lead down to a point. Take your time when sanding, rotating the pencil so that you get a good, evenly tapered point. After sanding, wipe the pencil on a rag to remove any graphite particles that remain on the shaft. When you finish carving and sanding, your pencil's lead should look like a long spear. This shape lets you make several different kinds of marks: the tip for fine lines, the edge of the point for broader marks, and the side of the lead for large marks.

The kneaded eraser is a very pliable tool. I use it almost as much as I use my pencil. It can be sculpted into a point or formed into any size or shape of eraser you need. White plastic erasers are handy as well. They're harder than kneaded erasers and can dig into the paper to remove darker lines. These also come as pencil-like eraser sticks that are super handy for getting rid of marks that are deeply embedded in the paper.

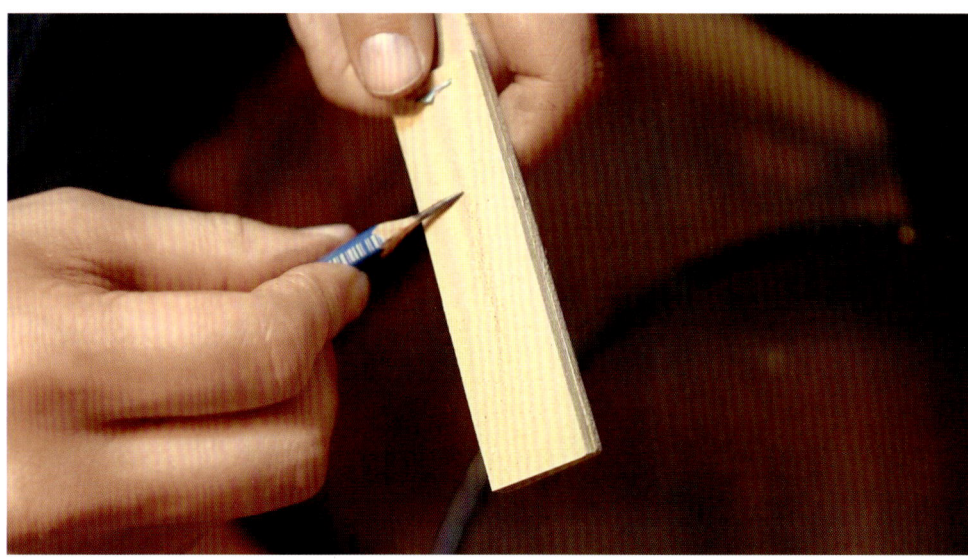

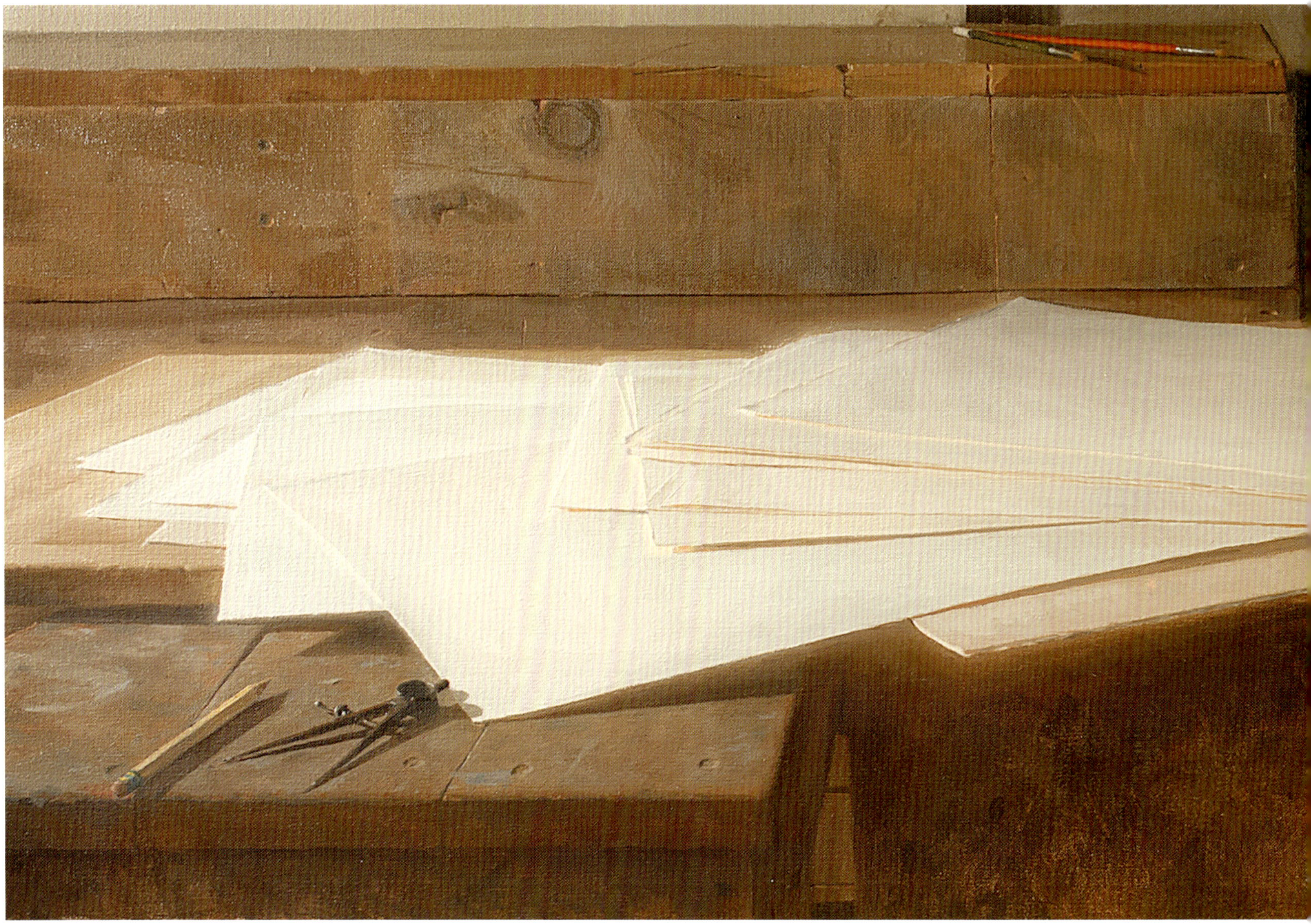

CHARCOAL

You may prefer to draw directly on your canvas rather than doing a preliminary drawing on paper. If you like, you can do this with a soft graphite pencil, but many artists prefer working with charcoal. Choose a medium vine charcoal like the Winsor & Newton willow charcoal shown. It's neither too hard nor too soft, so the mark it makes on your surface can easily be wiped away if you need to fix a mistake. If you use charcoal, you will want to paint over the lines after drawing with either waterproof ink or thinned oil paint. The charcoal can then be wiped off when the ink or paint is dry. If you don't do this, you'll get the charcoal in your paint.

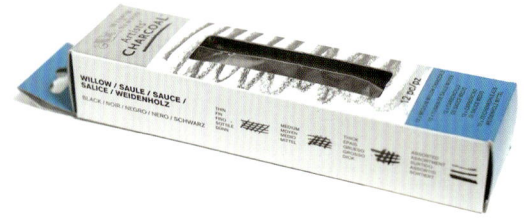

These Winsor & Newton medium willow charcoal sticks are a good choice for drawing directly on your canvas.

Photo by James Leocadi.

OTHER DRAWING SUPPLIES

Hold your drawing in place with blue painter's tape, which is a great adhesive that doesn't leave glue residue behind when lifted from the paper. I like to keep all of my drawing supplies in their own plastic bin, separate from my painting supplies. Bins like the one shown below are easy to take along when traveling.

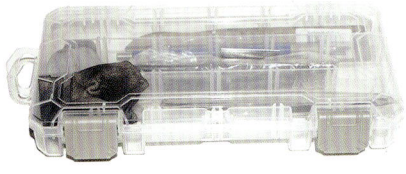

Storage bins keep all your drawing materials tidily in one place.

Paper and Drawing Boards

I recommend using Strathmore 400 series drawing paper pads, as they work well and are widely available. This 80 lb. paper is off-white in color, has a nice tooth, and stands up well to erasing. I've been using this paper for years. Invest in a few different-size pads—9 × 12, 11 × 14, and 18 × 24 inches.

I always back the pad with a drawing board to make the surface more rigid. Traditional drawing boards from art stores work well, but a piece of hardboard from a hardware store cut down to the size of the pad is just as good. Pick up some bulldog clips and extra-long rubber bands to secure your drawing pad to the board.

It's also a great idea to be actively sketching from life as often as possible. If you always carry a sketchbook with you, you can note anything that inspires you at any time.

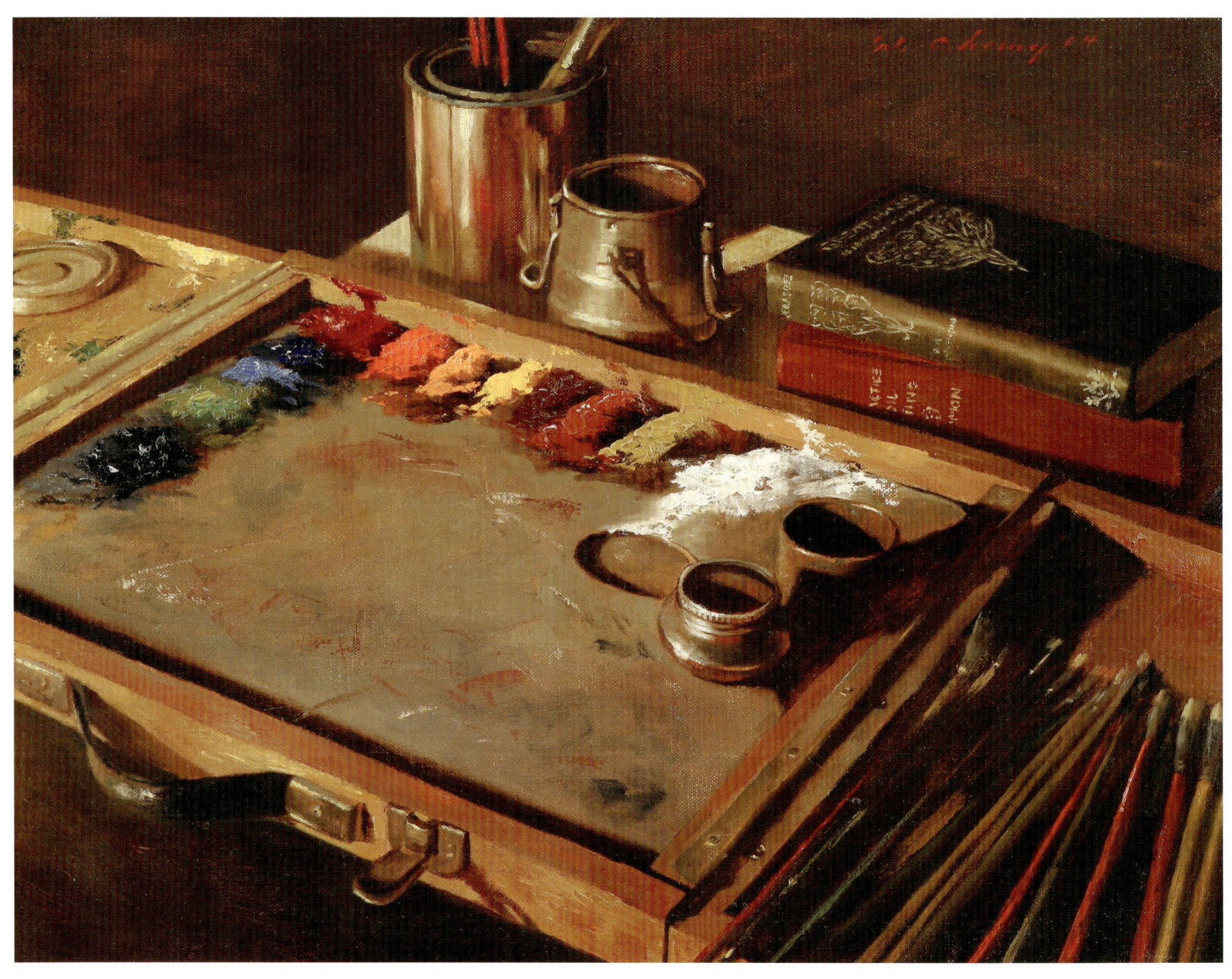

PAINTING TOOLS AND MATERIALS

There are countless oil-painting tools and materials on the market. In what follows, I've tried to stay with the basics—the things a beginning still life painter is most likely to need.

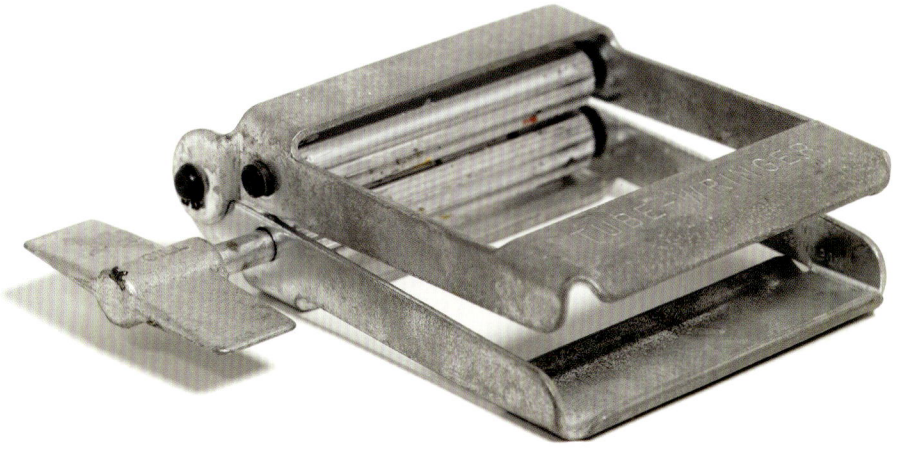

Oil Paint

Each painting medium has its strengths and weaknesses. I dabble in all of them, as still life paintings can be beautiful in any medium. But I predominantly work in oil paints, as I find oil to be the most versatile medium. It has great layering properties, and the colors will remain vivid over centuries.

Most oil paints are made of just two components: pigment and linseed oil as a binding agent. If the tube's label lists any other ingredient—such as safflower oil, walnut oil, or alkyds—I would not buy the paint. There are many good brands of oil paint, but for the beginner I recommend Gamblin, which is the least expensive of the high-end brands. Once you choose a brand, I recommend sticking with it to avoid variability, since oil paint colors can differ from brand to brand.

Do stay away from cheaper "student-grade" paints, whose colors are less concentrated because they have a higher oil-to-pigment ratio or have fillers or other additives (chalk, aluminum, magnesium stearates, etc.). Also, you should generally steer clear of paints whose color names include the word *hue* (for example, cadmium yellow hue), because a "hue" is a mixture of colors other than the true pigment.

For suggestions on which oil colors to choose when setting up your basic palette, see pages 226–227.

ABOVE: A tube wringer will help you get every last bit of paint out of a tube. This isn't a must-have, but it can save you some money, because oil paints can be expensive.

READING AN OIL PAINT LABEL

The labels on tubes of paint contain important pieces of information. Here are some of the things you can learn from reading an oil paint label:

Color Name

Pigments are referred to as either organic or inorganic. Organic pigments are carbon-based; modern synthetic organic pigments include azo, lake, phthalocyanine, and quinacridone pigments. Inorganic, or mineral, pigments include pigments based on heavy metals such as cadmium, chromium, cobalt, and iron. (This is important, because organic and inorganic pigments have different properties when mixed.) The names of some colors refer to the place the pigment originated from; examples include raw and burnt sienna, which are named for the Italian city of Siena, which produced these earth colors during the Renaissance.

Lightfastness Rating

The lightfastness of a pigment has to do with how stable it is when exposed to light. (Think of fabric dye: if a T-shirt fades when left out in the sun, the dye is not very lightfast.)

The labels of high-quality oil paints give their lightfastness rating, as determined by the American Society for Testing Materials (ASTM). The system ranges from class I (very lightfast) to class V (not lightfast). I avoid using any paints with an ASTM rating of V except in an underpainting.

Colour Index Name (CIN)

The Colour Index name, or CIN, is a universal guide to paint color. This code is more accurate at identifying a specific color than is the name of the color on the tube. For example, the CIN code PR108 can be broken down like this:

P = pigment
R = the red hue
108 = the specific number assigned to cadmium red pigment

The CIN system identifies ten hues: Yellow (Y), Orange (O), Red (R), Violet (V), Blue (B), Green (G), Brown (Br), Black (Bk), White (W), and Metallic (M).

Series Number

The series number on a tube of paint indicates how expensive it is relative to other paints produced by the same manufacturer. (The price has to do with how rare, and therefore how expensive, a given pigment is.) Usually, the higher the series number the more expensive the paint.

Toxicity

Some oil paints contain heavy metals—cadmium, cobalt, chromium, and lead—and should be used with caution. Try to avoid skin contact with these colors. (Using gloves while painting or washing your hands often is highly recommended.) I would also avoid sanding any of these paints, but if you choose to, use a respirator.

OPPOSITE, TOP: Paint-tube labels contain lots of information on the properties of the paint. I recommend reading the label before purchasing a tube of paint.

Image courtesy of Gamblin Artist's Oil Colors.

OPPOSITE, BOTTOM: Pigments are either organic (carbon-based) or inorganic (mineral).

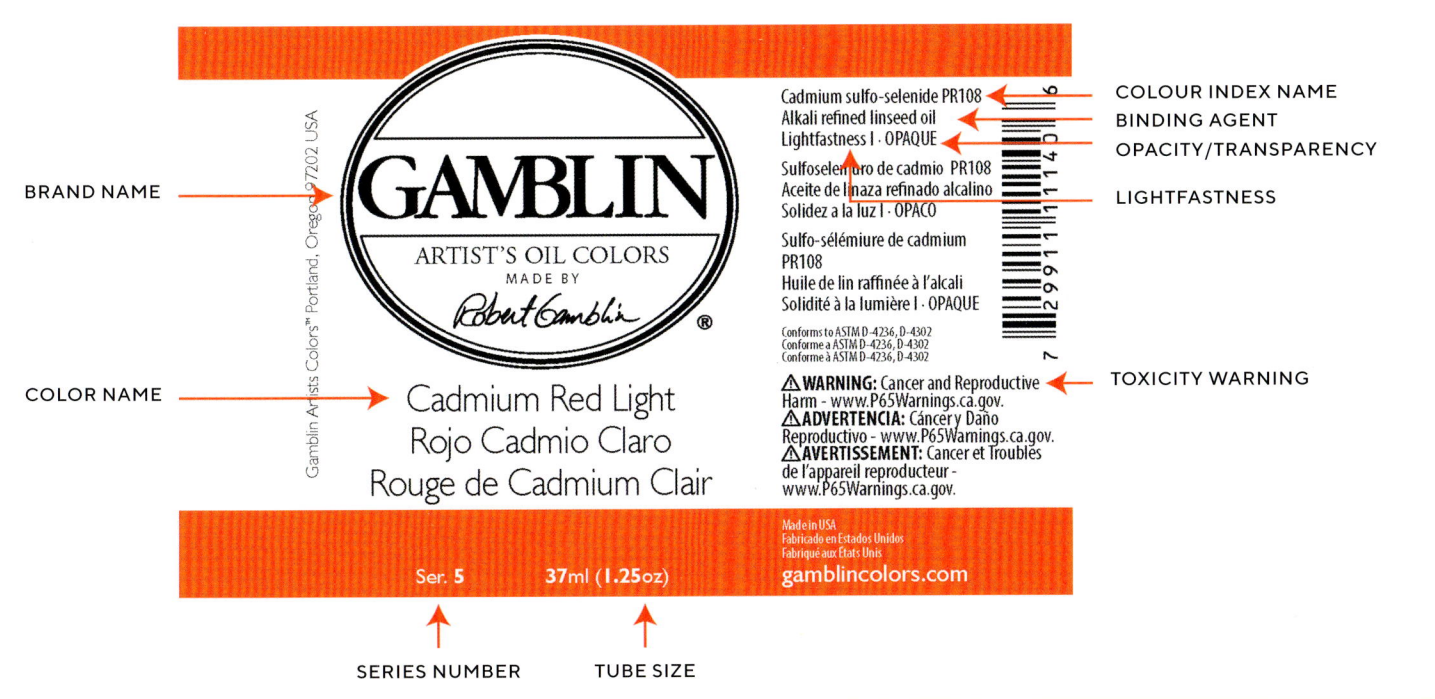

BRAND NAME

COLOR NAME

Gamblin Artists Colors™ Portland, Oregon 97202 USA

GAMBLIN
ARTIST'S OIL COLORS
MADE BY
Robert Gamblin ®

Cadmium Red Light
Rojo Cadmio Claro
Rouge de Cadmium Clair

Ser. 5   37ml (1.25oz)

SERIES NUMBER   TUBE SIZE

Cadmium sulfo-selenide PR108   COLOUR INDEX NAME
Alkali refined linseed oil   BINDING AGENT
Lightfastness I · OPAQUE   OPACITY/TRANSPARENCY

Sulfoseleniuro de cadmio PR108   LIGHTFASTNESS
Aceite de linaza refinado alcalino
Solidez a la luz I · OPACO

Sulfo-sélémiure de cadmium
PR108
Huile de lin raffinée à l'alcali
Solidité à la lumière I · OPAQUE

Conforms to ASTM D-4236, D-4302
Conforme a ASTM D-4236, D-4302
Conforme à ASTM D-4236, D-4302

⚠WARNING: Cancer and Reproductive   TOXICITY WARNING
Harm - www.P65Warnings.ca.gov.
⚠ADVERTENCIA: Cáncer y Daño
Reproductivo - www.P65Warnings.ca.gov.
⚠AVERTISSEMENT: Cancer et Troubles
de l'appareil reproducteur -
www.P65Warnings.ca.gov.

Made in USA
Fabricado en Estados Unidos
Fabriqué aux États Unis

gamblincolors.com

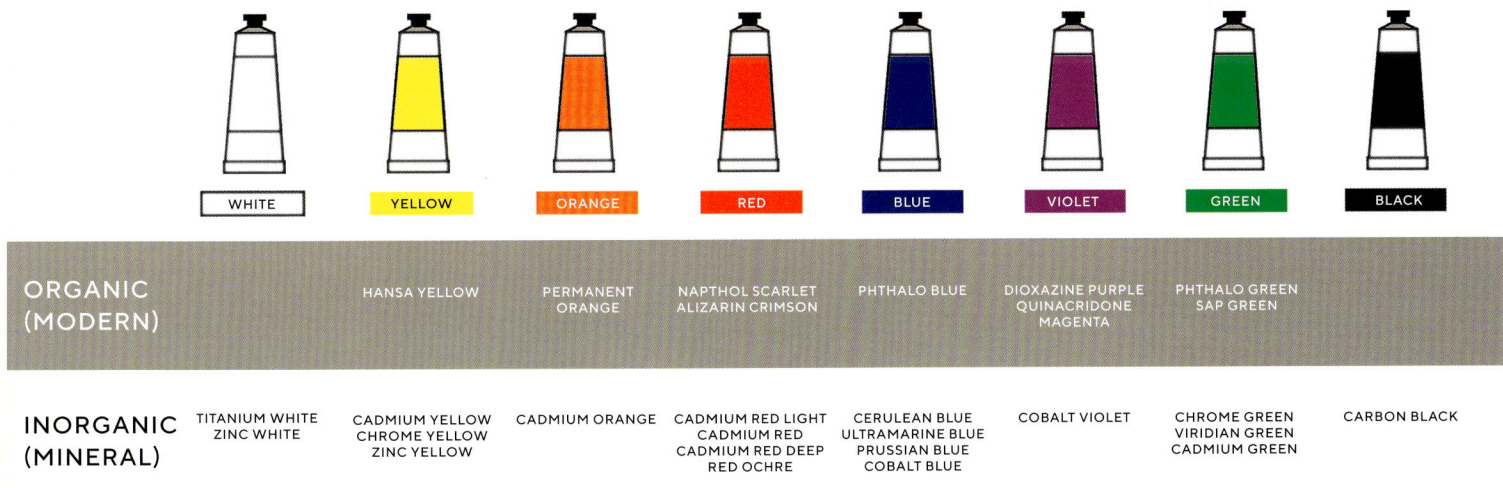

	WHITE	YELLOW	ORANGE	RED	BLUE	VIOLET	GREEN	BLACK
ORGANIC (MODERN)		HANSA YELLOW	PERMANENT ORANGE	NAPTHOL SCARLET ALIZARIN CRIMSON	PHTHALO BLUE	DIOXAZINE PURPLE QUINACRIDONE MAGENTA	PHTHALO GREEN SAP GREEN	
INORGANIC (MINERAL)	TITANIUM WHITE ZINC WHITE	CADMIUM YELLOW CHROME YELLOW ZINC YELLOW	CADMIUM ORANGE	CADMIUM RED LIGHT CADMIUM RED CADMIUM RED DEEP RED OCHRE	CERULEAN BLUE ULTRAMARINE BLUE PRUSSIAN BLUE COBALT BLUE	COBALT VIOLET	CHROME GREEN VIRIDIAN GREEN CADMIUM GREEN	CARBON BLACK

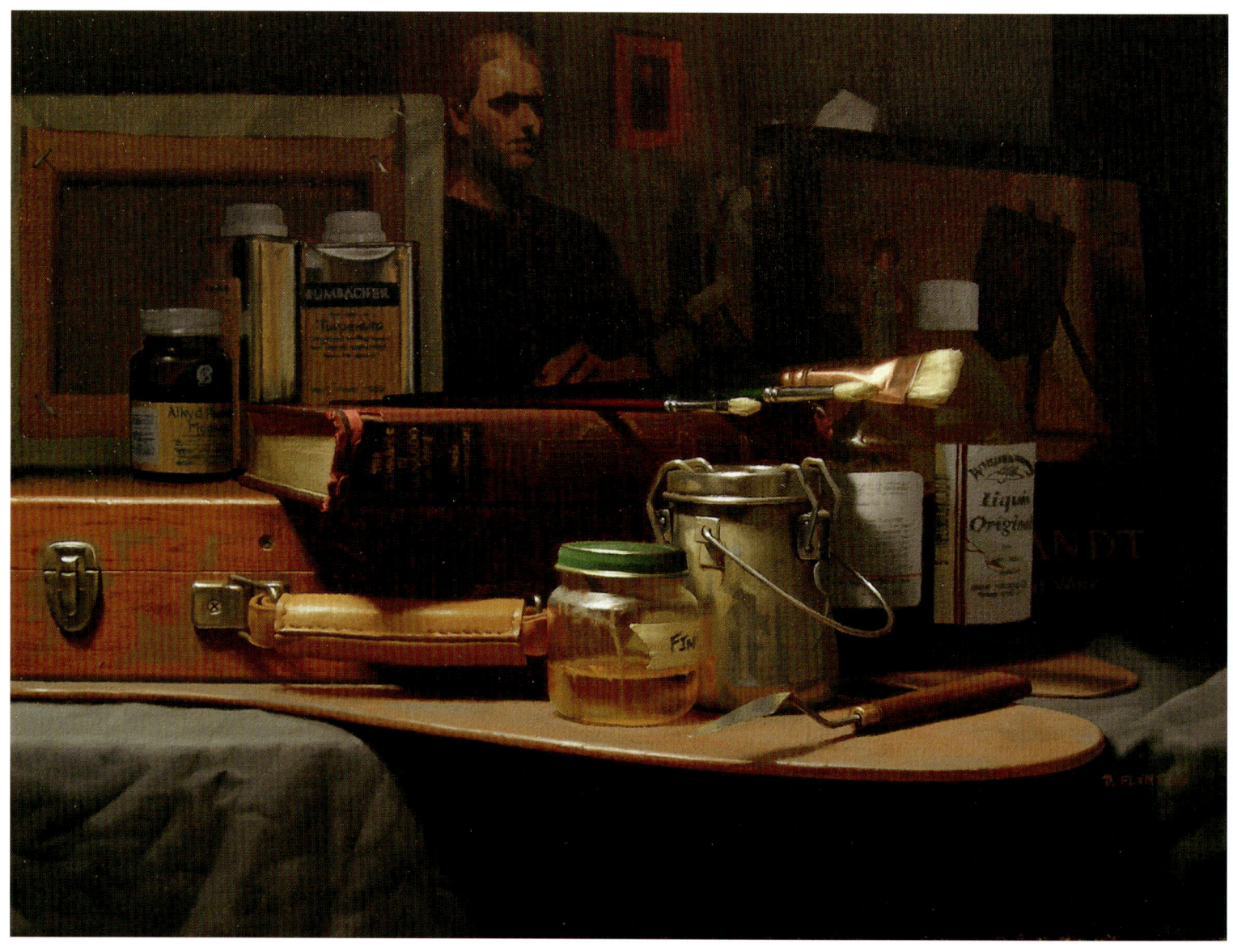

Mediums

Mediums have been used throughout the history of oil painting. They change the drying time of oil paint, slowing it down or speeding it up, as well as affecting the consistency of the paint. I like to keep the chemistry simple when painting, not adding too many things to my paint. That said, you will need to use a medium for some techniques, like glazing.

Some commonly used mediums are alkyd resin–based products, like Gamblin's Galkyd mediums, that speed up drying time. Cobalt-based mediums such as Grumbacher's Cobalt Drier accelerate drying time as well. Other mediums, such as poppy

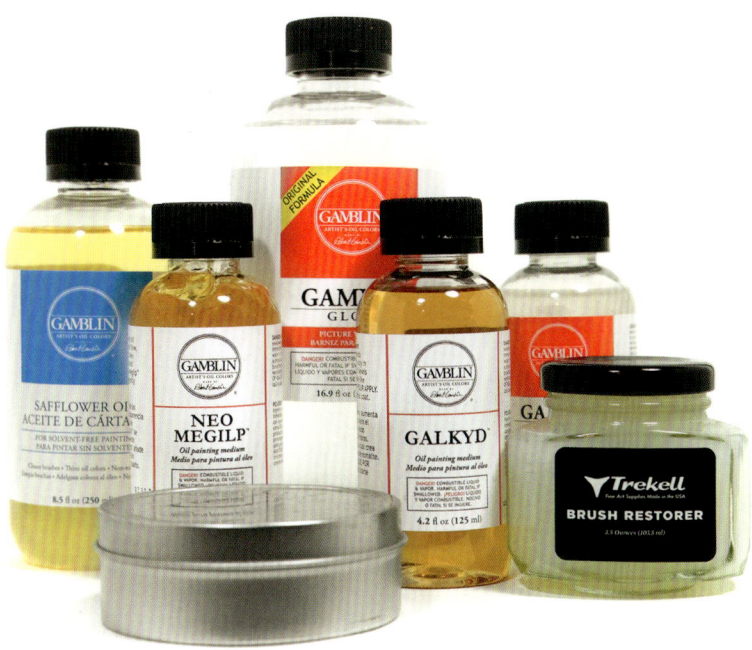

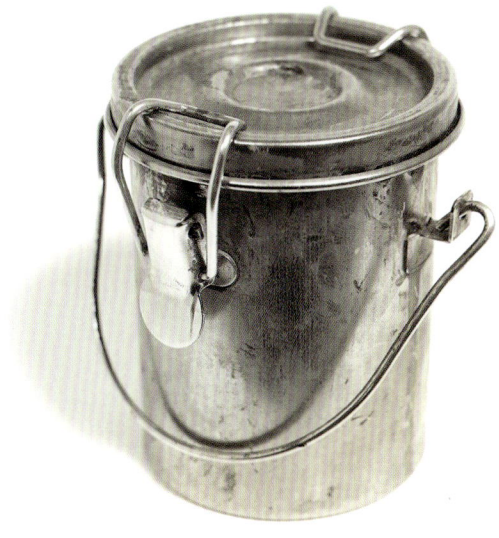

seed oil and walnut oil, slow drying time. Note that adding any medium to paint out of a tube will change the paint's consistency. I encourage you to experiment with mediums, but, like a good scientist, take notes along the way. However, don't begin your experimentation until after you've grasped the basic concepts regarding how to paint; till then, I advise you not to use any mediums except mineral spirits (used to thin paint).

Solvents

Solvents are mineral spirits. They are used for several purposes, including cleaning brushes and thinning paint for underpaintings. Modern solvents like Gamsol are odorless, but even though you can't smell the fumes you're still inhaling them when the solvent is exposed to the air. Therefore you should store solvents in containers that can be tightly sealed and should make sure that your painting environment is well ventilated whenever you're using a solvent.

A stainless steel brush washer makes a great container for mineral spirits. The lid has a seal inside so you can carry your solvent without any danger of its leaking or spilling. The container allows the paint to settle to the bottom, so the solvent can be used for multiple brush cleanings.

LEFT: Feel free to experiment with different mediums.

Photo by James Leocadi.

ABOVE: Brush washers are excellent for transporting mineral spirits.

TIP

Make sure your studio is stocked with lots of paper towels and rags for cleanup. Blue shop towels (there are several brands) are the best paper towels for painting because they are so absorbent. I use old T-shirts as paint rags. I always keep a rag in my hand while painting to wipe excess paint off my brush, as well as to wipe off excess mineral spirits after cleaning a brush.

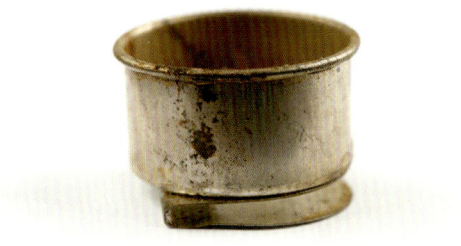

ABOVE: A medium cup hooks onto your palette, holding clean mineral spirits or a medium for you to use while painting.

Photo courtesy of Jessy Dunn.

Medium cups are little vessels that clip onto your palette to keep your mediums or solvents handy while painting. When you use mineral spirits as a medium, it's imperative that they be clean. I therefore have separate medium cups for cleaning my brushes and for the mineral spirits I use as a medium.

Brushes and Palette Knives

When choosing brushes, you have a lot of options. Each type of brush produces a distinctive set of marks. I recommend trying brushes of as many different shapes, sizes, and materials as possible to see which feel most comfortable to you. But to begin with, you might consider the starter set of Trekell brushes pictured opposite.

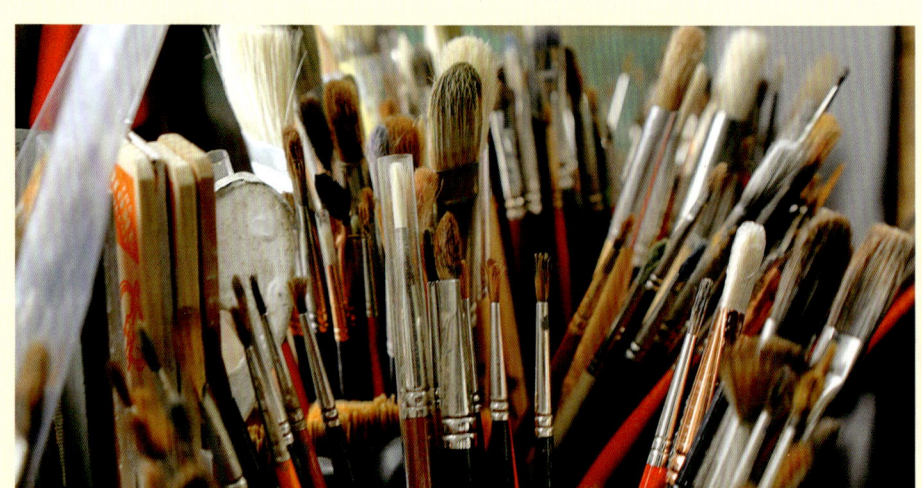

TIP

It's good to get into the habit of cleaning your brushes after every painting session. There are many brush cleaners that will extend the life of your brushes, such as Trekell Brush Restorer. But soap—Trekell Linseed Oil Soap, Murphy's Oil Soap, or plain old Ivory Soap—is also good for getting paint out of brushes. To clean a brush, run the brush back and forth across the bar of soap as if you were painting on it. Then use your fingers to rub the soap into the hairs. Run the brush under warm water, continuing to work the soap into the hairs. Lastly, rub the hairs into your palm as you rinse the brush under warm water. Store your brushes brush side up in a cup or jar so that their tips don't touch each other.

Brushes for oil painting are made of several different kinds of hairs, natural and synthetic. Natural-hair brushes include bristle brushes, which are made from the hairs of a hog. I use a variety of hog-bristle round brushes ranging from size 1 to size 8. Bristle brushes tend to leave a textured stroke. I find I use more paint when I use them.

Sable brushes are the softest of all brushes. Made of natural hair from minks or martens (a kind of weasel), they hold their points extremely well. They are known as finishing brushes because they are often used for lettering and for adding details to paintings. They also are great for blending paint.

Synthetic brushes leave a smoother, less textural mark than other brushes. They are very good for detail work, and when they get old and frayed they're great for the initial wash-in stage of a painting. I use Golden Taklon round synthetic brushes from Trekell Professional Art Supplies.

Palette knives are used for mixing paint on the palette (and also for poking into piles of paint that have begun to dry and formed a skin). They can be used to scrape excess paint off the palette at the end of a painting session. Some artists use them to apply paint to the canvas in the technique known as *impasto*.

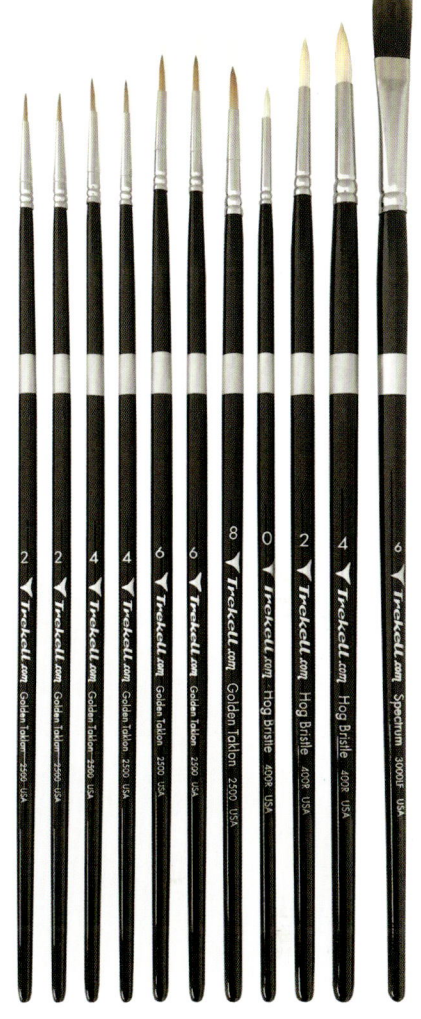

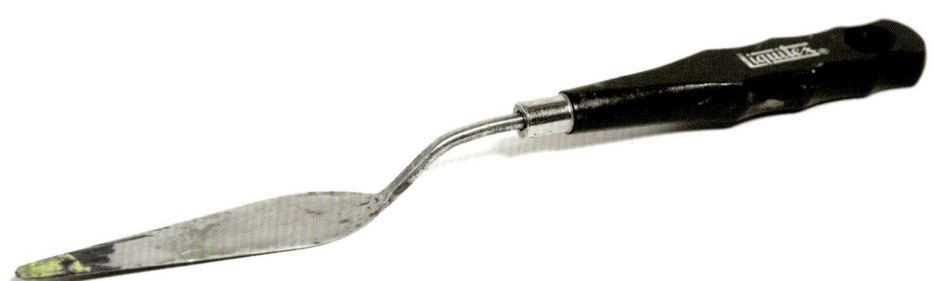

ABOVE: Trekell makes a useful starter set of brushes.

Image courtesy of Trekell Professional Art Supplies.

LEFT: Make sure you buy a palette knife whose blade is one solid piece. Blades made of two pieces welded together tend to break.

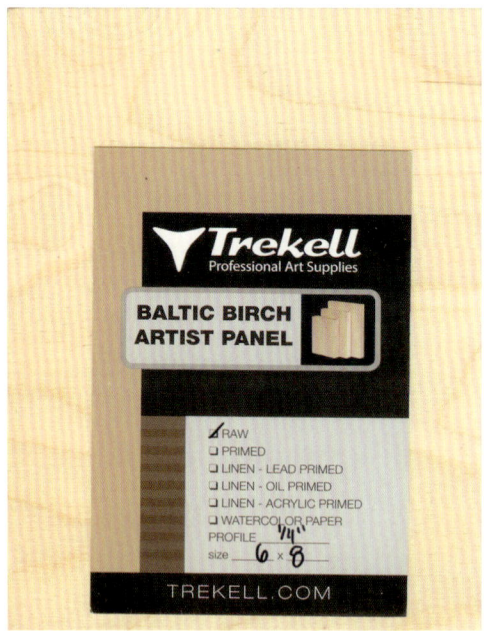

ABOVE: Raw wood panels allow you to gesso the surface yourself.

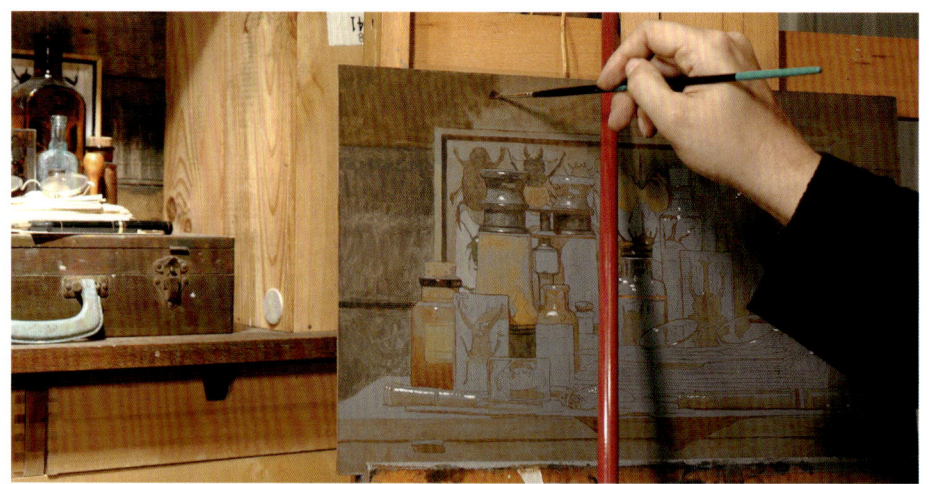

MAHL STICK

A mahl stick steadies the hand, helping you to avoid putting your hand on a wet surface when painting. You can make your own mahl stick with a dowel from a hardware store or buy one from an art-supplies vendor.

ABOVE: Here I am painting with a mahl stick, which keeps my painting hand off the surface of the painting.

Photo by Alex Archimbaud.

Surfaces

Cotton canvas and linen are the most traditional surfaces for oil painting. Canvas, however, is not a great surface for still life painting, and I recommend using linen instead. High-quality Belgian linen is best. Linen can be bought in pads (Centurion Oil Primed Linen Pads), or prestretched on wooden stretchers, or in rolls that enable you to cut pieces to your desired size for stretching or gluing on panels. Linen comes in a range of weaves, depending on whether you want a smoother surface (thinner weave) or rougher surface (thicker weave). Note: The word *canvas* is sometimes used loosely to mean any cloth painting surface, and, in fact, I sometimes use it that way in this book. But when I say "canvas," I mean *linen*.

Wood panels are readily available and fairly inexpensive. Panels such as those made from Baltic birch provide a firmer support than linen or canvas, as they won't expand or contract so much from humidity in the air. I paint on many different surfaces but mostly prefer panels. If you do choose to paint on linen, fixing the fabric to a panel is a good idea.

You can buy linen or panels that are presized and pregessoed or choose to do this yourself. Sizing and gessoing your own panels is not only cheaper, but it also gives you more control over how the surface will feel and behave. Sizing—traditionally done with rabbit skin glue but now with acrylic polymers such as Golden's GAC 100—acts as a barrier so that if the paint penetrates through the gesso, it will not infiltrate the linen or panel. If a surface is not prepared correctly, the paint will eventually eat through the surface (though this takes a very long time to happen).

After a surface has been sized, four to six coats of gesso are applied on top. Traditional oil gesso is a mixture of glue (usually rabbit skin glue), water, and chalk (calcium carbonate) that creates a flexible, absorbent surface for the oil paint. I prepare my own panels because it is much cheaper, and I can cut them to any size I want. I have sometimes mixed my own gesso, but I typically use acrylic gesso from Liquitex or Golden Paints, as it is much more convenient.

Tools for Measuring and Composing

Finding a sturdy measuring tool is very important. You can use a pencil or paintbrush for comparative measuring, but their thickness can get in the way. I prefer a thinner tool, like a knitting needle or a spoke from a bicycle wheel. For tips on measuring, see page 159.

A plumb line can be useful when drawing, as it will help you determine vertical lines. If you tie a string to a washer and just let it hang, gravity will reveal an absolute vertical line.

You can find yourself staring at a piece you're working on for so long that you can no longer see what is "off," or not working. But a mirror can help you evaluate your work more objectively. When you look at your painting in a mirror, the image appears flipped, letting you see any compositional flaws more easily.

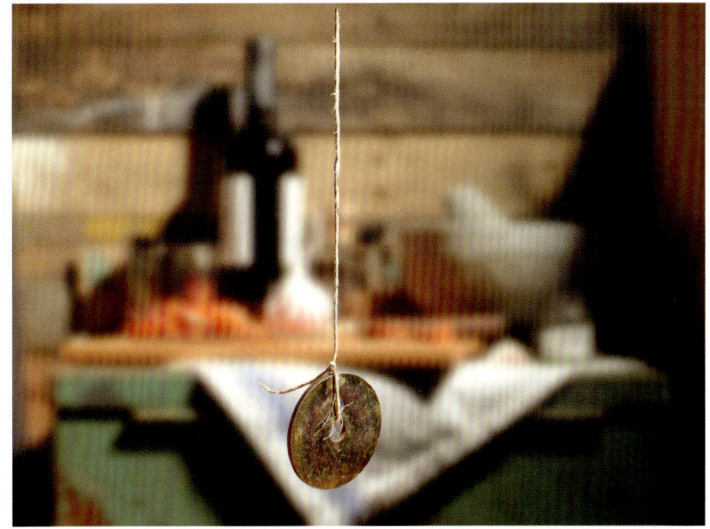

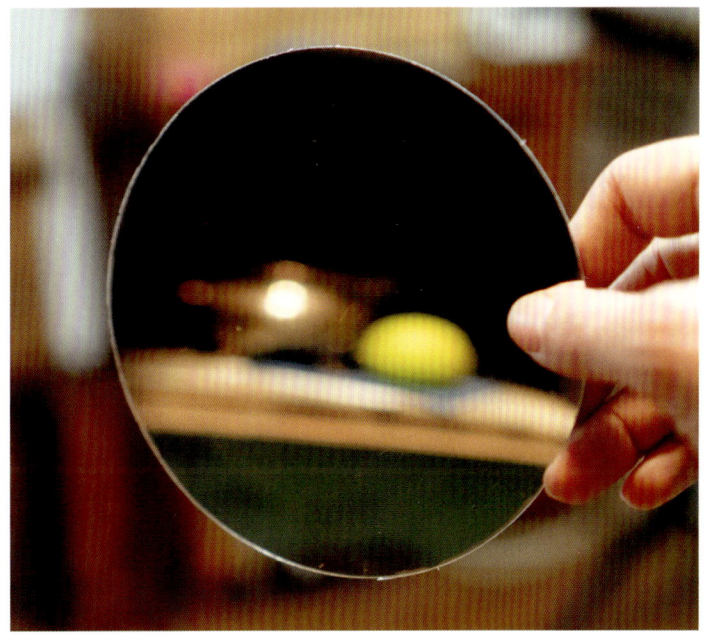

TOP: A plumb line can be made from a washer and any kind of string or twine.

ABOVE: Holding a mirror up to your painting lets you see it in reverse, helping you to look at it more objectively.

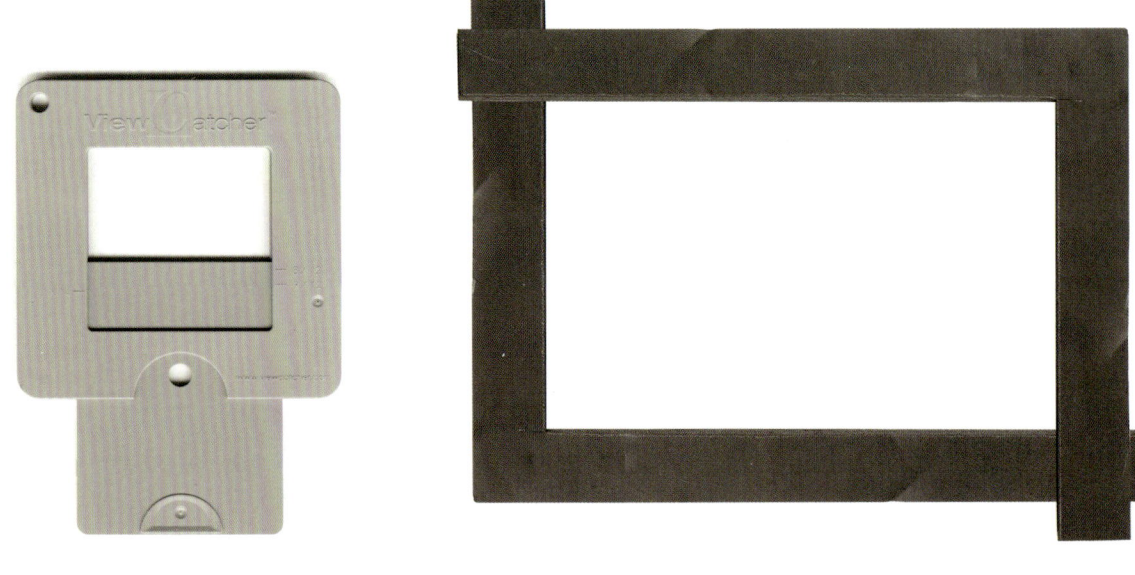

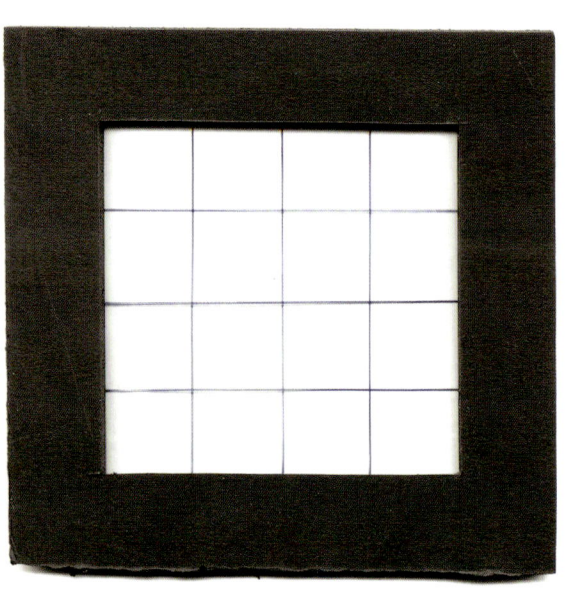

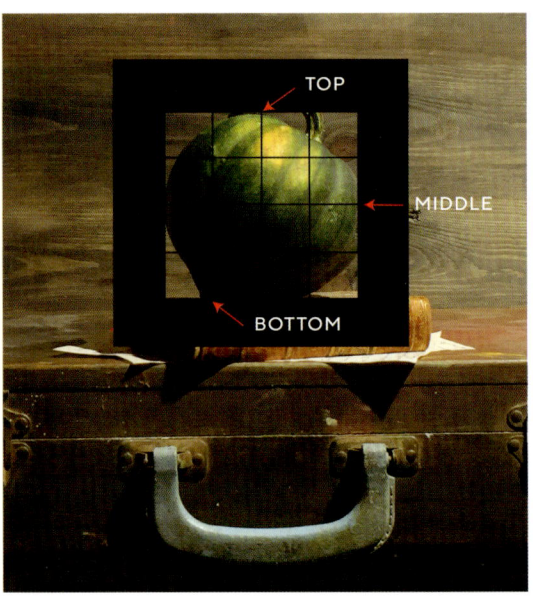

Holding a viewfinder up to your subject lets you crop the image and decide what to include in the picture's "frame" and what to leave out. You can buy an inexpensive plastic viewfinder or create one for yourself by cutting two square corners out of pieces of cardboard or foamcore (as in the photo at top right) and holding them out in front of your setup. You can move the two corners up and down and left and right to vary the proportions and to consider all different cropping options. When you find the right composition, clip the viewfinder in place and take note of the dimensions with a ruler.

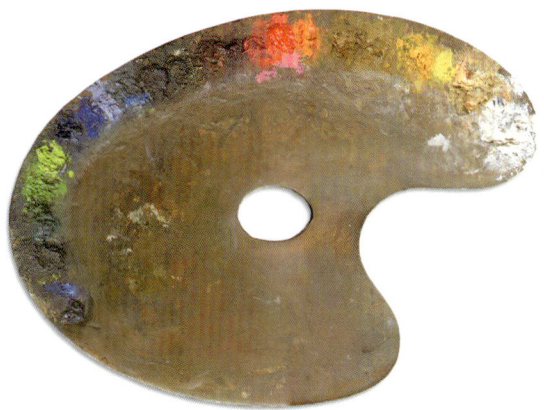
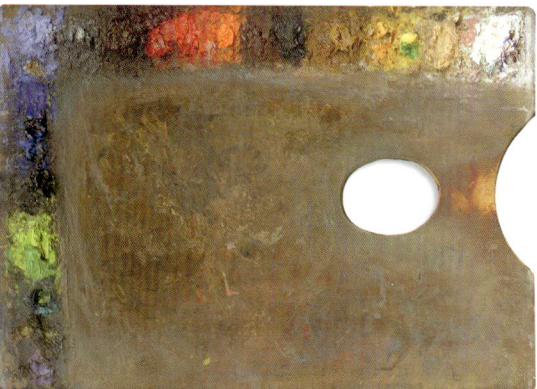
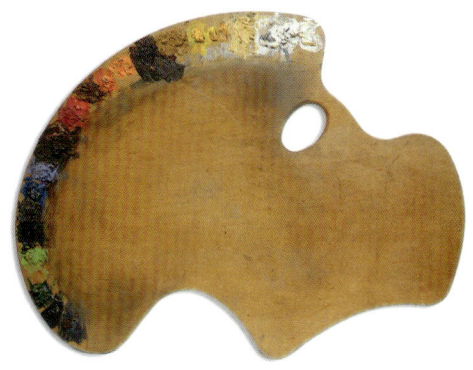

Palettes

It's helpful to have a range of different-sized palettes in your studio. When working on a small painting, I just use the palette in my pochade box because I don't have to hold it. When working larger, I grab a larger palette so I have more area to mix paint on. A larger palette also allows me to mix larger amounts of paint.

One of the most important considerations when choosing a palette is its weight. A lightweight palette won't put a strain on your muscles. Make sure your palette is counterbalanced with a weight glued to the bottom so that the weight distribution is equal. If the palette is not balanced, your arm, shoulder, and back may ache over time. The palettes made by New Wave Fine Art Products are my favorites—they're lightweight, sturdy, balanced, and attractively designed.

TOP: It's great to have a variety of palettes in different shapes and sizes.

RIGHT: Artist Dorothy Lorenze places her palette vertically just below the painting surface on her easel. Hanging your palette vertically like this lets your painting and palette receive the same amount of light from the same direction—making it easier to get values and hues right when transferring paint from the palette to the picture. Also, with a setup like this, you don't have to turn your body as your hand moves from palette to painting.

Photo courtesy of Dorothy Lorenze.

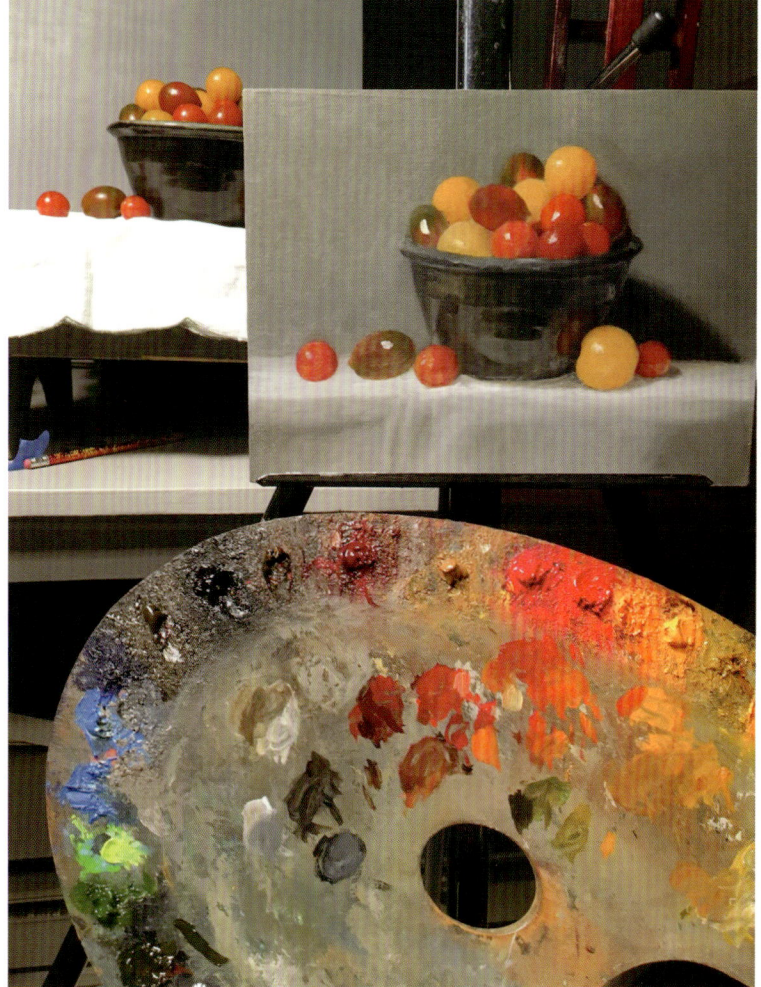

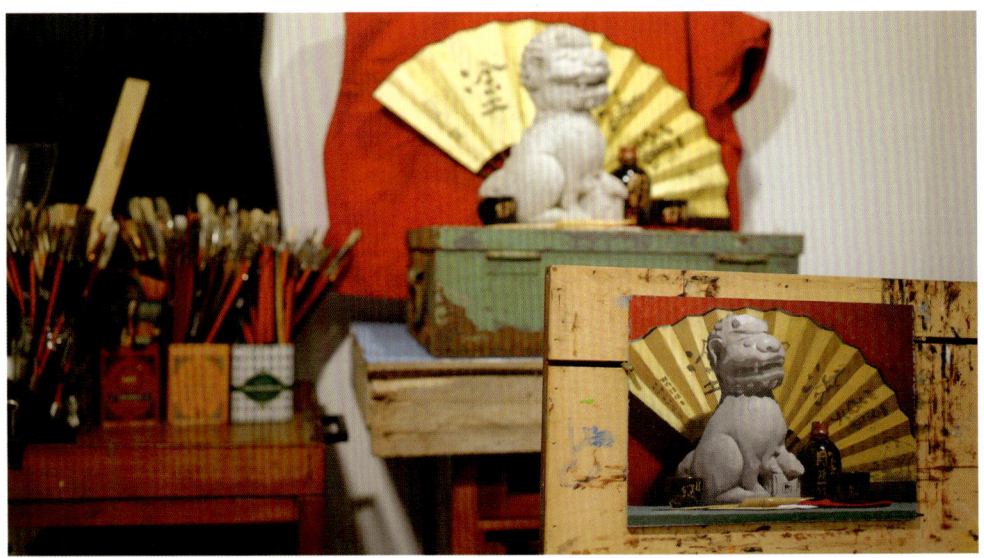

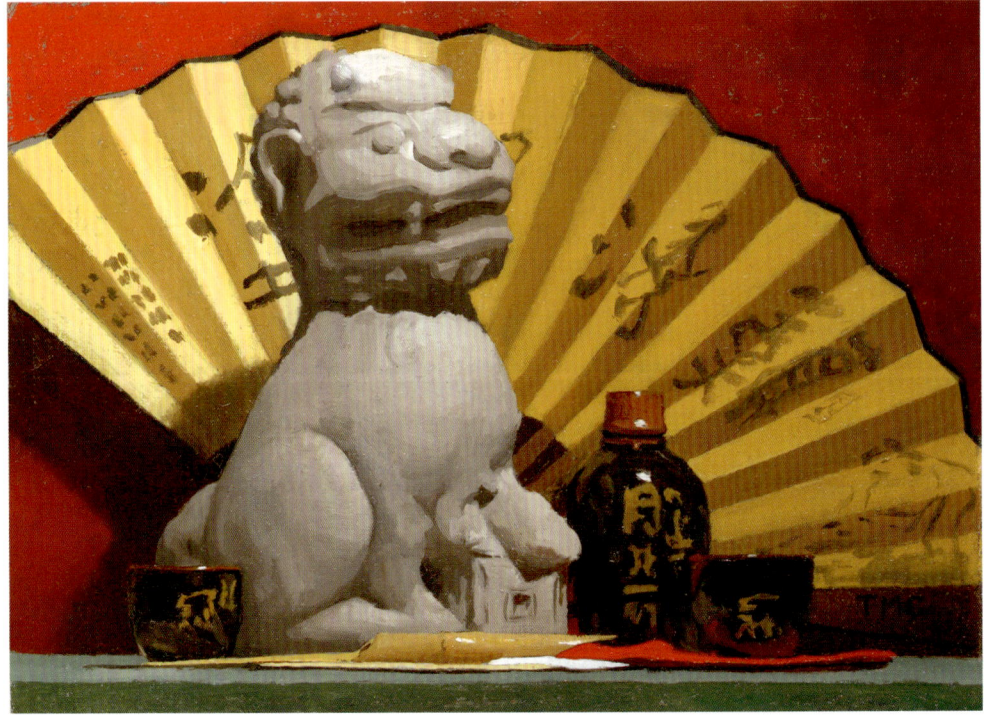

Pochade Boxes and Easels

A pochade box is a "portable studio" that combines an easel and a palette, and sometimes a compartment for supplies and a place to hold (and protect) a wet painting. The word *pochade* (pronounced poh-SHAHD) comes from French and means a rough or quick sketch or study. Most modern pochade boxes come with a tripod mount. I paint most of my small work (up to 11 × 14 inches) on a pochade box made by Open Box M.

One of the best things about a pochade box is that you can close it with wet paint inside, meaning you don't have to clean your palette all the time. The cover also protects the paint from dust particles. The drawback is that pochade boxes are rather expensive. A small, portable aluminum easel is a cheaper alternative.

For any painting over 11 × 14 inches I work on a larger wooden easel. Wooden easels are very sturdy and can hold the weight of a large panel or canvas. They're fairly inexpensive and are available from most art-supplies vendors.

Other Studio Furniture

You may stand or sit while painting—whichever works best for you. If you do choose to sit, a comfortable chair or stool is very important.

There are many different ways to store paint; I prefer to keep mine in a paint box. Paint boxes allow you to keep all your paints, palettes, and brushes in one place. The Impressionists actually painted right out of their paint boxes.

In my studio, I keep my paint box on top of a taboret—which is a small cabinet or stand designed to hold your art supplies. I keep the taboret by my side the whole time I paint, so that I can access my supplies easily.

SETTING UP YOUR STUDIO

You must have a room, or a certain hour or so a day, where you don't know what was in the newspapers that morning, you don't know who your friends are, you don't know what you owe anybody, you don't know what anybody owes to you. This is a place where you can simply experience and bring forth what you are and what you might be. This is the place of creative incubation. At first you may find that nothing happens there. But if you have a sacred place and use it, something eventually will happen.

—JOSEPH CAMPBELL

Once you have all of your materials, it's time to set them up in your studio. Setting up your studio correctly is the first step in making a successful painting. For years, I didn't understand how the Old Masters achieved such spectacular results. One of the most overlooked aspects of their success is that they understood how lighting and space considerations—for example, the distance between an easel and the subject being painted—affect perception. They set up their studios properly, and so should we.

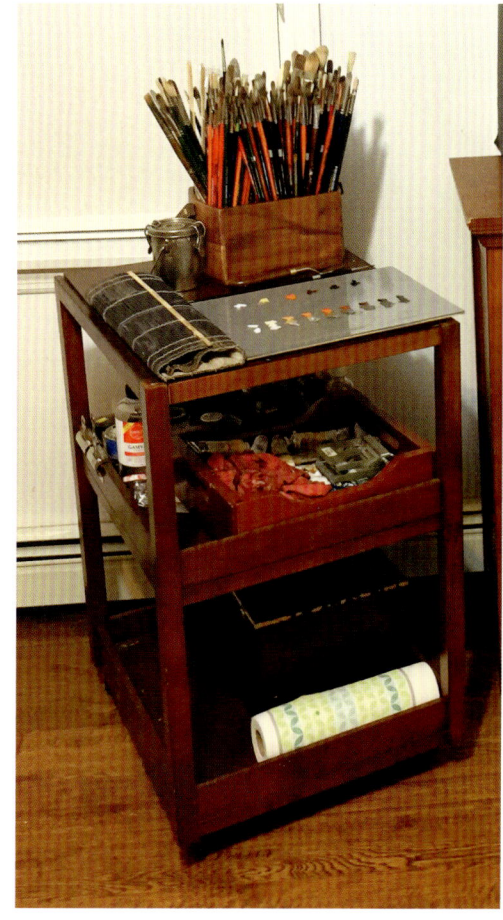

A taboret will hold all your painting supplies, keeping them within easy reach.

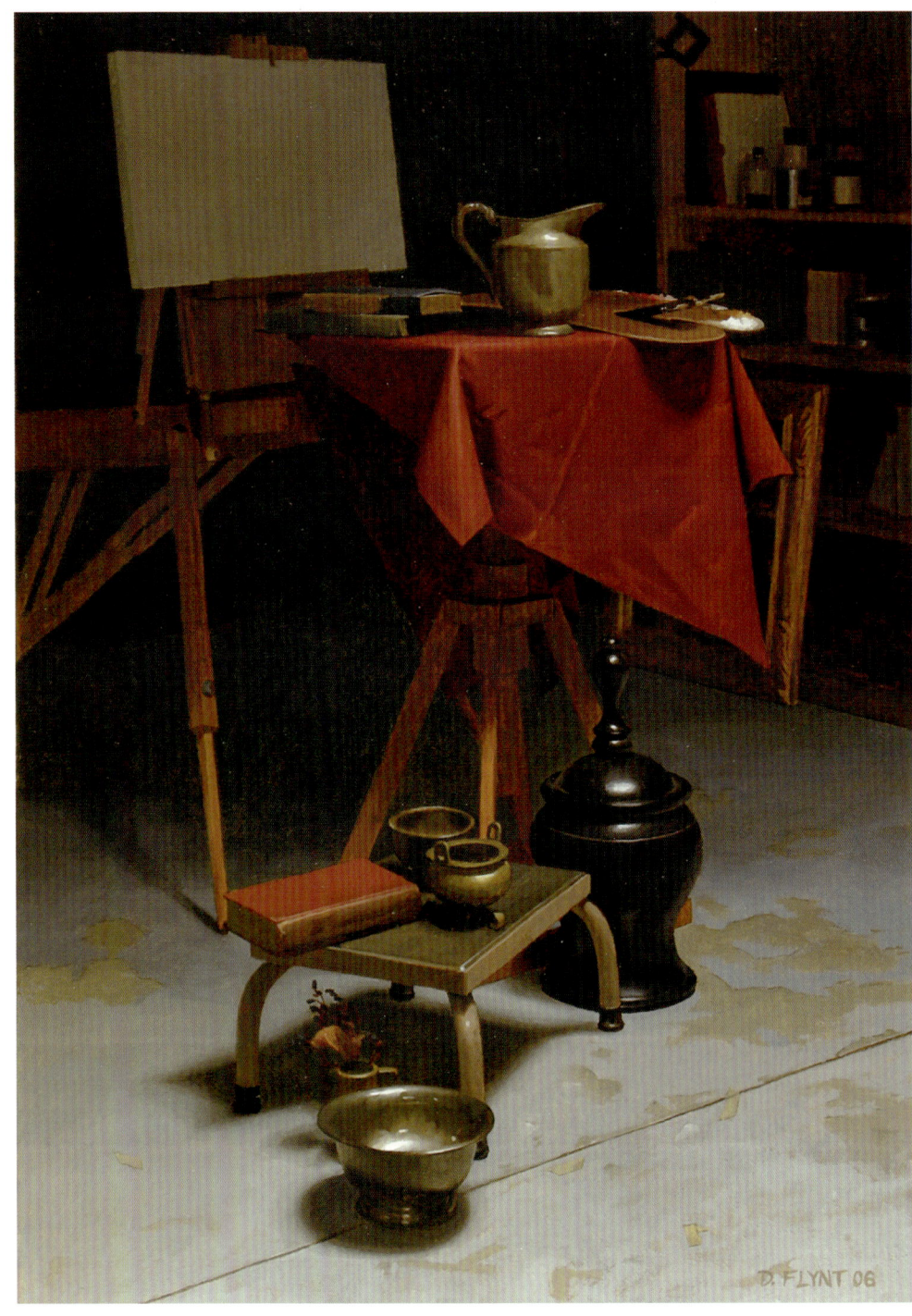

A Dedicated Space for Painting

If at all possible, you should dedicate a space for your still life painting. It can be a room in your home, a separate studio, or even a studio space you share with another artist—anywhere you're able to focus solely on your art. I strongly suggest that your studio have a door that can be closed to help you stay focused on the task at hand. I like to think of my studio as similar to a meditation or yoga space. Painting can be frustrating, since you're solving problems over and over again. The more focused you are, the more productive you will be.

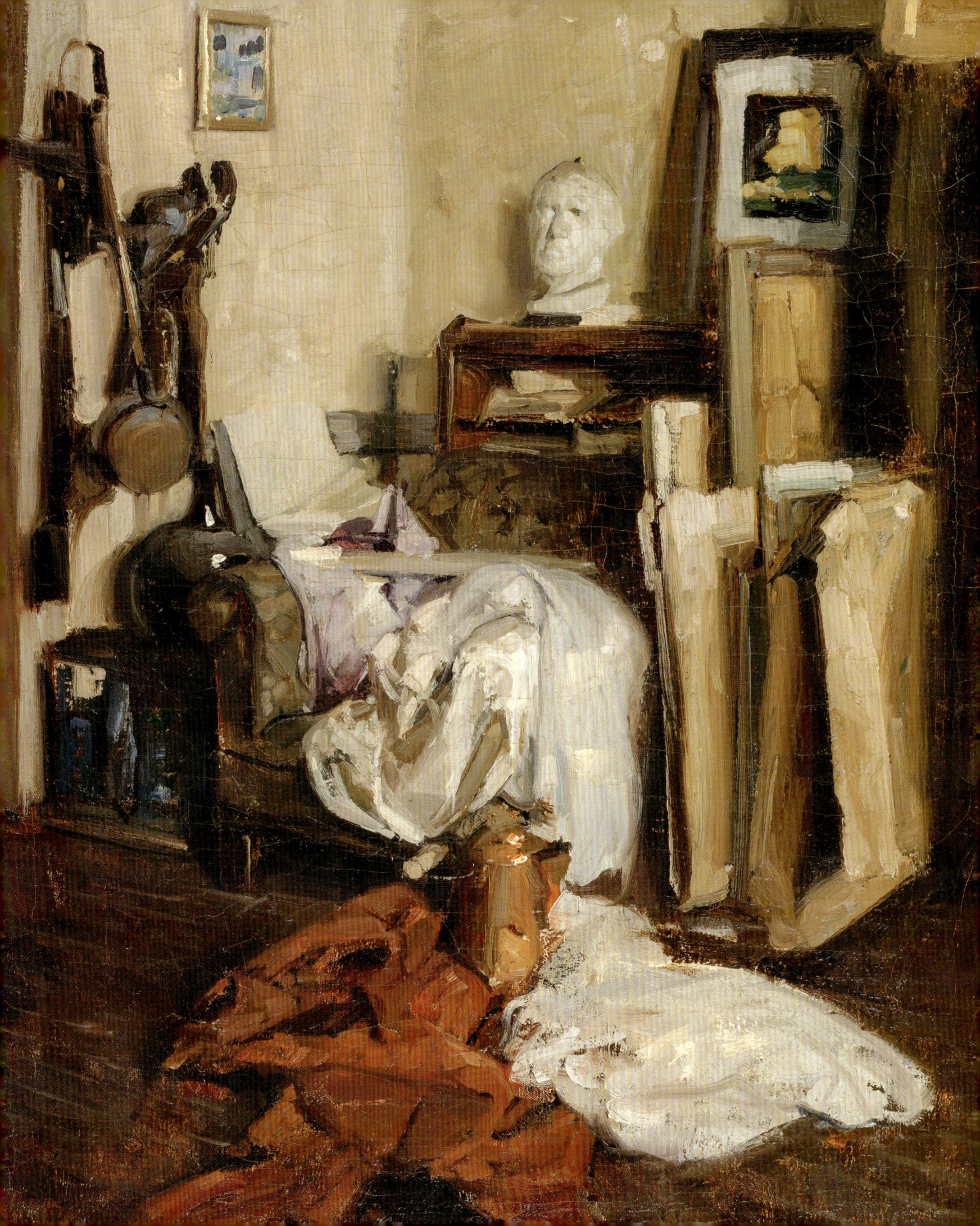

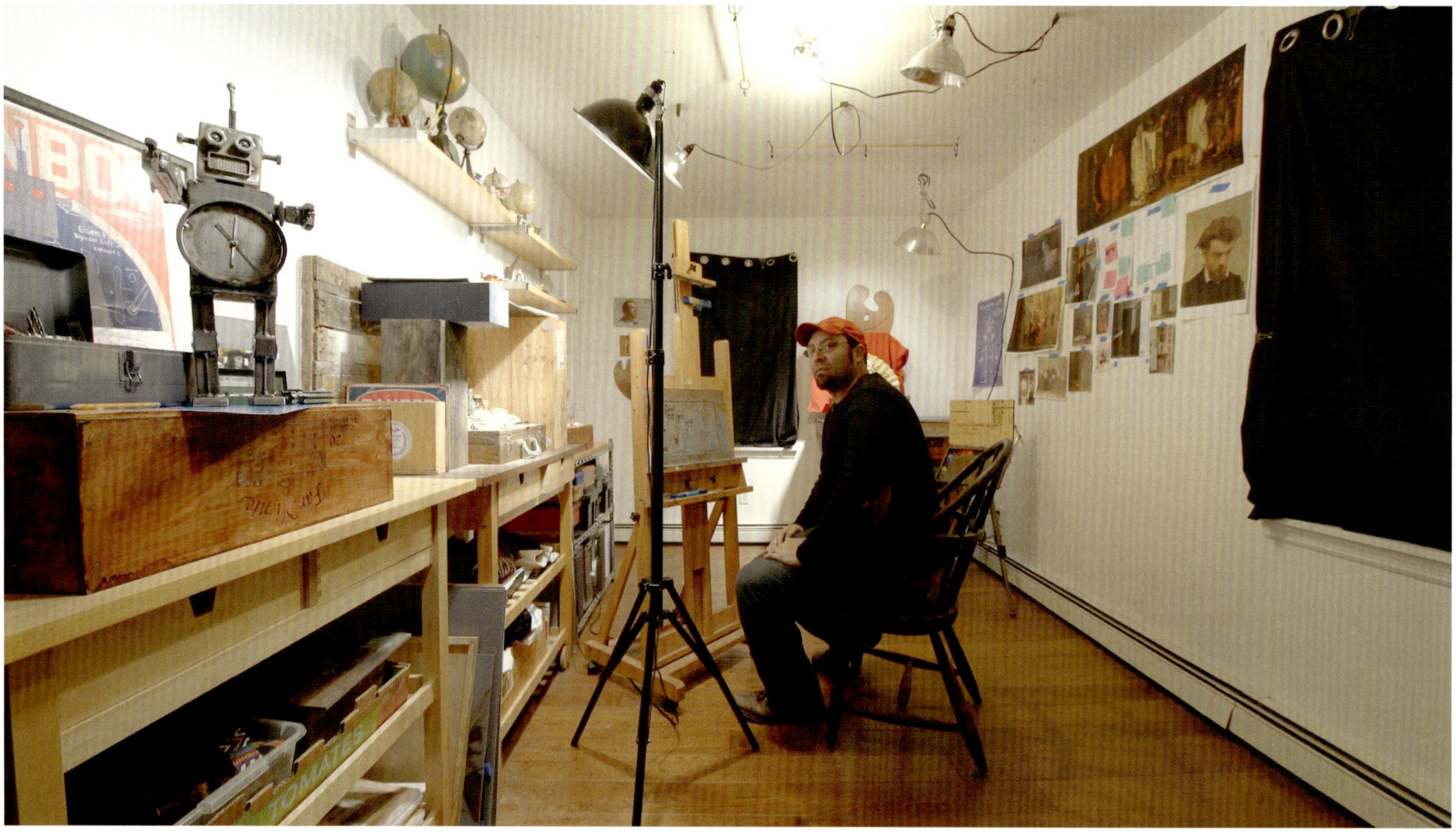

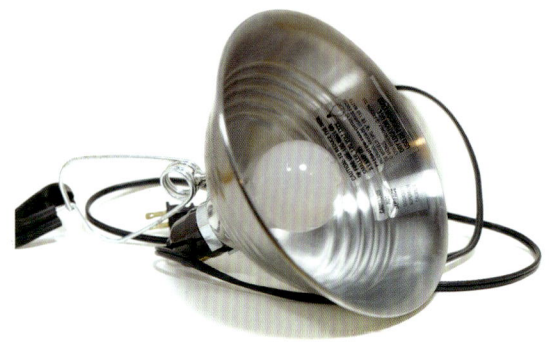

Proper Ventilation

Working with oil paints can be risky, since some paints and all mineral spirits (even the odorless ones) are toxic. So I highly recommend that you work in a well-ventilated space. At the very least, always have a window cracked or use a two-way fan that constantly circulates air in and out of your studio.

Lighting Considerations

The lights you choose and how you set them up will greatly affect your painting. If you paint in natural light, you will most likely have a single source illuminating both your setup and your easel. North light is best, as it stays more consistent over the course of the day and from season to season. It's more optimal if the light comes from overhead through a skylight rather than from the side through a window on the wall, because the shadows will fall downward instead of sideways.

If you paint under artificial light, you need to control the light as best you can. Ideally, you'll have a single light that is large enough to illuminate both your setup and your painting surface. If that cannot be achieved, I recommend using two lights, each

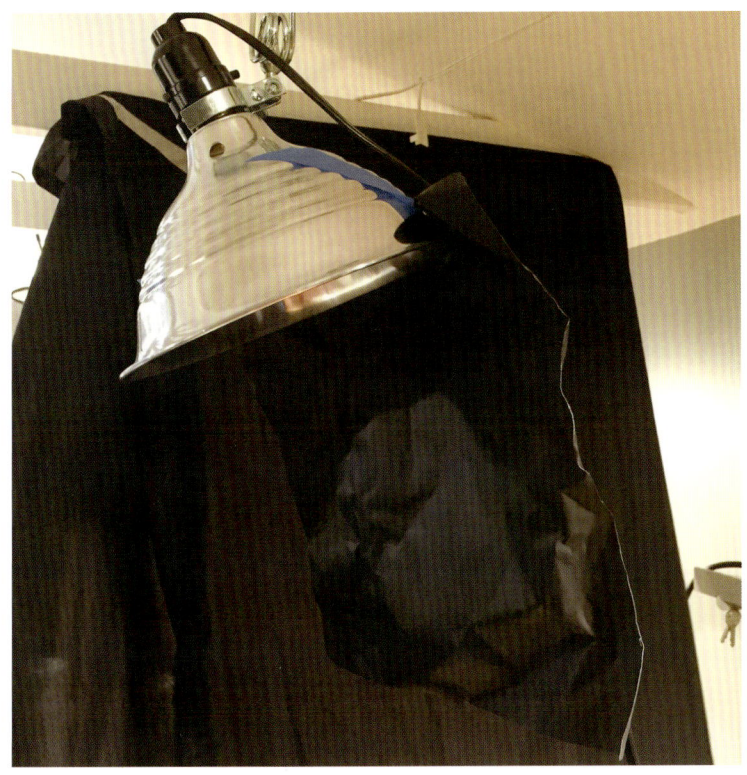

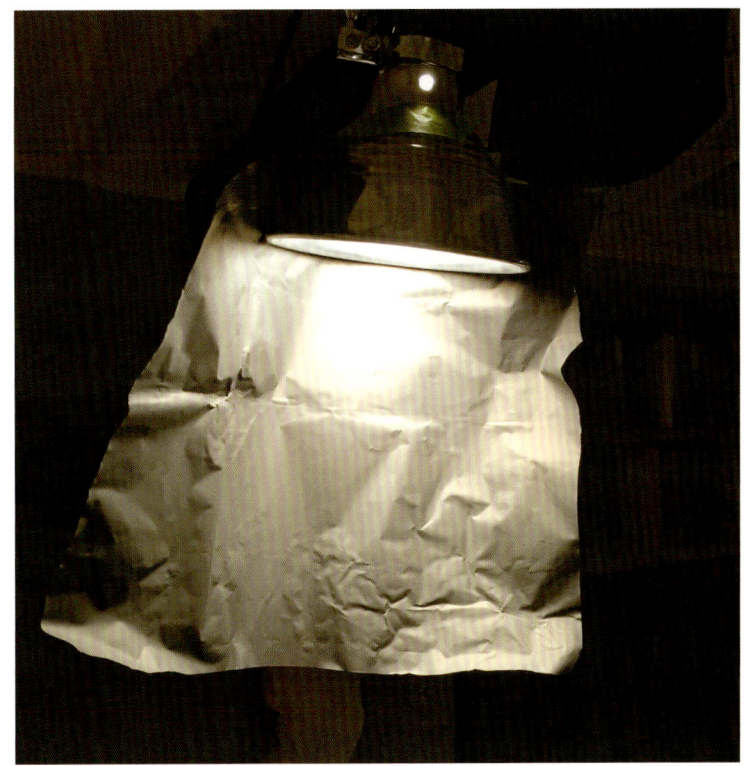

containing a bulb of the same type and wattage. Direct one at your setup and the other at your easel. The distance of the first light from the setup should be the same as the distance from the other light to the easel so that the degree of illumination is the same. Note that it is very important that the shadow of your painting arm does not fall across your canvas, because this will interfere with your ability to see what you are painting.

It is very important that you avoid raking light—light that falls on a surface and is nearly parallel to the light source. If you paint under raking light, you may almost feel as if you are working in the dark. Also, the raking light will emphasize the surface texture of your canvas or panel in a distracting way. Tipping your easel back slightly so that the light falls more directly on the painting surface will fix the problem.

If you paint under artificial light as I do, I also recommend that you block any excess light from coming into your studio. Excess light will interfere with how you perceive everything in your setup. Black foamcore boards are excellent for blocking out light. I also cover my studio's windows with black curtains.

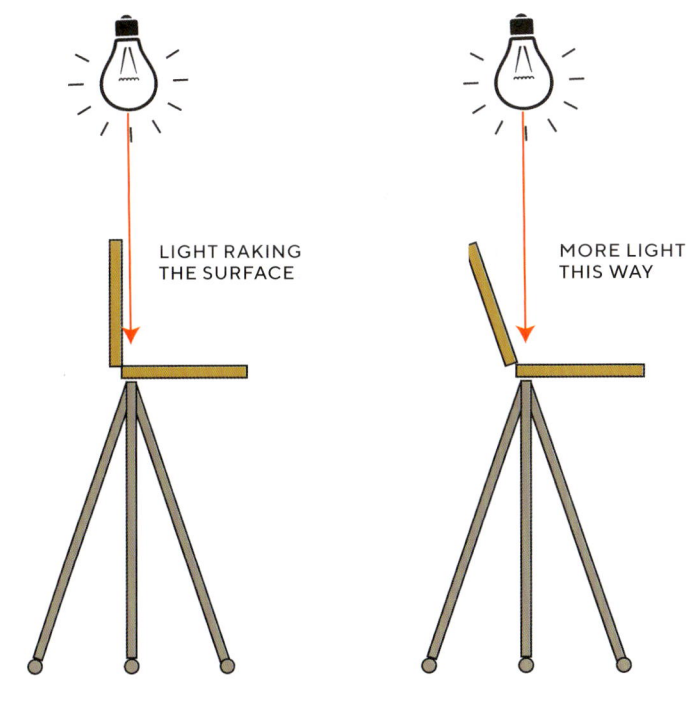

LIGHT RAKING THE SURFACE

MORE LIGHT THIS WAY

TOP: Black foil can be placed over a light to direct it where you want.

ABOVE: It's best not to place your painting in raking light, as it will make it hard to view your painting surface and will negatively affect the decisions you make.

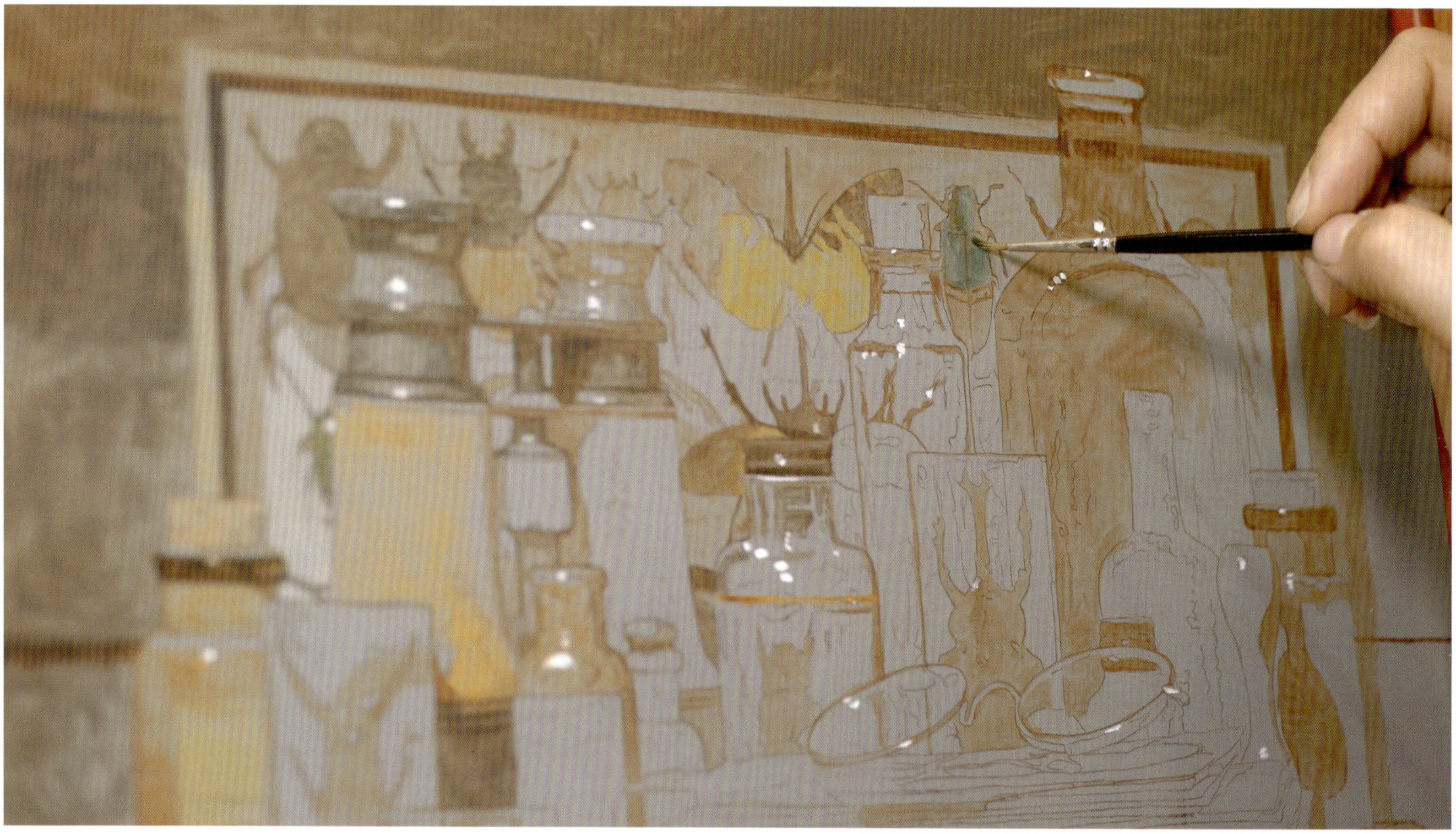

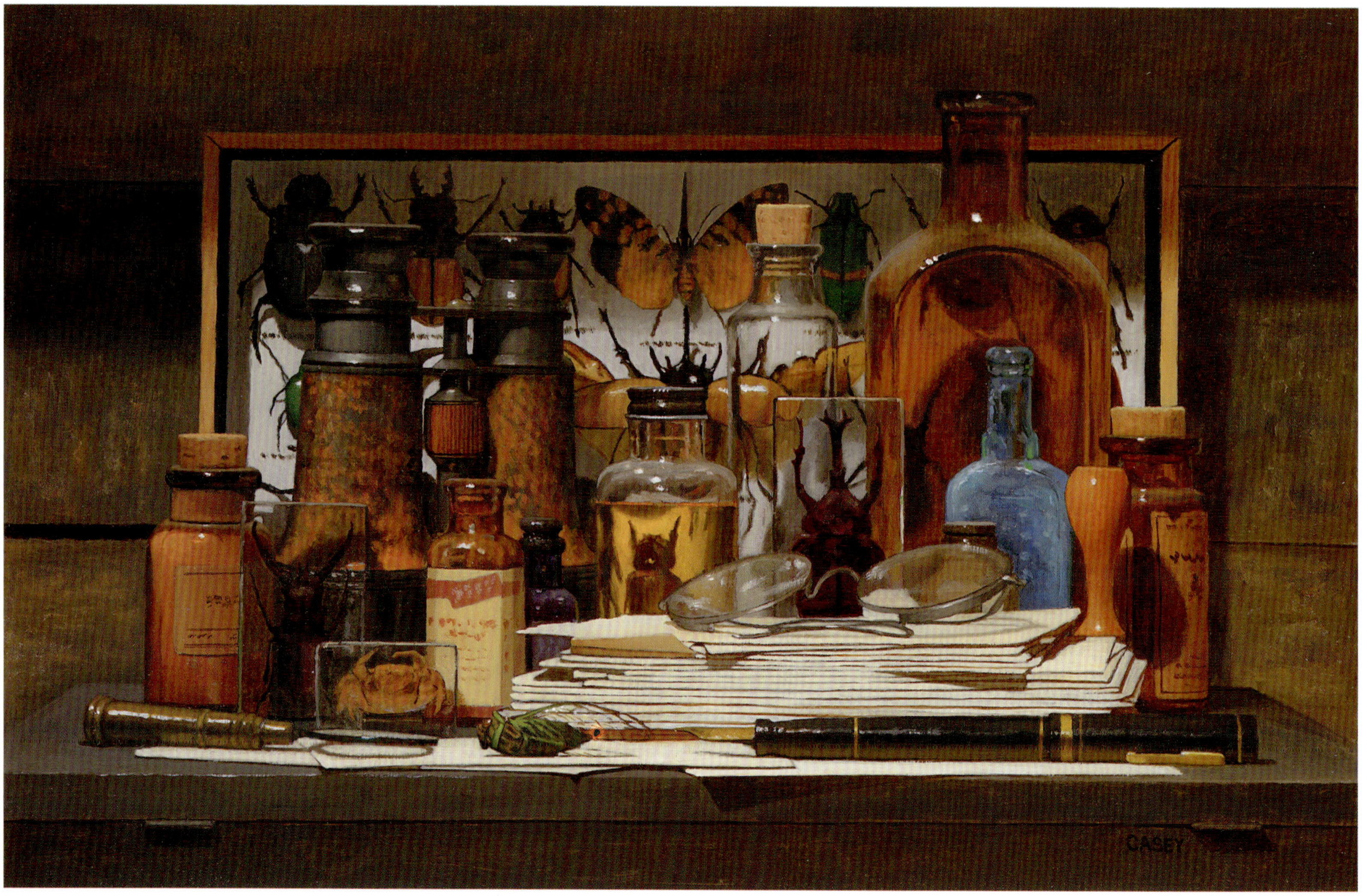
CASEY

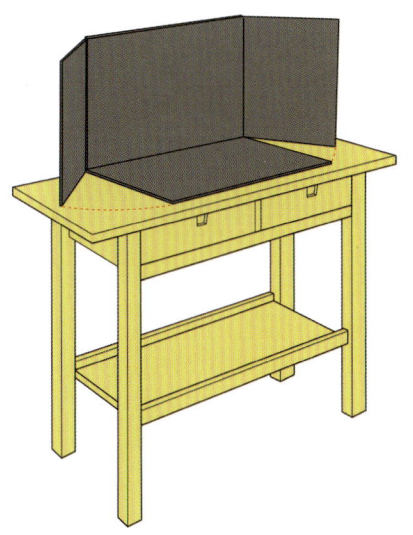

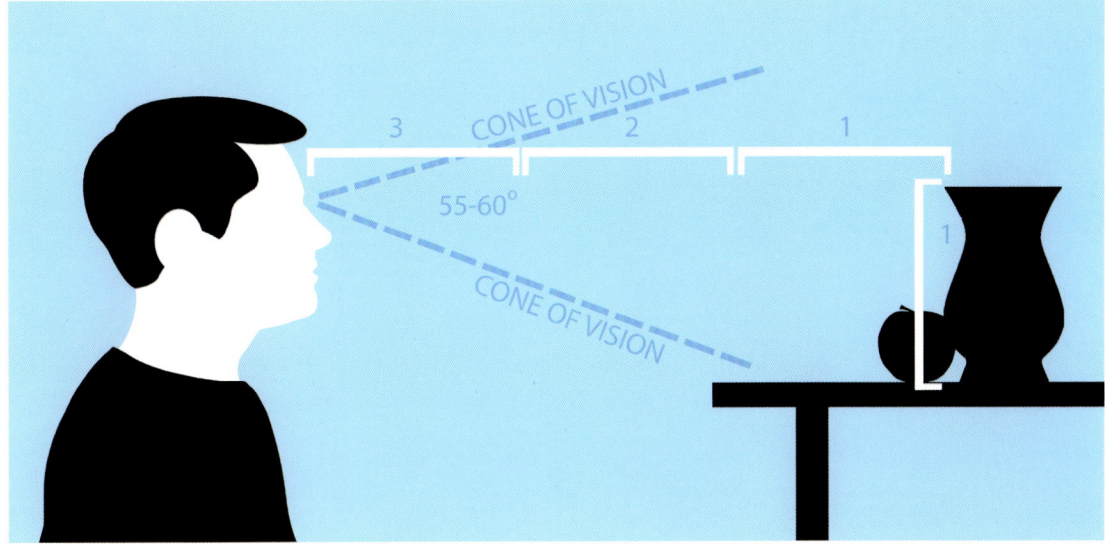

Wall Color

Everything in your painting environment affects your setup and therefore your painting. The color of your studio's walls (and everything else in your studio) will influence everything you observe. White walls reflect a lot of light, so I would at least try to tone them down a bit. A mid-gray value is recommended.

The Setup

I recommend getting a table, dresser, or a kitchen cart to devote specifically to your still life setups. If the piece has space for storing materials or props, so much the better.

If you don't control the light in your painting environment, you might have to contend with a lot of light bouncing off adjacent walls. A shadow box can help you control the light. I make simple shadow boxes out of black foamcore boards pieced together and hinged with tape.

Your distance from the setup while painting is an important consideration. If you sit too close to an object, you can't view the whole object without distortion. To avoid this, measure the height of your setup and locate yourself three times as far away. (For example, if your setup is two feet tall, you should paint from a distance of six feet away.)

One thing we tend to do naturally is to place ourselves in a position that caters to our dominant eye. My left eye is dominant, so I set my easel to my right when I paint. This allows me just to flash my eyes back and forth across the setup instead of moving my head from left to right as I paint. The more you turn your head while painting, the more you'll have to draw from memory instead of recording what you observe.

TIP

If you work under warm lights you may want to wear a cap with a bill, or visor. This will cut down on the raking light that can get into your eyes, causing them to tire. (It can also help prevent the retinal damage that can result from looking at light for too long.)

OPPOSITE, TOP: Here I am working on the wash-in stage of my painting *The Entomologist*. Notice how the cast shadows from my hand and brush fall away from the objects being painted.

Photo by Alex Archimbaud.

OPPOSITE, BOTTOM: Todd M. Casey, *The Entomologist*, 2018, oil on panel, 12 × 18 inches (30.48 × 45.72 cm). Courtesy of Rehs Contemporary Galleries, New York.

ABOVE, LEFT: Still life arrangements are often set up on a table with a shadow box.

ABOVE, RIGHT: To avoid distortion, the distance of your eye from the setup should be three times the height of the setup.

Illustration by James Decker.

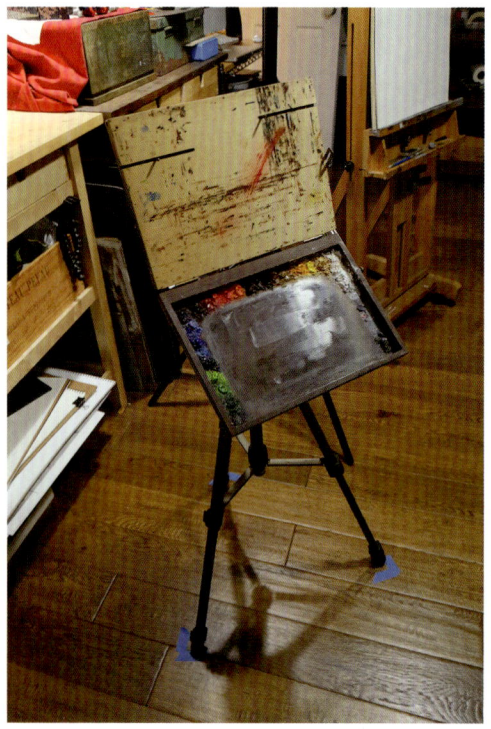

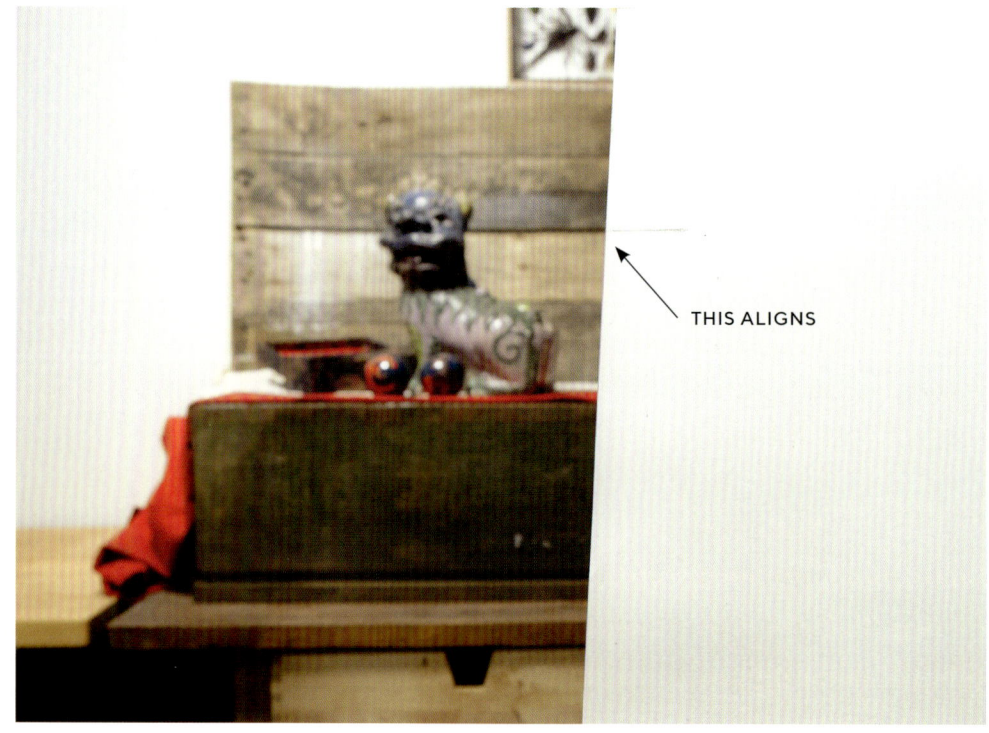

THIS ALIGNS

Since you'll be working on a painting over several sessions, you need to make sure that you return to exactly the same spot each time you paint. I highly recommend that you put tape marks around the feet of your easel and also mark your chair's position on the floor with tape. If you stand while painting, use tape to mark the position of your feet.

In addition to taping the positions of your easel and chair, I recommend aligning something on your drawing or painting with something in the setup. The position from which you paint will determine the perspective in your piece. If you move up or down, the perspective will change. Placing a mark on your paper or painting surface that aligns with something in the setup's background will get you back in the same spot each time.

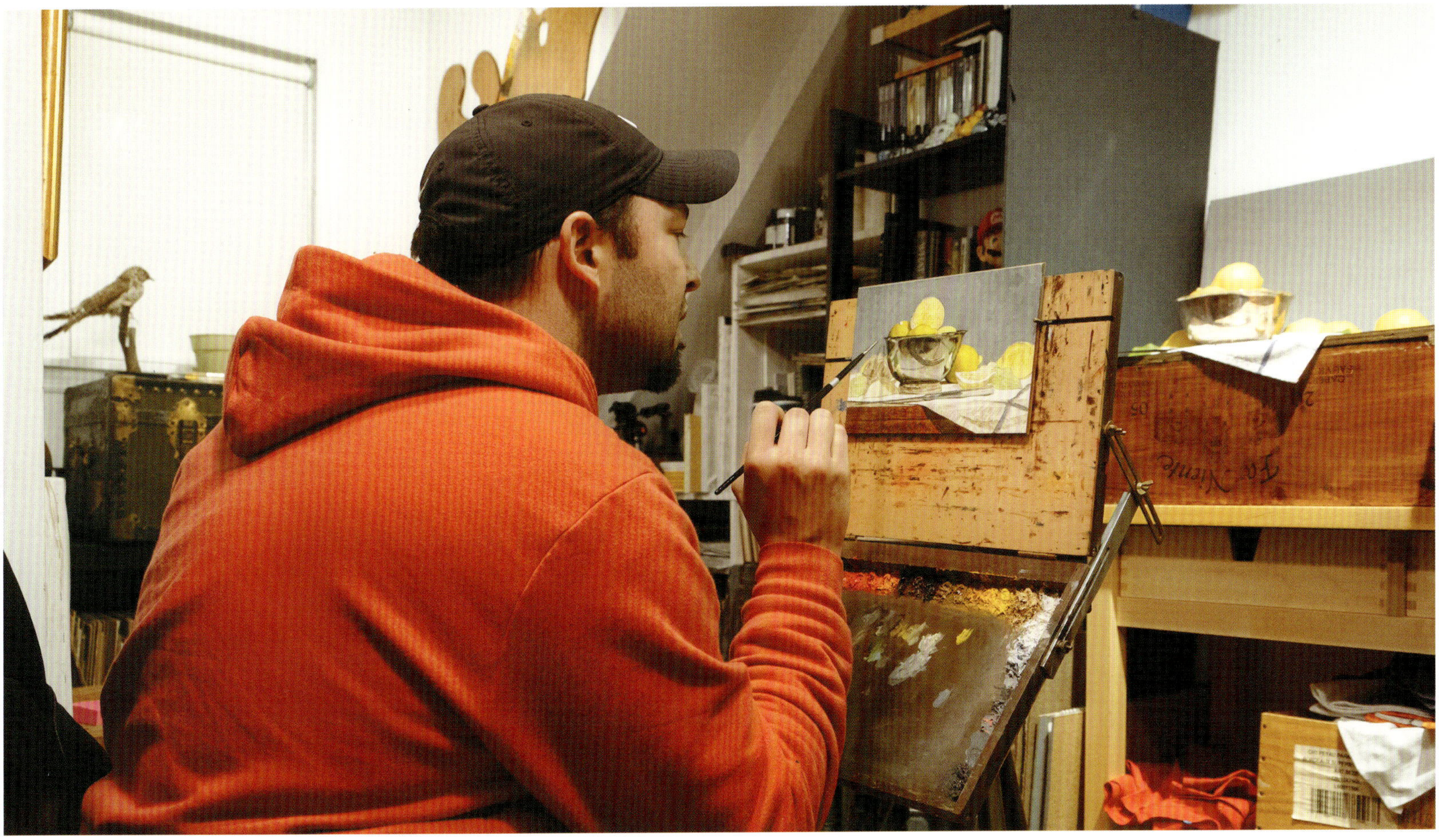

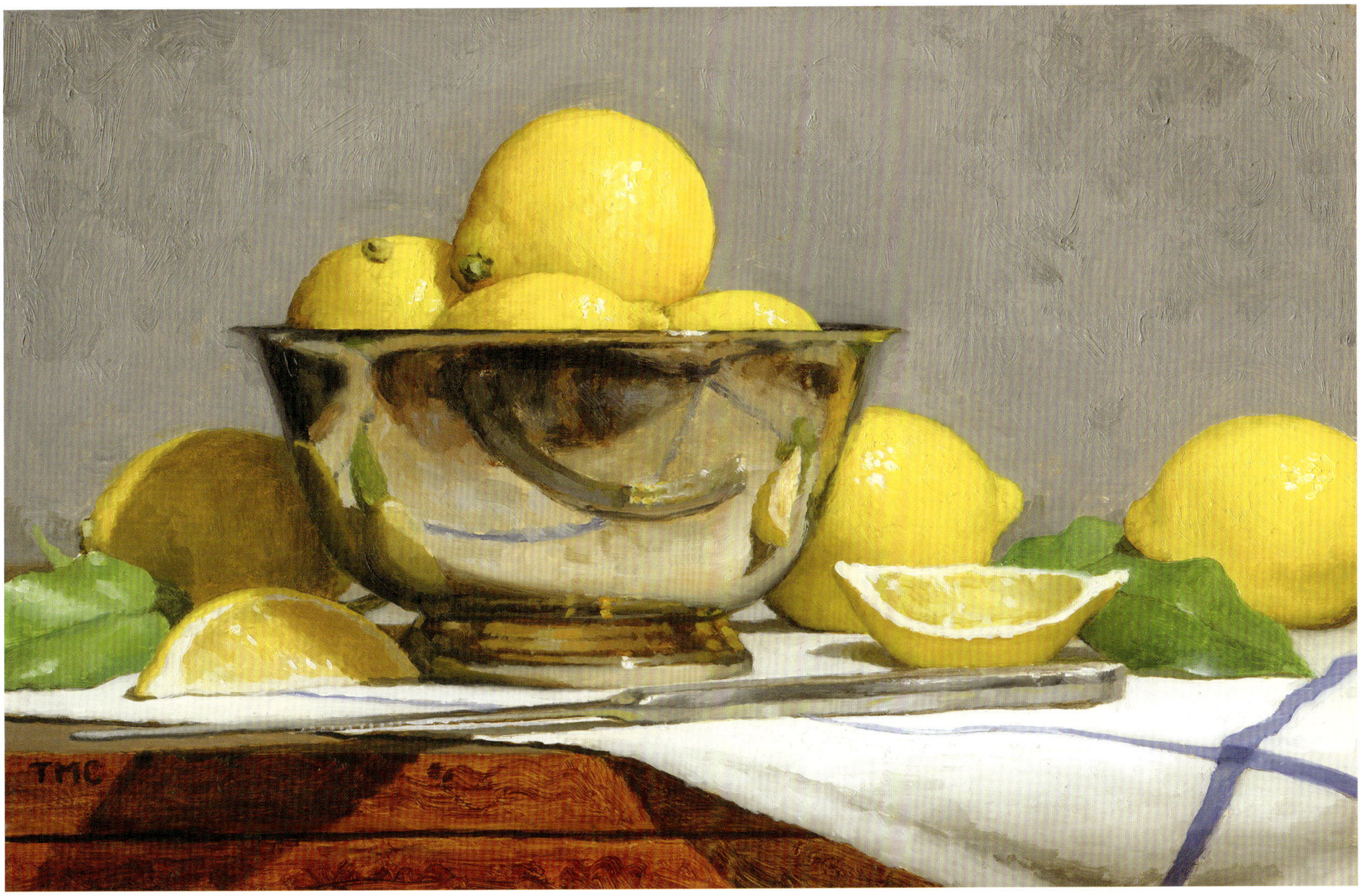
TMC

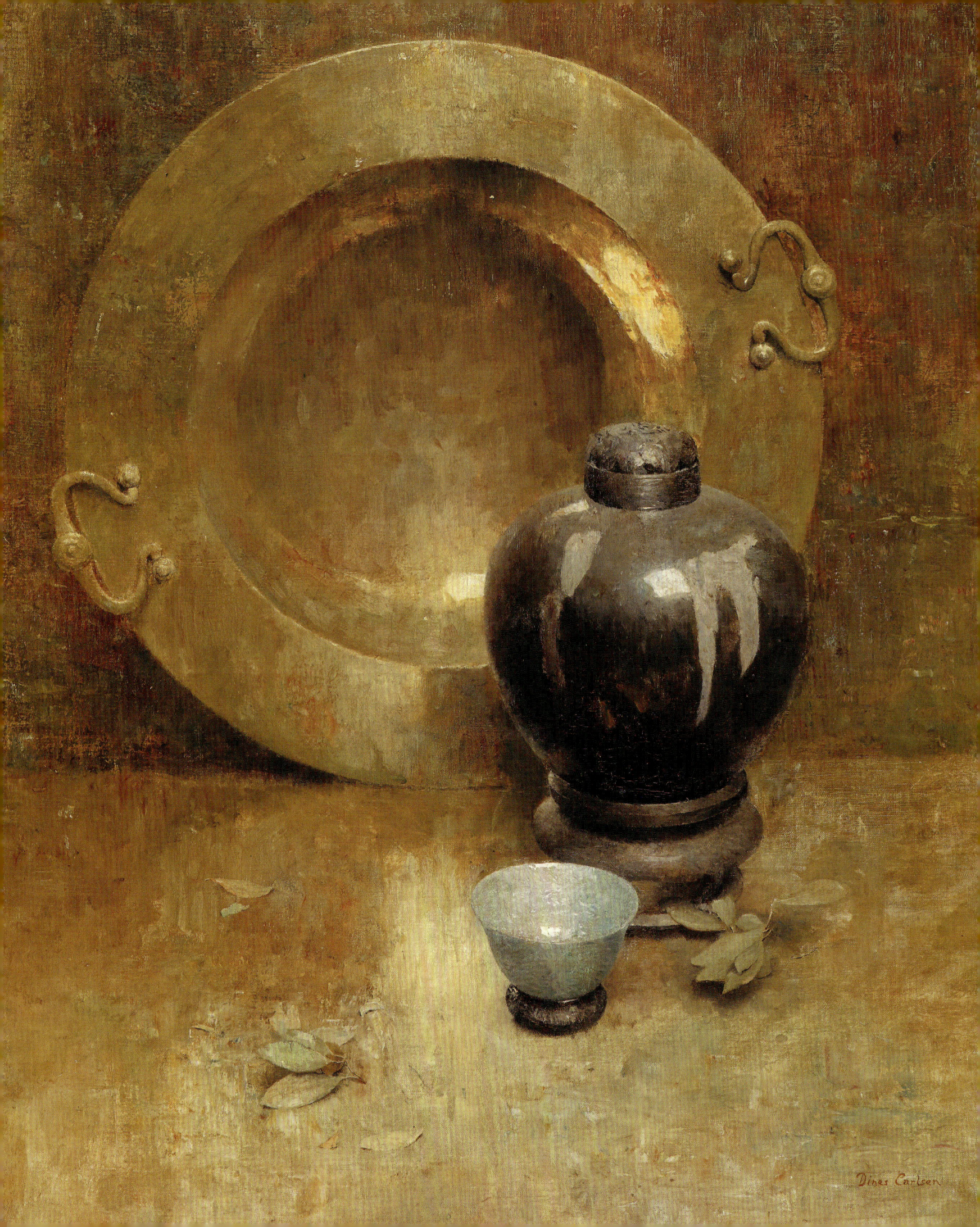

CHAPTER 2

WHAT TO PAINT: YOUR IDEA OR VISION

*What moves men of genius, or rather what inspires their work,
is not new ideas, but their obsession with the idea that
what has already been said is still not enough.*

EUGÈNE DELACROIX

Throughout time, artists have found inspiration in poetry, mythology, religion, politics, and everyday life. Some paintings feel timeless, while others define their time with the objects depicted.

Most still life paintings show an arrangement of objects sitting on a table or other surface. The great Dutch still life painters of the seventeenth century focused on displays of objects that celebrated wealth. (The Dutch word for this genre, *pronkstilleven*, means "ostentatious still life.") In French, the still life is referred to as *nature morte*, or "dead nature."

Objects can have a deep meaning that resonates with the artist and audience. We interact with objects throughout the day, and we often surround ourselves with things of personal interest. But unfamiliar objects can also attract us: you may walk by something that grabs

OPPOSITE: Dines Carlsen (American, 1901–1966), *The Jade Bowl*, c. 1919, oil on canvas, 35 ¼ × 30 ½ inches (89.53 × 77.47 cm). The Indianapolis Museum of Art at Newfields. Gift of the Friends of American Art, 20.140.

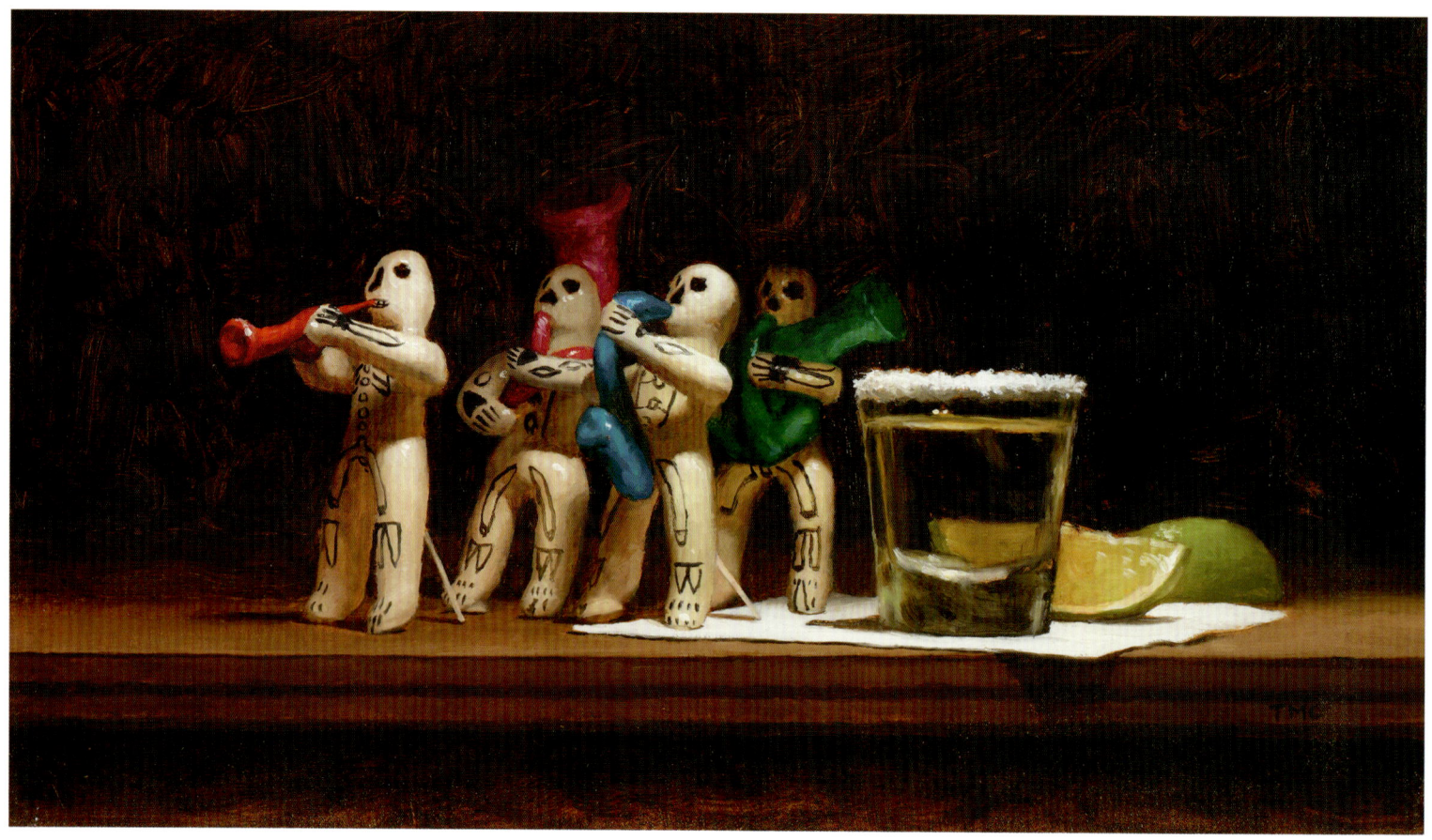

ABOVE: Todd M. Casey, *Where Inspiration Often Begins*, 2016, oil on panel, 7 × 12 inches (17.78 × 30.48 cm). Private collection.

your attention without your knowing why. You should therefore always be on the lookout for inspiration.

In this chapter, we will look at the question of what to paint and how to find inspiration. I'll show you some common subjects and themes and then give you some tips for working out your ideas. I'll also offer some ideas on how to be continually inspired.

COMMON STILL LIFE SUBJECTS

Deciding what to paint is an essential step in the process of image-making. It's crucial that you be interested in the objects you are painting. If they are not that interesting to you, you may not see the painting through to the end—or you won't feel the need to do a great painting. Finding the right objects to paint is therefore very important to keeping the artist—and, ultimately, the viewer—interested in the painting.

The world is your oyster, and there is no wrong thing to paint. But there are so many different subjects to consider that making a decision can seem overwhelming. Some painters choose to tell stories with their paintings, while others choose to depict objects with powerful symbolic meanings or simply to document the objects in their lives. But the choice doesn't have to be all that intentional—sometimes you might stumble onto a setup that just *has to be* painted.

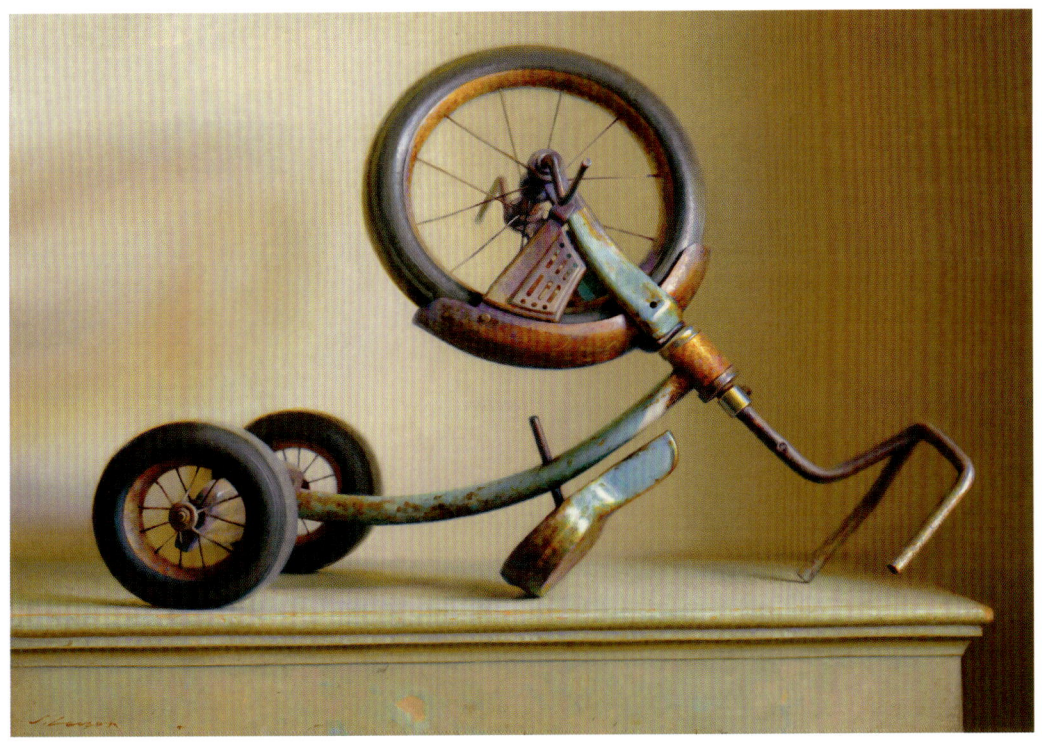

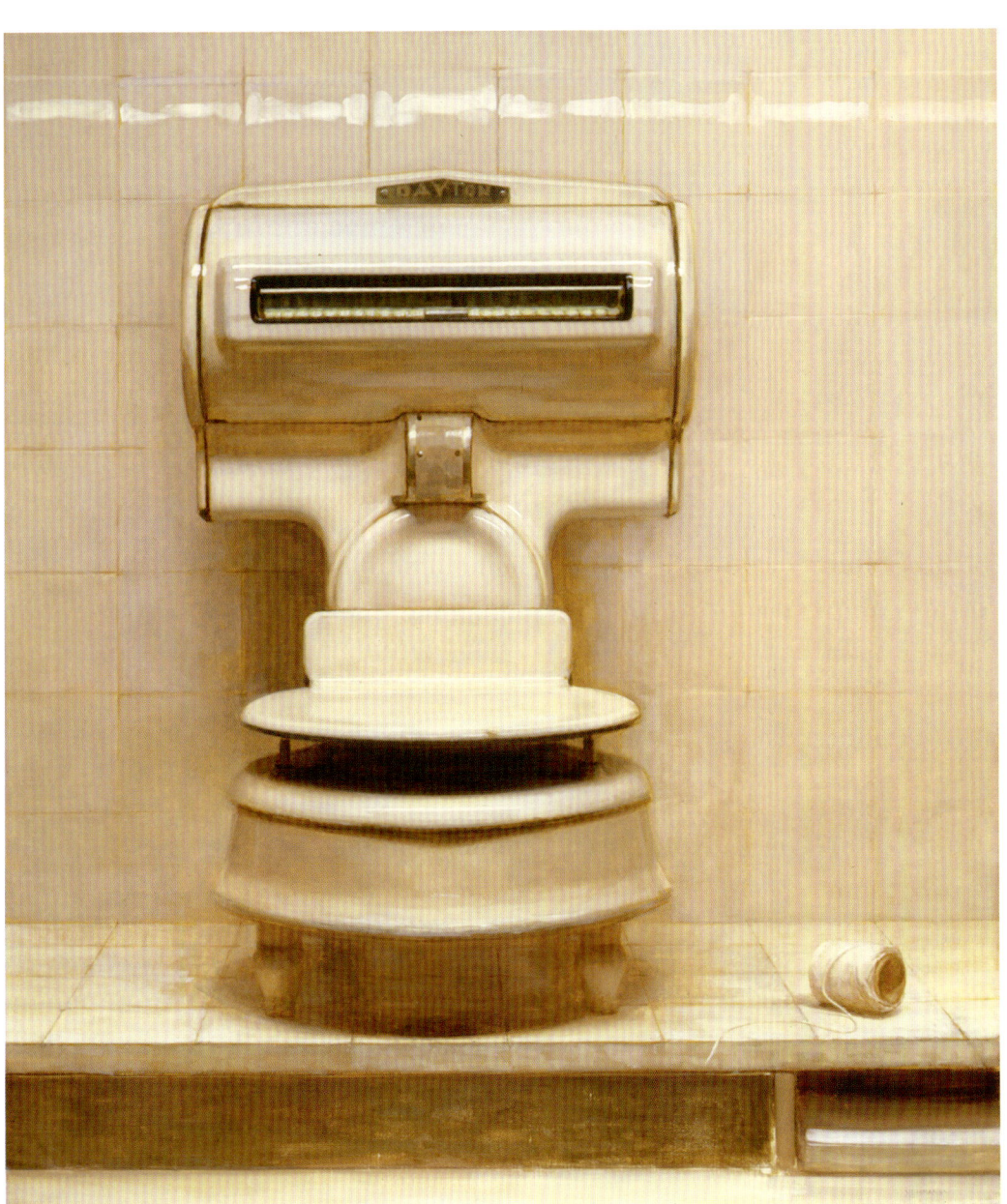

TOP: Jeffrey T. Larson, *Inner Child,* 2018, oil on linen, 30 × 42 inches (76.2 x 106.68 cm). Courtesy of the artist.

In Jeffrey Larson's painting, a child's tricycle has been turned upside down and placed on a chest. Focusing on a single thing in a painting forces the viewer to consider the poetry of a simple object.

LEFT: Kate Lehman, *The Scale (White),* 2003, oil on canvas, 34 × 28 inches (86.36 × 71.12 cm). Courtesy of the artist.

You might be inspired by any sort of object in any sort of setting, as Kate Lehman was for her painting *The Scale.*

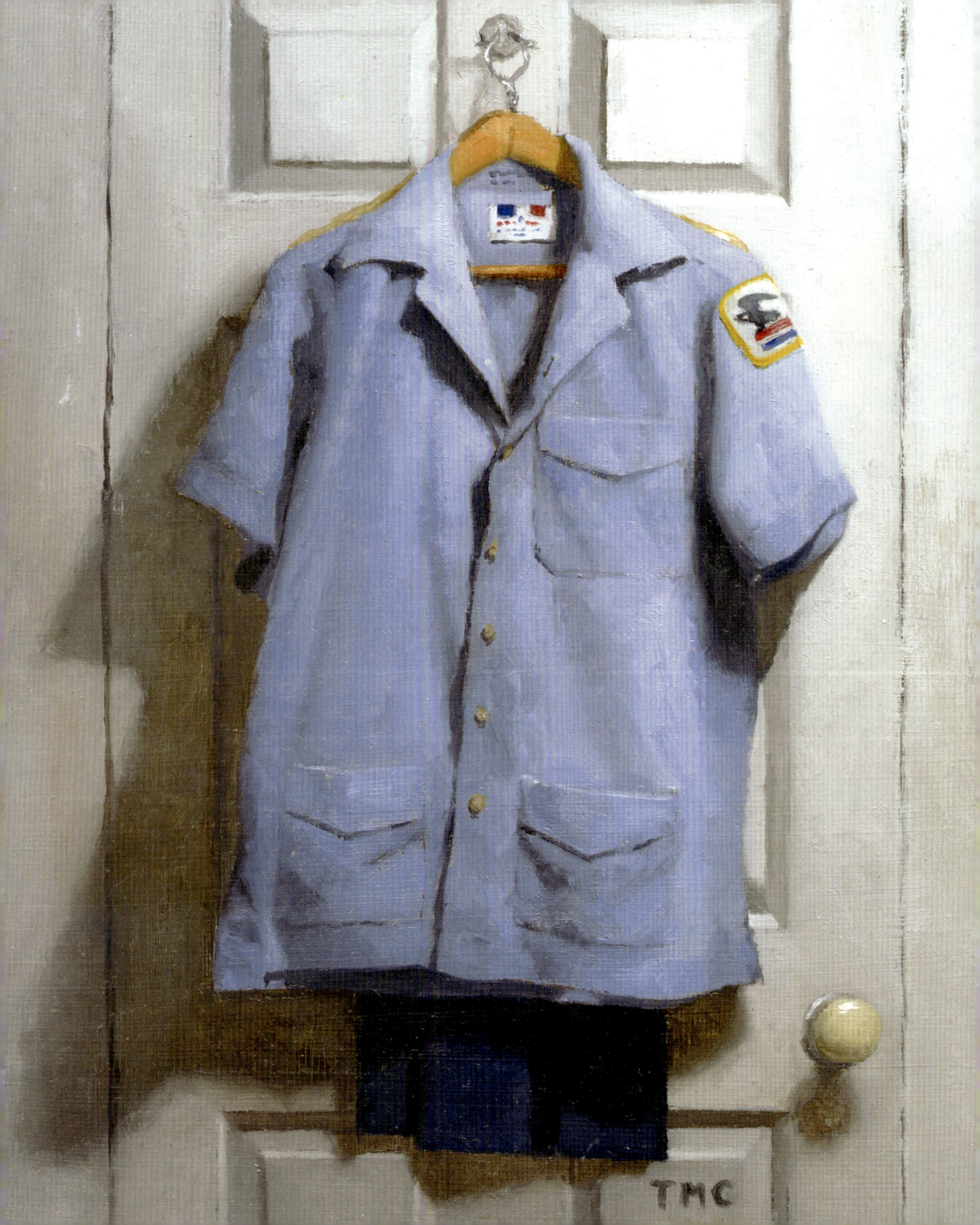

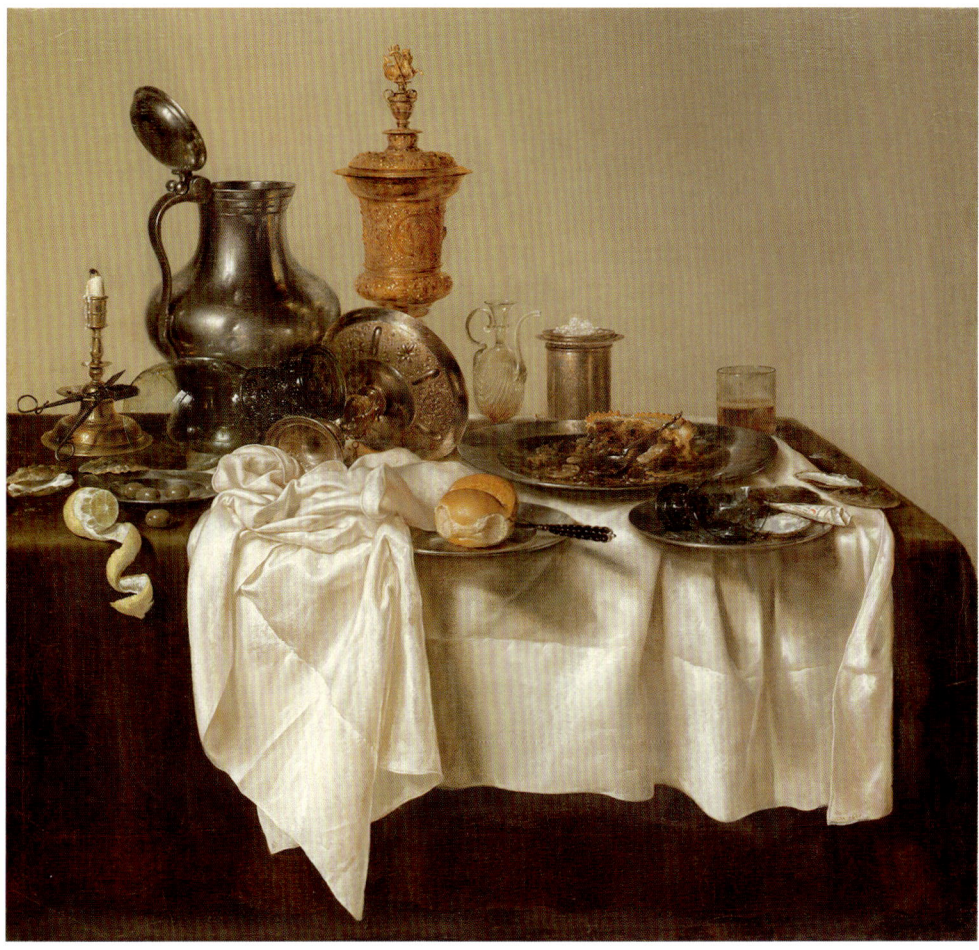

Historically, many painters have been interested in certain kinds of subjects, including nonorganic inanimate objects like books, bags, drinking glasses, plates, bottles, and cutlery. Such objects are perfect for both beginners and advanced still life painters because they don't move or change, so you can take as much time as you need to paint them.

Clothing and drapery are also traditional subjects. Sometimes clothing can have a deep personal meaning, since we are often defined by the clothes or uniforms we wear. But fabric can also provide a fluid line that can carry the viewer's eye through the composition. A cloth can even be the focal point of a painting, as in the Dutch master Willem Claesz. Heda's *Banquet Piece with Mince Pie*, above.

Food is also a perennially popular subject of still life painting. Sometimes fancy foods like lobsters or oysters are depicted, showing off the high social status of the artist or the people who commissioned the work. But humbler, more common foods like fruits and vegetables are often painted, too.

Food can be used compositionally to add color to a painting. And the shapes of many fruits and vegetables are simple forms similar to spheres and cones, giving the beginning still life painter a great place to start. But there's a problem with using fresh food as your subject: it's perishable. So you should definitely consider whether the fruits, vegetables, or other foods you want to paint will rot quickly or slowly. The

TIP

Remember, less can be more when painting inanimate objects.

OPPOSITE: Todd M. Casey, *Dad's Uniform— Spring,* 2017, oil on panel, 8 × 6 inches (20.32 × 15.24 cm).

ABOVE: Willem Claesz. Heda (Dutch, 1594–1680), *Banquet Piece with Mince Pie,* 1635, oil on canvas, 42 × 43 ¾ inches (106.7 × 111.1 cm). The National Gallery of Art, Washington, D.C. Patron's Permanent Fund.

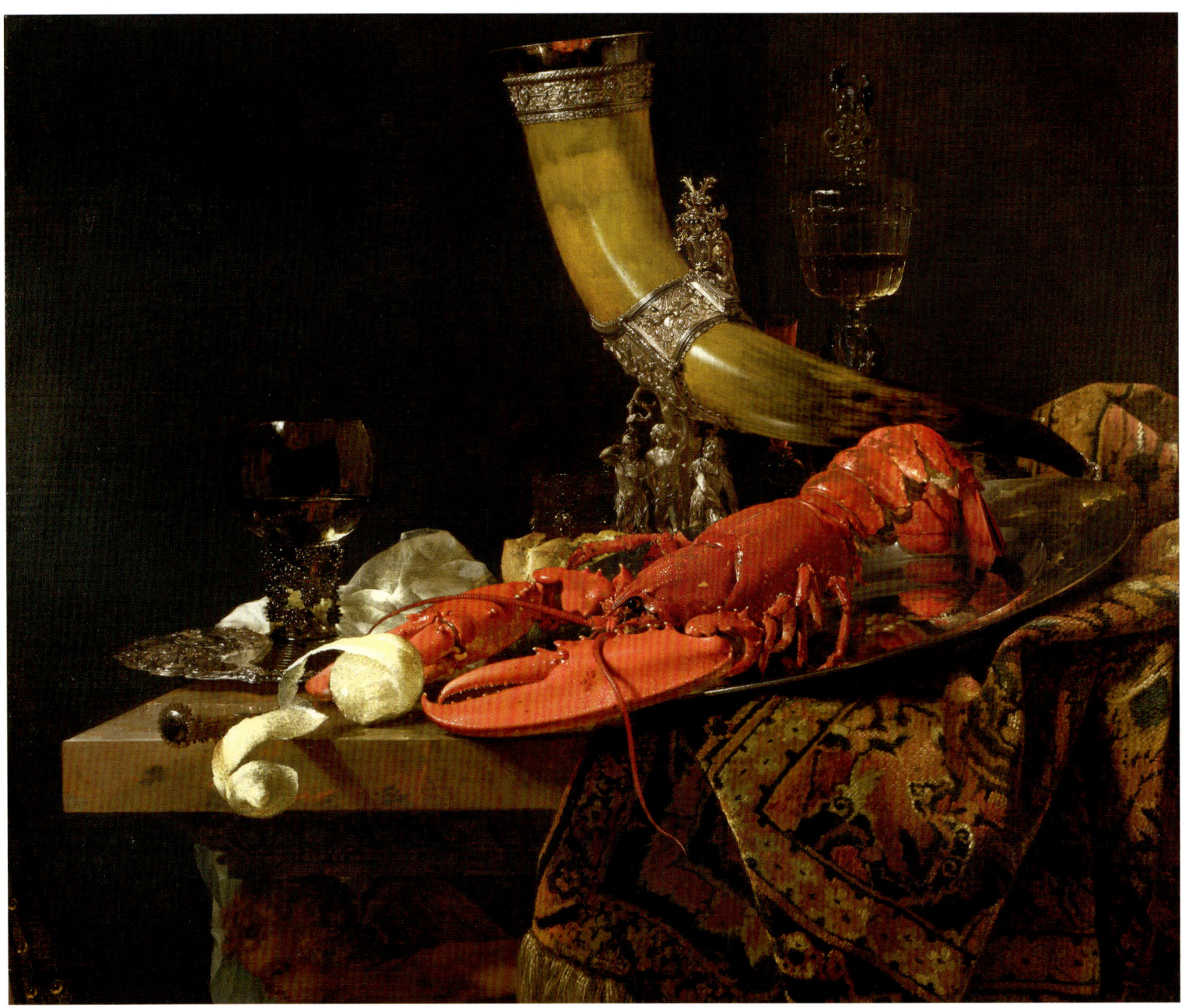

winter gourds (cucurbit family)—including pumpkins, butternut squash, and acorn squash—are great for painting sessions that stretch over several days because they decay very slowly. Lemons and limes decay fairly slowly, too. But some fruits, like figs and berries, begin to rot much faster. And when you slice open a fruit like an apple or avocado, it will begin to oxidize and turn brown very quickly. When a setup contains something that will oxidize, I try to paint it first. I also recommend purchasing more than one of the fruit, finding a few that are similar in size and color. Then, if you need to paint the fruit over more than one session, you can just slice open another one and paint from observation.

If you're worried about fruit rotting, plastic fruit might be a good option—if the quality is good enough that you cannot tell it's fake.

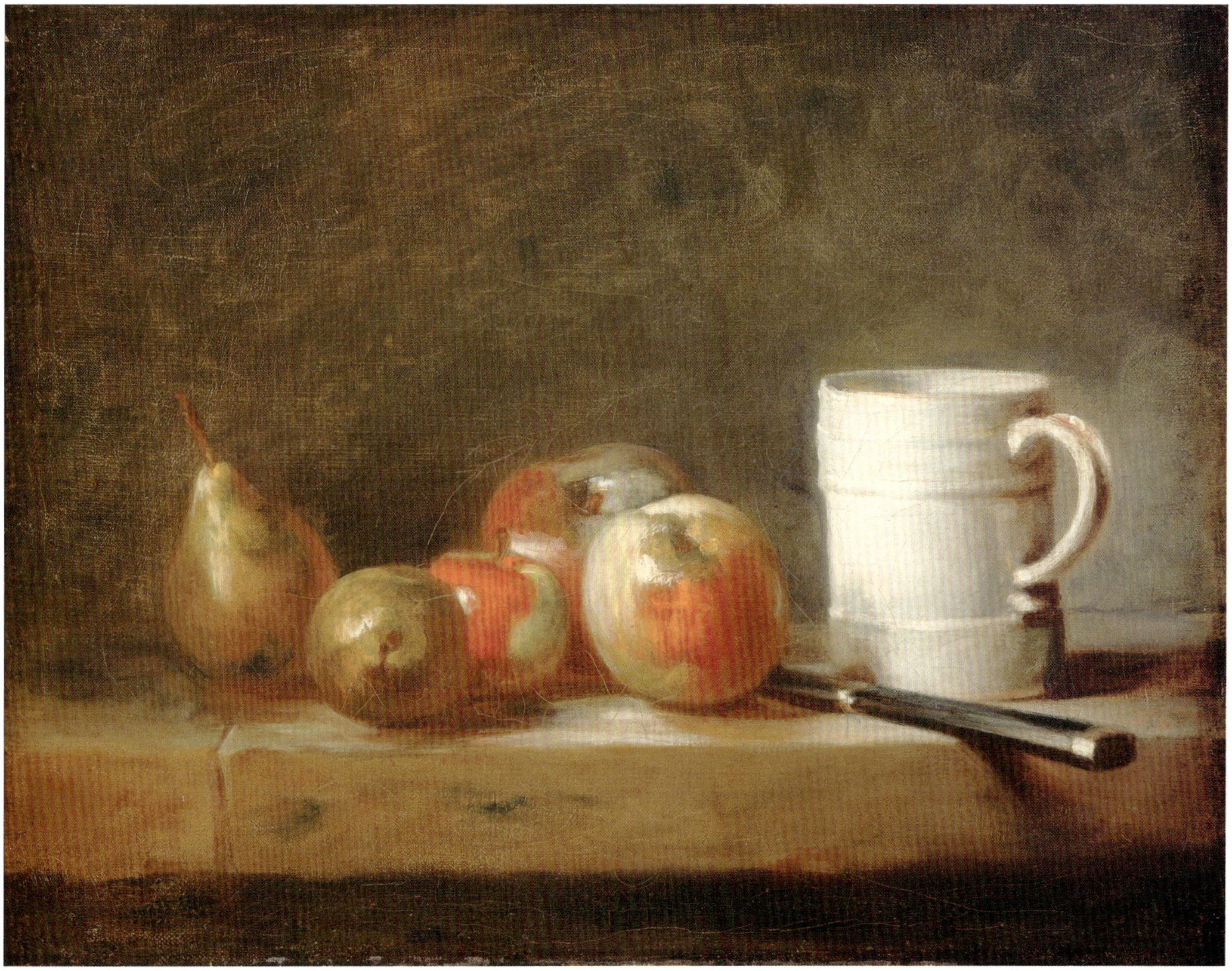

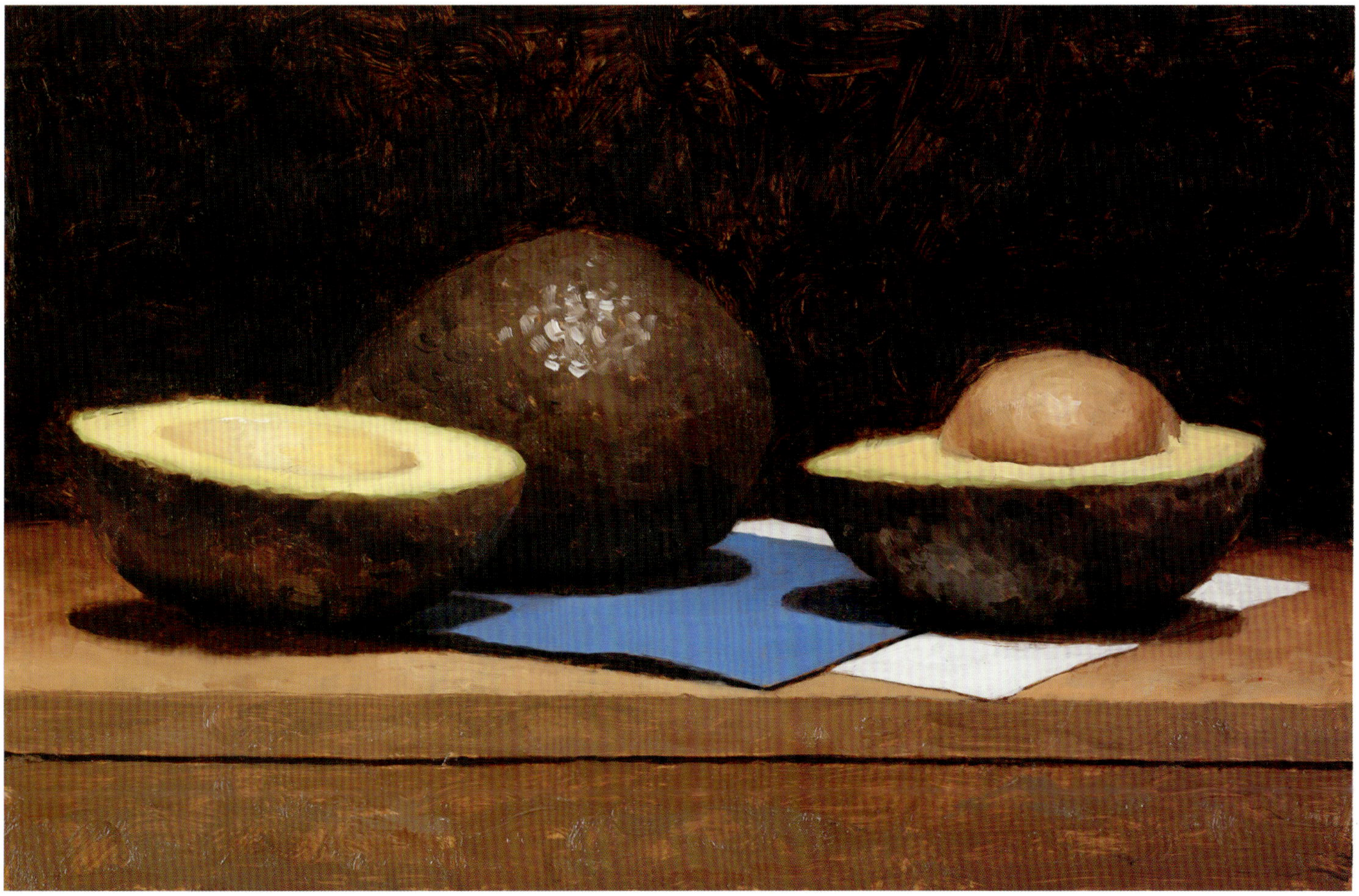

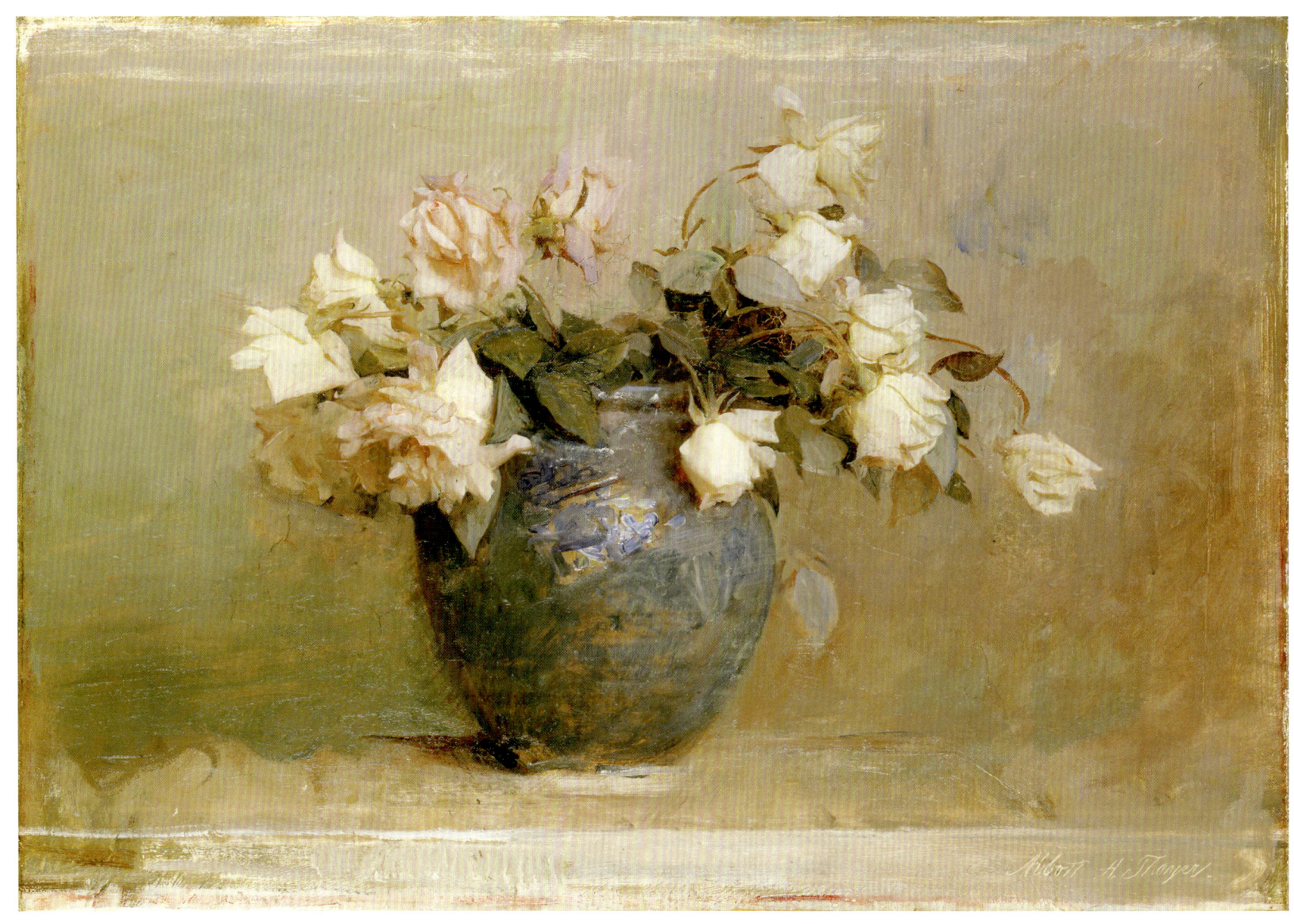

Flowers have been a common subject through centuries of art history. Historically, in the training of an artist, flower painting came after the artist had become fluent in the painting process. Flowers are very challenging yet very rewarding because they can change rather quickly, sometimes within minutes.

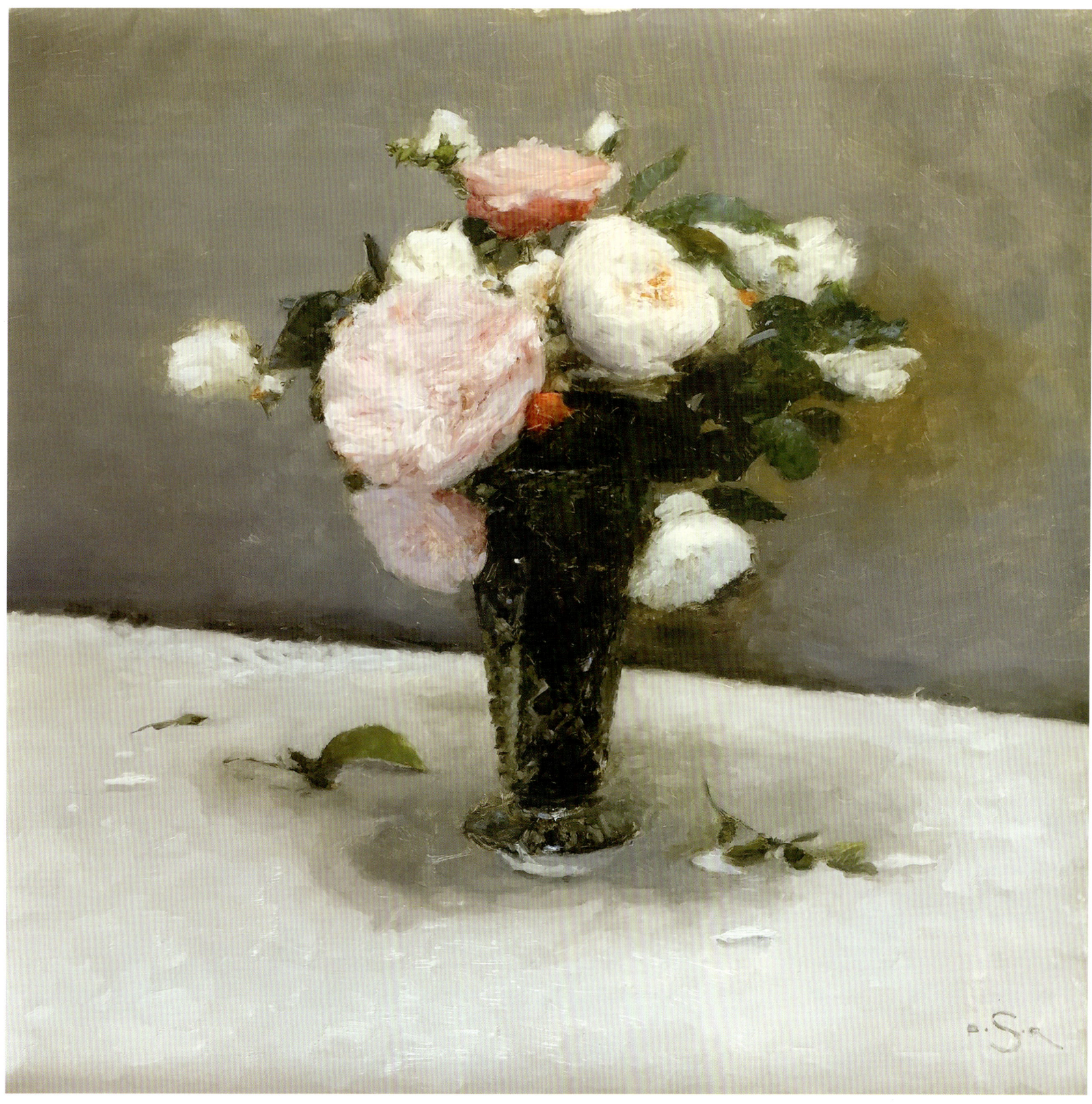

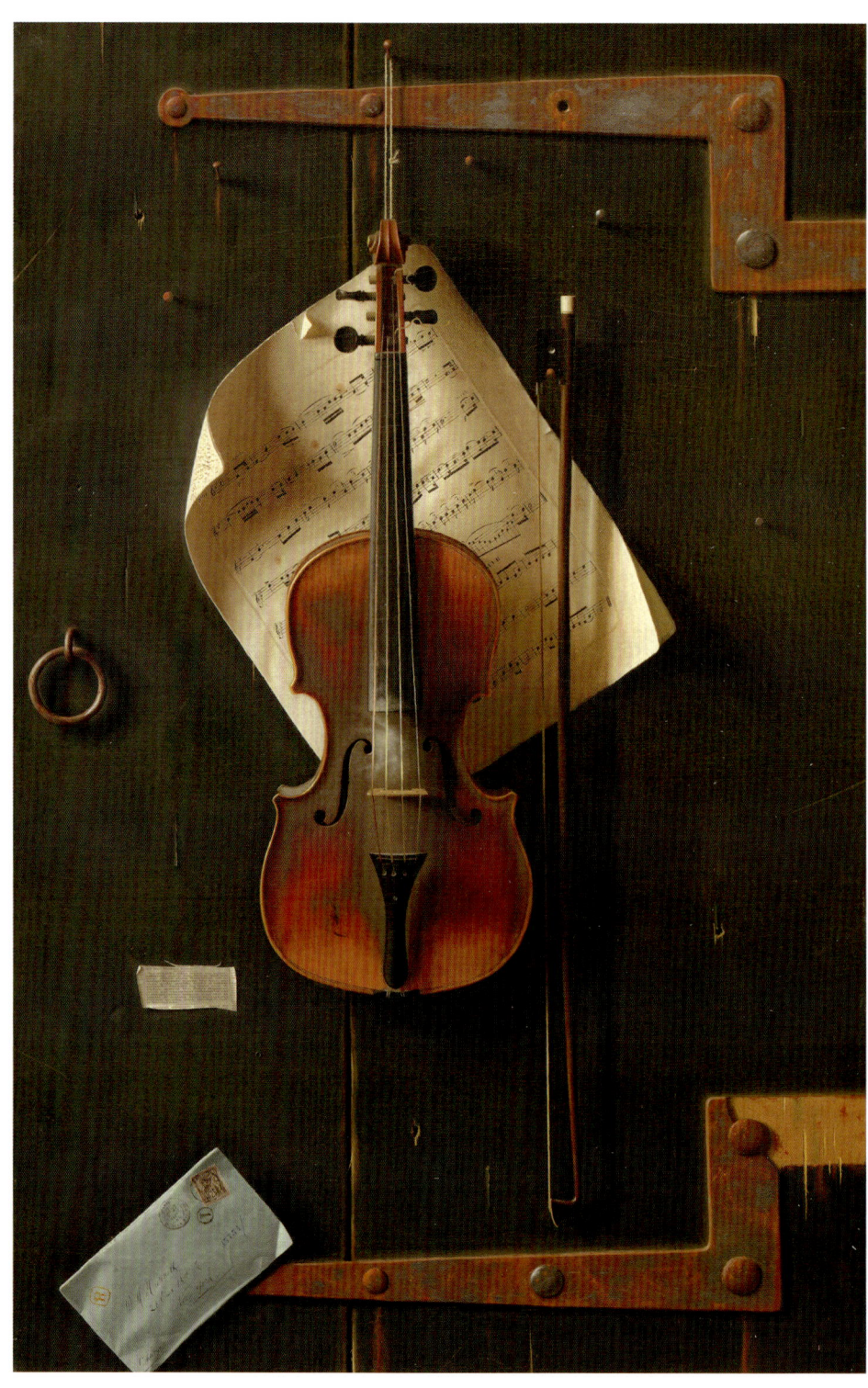

Another familiar theme in still life painting is trompe l'oeil, which is a French phrase meaning "fool the eye." The depth in a trompe l'oeil picture is usually shallow, and the illusion of three-dimensionality is so sharp that it seems as if the objects depicted are really right there in front of the viewer. Nineteenth-century American painter William Harnett was a master of trompe l'oeil, as you can see from his painting *The Old Violin*, above. Some contemporary artists, like Tony Curanaj, continue to work in this traditional genre.

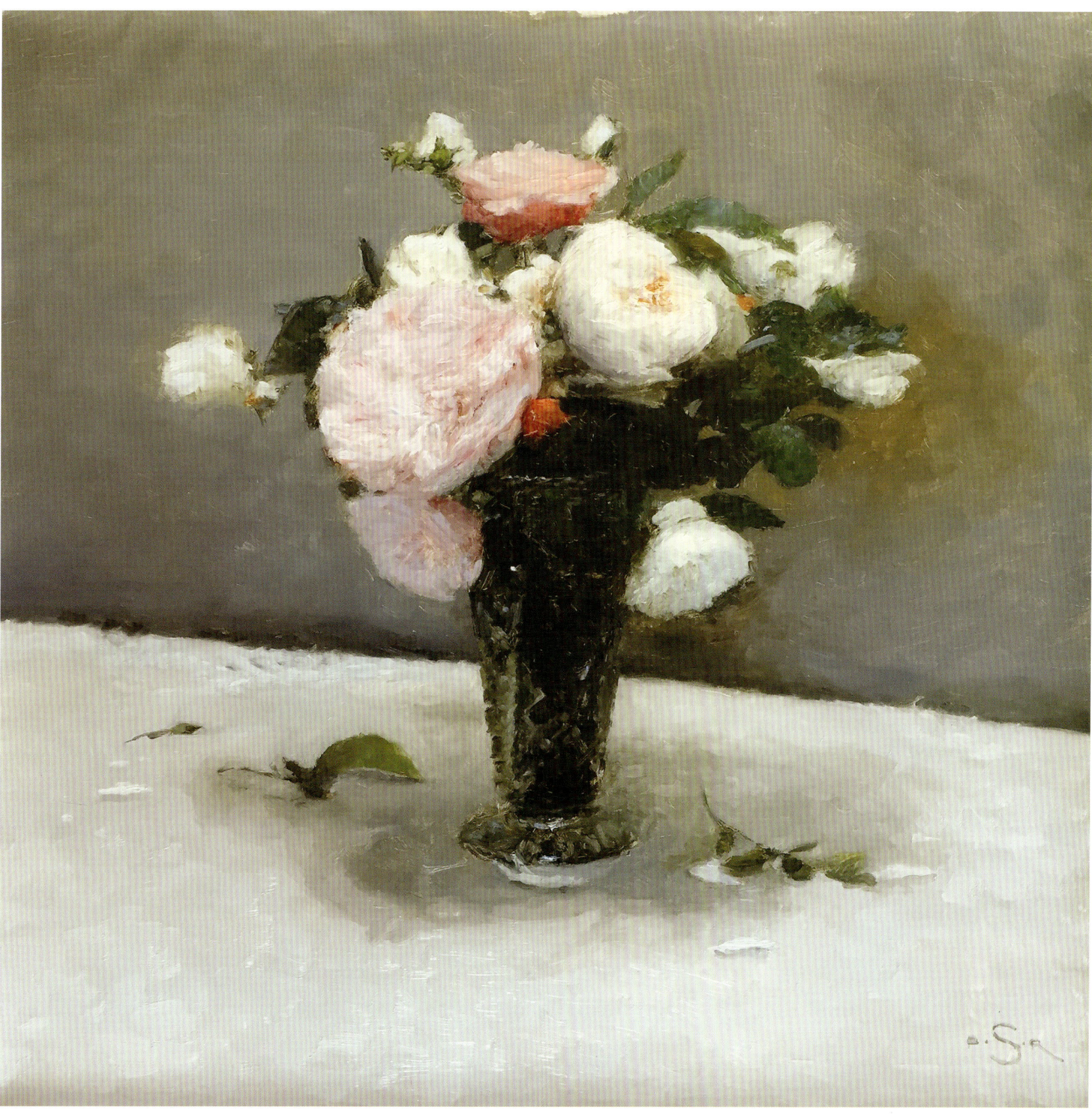

FISH, BIRDS, AND GAME

Dead animals—fish, birds, and game—have also been subjects for still lifes for centuries. In the days before meat came prepackaged and refrigerated in the supermarket case, these subjects were things the artists would have seen on a daily basis. The great American painter William Merritt Chase once wrote of game as "an uninteresting subject so inviting and entertaining by means of fine technique that people will be charmed at the way you've done it."

TOP TO BOTTOM: Emil Carlsen, *Still Life (Mallard, Grouse, Small Game Birds and Copper Pots)*, 1897, oil on canvas, 17 × 29 inches (43.18 × 73.66 cm). Courtesy of Emil Carlsen Archives (emilcarlsen.org).

Jean-Baptiste-Siméon Chardin, *Still Life with a Hare*, 1730, oil on canvas, 24 ⅝ × 32 inches (65.1 × 81.3 cm). The National Gallery of Art, Washington, D.C. Gift of Henry P. McIlhenny, 1958.

William Merritt Chase (American, 1849–1916), *Still Life: Fish*, by 1908, oil on canvas, 40 ⅛ × 45 ¹⁄₁₆ inches (101.9 × 114.5 cm). The Metropolitan Museum of Art, New York, N.Y. George A. Hearn Fund, 1908.

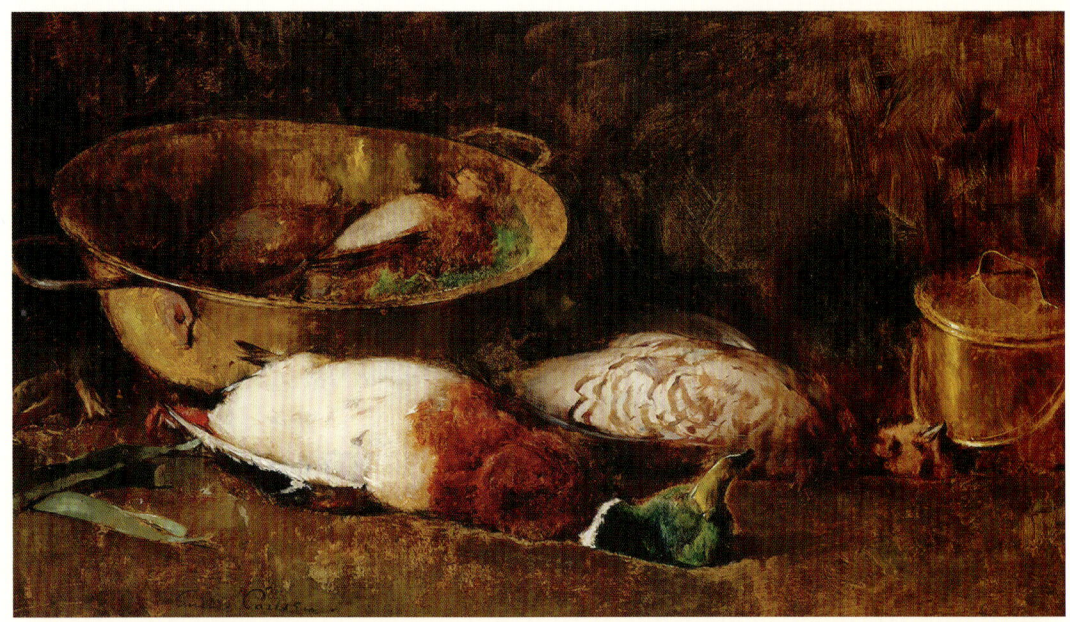

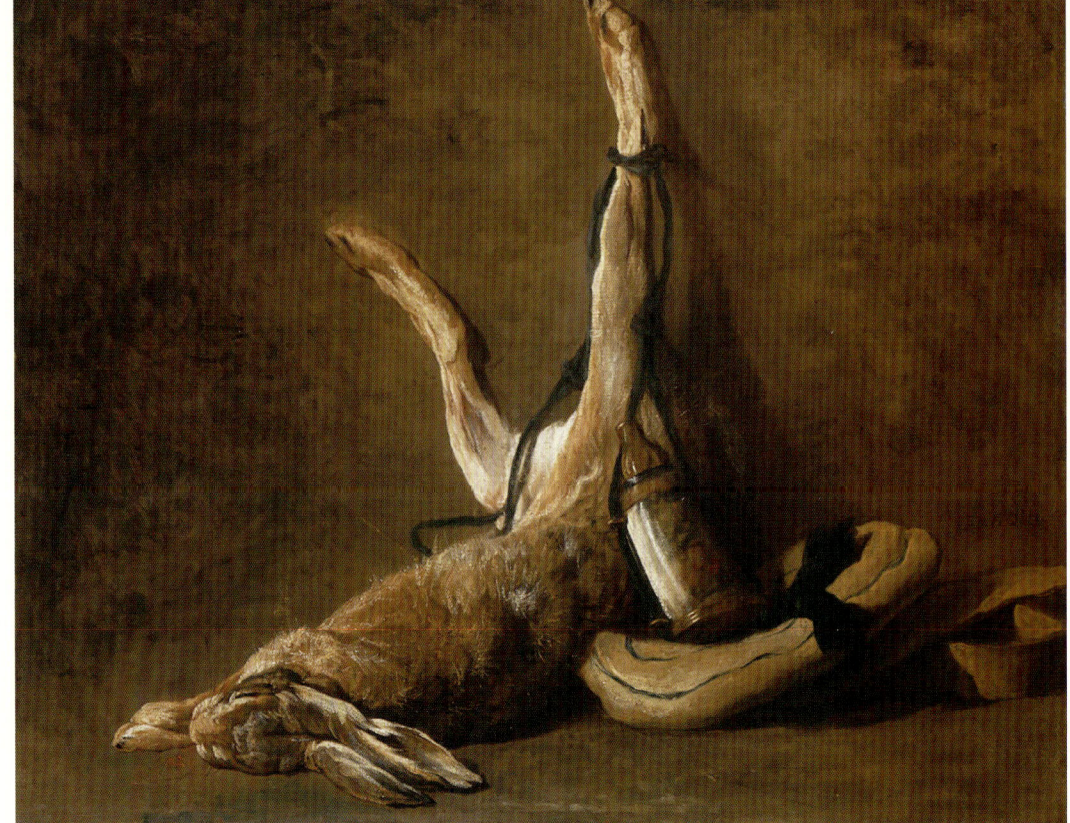

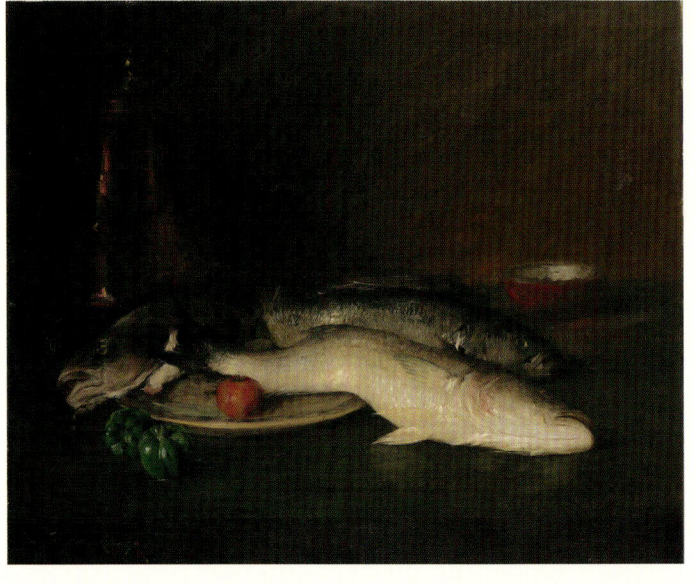

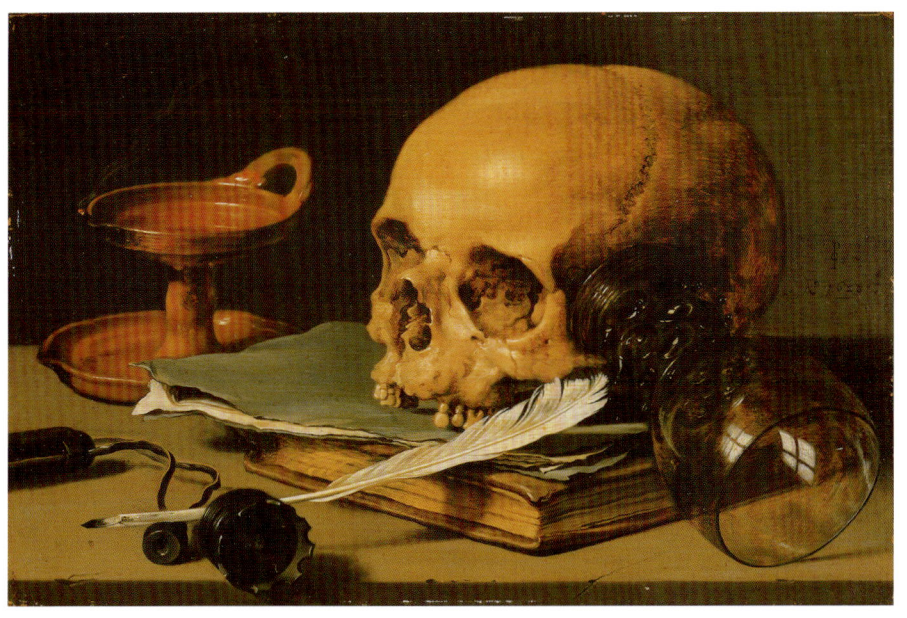

COMMON NARRATIVE THEMES

Because some objects carry symbolic weight, they can suggest a story, especially when juxtaposed with other objects. Thus some still life paintings can possess a narrative theme.

The so-called Vanitas theme was very popular among seventeenth-century Dutch still life painters. *Vanitas* is Latin for "vanity," and this narrative theme emphasizes human mortality and the vanity—emptiness or meaninglessness—of human life. Vanitas paintings are dominated by objects that symbolize death, such as skulls, bubbles, and perishable objects, echoing the idea that life is fleeting.

ABOVE: Pieter Claesz (Dutch, 1597–1660), *Still Life with a Skull and a Writing Quill*, 1628, oil on wood, 9 ½ × 14 ⅛ inches (24.1 × 35.9 cm). The Metropolitan Museum of Art, New York, Rogers Fund, 1949.

The objects in this painting by Pieter Claesz are symbols of death, with the skull being the most prominent and obvious.

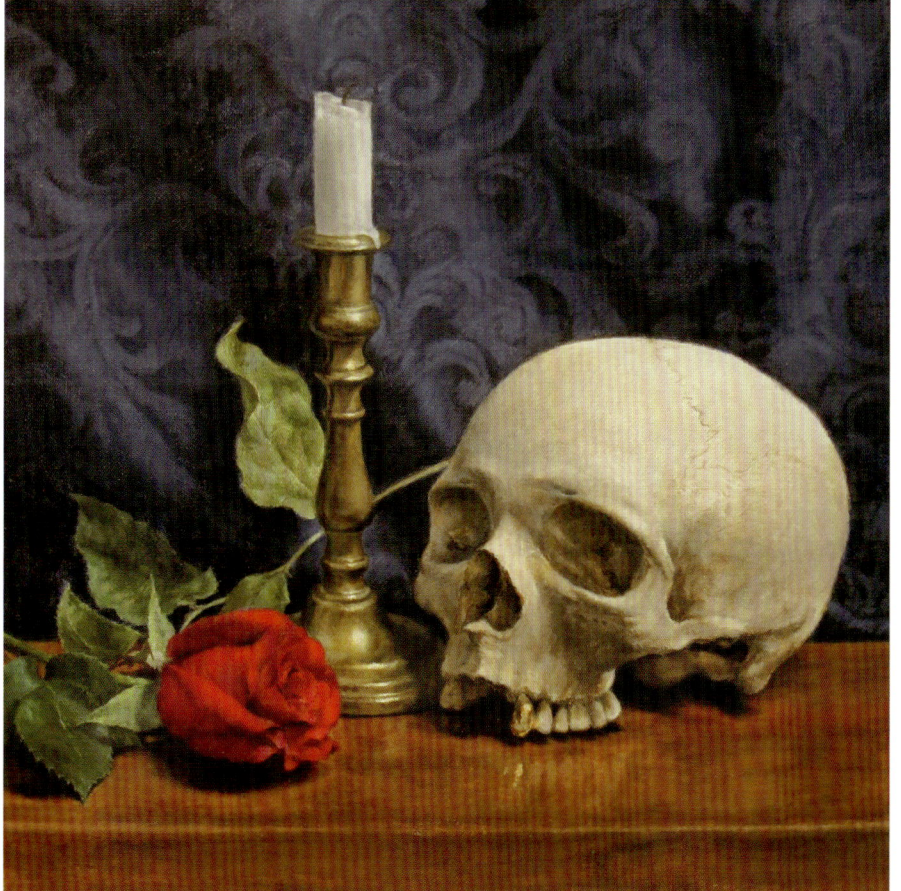

LEFT: John Reger, *Vanitas with Gold Tooth,* 2012, oil on canvas, 12 × 12 inches (30.48 × 30.48 cm). Courtesy of the artist.

Some contemporary artists have also explored the Vanitas theme, as shown by this painting by John Reger.

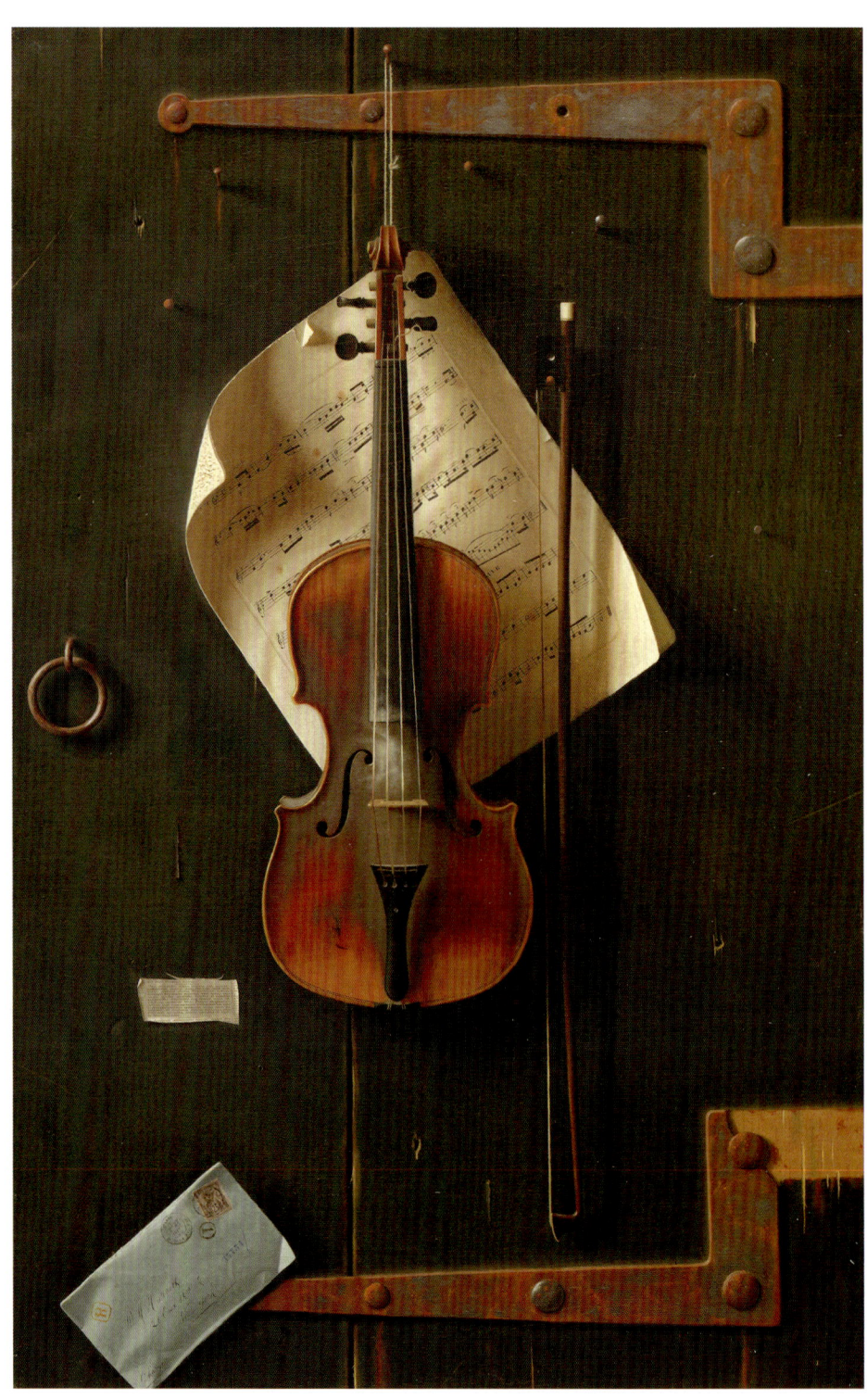

Another familiar theme in still life painting is trompe l'oeil, which is a French phrase meaning "fool the eye." The depth in a trompe l'oeil picture is usually shallow, and the illusion of three-dimensionality is so sharp that it seems as if the objects depicted are really right there in front of the viewer. Nineteenth-century American painter William Harnett was a master of trompe l'oeil, as you can see from his painting *The Old Violin*, above. Some contemporary artists, like Tony Curanaj, continue to work in this traditional genre.

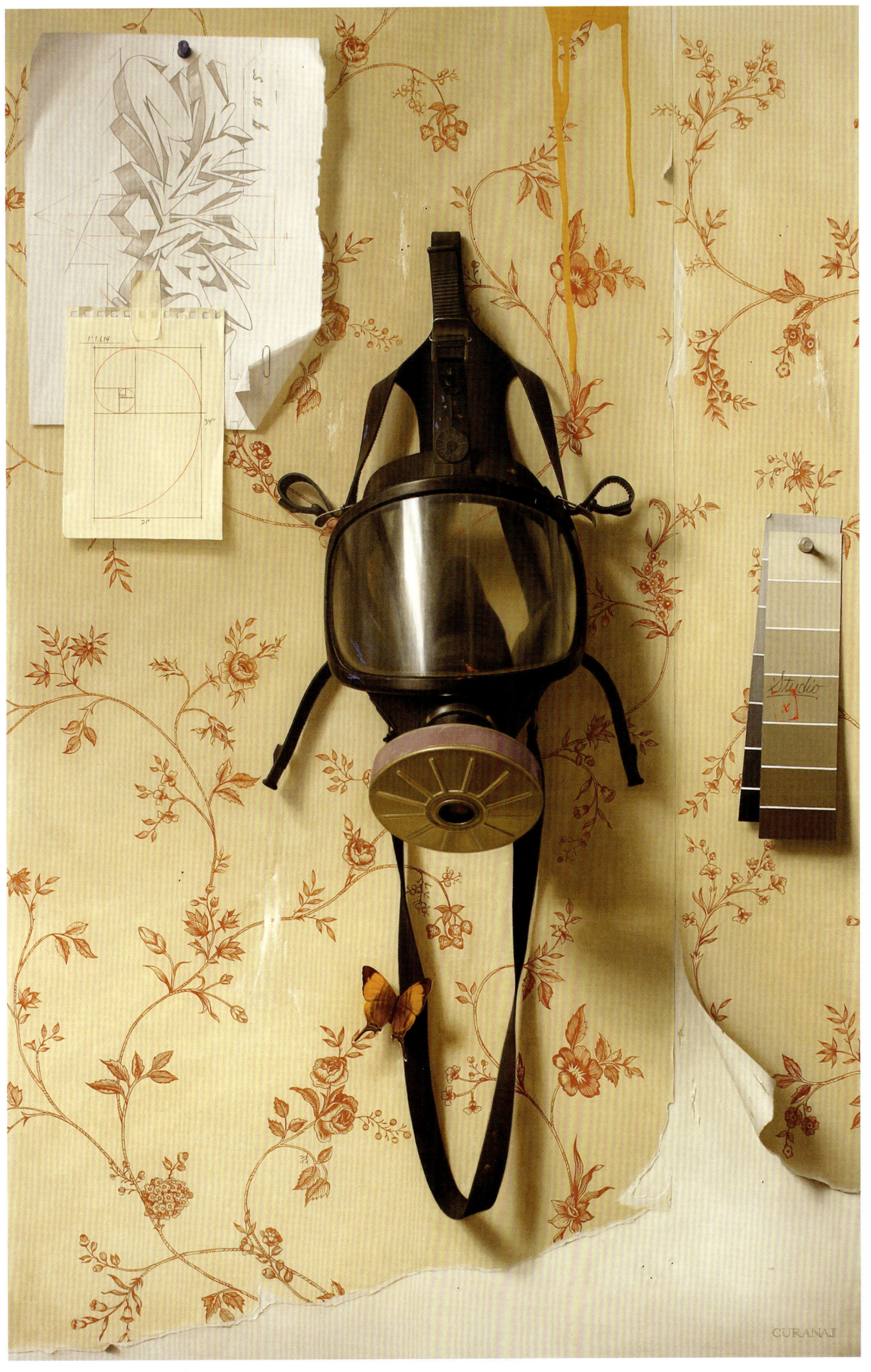

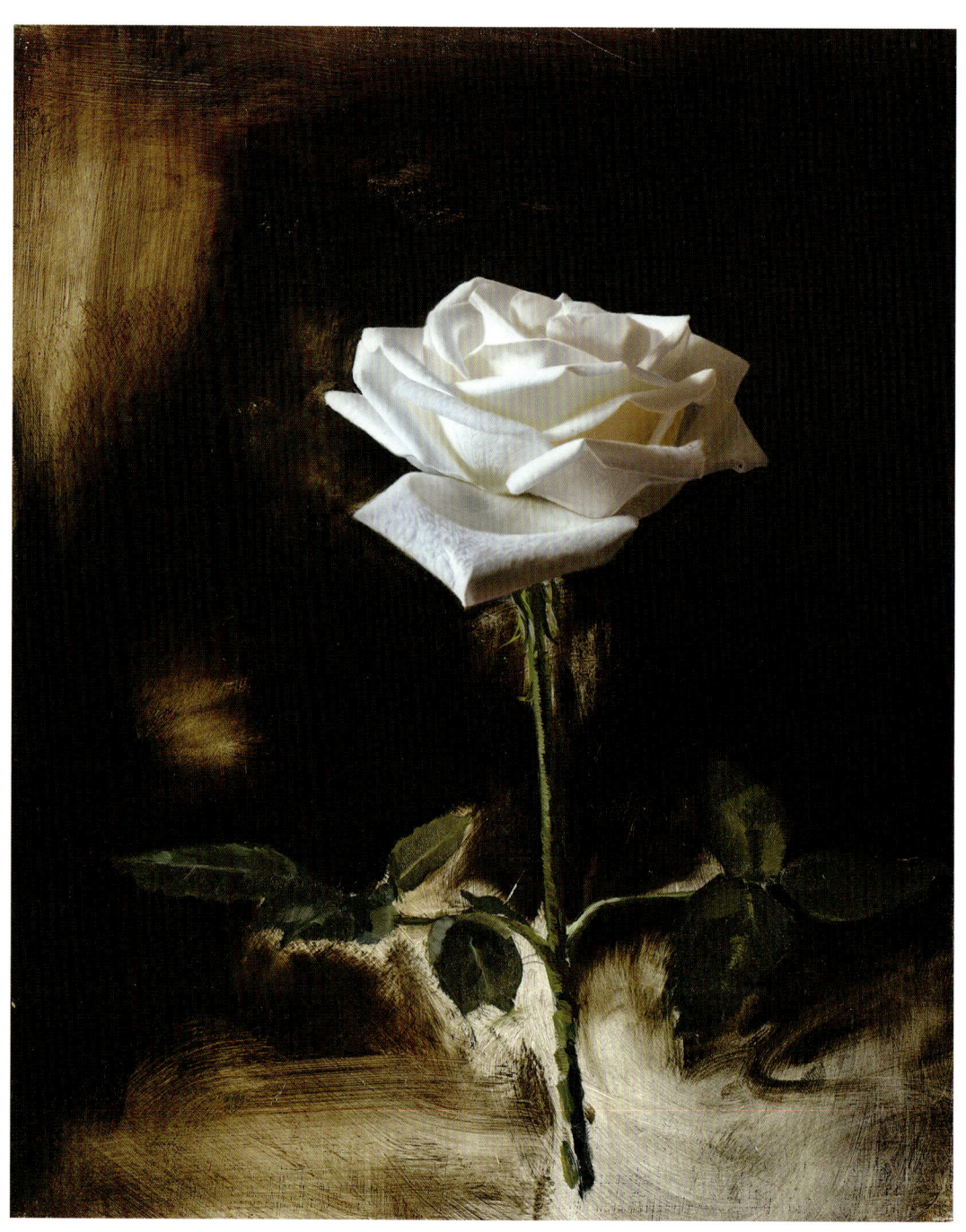

Here are two paintings—the before and after—from a series by Rodney Davis. According to Greek mythology, white roses turned red from the blood of Aphrodite.

Stories, whether historical or fictional, can also be great sources of inspiration for still life painting. Mythology has always been a theme in figurative paintings, including still life. As Rodney Davis writes about his painting *A Gift from Aphrodite* (opposite): "There is an ancient myth that all roses were white until Aphrodite pricked her finger on a thorn and turned them all red with her blood."

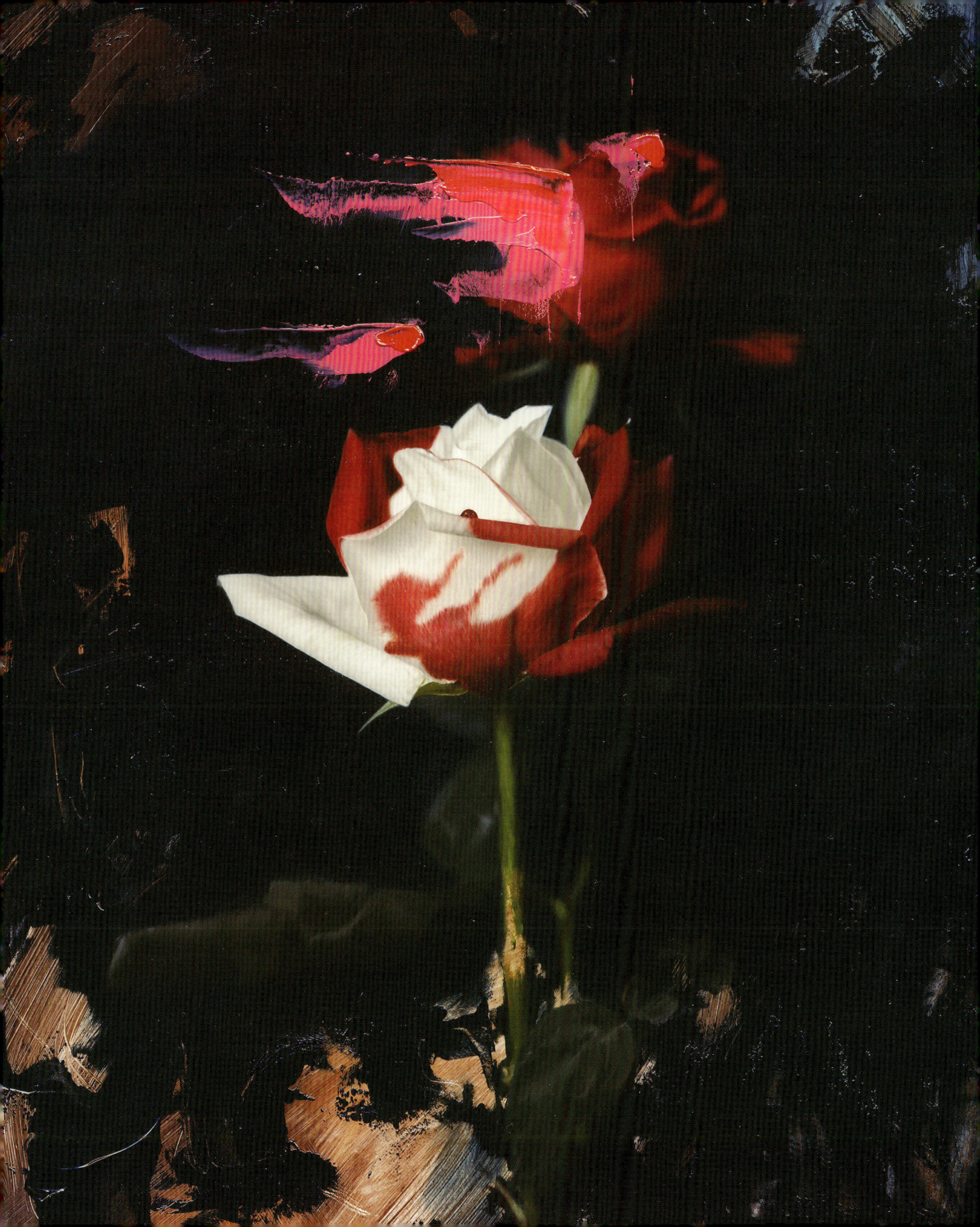

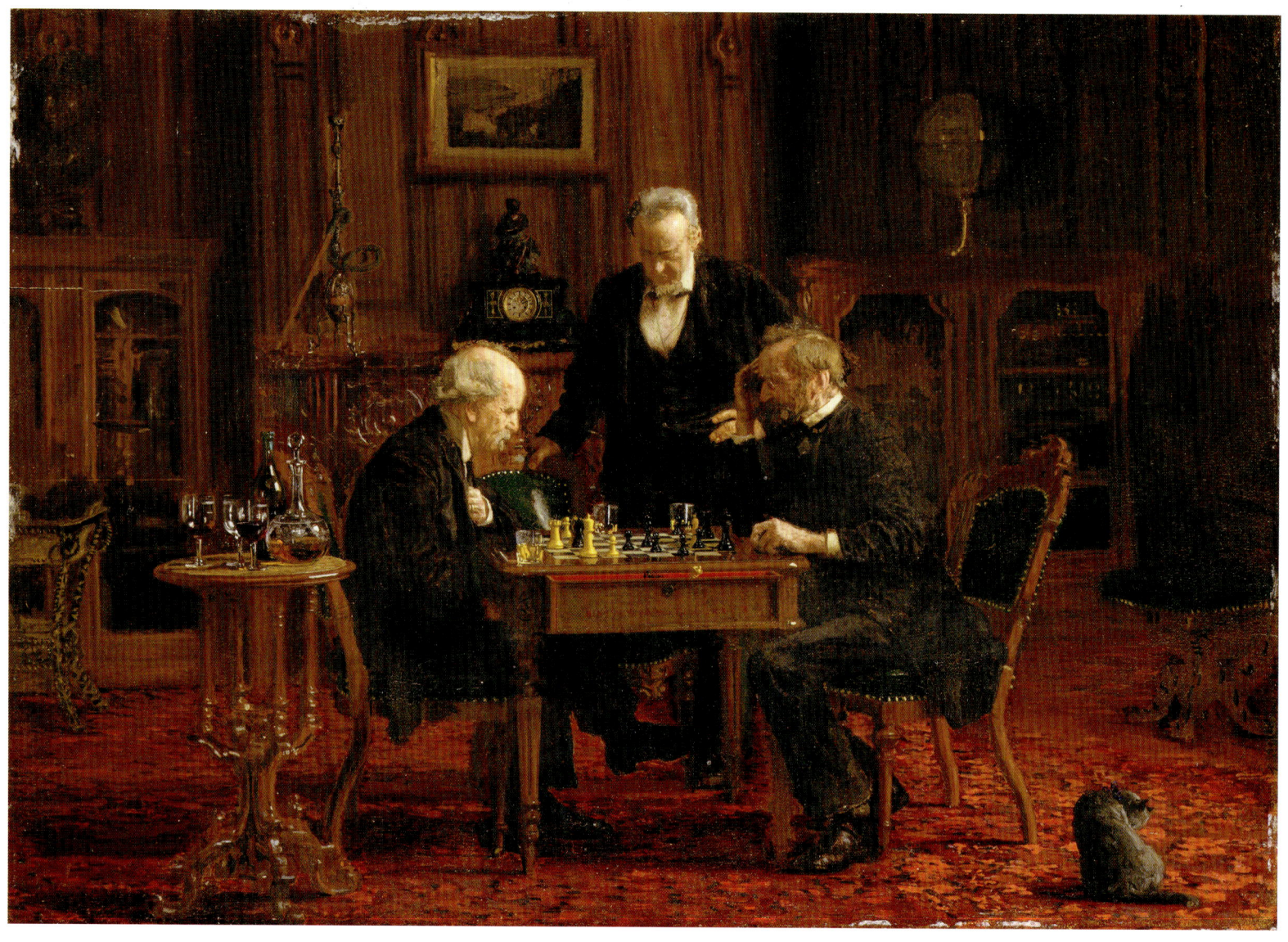

ABOVE: Thomas Eakins (American, 1844–1916), *The Chess Players,* 1876, oil on wood, 11 ¾ × 16 ¾ inches (29.8 × 42.6 cm). The Metropolitan Museum of Art, New York. Gift of the artist, 1881.

OPPOSITE: Henri Fantin-Latour (French, 1836–1904) *Still Life with Torso and Flowers,* 1874, oil on canvas, 45 ½ × 35 ¼ inches (116 × 90 cm). Gothenburg Museum of Art, Gothenburg, Sweden. Photo courtesy of the Art Renewal Center.

STILL LIFE IN A SETTING (INTERIORS)

Larger narrative figure paintings often contain arrangements of objects. If you zoom in on a section of a painting such as Thomas Eakins's *The Chess Players*, you see a still life. Artists have also expanded still lifes to show the surrounding environment, as in *Still Life with Torso and Flowers*, by Henri Fantin-Latour.

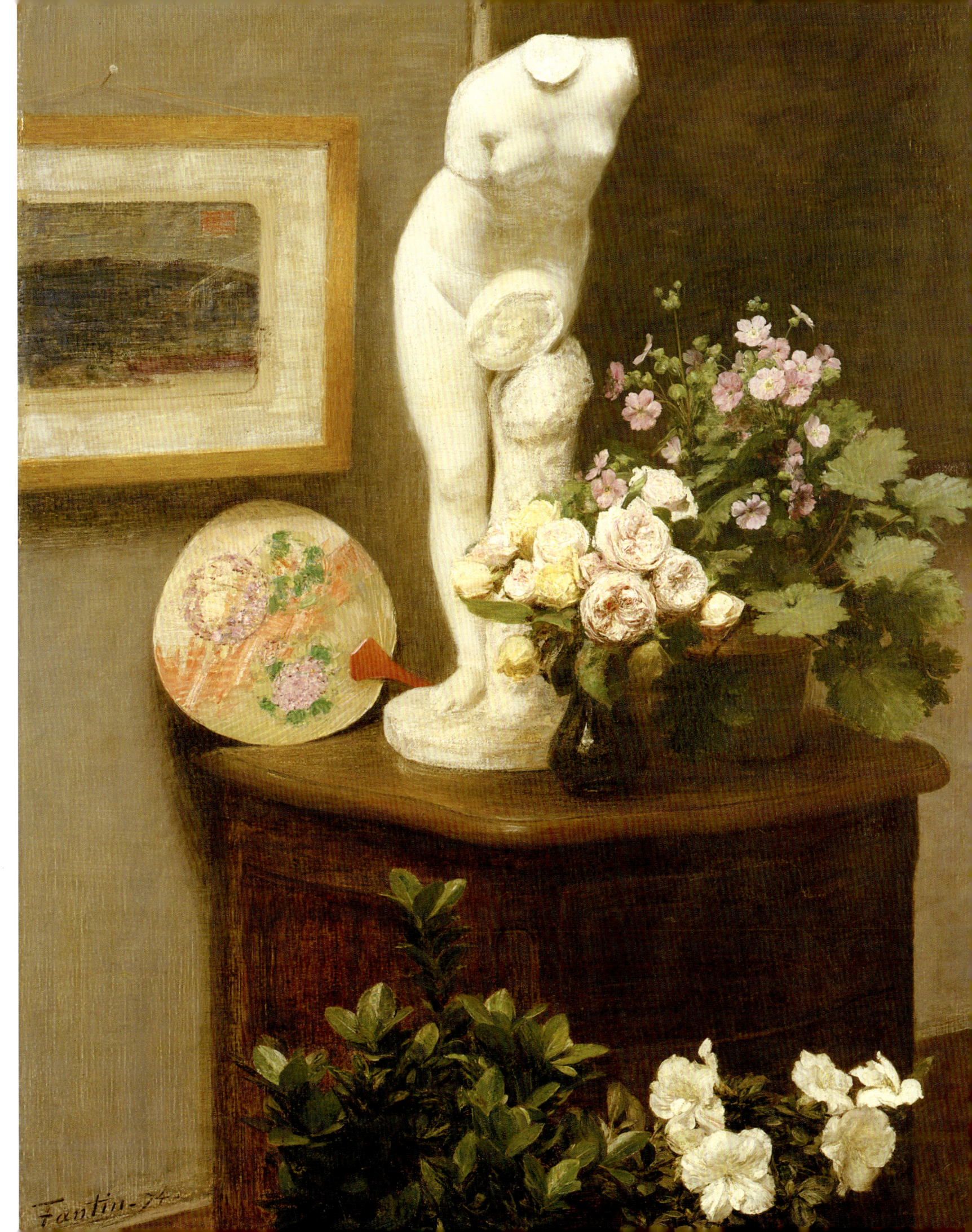

BACKGROUND COLORS— TRADITIONAL VERSUS CONTEMPORARY

Traditional still lifes often have dark backgrounds, as in the François Bonvin painting at right. In the days of the Old Masters, there were far fewer pigments than are available today, so colorful backgrounds like that in my painting *Sake*, below, tend to feel more contemporary. Cadmium-based colors were introduced around the time of the industrial revolution (1820s–1840s). Before the cadmiums were introduced, it was hard to get a high-chroma yellow, orange, or red color. (Vermilion was traditionally used.)

TOP: François Bonvin, *Nature morte aux cartes et à la mappemonde* (*Still Life with Maps and a Globe*), 1880, oil on panel, 7 ¼ × 9 ⅛ inches (18.3 × 23.2 cm). Photo courtesy of Sotheby's, Inc. © 2016.

RIGHT: Todd M. Casey, *Sake*, 2018, oil on panel, 6 × 9 inches (15.24 × 22.86 cm). Private collection.

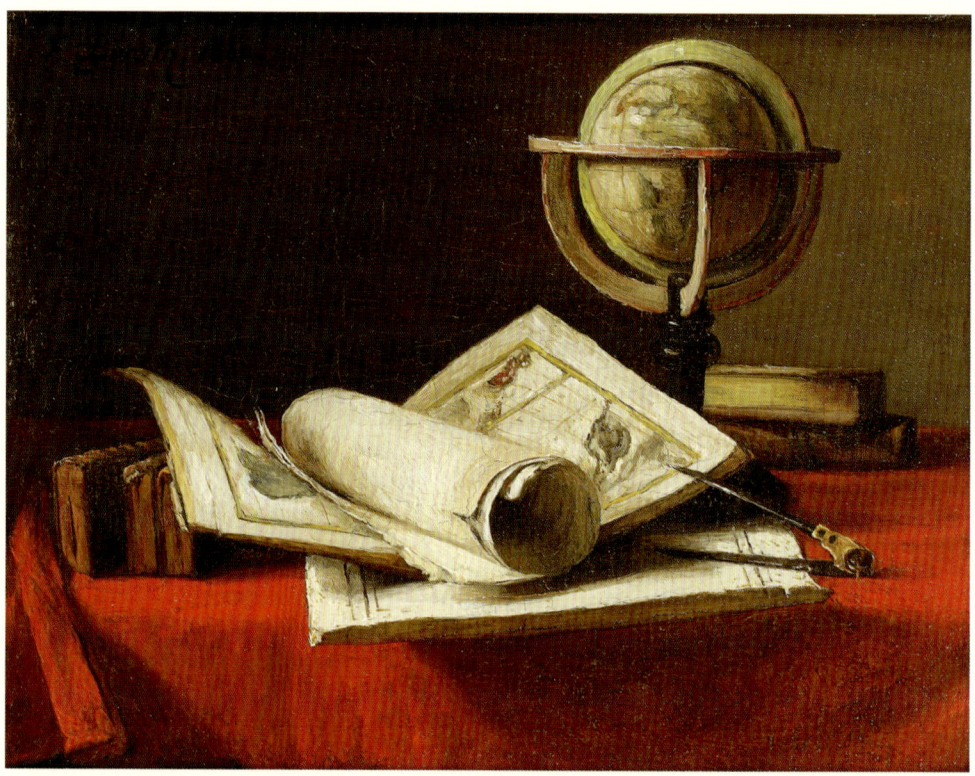

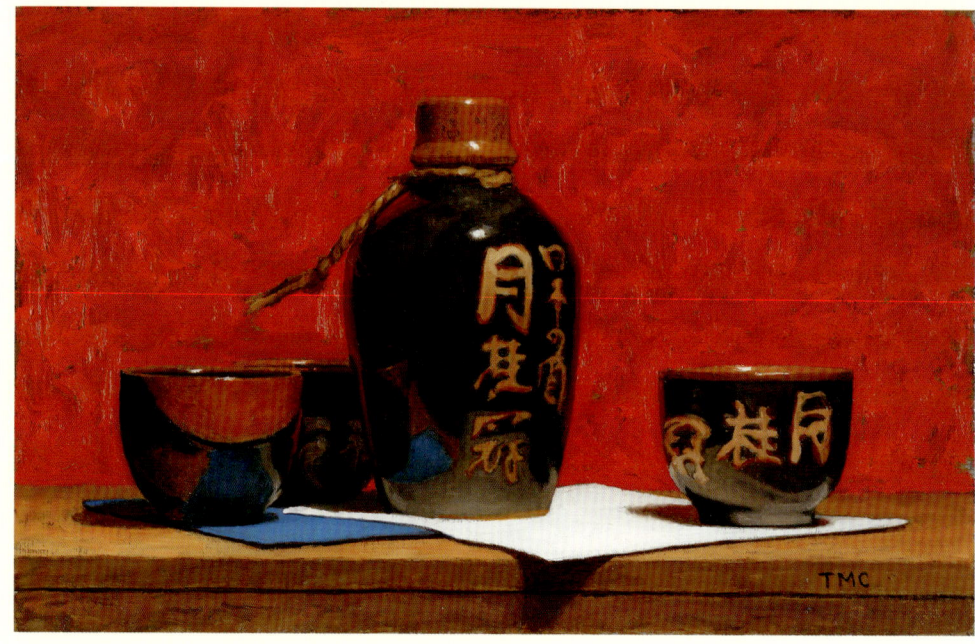

RECOMMENDED PROPS

Having a lot of props is a must for a still life painter. As you progress, you'll find that you're always on the hunt for interesting props.

I recommend, though, that you start by painting just a few simple things. Fruits are a great place to start because most have relatively simple forms—spheres, cylinders, etc. Fake fruit is perfect for beginners, because it's not perishable like real fruit, so you don't have to impose a time limit on finishing your painting. Arts and crafts stores sell plastic fruit that is so believable you'd think it's real.

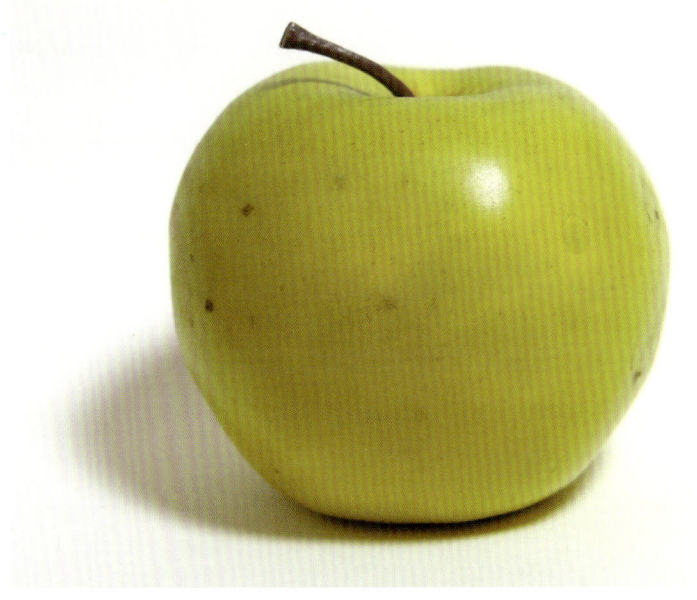

TOP: Artificial fruit, like this plastic apple, can look extremely real.

RIGHT: Hannah Brown Skeele (American, 1829–1901), *Fruit Piece,* 1860, oil on canvas, 20 × 23 ⅞ inches (50.8 × 60.6 cm). The Art Institute of Chicago. Restricted gifts of Charles C. Haffner III, Mrs. Harold T. Martin, Mrs. Herbert A. Vance, and Jill Burnside Zeno; through prior acquisition of the George F. Harding Collection.

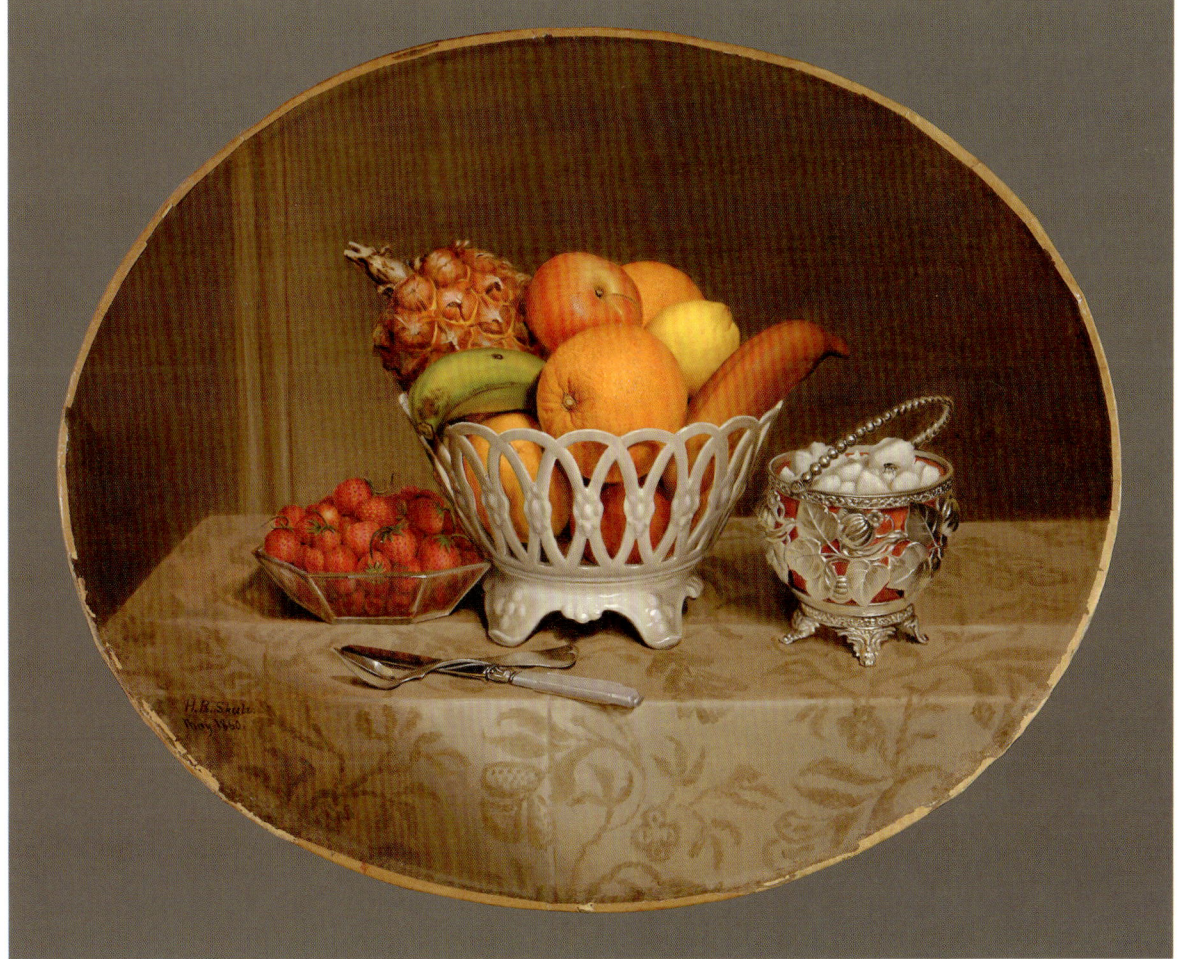

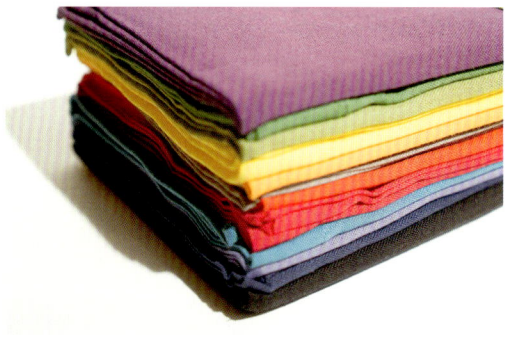

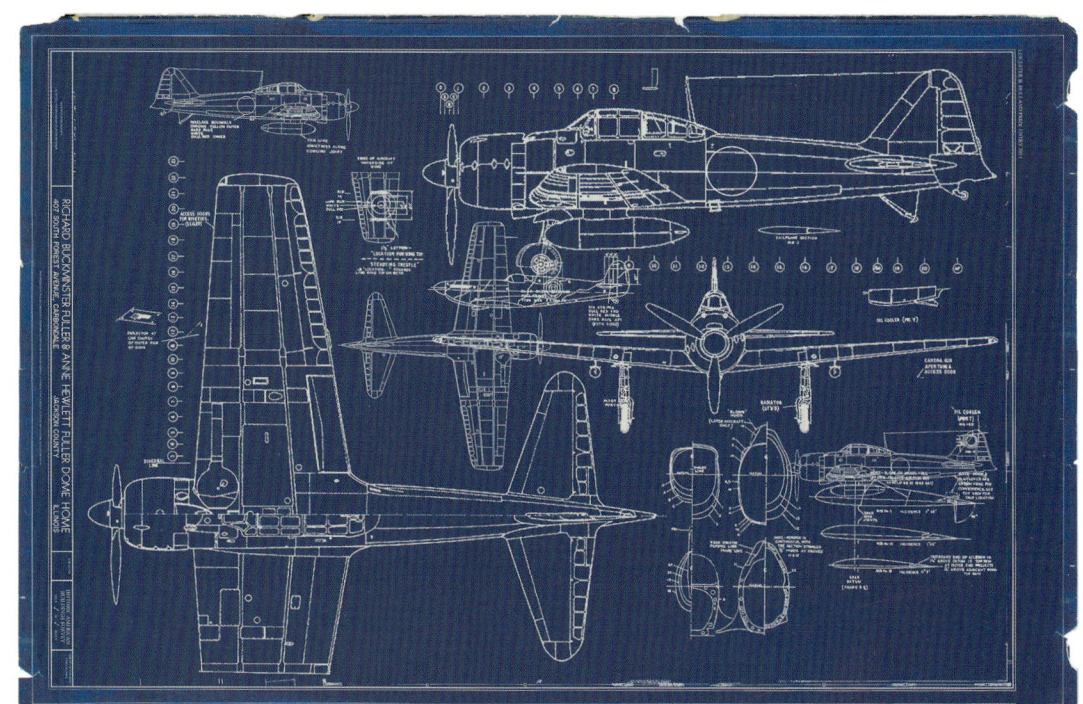

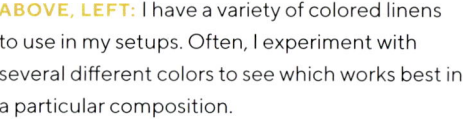

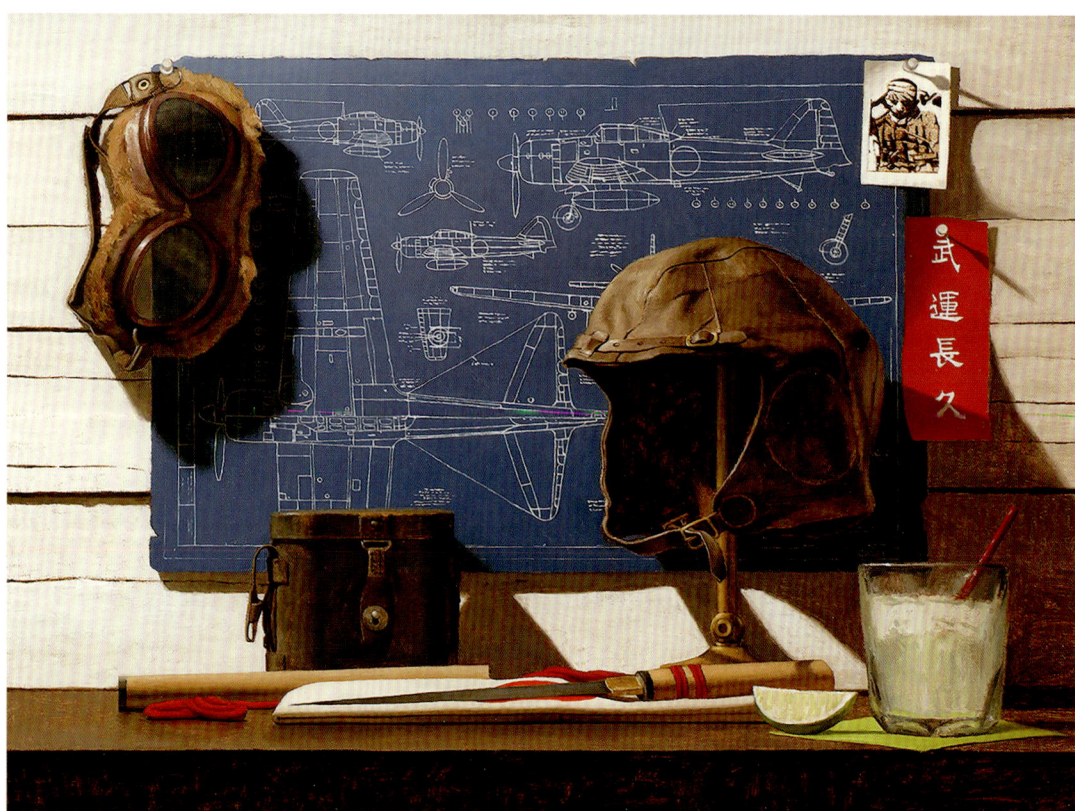

ABOVE, LEFT: I have a variety of colored linens to use in my setups. Often, I experiment with several different colors to see which works best in a particular composition.

ABOVE, RIGHT: I created this blueprint from artwork of World War II kamikaze planes that I found on the internet.

RIGHT: Todd M. Casey, *Birth of a Kamikaze,* 2015, oil on linen, 18 × 24 inches (45.72 × 60.96 cm). Collection of Howard and Amy Rehs.

A range of colors will make your compositions more interesting. I keep a large variety of cloths and papers of different colors and objects of different textures in my studio. I encourage you to collect wood, metal, and ceramic objects to use in your paintings—anything that speaks to you. Wooden boxes make great platforms for your setups.

If I can't find a prop I need, I sometimes make it myself—especially maps and other images that I can create digitally and then print out. For example, one of my clients wanted a painting built around the idea of a kamikaze cocktail. I didn't have any props related to kamikazes—the Japanese suicide pilots of World War II—but I was able to find some that I could buy. I wanted a blueprint in the background, but I couldn't find one of a kamikaze airplane. So I just made one from images I found online, printing it out and weathering the edges to make it look old. (That was a technique I learned when I worked for the art department at Ralph Lauren; we would often make new stuff look old or "antiqued" for our showroom.) The blueprint and the finished painting in which it appears are opposite.

WORKING OUT YOUR IDEAS

Once you decide what you want to paint, you should work out your idea on paper. I recommend always carrying a sketchbook or notebook with you so that you can jot down your thoughts about subjects and compositions whenever they occur to you. You don't want to censor or filter your thoughts at this point. Just write down or sketch out whatever you think of. Not every idea has to lead to a painting.

The things you sketch will stick with you. Sketching is similar to taking notes in longhand as opposed to typing them on a keyboard. It's a much more intentional process. When we physically write something out, we tend to emphasize certain words or edit things out. This is similar to what we do when drawing. Observing all the information in front of you takes some time, but it also makes you consider various options. You also connect with what you're observing on an emotional level. Sketching is an experience, not just an observation. You observe something and re-create what you're inspired by, gaining a deeper understanding of it.

Exploring ideas on paper can often lead you to arrange your setup in a different way than you might do with the objects in front of you. It's easier to play with light and abstractly see how the shapes interact.

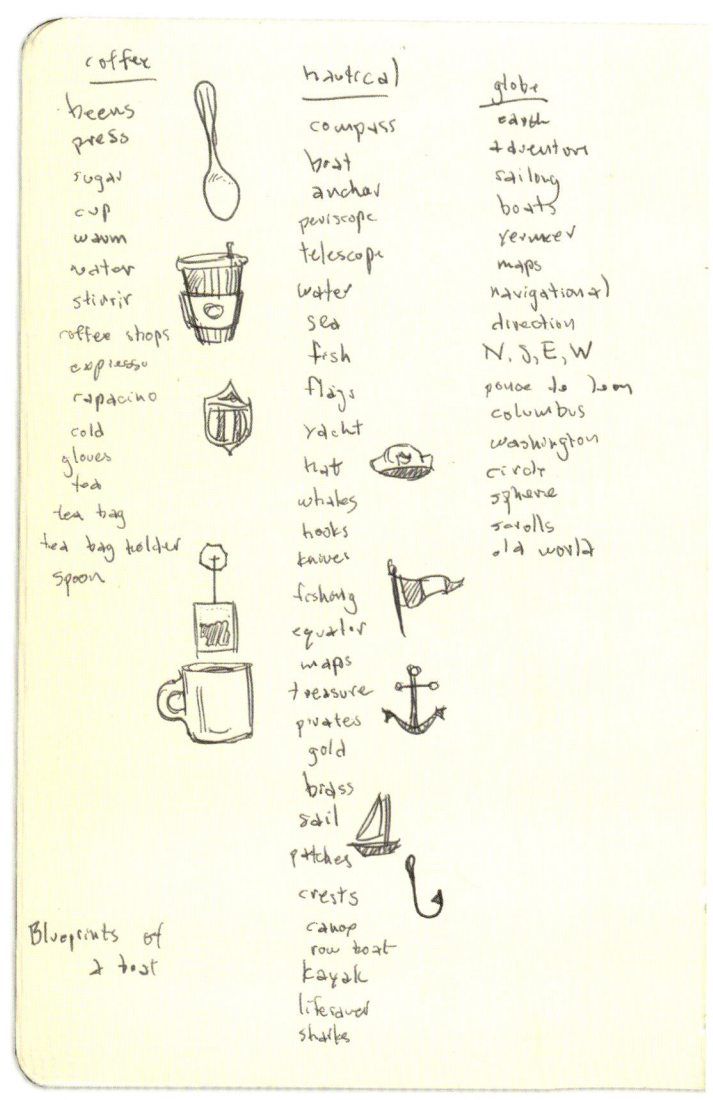

ABOVE: Todd M. Casey, word list in sketchbook, 2012.

These are some word lists (and little sketches) I made around the ideas of "coffee," "nautical," and "globe." The resulting variety of concepts might ultimately add depth to a composition.

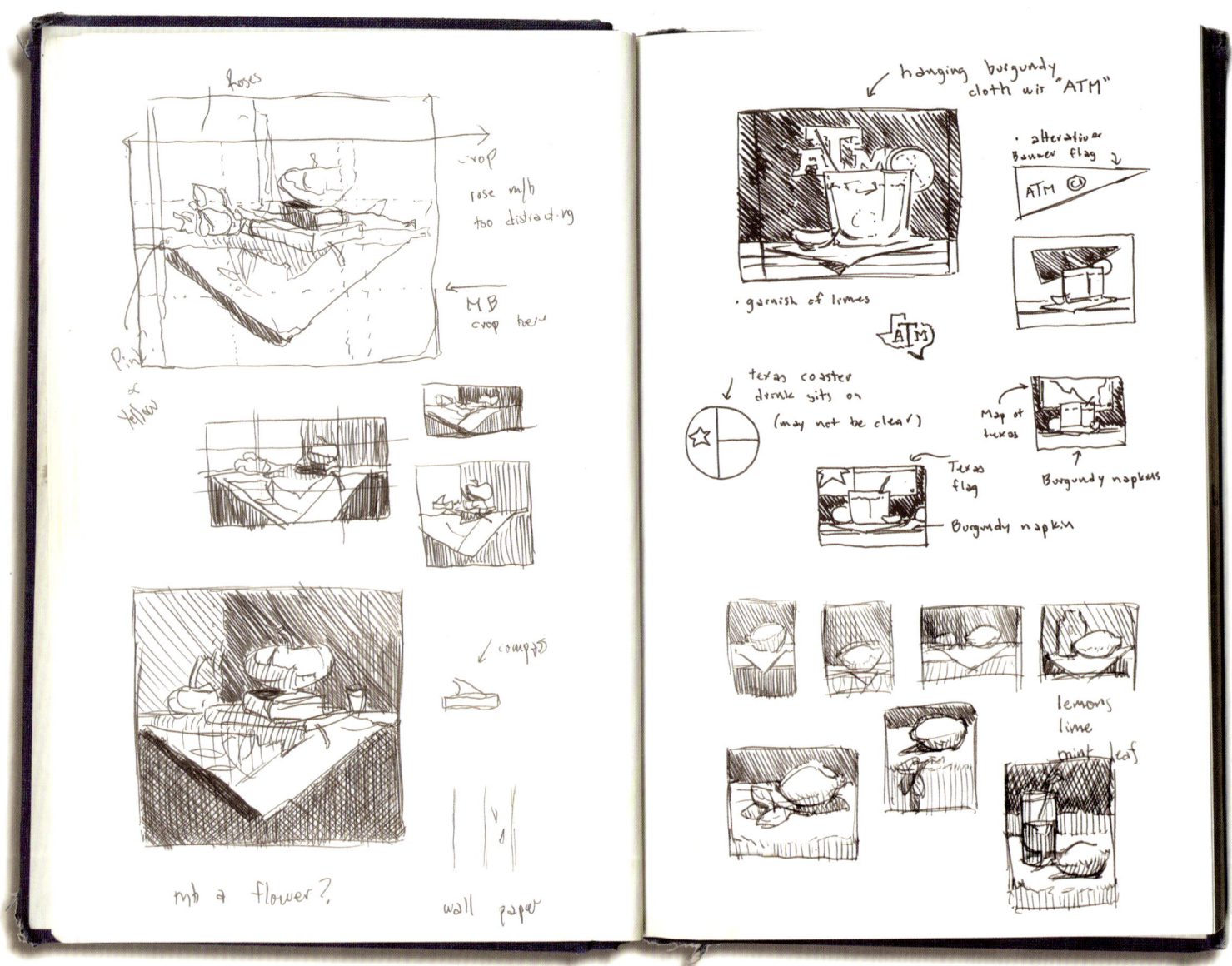

In my sketchbook, I often write word maps or jot down word associations in a stream-of-consciousness way. This helps me come up with ideas, off the top of my head, around one word or concept. You can often get confined in your thinking, and this kind of process helps steer you in your own direction.

After creating a word map, I usually build some ideas through small studies called thumbnail sketches. These aren't based on setups—they're just ideas about how a setup might be arranged. I'll also often draw icons to start thinking about the shapes and how they may interact with one another. Sometimes working an idea out on paper can help further a concept; you don't need to be bound by what is set up in front of you.

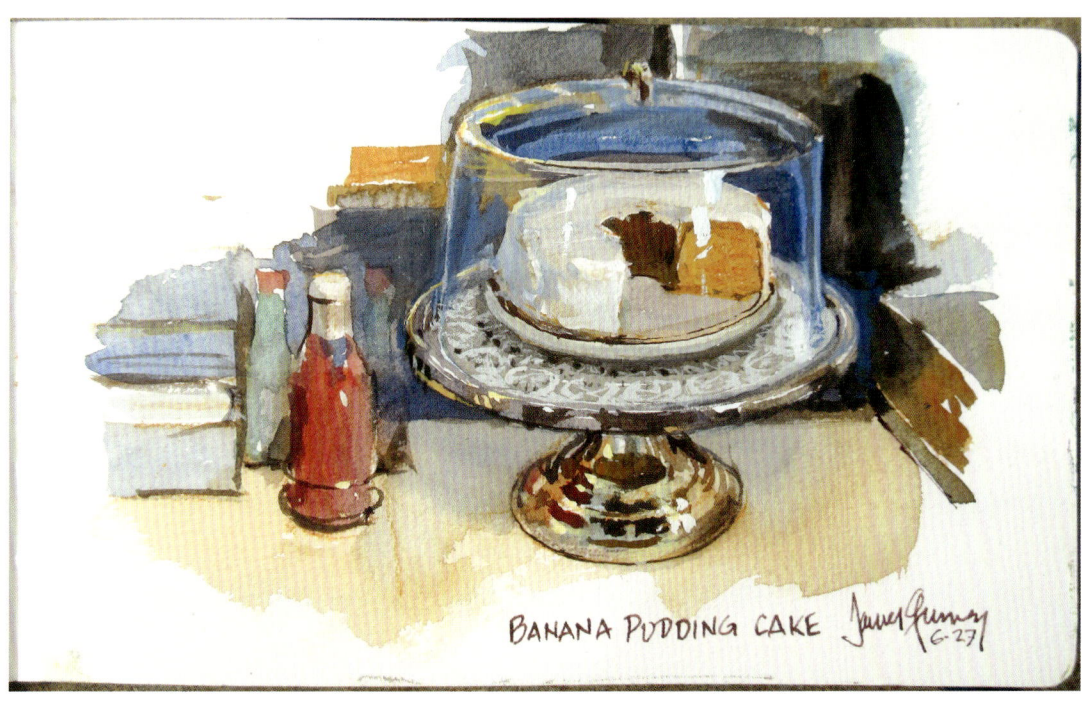

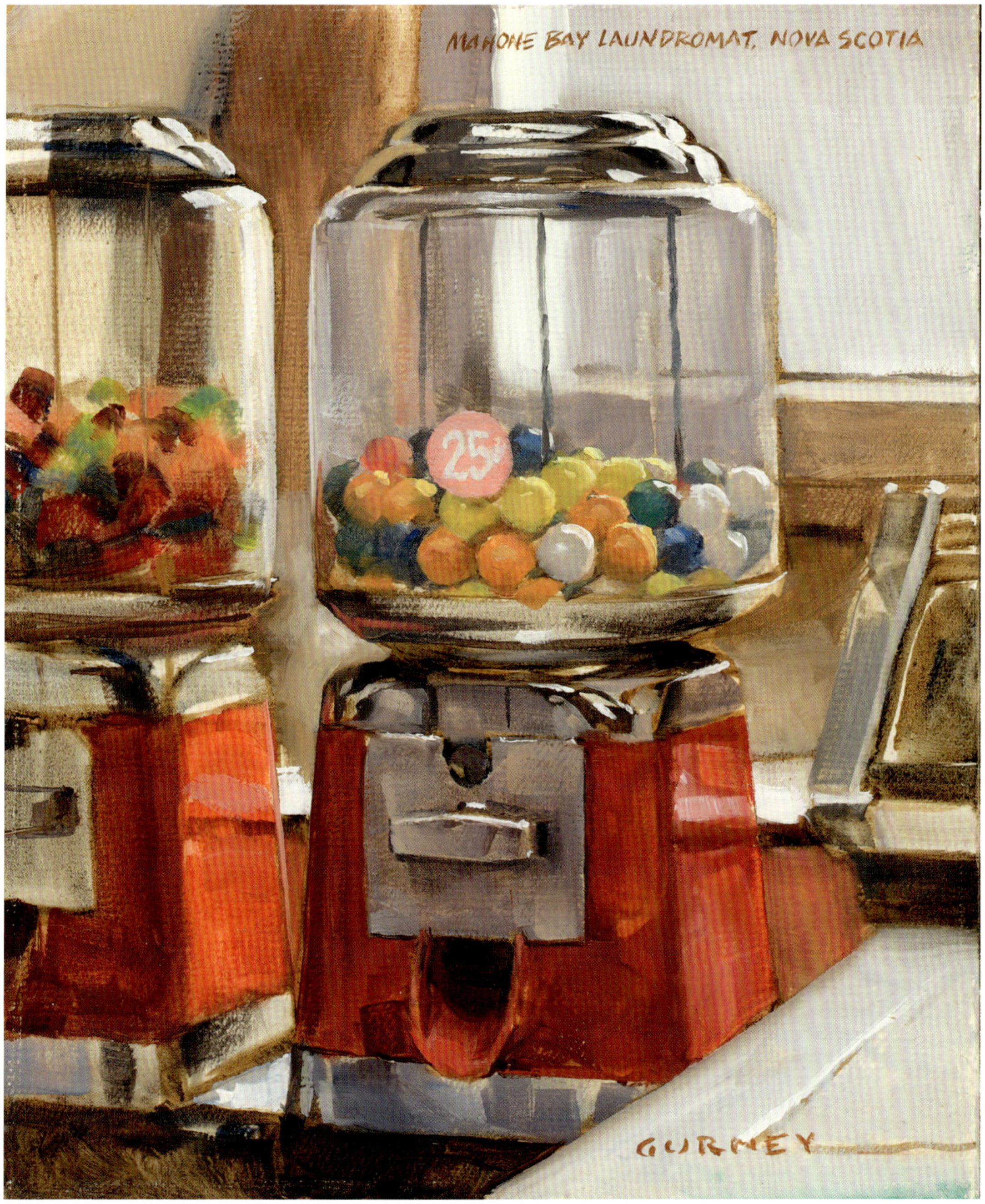

BANANA PUDDING CAKE

MAHONE BAY LAUNDROMAT, NOVA SCOTIA

GURNEY

ABOVE: James Gurney, *Banana Pudding Cake Study,* 2015, gouache on paper, 5 × 8 inches (12.7 × 20.32 cm). Courtesy of the artist.

LEFT: James Gurney, *Gumball Machine,* 1995, oil on canvas, 10 × 8 inches (25.4 × 20.32 cm). Courtesy of the artist.

As long as you have a sketchbook with you, you can do studies whenever and wherever you like. James Gurney does gouache and oil studies of objects he comes into contact with in everyday life.

WAYS TO GET INSPIRED

If you are not going to get a thrill, how can you give someone else one? You must feel the beauty of the thing before you start.
—CHARLES HAWTHORNE, FROM *HAWTHORNE ON PAINTING*

I spend a lot of time looking at objects and thinking of the stories I'd like to tell in a painting. I know that inspiration can come from anywhere. Sometimes an idea can start with an object that speaks to you.

You can find inspiration—for color, theme, mood, composition—in other artists' work. I collect postcards and posters from museums and put them up on a wall in my studio. Not all the images are still lifes—there are portraits, figure paintings, landscapes, and interiors. But they all consciously or subconsciously work their way into my ideas.

You may want to start an image collection of your own. You don't have to tape pictures to a wall—you can collect them on your computer or in a binder. But always try to discover what it is that draws you to an image. Always dig for the deeper meaning.

One of the best places to look for inspiration is the work of the Old Masters. We all have our off days when we don't feel inspired or just don't know what to paint. On such a day, why not visit a museum and experience the work of other artists? (But take note: it's fine to be inspired by the Old Masters and to continually try to achieve that kind of depth in your work, but don't do versions of their paintings. Your work needs to be an extension of who you are.)

The film director Ridley Scott has said that when he created *Gladiator* he was inspired by the scenes from ancient history painted by nineteenth-century painters like Jean-Léon Gérôme. In fact, you can find inspiration in all the arts. Don't just look at paintings—study all forms of art and nature, as well. Nature has always been human beings' biggest source of inspiration.

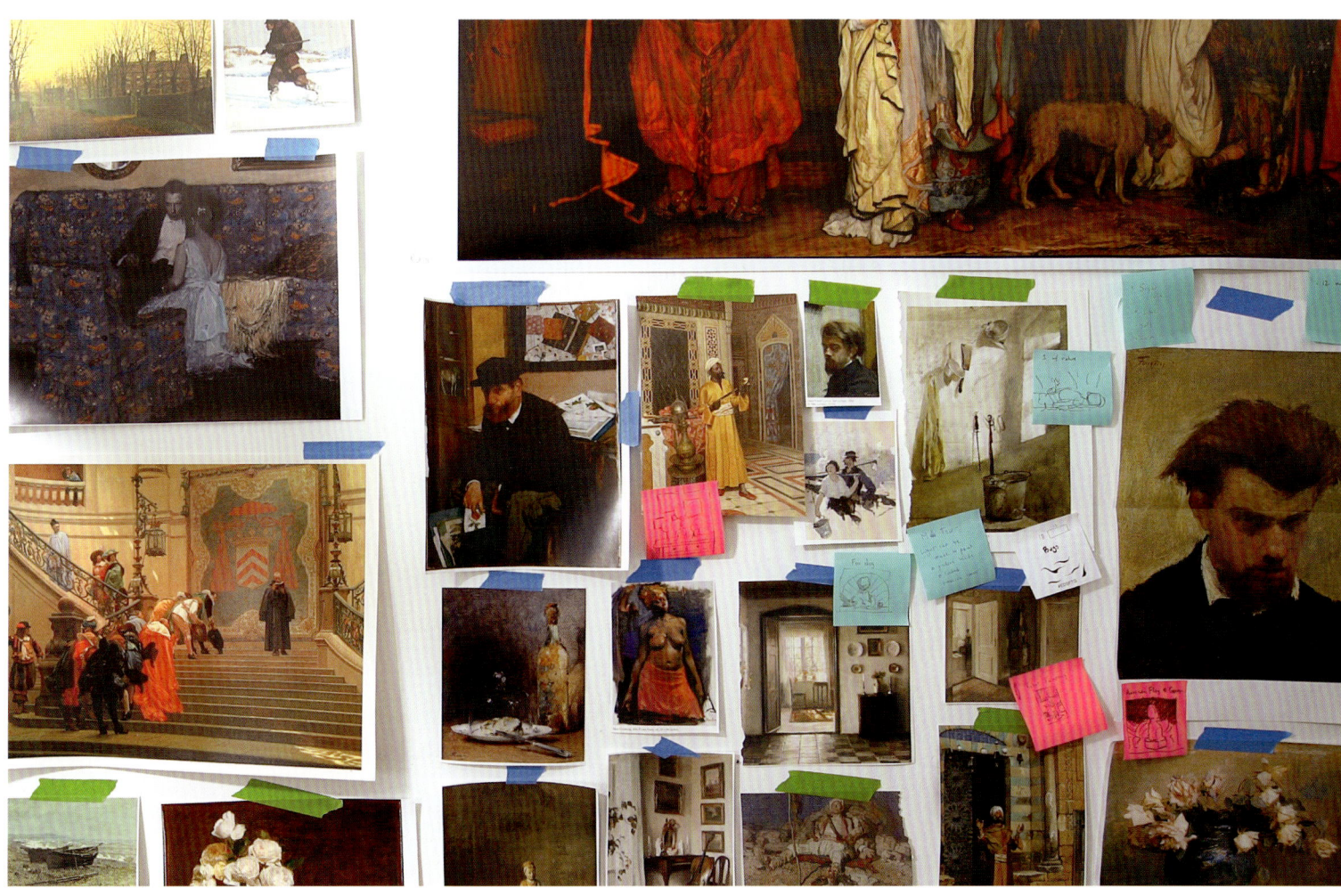

ON OTHERS' PERCEPTION

No matter how hard you try to control how your art is perceived, viewers will experience your work in their own unique ways. Sometimes the response will be intellectual: viewers will develop their own interpretations of your paintings and the meanings of the symbols you use. But a painting might also evoke a visceral response—a gut reaction—meaning that the viewer doesn't quite know why they feel the way they do. The only thing you, as an artist, can do is to embrace the reality that different people will respond differently to the work you do. Don't worry about how your work is received. Paint in bliss.

ABOVE: I have a wide range of images taped to my studio wall, by artists such as Dean Cornwell, Edwin Austin Abbey, Henri Fantin-Latour, Jean-Léon Gérôme, Andrew Wyeth, Vilhelm Hammershoi, Edgar Degas, and Max Ginsburg. They're very different from each other, but all are equally interesting to me. I'm constantly challenging myself to understand why I like these images.

Photo by Alex Archimbaud.

TAKING YOUR TIME

Ideas sometimes take a long time to develop. I find that my best paintings usually result when I ponder over them for a long while. With a few of my paintings, it's taken years to work out the concept/narrative. If you are telling a story in your work, you, too, should take your time in building the narrative. I feel that the integrity of a work of art can be compromised if you're painting under time pressure (though such pressure can't always be avoided).

I worked on my painting *The Shamrock* mentally and visually for about four years before I did the final version. Back when I was working at Ralph Lauren, there was a beautiful shipbuilder's blueprint hanging on the office wall, and I asked my boss if I could borrow it for a possible painting. He said I could. So then I had the blueprint but didn't know what other objects I would use with it to make a compelling image. When I was on Nantucket the following summer, I saw a model boat and decided to buy it. Then I gradually put together the other elements to build a narrative based around Nantucket. I worked out the concept through many studies—you can see a few of them opposite—before doing the final painting.

OPPOSITE, TOP LEFT: Todd M. Casey, sketch for *The Shamrock,* 2010, oil on panel, 5 ¼ × 4 ½ inches (13.33 × 11.43 cm). Courtesy of Rehs Contemporary Galleries, New York.

OPPOSITE, TOP RIGHT: Todd M. Casey, sketch for *The Shamrock,* 2010, oil on panel, 4 ¼ × 3 ¾ inches (10.8 × 9.52 cm). Courtesy of Rehs Contemporary Galleries, New York.

OPPOSITE, BOTTOM LEFT: Todd M. Casey, sketch for *The Shamrock,* 2014, oil on panel, 8 × 6 inches (20.32 × 15.24 cm). Private collection.

OPPOSITE, BOTTOM RIGHT: Todd M. Casey, *The Shamrock,* 2014, oil on canvas, 30 × 27 inches (76.2 × 68.58 cm). Private collection.

THE PURPLE COW

Early in my career as an illustrator I was called out by one of my mentors for doing predictable stuff. Something that really made me rethink the way that I approach painting was motivational writer Seth Godin's book *Purple Cow.* In the book, Godin says that if you were to drive by a field of cows, you probably would not stop and take a look at any old cow because they're pretty common to see. But if you saw a *purple* cow, you would absolutely stop and take a look. Thinking about this helps me to push the concept and think a little outside the box.

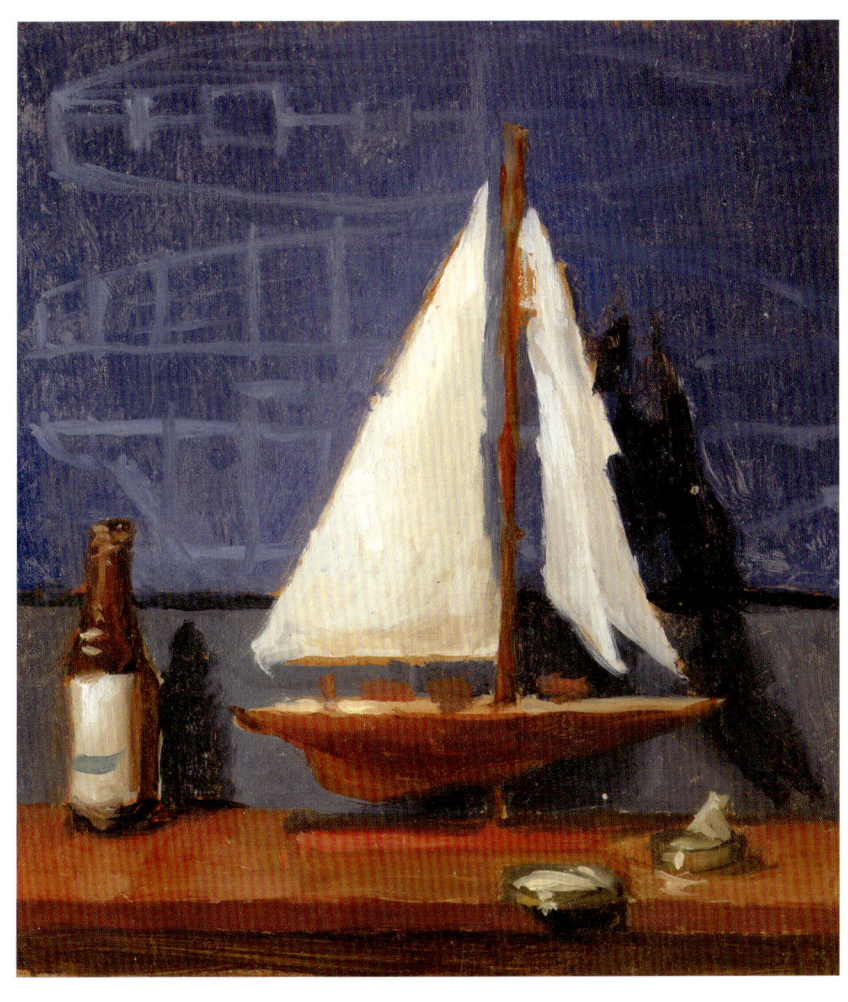

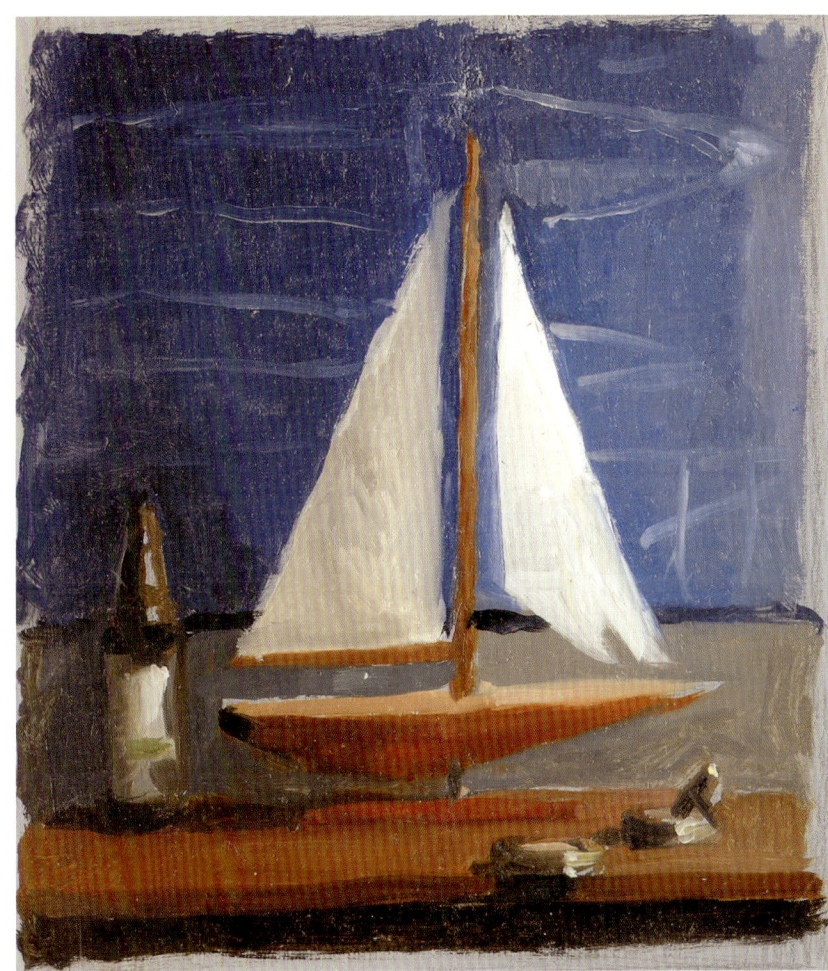

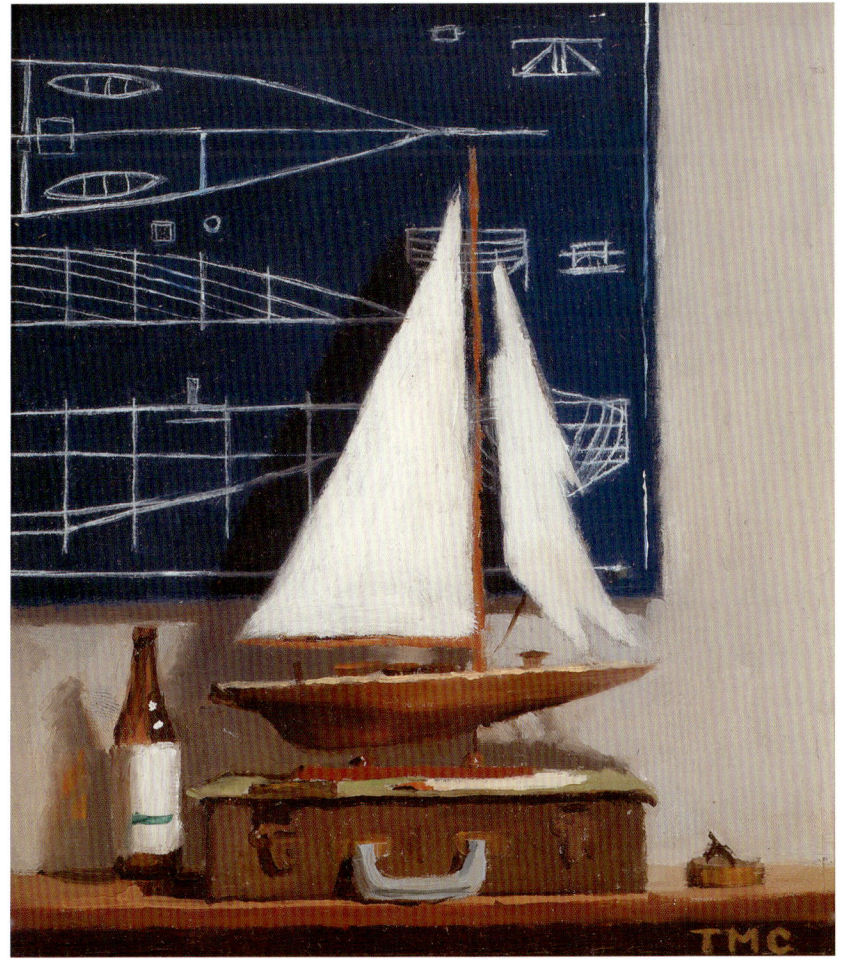

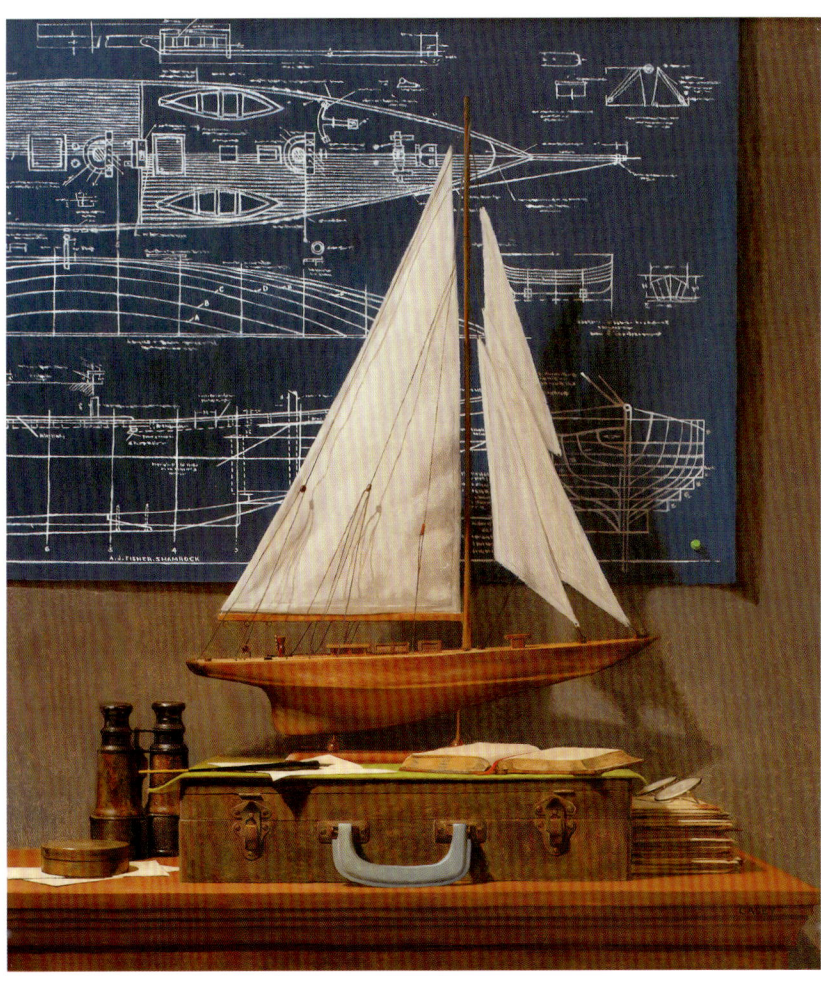

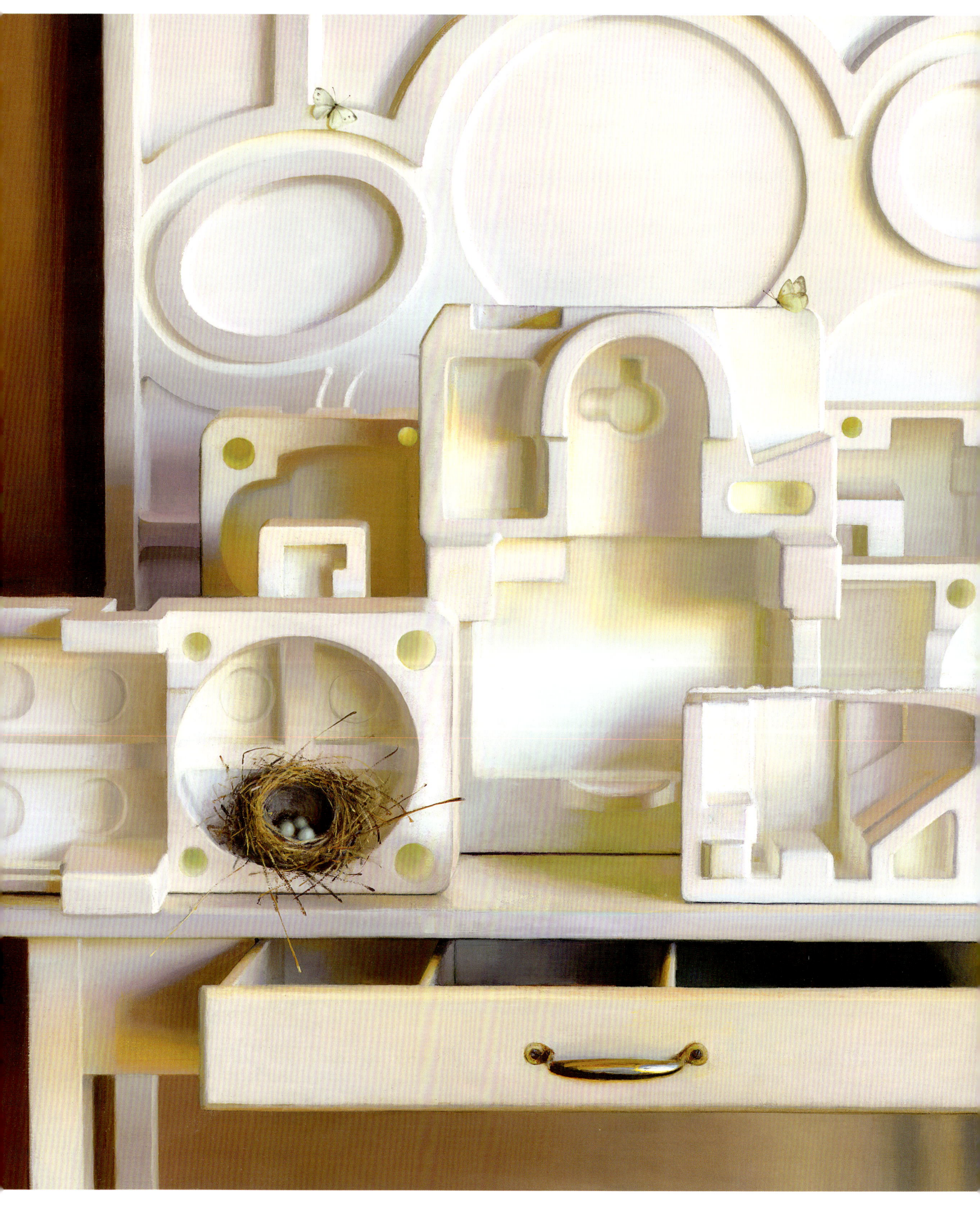

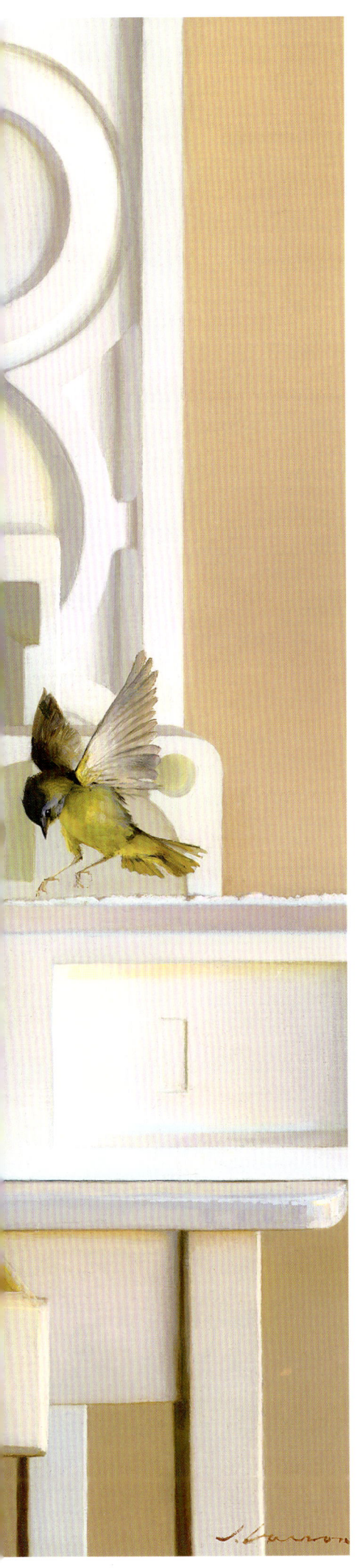

CHAPTER 3

COMPOSITION: CREATING UNITY

You must make the main thing in your picture appear most important. If anyone tells me my hat is more important than my head— by God I'm taking off my hat.

HARVEY DUNN

Once you have collected some objects you want to paint, it's time to organize them in a cohesive way that pleases the eye. In all the arts—literature, music, and the performing arts as well as the visual arts—composition refers to an arrangement of elements that organizes, harmonizes, and unites the work. By carefully composing a picture, you place emphasis on the most important element and guide your viewers through your painting so that they see the objects in the order you want them to.

LEFT: Jeffrey T. Larson, *In the Light of Life*, 2011, oil on linen, 36 x 40 inches (91.4 x 101.6cm). Courtesy of the artist.

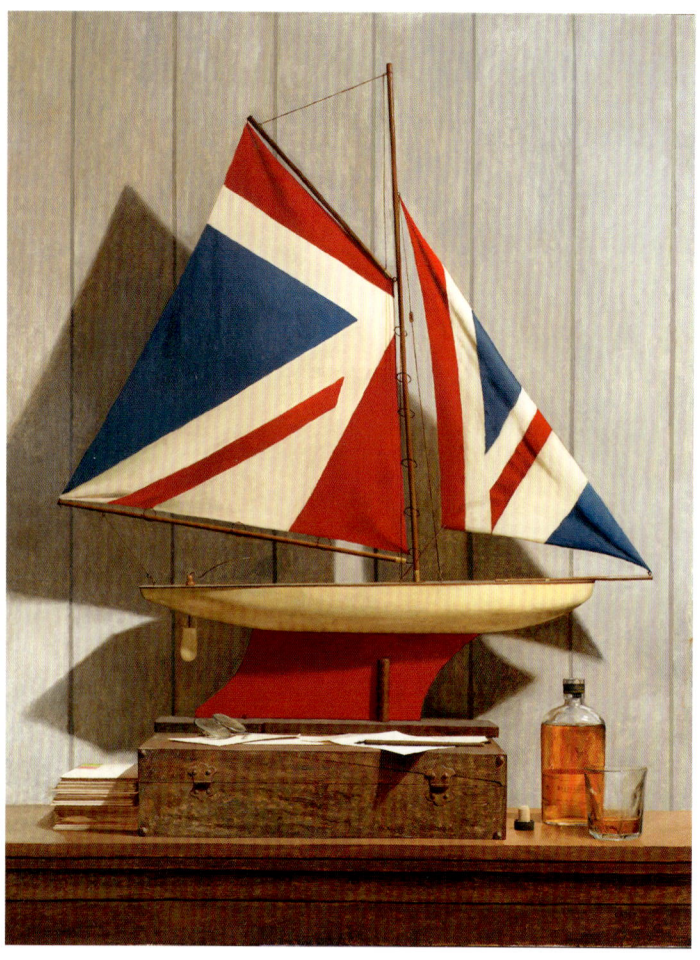

I used lots of big shapes to compose this scene. The dominant triangular shape of the boat sail is balanced by the rectangular shape at the bottom. Overall, the painting has a highly graphic quality.

THE SEVEN PRINCIPLES OF DESIGN

In his classic book *The Art of Color and Design*, Maitland E. Graves says that all good designs are built on seven basic principles: balance, movement, pattern, emphasis, contrast, rhythm, and unity. When you're composing a picture, these principles can act as a checklist to help you make sure your composition is as rich and engaging as it can be. Let's look a little more closely at each.

Principle 1: Balance

Every well-thought-out composition should feel balanced. There are three ways to classify balance: symmetry, asymmetry, and radial symmetry.

Symmetry means that if you were to draw a line down the center of an object, you would see that the left and right sides are exactly equal—mirror images of each other. A very symmetrical composition is one in which the balance is equal if divided by a center line. There is no dominant side, and the composition is rather static. If both sides are the same, the picture tends to be uninteresting, and the viewer may get bored.

Although we tend to idealize many objects, thinking of them as symmetrical, nearly everything organic is actually asymmetrical. *Asymmetry* means that if you were to draw a line down the center of an object, the left and right sides would not be perfectly equal. Asymmetry is very important in composition because it adds movement to a piece. Adding just a touch of asymmetry gives more weight to one side of a composition, drawing the viewer's eye to the element that creates that difference.

In *radial symmetry*, visual information is organized such that it is symmetrical in every direction—from the center out to the edges

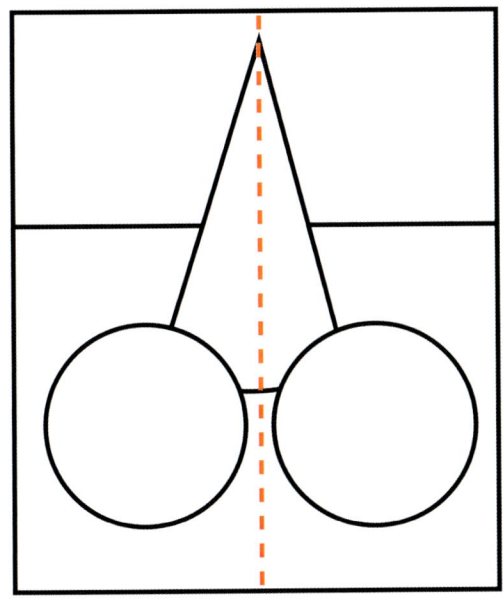

Symmetry

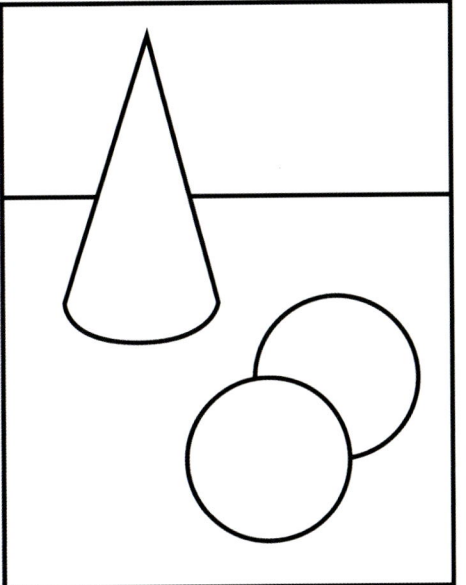

Asymmetry

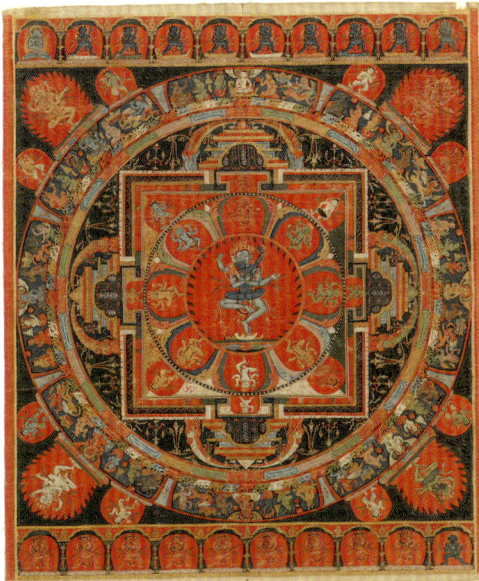

Radial symmetry

ABOVE: *Hevajara Mandala,* Tibet, 15th century, distemper on cloth, 21 ½ × 17 ½ inches (54.6 × 44.5 cm). The Metropolitan Museum of Art, New York. Gift of Stephen and Sharon Davies Collection, 2015.

TIP

You need to love your composition. Find the right objects, and work out a compelling setup that you will be excited to paint. Get it right, since you're going to spend a lot of time working on the painting and need to see it through to the end. Always look for new ways to compose so you don't get too repetitive. Some of my paintings are composed very easily, but some take a lot of time. Find what works for you and don't rush the process of loving your setup.

of a design, as in a snowflake. Radial symmetry is rare in Western composition—with the exception of the work of Dutch artist M. C. Escher—but it is common in some Eastern art, as in the Tibetan mandala above right.

Balancing a composition is similar to moving a seesaw: the only way to get the seesaw to move is to shift the weight to one side or the other. I like to make all my compositions asymmetrical, even if that means making one side of the image a hair more dominant than the other.

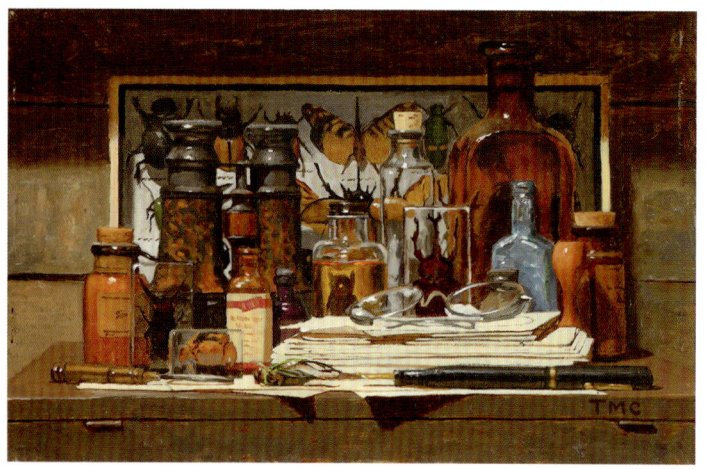

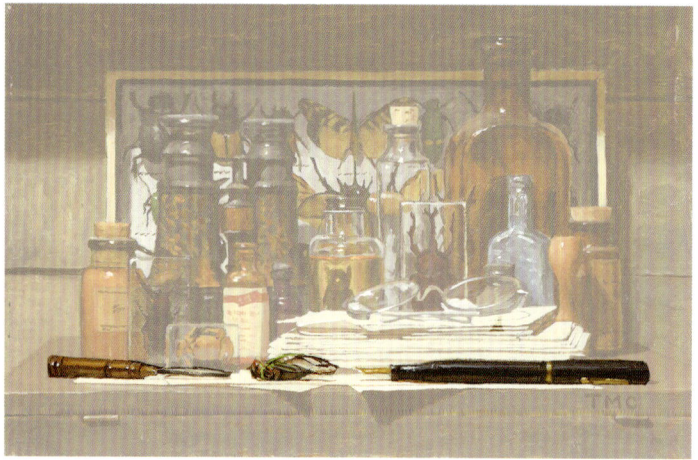

Principle 2: Movement

Some objects can imply action and move the eye through a design. In my study for my painting *The Entomologist*, at left, the scene is really busy, with lots of objects whose brown color builds unity. This composition, however, was built around the green cicada near the bottom of the image. It was not the intended focal point, so it was placed in the design in a very subtle way. To direct the viewer's eye to look at it, I used the directional shapes of the pen and the magnifying glass.

Principle 3: Pattern/Repetition

Pattern refers to the repetition of color or shapes within a composition. This repetition brings unity to the piece. One great way to balance areas with large dominant shapes is to incorporate a patterned textile into the composition. In *Moon and Star*, by Carol Broman, at top opposite, the pattern of embroidered stars on the cloth (and its reflection in the jug) carries the eye through the piece. It also echoes the starfish shape, helping to tie all the elements together.

The texture of brushstrokes can act as a pattern as well. In his painting *Fish with White Onions*, Travis Schlaht creates a texture in the upper right background that feels like an organic pattern. This helps balance the nontextural objects such as the red pepper, onions, and fish.

Too much pattern can confuse viewers, not letting them know where you want them to look. Too much flat, open area can do the same thing, so I always try to balance flat, open areas with patterned/textural areas.

ABOVE: Todd M. Casey, study for *The Entomologist*, 2017, oil on panel, 6 × 9 inches (15.24 × 20.32 cm). Private collection.

In this design, the magnifying glass and pen act as pointing devices to lead the viewer to look at the cicada.

OPPOSITE, TOP: Carol Broman, *Moon and Star*, 2010, oil on linen, 14 × 18 inches (35.56 × 45.72 cm). Courtesy of the artist.

OPPOSITE, BOTTOM: Travis Schlaht, *Fish with White Onions*, 2010, oil on linen, 12 × 16 inches (30.48 × 40.64 cm). Courtesy of the artist.

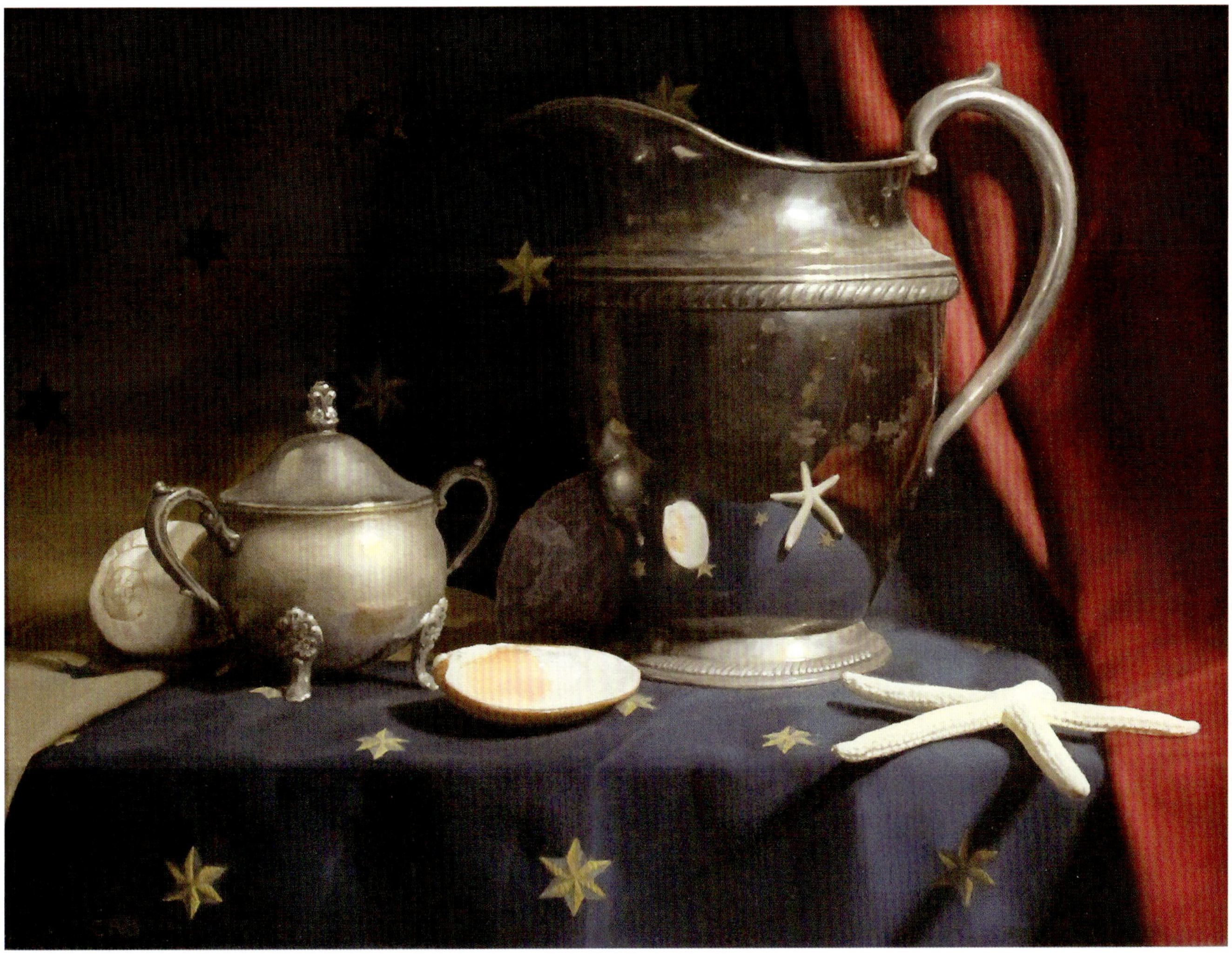

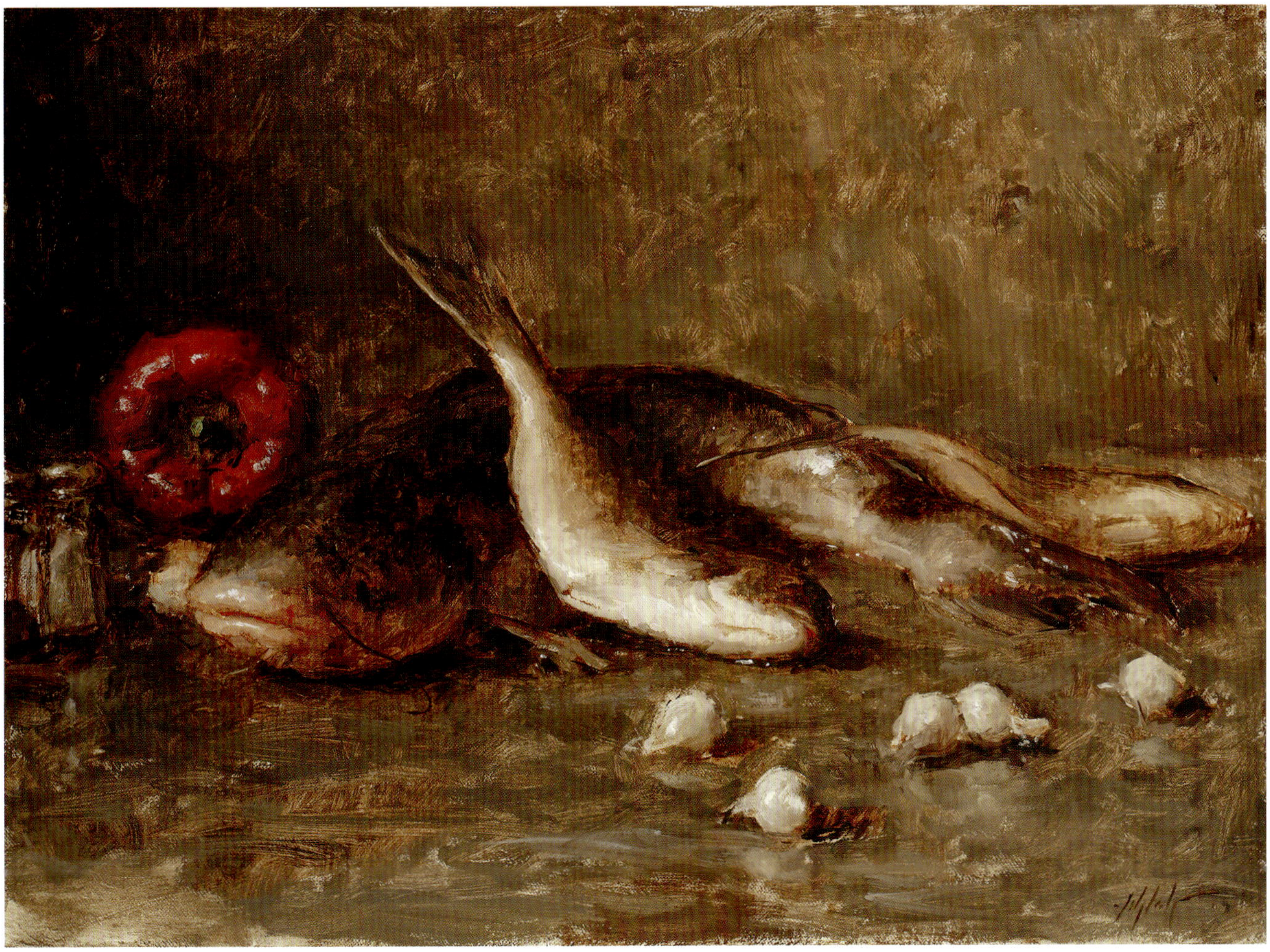

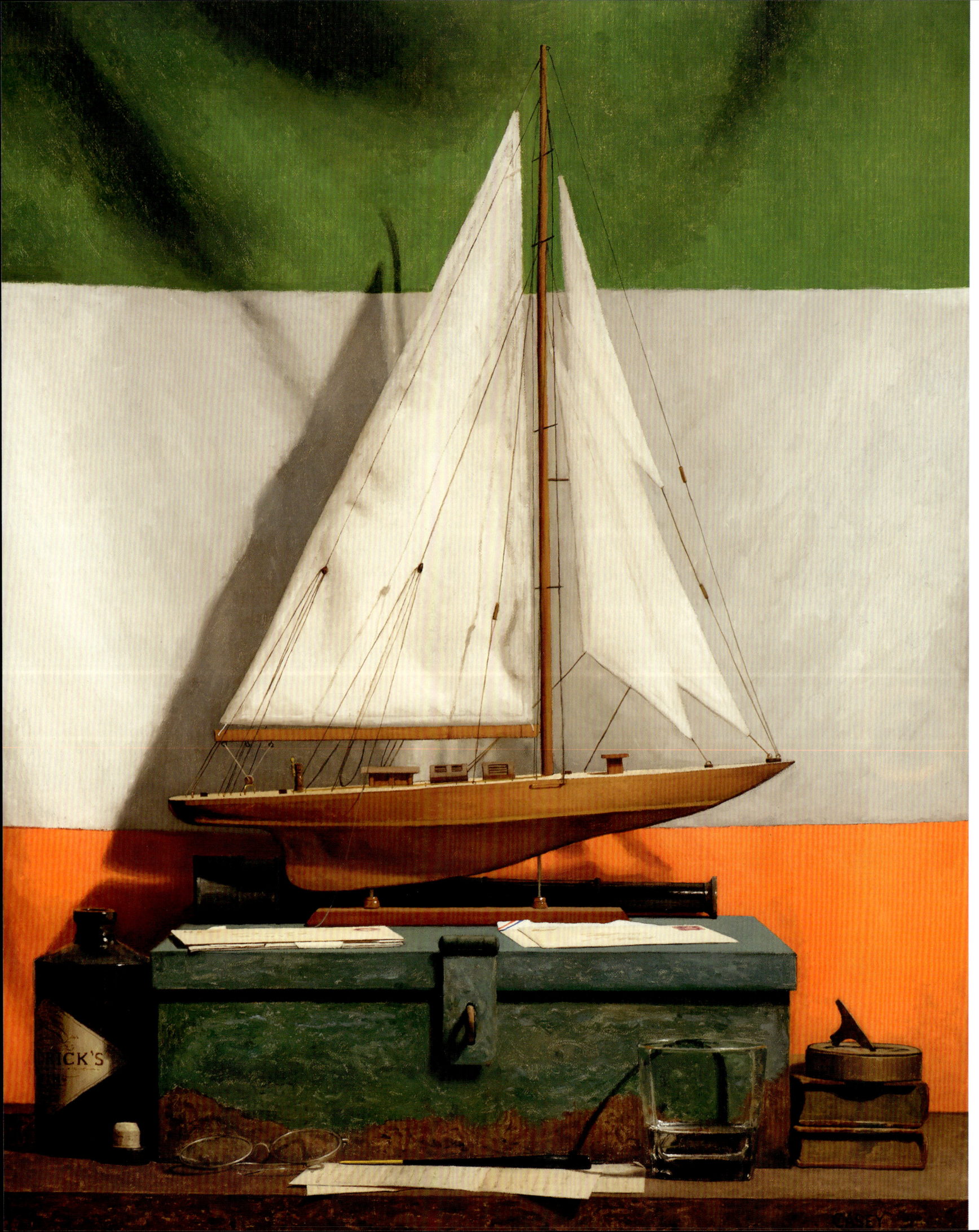

Principle 4: Emphasis, or Hierarchy

An emphasis, or hierarchy, should be considered when designing a composition so that the viewer knows where to look. Emphasis can be built in a couple of ways: through a dominant shape or a high-contrast focal point.

DOMINANT SHAPE

One way to have a clear hierarchy in your painting is to have one "star"—a large, dominant shape that will grab the attention of the viewer first. The examples here show the use of a triangle, rectangle, and circle as the dominant shape.

OPPOSITE: Todd M. Casey, *Against the Wind,* 2016, oil on linen, 36 × 28 inches (91.44 × 71.12 cm). Courtesy of Rehs Contemporary Galleries, New York.

Large shapes build hierarchy. In this boat painting, the triangular sail dominates the picture. I wanted to add shapes to the design that were not on a diagonal, so I went with some geometric squares and rectangles along the bottom to contrast with the triangle.

ABOVE, RIGHT: Todd M. Casey, *Cape Codder,* 2017, oil on panel, 9 × 12 inches (22.86 × 30.48 cm). Private collection.

RIGHT: Emil Carlsen, *Still Life with Brazier, Silver Tea and Quinces,* 1918, oil on canvas, 24 × 20 inches (60.96 × 50.8 cm). Courtesy of Emil Carlsen Archives (emilcarlsen.org).

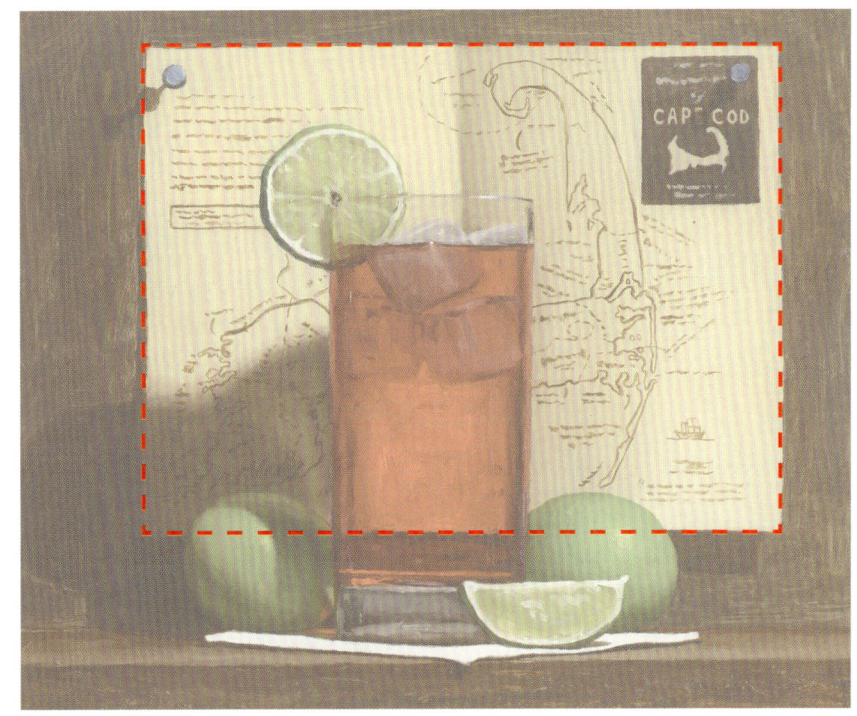

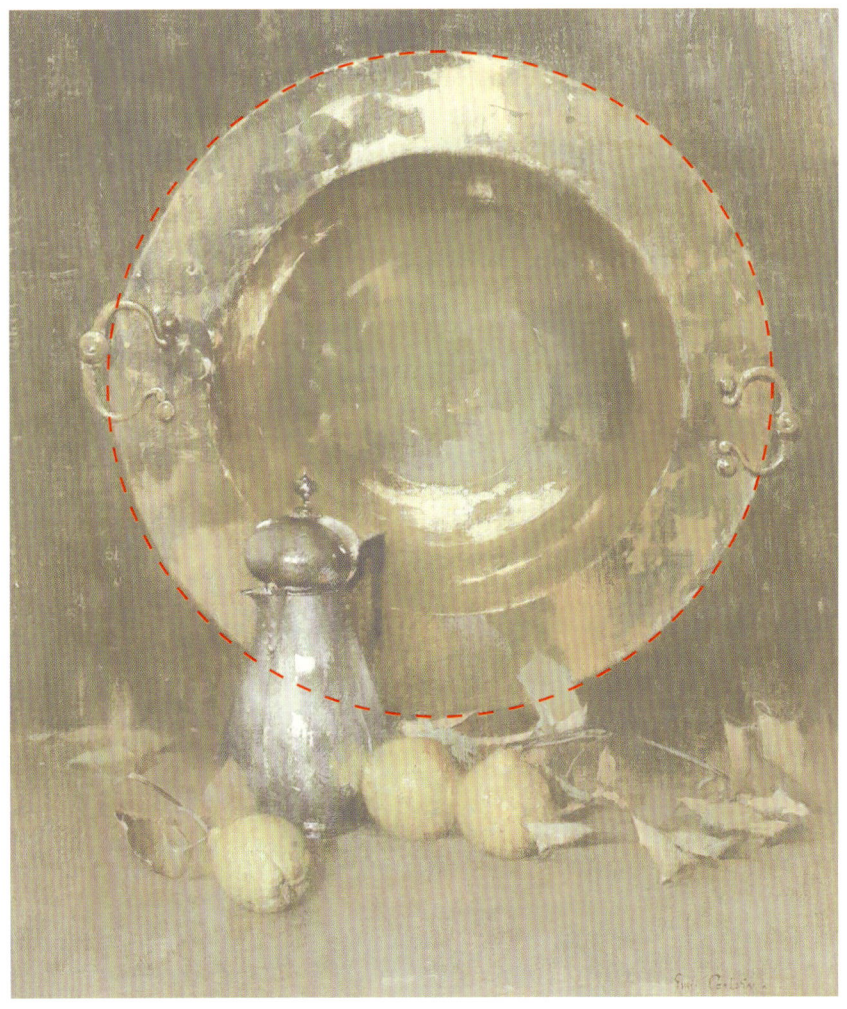

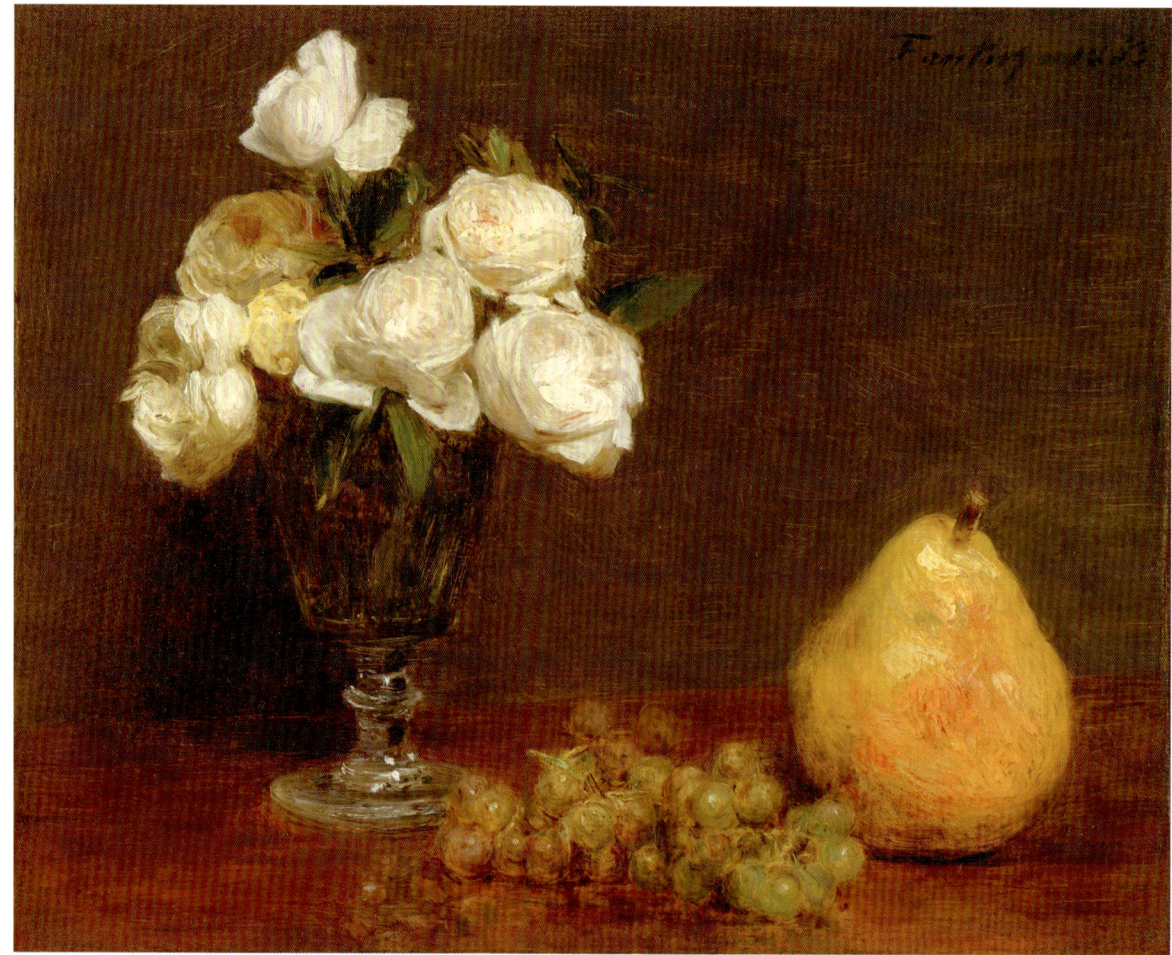

In *Still Life with Roses and Fruit,* Henri Fantin-Latour uses white roses contrasting against the dark background to bring the eye right to this area of the painting.

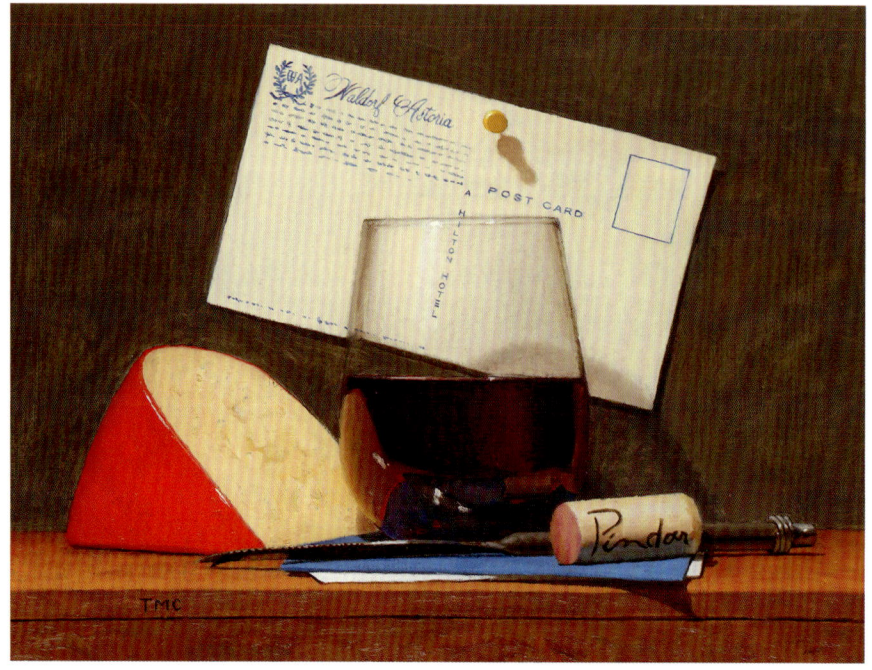

HIGH CHROMA

A high-chroma color such as an intense red, orange, or yellow can grab the viewer, forcing the eye to look at that area of the painting first. Sometimes color can override our instinct to look at high contrast. Here, we see that the eye goes right to the red cheese and not to the high contrast between the wine glass and the postcard.

HIGH-CONTRAST FOCAL POINT

The focal point is the area of a painting that you want the viewer to look at first—the entry into the total design. Often, this area has the highest contrast in the painting—the lightest value alongside the darkest value.

Principle 5: Contrast

I'm always thinking in terms of opposites and how opposites attract. If a composition is too dominated by one shape it's nice to add the complement of the shape into the design to balance it. If you have a lot of large objects, try to add some interesting small objects to the composition. If a composition is too busy, balance it with some passive areas to let the eye take a break. If one color is too dominant, balance it with its complement (see page 215 on complementary colors).

BELOW: Sadie Valeri, *Black Jug,* 2010, oil on panel, 8 × 10 inches (20.32 × 25.4 cm). Courtesy of the artist.

In *Black Jug,* Sadie Valeri achieves contrast through a difference in scale.

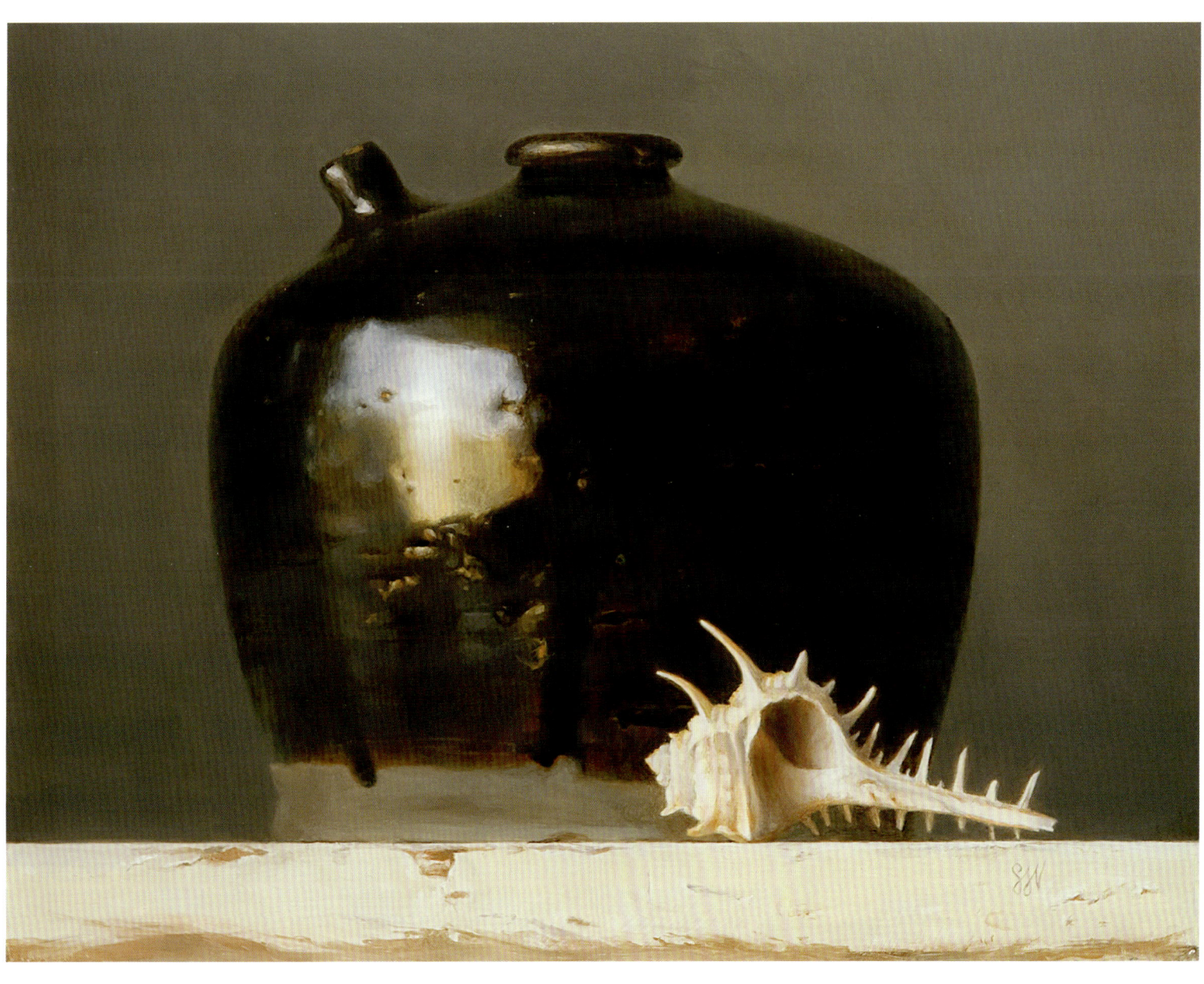

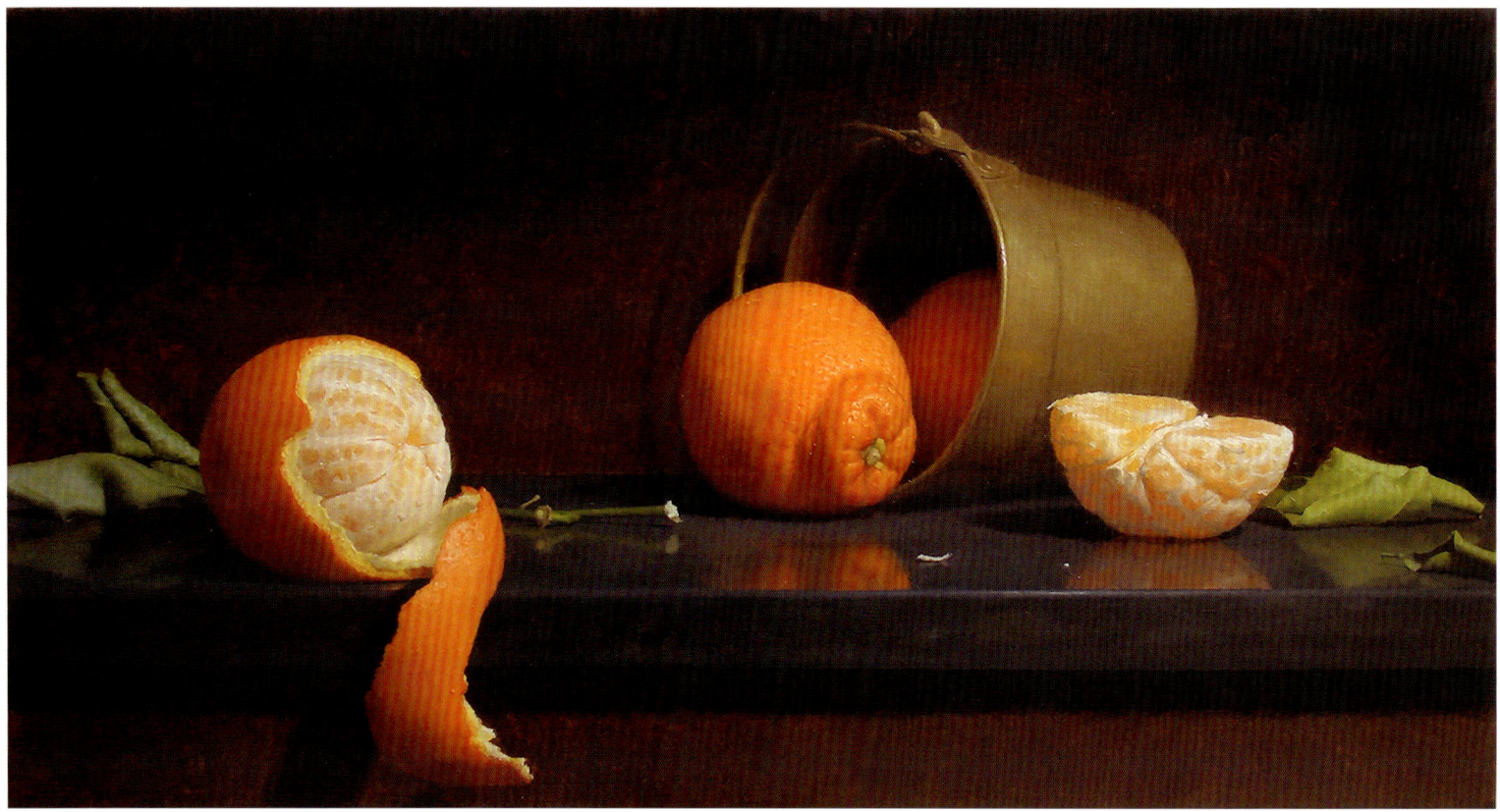

In this painting, the grouping of the bucket and oranges is contrasted by the half-peeled orange on the left. The objects are still united through color and repetition of the shapes but are contrasted by grouping and isolating.

In this Dutch still life, variety is achieved by a mixture of organic and inorganic objects. The composition remains unified by the colors.

Balancing isolated objects with grouped objects is another way to create contrast. If one area of the image has a lot of overlapping shapes, another area might have just one isolated object. The "busy" part of the design is balanced against a much more passive part.

Variety in a composition can also be key to a successful painting. Variety really is the spice of life, as too much of anything can get boring. A nice variety of shapes is a great way to spice up your composition. If you have a lot of circular shapes, a contrasting angular shape can help balance the composition.

TIP

Edit wisely. Placing the wrong object in a setup can change the whole story tremendously. The trick is to find the sweet spot where if you add one more thing to the composition it will be too much and if you subtract one thing the design will fall apart. I always tell my students to collect the elements they want to use in a picture, create a setup using all of them, and then slowly remove one item at a time. When it seems like you've taken out one element too many, put that last thing back—you've found what's needed to tell your story in its simplest form.

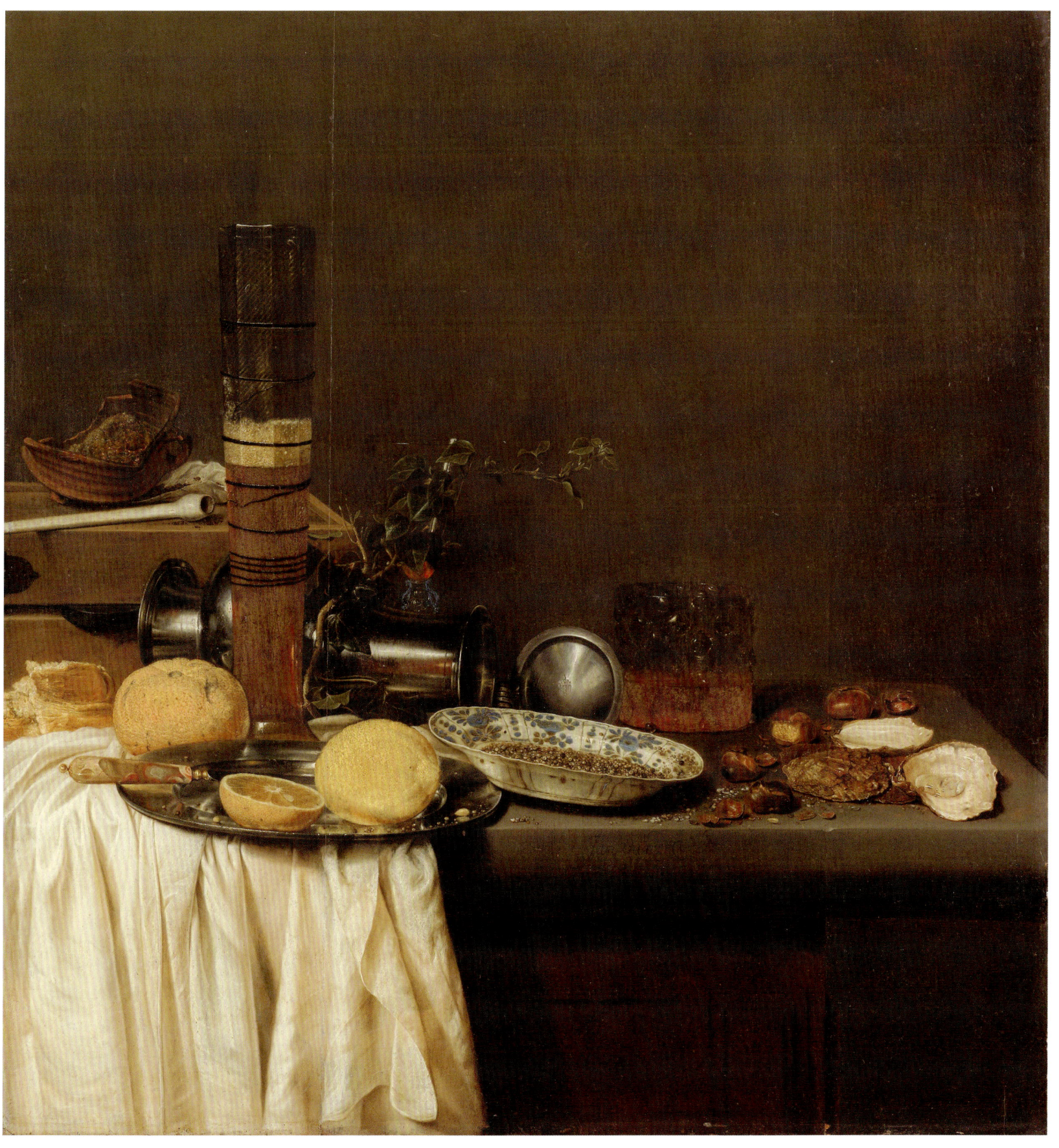

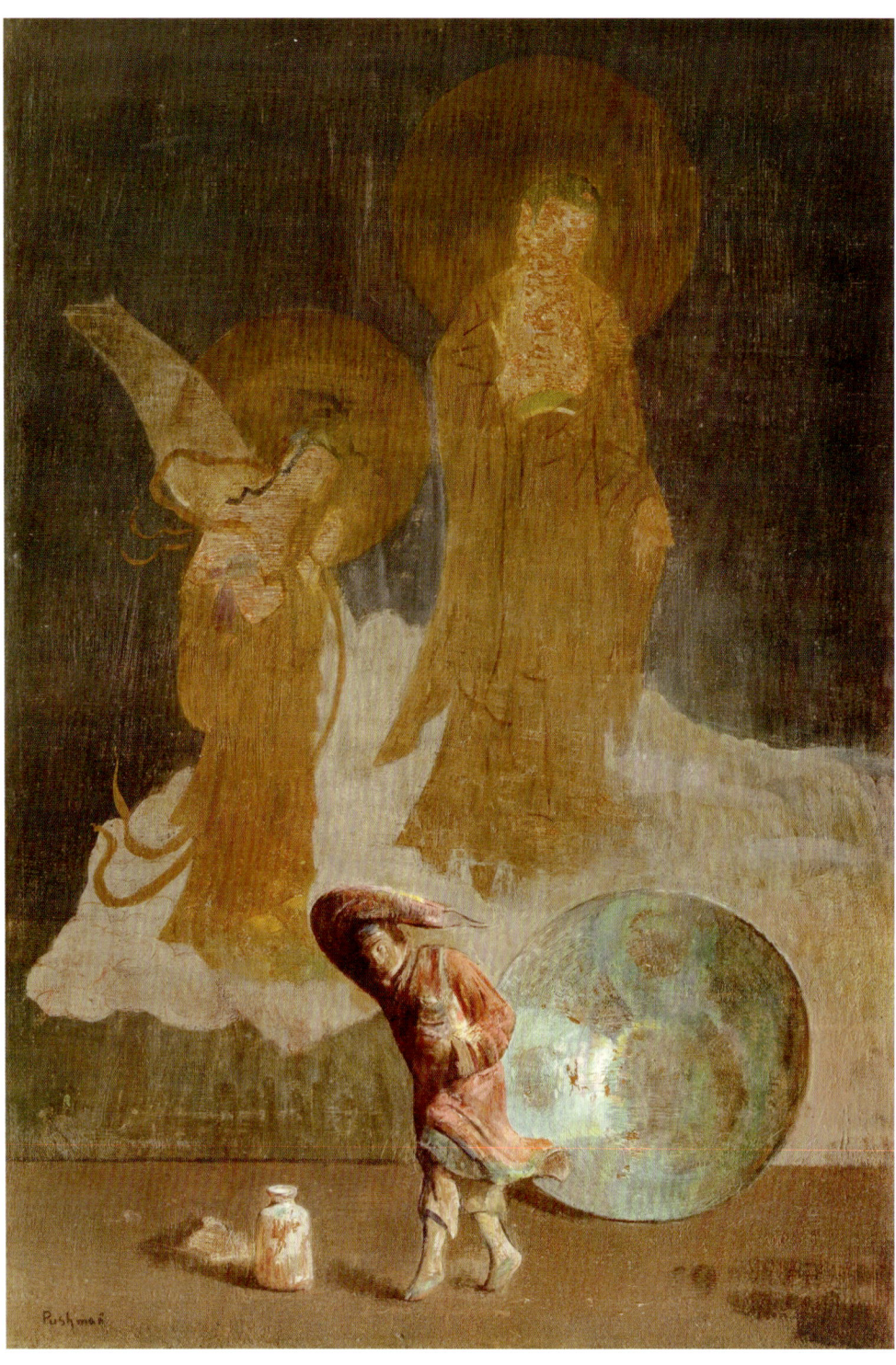

In Hovsep Pushman's *Eternal Compassion,* the similar shapes of the figurine and the two figures in the background create a unifying rhythm.

Principle 6: Rhythm

We usually think of rhythm as a characteristic of music—a strong, regular, repeated pattern of sound. But rhythm can be visual, too. Rhythm occurs in a composition when elements are repeated in a non-uniform way that feels organized and creates movement. For instance, you might repeat shapes that are not identical but belong to the same "family" of shapes, as in the painting above.

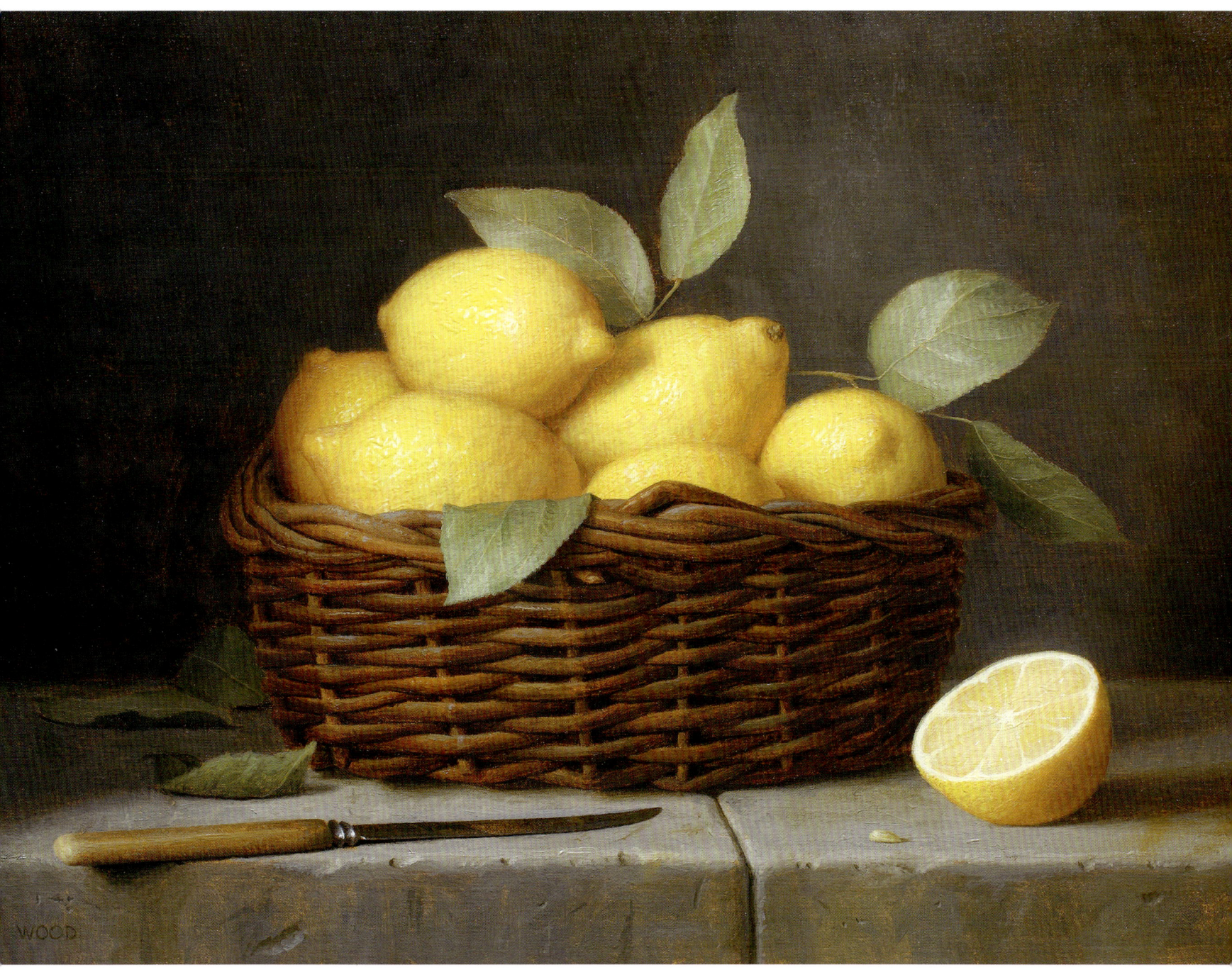

Principle 7: Unity, or Harmony

All compositions should strive for some sort of cohesiveness. Without unity, a picture may feel disjointed, as the elements will not feel tied to one another. Unity can be achieved in several different ways: through color (for example, through the use of analogous colors; see page 204), through complementary shapes, or through pattern and repetition. However you set up your composition, unity is one of the most important things to consider.

ABOVE: Justin Wood, *Basket of Lemons*, 2018, oil on canvas, 12 × 16 inches (30.48 × 40.64 cm). Courtesy of the artist.

In this painting, unity is achieved through the repetition of color and also through the use of analogous colors in the lemon, brown basket, and green leaves. Plus, the painting also has a nice contrast of warm and cool.

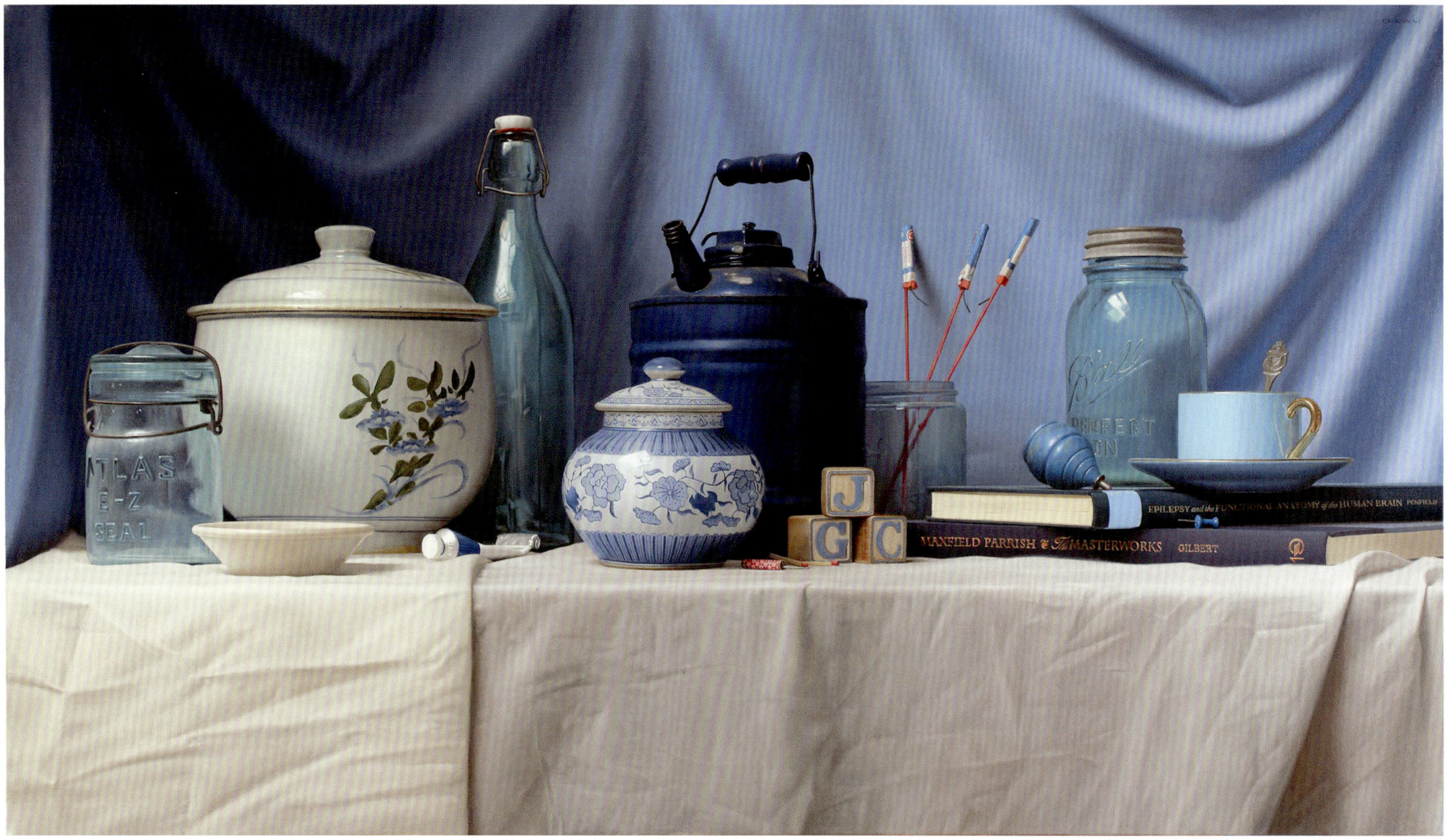

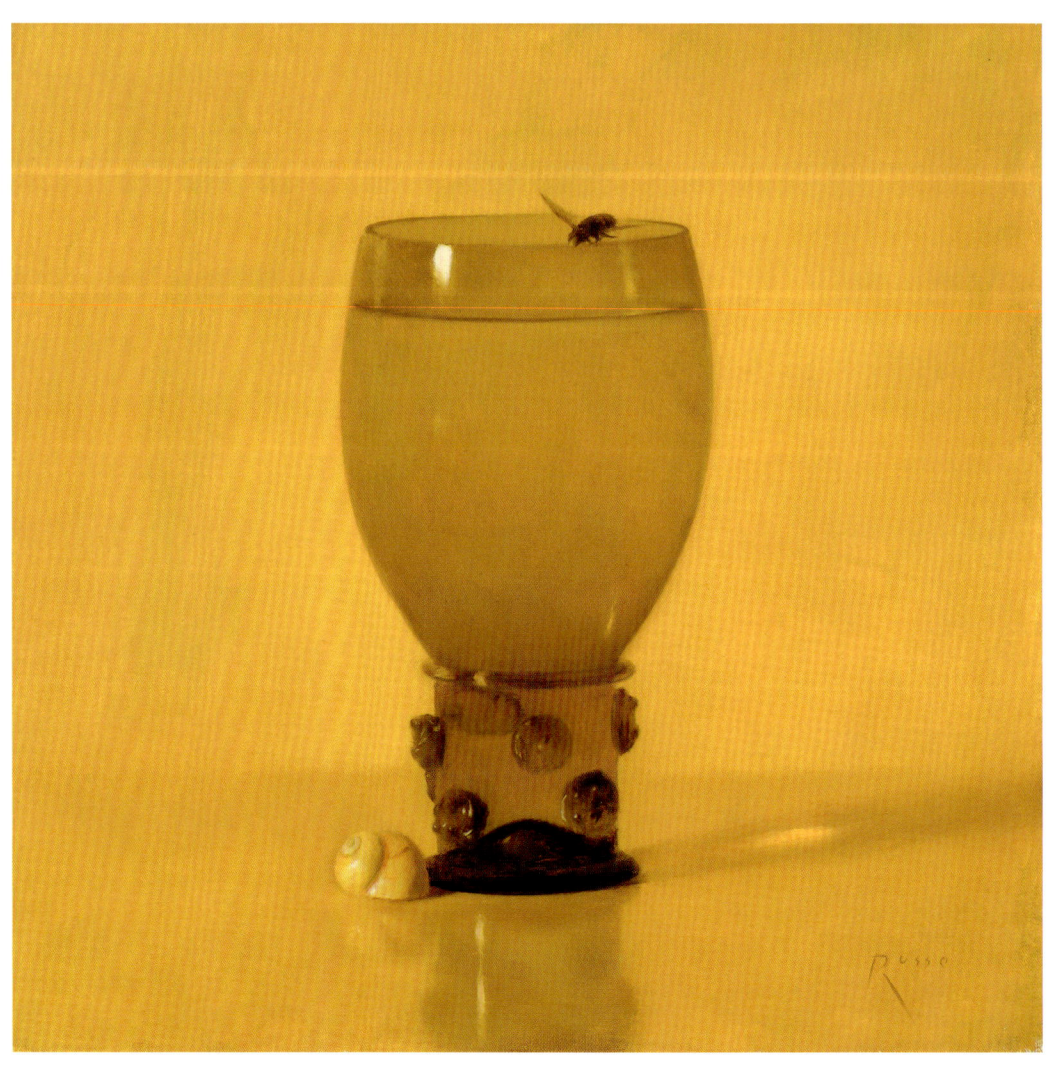

ABOVE: Tony Curanaj, *Kind of Blue,* 2014, oil on linen, 22 × 37 inches (55.88 × 93.98 cm). Courtesy of the artist.

Color can be used to unite all the elements in a picture. Here, the repeated use of blue creates unity throughout the design.

RIGHT: Carlo Russo, *Amber and Gold,* 2017, oil on linen, 9 × 9 inches (22.86 × 22.86 cm). Courtesy of the artist.

An amber/gold color dominates this painting by Carlo Russo, making it seem as if a yellow gel or film covers the composition, unifying the elements.

Tying together the different parts of a painting with hues of the same family will create a cohesive feel. You can have one color dominate a painting, which is referred to as color dominance.

DEPTH IN COMPOSITION

The seven elements of design are a great checklist, but there are some additional things to consider when composing. Depth is one of the most important, as it adds to the illusion of space. One way depth can be created is with overlapping shapes (sometimes referred to as *form over form*), in which closer objects partly obscure objects that are farther away.

Trompe l'oeil paintings (see page 72) traditionally have a very shallow depth of field—although the illusion of depth can be even more convincing than in a painting with a deeper depth of field. Certain tricks—like folded paper—enhance the illusion of depth, making the objects seem as if they're sitting right there on the surface of the painting.

BELOW: Julian Alden Weir (American, 1852–1919), *Still Life in the Studio*, 1878–80, oil on canvas, 30 × 48 inches (76.2 × 121.9 cm). Yale University Art Gallery.

Not only do the forms in Julian Alden Weir's *Still Life in the Studio* overlap, but we also see a full range of values, from light in the foreground to dark in the background. Both of these techniques heighten the illusion of depth in the painting.

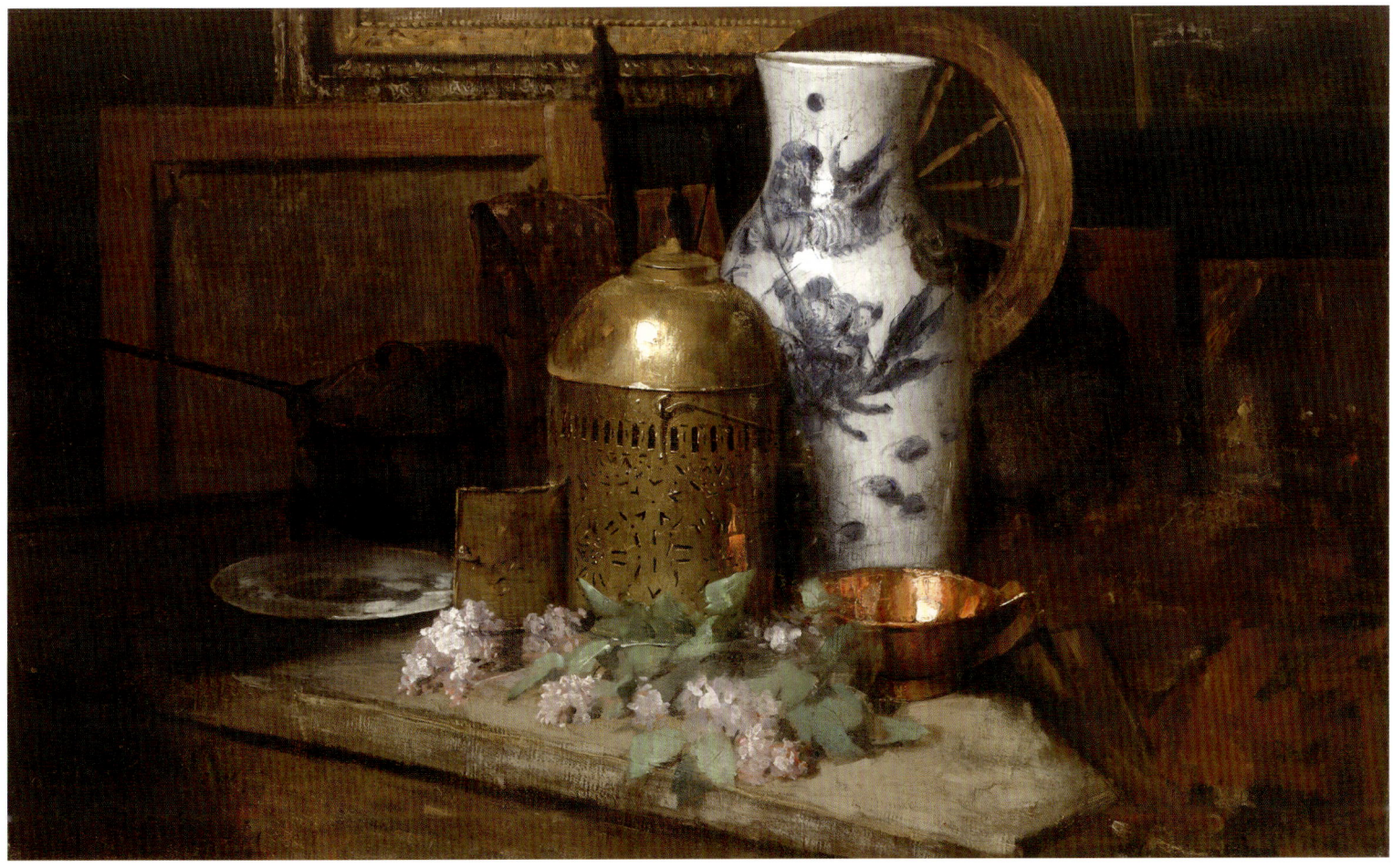

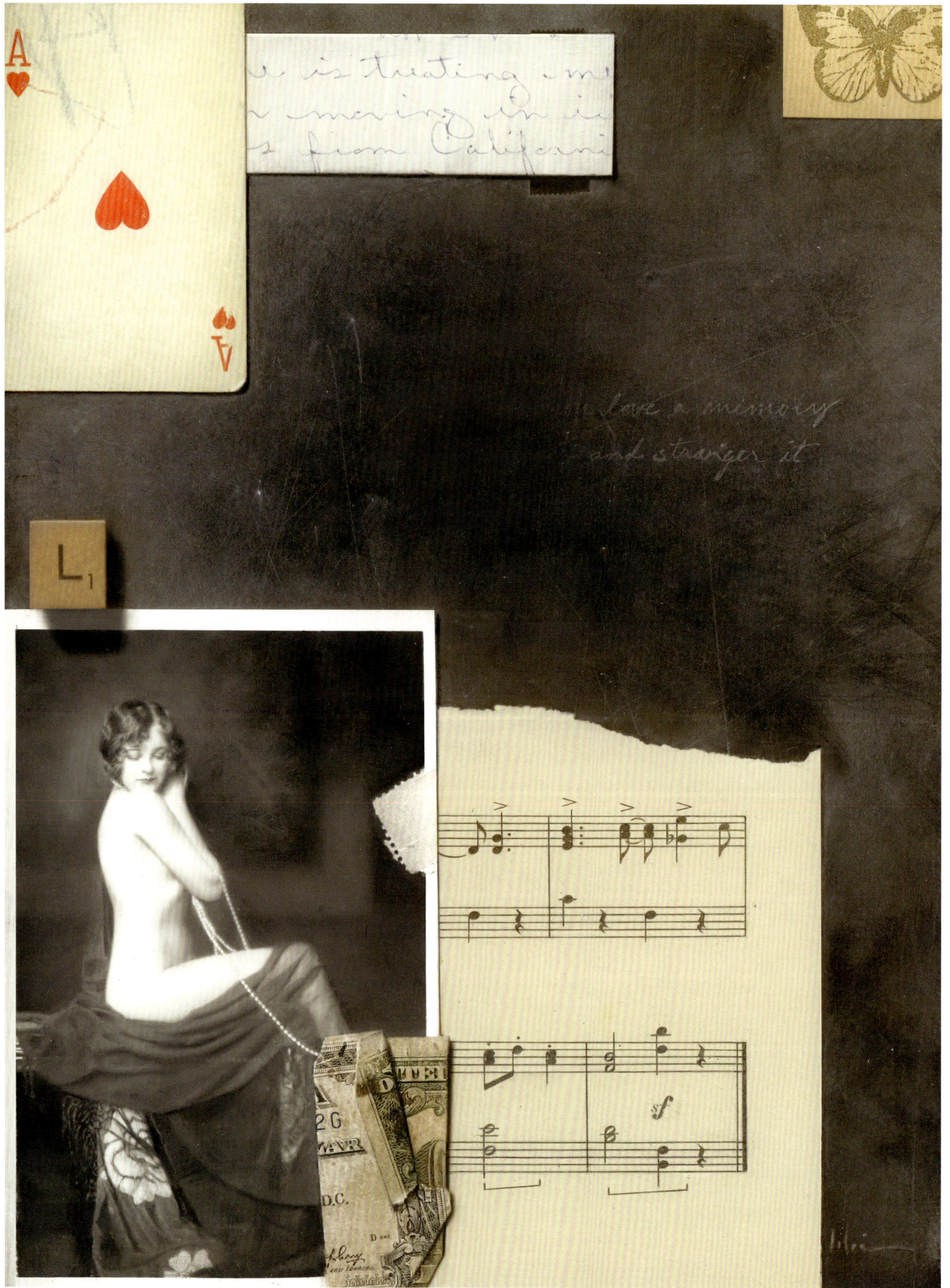

POINT OF VIEW IN COMPOSITION

It's also important to consider point of view when composing. The perspective from which you, as the artist, are looking at your setup is also the perspective from which the viewer will see the scene. There are essentially three points of view in still life:

1. The setup is at eye level.

2. You are looking down at the setup.

3. You are looking up at the setup.

The most common point of view is the eye-level, or straight-on, view. In this view, the surface that the objects are sitting on is very foreshortened (see page 180). This viewpoint takes the focus off perspective (depth) and places it on the objects' interaction with one another.

Looking down at a setup gives viewers the sense that they, too, are standing above it, looking down. Because you can see more of the plane that the objects are sitting on, there is a greater sense of depth than in the eye-level point of view.

The last of the three points of view is that from below the horizon line, where you are looking up at the setup. This is evident in Jeffrey T. Larson's painting *Fish and Crackers* (next page).

OPPOSITE: Anthony Waichulis, *Mémoire,* 2018, oil on panel, 12 × 9 inches (30.5 × 22.9 cm). Courtesy of the artist.

Painstakingly rendered objects, overlapping, and precisely painted shadows create a shallow—but very real-seeming—depth of field in this trompe l'oeil painting.

BELOW, LEFT: Sadie Valeri, *Wax Paper,* 2008, oil on panel, 11 × 14 inches (27.94 × 35.56 cm). Courtesy of the artist.

In this painting by Sadie Valeri, the viewer is just about at eye level with the setup.

BELOW, RIGHT: Kate Lehman, *Blue,* 2006, oil on canvas, 24 × 24 inches (60.96 × 60.96 cm). Courtesy of the artist.

The viewpoint here is from above the setup. Things diminish in size as they go back in space, creating depth.

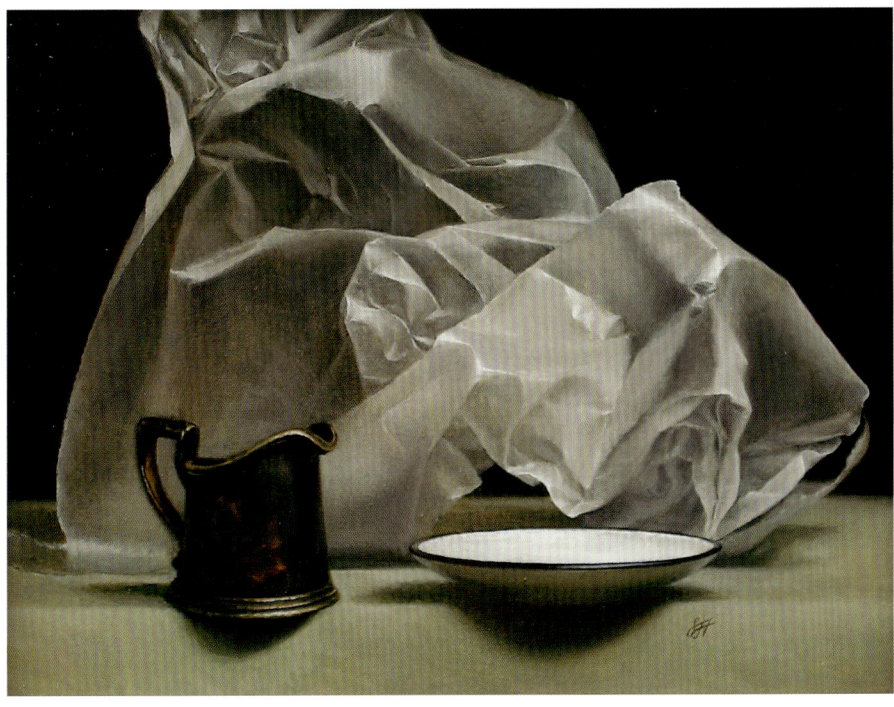

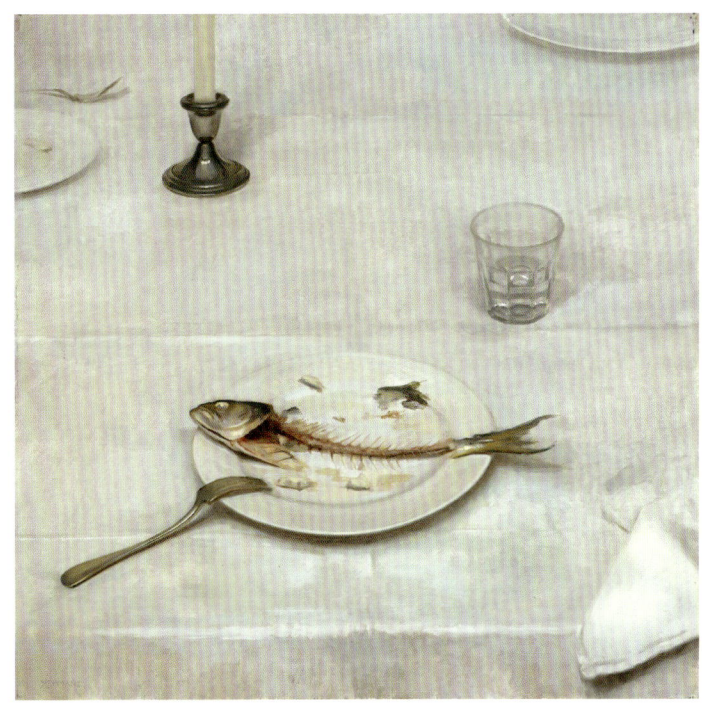

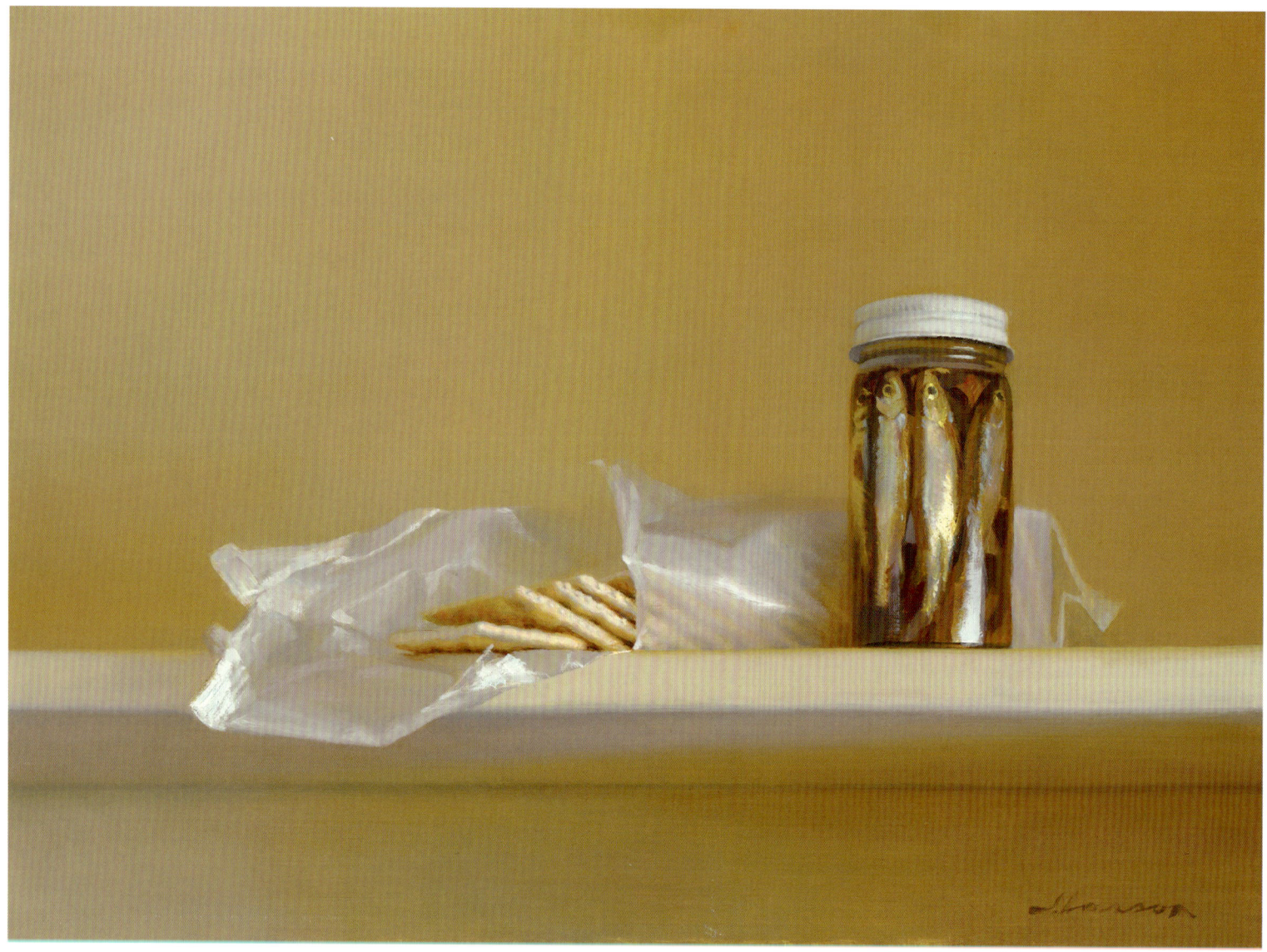

ABOVE: Jeffrey T. Larson, *Fish and Crackers*, 2009, oil on linen, 12 × 16 inches (30.48 × 40.64 cm). Courtesy of the artist.

Here, we see the lower side of the shelf, indicating that we're below the setup.

OPPOSITE, TOP: Todd M. Casey, *Pumpkin with Globe and Books*, 2012, oil on linen, 11 × 16 inches (27.94 × 40.64 cm). Courtesy of Rehs Contemporary Galleries, New York.

Lighting a still life from below can have an interesting effect on mood. This bottom-lit composition feels creepy and scary—probably because we associate this kind of lighting with horror movies in which monsters and villains are lit from beneath.

OPPOSITE, BOTTOM: Edward Minoff, *Mozzarella di Bufala*, 2010, oil on linen, 18 × 24 inches (45.72 × 60.96 cm). Courtesy of the artist.

The cast shadow breaks up this painting's background by adding a triangle shape to the design.

USING LIGHT TO COMPOSE

The direction of the light and the cast shadows it creates can have a major effect on a composition, creating abstract light and shadow shapes. Traditionally, still life setups are lit from the top. You can always play around, however, with how your setup is lit.

A cast shadow can be used to break up a big area or to create a large abstract shape. This can add variety to a design in which many of the shapes are vertical or horizontal.

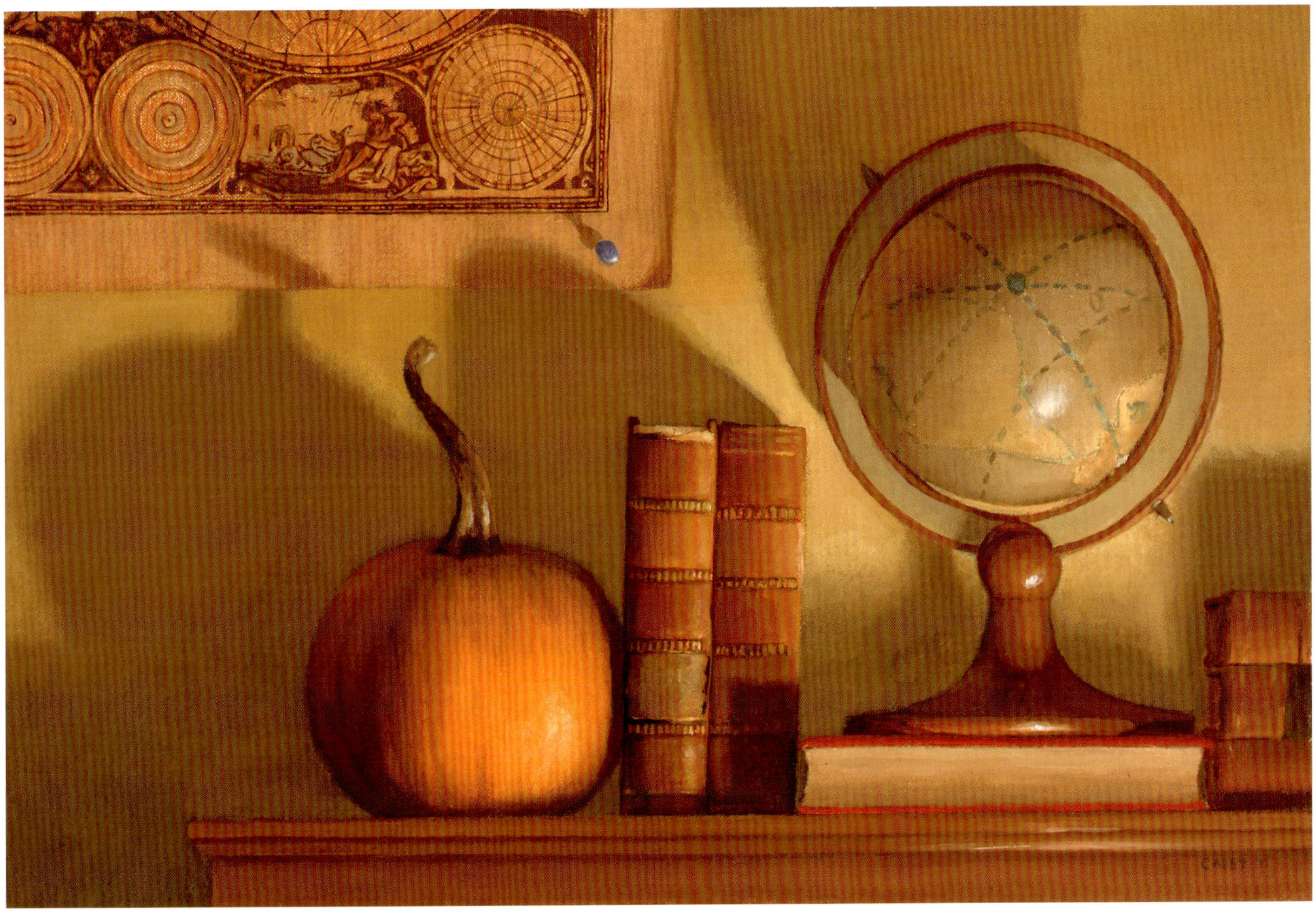

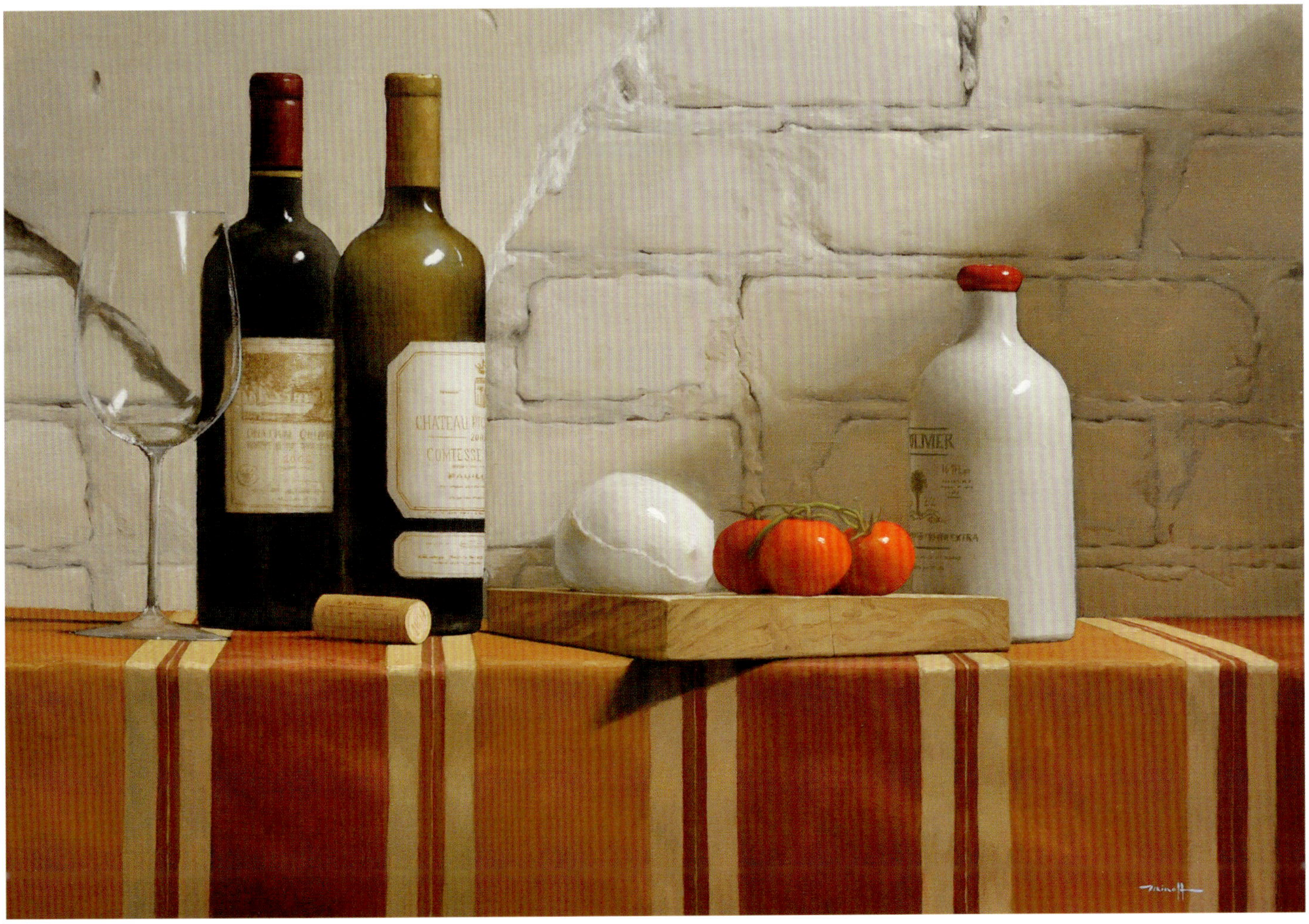
CHATEAU

THE RULE OF THIRDS

Over the centuries, artists have devised many tools to help them when composing. If you take pictures with a smart phone, you may be familiar with one of these—the rule of thirds. Android and iPhone phones allow you to impose a simple grid over the camera's viewing screen—a grid that divides the image into thirds vertically and horizontally. The four points where the horizontals and verticals intersect are called the "power points." If you place your image's focal point at or near one of these junctions, the composition will be more pleasing. This compositional tool also prevents you from putting objects too close to the edges of the image, which can create tension.

ABOVE: This rectangle has been divided into thirds vertically and horizontally. The "power points" where the lines intersect are circled in red.

RIGHT: Todd M. Casey, *Bar Study 1,* 2016, oil on panel, 6 × 9 inches (15.24 × 20.32 cm). Private collection.

Here we see the rule of thirds applied to a painting. The power points show high contrast and high saturation of color.

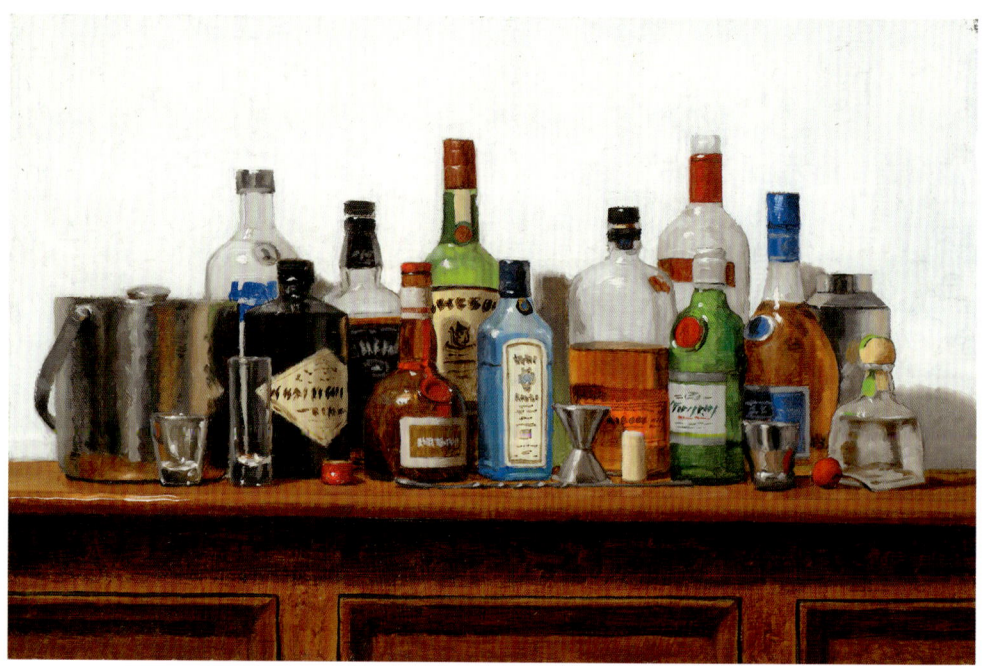

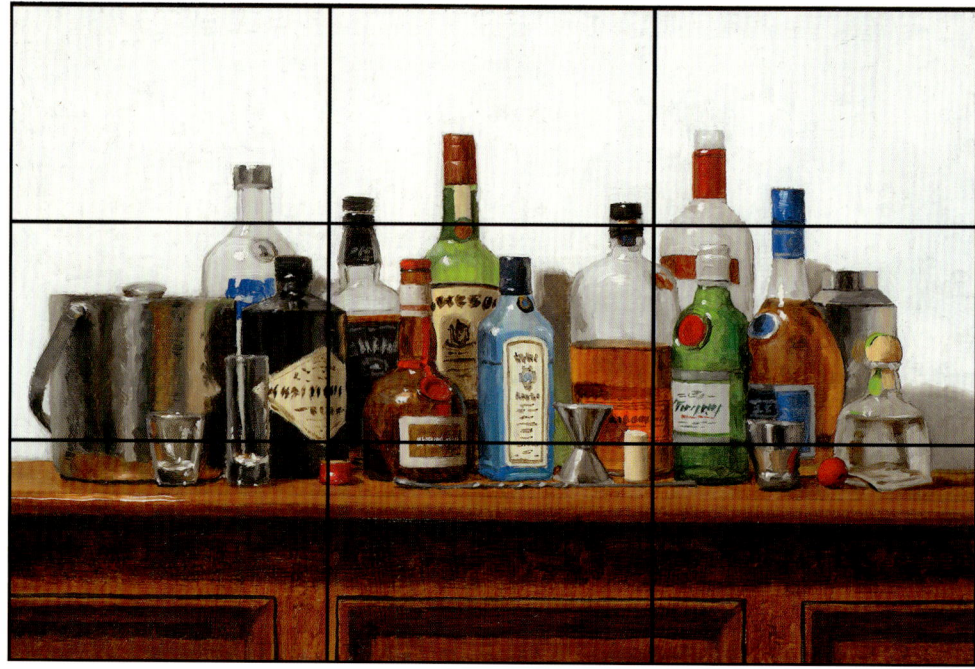

LOSING
YOUR EDGES

When you frame a painting with a traditional frame, you lose about one-quarter of an inch all around the image because of the rabbet—the lip of the frame that holds the painting in place. Therefore, you should keep any important element at least an eighth of an inch away from the edge. I plan for this loss from the beginning. Being aware of it means you won't be surprised when the work is framed.

TOP: The red line marks off the area that will be lost to the rabbet of a frame.

BOTTOM: When a picture is framed, approximately one-quarter of an inch is lost all around the outside edge.

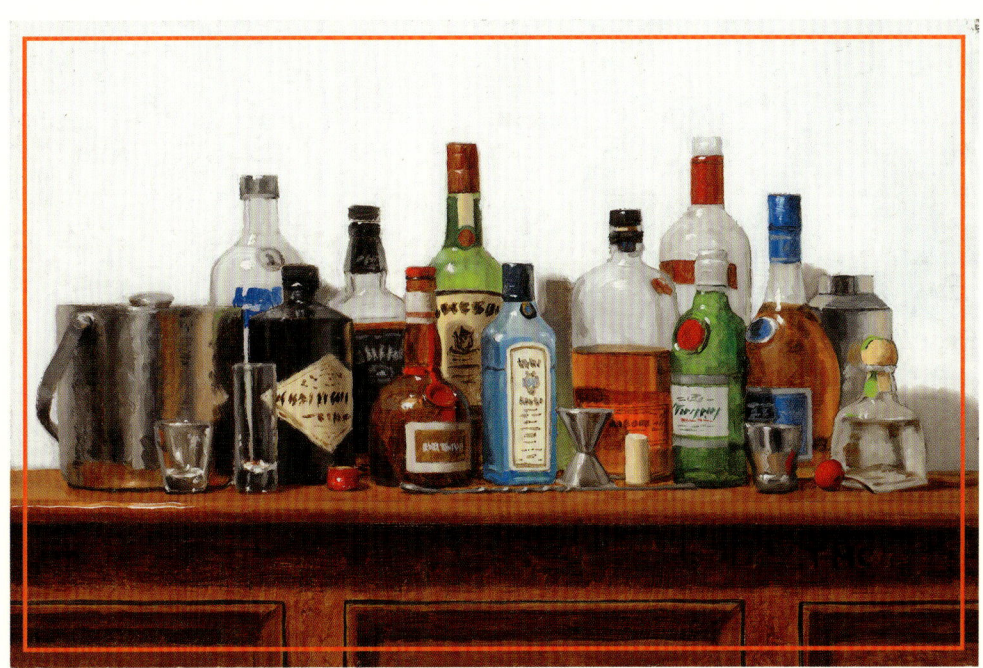

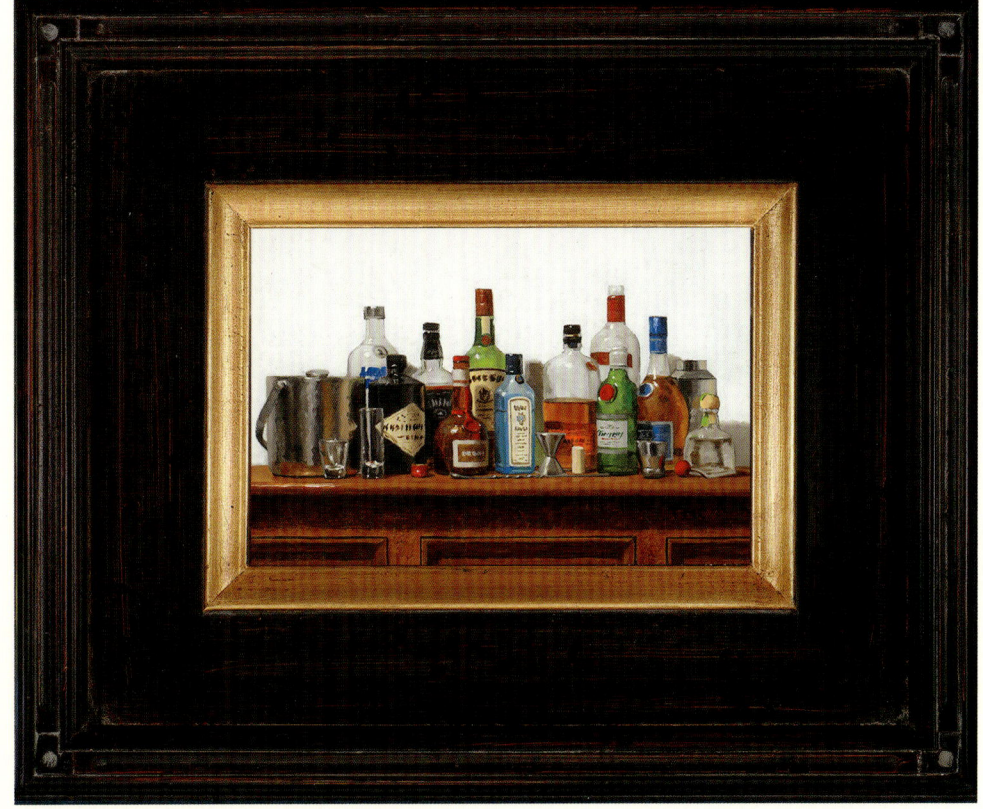

COMPOSITIONAL FORMATS

Portrait, landscape, circular (or oval), and square are the four traditional formats for still life. I like to approach a painting with an open mind and to figure out what the best format will be after setting up my composition.

My favorite of all the formats for still life is landscape because it emulates the way we pan a scene when watching a film. For the painting at bottom opposite, I worked with a client who was a big fan of the format typically used in film. He wanted the painting to reflect his love for this cinematic format, so I worked on a surface measuring 9 inches high by 16 inches wide, which has the same proportions.

ABOVE: Travis Seymour, *Still Life with Glasses,* 2012, oil on linen mounted on canvas, 24 × 20 inches (60.96 × 50.8 cm). Courtesy of the artist.

Portrait format

BELOW: John Douglas Patrick (American, 1863– 1937), *Dry Sink,* 1890–1900, oil on canvas, 10 × 20 inches (25.4 × 50.8 cm). Photo courtesy of Heritage Auctions, HA.com.

Landscape format

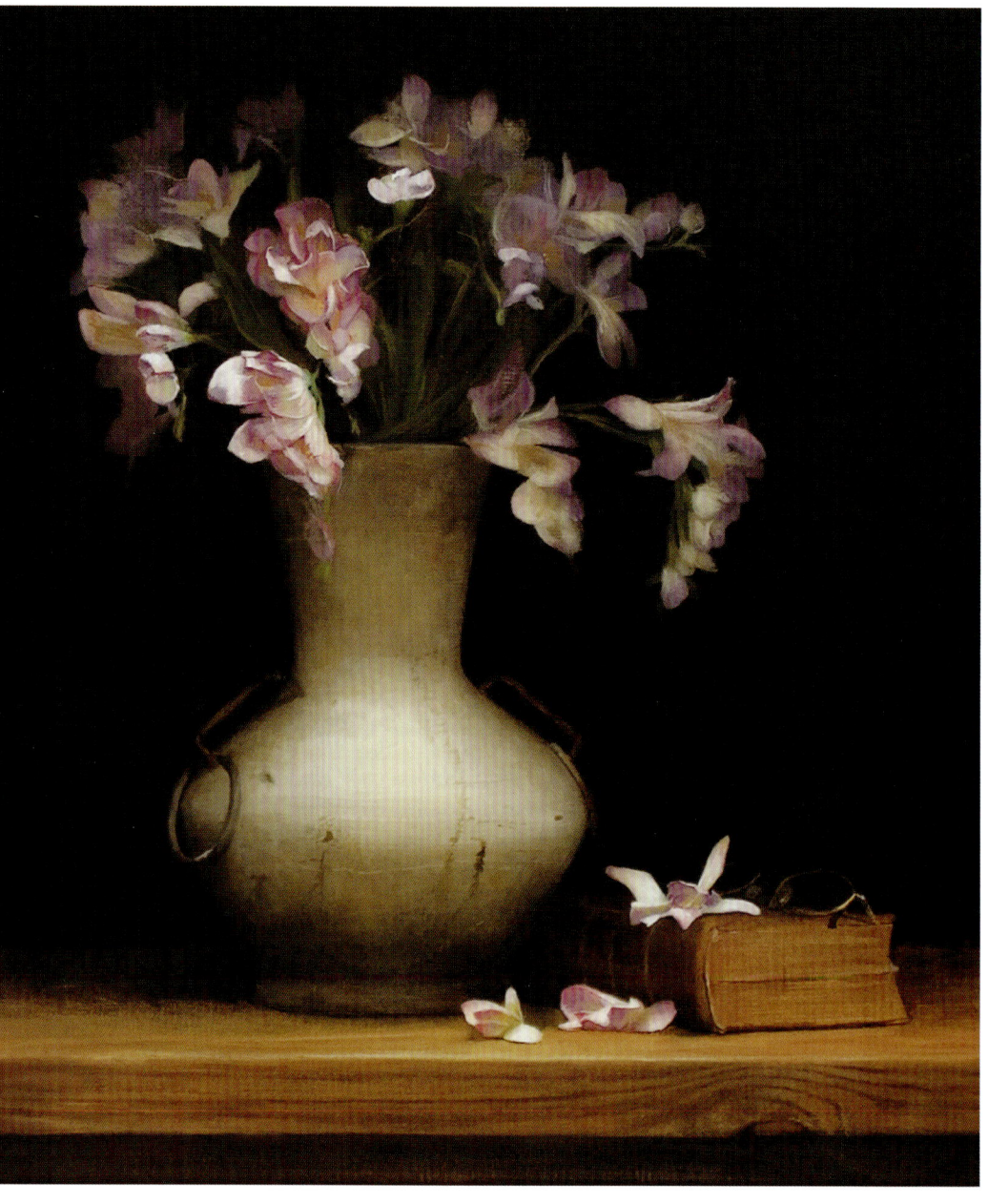

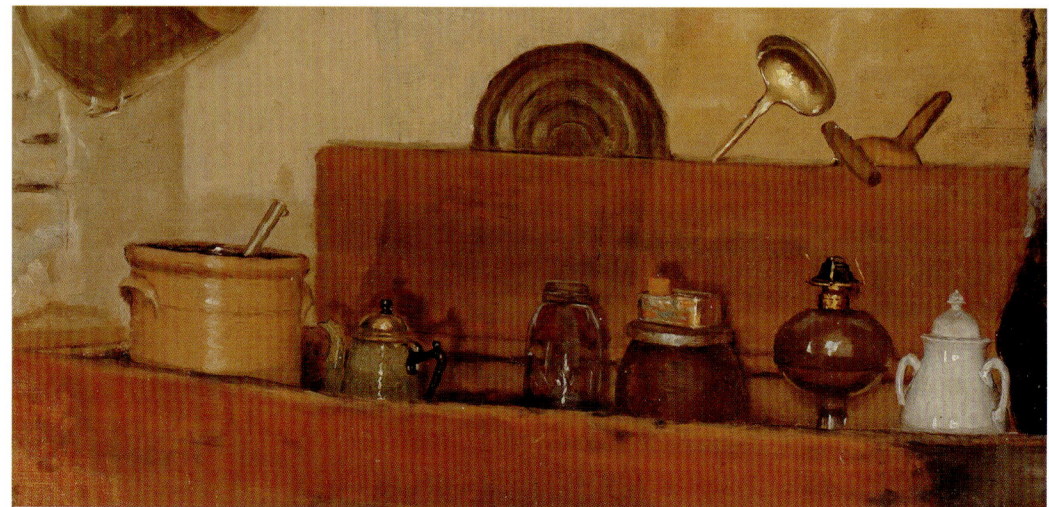

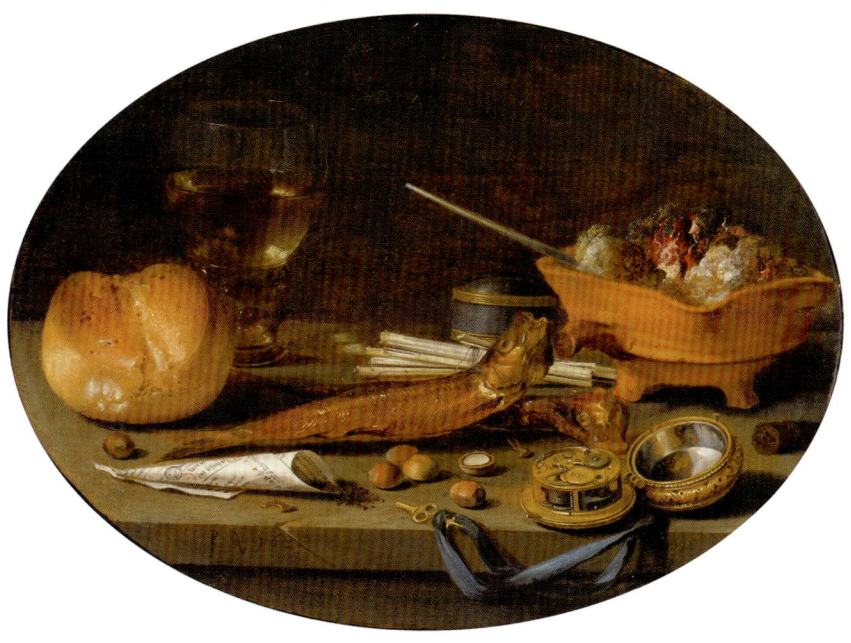

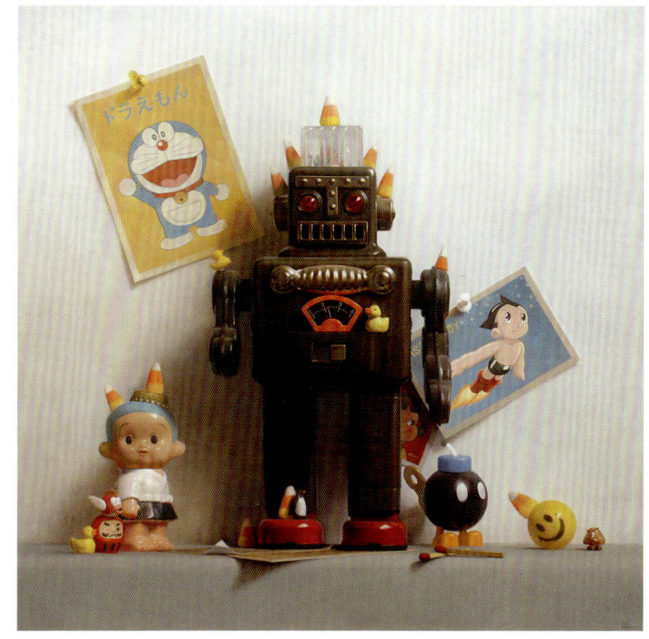

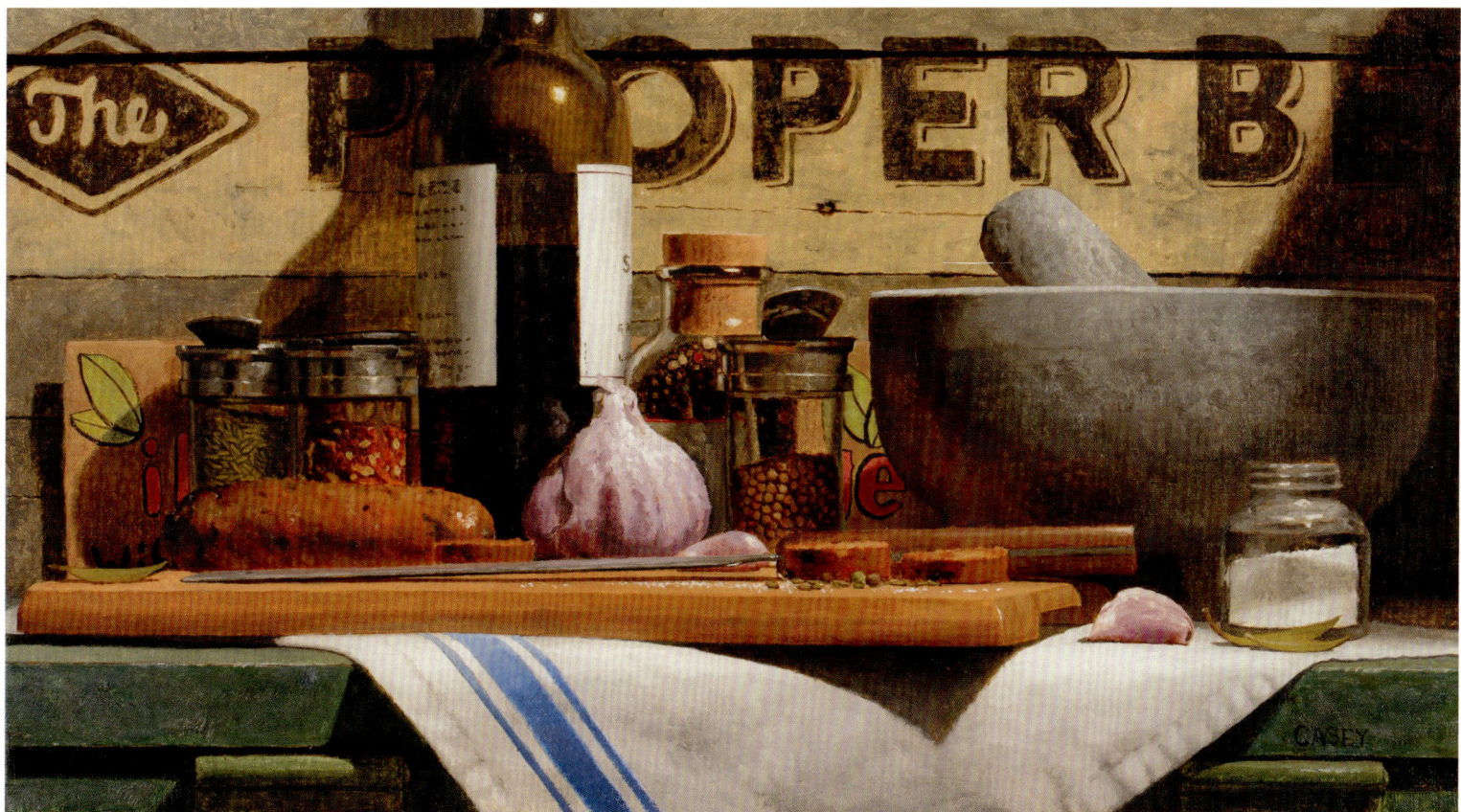

ABOVE, CLOCKWISE FROM TOP LEFT:
Pieter Claesz, *Still Life with a Roemer, a Roll, Smoked Herring, a Watch, Smoker's Requisites, Hazelnuts and a Brazier,* 17th century, oil on panel, 11 ½ × 15 ⅜ inches (29.3 × 39.2 cm). Photo courtesy of Sotheby's, Inc. ©2019.

Circular (oval) format

Samuel Hung, *Smoking Robot,* 2017, oil on panel, 36 × 36 inches (91.44 × 91.44 cm). Courtesy of the artist.

Square format

Todd M. Casey, *The Proper Beast: Italian Sausage,* 2018, oil on linen, 9 × 16 inches (22.86 × 40.64 cm). Collection of Thom Barbour and Brian Hines.

"Cinematic" format

TANGENTS AND SIMILAR PROBLEMS

In painting, a tangent occurs when a shape is placed right on the edge of the page or shares an edge with another shape. Tangents create tension in a design and should be avoided if at all possible. They can cause visual confusion, as the viewer may not be able to tell where a shape begins or ends.

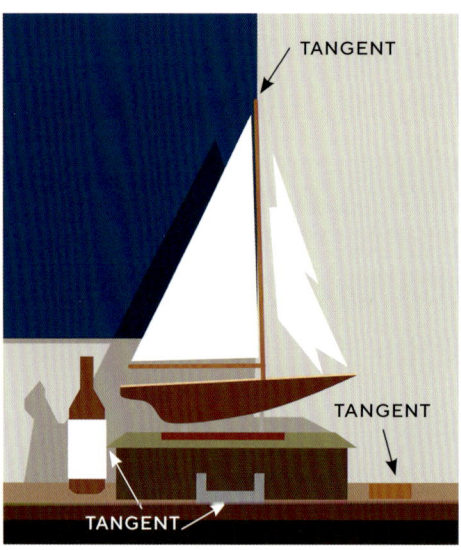 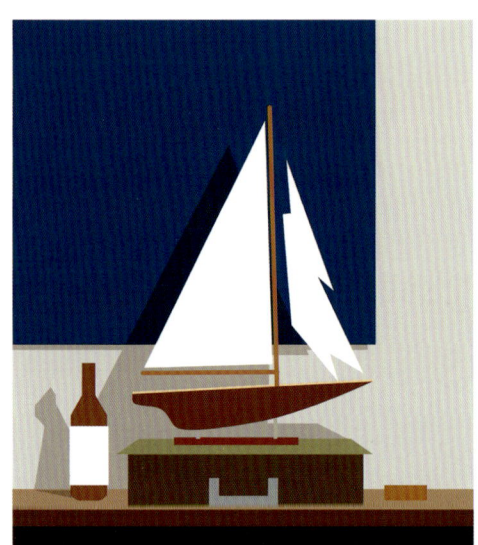

RIGHT: The composition on the left has several tangents, which flatten depth and create visual tension. Slight adjustments to the placement of the objects eliminate the tangents, producing a much more satisfying arrangement.

Relatedly, you should avoid putting one object right under another in the picture plane, which robs the composition of depth. Instead, overlap the objects.

Finally, you should avoid grouping all the objects together in one corner of a design. When composing, use all the available space to give the viewer a reason to look at the entire painting. Spreading the objects around engages the whole space and creates movement.

TIP

Sometimes the best advice I can give a student is to *take a break*. You need to walk away from your setup and come back to it with fresh eyes every so often. If you stare at your artwork for too long or work when you are tired, you may begin to make bad decisions. So be sure to take breaks often.

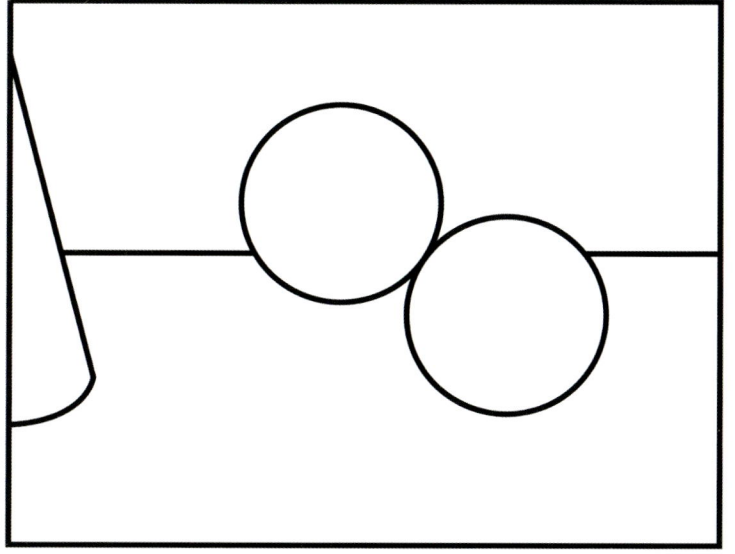

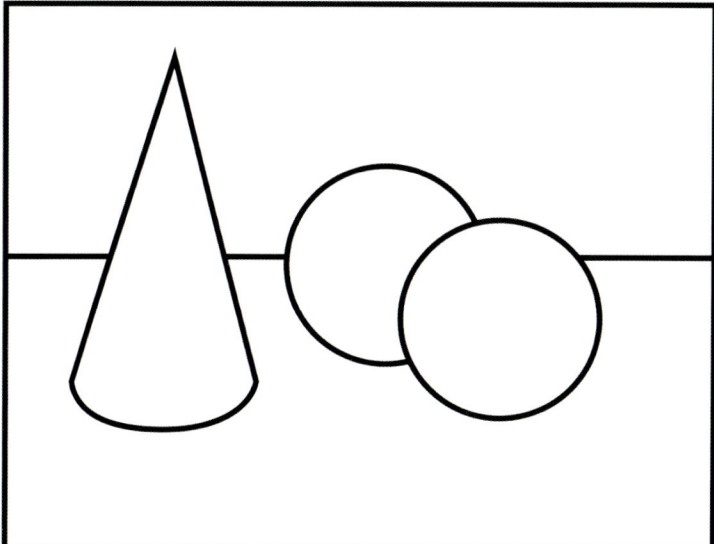

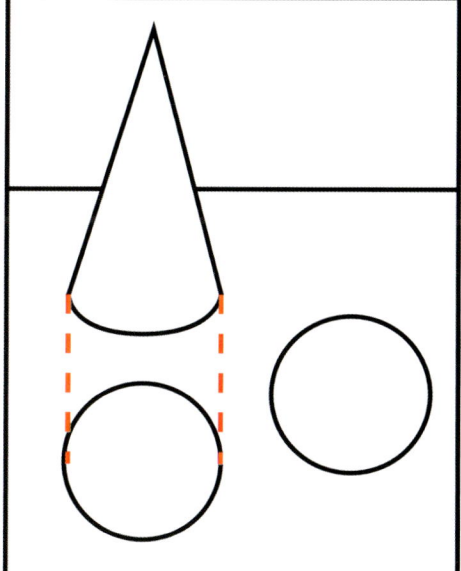

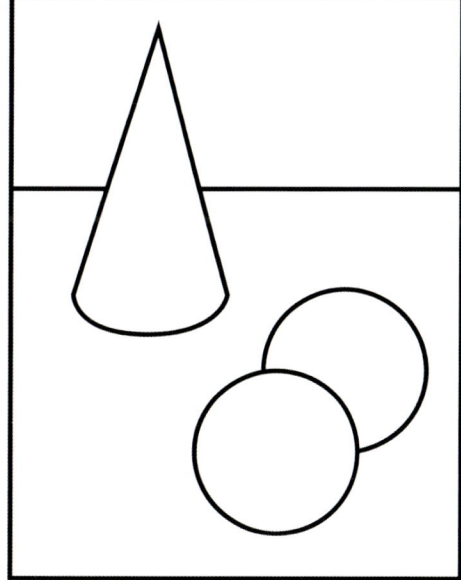

ABOVE: The image on the left has some bad tangents: the cone is cut off at the left edge and the two circles touch each other at their circumferences. The image on the right shows a much better placement of the cone and the circles. The cone is not cut off down the middle, and the circles do not share an edge.

LEFT: In the image at far left, one of the circles is aligned directly under the cone, which flattens out the picture. Moving it to overlap the other circle builds depth, as at near left.

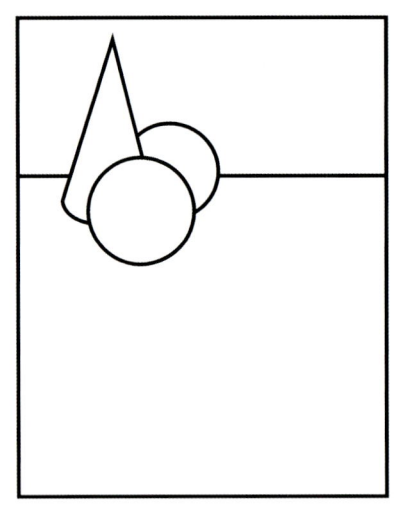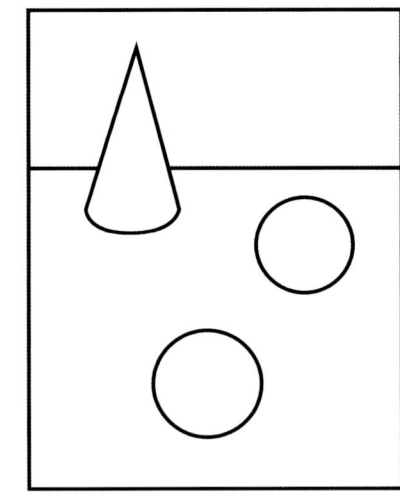

RIGHT: The composition on the left does not make great use of space. All the objects are in one corner, and the piece has no movement. A better solution appears at far right.

BELOW: Photo courtesy of Rehs Contemporary Galleries, New York.

For a show called "Skin and Tonic" at Rehs Galleries in New York, I did a series of fifty paintings. With that many images on view, it was really important not to repeat the same composition over and over.

OPPOSITE, CLOCKWISE FROM TOP LEFT: Todd M. Casey, *Bloody Mary,* 2016, oil on panel, 8 × 6 inches (20.32 × 15.24 cm). Private collection.

Todd M. Casey, *Dirty Martini,* 2016, oil on panel, 8 × 6 inches (20.32 × 15.24 cm). Private collection.

Todd M. Casey, *Old Fashioned,* 2017, oil on panel, 6 × 8 inches (15.24 × 20.32 cm). Private collection.

COMPOSING A SERIES OF PAINTINGS

Another thing to consider is how your work will look when you show a number of paintings together. It's a daunting task to create a body of work that feels unified but not repetitive. A successful series offers consistency (for example, of subject matter or theme) but also variety (for example, of color or size). To achieve the desired unity-in-variety, you'll need to imagine how the individual works will look when hung together—either side by side or in some other arrangement. The image below shows how I approached this challenge for a show of my work at New York's Rehs Contemporary Galleries in 2017.

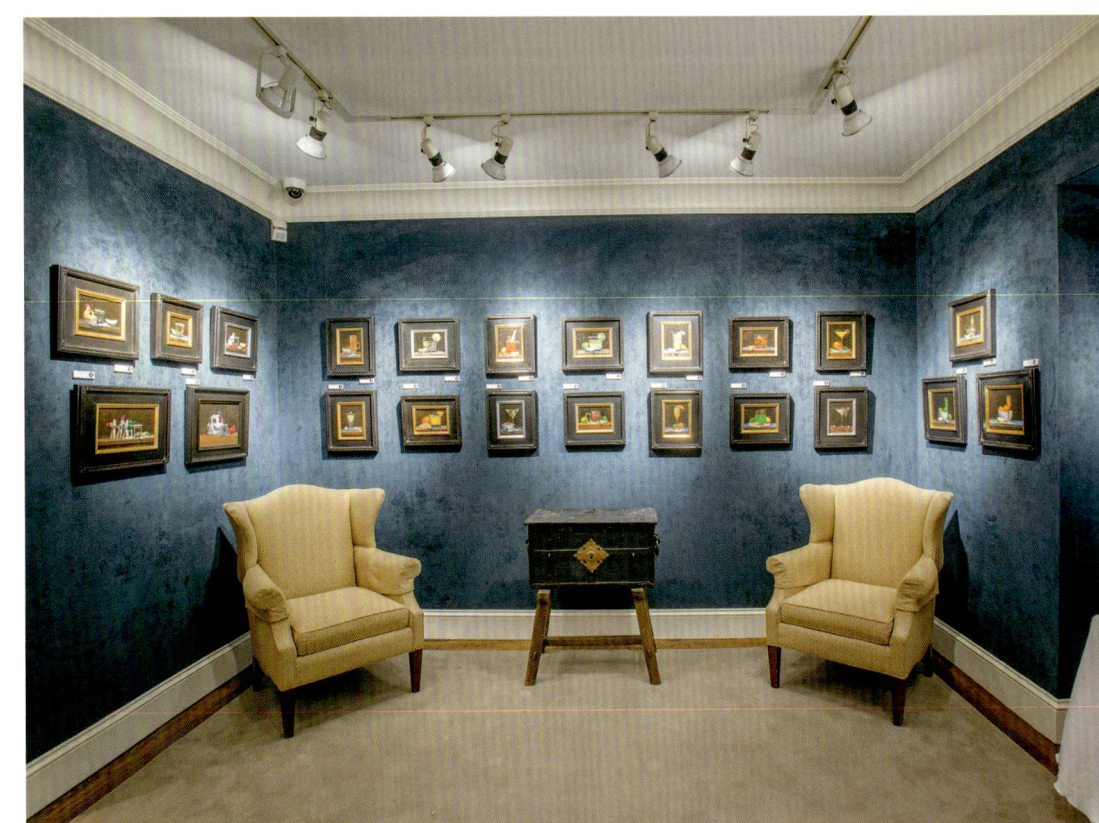

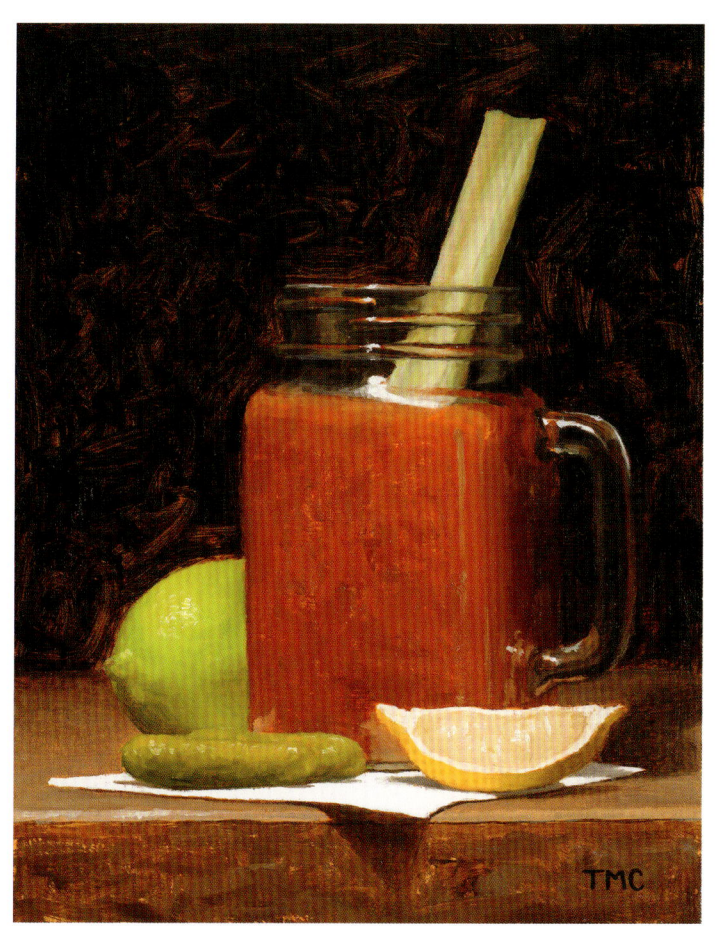
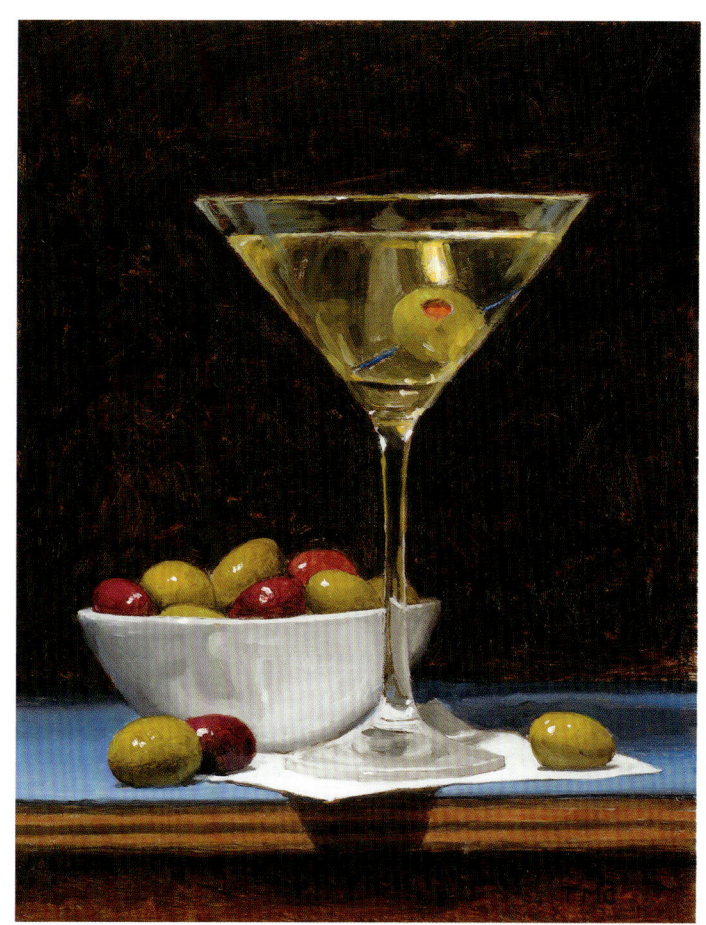

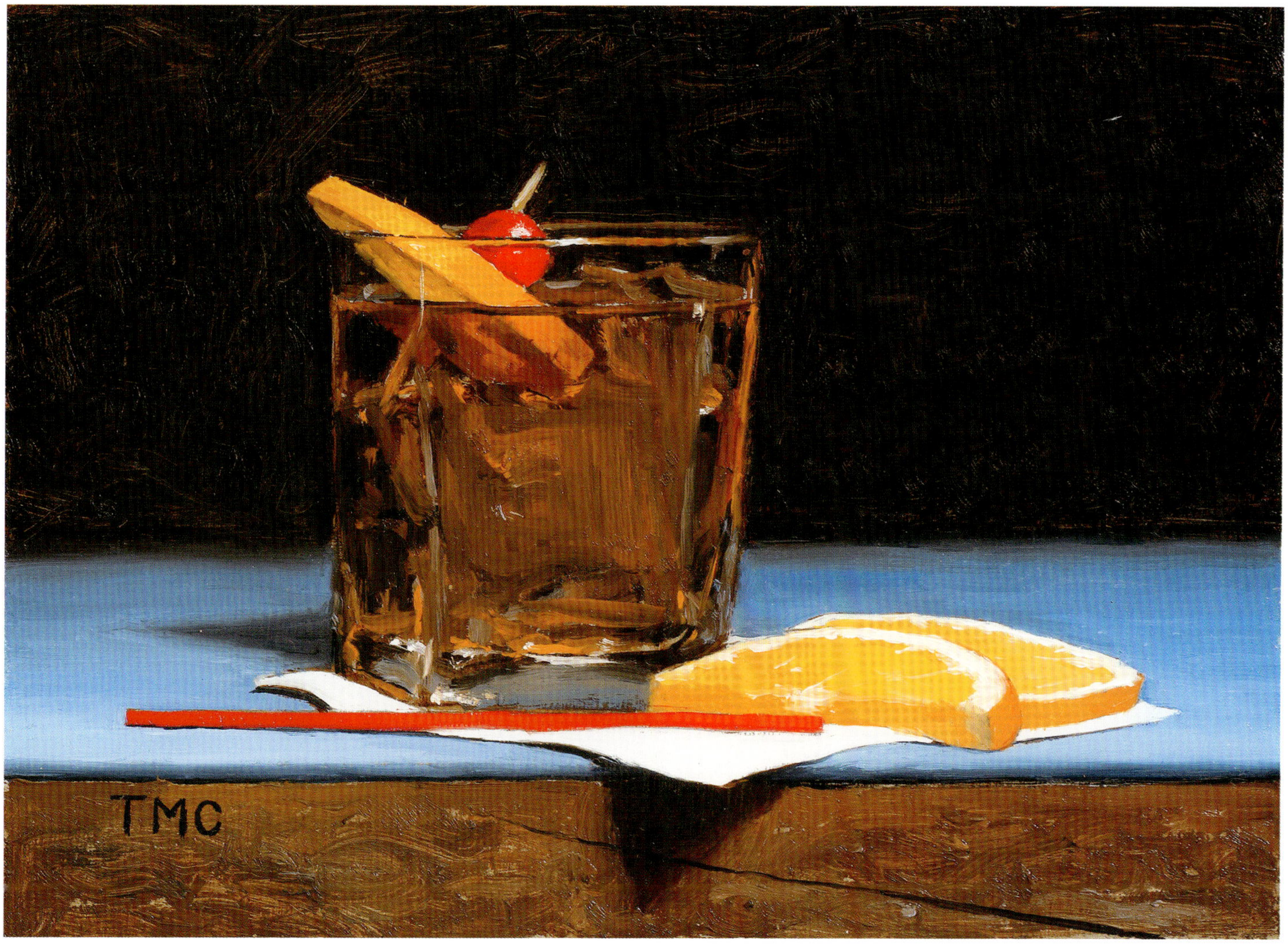

OPPOSITE: Todd M. Casey, *Death in the Afternoon,* 2016, oil on panel, 12 × 12 inches (30.48 × 30.48 cm). Courtesy of Rehs Contemporary Galleries, New York.

The concept for this painting was based on Ernest Hemingway's book on bullfighting, *Death in the Afternoon,* and the fact that the cocktail portrayed—the absinthe drip—is a very potent drink. Having Hemingway in mind helped me to find the right props to tell the story.

YOUR PICTURE IS YOUR STAGE

When composing a still life, I sometimes imagine I'm the director of a Broadway play and that my setup is the play's set. After all, there are a lot of parallels between theater and painting:

- The stage: the platform on which the objects stand
- The main character(s): the objects on which most attention is focused
- The supporting cast: the other, smaller objects throughout the piece
- The lighting: the way the light falls on the characters/objects

Lighting is a huge part of a stage production, and I often try to emulate theatrical lighting—for instance, by "spotlighting" a main character/object, bringing the audience's attention to the highest-contrast area. Once you've grabbed the attention of the audience, you can pull them into your story. Like a theater director, your goal as a painter should be to strike a chord with your audience, to really connect with them.

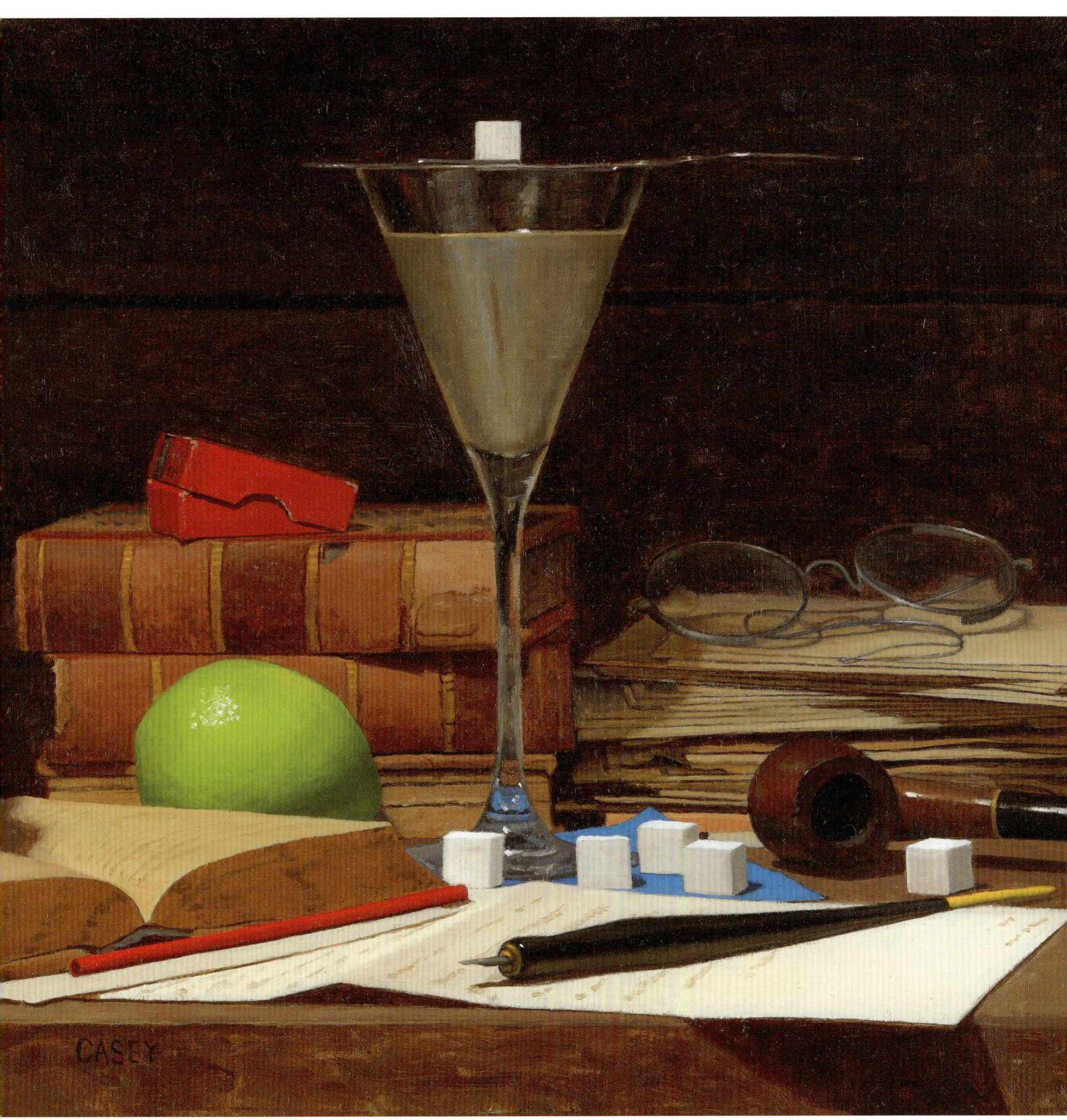

GUIDELINES—NOT RULES

Use the rules, don't be used by the rules.
—JOSEPH CAMPBELL

In 1967, Russian psychologist Alfred Yarbus published the book *Eye Movements and Vision*, based on the experiments on eye tracking he'd done at the Soviet Union's Academy of Sciences. Yarbus observed people looking at art, tracking their eye movements as they interacted with a painting. What he found was that individuals didn't necessarily look at a painting the way the artist intended. People's preferences sometimes directed them to look somewhere else. That's good to keep in mind, since it means that the "rules" of composition aren't hard and fast. You should use all the information in this chapter as a set of guidelines rather than a list of unbreakable rules.

I try not to force my compositions to fit into a set of rules. I don't want my compositions to look mechanical. Rather, I focus on the essence of what I want to convey, and I gather elements that help tell the story. As I set up the composition, I try to be aware of some of these guides. If the setup is not coming together well enough, it's often because a principle of design was overlooked.

By the way, Alfred Yarbus's eye-tracking experiments revealed something else that's very interesting—that a picture's title has a major influence on how the viewer interacts with the image. If the name of the painting mentions an action or person, the viewer's eye will move to that part of the painting right away. Therefore, choose your titles wisely—they're an important part of your viewers' experience of your work.

EXERCISE

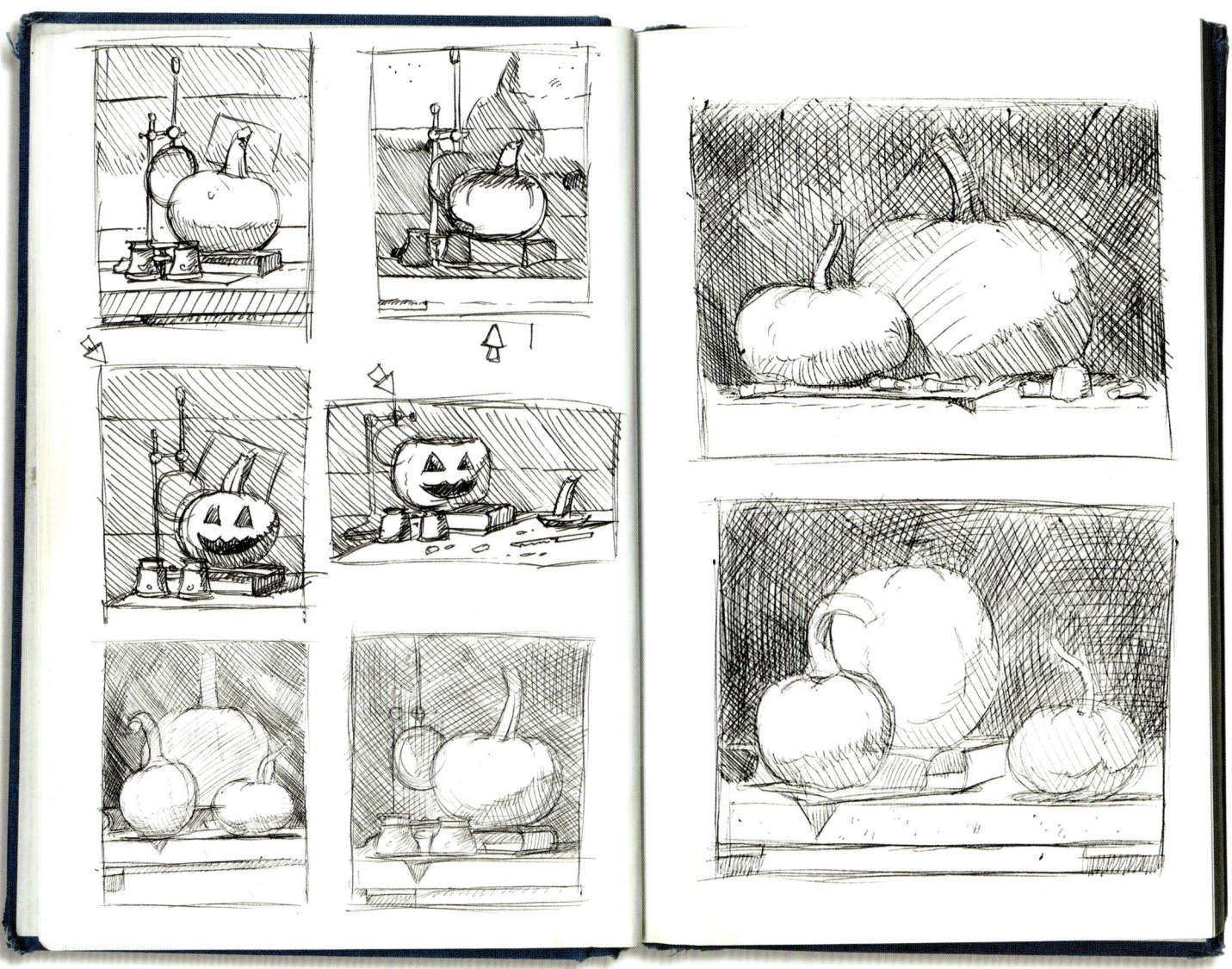

EXERCISE

Simple sketches in a sketchbook are a great way to work out ideas on paper. Using simple shapes, you can observe the direction of the light and also think about high-contrast areas for the focal point. Sketching lets you design the whole scene the way you envision it. Remember: for an artist, drawing and composing are equivalent to thinking. Actively sketching will make connections in your neural network to the objects that you're drawing.

ABOVE: These pages from my sketchbook show some quick compositional studies that didn't all make it past the idea stage. Just the act of sketching it out will help me decide if I really want to pursue an idea or not.

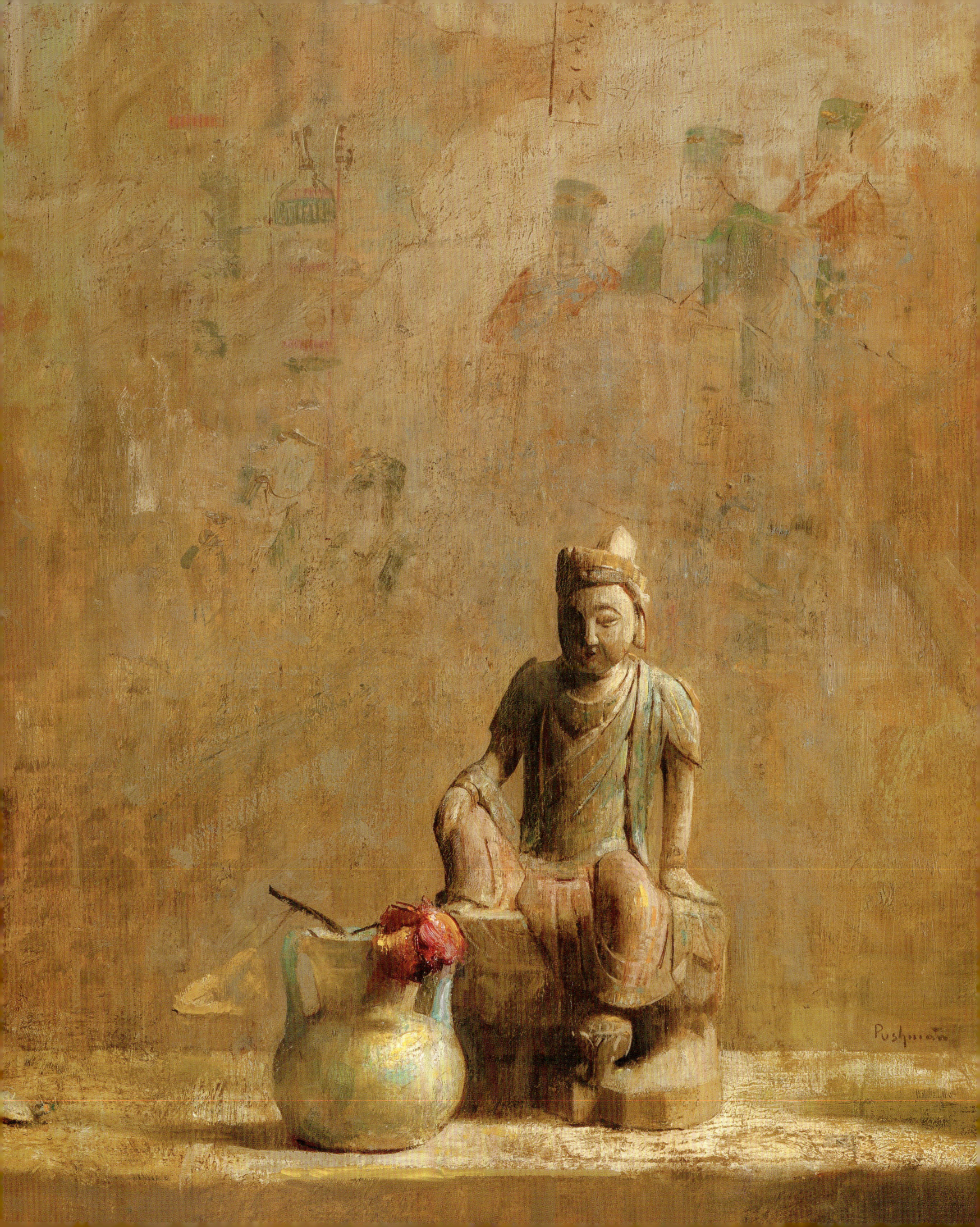

CHAPTER 4

LIGHT: ILLUMINATION AND SHADOW

Observation and study are necessary to achieve mastery of light and form.

ANDREW LOOMIS

Everything we observe is the play of light and shadow on forms. When light hits a form, it describes the surface and the volume of the body it is illuminating. Light interacts with the total environment, and all the illuminated elements in the environment affect each other. A basic grasp of the physics of light and simple geometry enables us to understand how light and shadow interact on a form and in an environment.

In this chapter, I delve a bit into science to help you see how light and shadow work and the properties of each. I also introduce some useful terminology. The more you know about light and shadow, the better you will be able to re-create their effects when painting.

OPPOSITE: Hovsep Pushman, *Eternal Destiny No. 2*, n.d., oil on board, 23 ¼ × 18 ½ inches (59.1 × 47 cm). Photo courtesy of Heritage Auctions, HA.com.

THE SCIENCE OF LIGHT

Light travels as a wave or particle (it behaves like both) from a source such as the sun or a light bulb. When we observe light hitting an object we are seeing wavelengths from the visible spectrum, which illuminate the object and are reemitted to our retinas.

When light strikes a form, the side of the form that faces the light is revealed. A shadow begins where the form turns away from the light source. On a sphere, this happens at 180 degrees from the light source. As the source of the light moves, so does the shadow in relation to the form. The shadow on a sphere, however, will always be perpendicular to the direction of the light.

The geometry of the light also determines where the cast shadow will fall on the surface that the object casting the shadow is sitting on. A cast shadow from one form will follow the form of an object the shadow is cast upon.

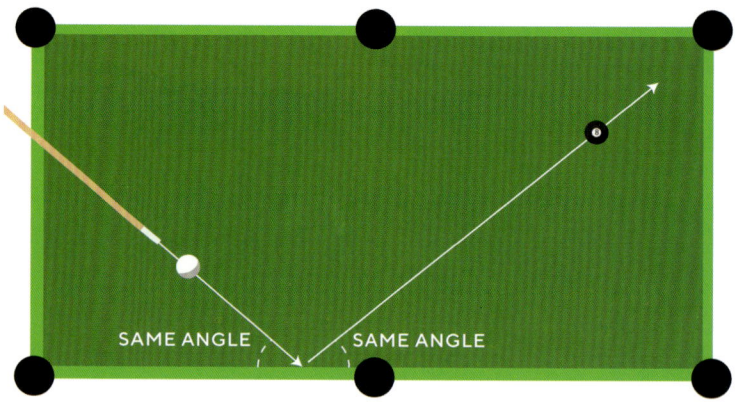

SAME ANGLE   SAME ANGLE

A light particle or wave, like a billiard ball, bounces off an object at the same angle at which it strikes the object. Or, to put it more technically: the angle of incidence equals the angle of reflection.

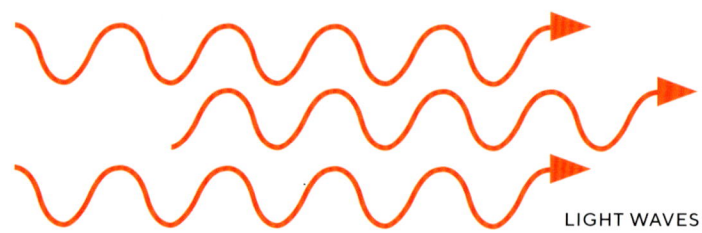

LIGHT WAVES

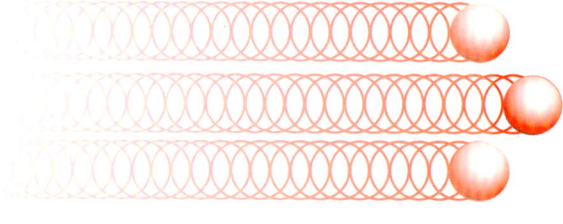

LIGHT PARTICLES

ELECTROMAGNETIC SPECTRUM

WAVELENGTH (APPROXIMATE)						

RADIATION TYPE	RADIO WAVES	MICROWAVES	INFRARED	ULTRAVIOLET	X-RAYS	GAMMA RAYS

VISIBLE SPECTRUM

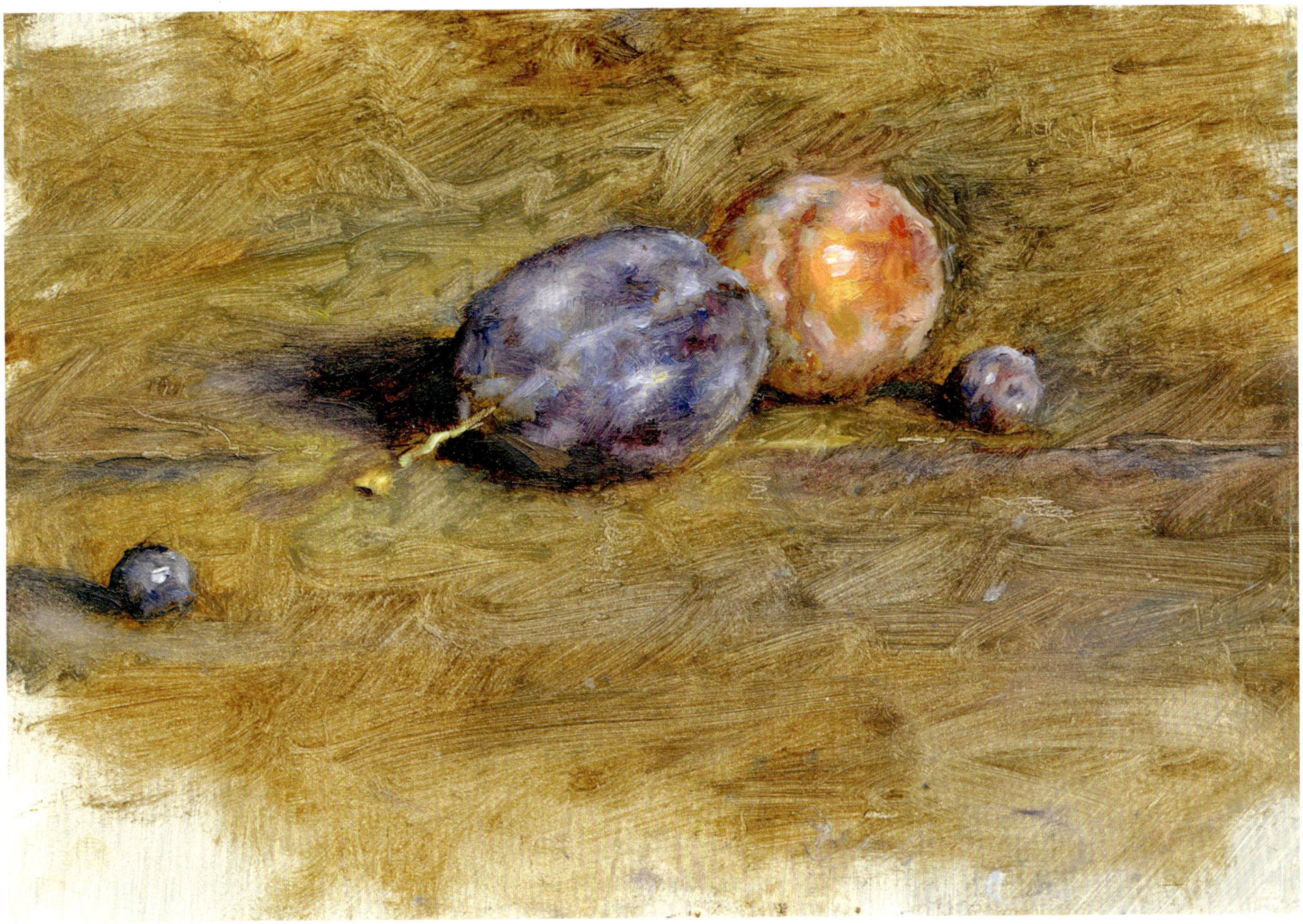

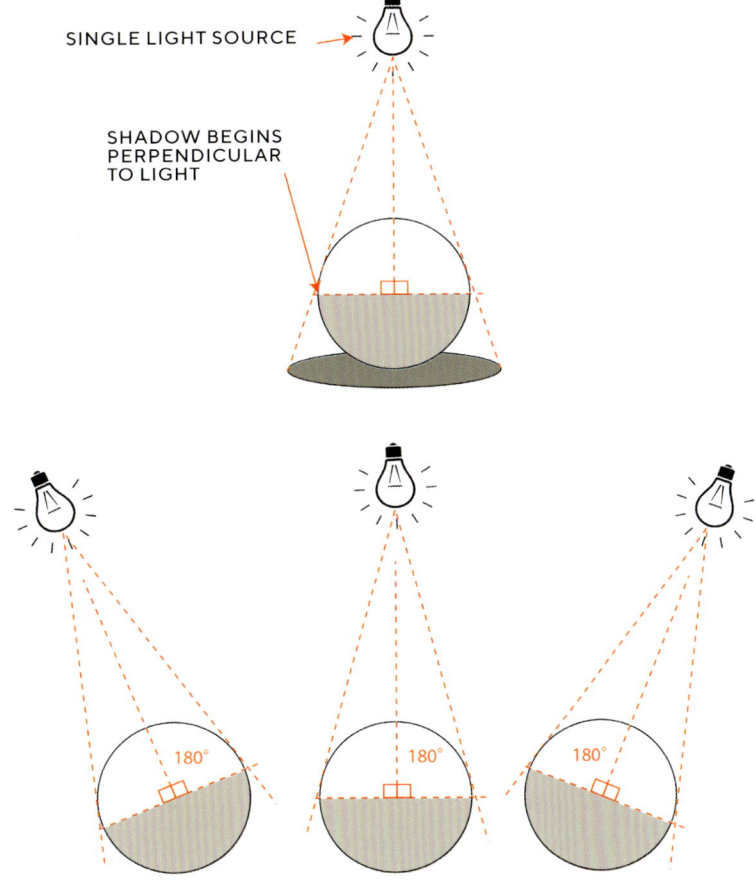

SINGLE LIGHT SOURCE →

SHADOW BEGINS
PERPENDICULAR
TO LIGHT

180°   180°   180°

ABOVE: Robert Liberace, *Still Life with Plums and Gooseberries,* 2011, oil on panel, 8 × 10 inches (20.32 × 25.4 cm). Courtesy of the artist.

Here we see a consistent light above and to the right of the viewer, which places the shadows to the left of each of these simple forms.

LEFT: Shadow falls on a sphere where the form turns away from the light source, at 180 degrees in relation to the light source. On a sphere, therefore, the shadow is perpendicular to the direction of the light.

BOTTOM: Here we see the light from three different angles. Notice that the shadow always begins as the form turns away from the light, no matter where the light source is. This is always at 180 degrees to the direction of the light on a sphere.

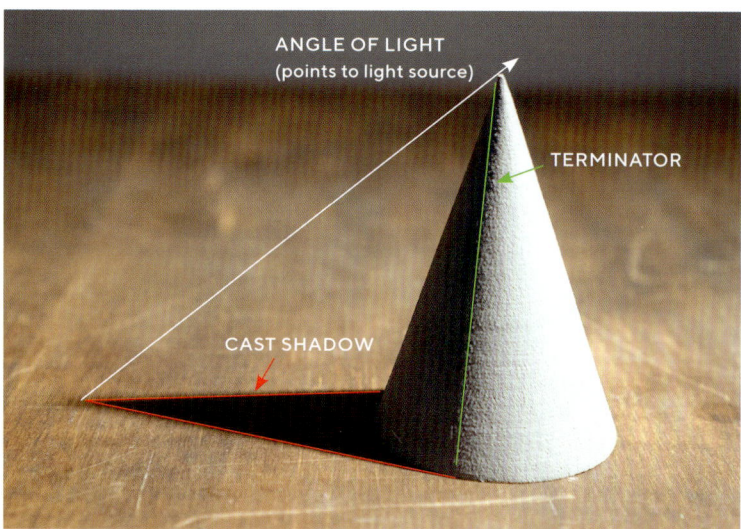

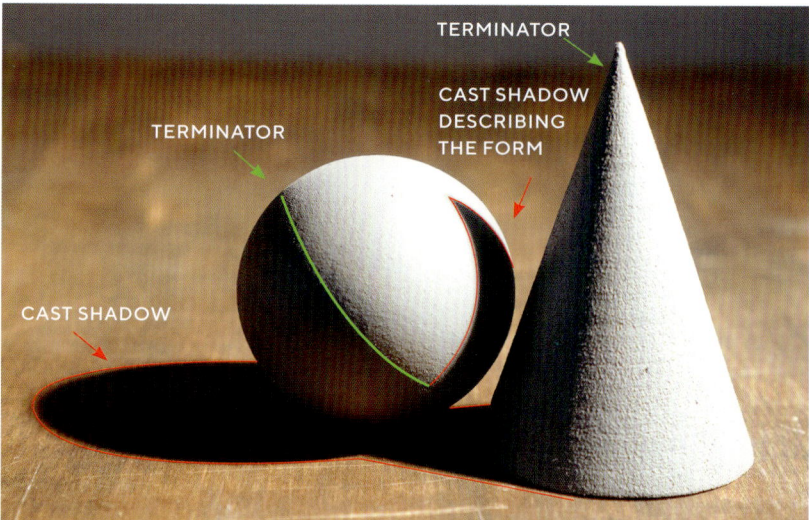

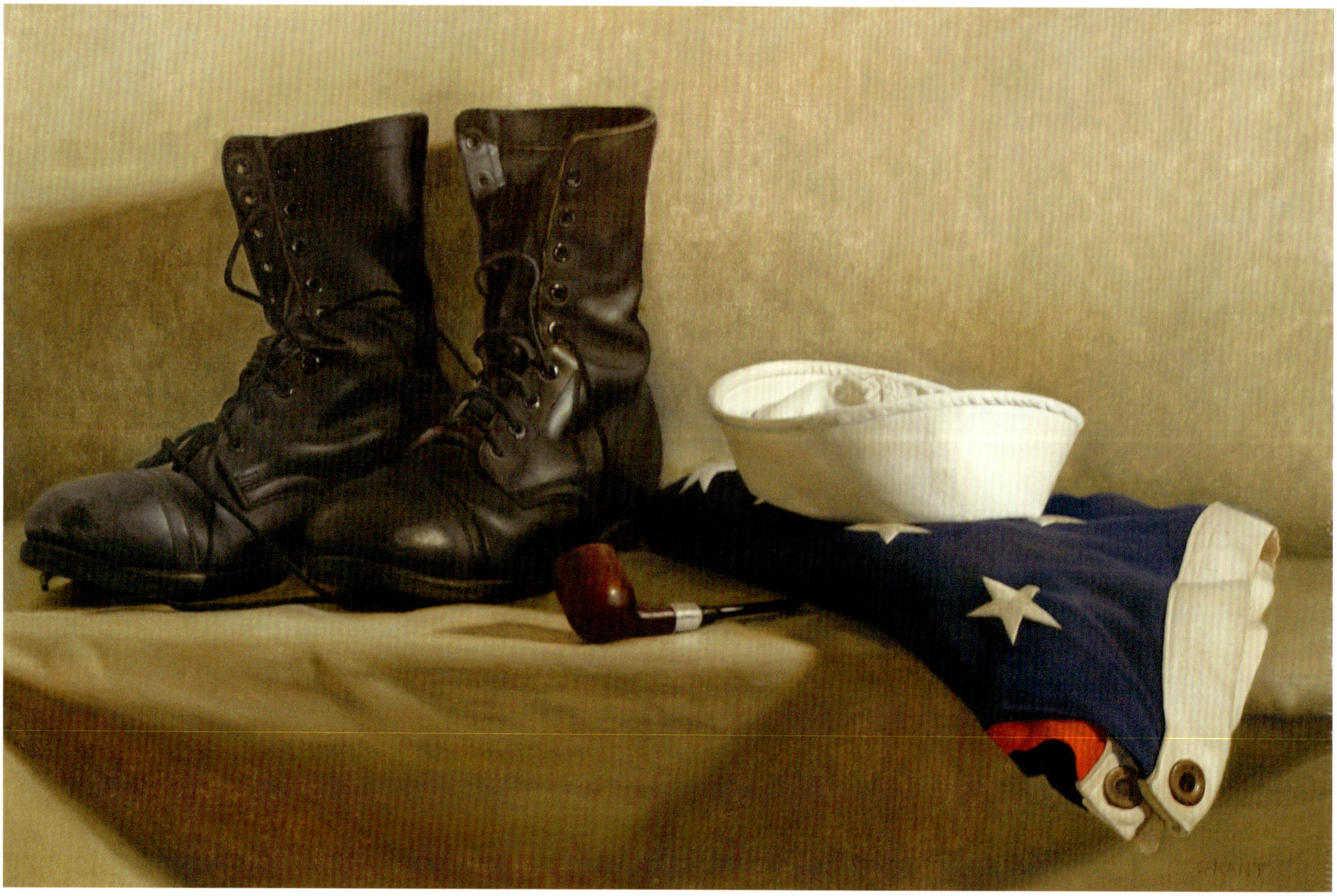

TOP: A cast shadow defines the form it is cast onto. On the left, the cone's long cast shadow shows that the surface the cone sits on is flat. On the right, the same cast shadow falls onto a sphere, which it wraps around, revealing the sphere's form.

ABOVE: Danny Grant, *Sailor's Tribute,* 2011, oil on linen, 16 × 24 inches (40.64 × 60.96 cm).

In this painting, the artist Danny Grant uses a light source coming from the right side. Each shadow is an elongated version of the form casting it.

THE TERMINOLOGY OF LIGHT AND SHADOW

The term *chiaroscuro*, which combines the Italian words *chiaro* ("clear") and *oscuro* ("obscure"), refers to the contrast and interplay between light and dark in painting. (In art history, it is often used specifically to describe the intense contrast between light and dark that can be found in the works of artists like the Baroque painters Caravaggio and Georges de la Tour.)

We can categorize all of the light side of a form as "light" and all of the dark side as "shadow." When we observe light on a sphere, half of the sphere is in light and half of the sphere is in shadow.

Form light is a general term for everything we see in the light. This is made up of the *light most facing plane* and the *halftone*. The light most facing plane is the part of an object that most directly faces the primary light source. It is sometimes called the "angle of light" because it refers to the direction of the light. The halftone is the darkest part of the light, which is the area just above the start of the shadow.

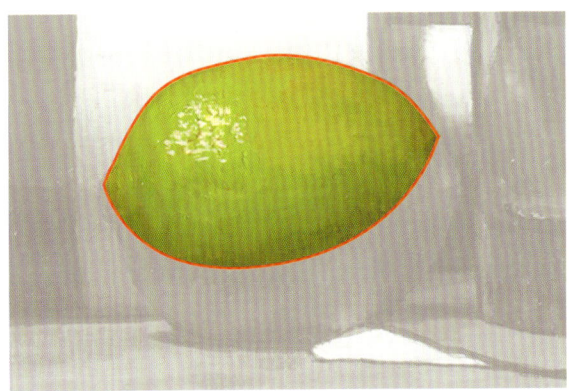

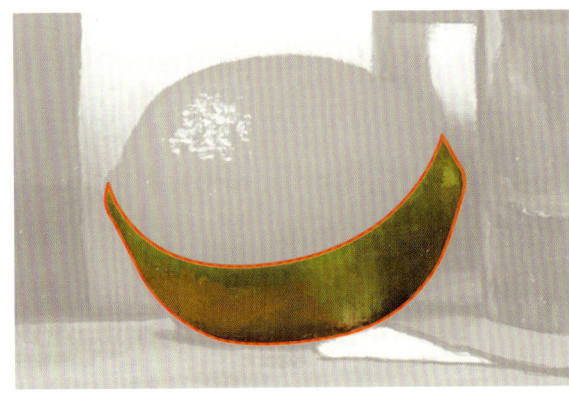

ABOVE: We see the light (top) and shadow (bottom) on a sphere-like object—a lime in a detail from my painting *Cape Codder*.

BELOW: Light and shadow terms

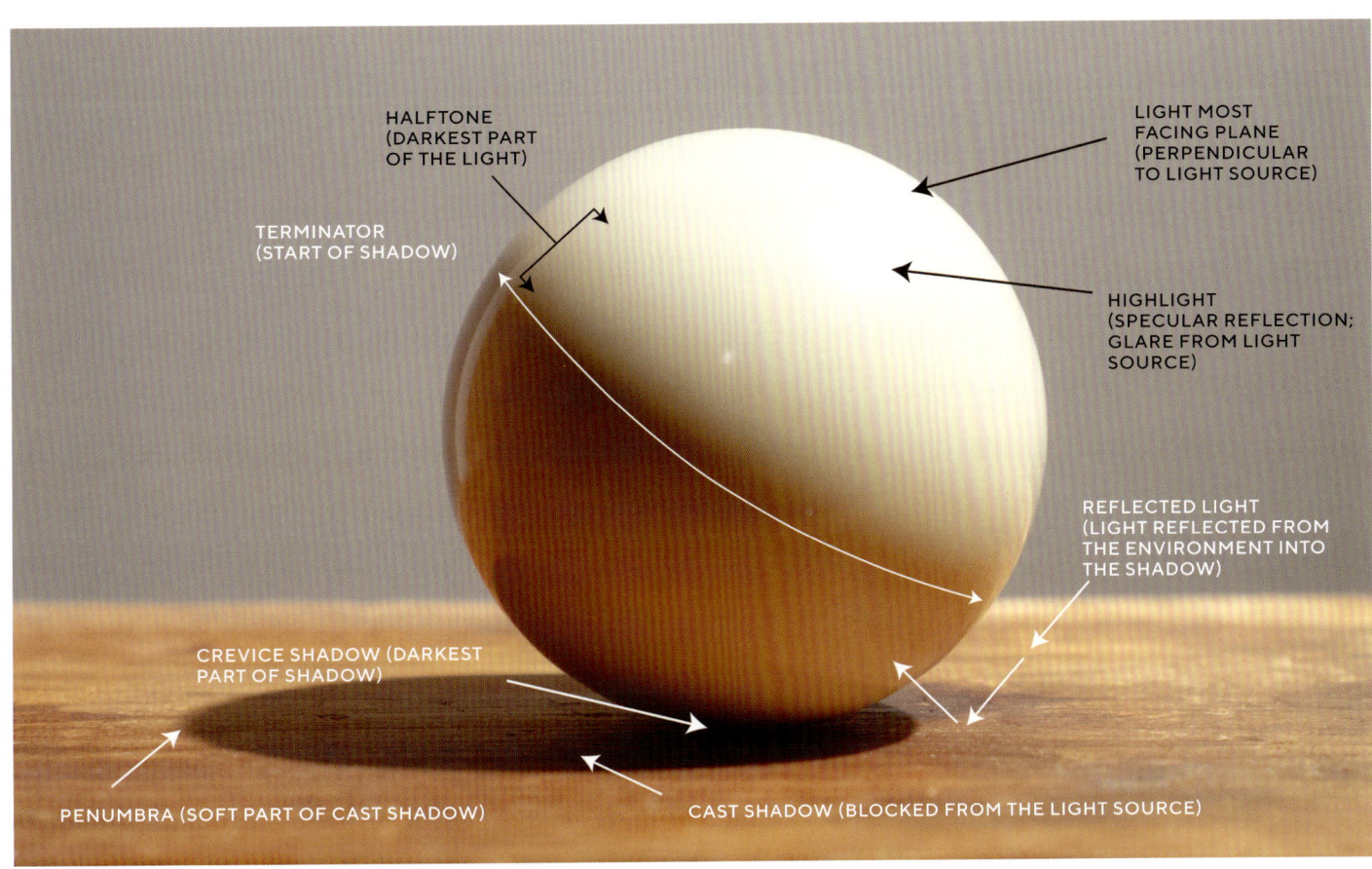

HALFTONE (DARKEST PART OF THE LIGHT)

LIGHT MOST FACING PLANE (PERPENDICULAR TO LIGHT SOURCE)

TERMINATOR (START OF SHADOW)

HIGHLIGHT (SPECULAR REFLECTION; GLARE FROM LIGHT SOURCE)

REFLECTED LIGHT (LIGHT REFLECTED FROM THE ENVIRONMENT INTO THE SHADOW)

CREVICE SHADOW (DARKEST PART OF SHADOW)

PENUMBRA (SOFT PART OF CAST SHADOW)

CAST SHADOW (BLOCKED FROM THE LIGHT SOURCE)

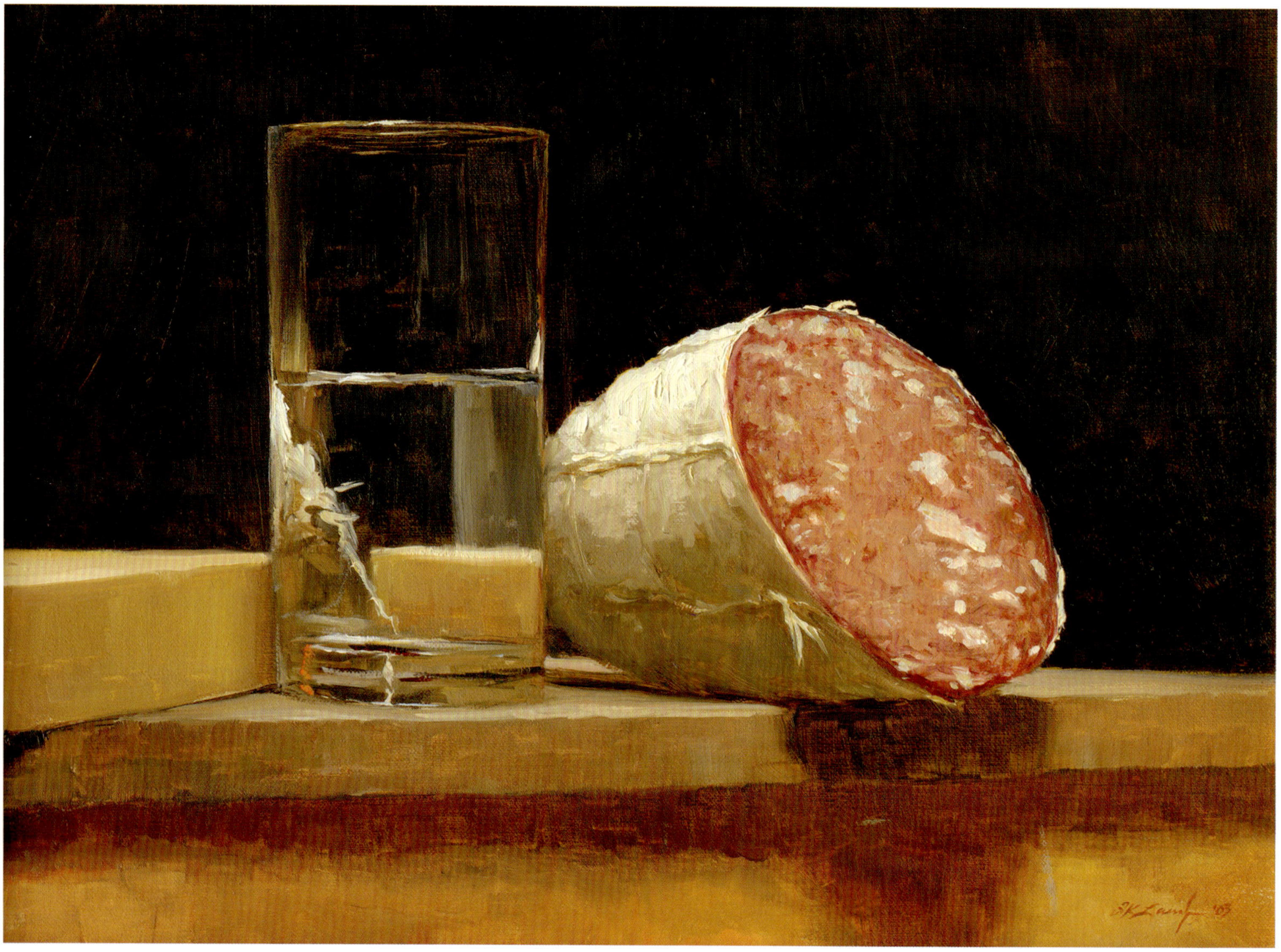

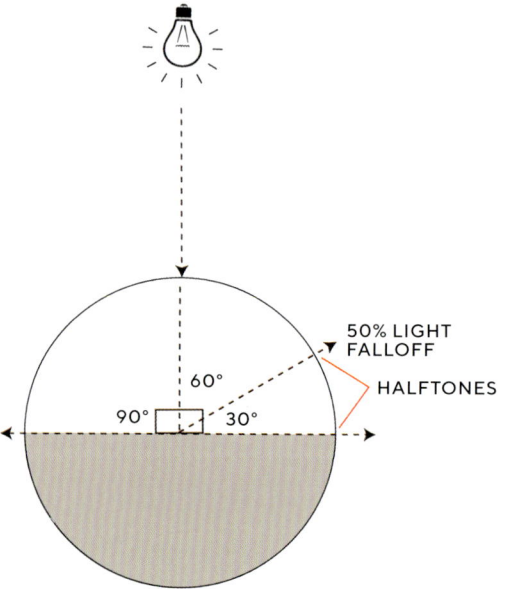

Form shadow is a general term for everything we see in the shadow. The form shadow starts at the *terminator* and ends at the *crevice shadow*. The terminator (an astronomy term) is the place where the light terminates—the beginning of the shadow. This is generally perceived as a soft line separating the area directly illuminated by the primary light source from the shadow. A little farther into the shadow, just beyond the terminator, is the *core shadow*—the darkest part of the shadow.

TOP: Sarah Lamb, *Still Life of Salami*, 2003, oil on linen, 12 × 16 inches (30.48 × 40.64 cm). Courtesy of the artist.

Each object in this still life has a crevice shadow that sits between forms and is the darkest part of the shadow. Crevice shadows help ground objects onto a surface.

LEFT: The halftone is usually where the largest noticeable change in value appears on a sphere.

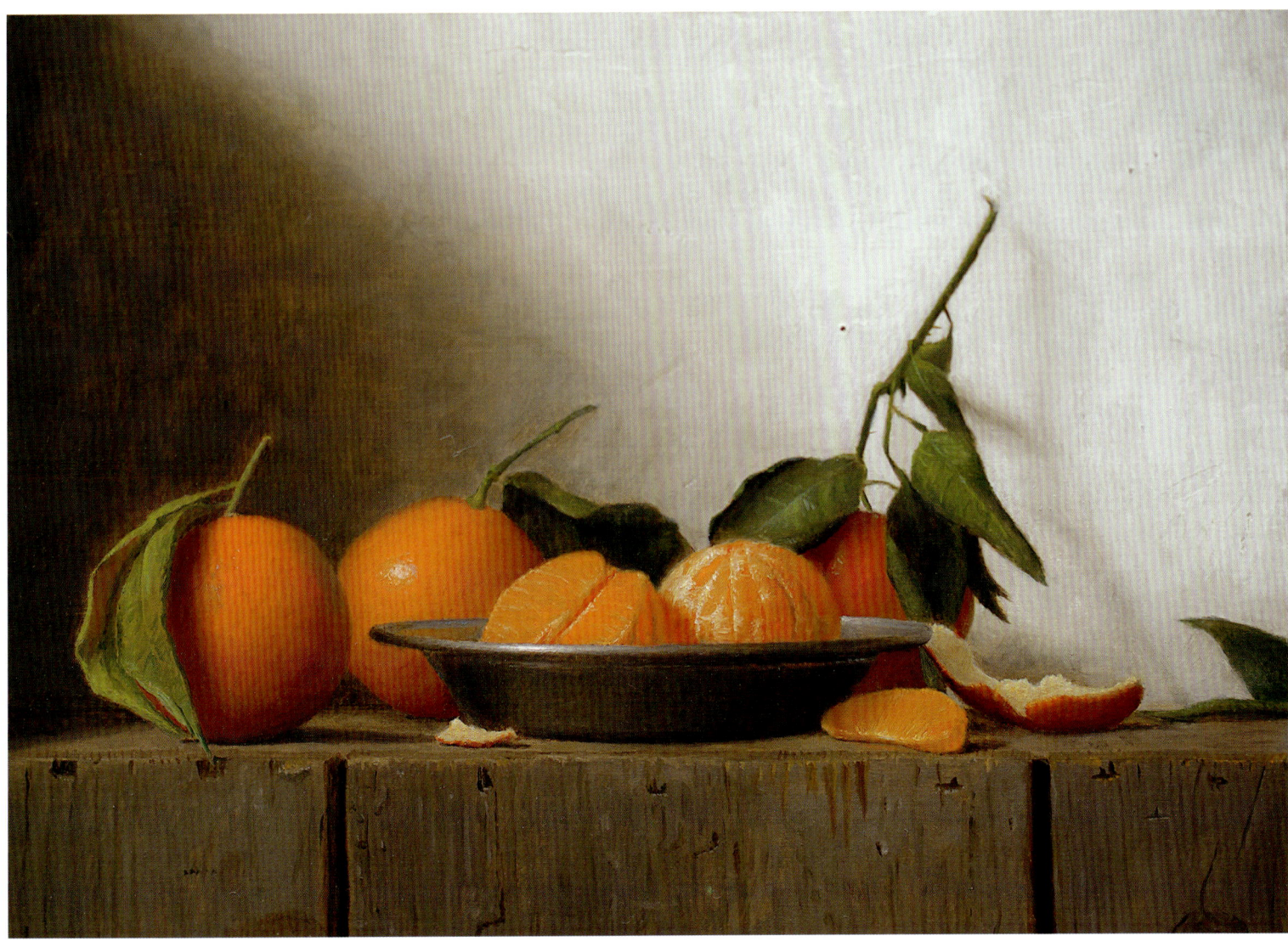

ABOVE: Justin Wood, *Satsuma Mandarins*, 2016, oil on panel, 11 × 14 inches (27.94 × 35.56 cm). Courtesy of the artist.

In Justin Wood's painting, reflected light from the table illuminates the shadows of the mandarin oranges.

In the form shadow there is almost always reflected light as well. Reflected light is caused by light particles (or waves) bouncing back from adjacent objects in an environment; it changes in appearance depending on the surface and color of those objects. Lighter and more chromatic colors tend to reflect more light than darker, more muted colors.

In most circumstances the darkest part of the shadow is the *crevice shadow*, which forms where two surfaces are in contact with another. The farther we go into the crevice, the less reflected light from the environment can reach. The crevice shadow is sometimes called the *accent shadow* or the *occlusion shadow*.

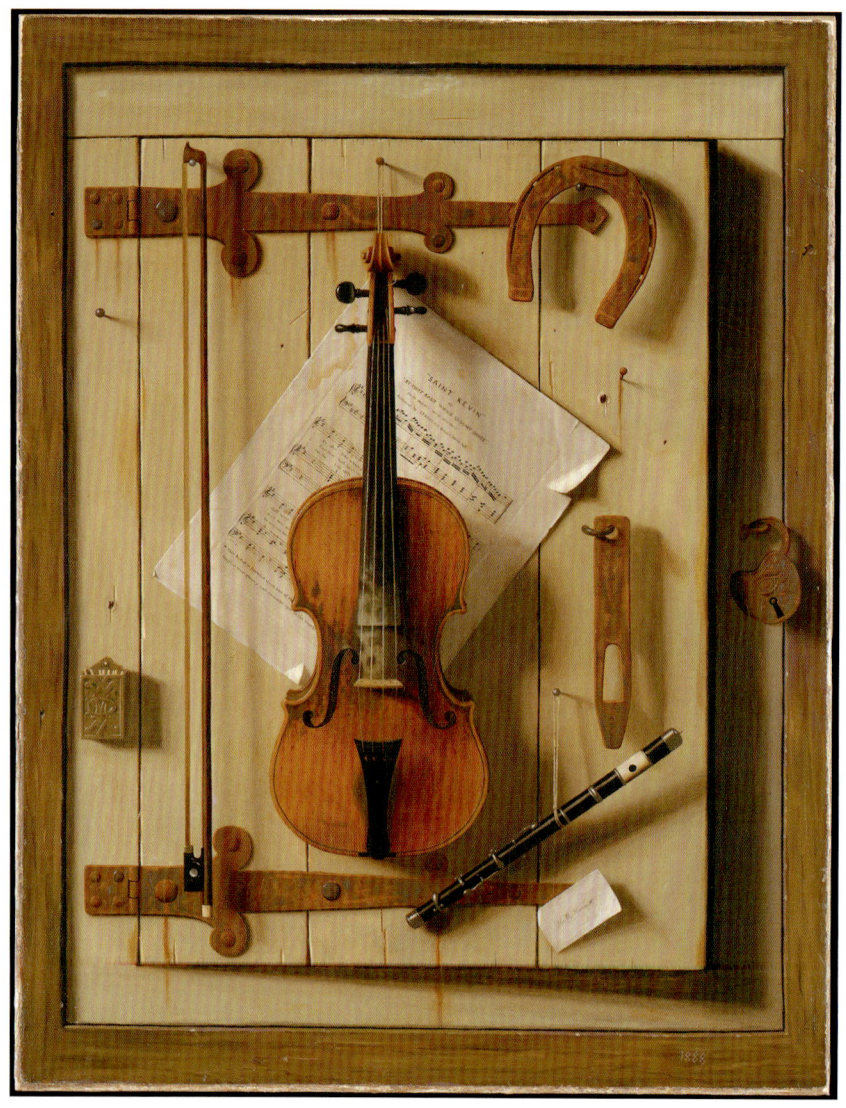

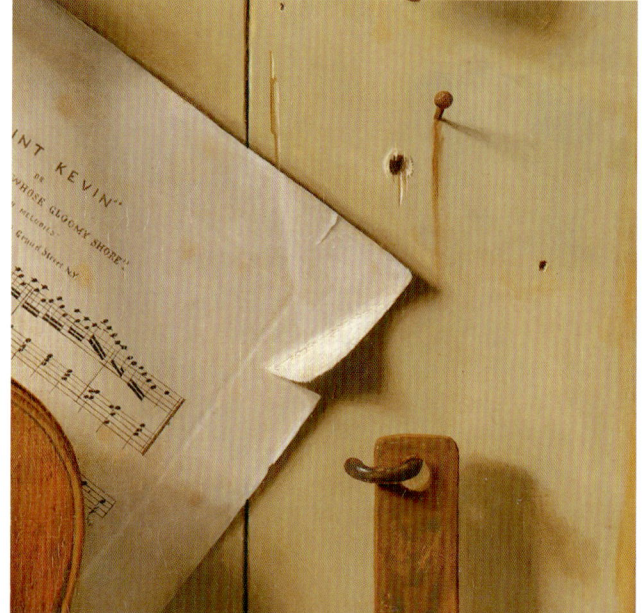

LEFT AND ABOVE: William Harnett, *Still Life—Violin and Music,* 1888, oil on canvas, 40 × 30 inches (101.6 × 76.2 cm). The Metropolitan Museum of Art, New York. Catharine Lorillard Wolfe Collection, Wolfe Fund, 1963.

The detail of William Harnett's painting clearly shows that cast shadows are sharper the closer they are to the objects casting them. They soften as they get farther from the objects.

BELOW: The outer portion of the cast shadow is in partial light, softening the outer edge.

Cast shadows occur when an object casts, or projects, a shadow onto another surface. Depending on the direction and proximity of the light source, cast shadows shorten or become elongated. They follow the shape of the forms they are cast upon.

The *penumbra* (another term borrowed from astronomy) refers to the softer edges of a cast shadow. Along its edges, the cast shadow is in partial light and therefore softer.

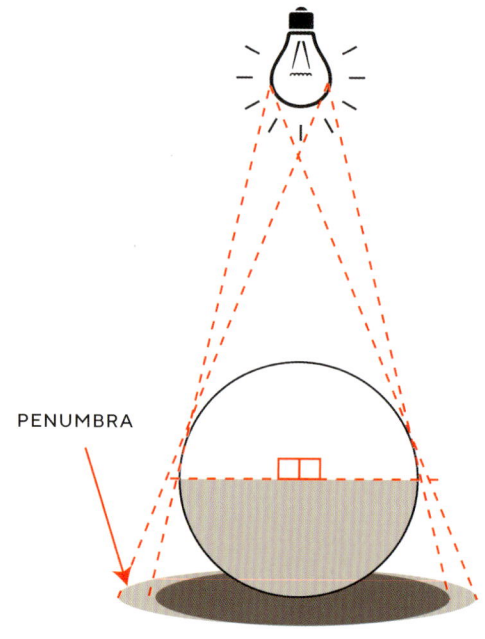

PENUMBRA

WHAT IS IN LIGHT
AND WHAT IS IN SHADOW?

It's often difficult to distinguish where the light ends and the shadow begins. Remember: the halftone is part of the light, but it can often get wrongly grouped with the shadow instead.

Holding a tool such as a pencil or paintbrush up to an object in your setup can help you quickly identify what is halftone and what is shadow. When the cast shadow from the paintbrush merges with the dark area on the squash, that's where the terminator—the beginning of the shadow—is.

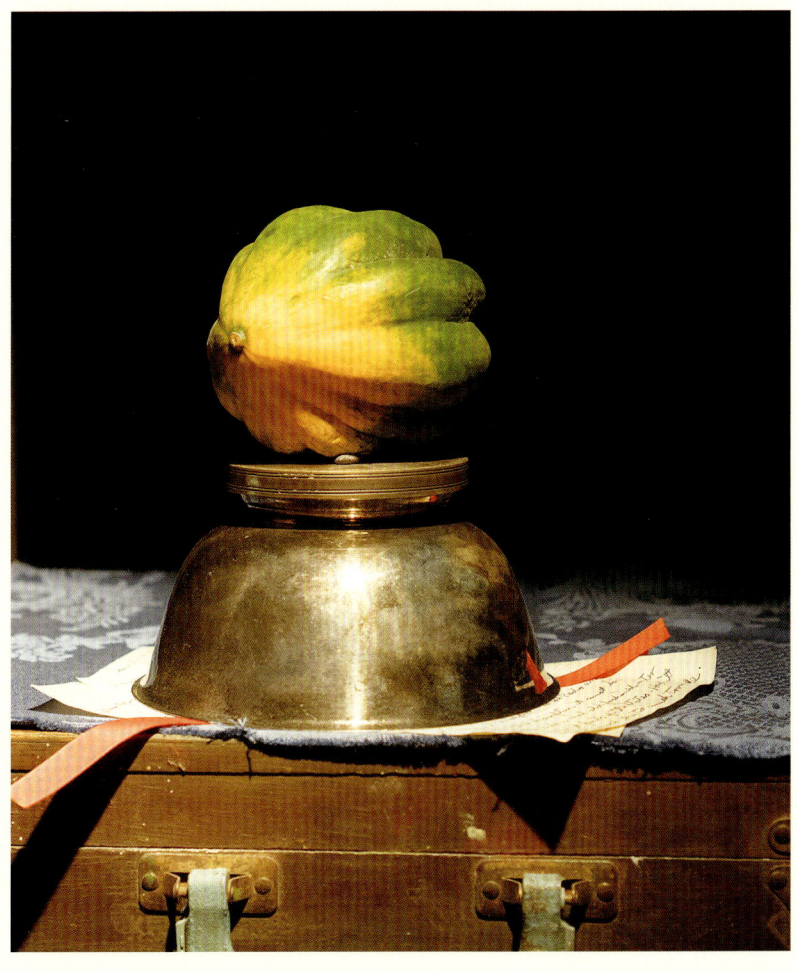
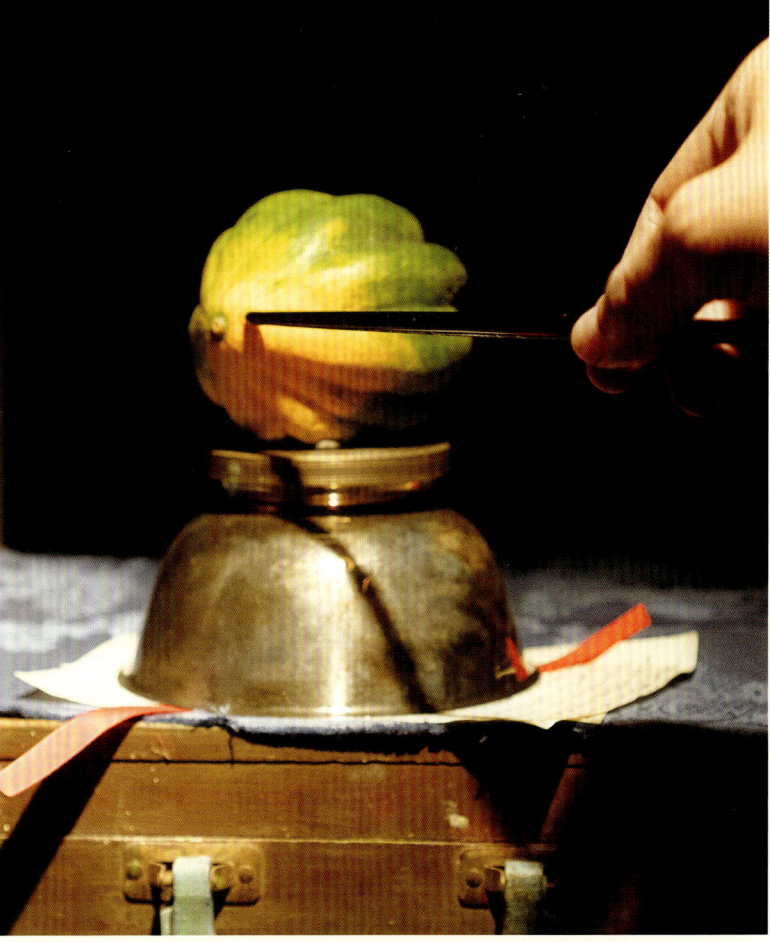

SURFACE REFLECTION AND BODY REFLECTION

When light strikes a surface it sheers into two components: *surface reflection* and *body reflection*. You can think of this as light either being reflected off the surface or absorbed into the body. These two components affect our entire visual perception of an object.

We observe a *highlight* when a light ray is reflected into our eyes off the surface we are looking at. The shinier the surface, the more obvious the highlight. The more matte the surface, the less obvious the highlight will appear. A rough or porous surface can break up the highlight, as can be seen on citrus fruits like lemons and limes. Only a surface that is 100 percent matte will reflect no light off the surface.

A *diffuse reflection* happens when light waves/particles are not reflected directly off the object but are redirected from the surface at different angles or are absorbed into the surface. A matte surface breaks up the reflection, which is therefore not as intense or prominent as a reflection on a glossy surface.

A glossy surface will produce a *specular highlight*—an obvious, bright spot on the form.

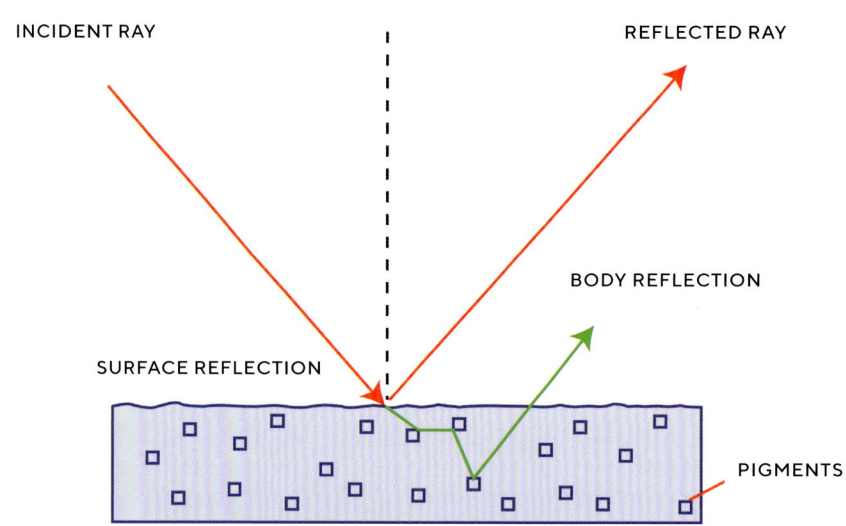

Surface reflection and body reflection.

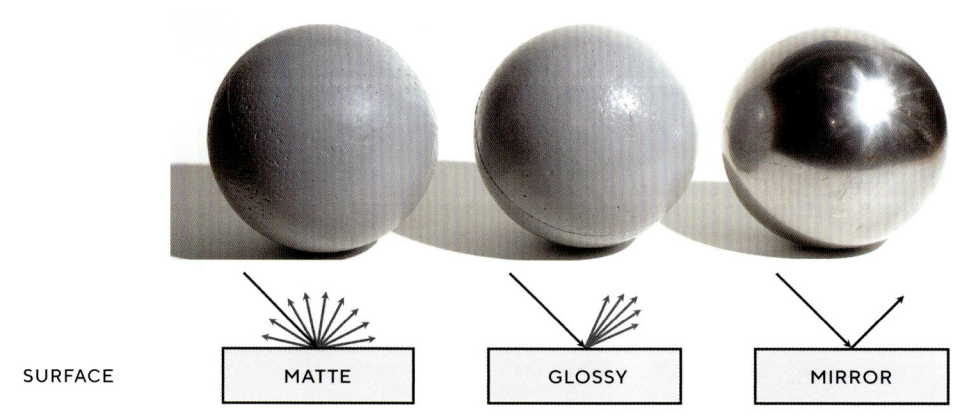

Reflection of light off matte, glossy, and mirrored surfaces.

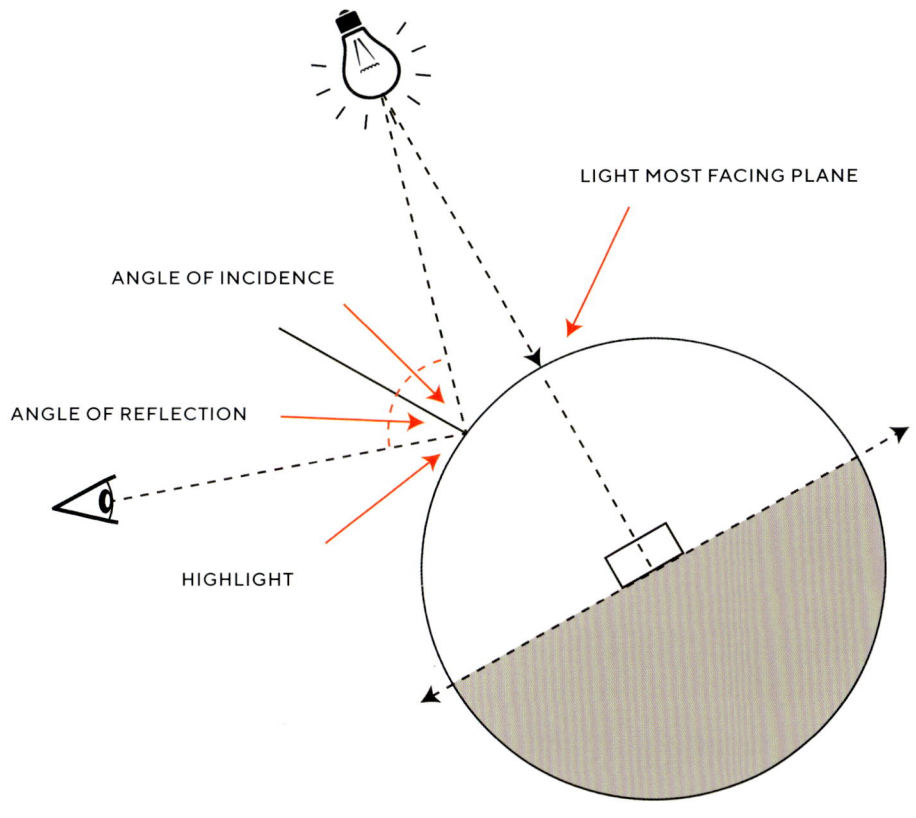

LIGHT MOST FACING PLANE

ANGLE OF INCIDENCE

ANGLE OF REFLECTION

HIGHLIGHT

A highlight is the glare from the primary light source bouncing off a surface. We normally observe a highlight on the surface between the viewer and the light source (on shiny surfaces). The action of the light is like that of a billiard ball in a game of pool: the ball bounces off a bank at the same angle at which it hit the bank. (The angle of incidence equals the angle of reflection.)

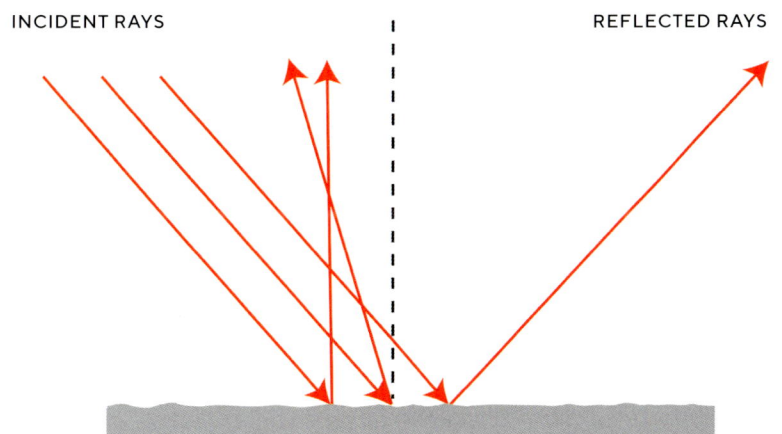

INCIDENT RAYS

REFLECTED RAYS

When an incident ray hits a matte surface, the light scatters and is less predictable than when light strikes a glossy or mirrored surface.

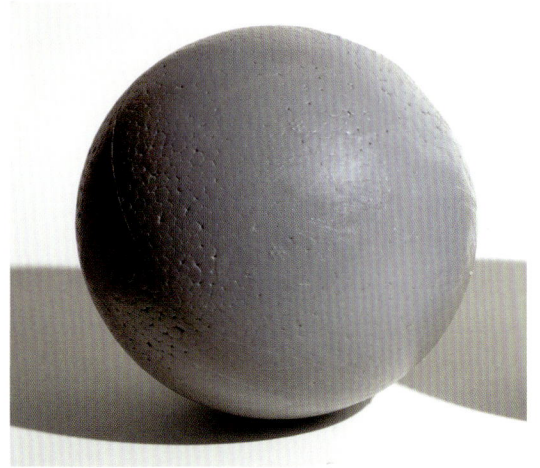

On this matte sphere, a highlight is still present, but it is less intense than it would be on a glossy surface.

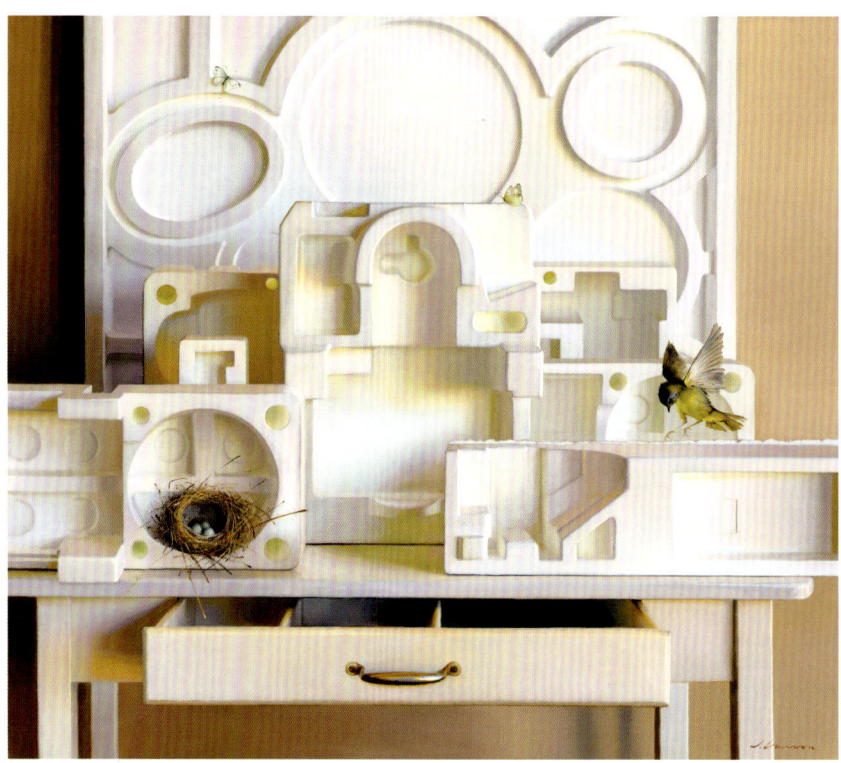

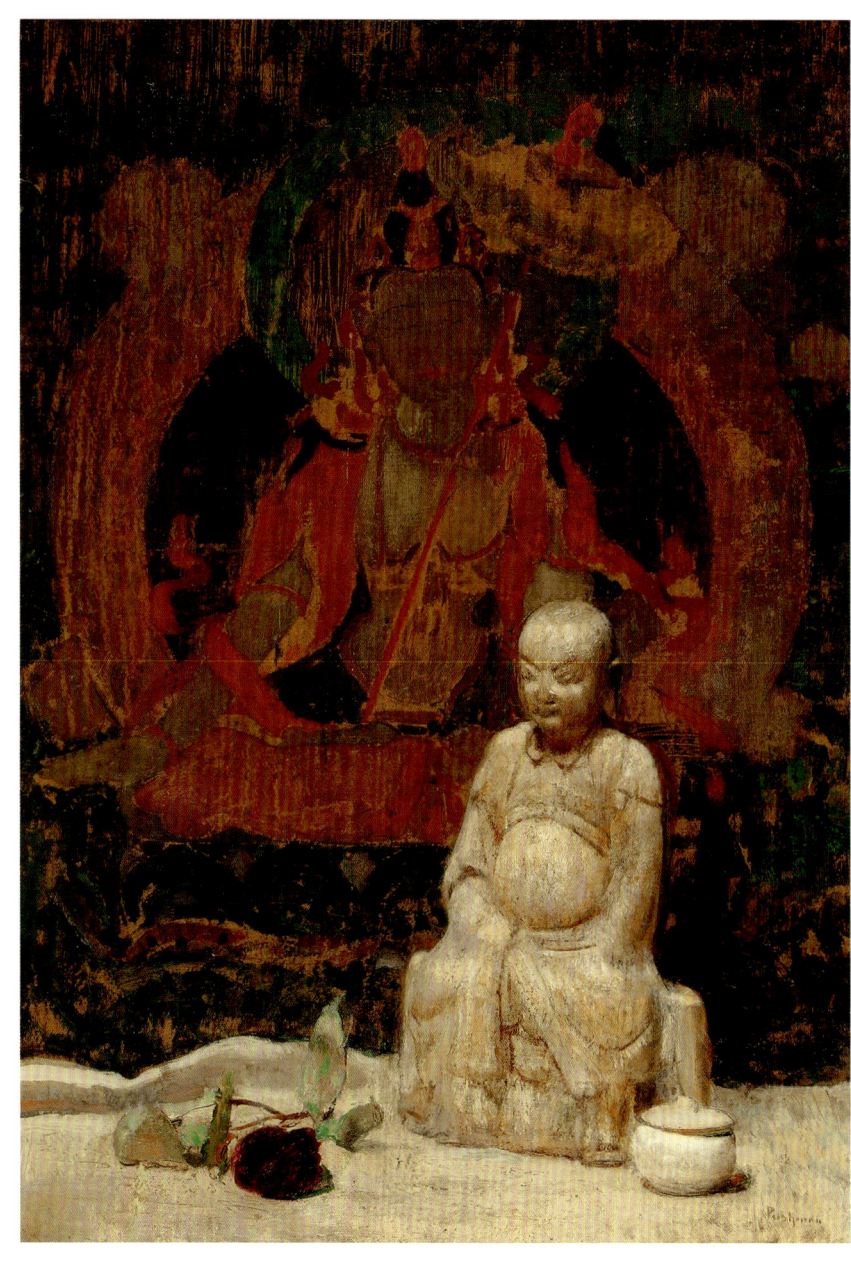

We see almost no highlights on the Styrofoam objects in Jeffrey T. Larson's painting, indicating that the forms have matte surfaces. We do, however, see a clear highlight on the shiny metal drawer handle.

The diffuse highlights on the forehead and shoulder of the seated figure in this painting indicate that the figure's surface is matte.

In Michael Klein's painting *Studio Bouquets*, the white specular highlight on the vase at right shows that its surface is glossy.

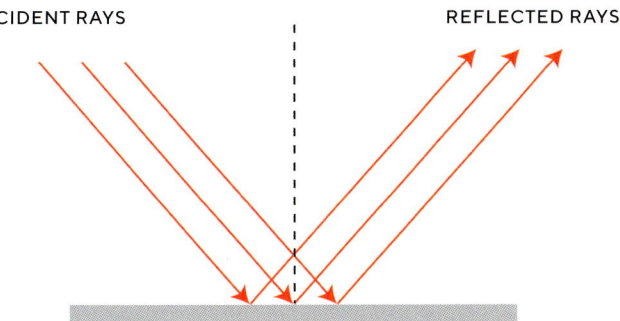

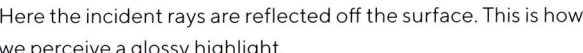

Here the incident rays are reflected off the surface. This is how we perceive a glossy highlight.

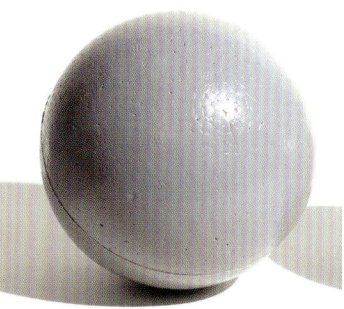

The perceived highlight on a glossy surface is more concentrated and intense than on a matte surface.

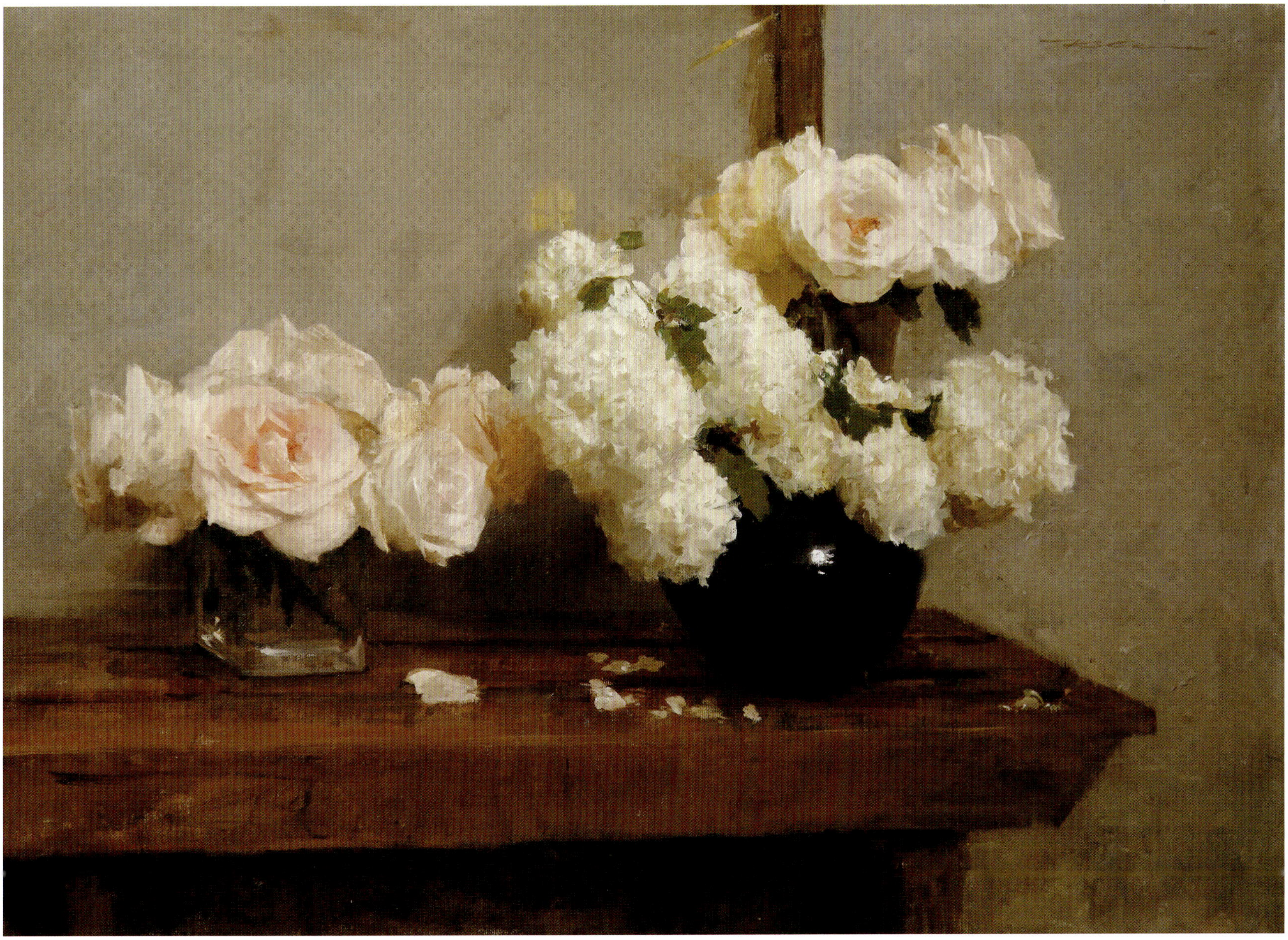

LIGHT ON SUBFORMS

Subforms are smaller forms that sit on larger forms. They are affected by light in the same way as larger forms. Highlights will be apparent on subforms, too.

OPPOSITE: Louis-Antoine Estachon (French, 1819–1857), *Still Life with Fruit,* 1851, oil on canvas, 33 × 26 inches (108.26 × 85.3 cm). Photo courtesy of Rehs Galleries, Inc., New York.

The many subforms on the surface of the larger form of the gourd in this painting are also affected by light.

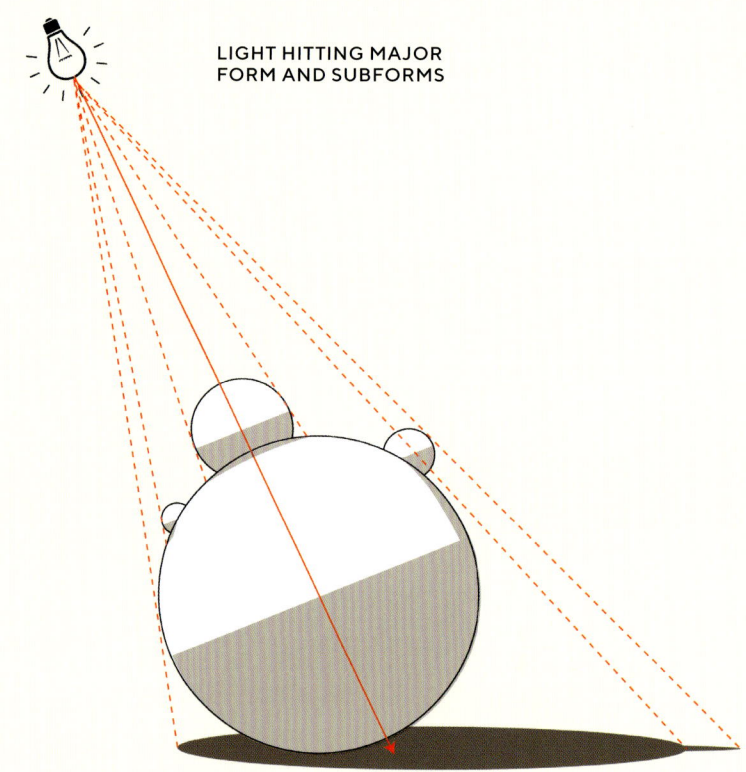

LIGHT HITTING MAJOR
FORM AND SUBFORMS

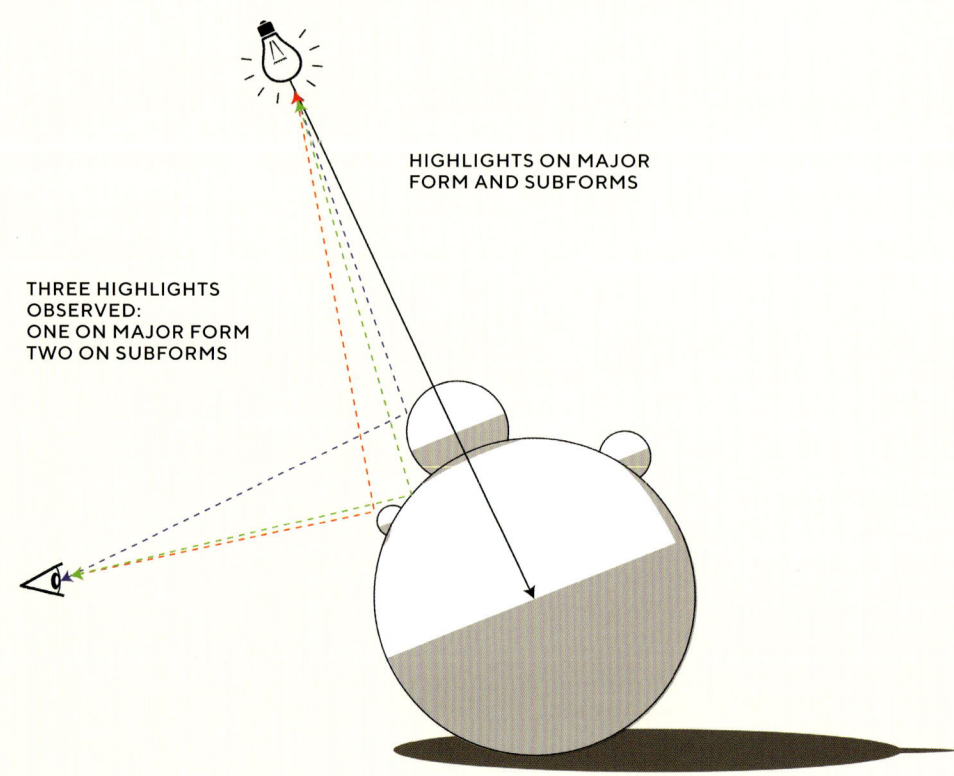

HIGHLIGHTS ON MAJOR
FORM AND SUBFORMS

THREE HIGHLIGHTS
OBSERVED:
ONE ON MAJOR FORM
TWO ON SUBFORMS

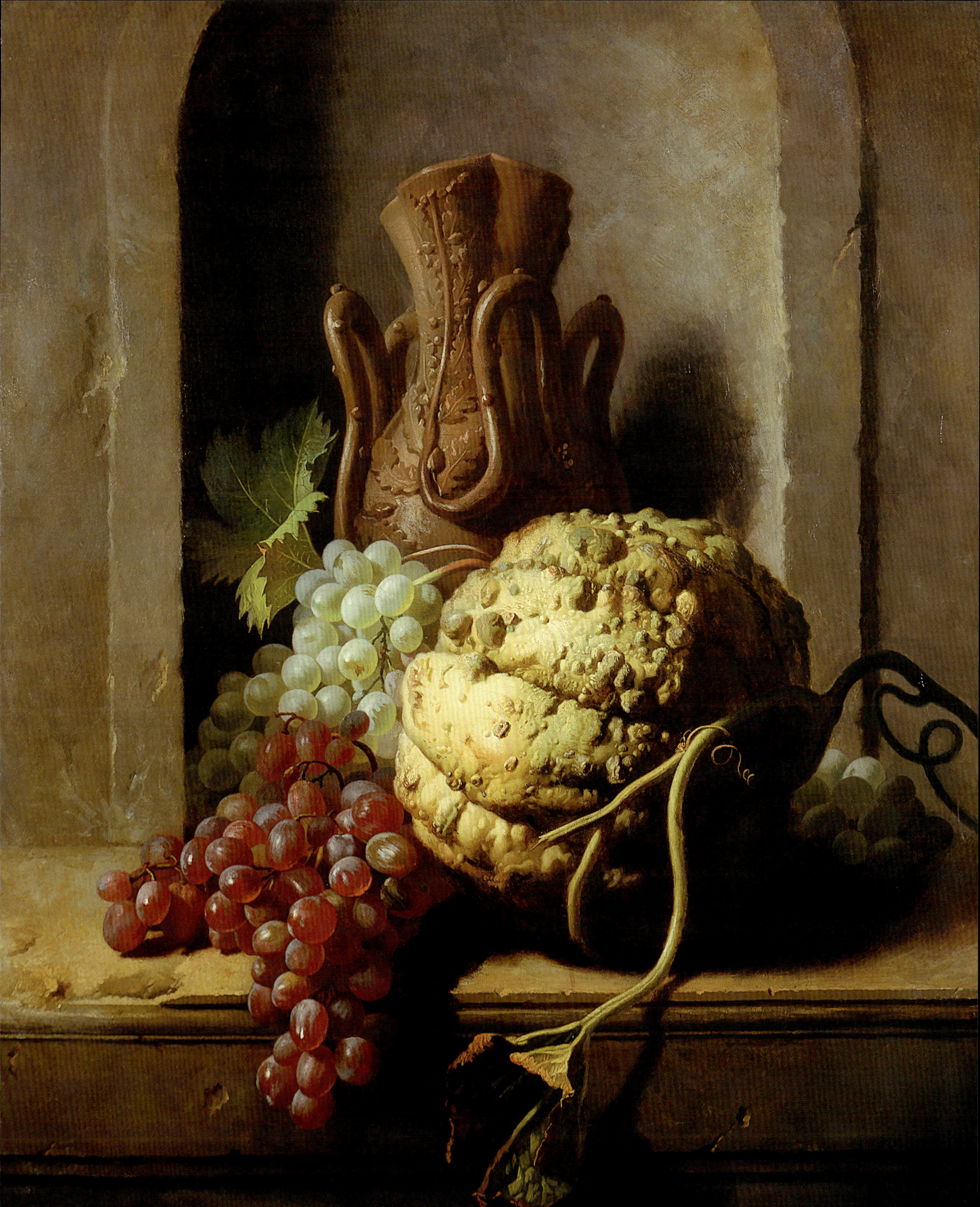

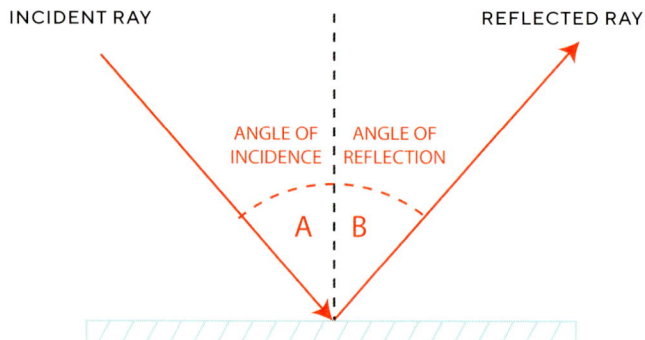

INCIDENT RAY   REFLECTED RAY

ANGLE OF   ANGLE OF
INCIDENCE   REFLECTION

A   B

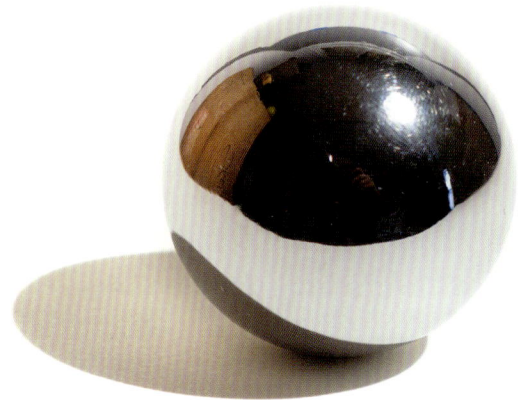

MIRROR REFLECTION

In a *mirror reflection*, the rays of light are reflected off a highly polished, extremely shiny surface. Rounded objects made of metals such as gold, platinum, chrome, stainless steel, and silver are common in still lifes; their surfaces act like a curved mirror. Because the surface is not flat, the reflection warps what it reflects as it follows the surface of the form.

If the reflective metal is highly polished, it may make the form of the object itself difficult to see because its mirrorlike surface reflects the surrounding environment. In still lifes incorporating such objects you will often see the artist's reflection in the mirrored surface. The only gradation of values will be the light falloff happening in the environment.

White metals like silver and steel have only surface reflection. Surfaces such as plastic and paint have both surface reflection and *body reflection*. Body reflection reveals the object's color as the light rays enter the surface and reemerge.

ABOVE: A steel ball bearing is like a mirror wrapped around a sphere. It reflects the surrounding environment, warping it. Light and shadow are not present except in the environment, not on the mirrored surface itself.

RIGHT: William Nicholson (English, 1872–1949), *The Silver Casket,* 1919, oil on canvas, 13 × 19 inches (33 × 40.5 cm). Photo courtesy of Kasmin Gallery, New York. © Desmond Banks. Private collection.

A good example of an obvious highlight appears in this painting by William Nicholson.

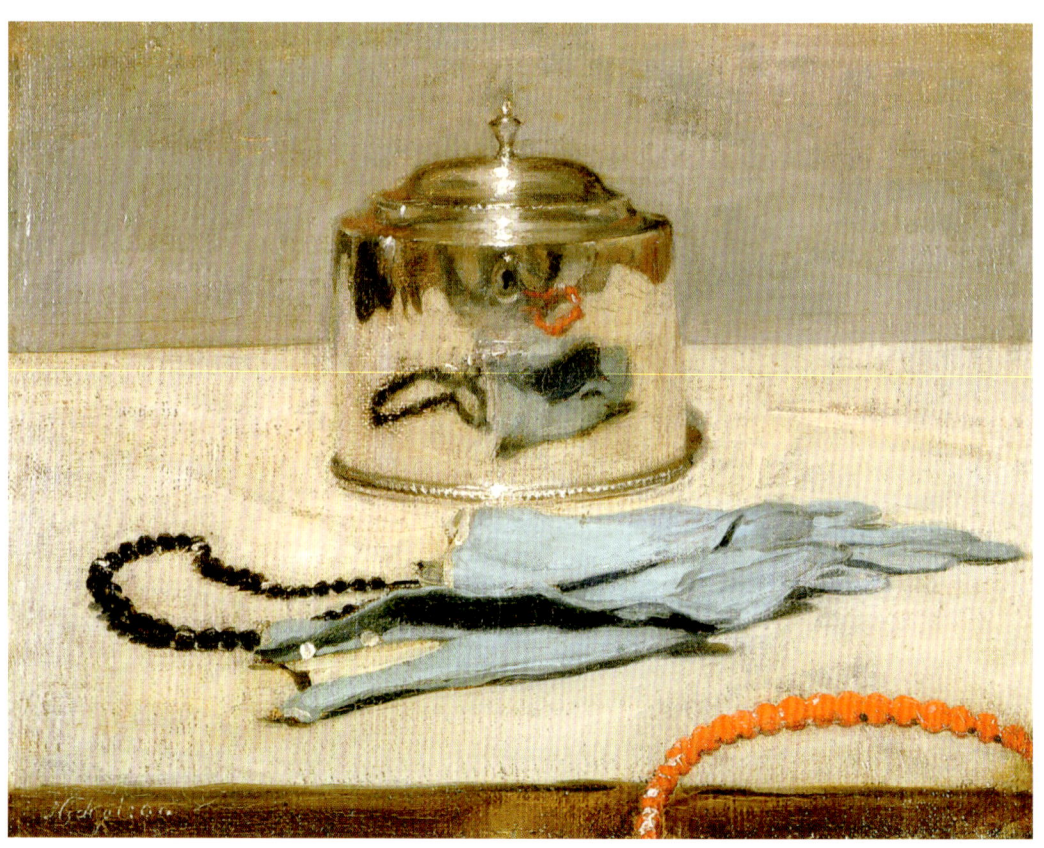

LIGHT ON GLASS

When light hits a transparent surface such as glass, you notice a clear highlight. A transparent object acts like a lens that bends or scatters light rays. (All transparent objects that are not flat have some degree of lens effect.) Some light will also pass through the surface, which distorts the light. The thicker the transparent material, the more the light will bend. Some form is apparent on the edges of a glass object, showing the thickness of the material.

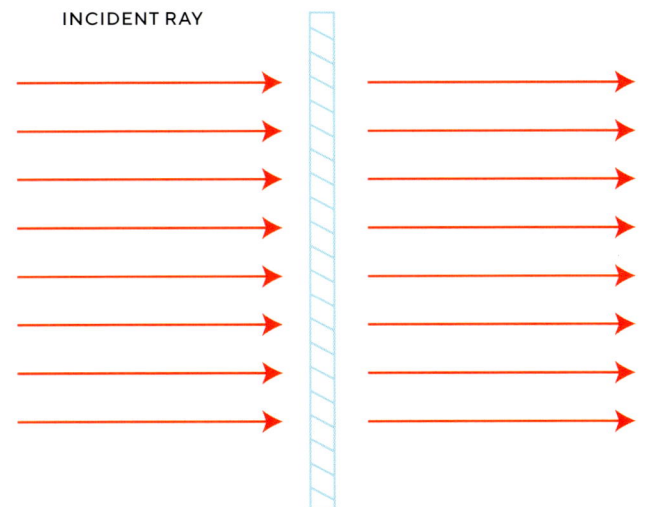

TRANSPARENT SURFACE

INCIDENT RAY

LIGHT PASSES THROUGH

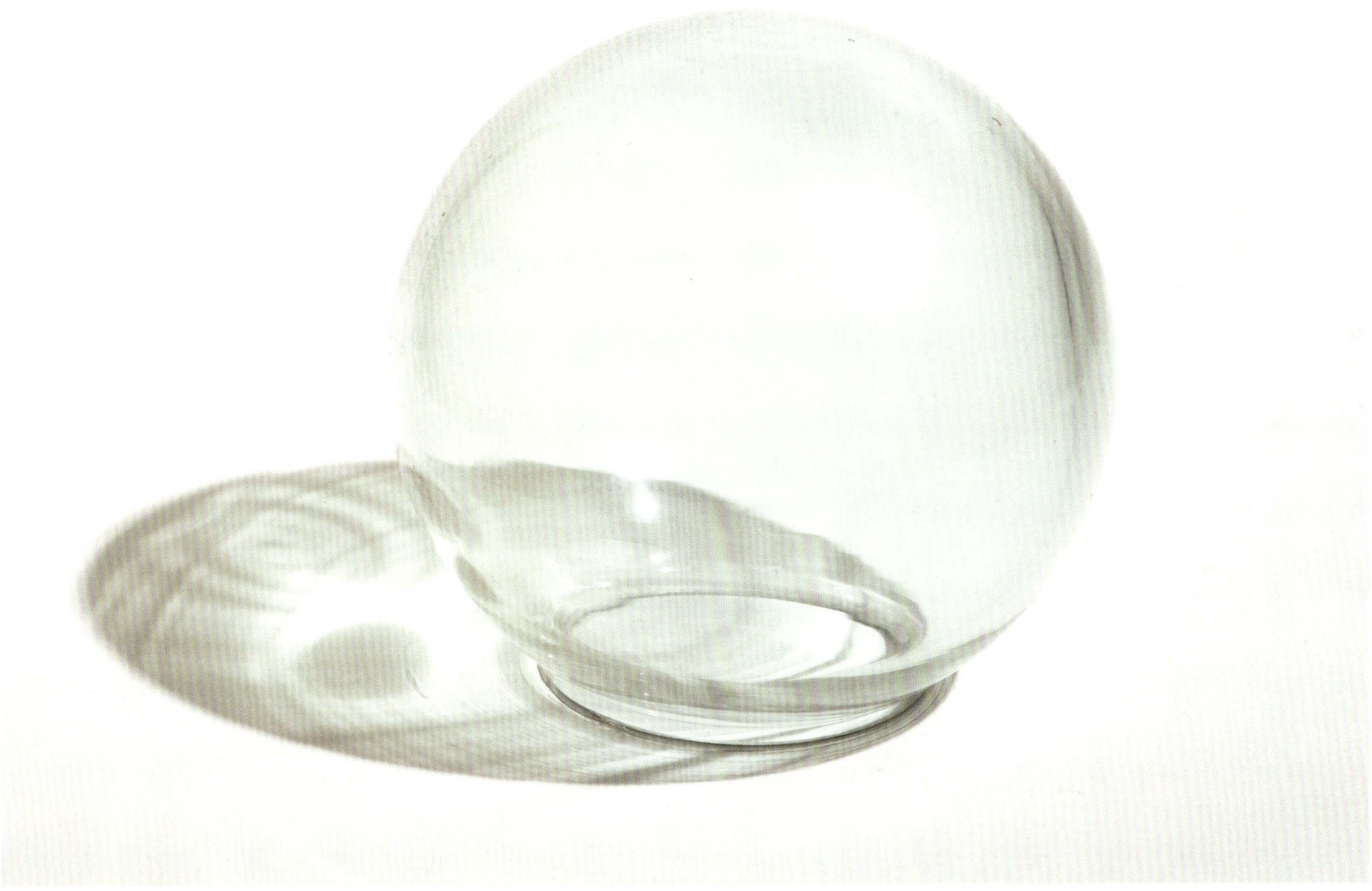

Light will pass through a transparent surface.

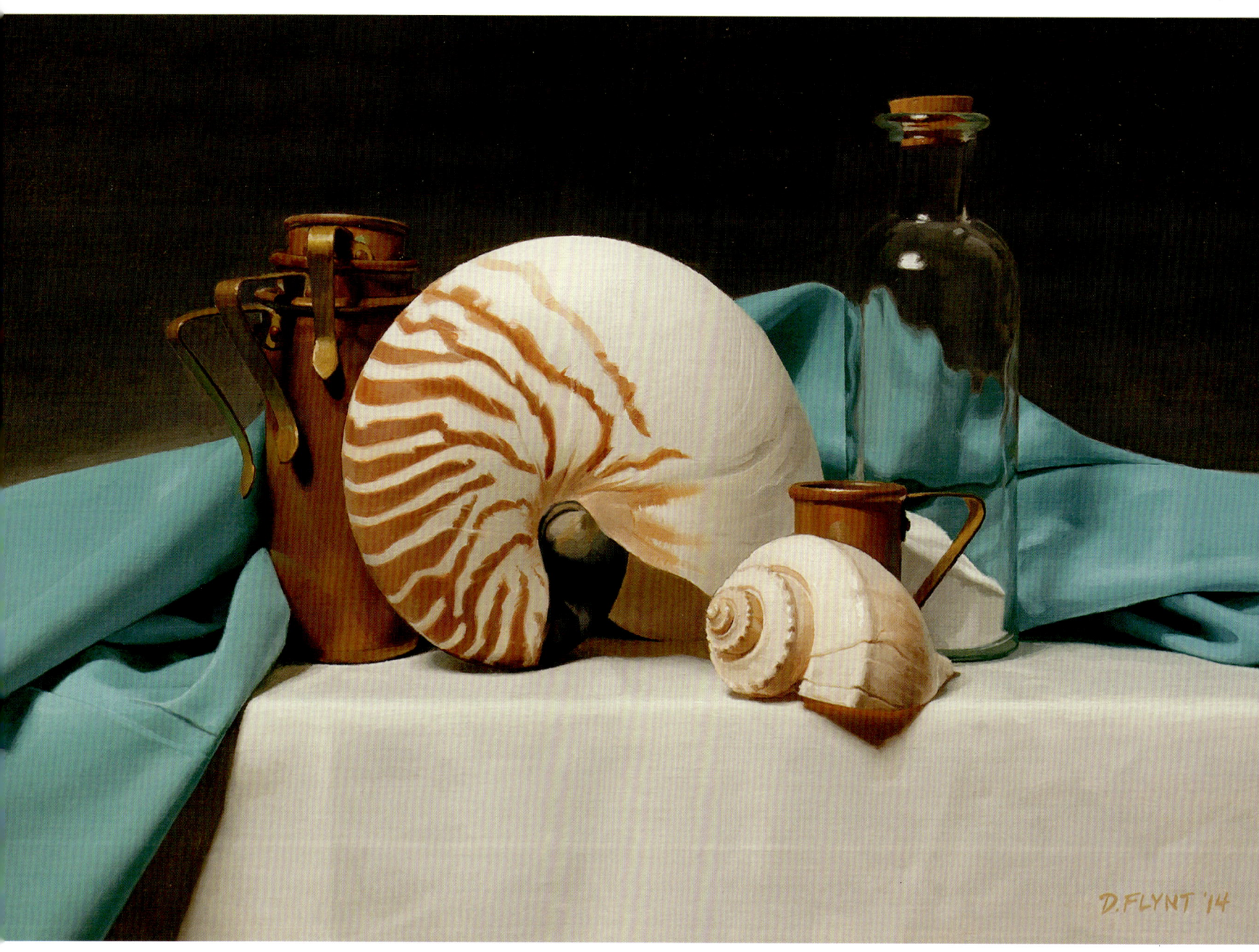

D.FLYNT '14

In Douglas Flynt's *Colors of the Sea*, light passes through the surface of the glass and shows the turquoise cloth behind it, revealing the glass's transparency.

Glass comes in several different forms: clear, colored, and opaque. Painting glass can be quite difficult. With clear glass, the thickness of the glass determines how the edges of the object are perceived, as these are the only forms of the object itself that you really see. You also need to focus on reflections from the environment and the highlights on the glass object's surface, since these are mostly what you are painting.

Transparent objects do cast shadows even though light is passing through them. When light is focused rather than scattered it casts a shadow. Semi-transparent colored glass behaves similarly, although it acts like a colored filter or gel.

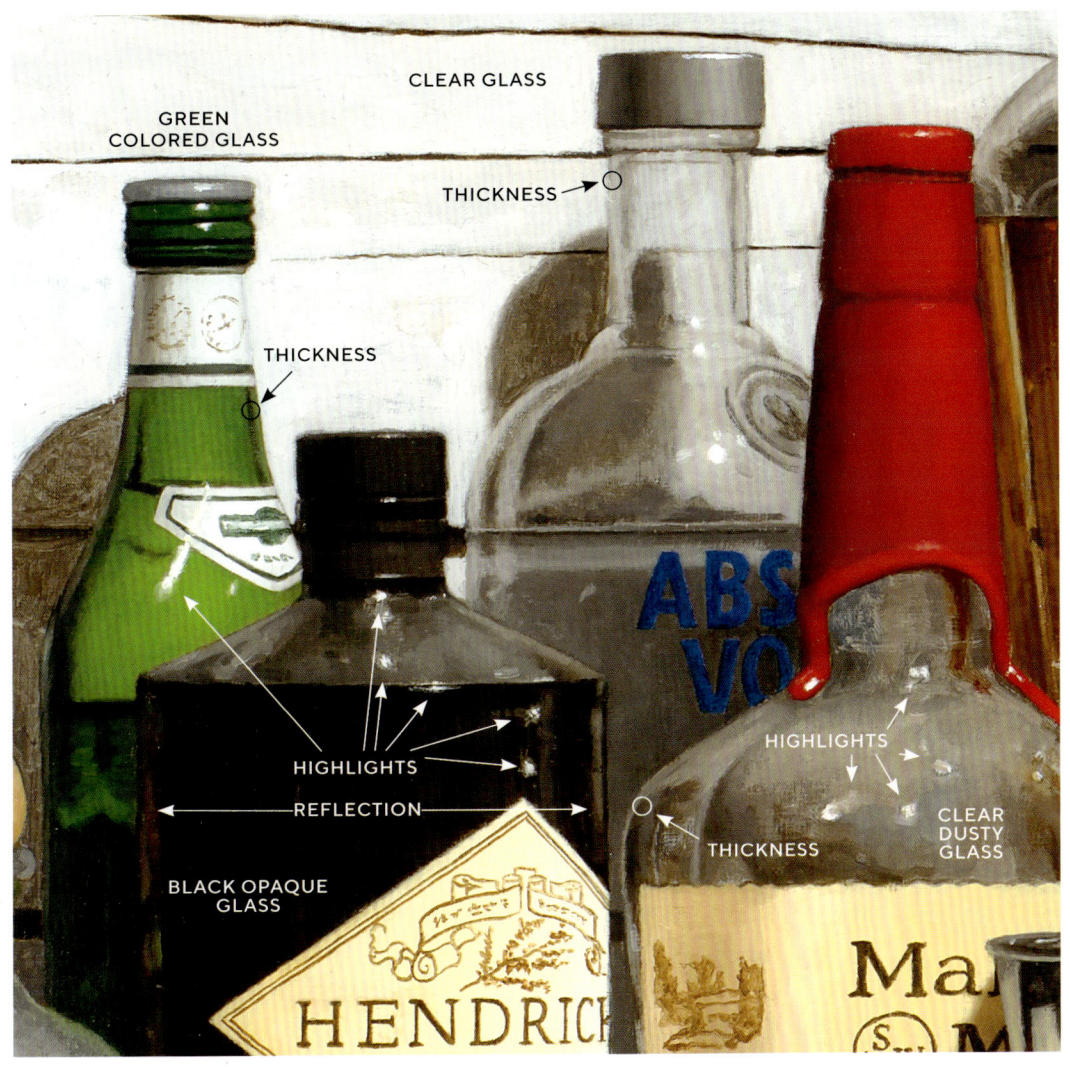

GREEN
COLORED GLASS

CLEAR GLASS

THICKNESS

THICKNESS

HIGHLIGHTS

REFLECTION

BLACK OPAQUE
GLASS

HIGHLIGHTS

CLEAR
DUSTY
GLASS

THICKNESS

HENDRIC

ABS
VO

Ma
M

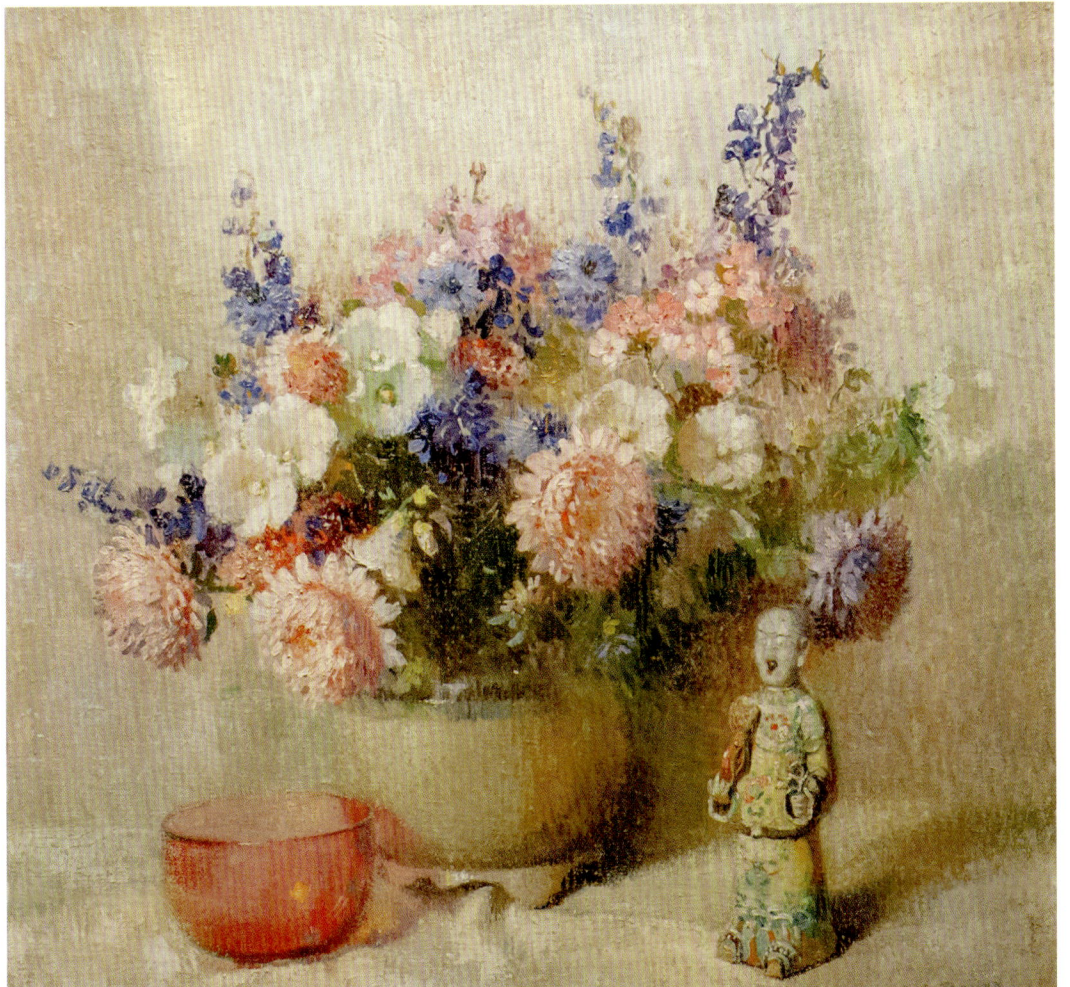

ABOVE: All glass shows highlights, as you can see in this detail from my painting *The Art of Mixology*. (The full painting appears on page 147.) If the glass is clear, you will be able to see the thickness of the glass at the edges of the forms.

LEFT: George Loftus Noyes (American, 1864–1954), *Old Time Bouquet*, n.d., oil on canvas, 24 × 25 inches (60.96 × 63.5 cm). Whistler House Museum of Art, Lowell, Mass. Gift of Miss Elizabeth Lambert, 1978 (for LAA 100th anniversary). Photo courtesy of Albert F. Casey.

Light mostly passes through the pink bowl at the bottom left. This makes the bowl appear brighter.

LIGHT ON A TRANSLUCENT OBJECT

A translucent object is neither opaque nor totally transparent. Some light will pass through the object, but the light will scatter through the material. As it does so, all the colors except for those we perceive are absorbed, and the chroma intensifies. The longer the light spends in the object, the more radiant the material will appear. This *diffuse transmission* of light can also be observed on thin clothes and, especially, on flower petals.

BELOW: Angela Cunningham, *Delicate,* 2013, oil on linen, 9 × 12 inches (22.86 × 30.48 cm). Courtesy of the artist.

Yellow light brightens up the shadow on the zygomatic bone of the skull in this painting. This diffuse transmission of light can also sometimes be observed on thin clothes, grapes, jelly, a peeled orange, and, especially, flower petals.

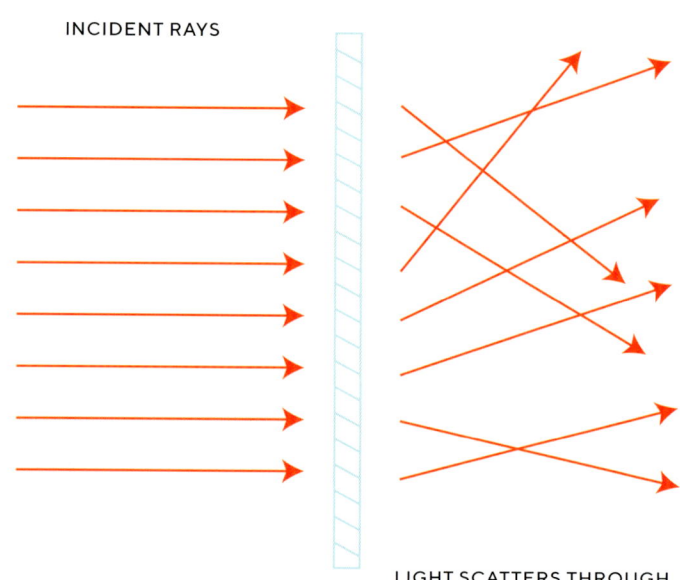

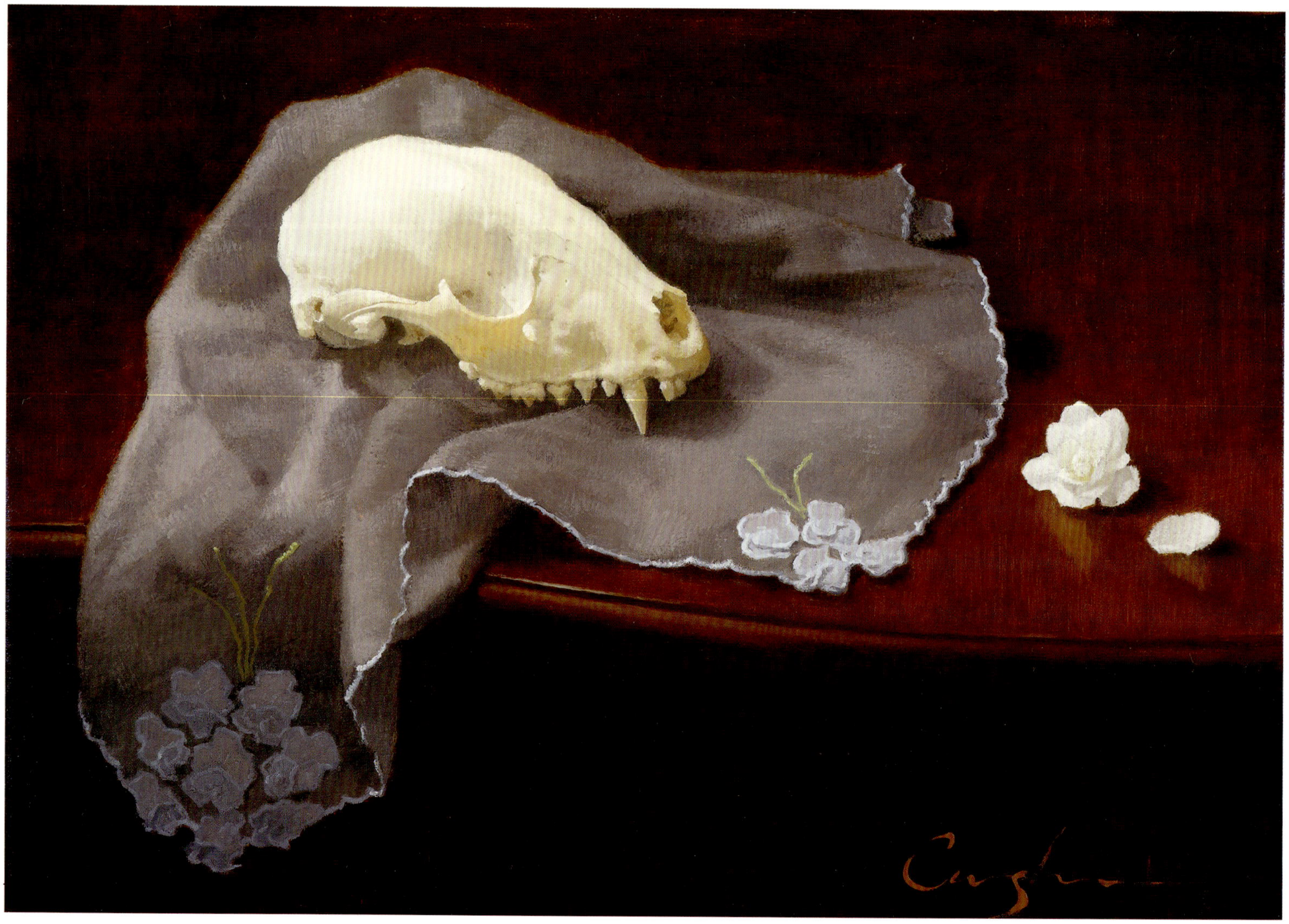

INCIDENT RAYS

TRANSLUCENT SURFACE

LIGHT SCATTERS THROUGH

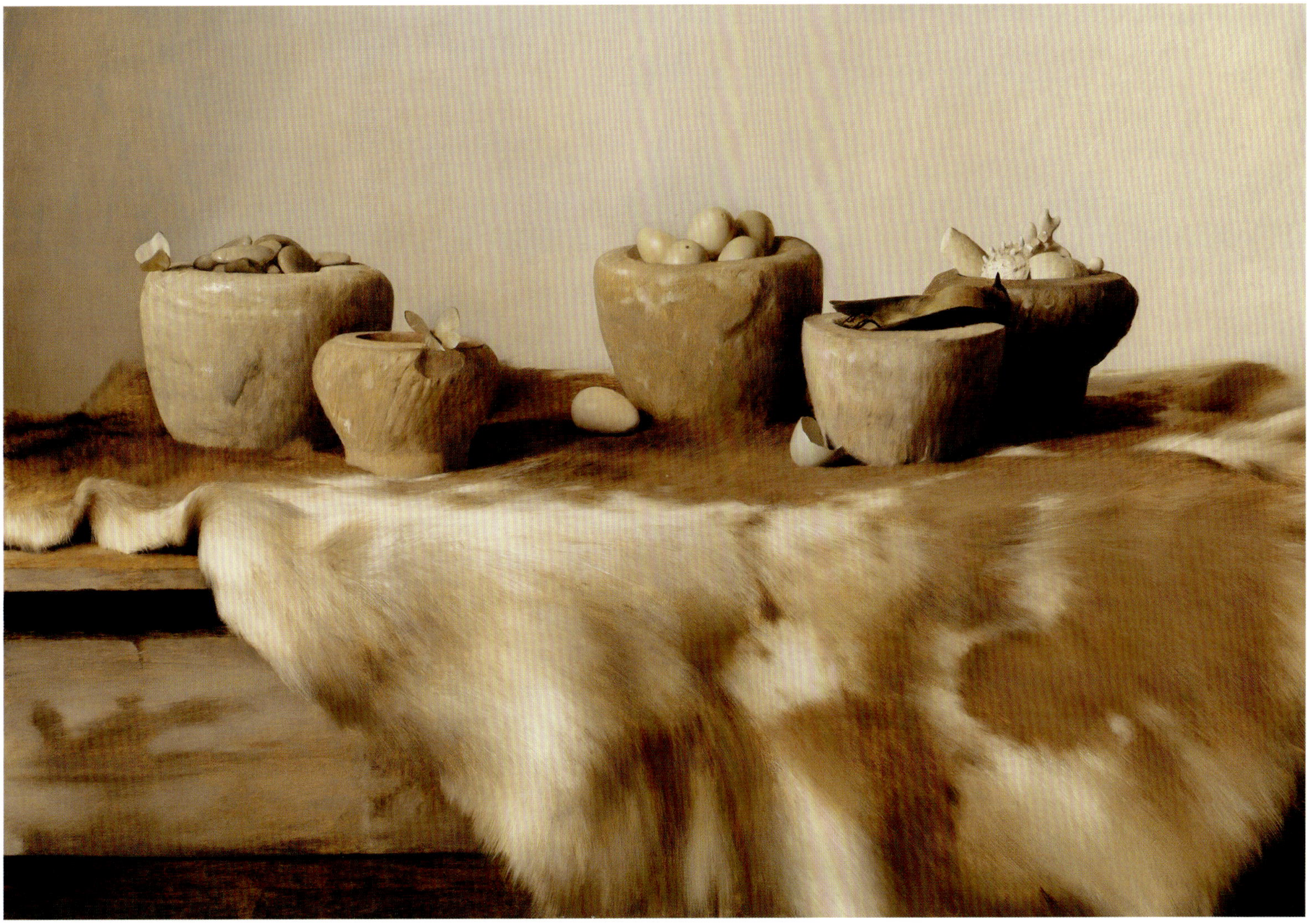

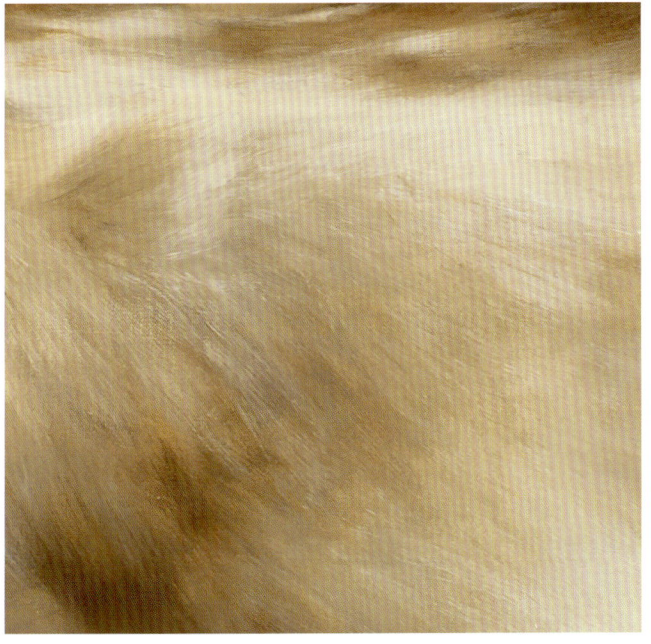

LIGHT ON HAIR, FUR, FABRIC, AND WOOD

Light can take on many different properties when hitting fabric. The surface texture will determine how the cloth is rendered. If the cloth is shiny, as with polyester, leather, silk, or rayon, the highlight will be more obvious. Fabrics such as wool, denim, cotton, and velvet, however, absorb most of the light and diffuse the highlight.

ABOVE AND LEFT: Carlo Russo, *The Beginning and the End,* 2017, oil on linen, 24 × 34 inches (60.96 × 86.36 cm). Courtesy of the artist.

We perceive the edges of the fur in Carlo Russo's painting *The Beginning and the End* as being really soft. If the edges had been hard, it would feel more like a pattern than like hair. Capturing light on hair or fur can be very difficult. Although composed of many strands, hair or fur has to be seen as a mass rather than as individual hairs. The transition from dark to light has a soft edge.

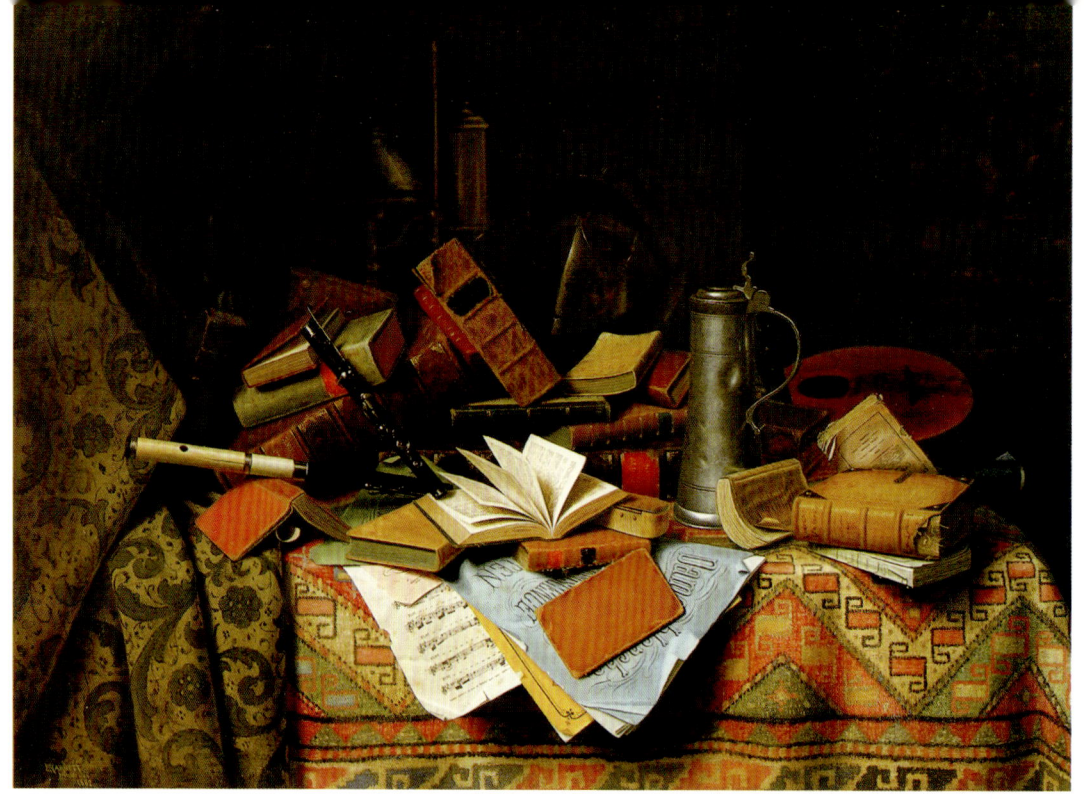

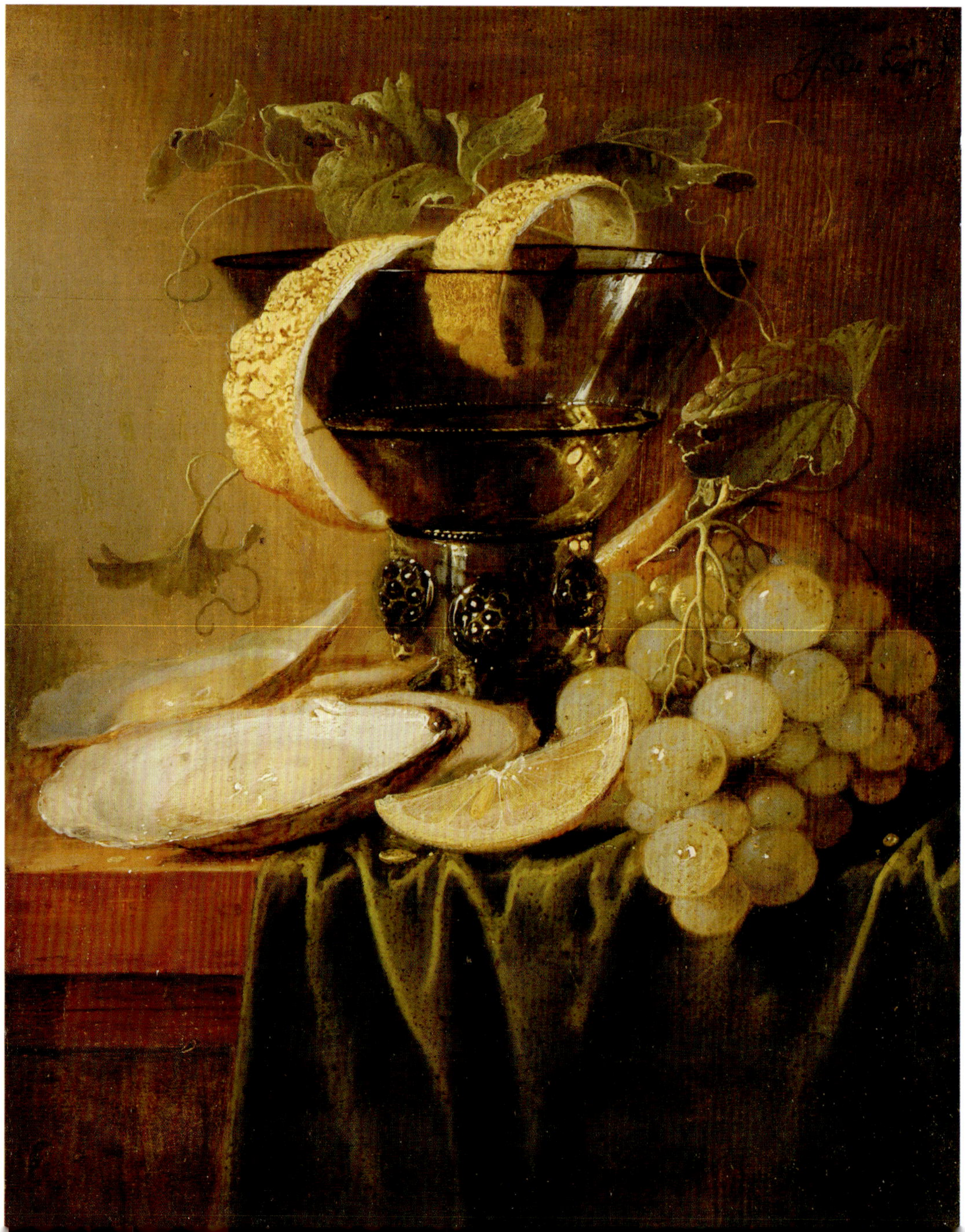

ABOVE: William Harnett, *A Study Table*, 1882, oil on canvas, 39 ¾ × 51 ¼ inches (101.2 × 130.4 cm). Museum of Art, Munson-Williams-Proctor Institute. Photo courtesy of the Art Renewal Center.

William Harnett's *A Study Table* shows draperies of two different cloths, neither of which has a clear highlight, which makes the fabric feel dense.

RIGHT: Jan Davidsz. de Heem (Dutch, 1606–1683/84), *Still Life with a Glass and Oysters,* c. 1640, oil on wood, 9 ⅞ × 7 ½ inches (25.1 × 19.1 cm). The Metropolitan Museum of Art, New York. Purchase, 1871.

In *Still Life with a Glass and Oysters,* the fabric seems more like silk because of the shiny highlights.

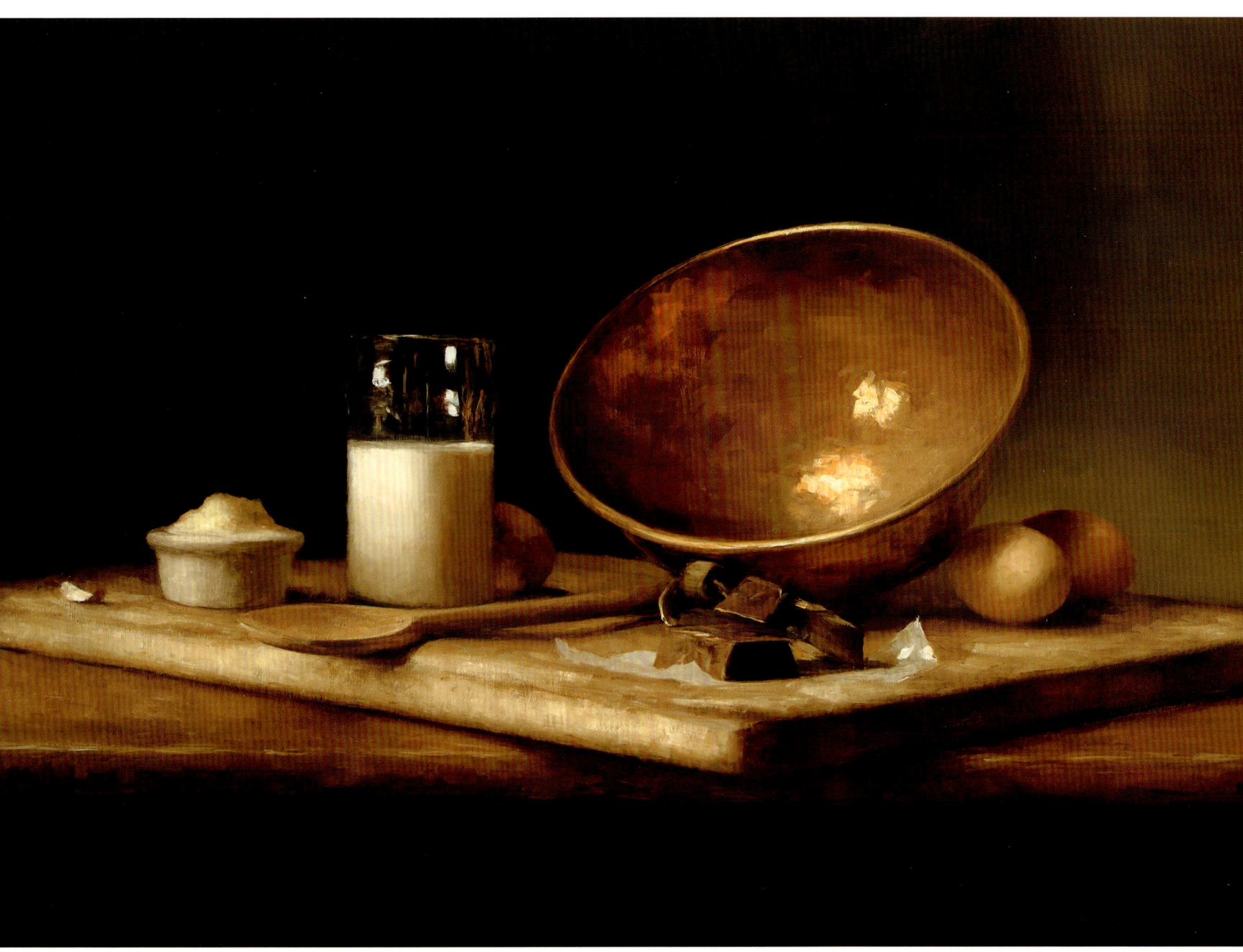

Wood can have an obvious or a broken-up highlight, depending on whether the surface is dry, polished, or wet. On dry or unvarnished wood, the highlight will be broken up because of the rough or matte surface. If the wood is polished, lacquered, or varnished, a clear, defined highlight will appear on the surface.

ABOVE: Sarah Lamb, *Chocolate Mousse,* 2010, oil on canvas, 18 × 25 inches (45.72 × 63.5 cm). Courtesy of the artist.

In Sarah Lamb's *Chocolate Mousse,* three different wood elements (tabletop, cutting board, spoon) interact differently with light.

A VERY COMMON MISTAKE

One of the most common mistakes I see students make is to render transitions of values to the highlight instead of to the light most facing plane.

The geometry of the light stays consistent no matter where you are standing in relation to an illuminated object, and it's that geometry that defines the light most facing plane. The highlight, however, does not stay constant as you move around an object. The highlight's position will change depending on where you are viewing the object from.

The light most facing plane and the highlight need to be separated and articulated correctly. When rolling form (see pages 246–251), the gradation of values should be applied to the light most facing plane, not to the highlight. The highlight merely shows where the artist was standing while creating the artwork. The difference can be clearly seen in the images here, which show how the highlights change as the viewer changes position while the light most facing plane always remains the same.

RIGHT, TOP TO BOTTOM: As we move around an object, the highlights change position as the geometry of the light most facing plane stays the same.

OPPOSITE: Todd M. Casey, *Mezcal Tequila,* 2018, oil on panel, 6 × 8 inches (15.24 × 20.32 cm). Private collection.

In my painting *Mezcal Tequila*, the transition of values is rendered to the light most facing plane.

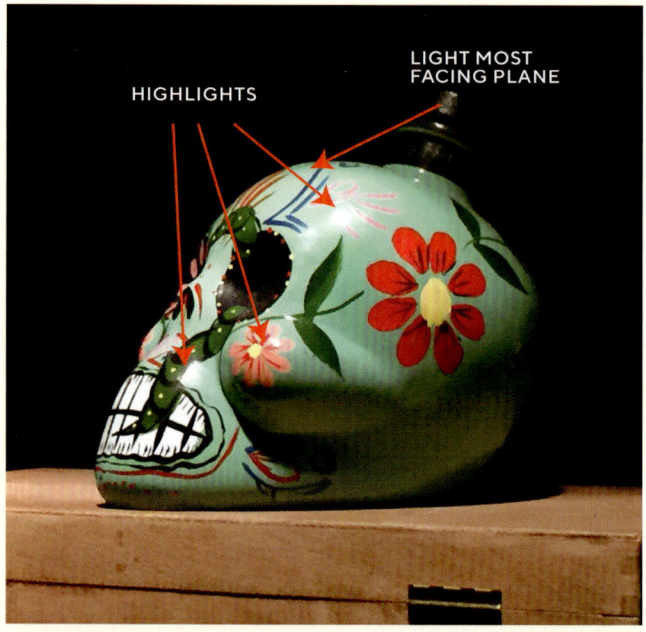

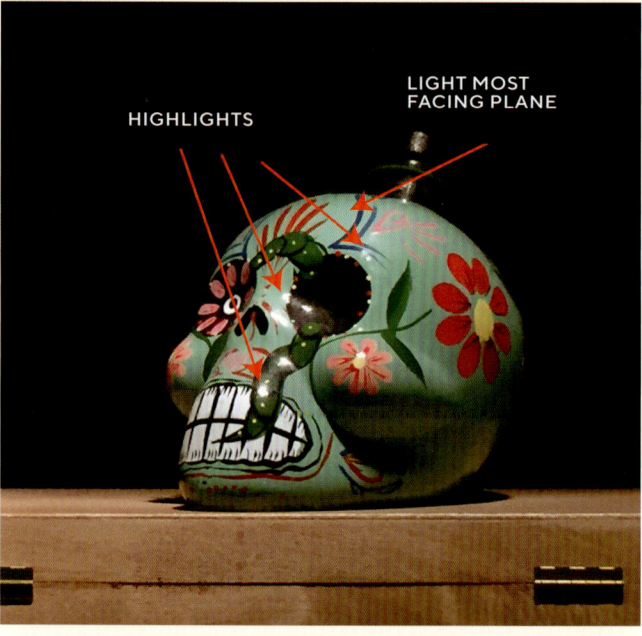

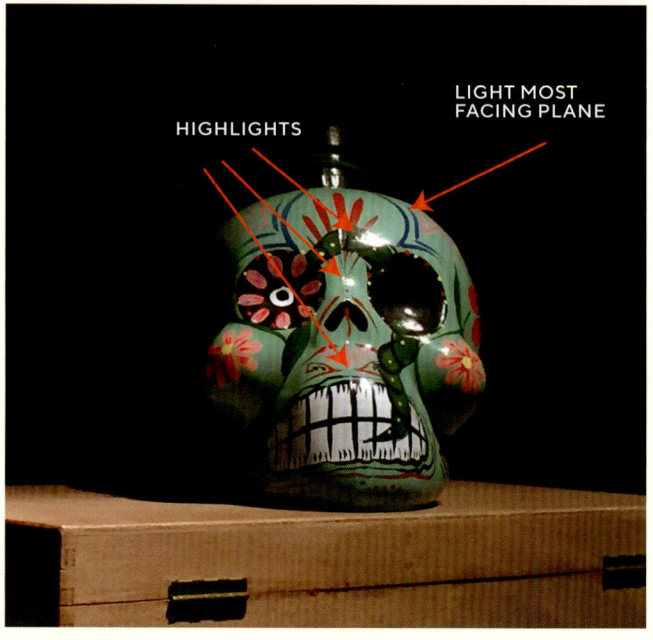

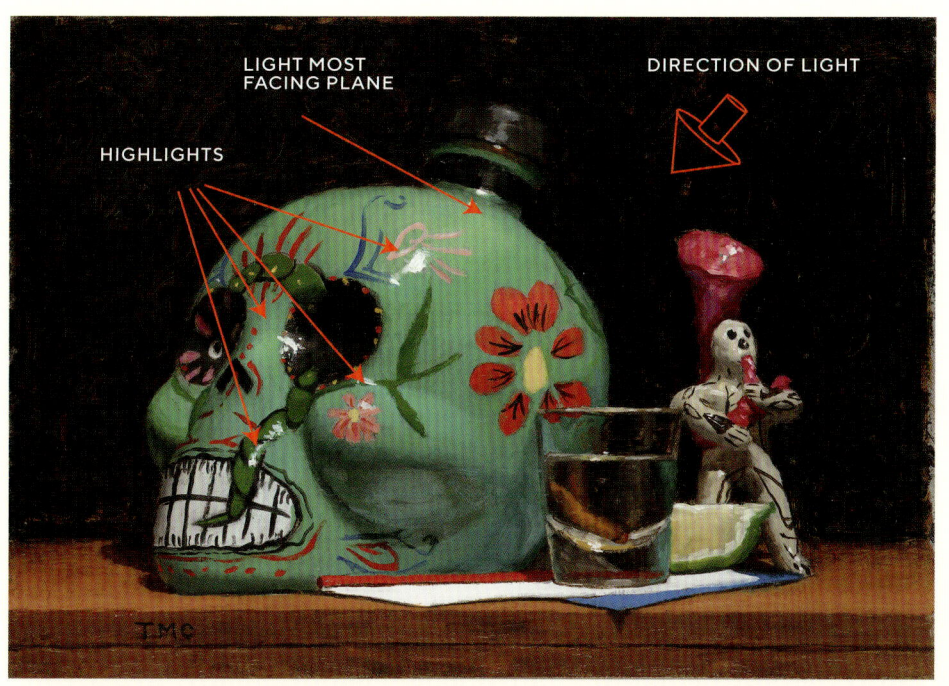

LIGHT MOST
FACING PLANE

DIRECTION OF LIGHT

HIGHLIGHTS

TMC

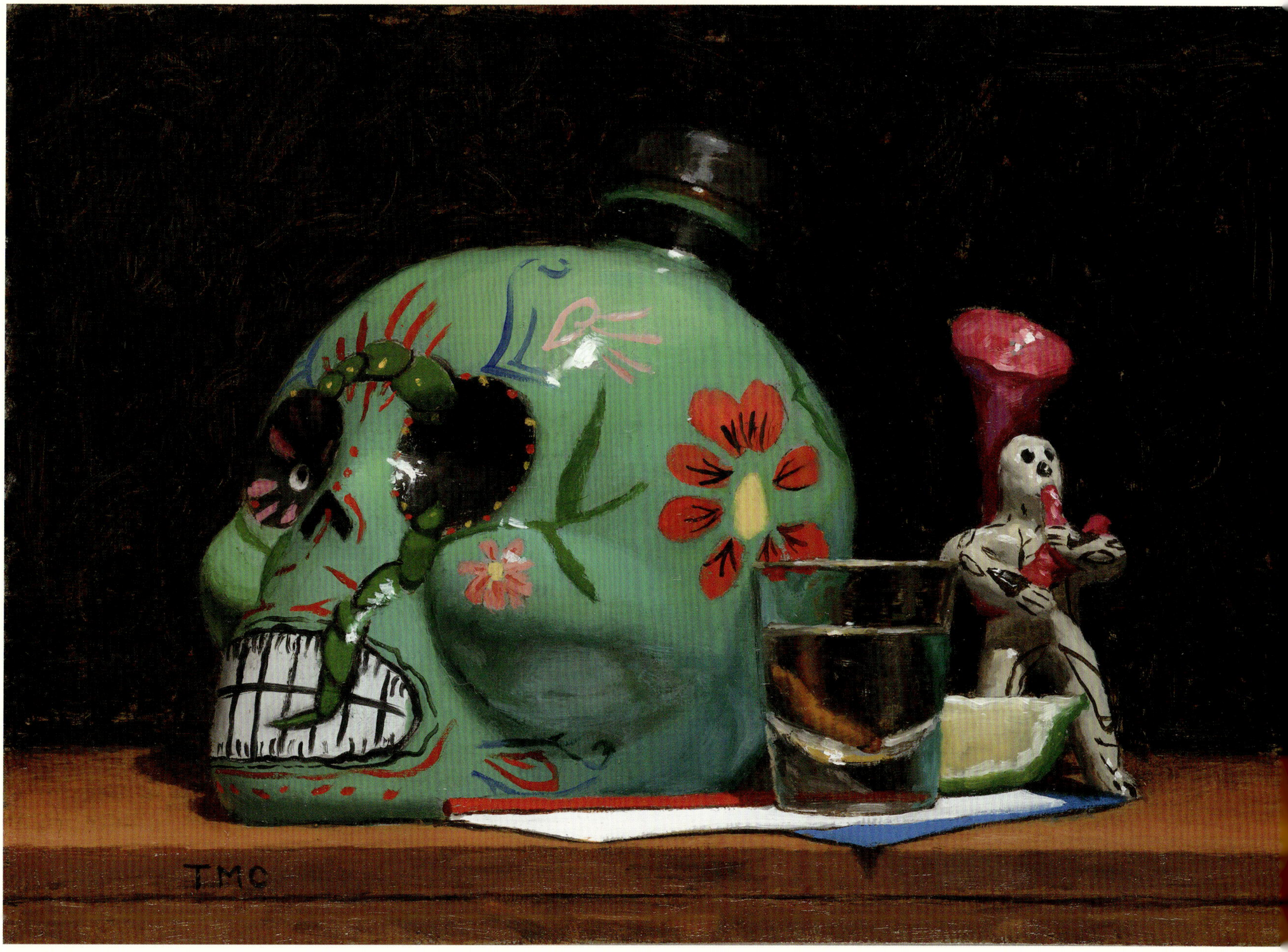

TMC

LIGHTING YOUR STUDIO

There are a number of factors to consider when setting up the lighting in your studio, including whether to use natural or artificial light, the light's size, the distance and angle of the light in relation to the setup, and the light's temperature. All these variables will affect how you see.

Natural versus Artificial Light

Your first lighting decision is whether to use natural or artificial light. Some artists prefer one over the other, but it's really up to you. You can make a nice painting with either. Your studio setup may determine which you choose to paint under: if the space doesn't have appropriate windows or skylights, you may only have the option of painting under artificial light.

The best sort of natural light for painting is northern light—sunlight coming through a north-facing window or skylight. Temperature-wise, northern light falls within the neutral range on the Kelvin scale (see page 148). It's cooler and more ambient than light from other directions because the light from the sun is reflected off the atmosphere. Yet another benefit is that northern light doesn't change all that much over the course of the day because it is not direct light. If your studio's windows don't face north, you can approximate the effect of northern light by using light bulbs whose temperature measures 5500–6500K (sometimes called "daylight" bulbs).

Artificial lights give you much more control over lighting effects. You can control the size of the light, the distance from your setup, the angle, and the temperature. If you set your light source close to your still life setup, the shadows will be crisply defined. Moving the light farther away will soften the shadows.

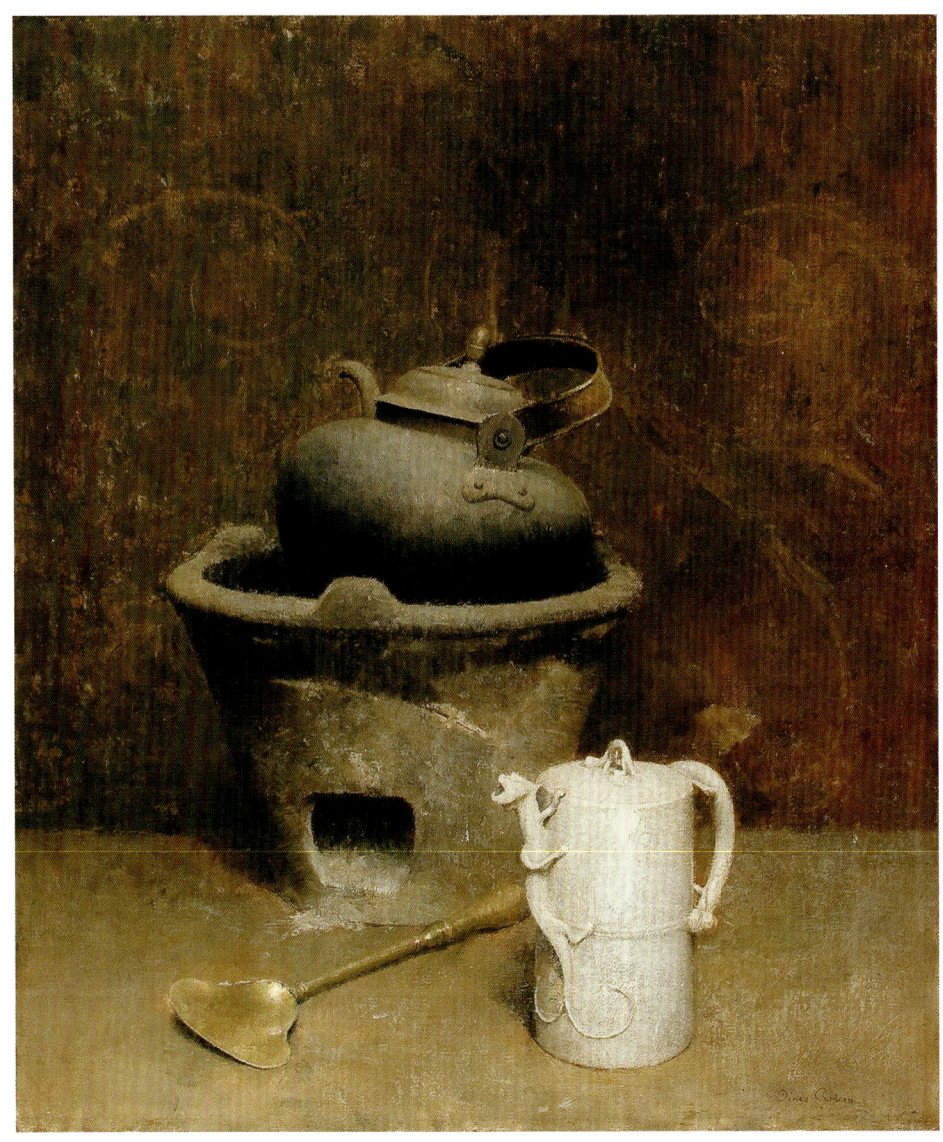

ABOVE: Dines Carlsen (American, 1902–1966), *Chinese Teapot and Pewter Kettle,* n.d., oil on canvas, 24 × 20 inches (61 × 50.8 cm). Photo courtesy of Joseph Bartolomeo, Shannon's Fine Art Auctioneers.

Dines Carlsen's *Chinese Teapot and Pewter Kettle* was painted under northern light, which softens the contrast between light and shadow.

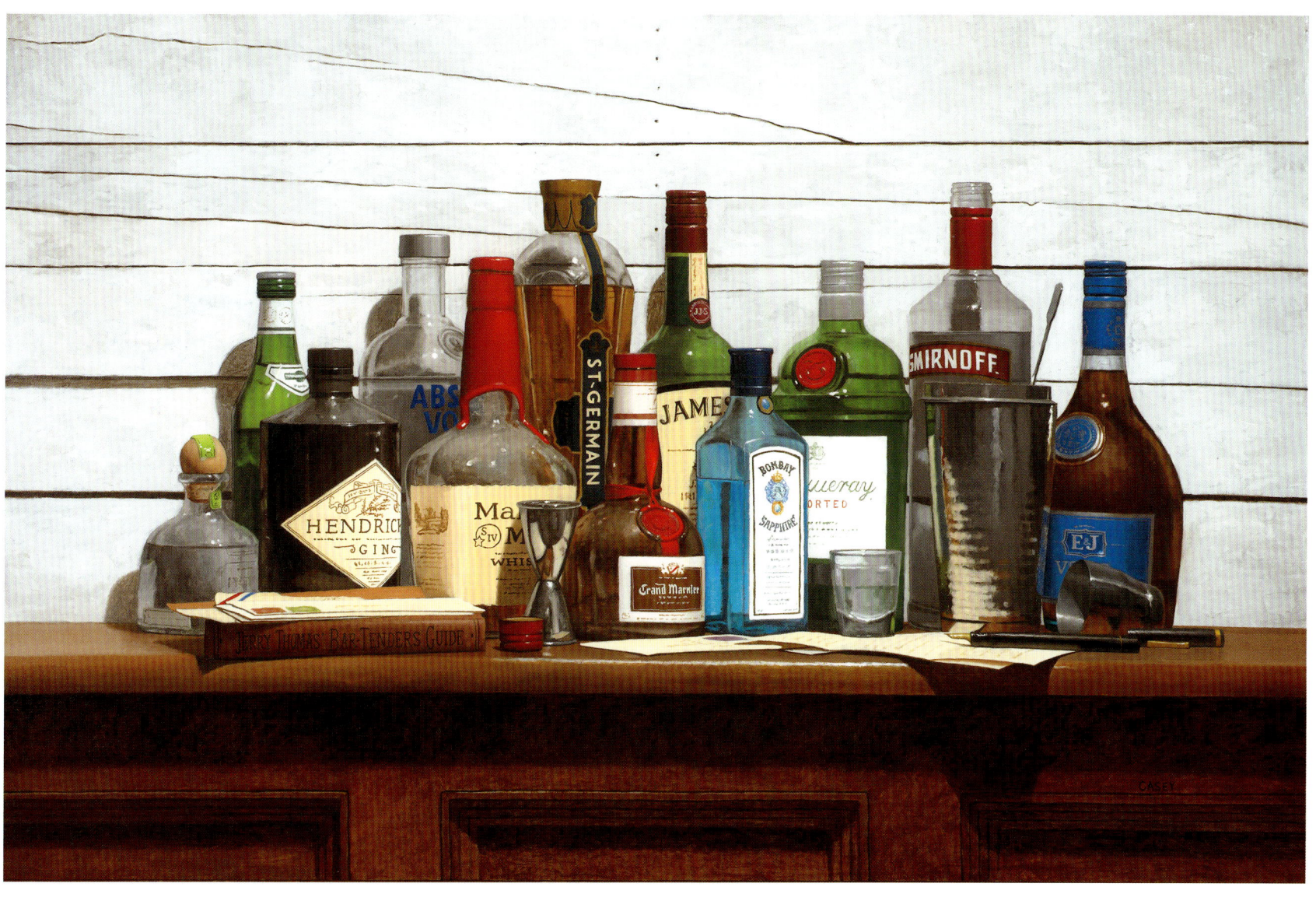

My painting *The Art of Mixology* was done under warm artificial light, as can be seen in the hard cast shadows.

Distance and Angle of the Light

The distance of the setup from the light source and the angle of the light play a big part in how we perceive light and shadow. The closer the light source is to the objects, the more light they will receive, and this often creates a higher contrast of light and shadow. Also, shadows tend to shorten or lengthen according to the angle of the light source in relation to the object. The farther away an object is from a light source, the lower the contrast.

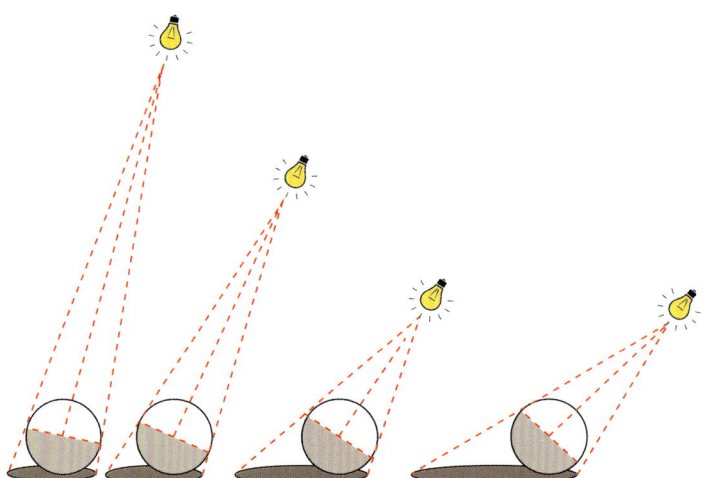

The angle of the light and the distance of the light from the setup are major factors in how you perceive light and shadow.

Temperature of the Light

Which lights you choose will vastly affect your paintings. When starting out, you may want to begin with a warm artificial light. Warm light produces a visual palette that's easier to work with than that produced by cooler light, which can give a "chalky" feel. It also results in greater contrast, making it easier to see changes in value. With artificial light, the contrast of light and shadow is greater than under natural light, meaning that it's easier for you to see light's effects on a form. Light temperature is measured in Kelvins (K), with a warm light being about 2500K, daylight being about 5500K, and cooler northern light measuring between 5500K and 6500K.

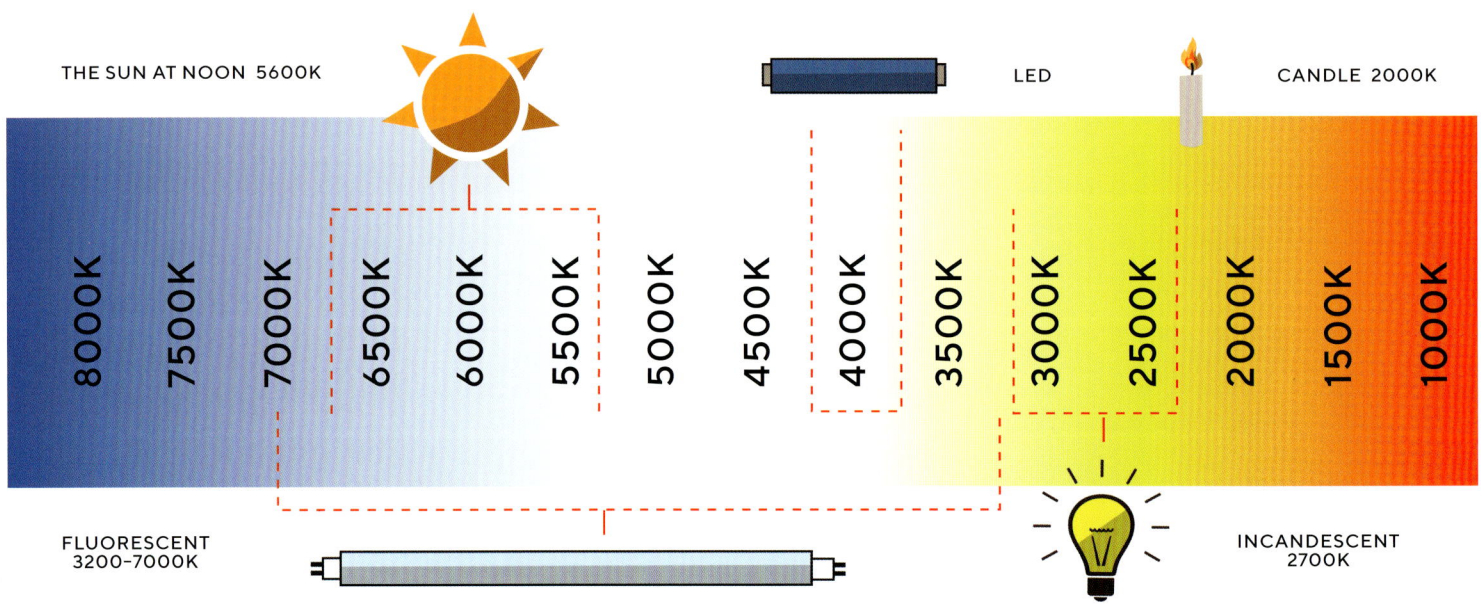

The Kelvin scale of light temperature.

THINKING OF LIGHT SPATIALLY

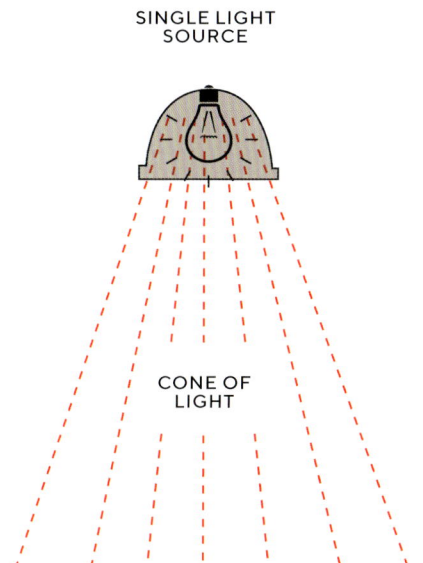

SINGLE LIGHT
SOURCE

CONE OF
LIGHT

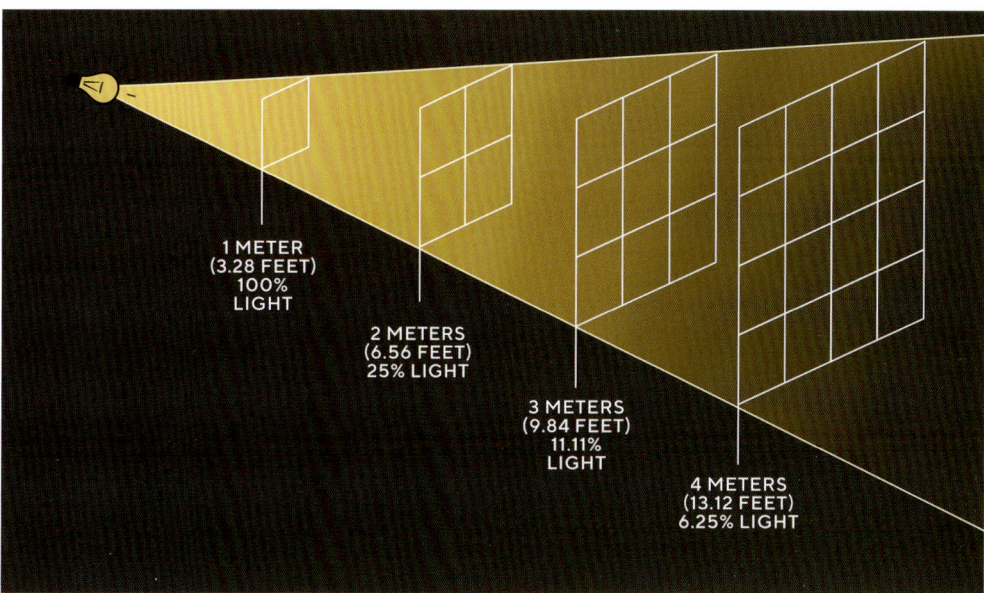

1 METER
(3.28 FEET)
100%
LIGHT

2 METERS
(6.56 FEET)
25% LIGHT

3 METERS
(9.84 FEET)
11.11%
LIGHT

4 METERS
(13.12 FEET)
6.25% LIGHT

The light falls off as the illumination spreads.

The sun emits light in all directions. But most indoor studio lights have a shade or hood that points the light in a specific direction. The opening gives the light a conical shape, and the light that's emitted is referred to as the *cone of light*.

Light diminishes as it travels away from the source emitting the light. Therefore, the farther an object is from the light source, the darker it will generally appear. This phenomenon is much more noticeable in artificial light and is referred to as the *falloff of light*. Light from a natural light source does not decay as rapidly as from an artificial light. It is, however, still happening—it's just more subtle. Whether you can observe it or not, you can still use the falloff of light to create more depth in a painting. I sometimes exaggerate the effect—for example, by making an area darker than what I actually observe. This makes that area more passive, so the viewer does not focus on it but focuses on the contrasting light area instead.

We often don't see all the transitions or value shifts that are happening when we look at an object or plane in space. If you were to scientifically measure the light and shadow, you would see that there are in fact gradual transitions of value on everything. Objects and surfaces do get darker as they move farther from the light, but our eyes don't always notice the shift because it's too subtle. As you gain knowledge and understanding of light, you'll be able to "push" the value a little more than you actually see it to create a greater sense of depth in your paintings.

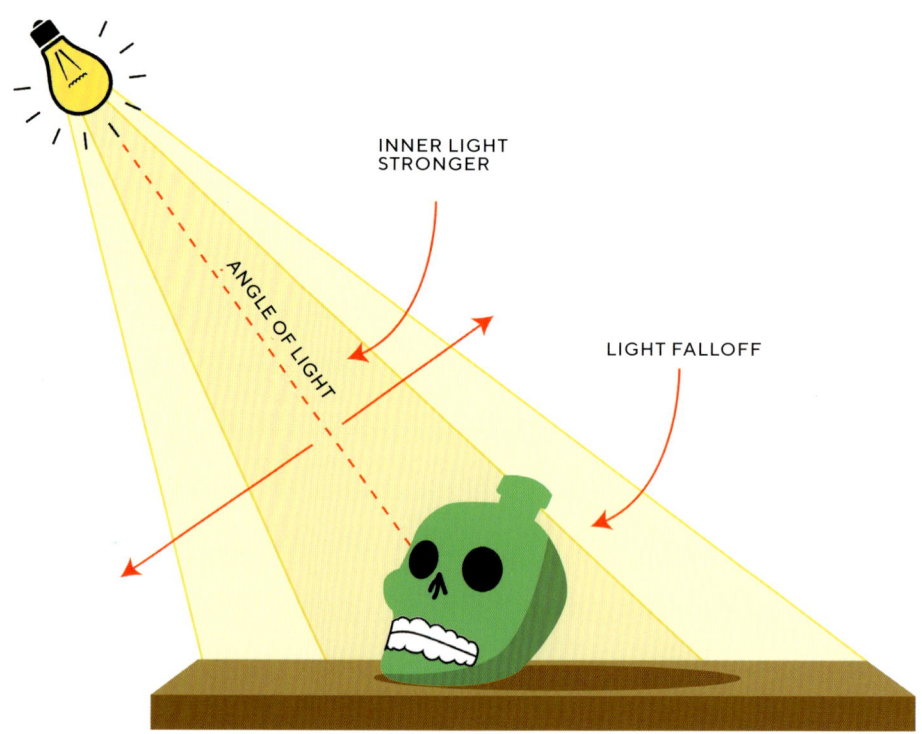

RIGHT: Light falloff is a function of distance, in both parallel and perpendicular directions, from the light source.

BELOW: Arturo García, *Rescue of a Dream Maker,* 2007, oil on linen, 15 × 20 inches (38.1 × 50.8 cm). Courtesy of the artist.

In his painting *Rescue of a Dream Maker*, Arturo Garcia places a much more intense light just under the handle in the center of the painting. As the light moves left and right, the light falloff is clear.

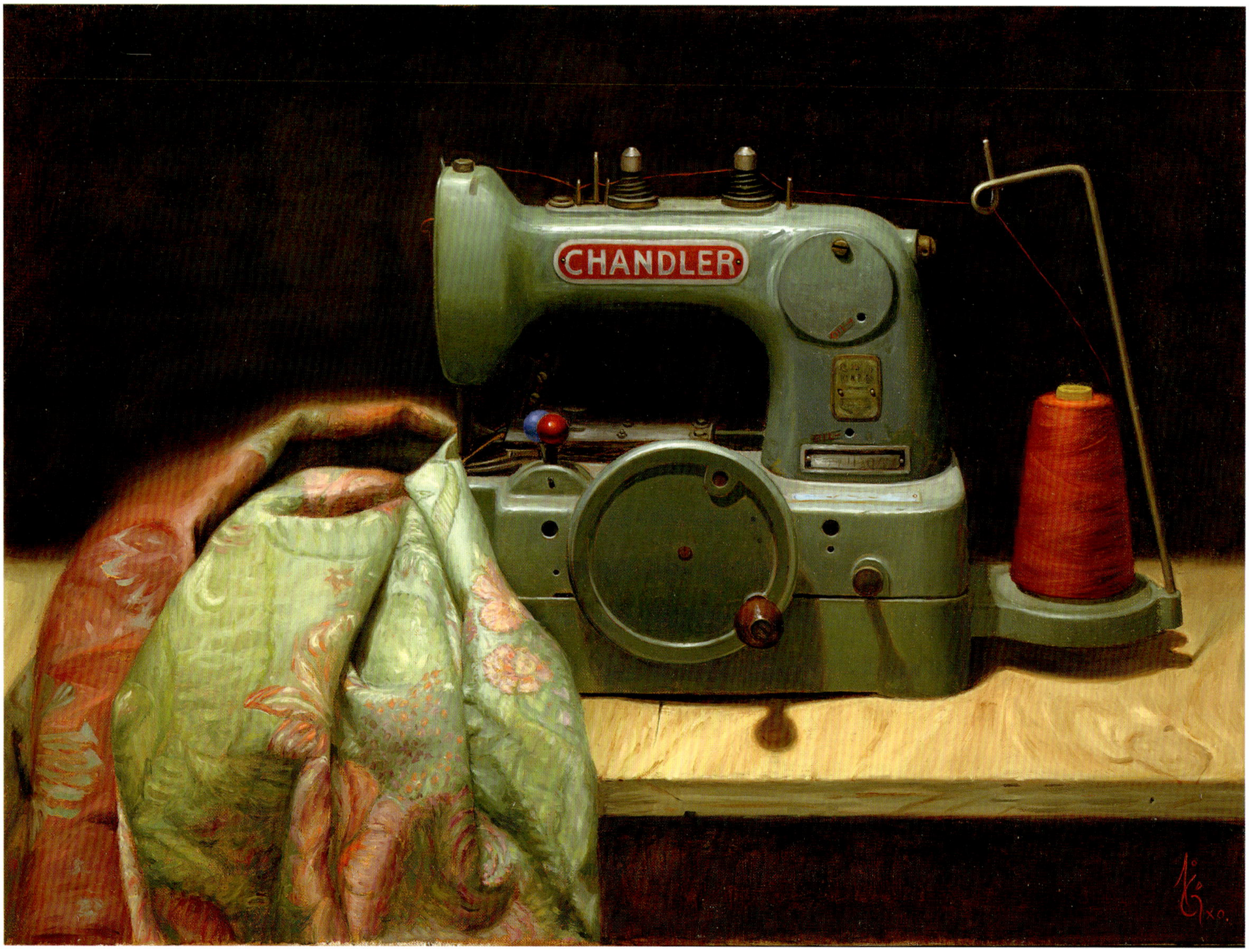

BOUNCE LIGHT INTO YOUR SHADOWS

If you find that your shadows are a little boring and you want to bring some life into them, try bouncing light into the shadows. I often do this by using an object outside the setup—a piece of cardboard or a high-chroma fabric—to brighten up a form shadow within the setup.

RIGHT: Todd M. Casey, *Old Forester,* 2018, oil on panel, 8 × 6 inches (20.32 × 15.24 cm). Private collection.

In my painting *Old Forester,* the form shadow on the left of the whiskey bottle is livened up by reflected light coming from outside the setup on the left. I bounced some warmth into the shadow with a piece of cardboard.

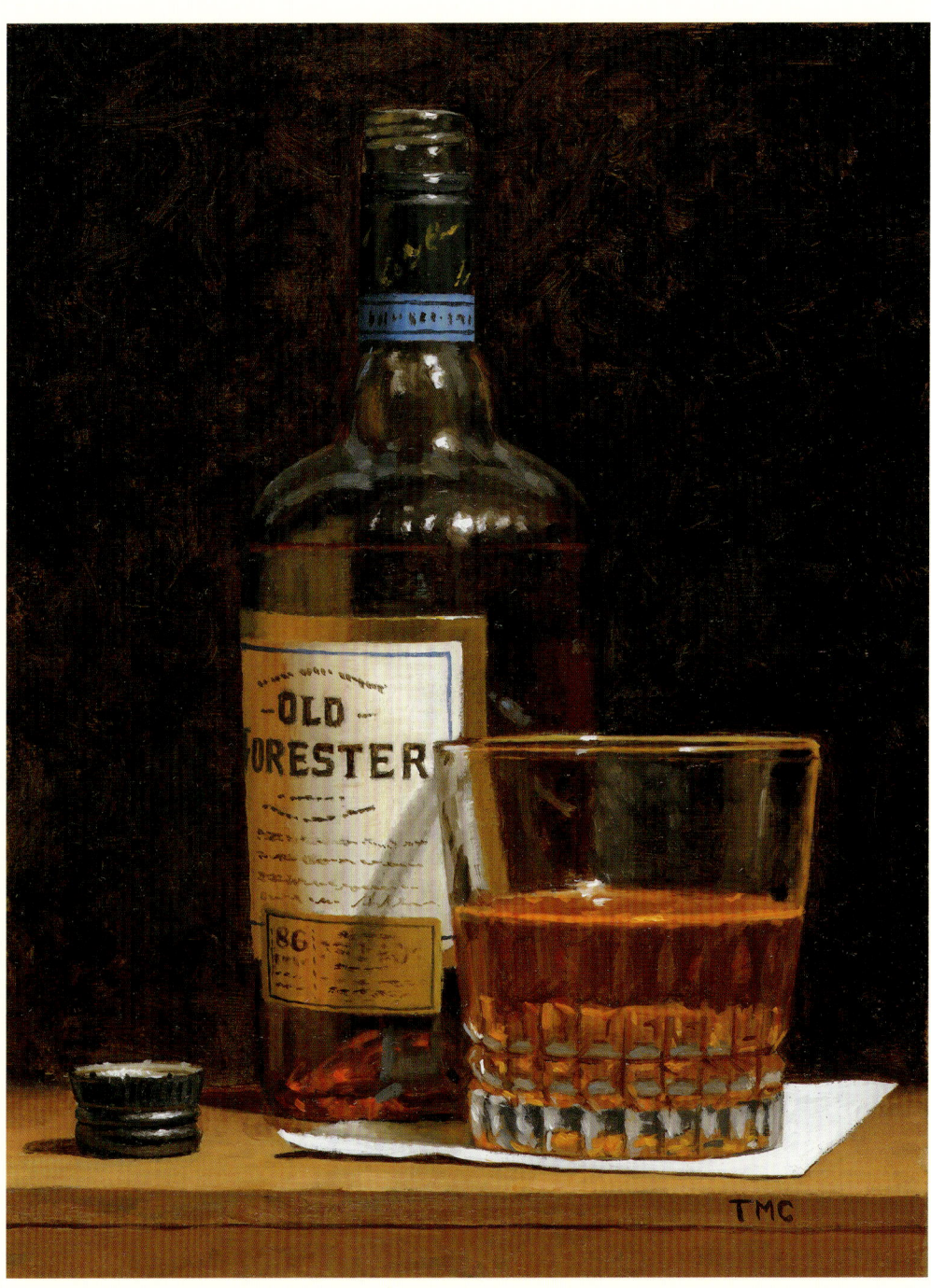

EXERCISES

EXERCISE 1: DRAW LIGHT ON FABRIC

A great exercise for observing light and shadow is to do a rendering of some fabric. With drapery, it's often hard to distinguish what is in light from what is in shadow. Doing a few such drawings will heighten your sense of the terminator versus cast shadows and of soft versus hard edges.

BELOW: Douglas Flynt, *In Remembrance of the Union,* 2015, oil on linen, 44 × 58 inches (111.76 × 147.32 cm). Courtesy of the artist.

In Douglas Flynt's painting *In Remembrance of the Union*, each ripple of fabric shows a clear division between light and shadow.

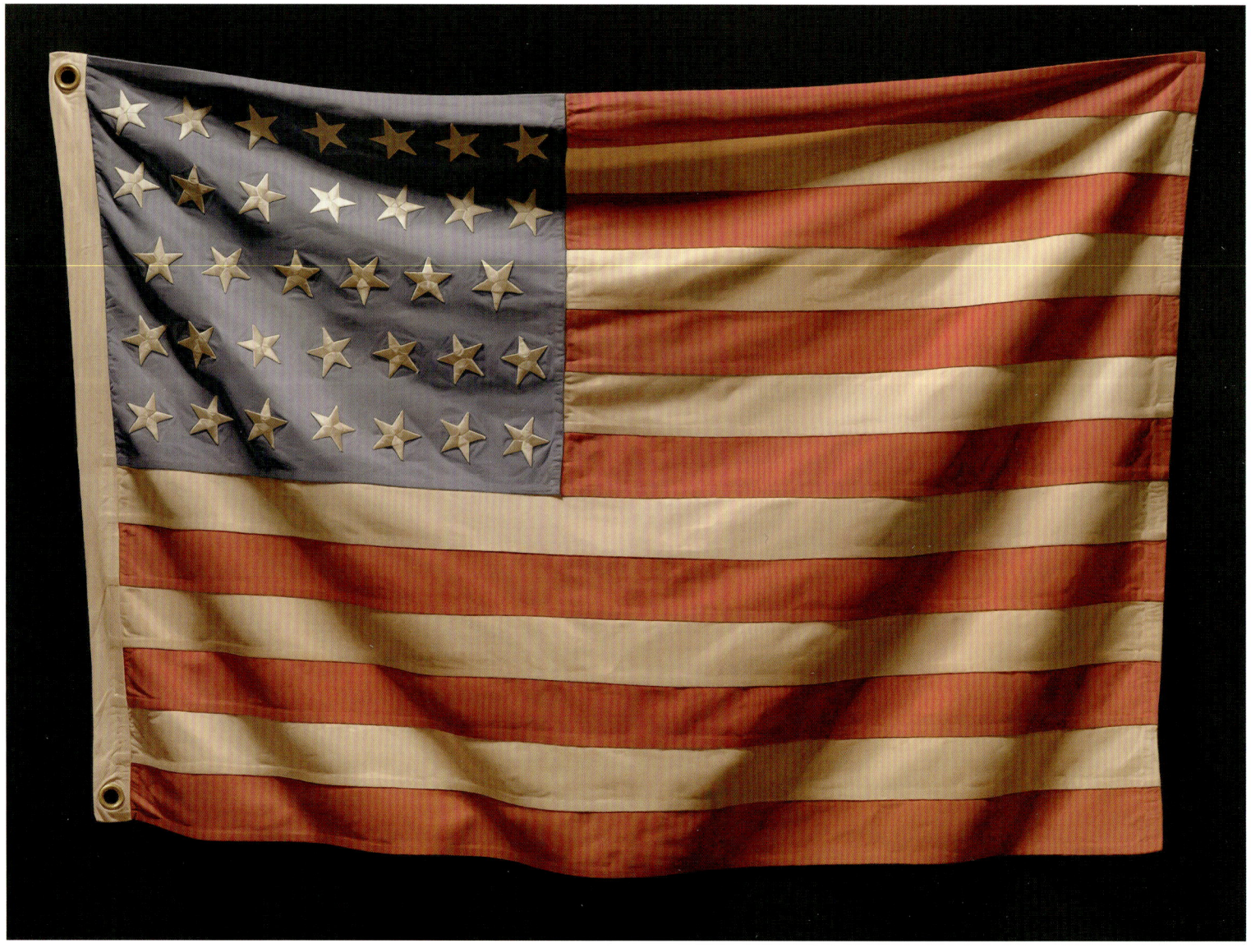

EXERCISE 2: PRACTICE DRAWING CHIAROSCURO

In your sketchbook, practice drawing light as it falls on a form. You can practice on objects, people, or anything you like, but keep it simple, using just light, shadow, and contour. With just two variations in mark-making, you can create a sense of light falling on a form. Let the mark for a terminator be a soft or a broken line, and make the cast shadow marks crisper in comparison.

BELOW: In these sketches from my sketchbook, you can see that just indicating the terminator, the cast shadow, and the contour can communicate the appearance of light on a form.

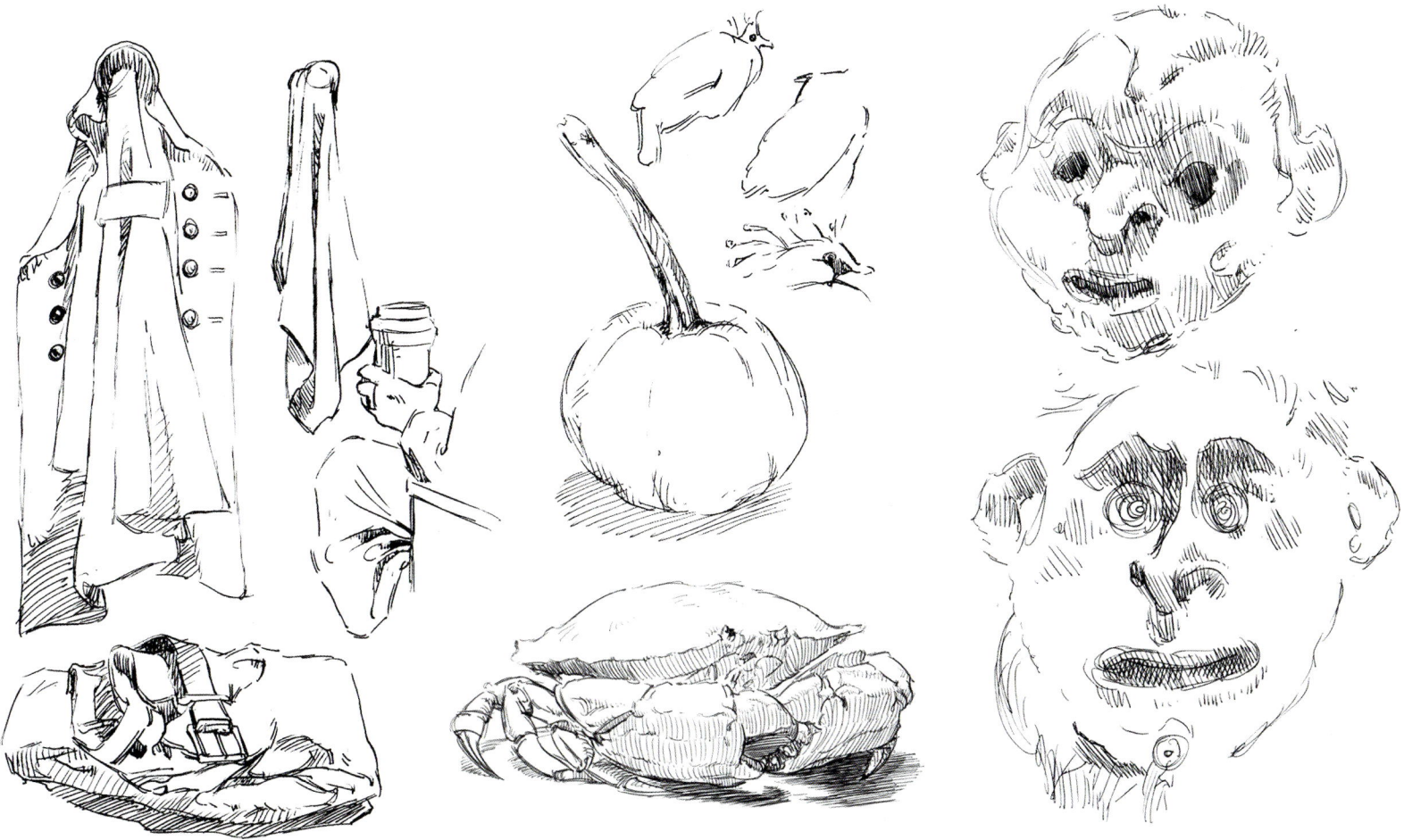

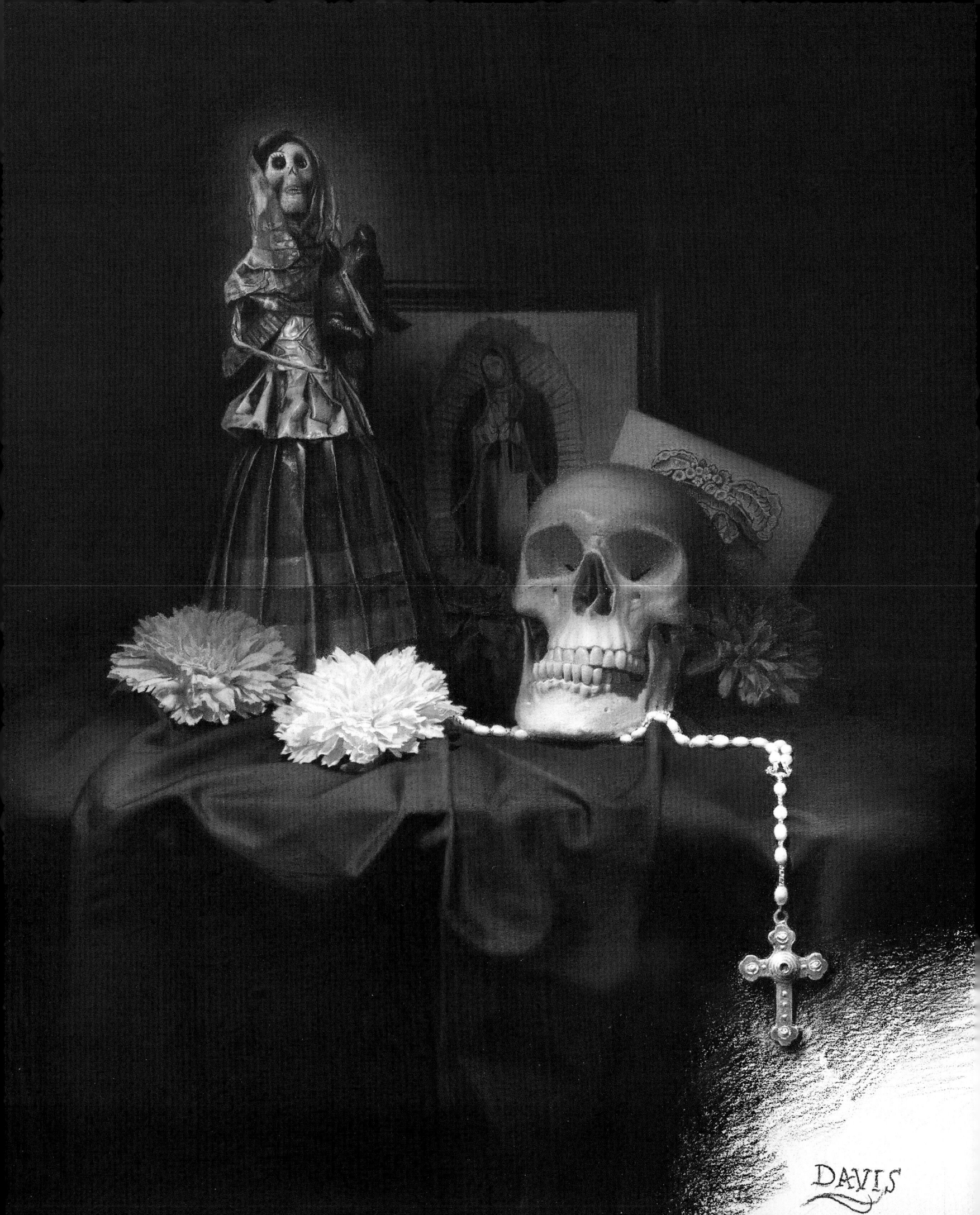

CHAPTER 5

DRAWING: THE STRUCTURE OF A PAINTING

I love the quality of pencil. It helps me to get to the core of a thing.

ANDREW WYETH

Like the foundation of a house, a drawing is the underlying structure that a painting is built upon. Under every good painting lies a solid drawing. An incorrect drawing will not be saved by good color because the application of color is itself guided by the drawing and by value.

Drawing is the most important foundational element in the training of an artist. In my training at an atelier, drawing and value had to be mastered before a student could move on to painting. I drew for a full year without painting at all. Good drawing is a product of patience.

Drawing is a constant back and forth between expression and accuracy. In the early stages of drawing, focus much more on accuracy and less on the expressive qualities in mark-making. Each of us has an individual way of making marks that is different from everyone else's. But, just as in handwriting, that individual expression will develop over time. To begin with, expression should not overpower the essence of the thing you are drawing.

OPPOSITE: Rodney O'Dell Davis, *All Saints Day,* 2015, charcoal on paper, 18 × 11 inches (45.72 × 27.94 cm). Courtesy of the artist.

DRAWING FOR PAINTING

This chapter focuses on drawing *for* painting—that is, drawing not as an independent pursuit but one that's specifically meant to provide a basis for painting. The approach to this kind of drawing has to focus on proportion, contour, light and shadow, and perspective. All these concepts will structure the final painting.

As Michelangelo once said, "An artist must have his measuring tools not in the hand, but in the eye." I believe that you can train your eyes to see in an accurate way that does not depend so much on measuring, but this only comes with a lot of practice. The ultimate goal is to have an accurate, solid drawing on which to base a painting. Don't be prideful about drawing without measuring tools, as the goal should be accuracy, not expression.

BELOW: Todd M. Casey, drawing for *Acorn Squash,* 2010, graphite on paper, 14 × 9 inches (35.56 × 22.86 cm).

A good preliminary drawing—one with correct proportions, well-defined contours, and a clear division of light and shadow—is the framework for a good painting.

BELOW RIGHT: Todd M. Casey, *Acorn Squash,* 2010, oil on linen, 14 × 9 inches (35.56 × 22.86 cm). Private collection.

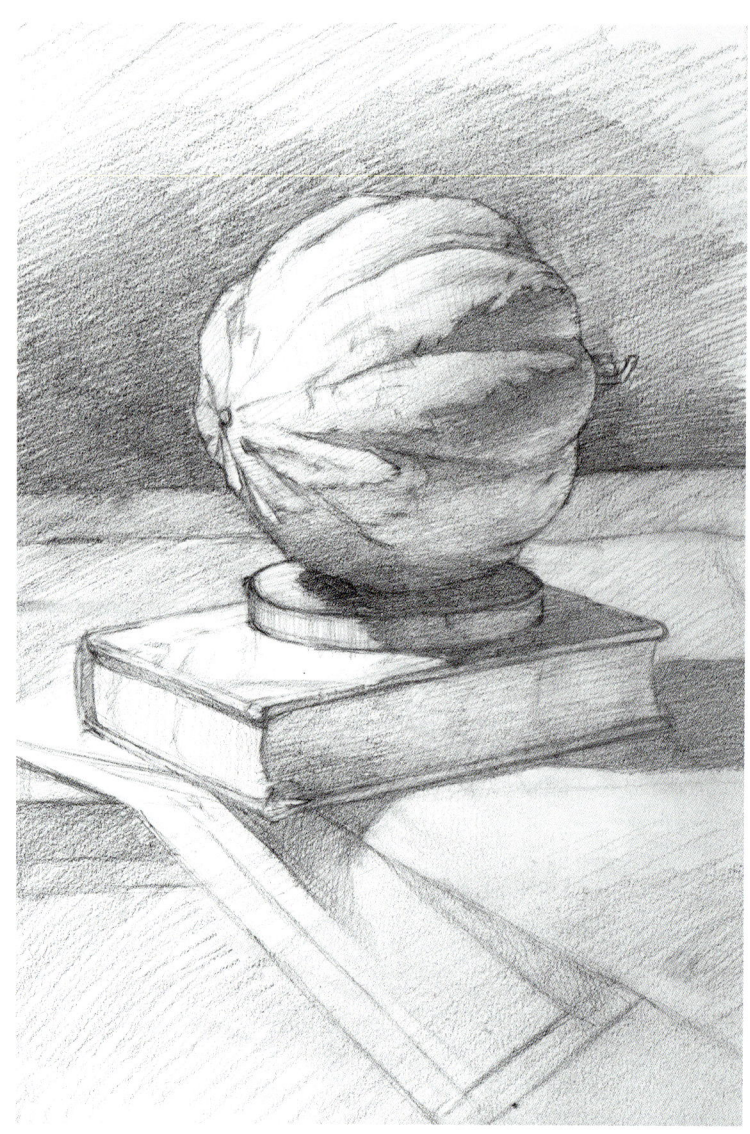

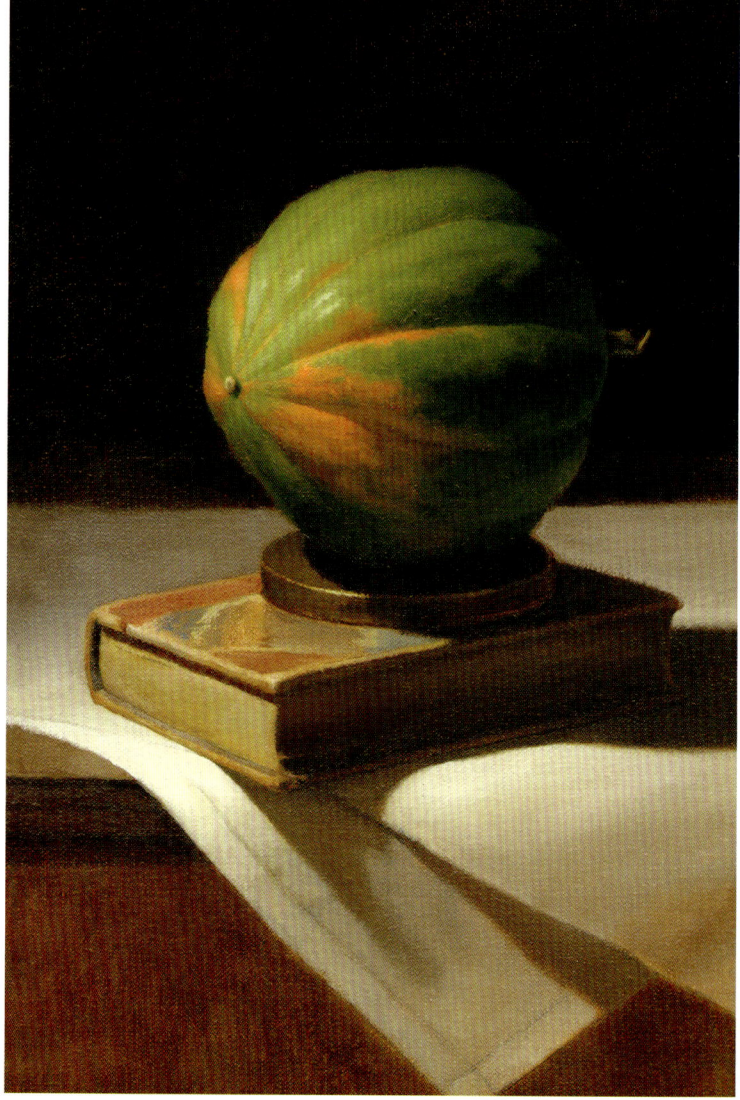

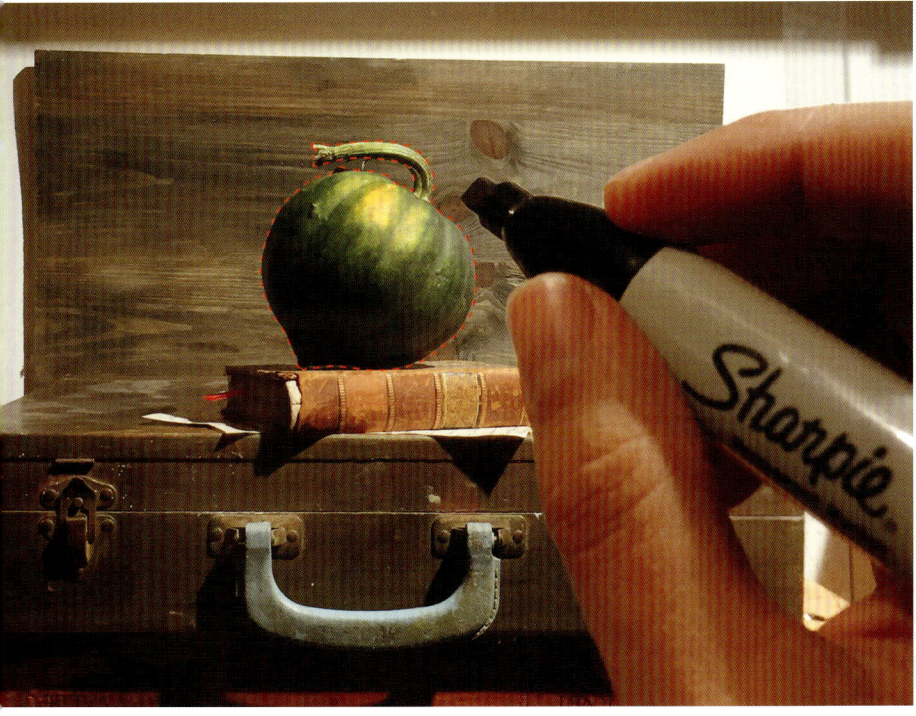
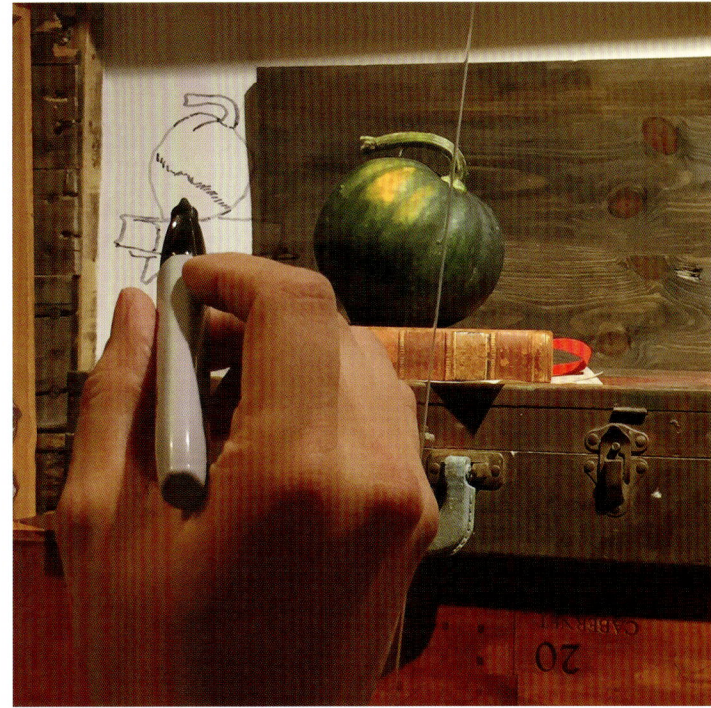

ABOVE: Imagine you had a sheet of glass in front of the setup you're drawing. If you could draw on the glass with a marker, you would be able to trace the contour of each object and the shapes of light and shadow. This is what we strive to do in creating preliminary drawings—though we work on paper (or the painting surface itself) instead of glass.

BELOW: Here are some common archetypal images: an apple, an eye, a banana, a light bulb, and a lemon. These are recognizable generalizations, but in reality every individual apple looks slightly different from every other apple.

PROBLEMS OF PERCEPTION

Preconceived notions can get in the way of truly seeing what is in front of you. One of the biggest challenges everyone faces when drawing has to do with the fact that we tend to draw what we *think* we see instead of what we actually *are* seeing. That is, we draw an archetype rather than the specific object in front of us. You have to undo this way of thinking—not drawing "an apple," but rather the very particular apple you see.

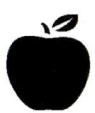 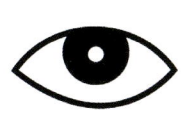   

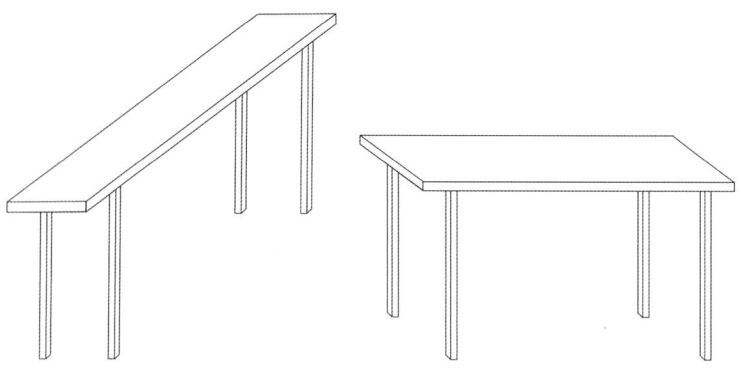

The length of the table on the left is the same as that of the table on the right.

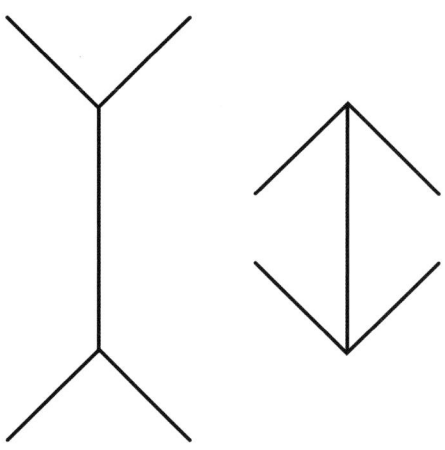

In this illusion (known as the Franz Carl Müller-Lyer illusion), the vertical lines between the arrows are the same length. Visual context plays a big role in how we perceive things.

The best way to approach a drawing is with the idea that "I have no idea what I'm drawing." By not attaching yourself to knowing anything, you find that all the information you need is sitting right in front of you. This helps you draw the individual characteristics of each object. Think of it like this: Imagine you are a paleontologist at a dig. You find a bone, and as you continue to dig you gradually reveal the skeleton of an animal. You collect the information—piece by piece, bone by bone—but you have no clear idea what you are uncovering. Then, when all the bones are unearthed and arranged together, you see that you have collected the remains of a woolly mammoth. This is like the "I have no idea what I am drawing" experience. The not-knowing helps you fight the urge to draw what you think you know instead of what you actually see.

Optical illusions can also create perceptual problems. We are all familiar with classic optical illusions, but real objects can also fool our eyes. For example, our eyes and brains have trouble judging the relative proportion of a height to a width. No matter how many times I look at the two tables shown in the diagram above left, I cannot convince myself that they are the same length—and yet they are!

We can also get confused about the length of an object because of its surroundings. The diagram at left shows two vertical lines that are the same length—although the line on the right looks much shorter. The way to avoid errors based on optical illusions is to use a measuring tool.

COMPARATIVE MEASURING

Some artists will always want to draw freely, without measuring. Drawing freely is expressive and fun, but it's guesswork. To make sure that your drawings are proportionally accurate, you've got to measure.

To find proportions, I use the *comparative measurement method*. With this method, the object you draw will always have the same height-to-width relationship, no matter how big or small you draw it on the page. The principle is very simple: if, for example, you're drawing a lime and determine by measuring that its shadow begins at the halfway mark between the top of the lime and the bottom, then the shadow will always begin halfway down, no matter how large or small your drawing.

Comparative measuring does not necessarily mean that your drawing has to be the same size as the actual observed setup. It can be, if you want it to, but what's important is that the proportions be the same no matter how large or small you make your drawing.

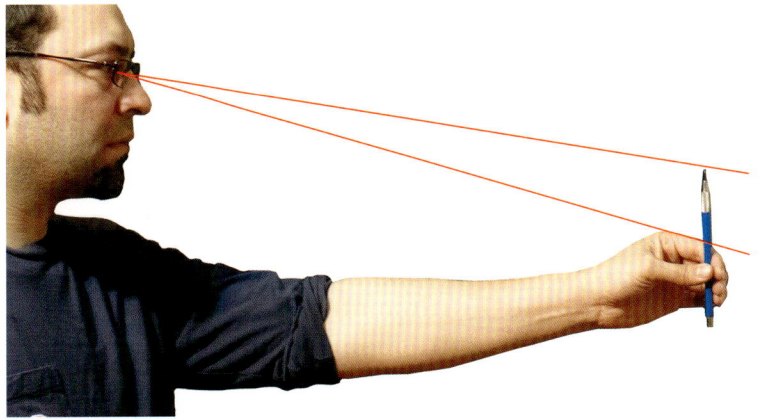

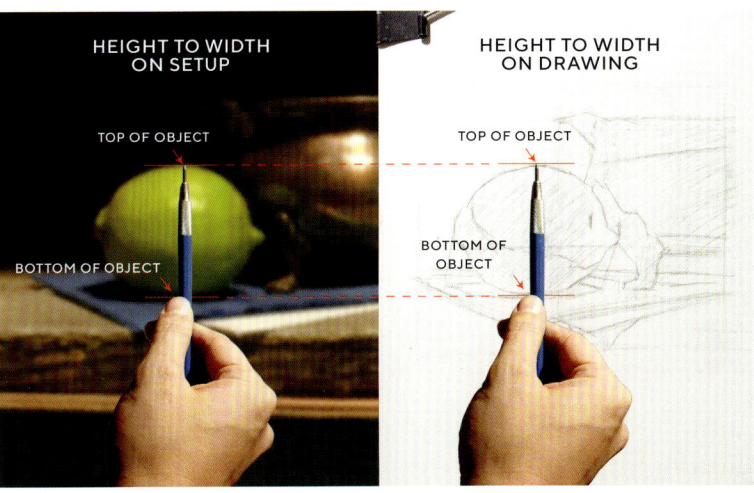

TOP RIGHT: When doing comparative measuring, fully extend your arm and hold your measuring tool (here, a mechanical pencil) as perfectly vertical as you can. Once you find a measurement, like the height or width of the lime in the images at right, make sure it matches the same measurement on your drawing.

CENTER RIGHT: I align the tip of my measuring tool with the top of the object I want to measure—here, a lime. Then I place my thumbnail where the tool aligns with the bottom of the object. This height measurement should square with the height of the lime in the drawing, as shown.

BOTTOM RIGHT: Now, I rotate the height measurement to find the *comparative* measurement of the lime's width from left to right. As you can see, the lime is wider than it is tall. When I take this measurement, I notice that the point marking the bottom of the vertical measurement aligns with where the lime overlaps the pewter vessel, so I make sure that these measurements relate in the same way in my drawing.

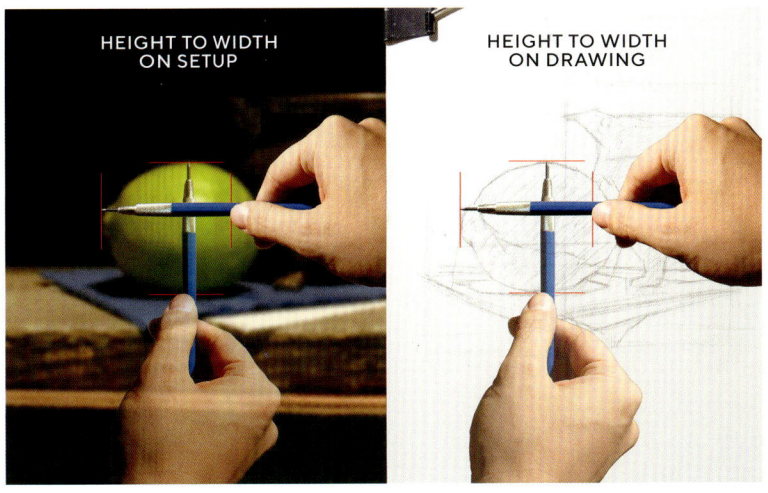

THE BLOCK-IN

I will now take you through the steps
needed to do an accurate drawing for a
painting. By the end, the drawing will
have an accurate contour and a clear
separation of light and shadow. But let's
begin with the essential first stage of the
drawing, known as the *block-in*. Think
of the block-in as *sculpting* the scene. If
you were sculpting the scene in clay, you'd
start with a hunk of clay for each object
and then carve into it. Before you begin
sculpting the shapes, however, you have
to make sure that they are in the correct
proportion in relation to one another.

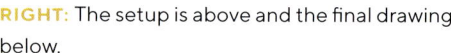

RIGHT: The setup is above and the final drawing
below.

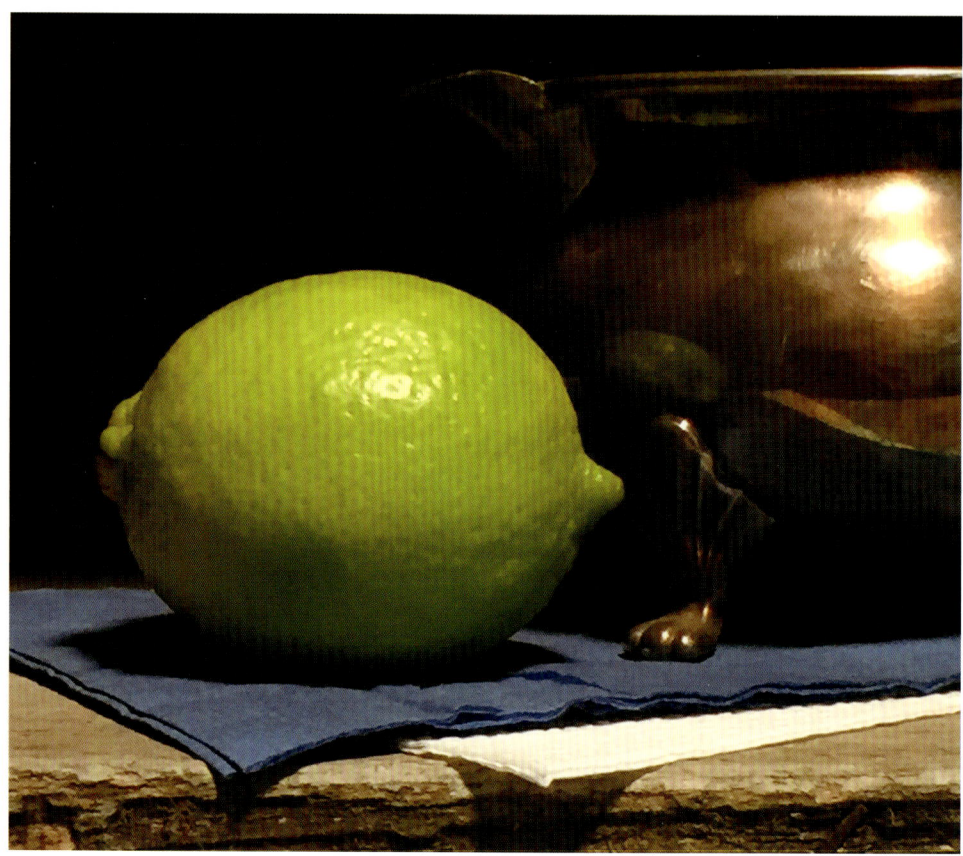

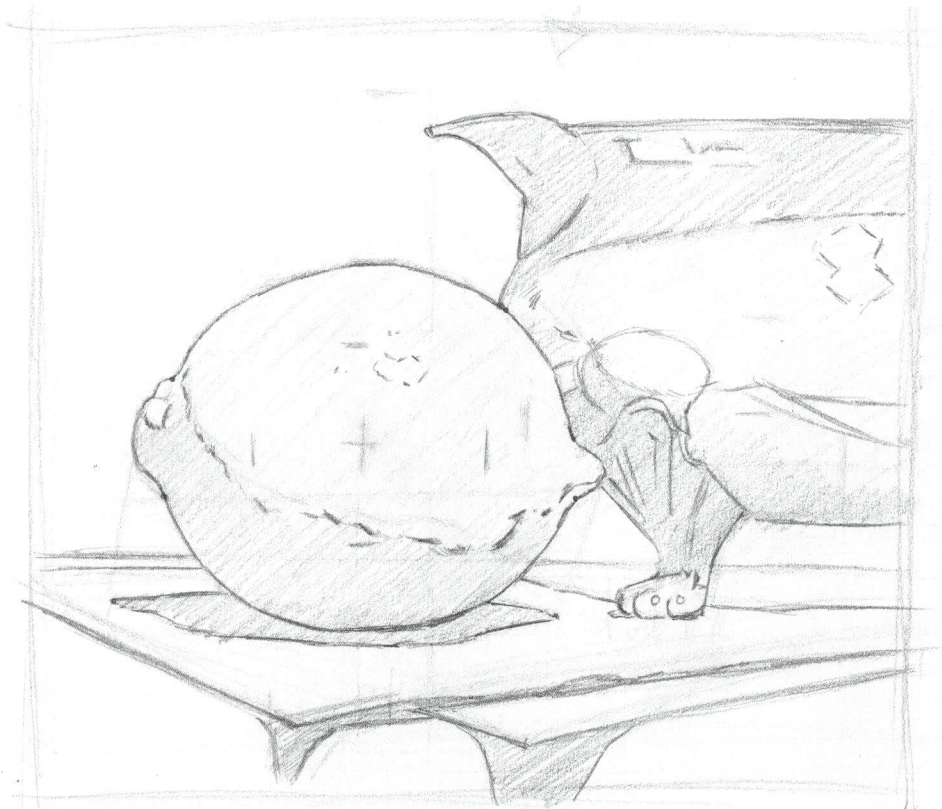

During the block-in stage, I go through a process consisting of the following steps:

1. Establish the scale and the large masses
2. Determine the relation of height to width
3. Align with the vertical and the horizontal
4. Draw the light and shadow shapes (and abstract them)
5. Find halfway points
6. Find the quarters
7. Do two-point comparisons
8. Do triangulations (three-point comparisons)

I run through this list each time to make sure that I have considered everything. If the drawing feels off somehow, I'll revisit all the steps, multiple times if necessary, to check my intuition. In the following pages, we'll look at each of these steps in more detail.

PLAN YOUR COMPOSITION

One of the most common mistakes I see students make is neglecting to plan how big or small a drawing is going to be. If you don't plan your composition, your drawing may go off the page. To avoid this, start with four lines that establish the parameters—top and bottom and the two side edges—of your drawing, as shown here. Leave a margin of at least an inch on each side of this box. This gives you room for the drawing to grow if needed.

HOLDING YOUR PENCIL

How your hold your pencil when drawing is important because it can dictate how light or dark you make your marks. You should start out with a very loose "baton" grip, holding the back end of the pencil to keep your lines big, wide, and light. You are drawing with your whole arm and shoulder at this stage.

Later, as you refine your drawing, you can move your hand in toward the pencil's lead, in the "handwriting" grip. At that point you'll be locking in your drawing and will use your wrist and elbow more than your shoulder.

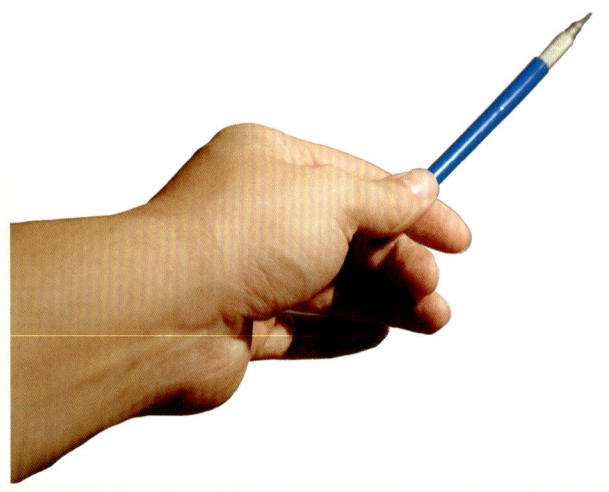

Use the baton grip as you start drawing.

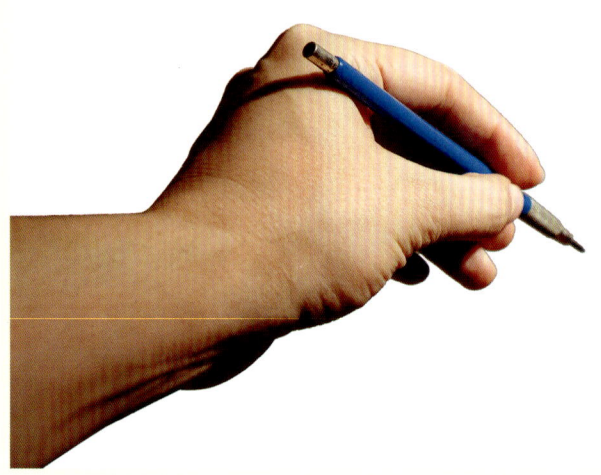

Use the handwriting grip as you refine the drawing.

Keeping the lines big and wide, as on the left, allows you to "carve" into them with an eraser to get the lines in the right spots, as on the right. Keeping them light lets you move the information around more easily.

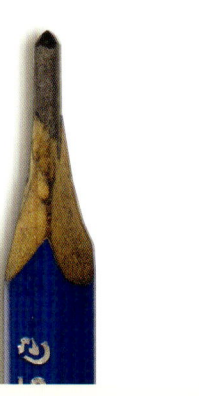

When starting your drawing, draw very lightly with a somewhat dull pencil point, as shown at left. You want to be able to move lines if necessary, but that's hard to do if the lines are dark and embedded in the paper. Resist the urge to draw dark with a sharper point until you know the proportions are correct.

1. Establish the Scale and the Large Masses

Start your drawing with the masses of the large shapes. This should be done lightly, loosely, and very fast, moving across the paper quickly.

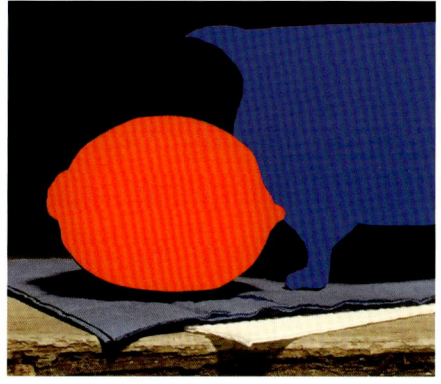 

LEFT: On the left are the masses of the two major shapes in this setup of a lime and a pewter vessel. On the right are those masses of the shapes quickly drawn on paper. Drawing the masses— sometimes referred to as the silhouette—gives you a nice place to start.

2. Determine the Relation of Height to Width

It is very important to determine an object's height in relation to its width because it's the first major relationship you set down on your paper and it locks in the scale of your drawing.

You may think that an object's height and width are equal, but don't trust your judgment—find the measurements!

Sometimes the measurement will align with something important in the setup, but not always. If there's no discernible alignment, approximate as best you can and place a mark there on your paper. If you need, make an abbreviated note (like *HW* for height-to-width) so you don't lose track of the meaning of the marks you make.

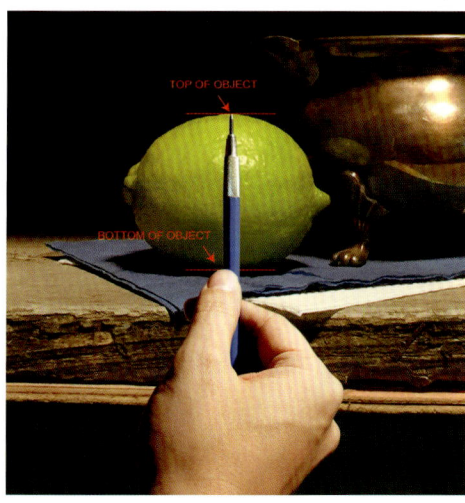 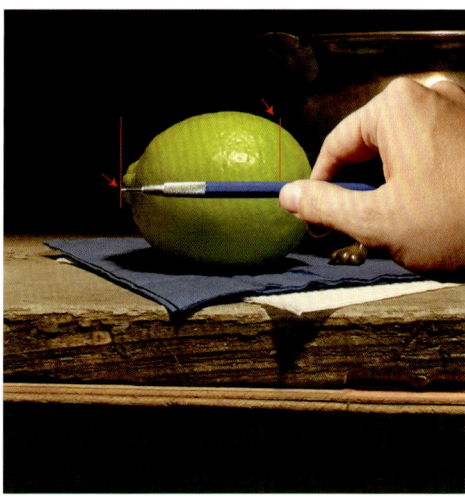

LEFT: First, I find the vertical measurement of the lime on the setup. I then rotate the measuring tool to find how the height relates to the width. In the case shown here, I find that the vertical measurement is nearly the same as the length from the left side of the lime to where the lime and pewter vessel overlap.

LEFT: I then put marks on my drawing to show all the vertical and horizontal measurements.

CENTER: In the image at left, the lime has been blocked in based on the height-to-width measurements. The pewter vessel is then blocked in based on these findings, as well.

BOTTOM: If you wish, you can check the measurements on the setup against those in your drawing by using a gridded viewfinder.

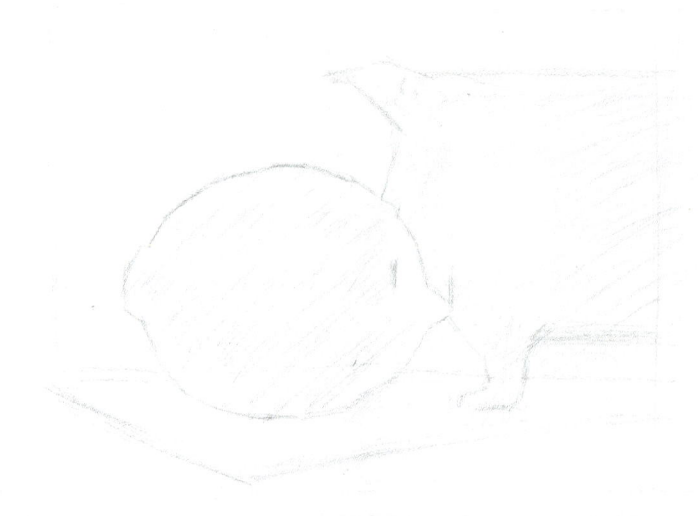

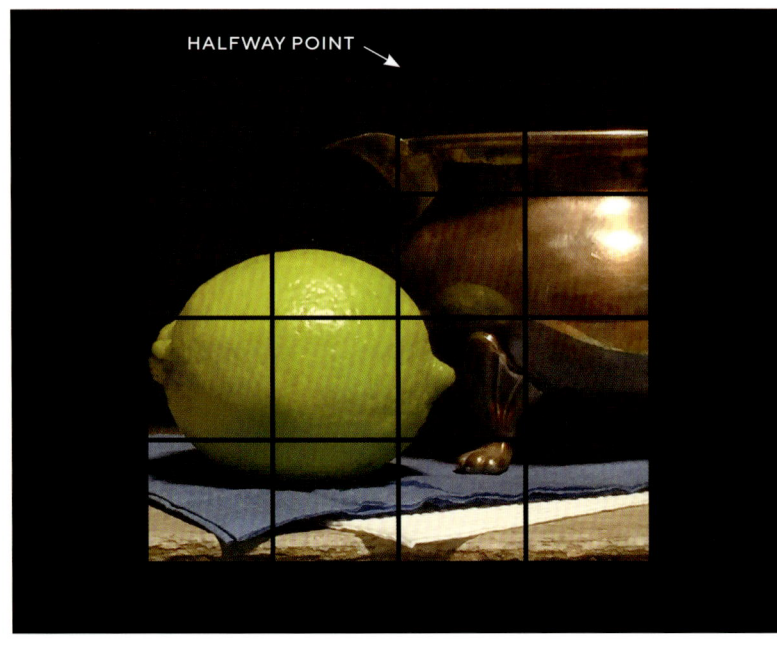

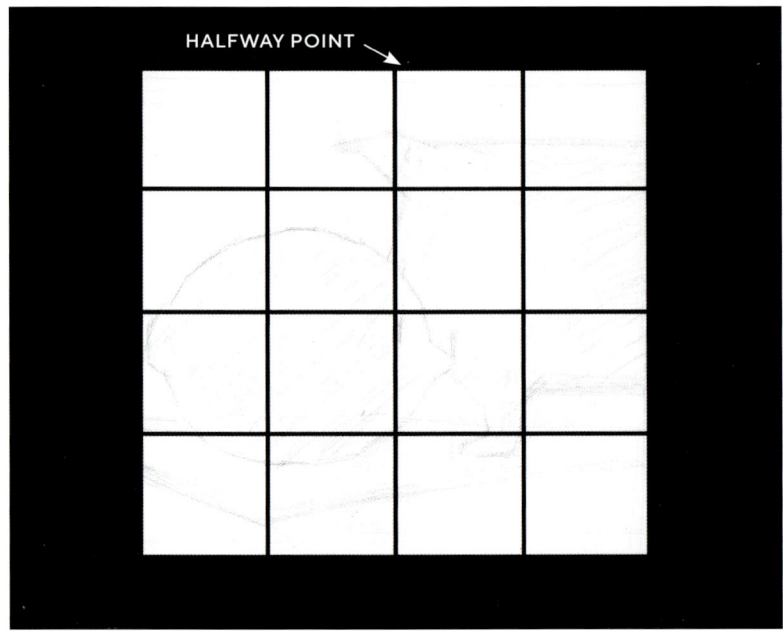

Once I've marked the height and width measurements on my drawing, I can use the marks to anchor the drawing. All other measurements will now relate to these marks. I then begin to block in the shape of the lime based on these findings.

3. Align with the Vertical and the Horizontal

A plumb line is useful for seeing how forms in the setup align vertically with one another—information you can then transfer to your drawing. You can check horizontal alignments with a pencil, paintbrush, or bike wheel spoke.

TOP ROW: When I hold a plumb line in front of the setup, I notice that the spout of the pewter vessel aligns vertically with the point where the two napkins overlap. I can then mark this on my drawing.

BOTTOM ROW: You can use a measuring rod (like my trusty bicycle-wheel spoke) to check the horizontals. Determining the verticals and horizontals is like imposing an imaginary grid on the setup.

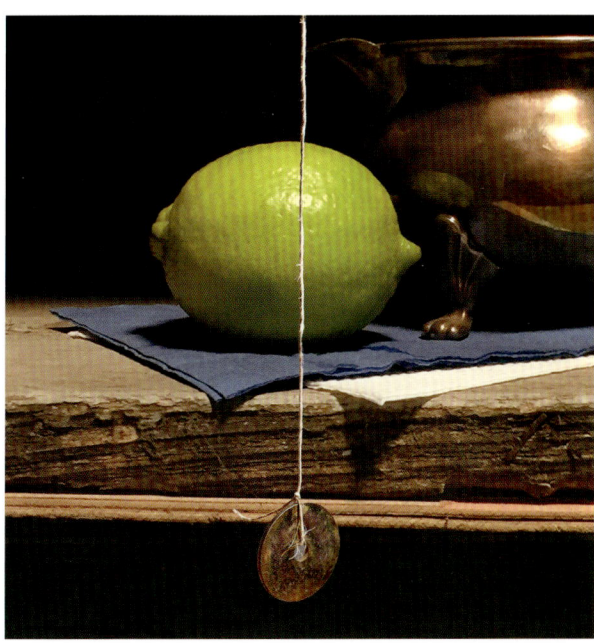

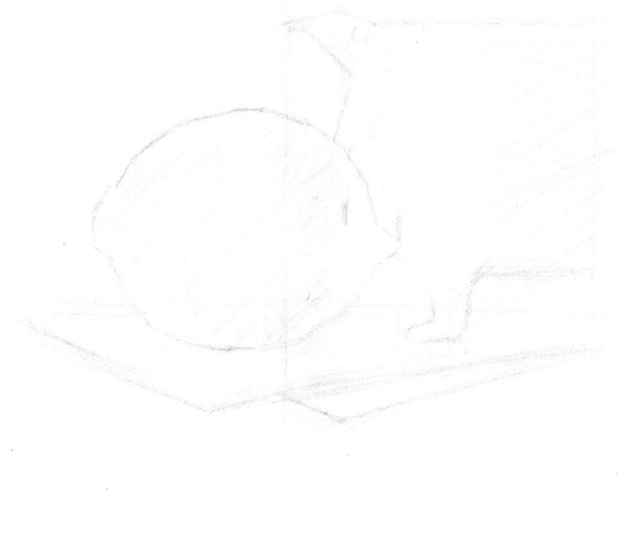

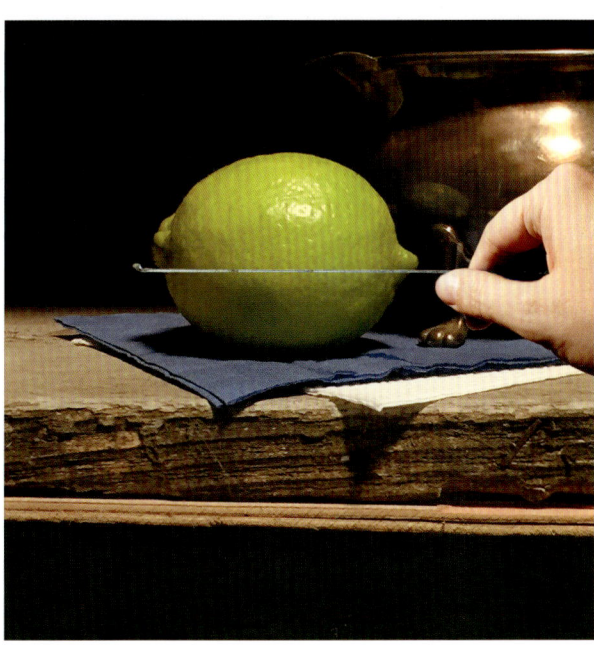

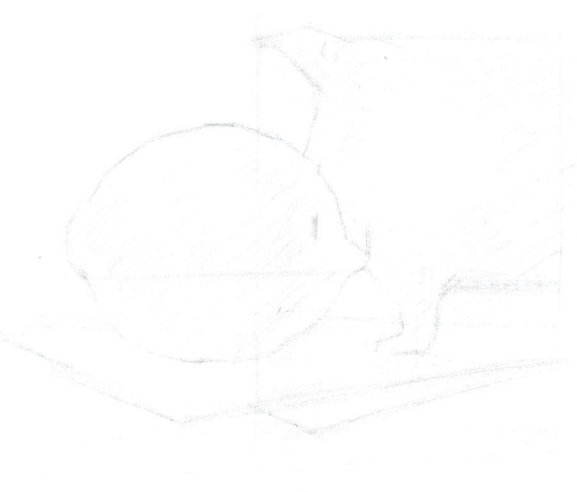

4. Draw the Light and Shadow Shapes
(and Abstract Them)

Once you have the shapes blocked in, you can start to loosely draw the light and shadow (chiaroscuro) on each shape. If you nail the shapes of light and shadow, the object will be there—you don't have to draw the thing.

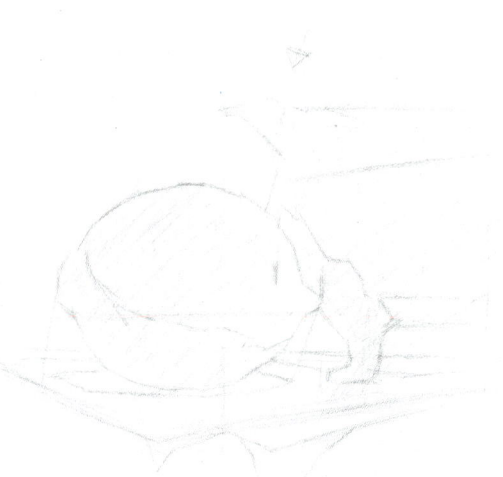

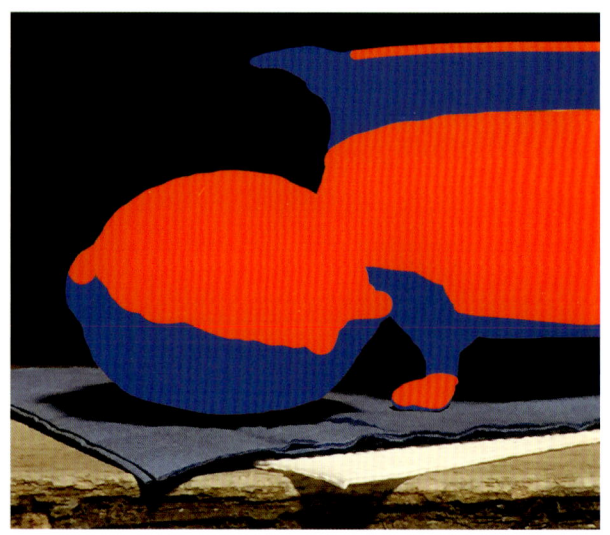

ABOVE: As you can see at left, I always place a big arrow at the top of my drawing to show where the light is coming from. At this stage, simply suggesting where the shadows will be can help the drawing turn a corner into three-dimensionality. The image on the right shows the separation of light (red) from shadow (blue).

RIGHT: With the line separating light from shadow indicated, the lime could be a cartoon head looking right. This creative way of looking really removes you conceptually from the object in front of you.

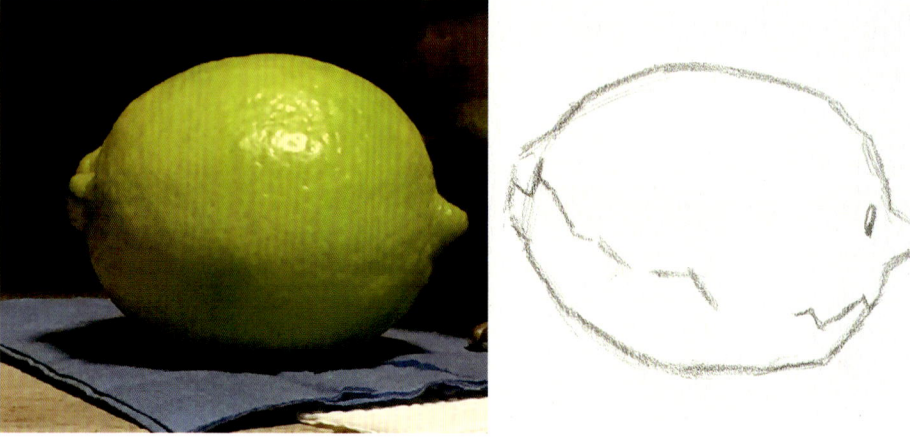

After you break a shape down into light and shadow, it's a good idea to "abstract" it or to relate it to something entirely different from the object in front of you. In my case, I relate the light/shadow shapes to cartoon shapes, as in the image above. This helps me draw the shapes accurately—not to draw what I think a shadow should look like.

This ability to see something as *something else* is related to the idea of multistability in Gestalt psychology, in which negative and positive shapes can be looked at alternately as one thing or as a completely different thing, as in the classic visual brainteaser known as Rubin's Vase, right.

5. Find Halfway Points

Next, you want to find the halfway points on each object, horizontally and vertically. This helps to further break down each shape to make all the measurements more accurate.

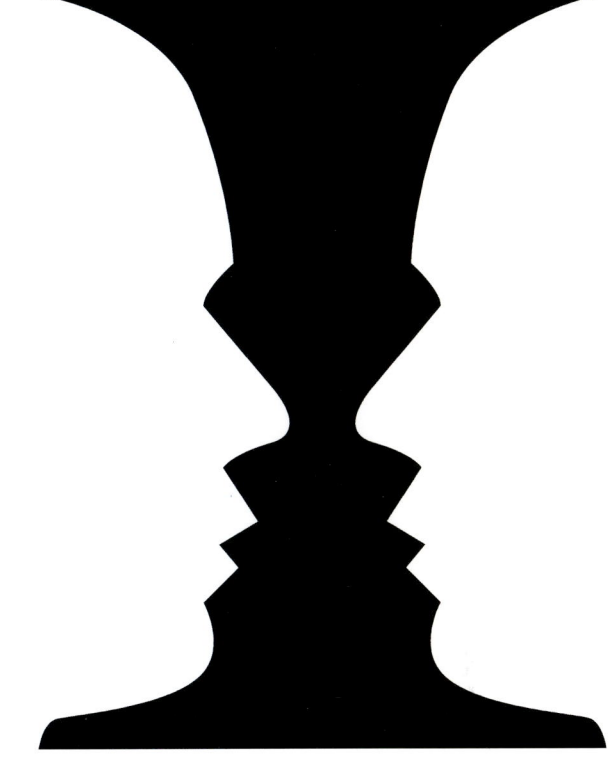

RIGHT: Looking at Rubin's Vase, the mind moves back and forth, perceiving the image either as the profiles of two people looking at one another or as a vase.

BELOW: In the image at left, the red dashed line marks the halfway vertical measurement of the lime. The halfway horizontal measurement is in blue. I mark both of these on my drawing to use as a reminder. (If you wish, you can write "HW"—for "halfway"—on the drawing as well.)

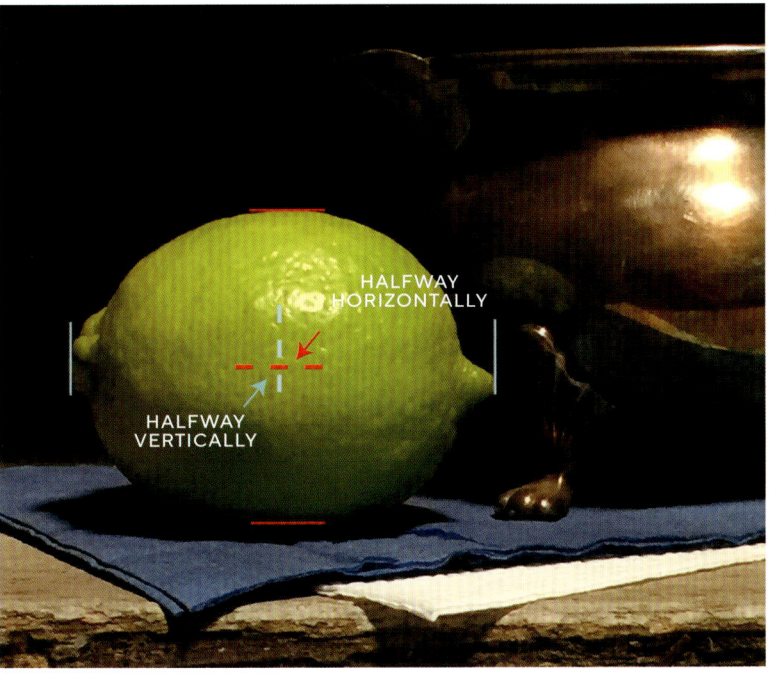

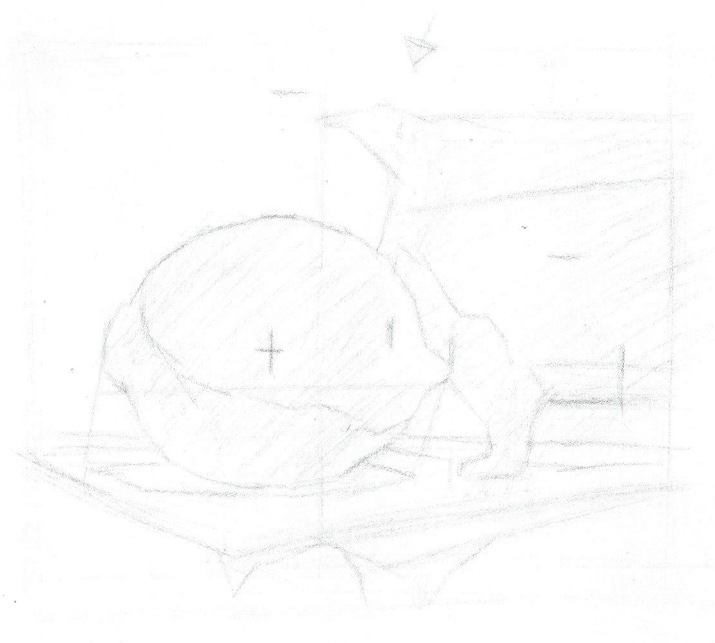

6. Find the Quarters

After finding the halfway points on each object, I then find the quarter measurements of the height and the width, breaking the vertical and horizontal measurements into four equal parts to see if there is something that the measurement aligns with.

BELOW: In the image at left, the red dashed lines mark quarter vertical measurements of the lime. The quarter horizontal measurements are in blue. I also mark these on my drawing as reminders. (If you wish, you can write Q—for "quarter"—on the drawing as well.)

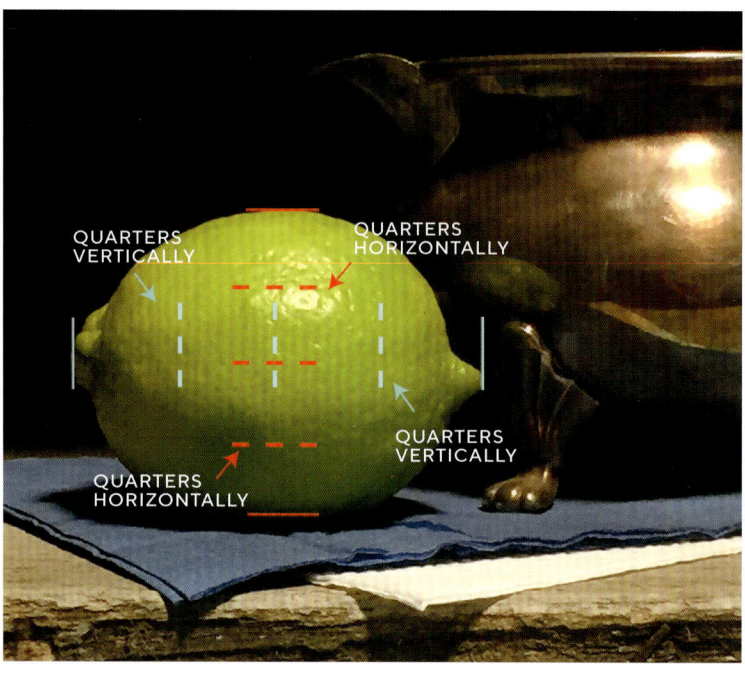

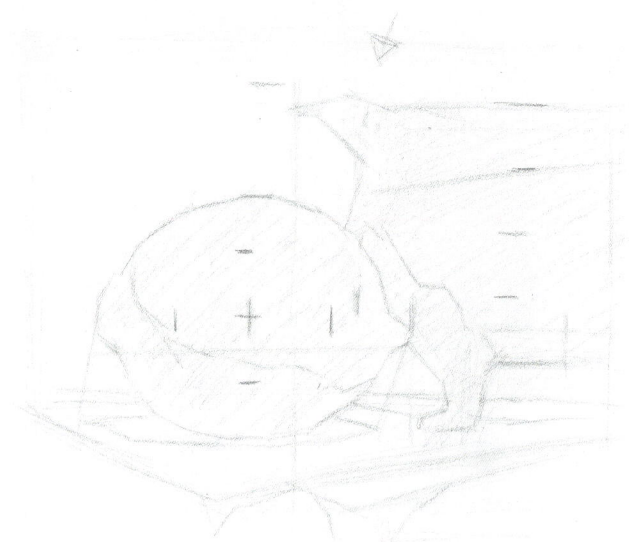

CURVES AND TILTS

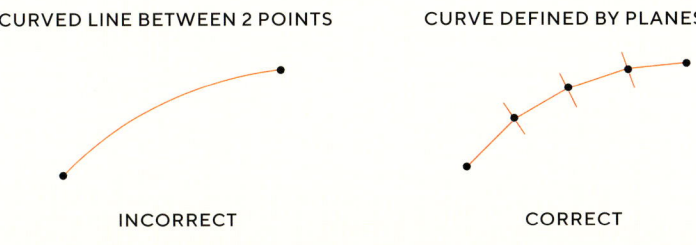

CURVED LINE BETWEEN 2 POINTS

CURVE DEFINED BY PLANES

INCORRECT

CORRECT

During the block-in, you should draw only straight lines—no curved lines. A series of straight lines can be broken down into smaller planes to represent a curve, and the curve can then be drawn based on this blocked-in version. Approaching curves this way will greatly improve your accuracy, because when you try to draw a curve freehand you can almost never get it perfectly right.

The angle between two points on your setup is referred to as a *tilt*. Align your measuring tool with the angle, or tilt, that is created between the two points. Then you can exactly re-create this angle by locking your arm to maintain the angle and moving the measuring tool over to your drawing. It may take some practice to perfect this process.

TOP: Draw a curved line as a series of straight lines and then redefine it as a curve within this framework of planes. If you try to draw a curved line freehand, it usually won't be accurate.

CENTER AND BOTTOM: Hold your measuring tool up to an angle in the setup. Then lock your arm and transfer this tilt to your drawing.

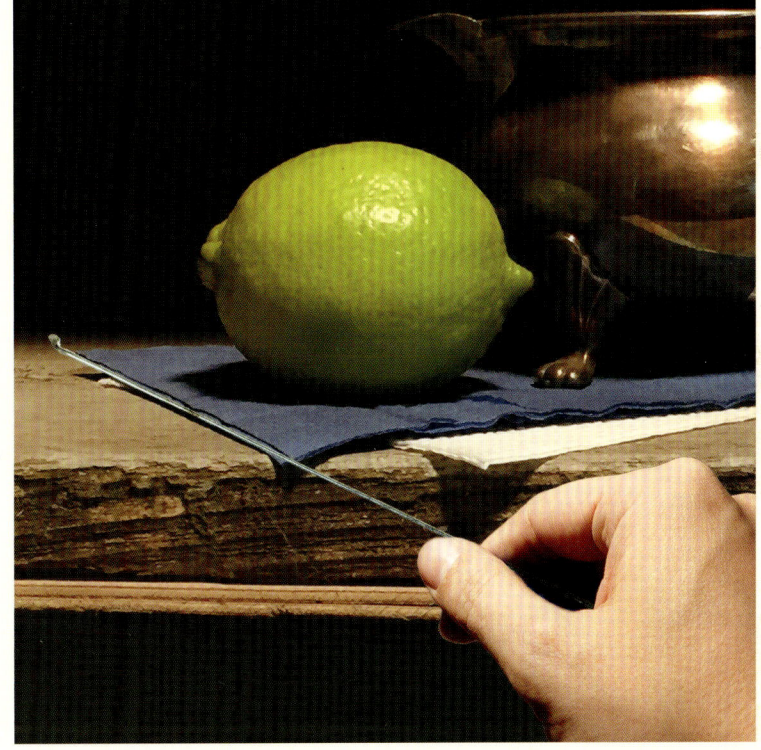

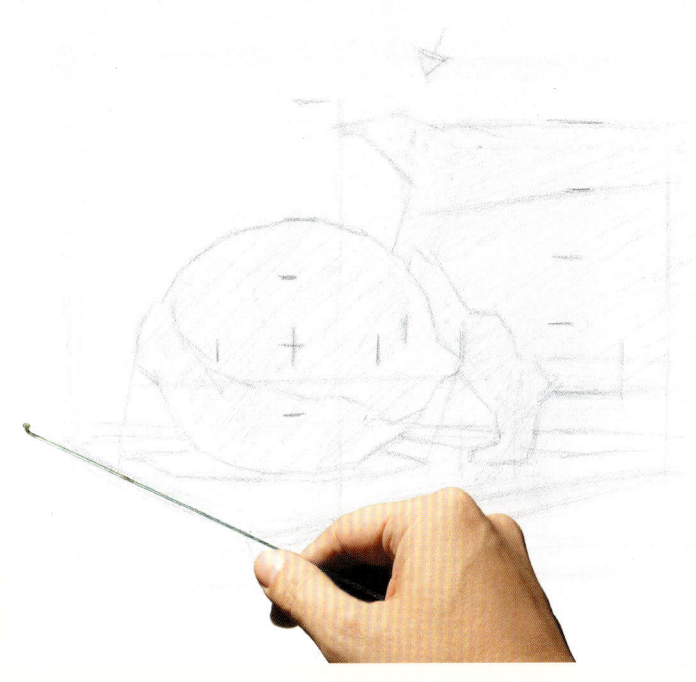

7. Do Two-Point Comparisons

In a two-point comparison, you take two points on the setup, draw an imaginary line between them, and then find another relationship between points on the setup that is of the same length. Then check to see if the distances between the pairs of points are the same on your drawing. This kind of comparison keeps you honest when drawing. "Close enough" isn't good enough. If something is off, it's off!

I connect two of the points on the setup and then look for another connection between two points that is the same length. I compare these relationships on my drawing to make sure that the measurements correspond.

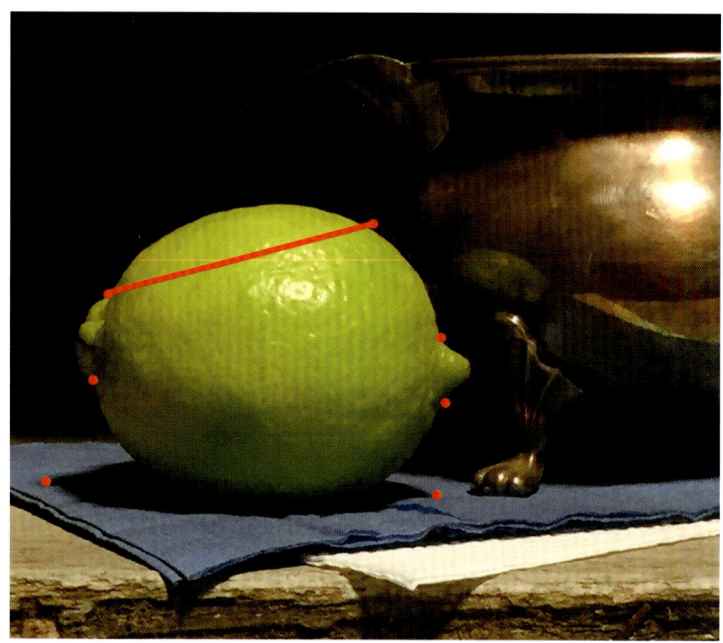

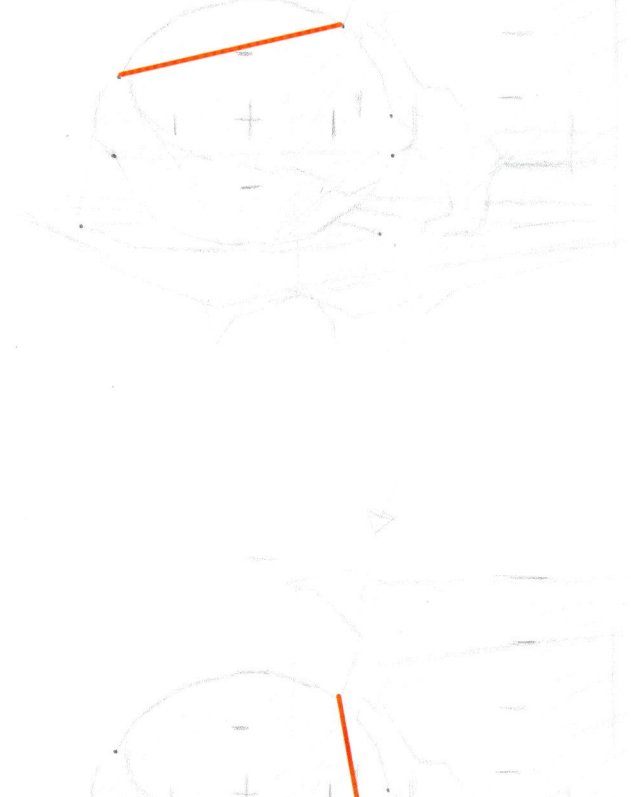

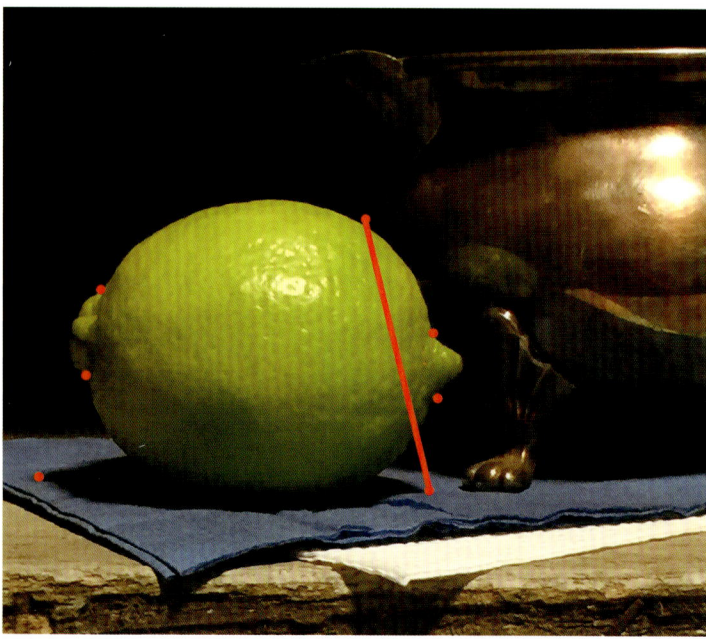

8. Do Triangulations (Three-Point Comparisons)

In a triangulation, you are taking three points in the setup and relating them to one another. I usually take three major points where forms overlap or where planes break or change direction. You can, however, pick any three arbitrary points; the goal is to make sure they relate to each other in the drawing the exact same way they do on the setup. The more you do this—and the more often everything checks out correctly—the better your drawing will be.

After going through all eight of these steps with each major shape, I start to refine the whole drawing, object by object. The drawing of the lime serves as an anchor for measuring everything else.

In the setup, point 1 sits in between points 2 and 3 horizontally. Point 3 sits between points 1 and 2 vertically. Make sure these relationships are precisely replicated on the drawing.

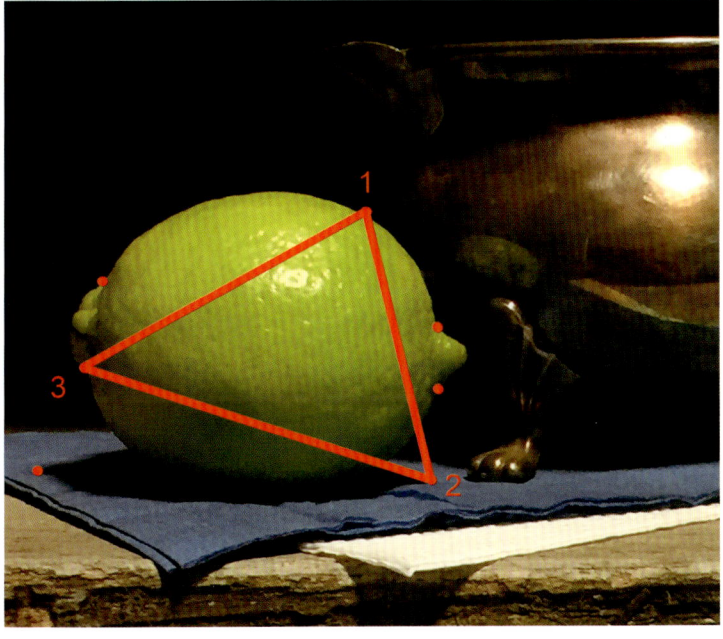

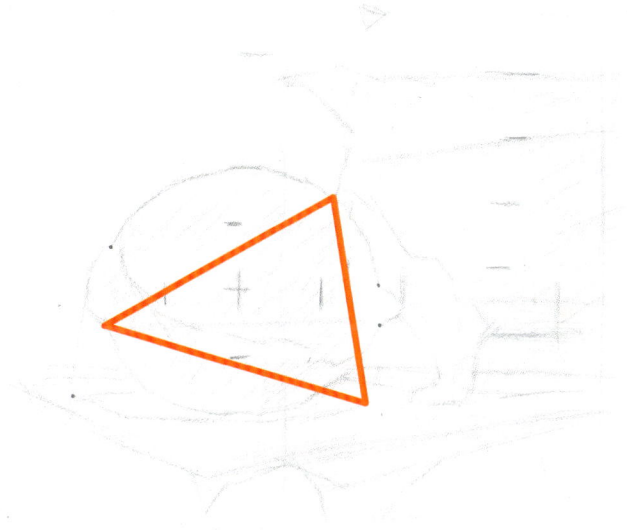

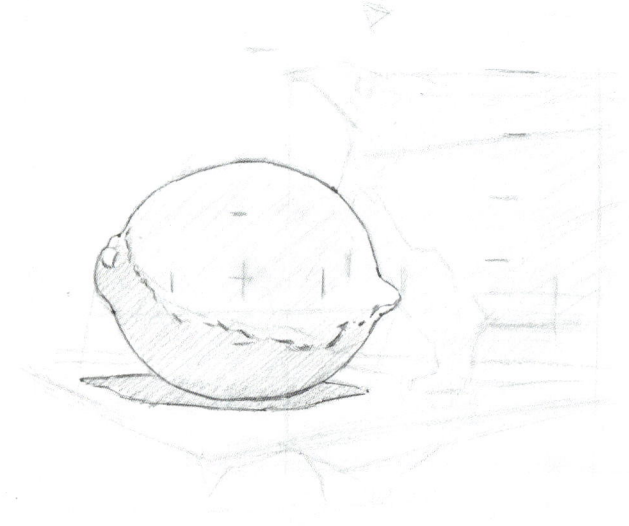

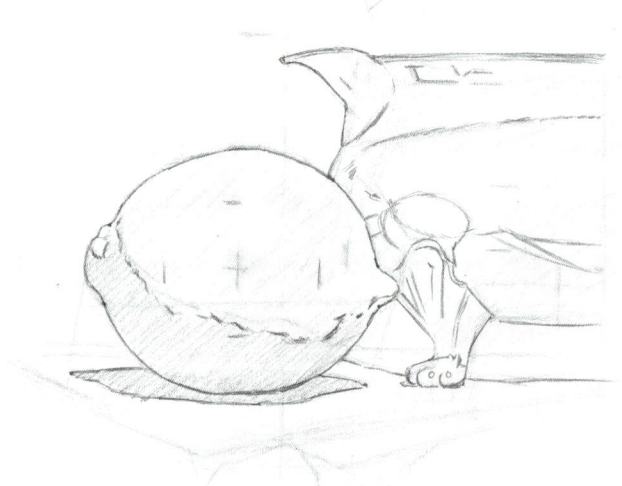

TOP: Once you have a shape locked in, like the lime in this drawing, use it as an anchor to measure everything else.

CENTER: Here, the pewter vessel has been refined, based on the lime.

BOTTOM: Finally, the napkins are added to the drawing, as well as just a little tone to define the light and shadow. I also make note of the highlights. You can leave your marks for the halfway and quarter points or clean up the drawing if you'd prefer.

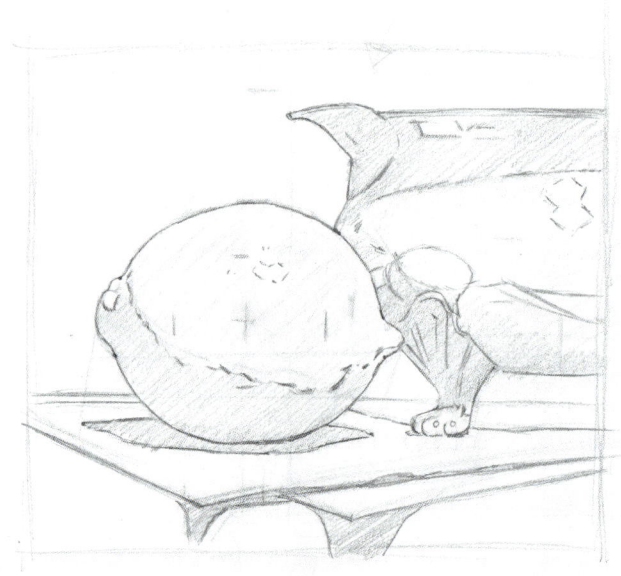

CONTOURS AND SIMPLE FORMS

The contour is the line around an object—similar to a silhouette. Contour lines don't really exist in nature, so the contour is more of an implied boundary indicating the edge of a form. Draw contours as two-dimensional shapes that interact with two-dimensional background shapes, like puzzle pieces that have to fit together perfectly.

Up until this stage of the drawing process, the drawing has only two-dimensional shapes. Now we must start to think of them three-dimensionally. Adding the dimension of depth takes the forms from two-dimensional flat shapes to three-dimensional forms.

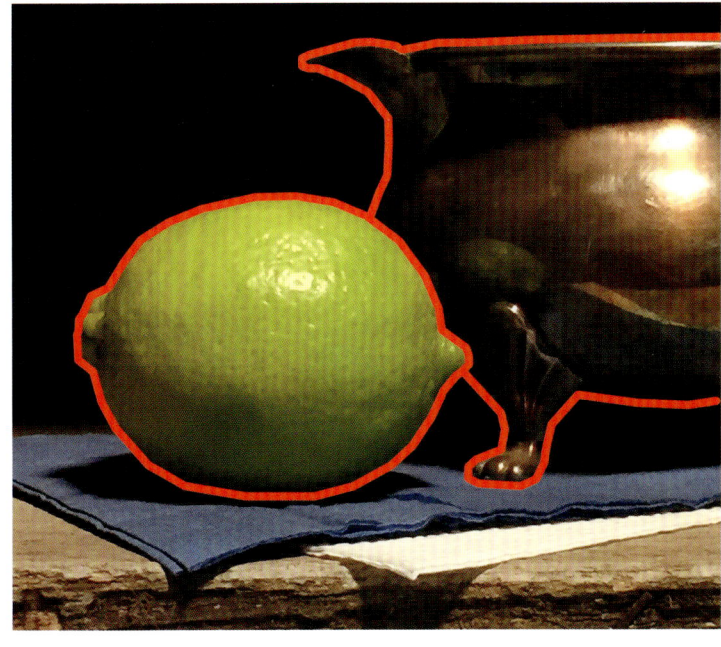

Here the contours around the shapes are articulated.

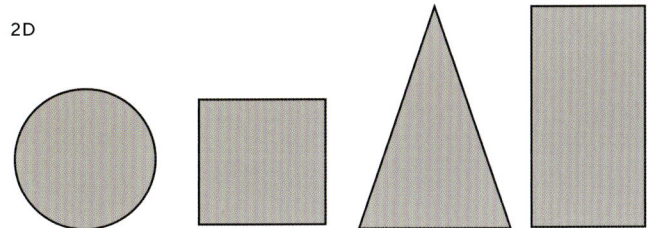

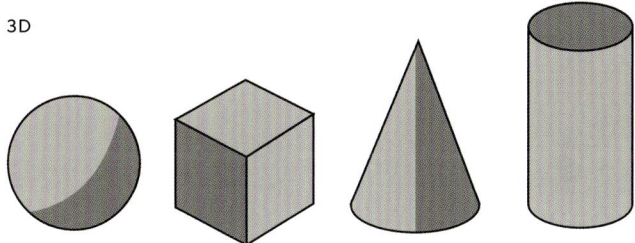

Here are two-dimensional and three-dimensional versions of the same shapes.

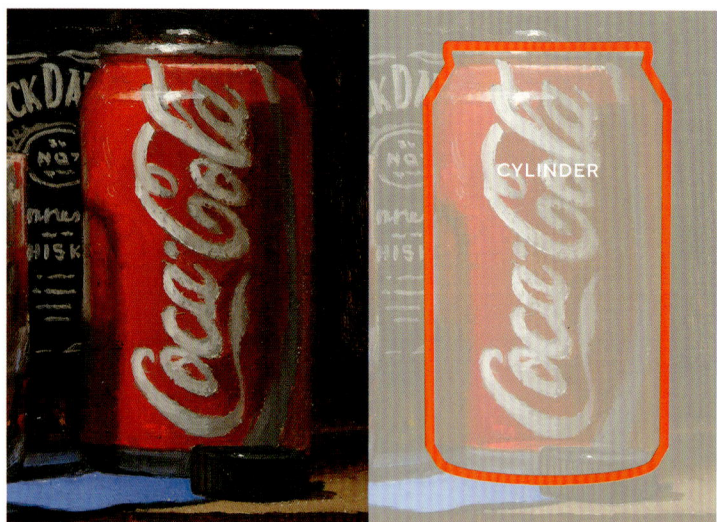

The form of this Coke can is basically a cylinder.

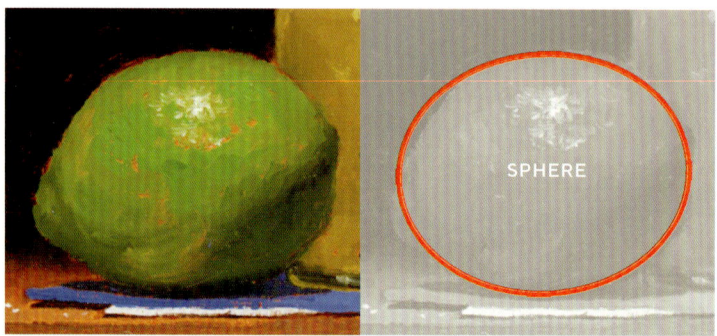

This lime's form is that of a slightly squashed sphere.

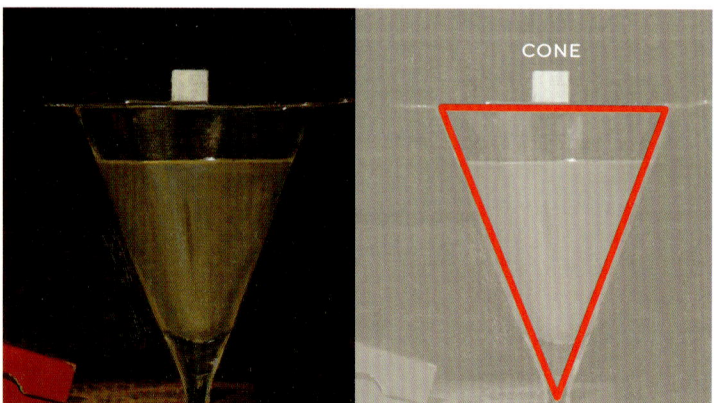

The bowl of this absinthe glass is an almost perfect cone.

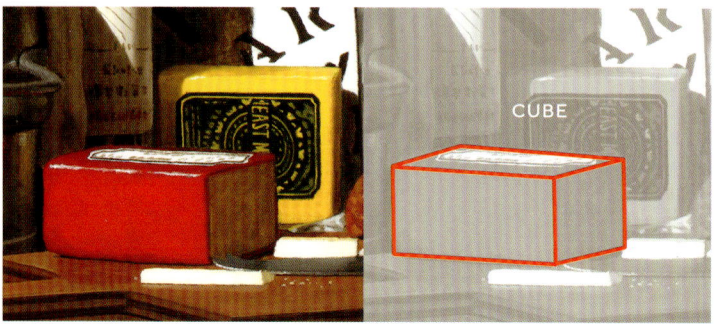

This hunk of cheese is cubical in shape.

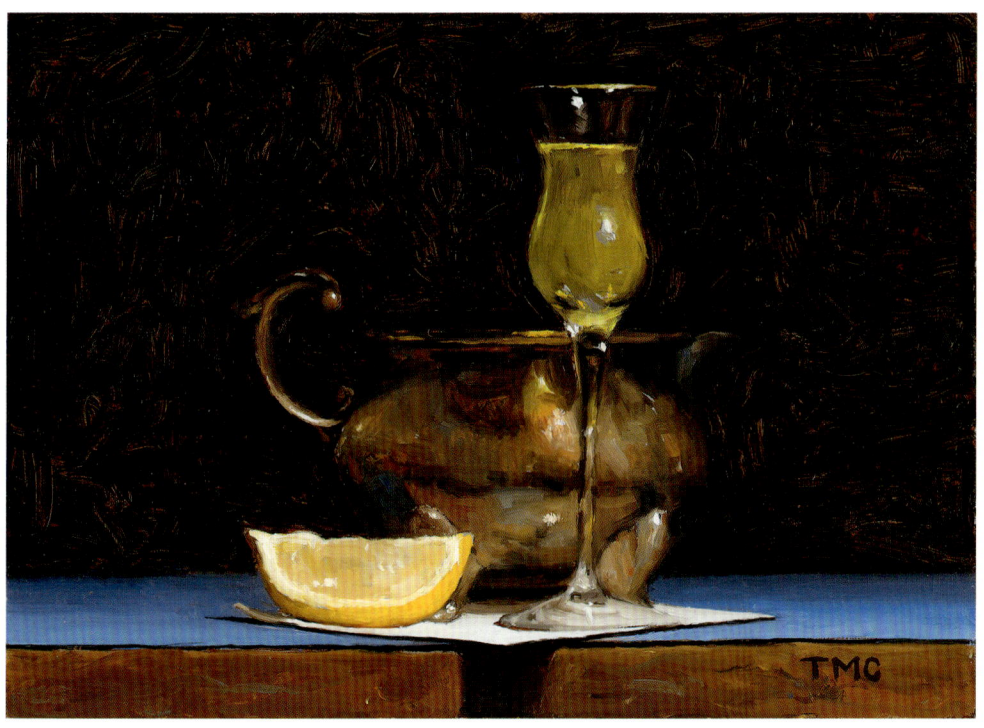

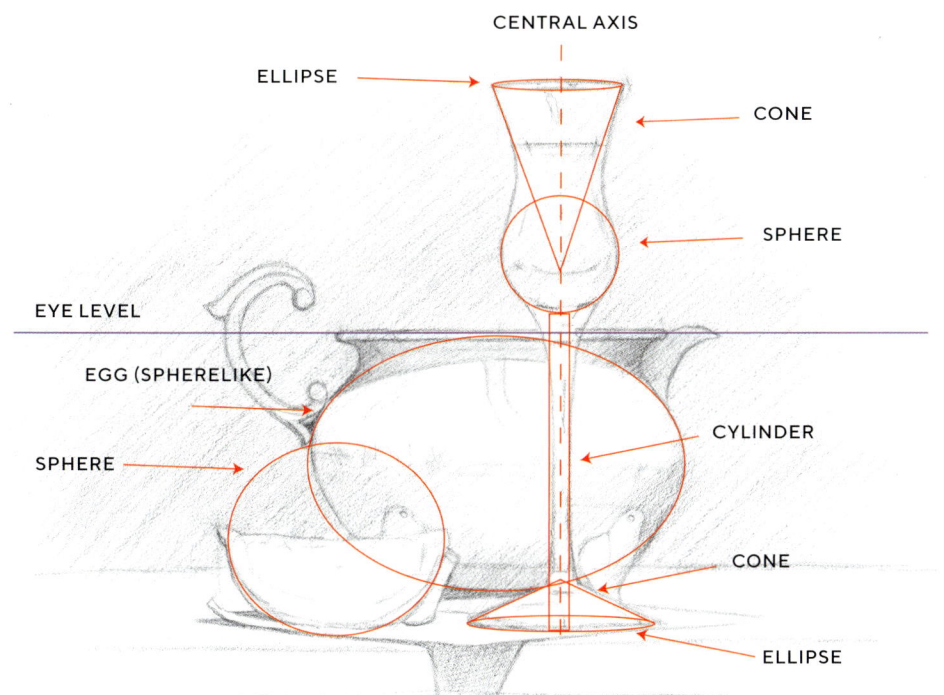

TOP: Todd M. Casey, *Limoncello*, 2015, oil on linen, 6 × 8 inches (15.24 × 20.32 cm). Private collection.

LEFT: On this drawing for my painting *Limoncello*, I've superimposed an analysis of the basic shapes of the objects depicted.

Every object either possesses one of the four basic shapes—cylinder, sphere, cone, cube—or is some combination of these shapes. Every complex shape can be broken down into a combination of simpler shapes.

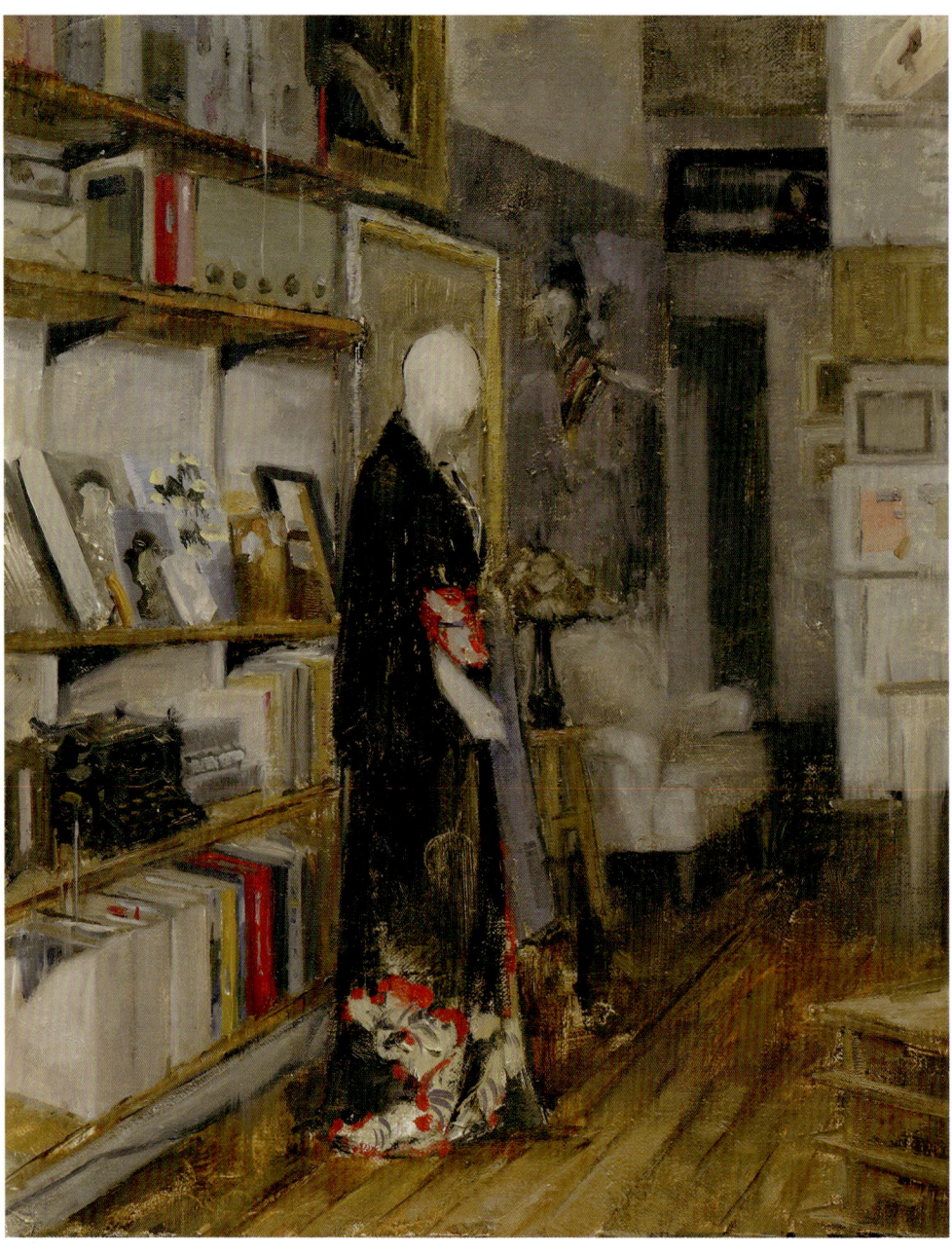

Hyeseung Marriage-Song, *Sunday Sketch in the Studio,* 2018, oil on linen on wood, 10 × 8 inches (25.4 × 20.32 cm). Courtesy of the artist.

In this painting by Hyeseung Marriage-Song, all the objects appear in two-point perspective.

PERSPECTIVE AND FORESHORTENING

If you intend to make a living at drawing, by all means learn [the rules of perspective] now, and do not have them bothering you and your work for the rest of your life.

—ANDREW LOOMIS

Once we have the basic shape of a form, we then have to place the form in space. We do so using perspective—the illusion of depth created in a picture plane as seen by the observer. The basic principle of perspective is that objects diminish in scale as they move back in space, away from the observer.

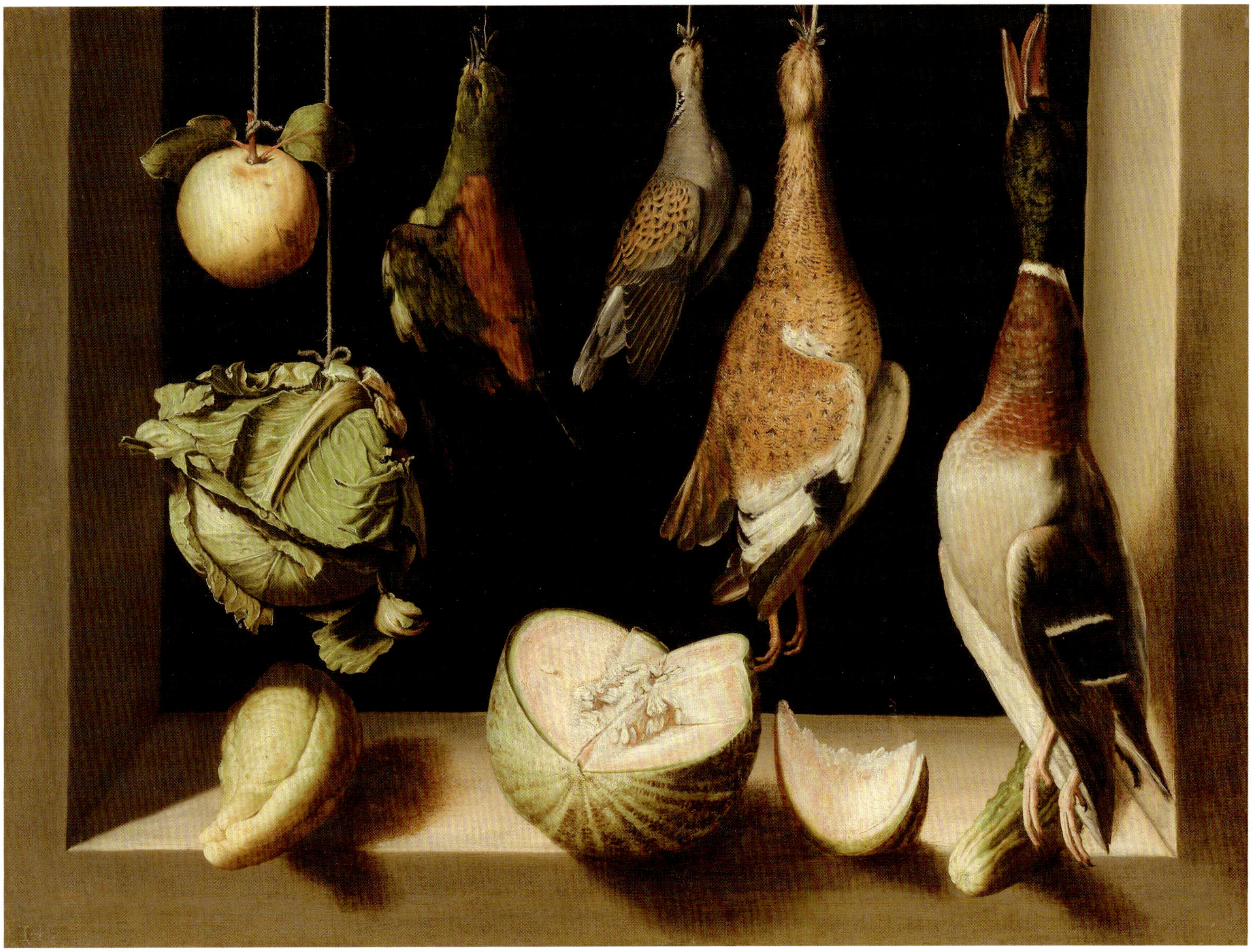

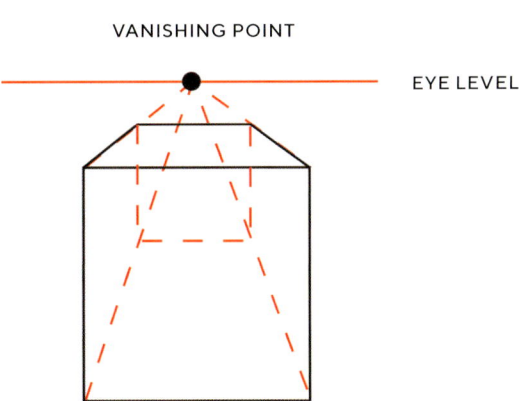

One-Point Perspective

One-point perspective exists when you are looking directly at something (such as the cube in the diagram below) and one of the object's planes is perpendicular to your line of sight. All the lines extending from the side edges of the object will converge at a single vanishing point at eye level (the horizon).

ABOVE: Juan Sánchez Cotán (Spanish, 1560– 1627), *Still Life with Game Fowl*, 1597–1607, oil on canvas, 26 ¹¹⁄₁₆ × 34 ¹⁵⁄₁₆ inches (67.8 × 88.7 cm). The Art Institute of Chicago. Gift of Mr. and Mrs. Leigh B. Block.

Juan Sánchez Cotán's *Still Life with Game Fowl* is in one-point perspective.

LEFT: One-point perspective

VANISHING POINT

EYE LEVEL

Two-Point Perspective

Two-point perspective applies when you see two sides of an object, neither of which is perpendicular to your line of sight. There are two vanishing points on the eye level, or horizon, and all the points on the object's vertices can be connected to both vanishing points with straight lines. You can find the approximate vanishing point(s) of any object seen in perspective by aligning a straightedge tool with the tilted edges of the observed planes. To find the absolute vanishing point(s), you would extend those lines to the horizon.

RIGHT: Kevin M. Wueste, *Paper Flower 2 (Whole Foods Bag),* 2016, oil on panel, 10 × 12 inches (25.4 × 30.48 cm). Courtesy of the artist.

This painting by Kevin Wueste is in two-point perspective.

BELOW: Two-point perspective

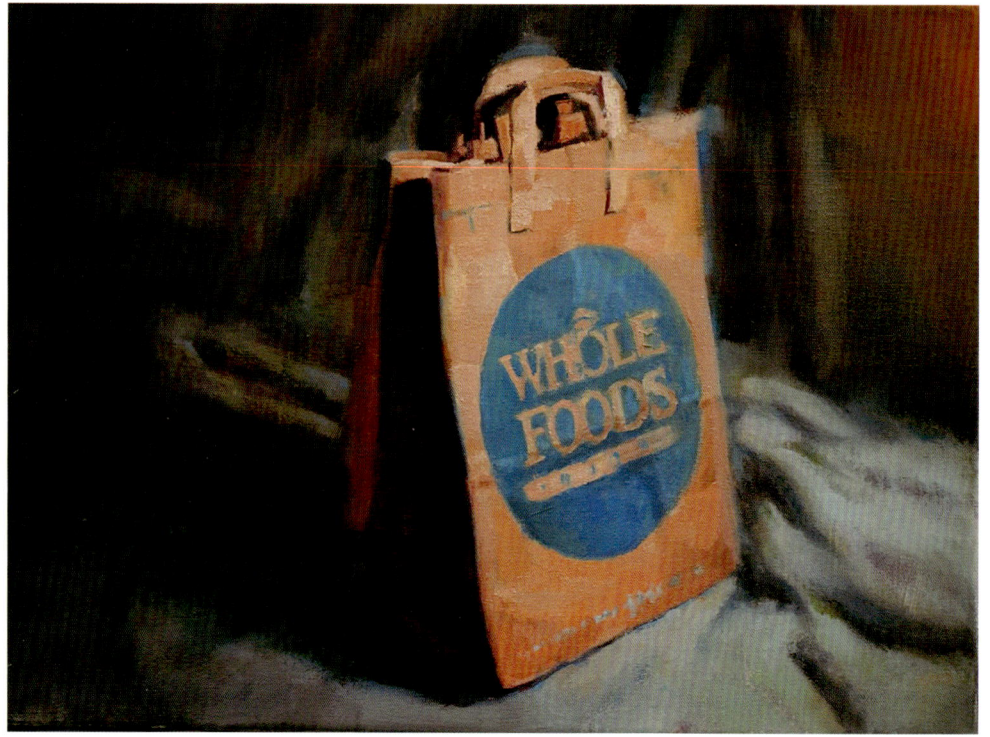

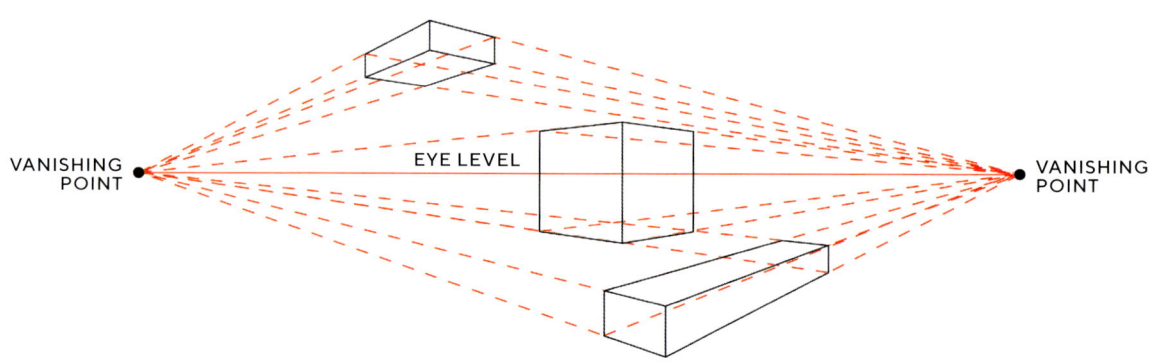

EYE LEVEL

All observed perspective is determined by eye level (or by the horizon line when outdoors). As you move up and down, your eye level changes and your observed perspective changes as well.

Eye level determines the degree of foreshortening observed in your setup. The only time we don't see foreshortening of the plane that the objects are sitting on is when we look at a setup from directly above. However, the perspective of being directly over a setup is very rare in still life painting. The painting *Red Mullets*, by Claude Monet, is one of those rare exceptions—the artist's eye is almost (not quite) directly above the setup.

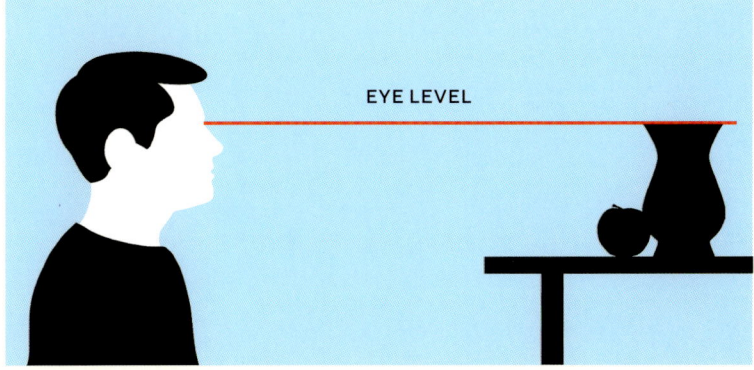

ABOVE: If I could shoot laser beams out of my eyes like Superman, the beams would determine my eye level. Illustration by James Decker.

BELOW: Claude Monet (French, 1840–1926), *Red Mullets,* 1870, oil on canvas, 12 ¼ × 18 ⅛ inches (31.1 × 46 cm). The Harvard Art Museums/Fogg Museum, Friends of the Fogg Art Museum Fund. © President and Fellows of Harvard College.

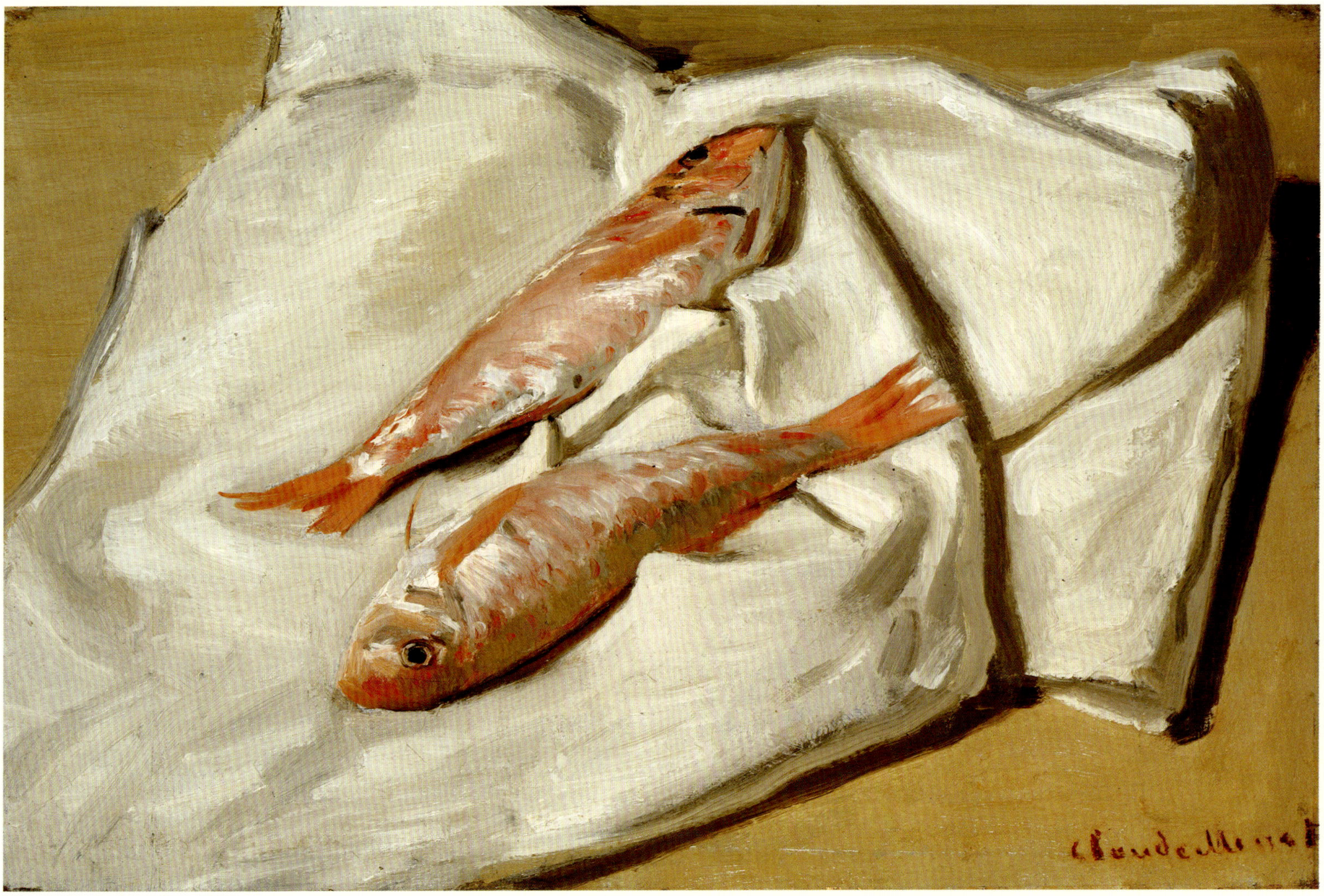

In this painting, Philippe Rousseau foreshortened the top plane of the table and all of the objects that sit flat on it, like the plates and cutlery. This helps create the illusion of depth as the tabletop recedes in space.

Foreshortening

Foreshortening is a perceived distortion of perspective such that an object or portion of an object appears larger or smaller than it actually is in relation to other objects. For example, suppose you are viewing a reclining human figure from the perspective of the soles of the figure's feet. In that case, the feet would appear much larger in relation to the other parts of the figure than they actually are. That's an extreme example, but, in fact, almost every plane we see—unless it is directly facing us—is foreshortened to some degree. Foreshortened forms are extremely hard to draw accurately.

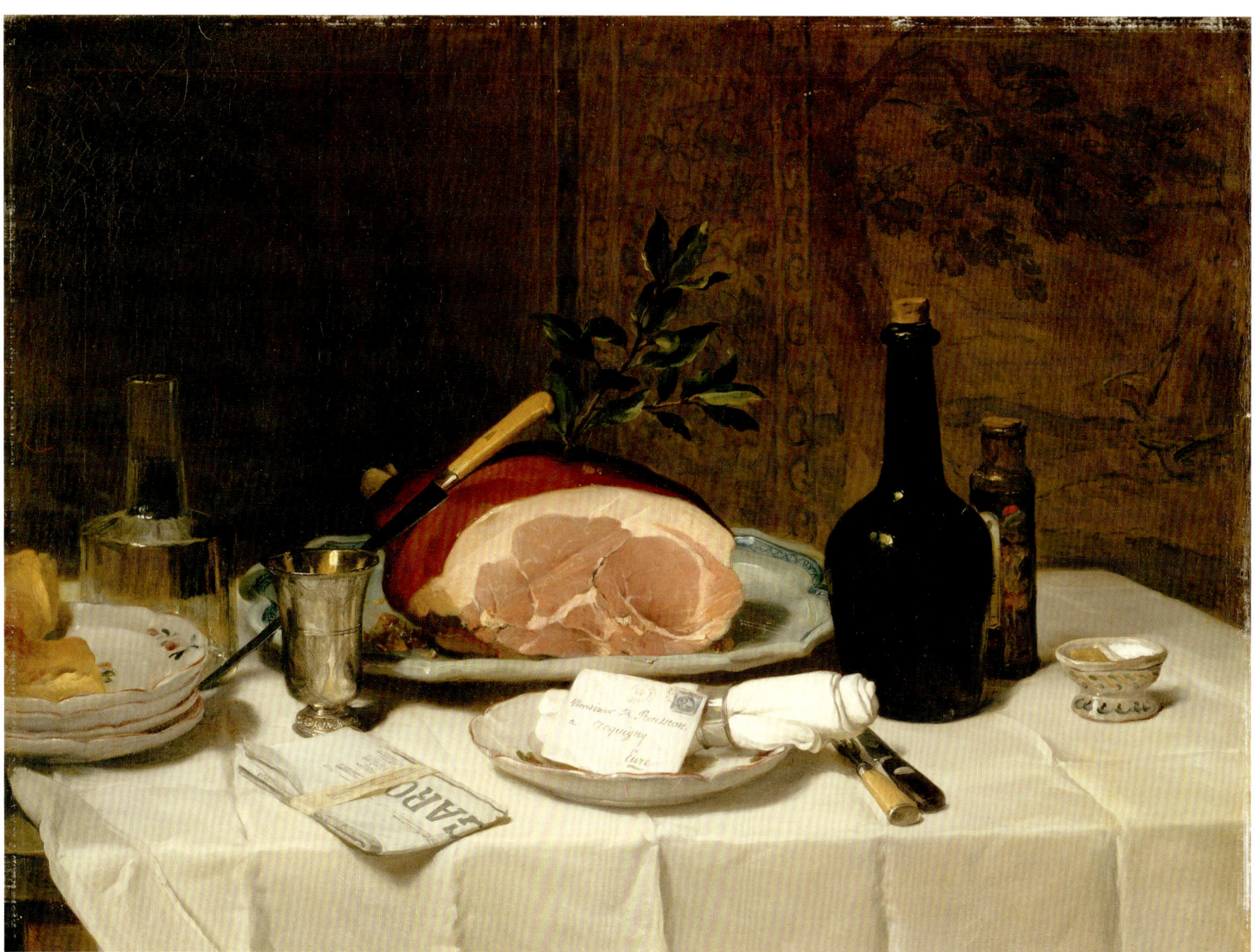

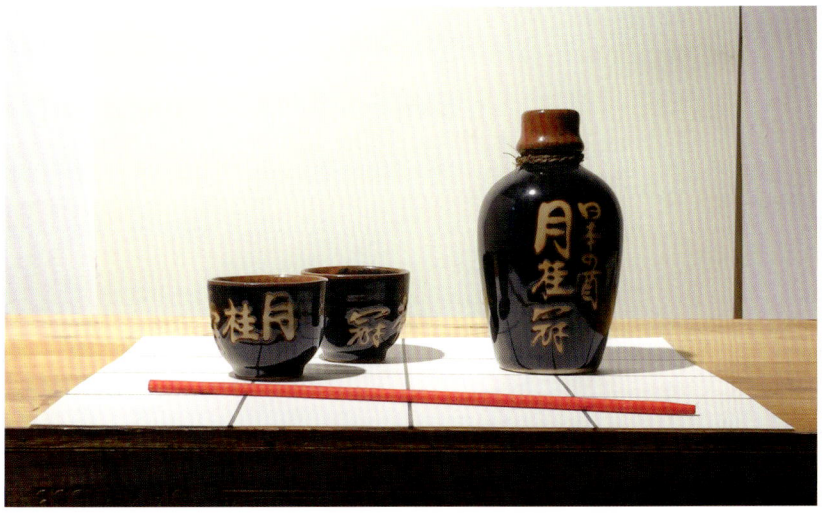
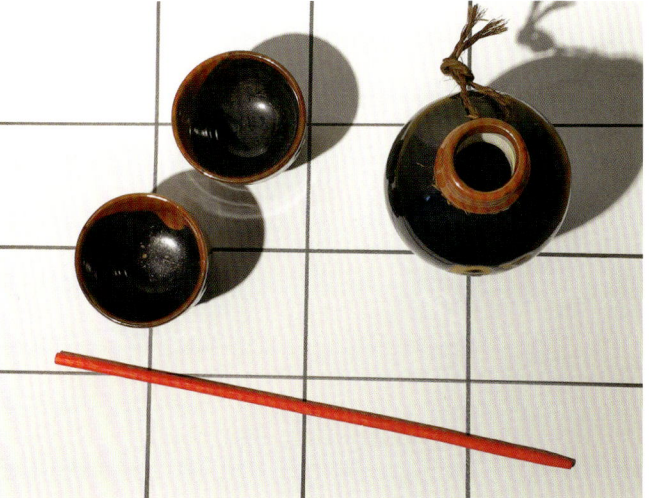

When drawing foreshortened forms, we tend to exaggerate, which causes the frontalization of foreshortened planes—meaning that we turn the planes more toward the viewer than they actually are. It's another example of our drawing what we *think* we see instead of the information that's really in front of us.

CONSTRUCTING SIMPLE FORMS

When constructing any of the four simple forms—cylinder, cone, sphere, or cube—you should begin by drawing the shape inside a box. You then "carve into" the box to find the form inside.

The box should be placed in one- or two-point perspective. Next, draw a line down the center of the box; this is the central axis.

ABOVE: In the photo at left, the setup is observed from the front. On the right, the same setup is seen from above, and the forms of the sake cups and bottle are greatly foreshortened.

BELOW LEFT: Begin by drawing each shape inside a box.

BELOW RIGHT: The sphere inside the box could be represented as a circle drawn on each plane of the cube. If a laser carved out a circle on each side of the cube, you would be left with a perfect sphere.

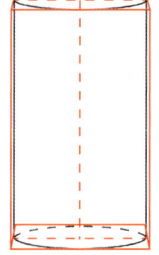
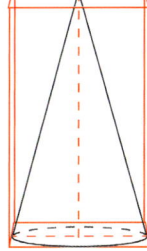
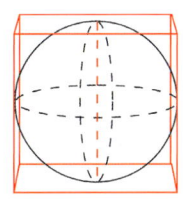
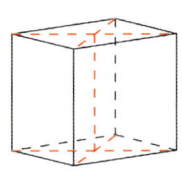
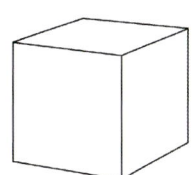
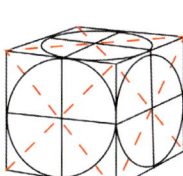
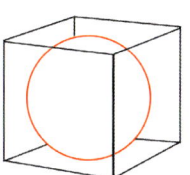

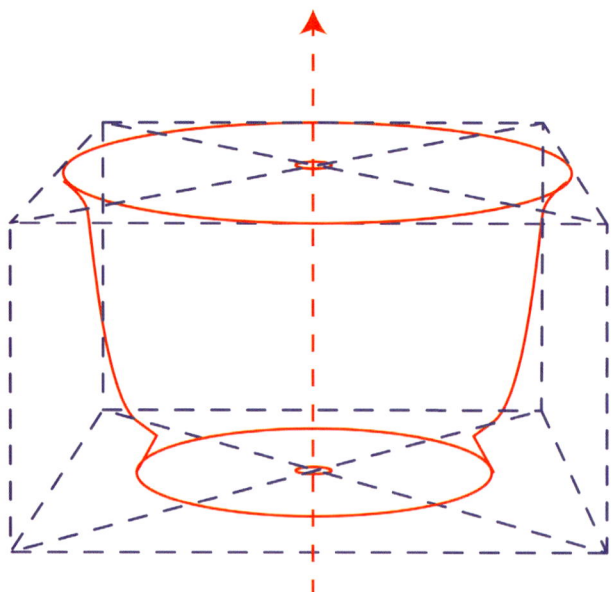

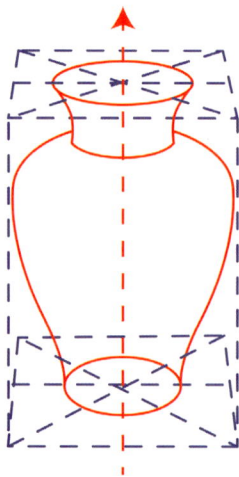

Every symmetrical shape has a central axis. Finding the central axis helps you make sure that every point on the object's contour is symmetrically aligned with the point at the same height on the opposite side of the object.

DRAWING ELLIPSES

When you observe the mouth of a round cup, bottle, or vase from directly overhead, you see a circle. But if you look at the object from the side, from any angle, you see its mouth as a foreshortened circle—that is, an ellipse. Ellipses are difficult to draw accurately—beginners tend to draw their outer corners as pointed rather than curved—but it becomes a little easier to draw them when you understand why we see them as we do.

An ellipse has two axes—the major axis and the minor axis. The major axis is its width from left to right, which doesn't vary as the observer's eye level moves up or down in relation to the object. The minor axis is its perceived height, which grows larger as the observer's eye level moves upward or downward, as you can see in the illustration at top left, opposite. If your eye is level with the object's mouth, the ellipse disappears, becoming a straight line. If your eye is directly above the mouth of the object, the major axis (width) and minor axis (height) are the same—meaning the ellipse has become a full circle.

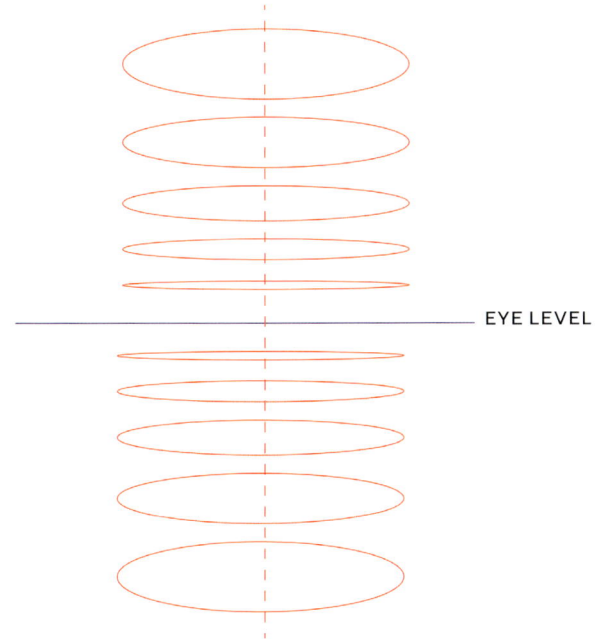

As eye level moves up or down, the shape of the ellipse changes.

EYE LEVEL

MINOR AXIS

MAJOR AXIS

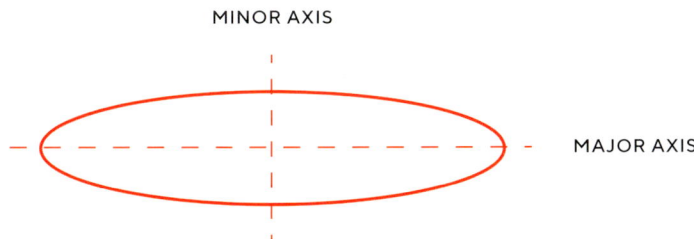

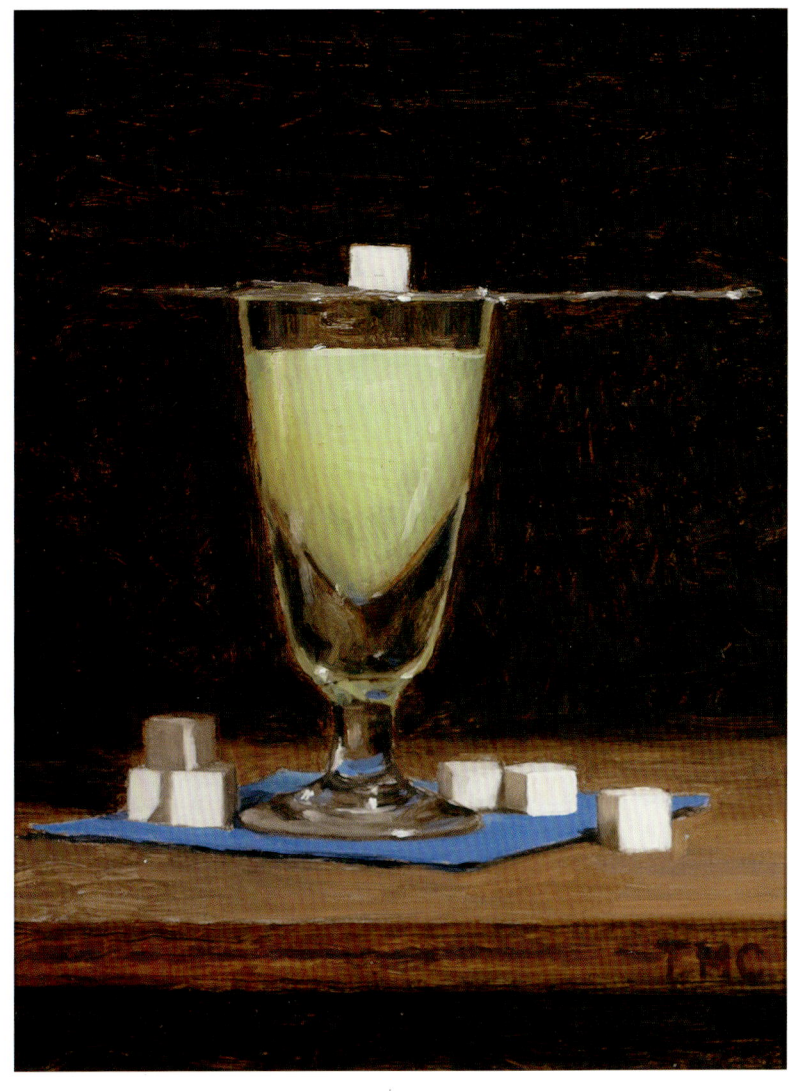

ABOVE: Todd M. Casey, *Absinthe,* 2013, oil on panel, 8 × 6 inches (20.32 × 15.24 cm). Courtesy of Rehs Contemporary Galleries, New York.

In my painting *Absinthe*, the eye level is right at the top of the glass, which therefore appears as a straight line.

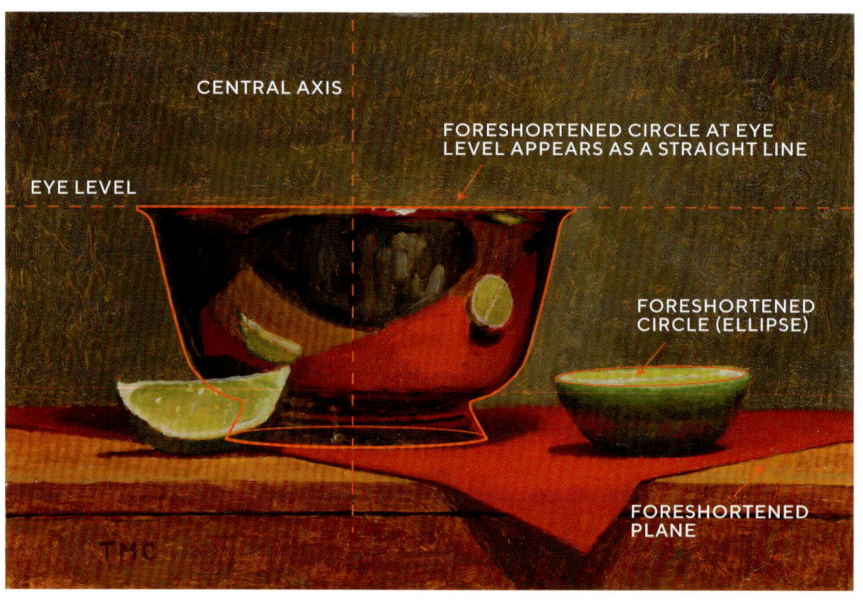

LEFT: Todd M. Casey, *Bowl with Limes,* 2018, oil on panel, 6 × 9 inches (15.24 × 22.86 cm). Courtesy of Rehs Contemporary Galleries, New York.

Here I've highlighted some of the foreshortening that's happening to the bowl, the lime on the right, and the ground plane in my painting *Bowl with Limes.*

BELOW, LEFT TO RIGHT: Justin Wood, *Silver Tumbler and Lemon,* 2018, oil on linen, 8 × 6.5 inches (20.32 × 16.51 cm). Courtesy of the artist.

Celeste Ryder, *A Painter's Tale,* 2016, oil on panel, 10 × 8 ¼ inches (25.4 × 20.95 cm). Collection of Dr. Philip Walls of Lutherville, Md.

When painting *Silver Tumbler and Lemon,* Justin Wood was sitting slightly above the setup and looking down at the ellipse at the mouth of the silver tumbler. In *A Painter's Tale,* artist Celeste Ryder places her eye level just below the mouth of the pitcher, so we look up at the ellipses that are higher on the pitcher and down at the ellipses that are lower on the pitcher.

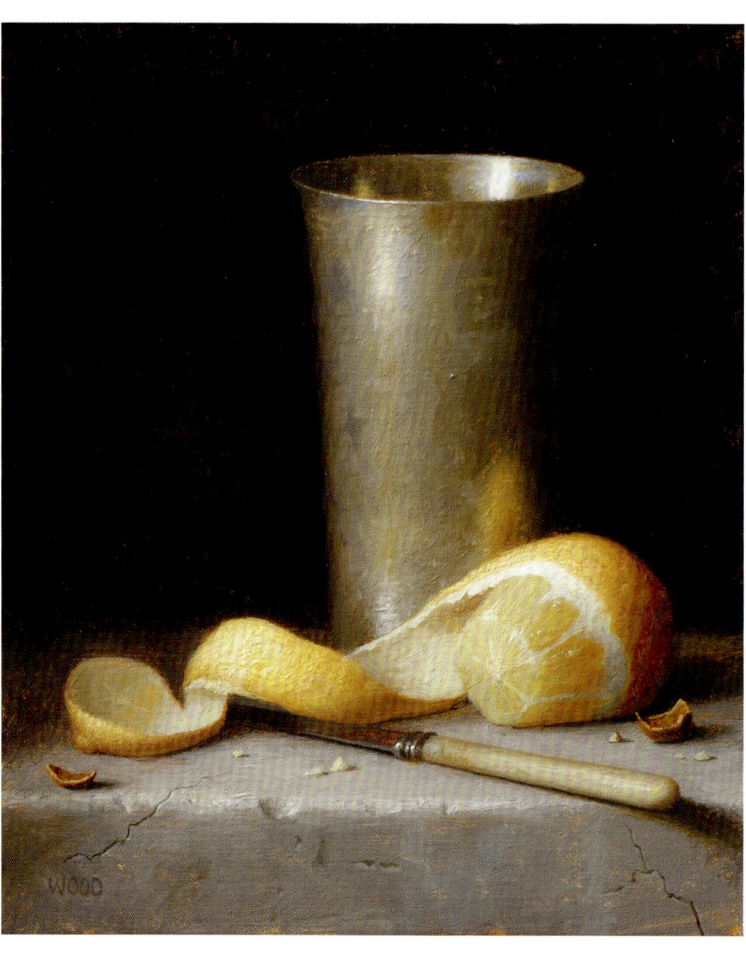

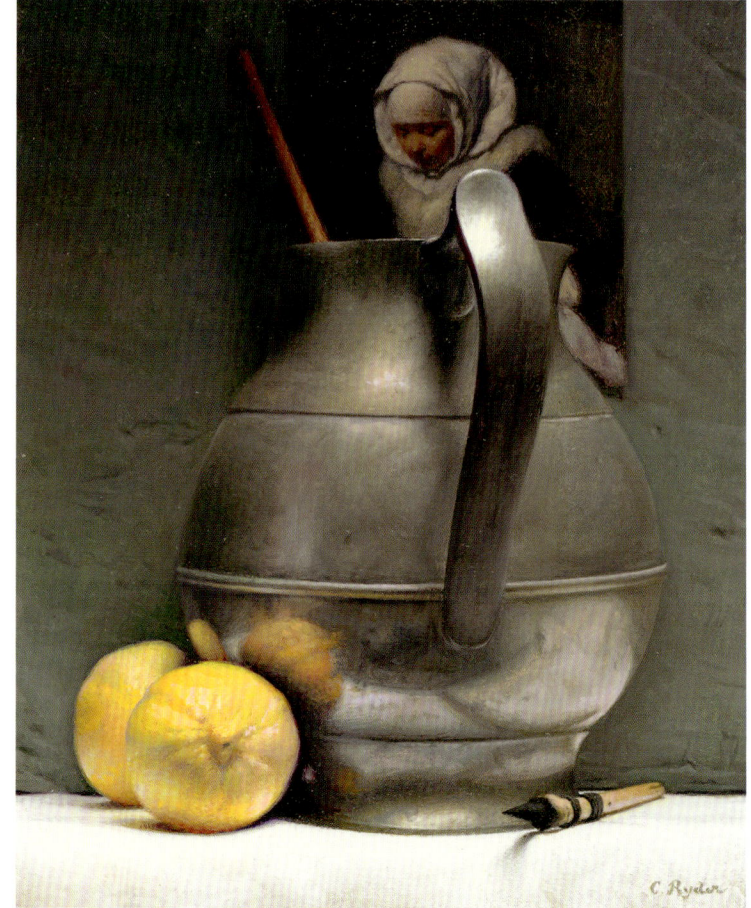

DIRECT AND INDIRECT APPROACHES TO DRAWING FOR PAINTING

When drawing for a painting, you may choose either to work directly, drawing on the painting surface itself, or indirectly, preparing a preliminary drawing on paper and then transferring it to the painting surface. Each approach has its pros and cons. Use whichever works best for you. The most important thing is to have an accurate drawing to build on.

The Direct Method

Many contemporary artists prefer to draw directly on the canvas or panel. This is a bit more difficult than working indirectly, but you will gain confidence and get better at it with each painting you do in this manner.

You can draw directly on the painting surface either with pencil or with paint. (Both work, and both are archival.) If you draw with paint, I recommend using a

TIP

A fun way to check your drawing is to quickly and repeatedly move your eyes back and forth from the drawing to the setup—almost as if you were flipping pages in a flipbook. As you do so, do any of your lines appear to move? If so, that area of your drawing may be off.

BELOW, LEFT TO RIGHT: For my painting *Bloody Mary*, I did the drawing directly on the panel.

Todd M. Casey, *Bloody Mary*, 2018, oil on panel, 9 × 6 inches (22.86 × 15.24 cm). Private collection.

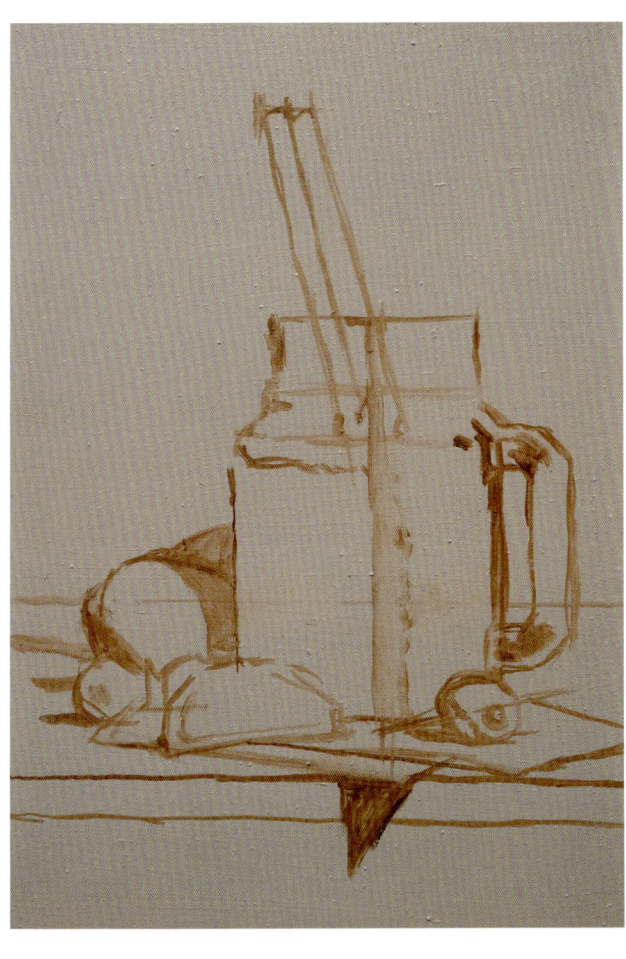

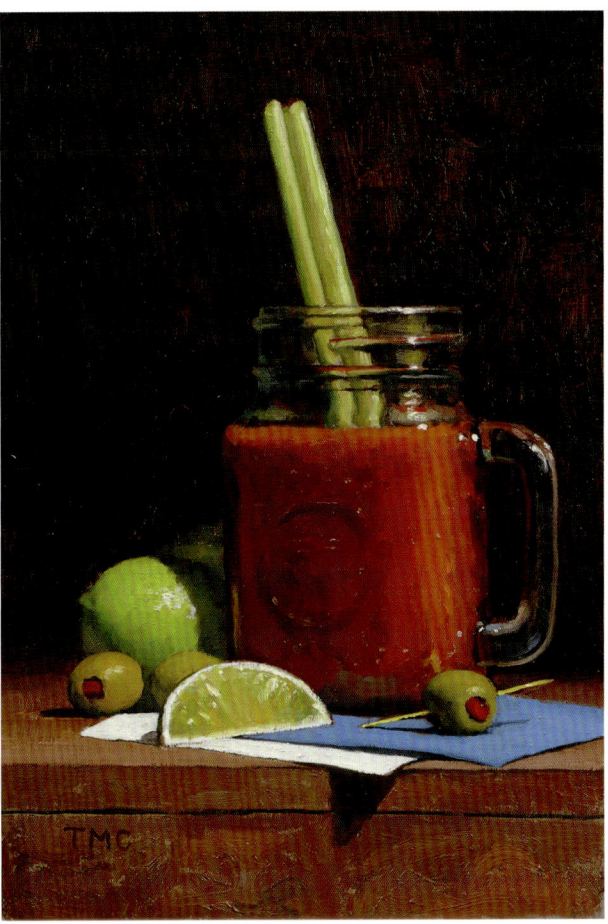

quick-drying color like burnt umber or raw umber. I like to mix some solvent with the paint to make my lines lighter so I can build my drawing slowly.

The Indirect Method

The indirect method, in which a preliminary drawing (sometimes referred to as a cartoon) is made and then transferred to the painting surface, is the more traditional approach, one that's been employed for centuries.

This type of drawing doesn't need to be fully rendered. All that's needed is contour, accurate proportions, and the separation of light and shadow. There is no need for hatching or value at this stage.

Among the important things to consider when drawing for painting is how the composition will fit on the painting surface. The indirect method allows me to play around with the scale of the drawing and consider different cropping scenarios. It also helps in working out complex compositions.

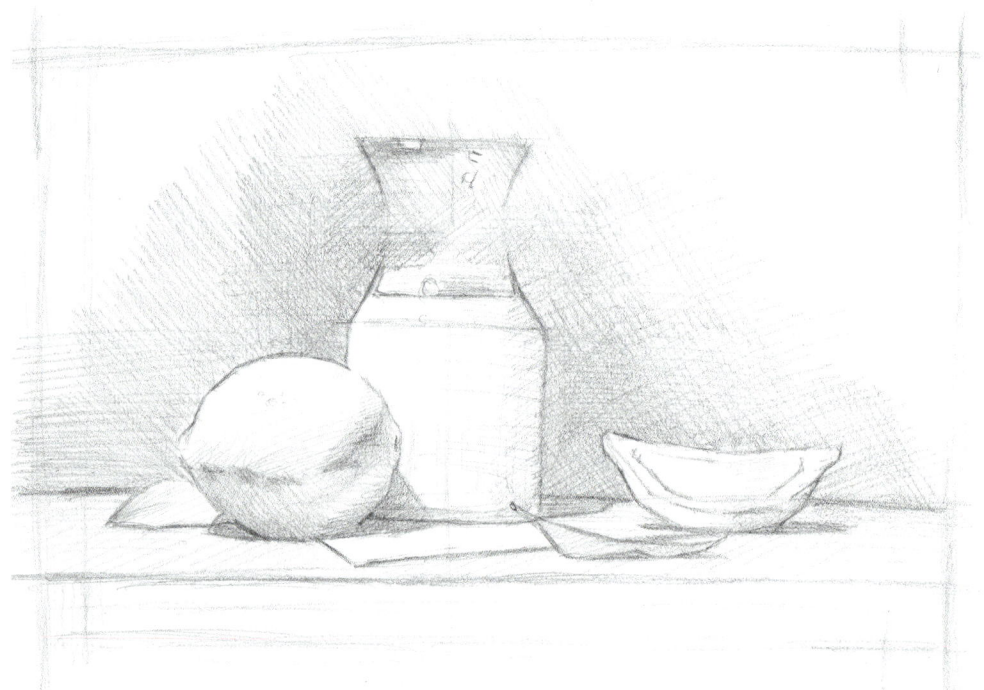

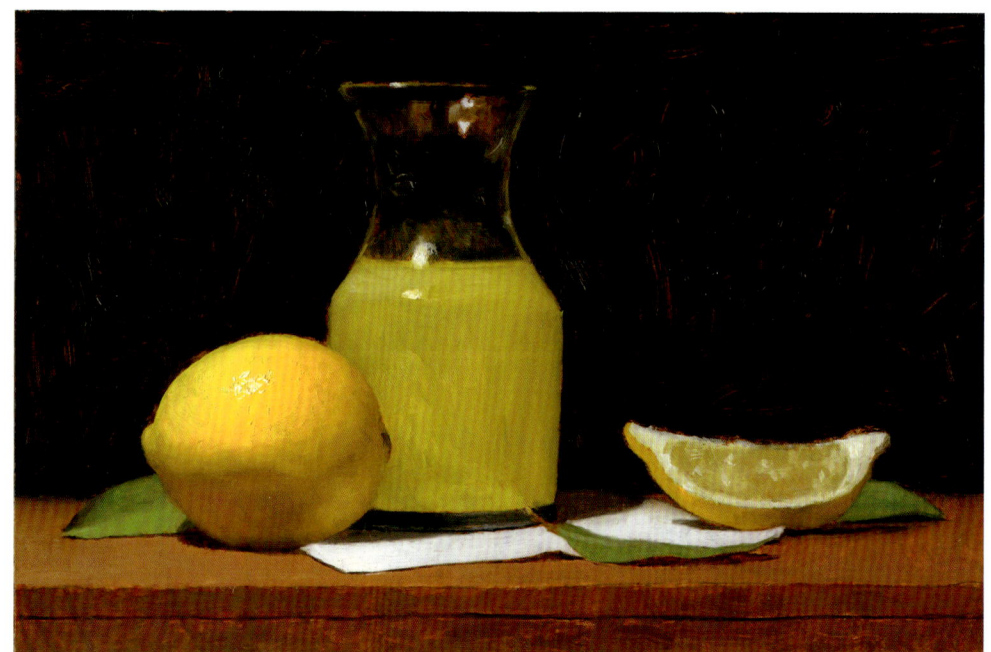

TOP: Here's the preliminary drawing I did for my painting *Limoncello with Lemons*.

RIGHT: Todd M. Casey, *Limoncello with Lemons*, 2017, oil on linen, 6 × 9 inches (15.24 × 22.86 cm). Private collection.

TRANSFERRING A PRELIMINARY DRAWING

When the drawing is complete, you need to get it onto your surface. The process is similar to how a carbon-paper transfer works. You can do it with oil paint scrubbed onto the back of a piece of paper, as I do here, or you can use transfer paper (such as Saral).

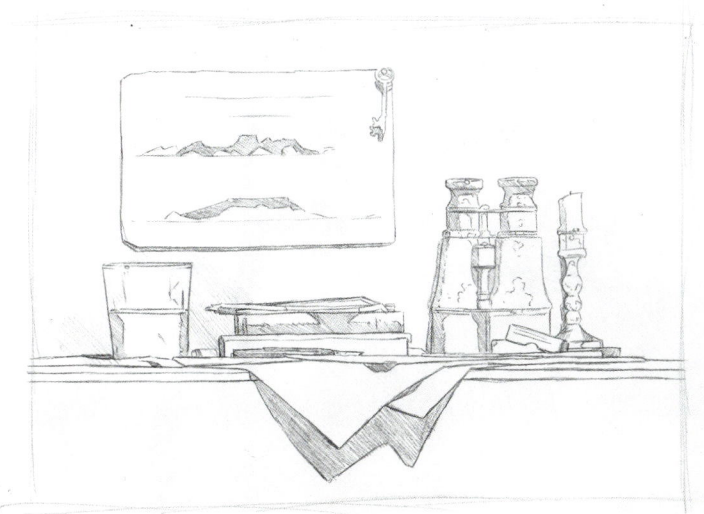

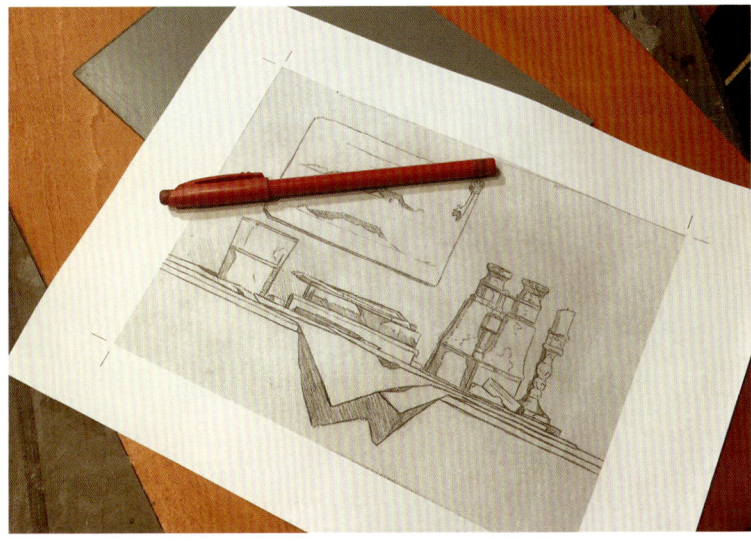

STEP 1

Start with an articulated drawing of your setup (top). The contours of each shape and the light and shadows should be clear. Scan the drawing and print it out at the scale of the painting you want to do.

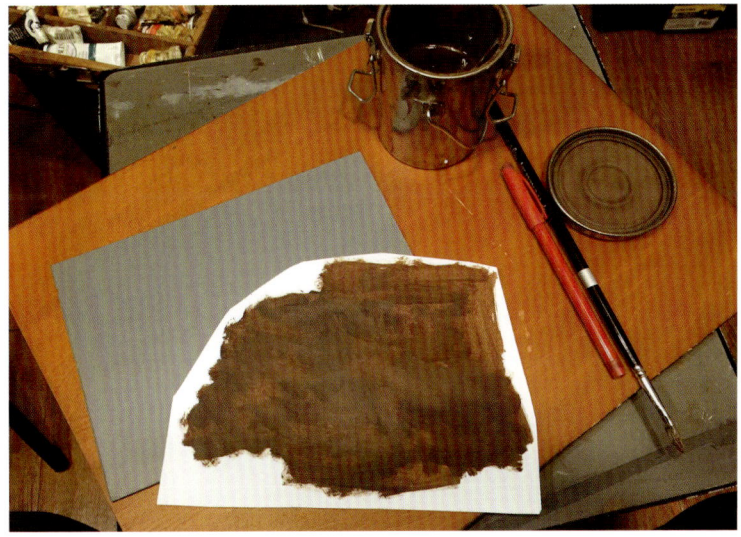

STEP 2

On your palette, mix burnt umber paint with a little solvent. Then paint the mixture onto the back of the printout of your drawing. Wait a minute or two for the Gamsol to evaporate before the next step. (In the photo, I've cut the drawing into an irregular shape so that it can easily be taped to a board; there was no information needing to be transferred in the areas that have been cut away.)

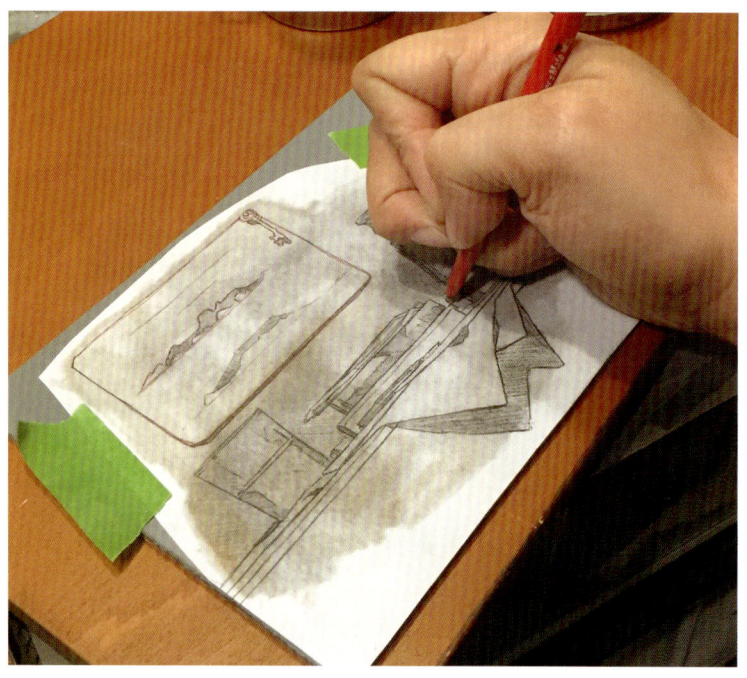

STEP 3

Tape the paper to your painting surface, being careful to center the composition. With a red ballpoint pen, trace over the lines of the drawing. Using a red pen helps you keep track of the lines you have already traced.

STEP 4

Untape one of the edges of your transfer and carefully lift it to see if you've transferred all of your lines.

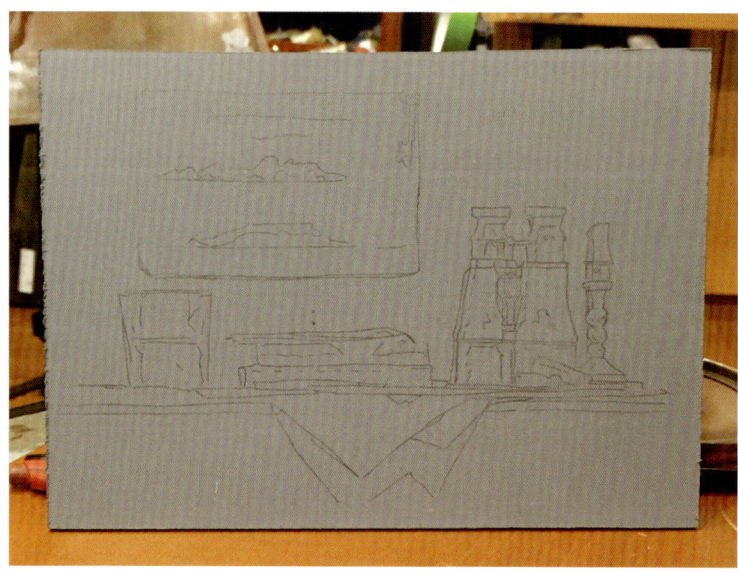

FINAL

Here, the drawing has been transferred to a panel using the oil paint transfer method.

AN ALTERNATIVE METHOD

You can also transfer a drawing using vine charcoal on the back of the paper rather than the oil paint mixture. Charcoal is easy to apply and easy to wipe off the painting surface if you need to make a change. After the lines are worked out, you can either ink them (lightly) or paint over them with oil paint mixed with solvent. If you don't ink or paint over them, the charcoal will smear and mix in with your oil paint.

When I work in larger formats (12 × 16 inches and up), I tend to draw directly on the canvas with charcoal rather than doing a separate drawing and transferring it. It's hard to print out a large transfer drawing because it usually requires tiling papers together.

EXERCISES

EXERCISE 1: COPY A BARGUE PLATE

Back in the nineteenth century, French painter Charles Bargue and his colleague Jean-Léon Gérôme created a drawing course in which students copied a series of lithographs that came to be known as the Bargue plates. These valuable exercises can be done with just a pencil, paper, an eraser, and a tool for measuring tilts and proportions.

Copying a Bargue plate helps you see big shapes and tilts right away, locking them into a drawing early. The rendering is then applied over this solid foundational drawing. The aim is to produce a perfectly accurate copy of the plate.

The Bargue drawing course is available as a book, *Charles Bargue: Drawing Course*, 3rd ed., by Gerald Ackerman (Paris: ACR, 2003). A reproduction of the book appears online, at archive.org/details/C.BargueDrawingCourse, and a number of tutorials in drawing Bargue plates can be viewed on YouTube.

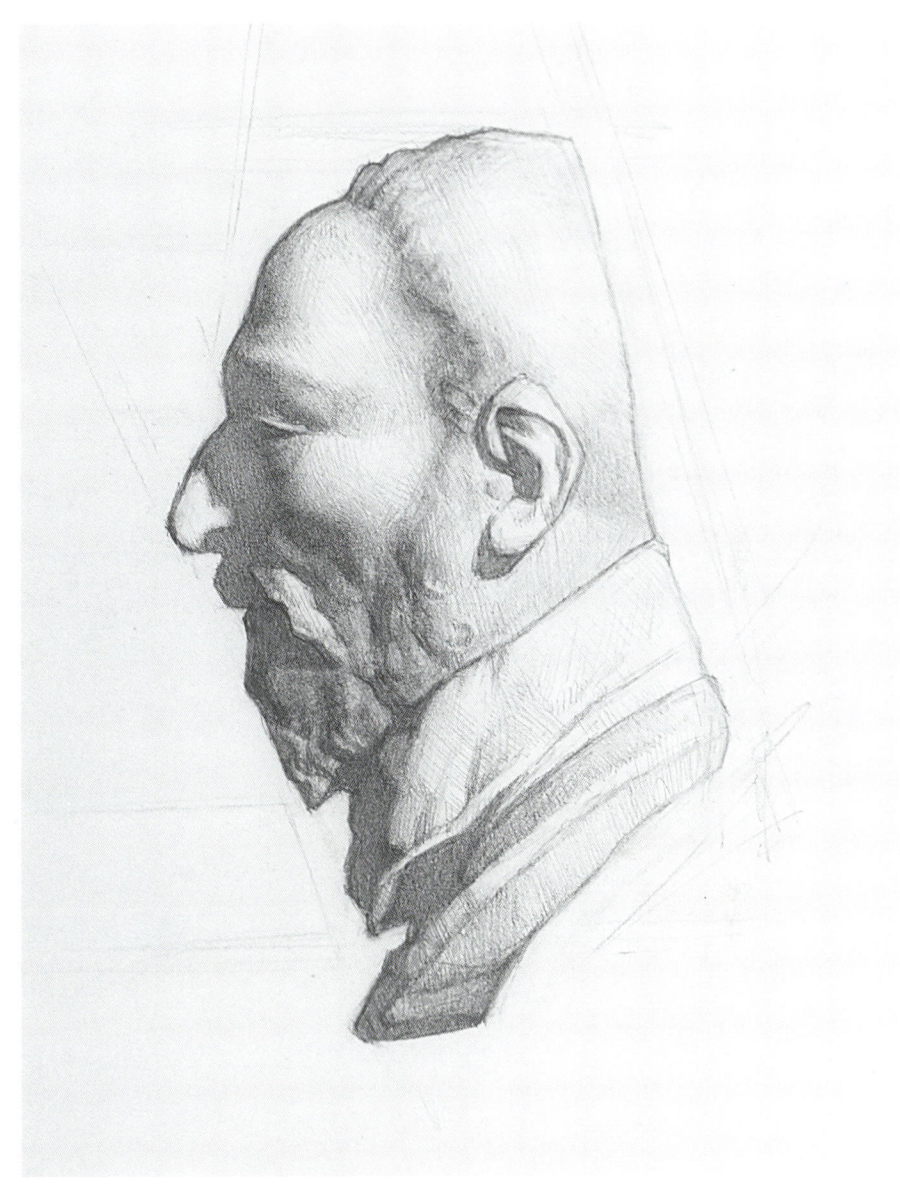

ABOVE, LEFT: Kevin M. Wueste, copy of a Bargue Plate of a profile, 2017, graphite on paper, 11 × 9 inches (27.94 × 22.86 cm). Courtesy of the artist.

EXERCISES

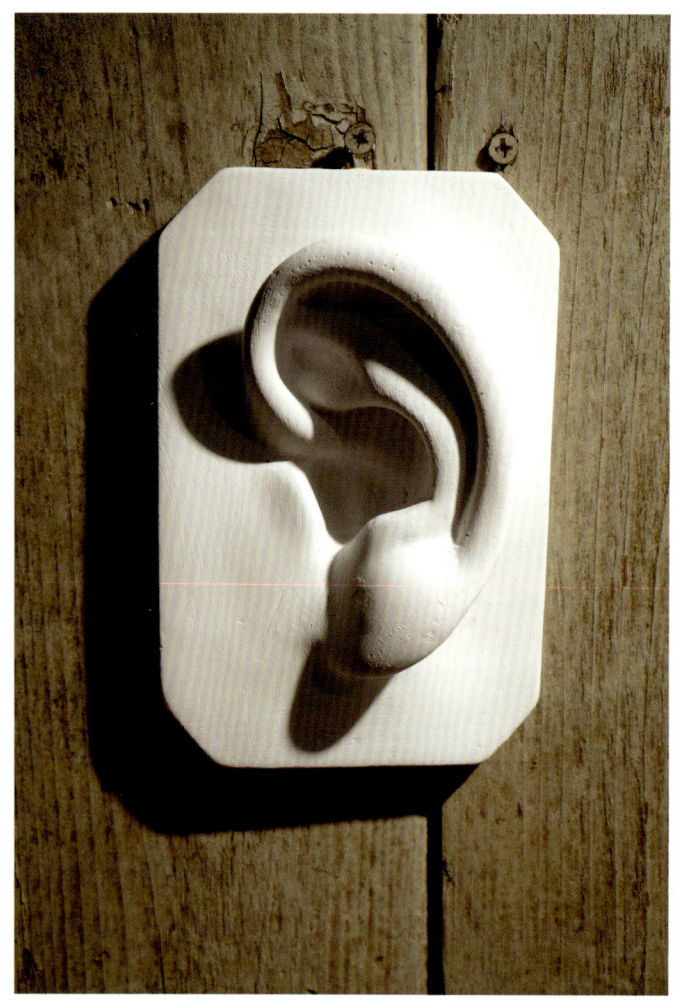

EXERCISE 2: DO A CAST DRAWING

Drawing plaster casts is a great way to cut your artistic teeth, and having a plaster cast on hand to study and work from is a great way to practice drawing in your studio. Plaster casts of sculptures can be purchased from several online retailers, including the Caproni Collection (capronicollection.com). Some of these casts are very expensive, but you can find one that's perfectly suitable for drawing for less than $200.

LEFT: This cast of an ear, which I used for my very first cast drawing, can be found in many art stores.

BELOW, LEFT: Irvin Rodriguez, *Equus,* 2010, graphite on paper, 22 × 22 inches (55.88 × 55.88 cm). Courtesy of the artist.

The first year of atelier study concludes with a difficult cast drawing. This was artist Irvin Rodriguez's final cast drawing.

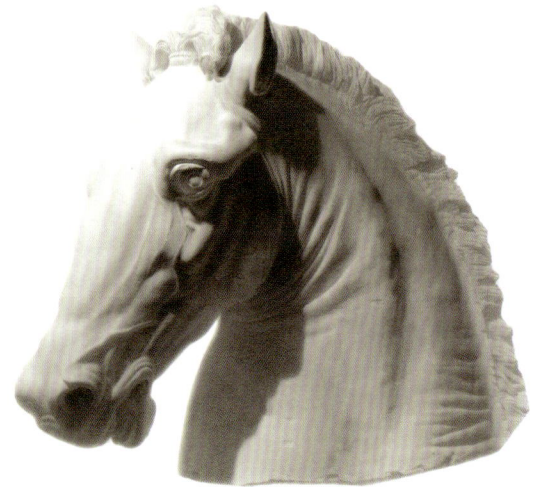

EXERCISE 3: DRAWING A FORESHORTENED OBJECT

One exercise that has helped me tremendously is to take a sculpture or any interestingly shaped three-dimensional object and lay it on its side, really foreshortening the planes, and then draw it from various angles. If you do such drawings whenever you can, you'll get very good at identifying and drawing foreshortened planes.

RIGHT: Because of foreshortening, my bust of George Washington looks very different when viewed from different angles.

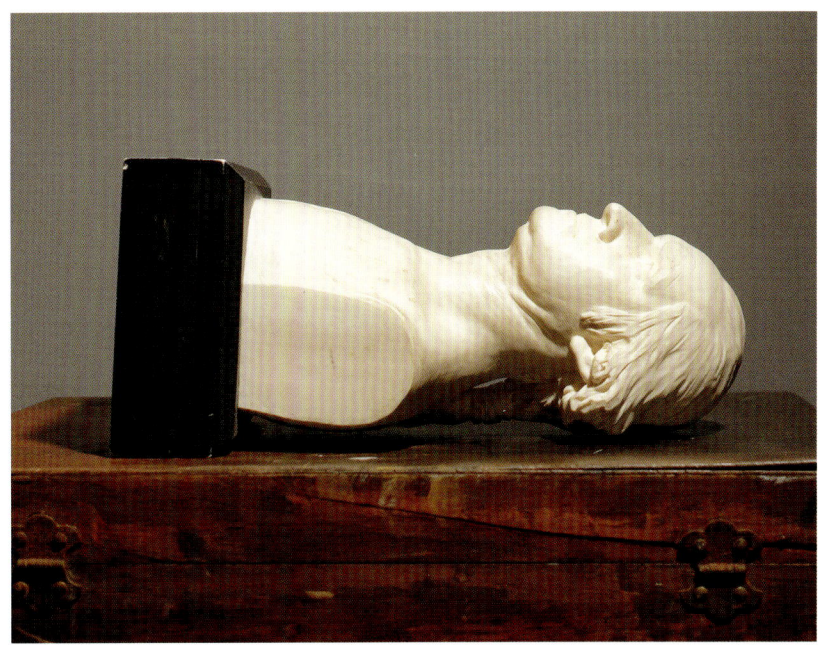

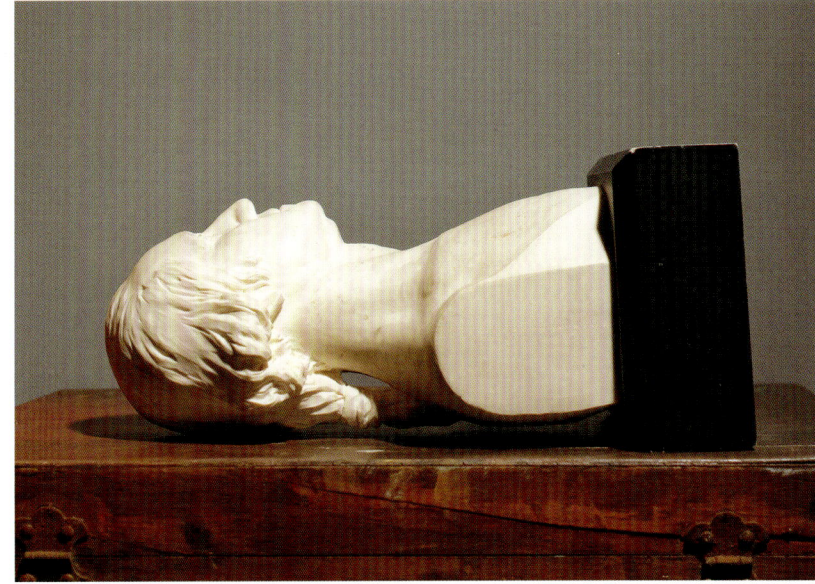

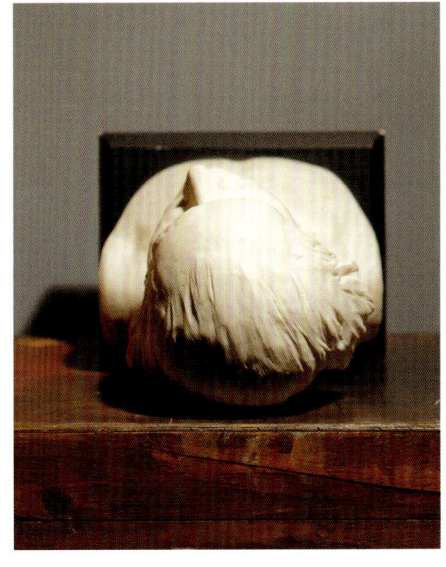

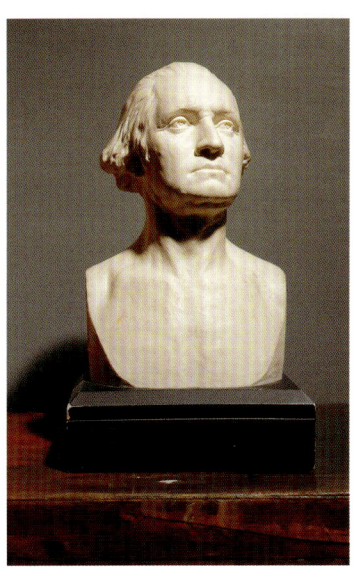

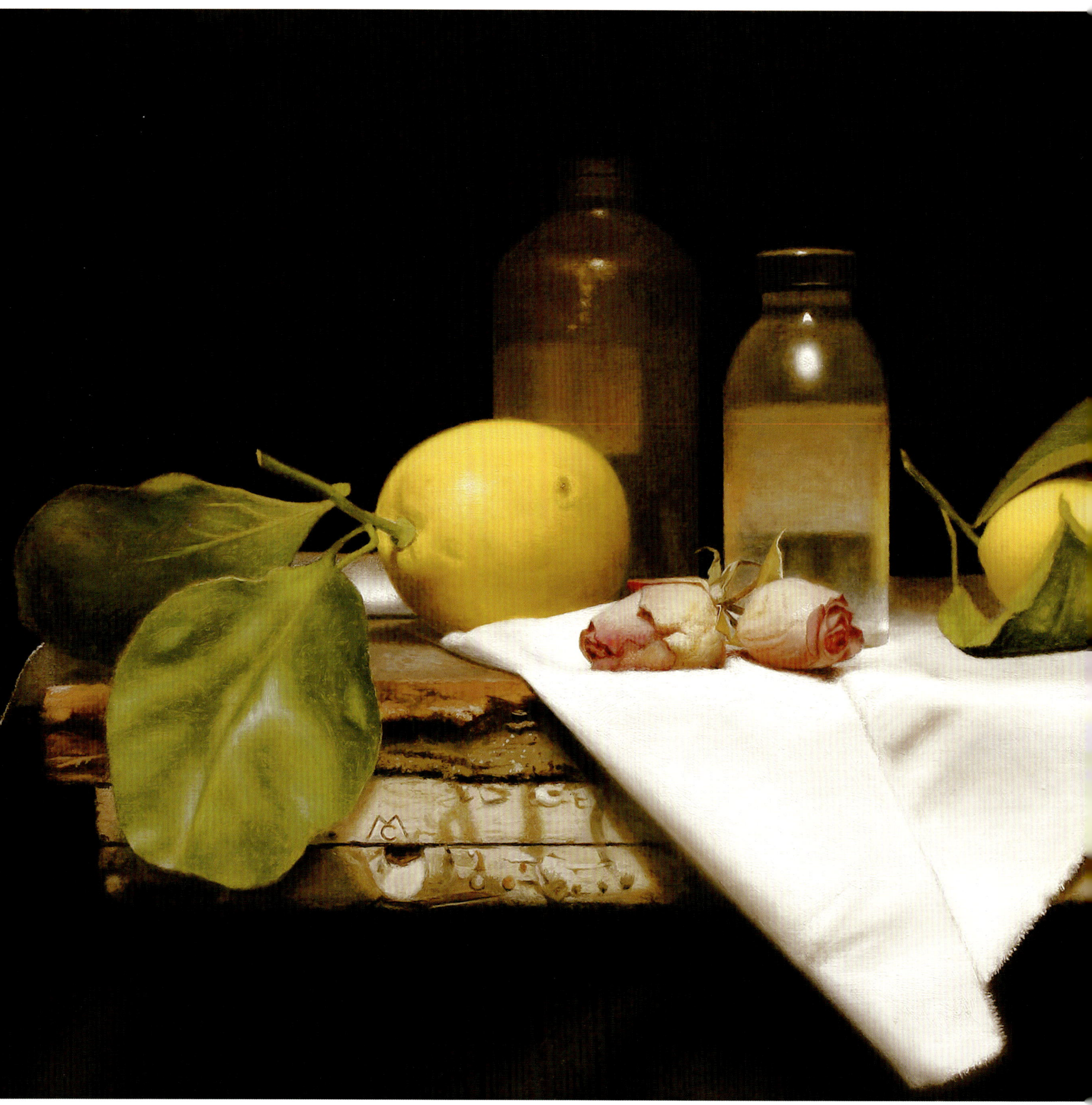

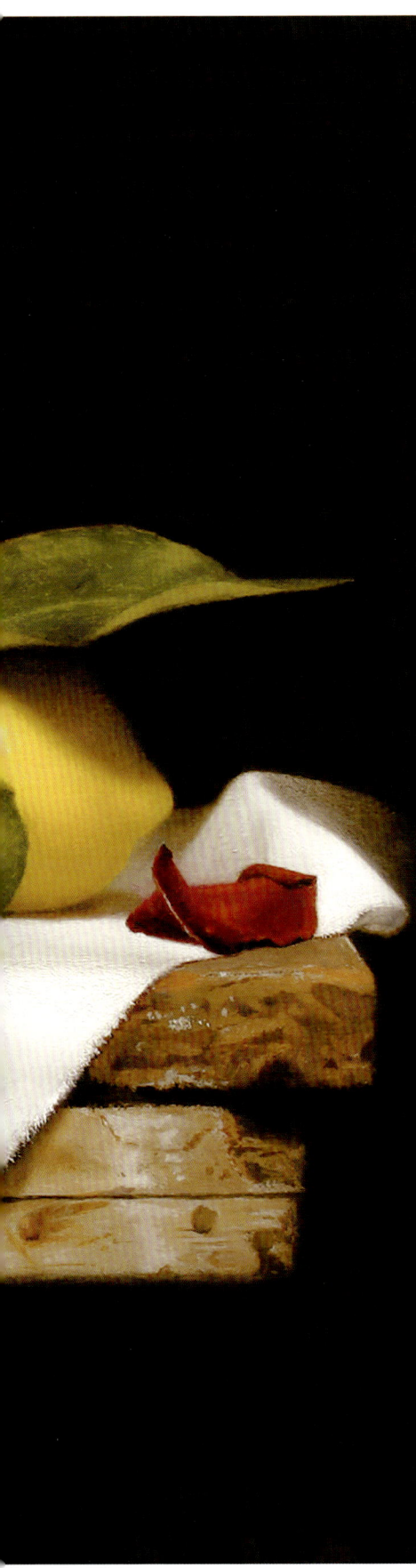

CHAPTER 6

COLOR: SCIENCE AND ART

In visual perception a color is almost never seen as it really is—
as it physically is. This fact makes color the most
relative medium in art.

JOSEF ALBERS

Color—its science, its expressiveness, its psychology—is one of the most fascinating aspects of creating art. Throughout the history of art, color was sometimes limited by the number of pigments available. But now we have access to many, many pigments, making a very wide range of colors available to artists. Not all artists use a full range of colors in their work, however. Often, artists enhance a mood or give a specific look to their paintings by limiting the colors they use.

This chapter covers the science of color, color terminology, and color schemes, as well as how to mix color and apply color to a painting.

LEFT: Carlos Madrid, *Composition with White Cloth and Bottles IV,* 2011, 13 × 17 inches (33.02 × 43.18 cm). Courtesy of the artist.

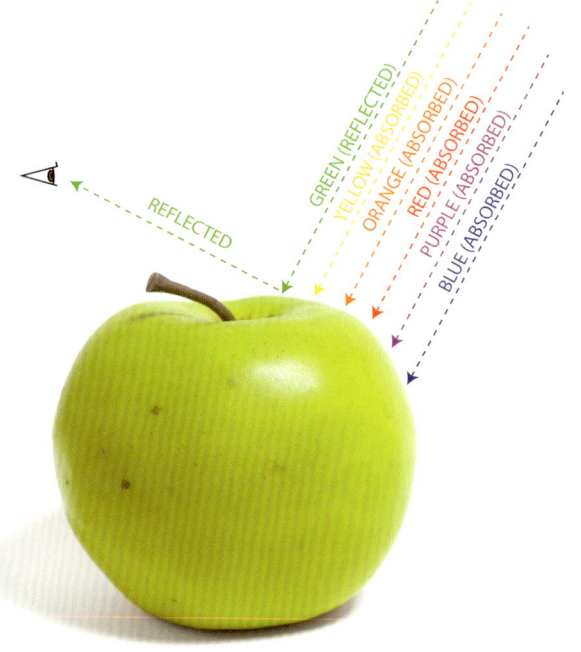

COLOR PERCEPTION

We perceive light through our optical system. Our eyes pick up light, which varies in wavelength, and transmit the information they receive to our brain. When we look at an object, we do not see the wavelengths of light that are absorbed into the object—just the wavelengths that are reflected. On a green apple, the green wavelength is reflected and that is what we observe as the apple's color.

The retina of an average human eye contains a set of photoreceptor cells called cones and rods. Cones enable us to see colors (red, green, and blue), and rods, which perceive only black and white, help us see in low light conditions. As light enters the eye, our photoreceptor cells send information from the retina to the brain. This is how we experience color.

ABOVE: When you see a green object, all the colors of the spectrum are being absorbed into the object's surface except green, which is reflected off the object.

RIGHT: Robert Liberace, *Tomatillos and Shallots,* 2010, oil on panel, 11 × 14 inches (27.94 × 35.56 cm). Courtesy of the artist.

In this painting by Robert Liberace, green and red light particles are reflecting off the objects, revealing their colors to the human eye.

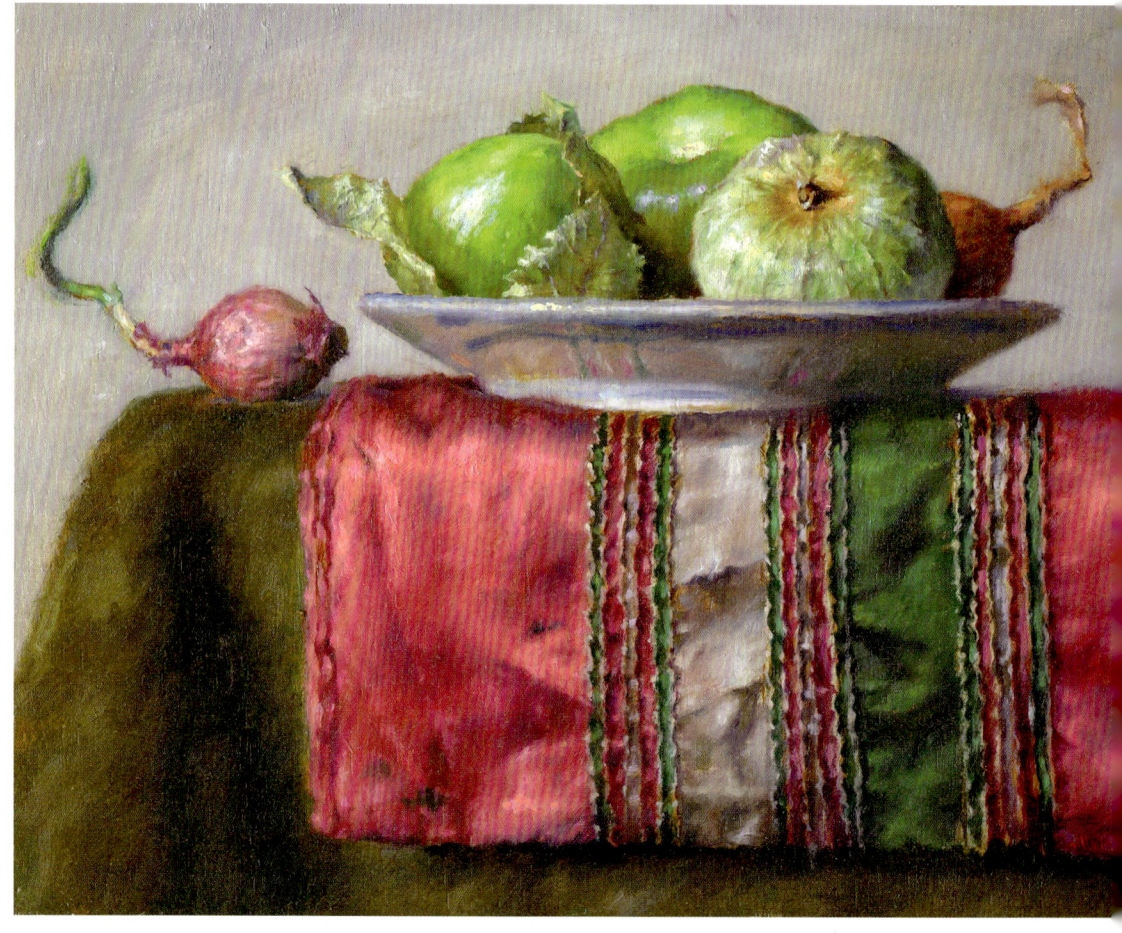

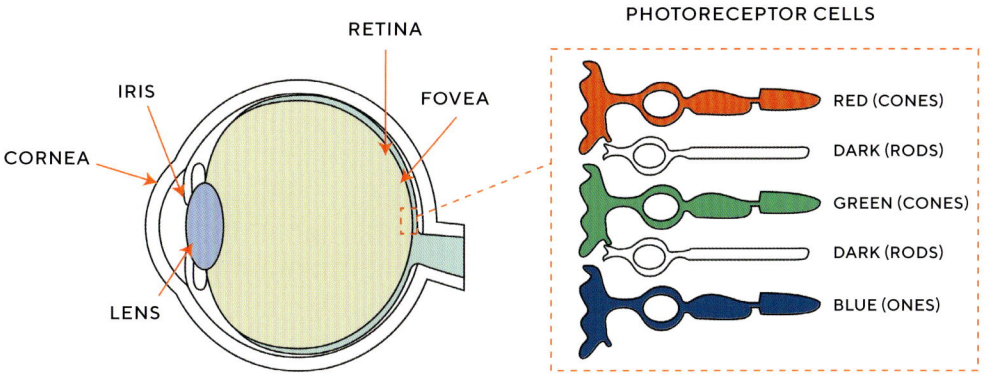

PHOTORECEPTOR CELLS

RETINA

IRIS

FOVEA

CORNEA

RED (CONES)

DARK (RODS)

GREEN (CONES)

DARK (RODS)

BLUE (ONES)

LENS

OBSERVED RANGE OF COLOR VERSUS PIGMENT RANGE

We see more colors in nature than we can see on a TV or computer screen. And we see more colors on a TV or computer screen than we can reproduce with pigments. Therefore, we cannot reproduce in paint the full range of color we see in nature or even on a screen. The range of values and colors achievable in paint is always a compression of what we can actually see. (That said, you can achieve a very wide range of color with pigments.)

ADDITIVE VERSUS SUBTRACTIVE COLOR

There are two common ways to create color images: additive color and subtractive color. Additive color is color that is emitted from a light source such as a computer monitor or TV screen. The three primary colors of additive color are red, green, and blue (RGB). When they are mixed together, they produce white light. Subtractive color is reflected color; its primaries are cyan, yellow, and magenta; when mixed, they produce black. (The CMYK system used in color printing adds black—symbolized by the letter *K*—to the three primaries.) When working with pigments, we're working with a subtractive color system.

ABOVE: Light enters the eye and stimulates the retina's rods and cones, which send messages to the brain.

BELOW: This diagram shows the hierarchy of how many colors we can see in nature or on a TV or computer screen compared to the range that can be achieved with pigment.

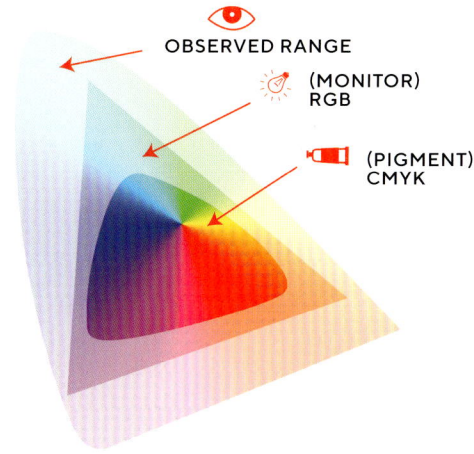

OBSERVED RANGE

(MONITOR)
RGB

(PIGMENT)
CMYK

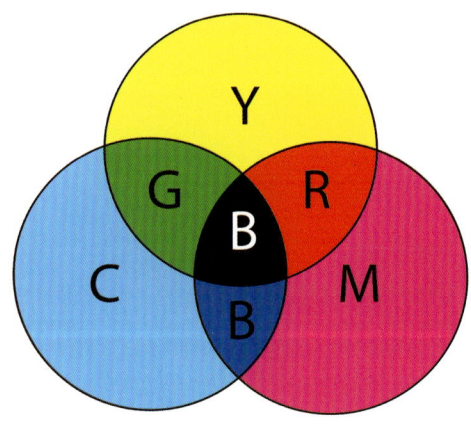

ADDITIVE COLORS
(LIGHT)

SUBTRACTIVE COLORS
(PIGMENTS)

TOP: Additive colors (light). A monitor (TV or computer screen) mixes red, green, and blue (RGB) to achieve the range of color.

ABOVE: Subtractive colors (pigments). In pigments, cyan, magenta, yellow, and black (CYMK) are mixed to achieve the range of color.

OPPOSITE, TOP TO BOTTOM: Todd M. Casey, *Lobster Study,* 2016, oil on panel, 6 × 8 inches (15.24 × 20.32 cm). Private collection.

John F. Peto (American, 1854–1907), *Still Life with Cake, Lemon, Strawberries, and Glass,* 1890, oil on canvas, 10 ⅛ × 13 ¹⁵⁄₁₆ inches (25.72 × 35.4 cm). The National Gallery of Art, Washington, D.C. Collection of Mr. and Mrs. Paul Mellon.

THE TWO-DIMENSIONAL COLOR WHEEL

All colors are the friends of their neighbors and the lovers of their opposites.
—MARC CHAGALL

The familiar color wheel takes the form of a two-dimensional circle. This color wheel can be used in painting to develop color schemes that limit the number of colors in a painting in order to build color unity. This unity can affect how the painting is perceived by viewers—the mood or feeling it evokes.

Primary Colors

The primary colors are the three colors that cannot be made by mixing other colors together. Traditionally, blue, yellow, and red have been considered the three primary colors, but a modern approach uses cyan, yellow, and magenta. The two still life paintings opposite both combine the three primary colors in their compositions—vividly in my *Lobster Study* and more subtly in John F. Peto's *Still Life with Cake, Lemon, Strawberries, and Glass.*

TIP

Keep your color mixtures simple. Try never to use more than three tube colors when mixing a color. Two is better: because there are only two variables, it's relatively easy to mix the same color again. When you mix three, it gets a bit tougher to arrive at the exact same color mixture. Taking notes about the amounts of tube colors you use can help.

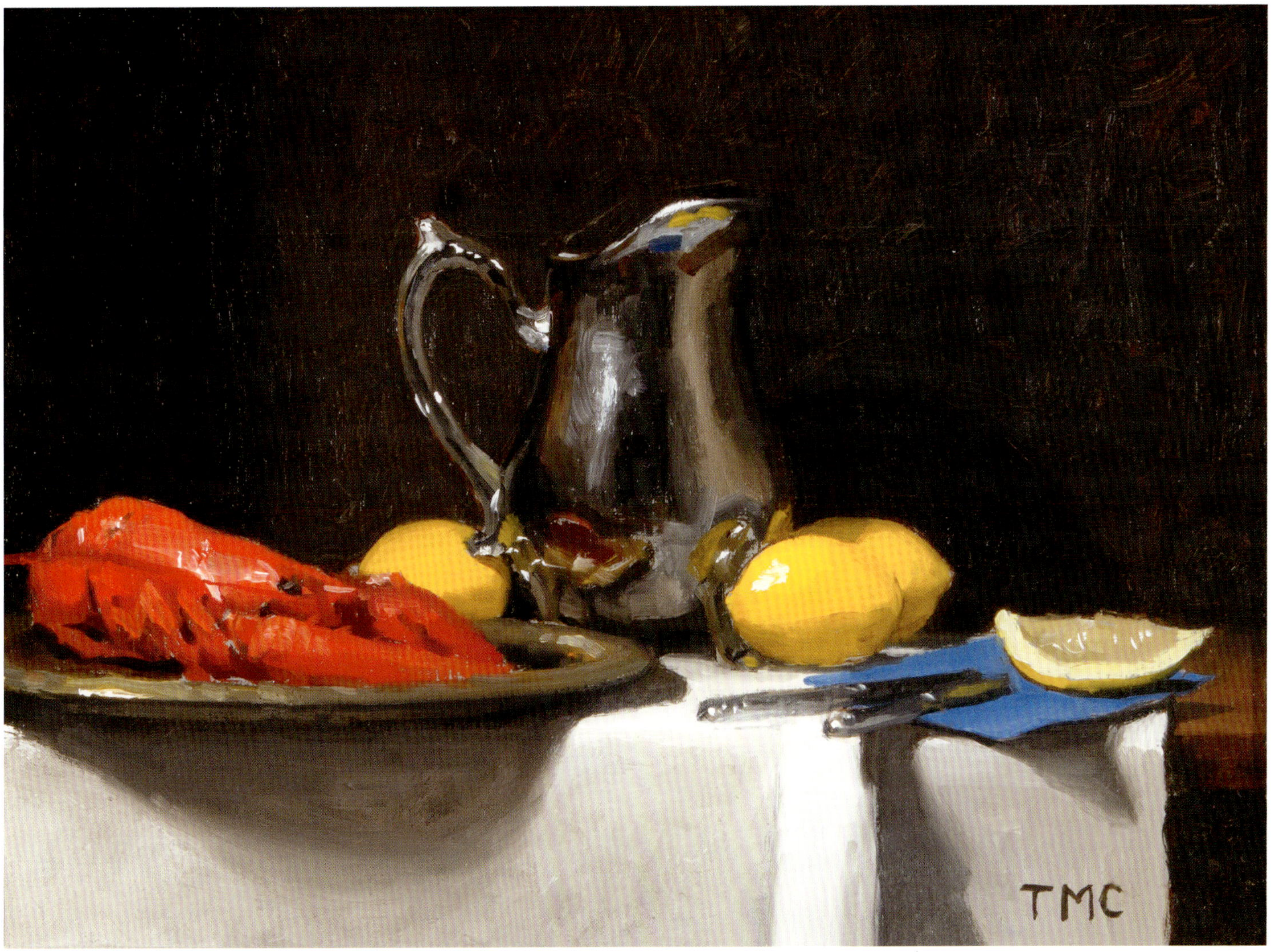
TMC

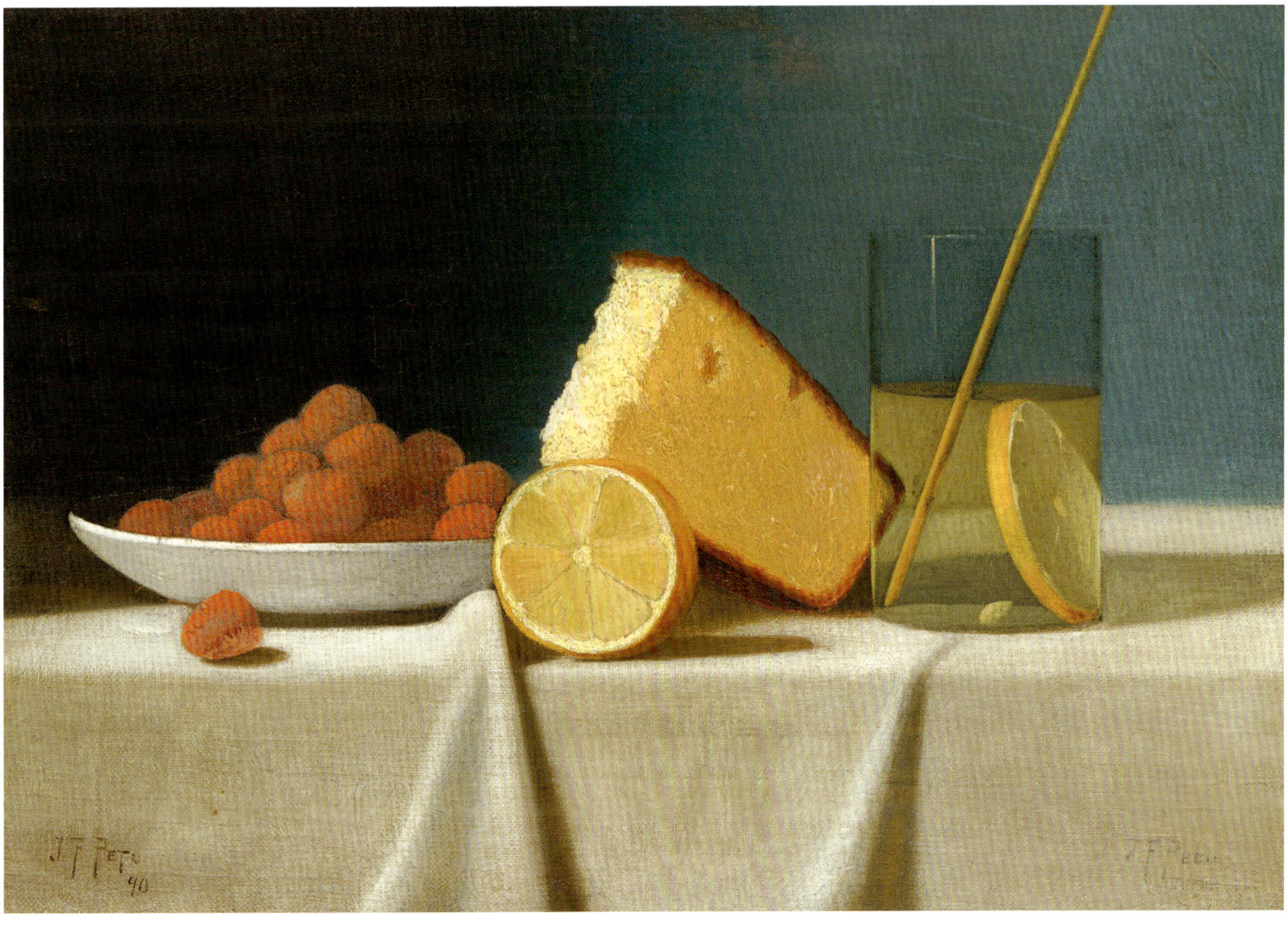

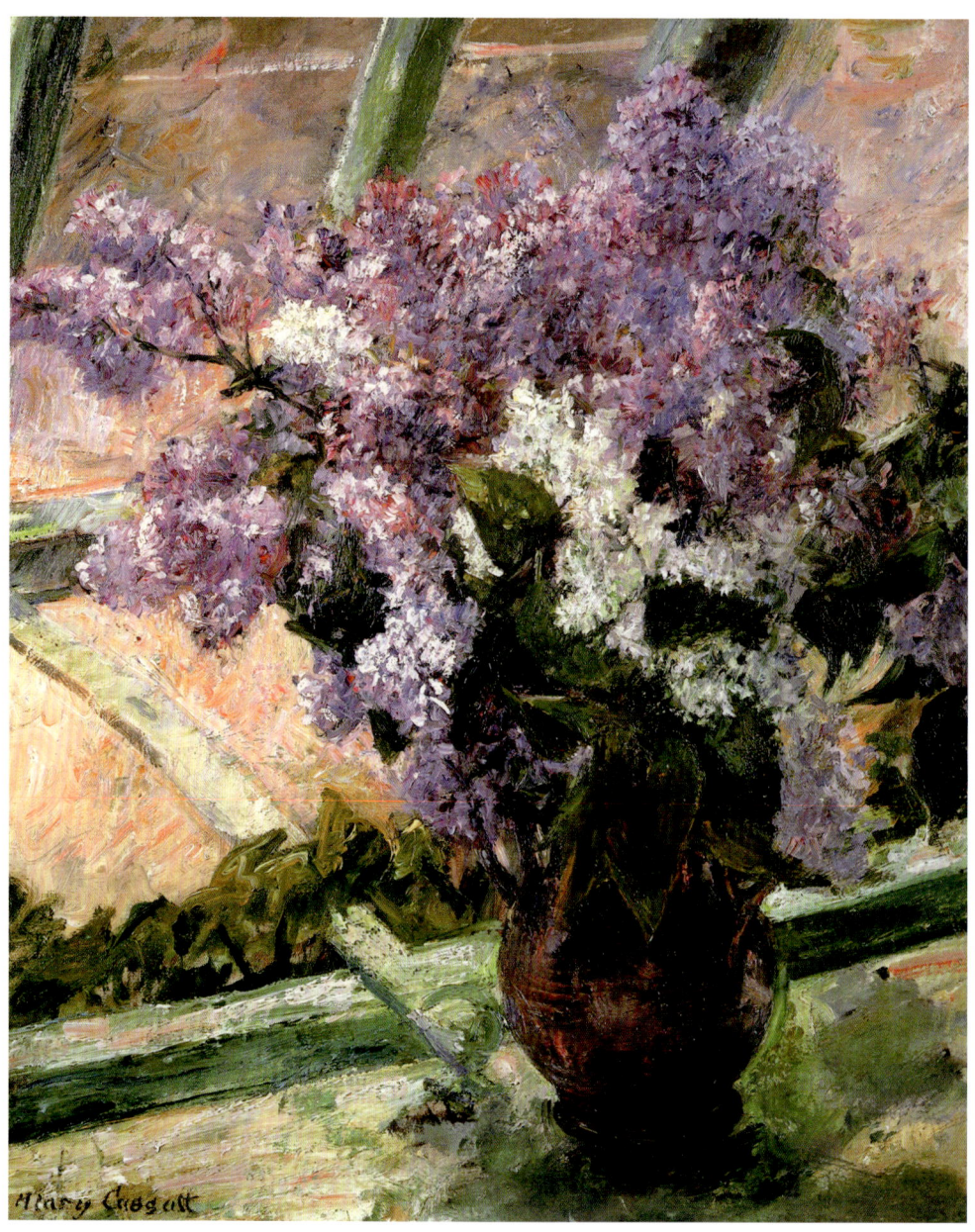

Two secondary colors—violet and green—dominate this still life by the American Impressionist Mary Cassatt.

Secondary Colors

Each of the three secondary colors is achieved by mixing two primaries together. The secondary colors are green (yellow + blue), violet (blue + red), and orange (red + yellow).

Y	+	B	=	G
B	+	R	=	V
R	+	Y	=	O

Each secondary color is a mixture of two primaries.

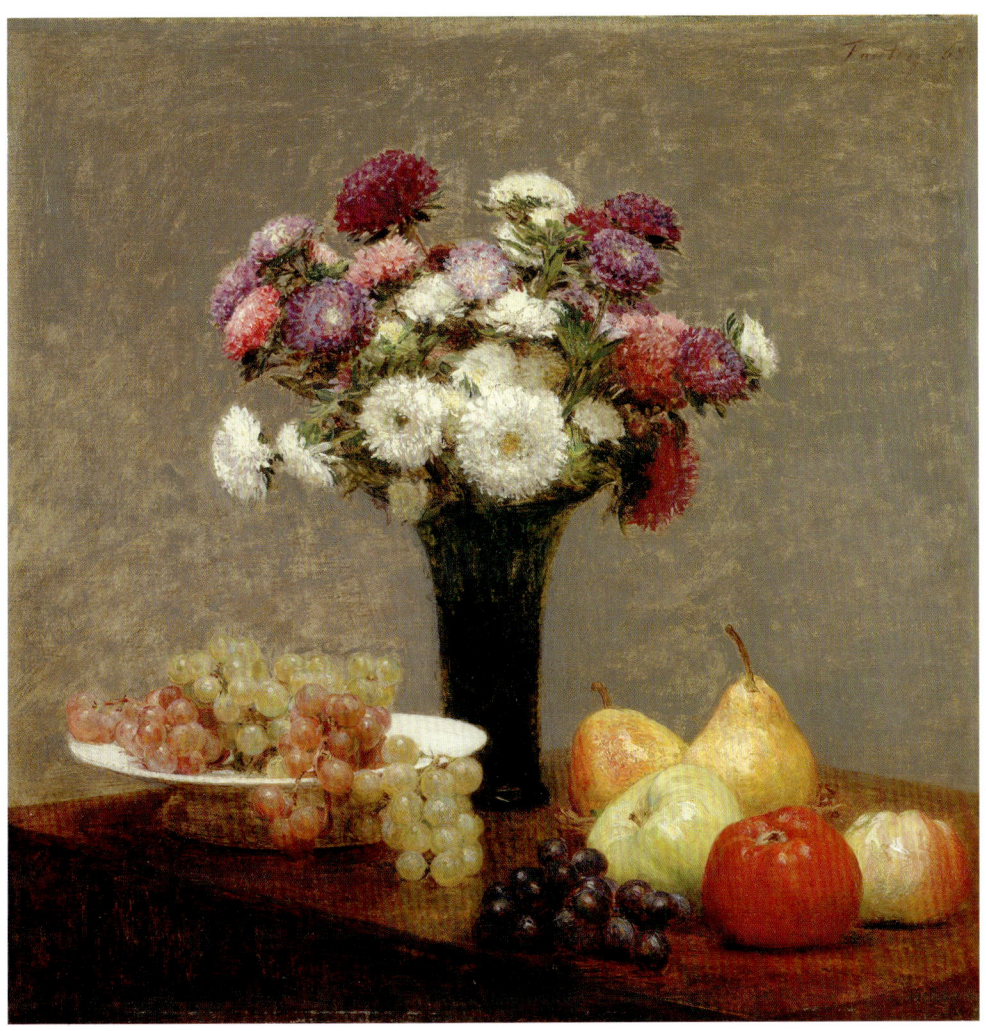

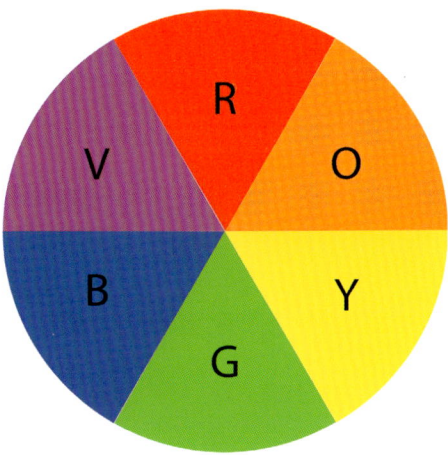

The basic color wheel is composed of the three primary and three secondary colors.

"ROYGBV"

When you put the primary and secondary colors together you get the basic color wheel. The acronym ROYGBV—pronounced "Roy G. Biv"—can help you remember the order of the colors on the wheel: red, orange, yellow, green, blue, and violet (purple).

This masterpiece of still life painting by Henri Fantin-Latour subtly incorporates all the primaries and secondaries.

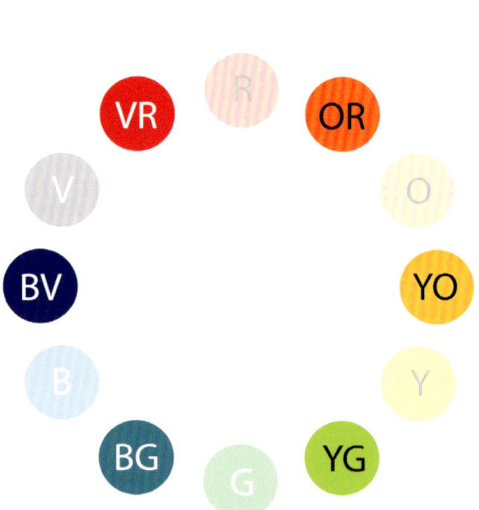

The six tertiary colors are orange-red (OR), yellow-orange (YO), yellow-green (YG), blue-green (BG), blue-violet (BV), and violet-red (VR).

RIGHT: Sarah Lamb, *Confit Pots and Pomegranates,* 2018, oil on panel, 25 × 37 inches (63.5 × 94 cm). Courtesy of the artist.

This painting by Sarah Lamb uses a tertiary color scheme balanced with some red-orange accents.

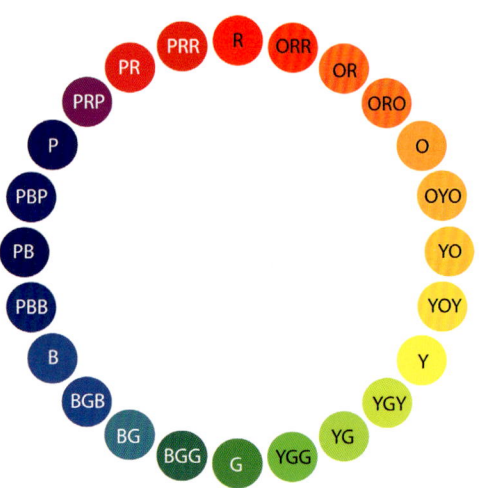

The 24-step color wheel

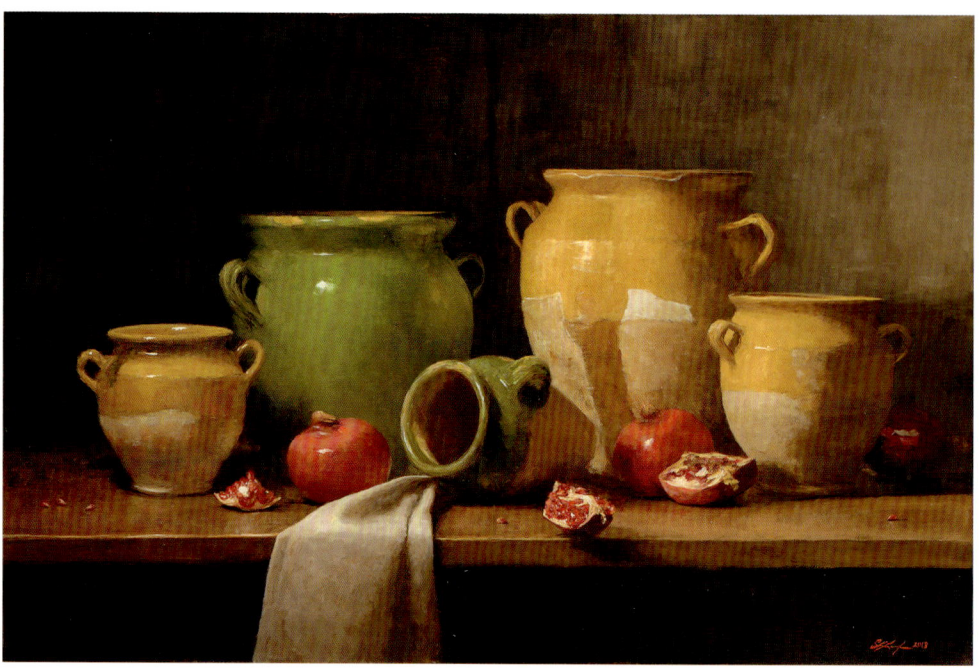

Tertiary Colors

Breaking down the color wheel even further, you reach the tertiary colors—the "in-betweens" linking the primaries and secondaries. Each tertiary color is referred to as a combination of the two colors on either side. Thus orange-red (OR) lies between red and orange.

The 24-Step Color Wheel

If we break down the wheel even further, putting one more color between every two tertiary colors, we have a 24-step color wheel. We name each new color according to the two colors on either side of it, so the color between red and orange-red is orange-red-red (ORR). Working with a 24-step wheel gives you the variety you need to get a wide range of colors and mixtures.

COLOR TEMPERATURE

Colors can be defined as warm or cool. If we split the wheel from yellow-green to violet-red, we separate the warm from the cool colors, as shown in the diagram on page 202. I tend to push my colors toward the warmer side, because we psychologically associate warmth with life and cold with death. Warm colors also come forward in space, while cool colors recede. In nature, because of moisture in the air, faraway objects tend to appear blue (i.e., cooler)—a phenomenon known as atmospheric perspective.

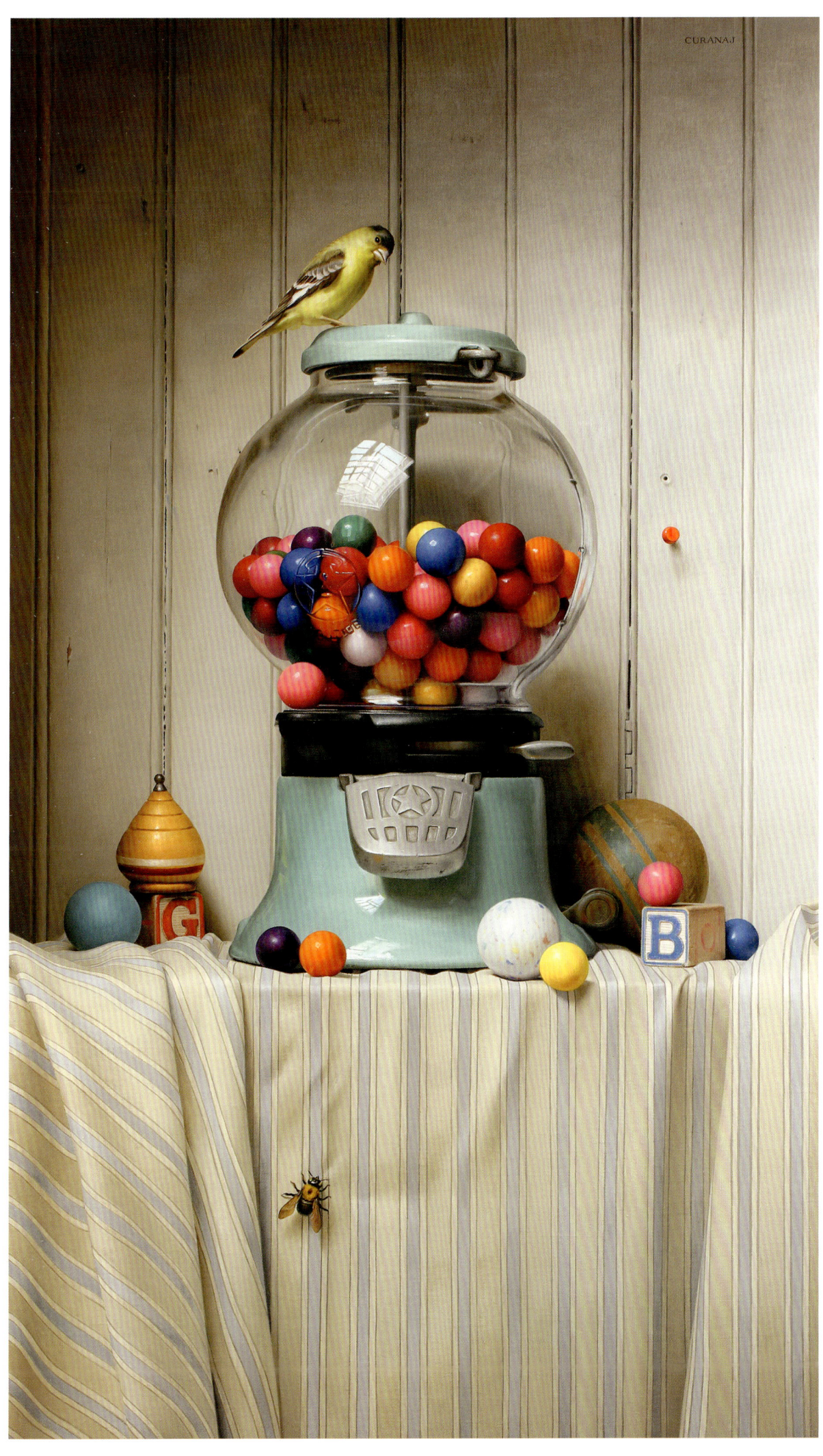

Tony Curanaj, *The Gumball Incident,* 2015, oil on canvas, 28 × 15 ½ inches (71.12 × 39.37 cm). Courtesy of the artist.

In his painting *The Gumball Incident,* Tony Curanaj uses nearly the whole color wheel but balances all the color with a light neutral background.

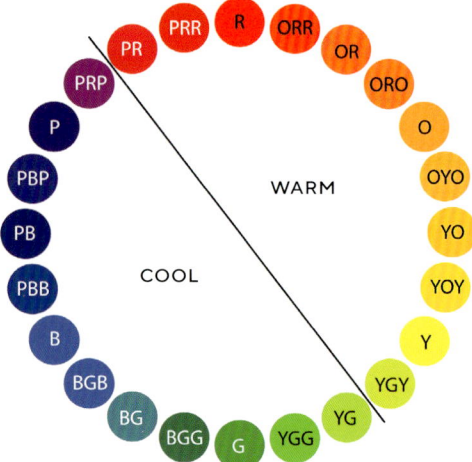

The 24-step color wheel divided into cool and warm colors

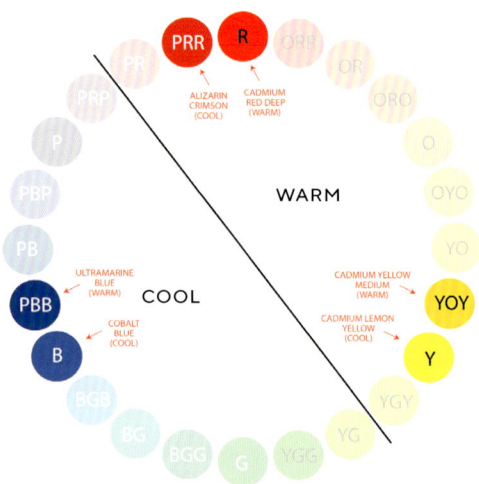

Colors are warmer or cooler in relation to one another. For example, alizarin crimson and cadmium red deep sit next to each other on the color wheel, but alizarin crimson is the cooler red because it is nearer the warm-cool dividing line.

ABOVE, RIGHT: Édouard Vuillard (French, 1868–1940), *Flowers,* 1906, oil on canvas, 21½ × 18 inches (54.61 × 45.72 cm). Indianapolis Museum of Art at Newfields. James E. Roberts Fund.

Édouard Vuillard's *Flowers* nicely balances warm and cool. It's good to balance the two temperatures, but one should dominate. Here, warm dominates the color scheme, which has blue accents.

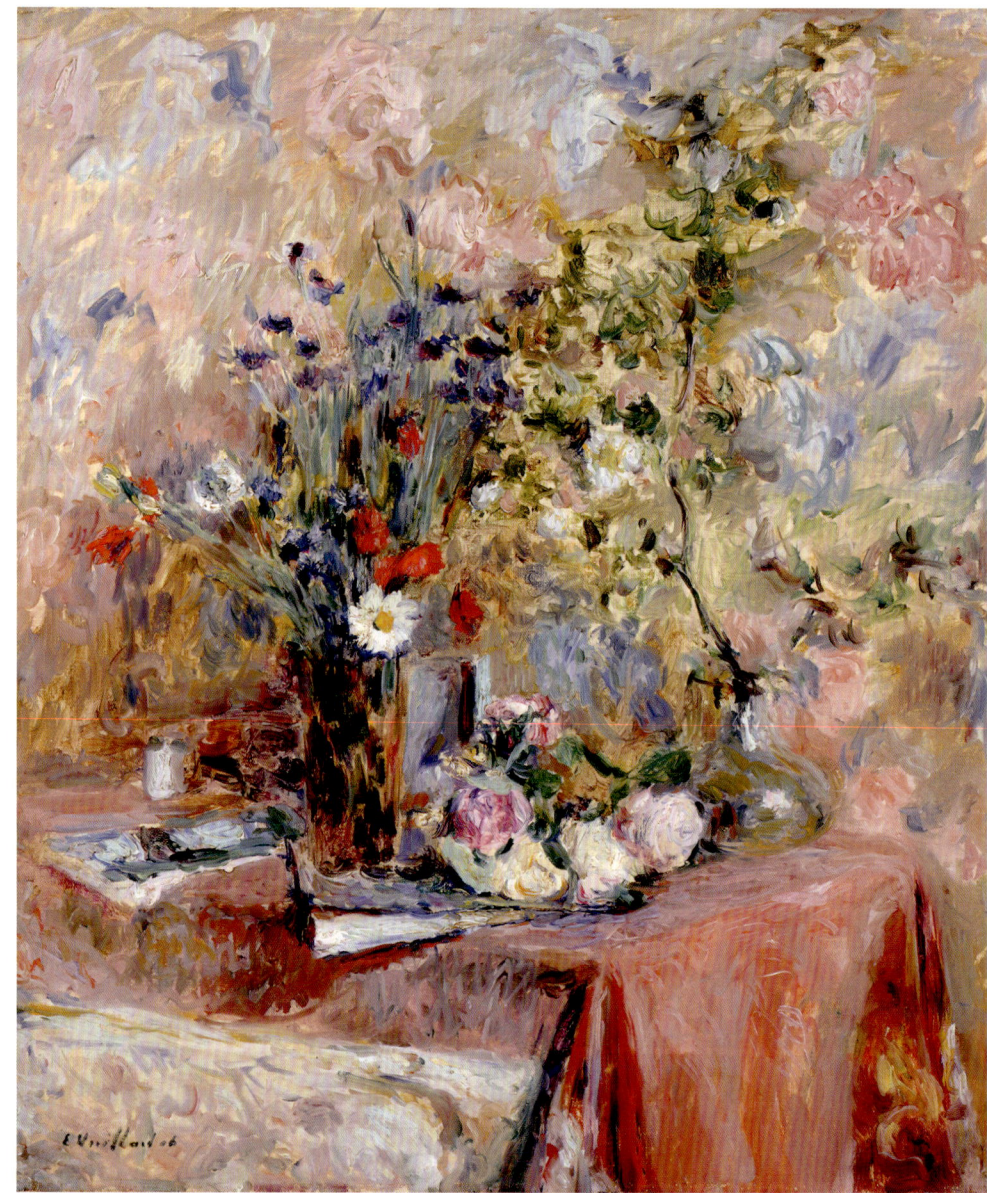

Color temperature, however, is a relative concept—colors are warm or cool in relation to and in contrast with one another. The difference depends on how close or far away the respective colors are from the temperature line drawn on the wheel. Of two colors, the color closer to the line would be considered the warmer or cooler of the two, as the diagram at left shows.

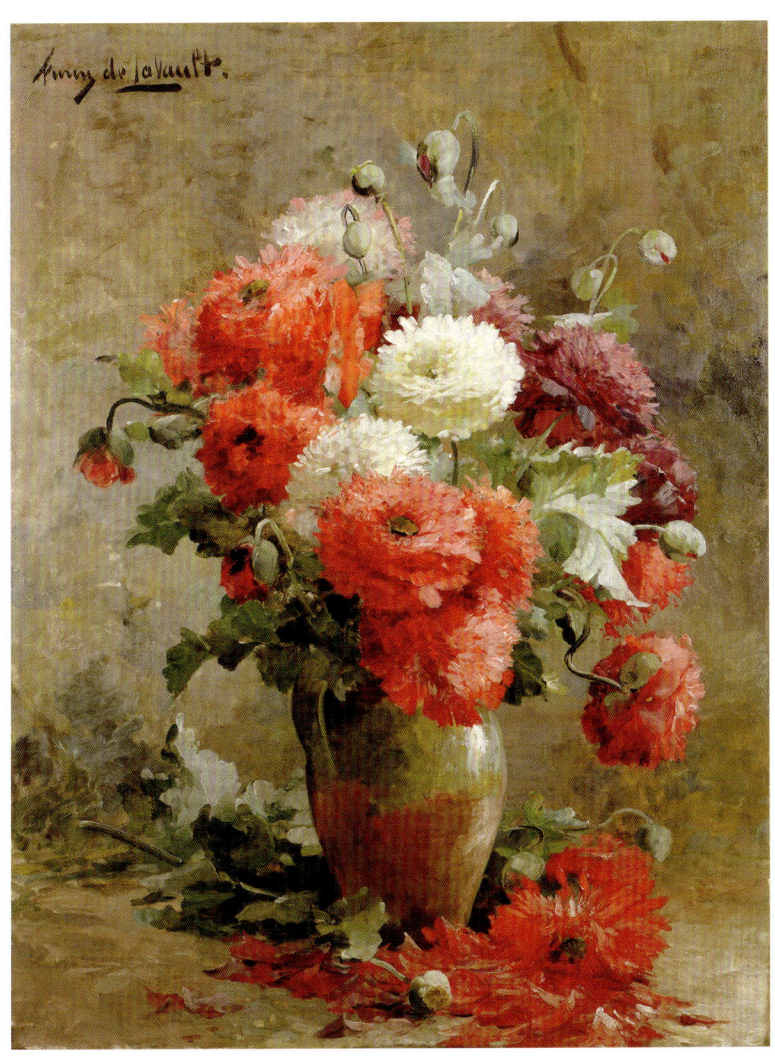

LEFT: Albert-Tibule Furcy de Lavault (French, 1847–1915) *Still Life with Peonies,* n.d., oil on canvas, 39 × 29 inches (99.06 × 73.66 cm). Courtesy of Rehs Galleries, New York.

In Albert-Tibule Furcy de Lavault's painting *Still Life with Peonies*, the three-dimensionality of the bouquet is enhanced by the artist's use of color temperature. The warmer red flowers at the front of the arrangement come forward in space, while the cooler violet-red flowers at the back recede.

THE COLOR OF A HIGHLIGHT

As I noted in the chapter on light and shadow, highlights are glare resulting from light hitting a surface. If you study highlights, you'll notice that they aren't actually pure white. The color of a highlight is determined by the color temperature of the light source and by the local color. Highlights almost always have an inner and an outer portion, or ring. The inner ring is the color of the light source, while the outer ring visually intermixes the color of the light source and the local color.

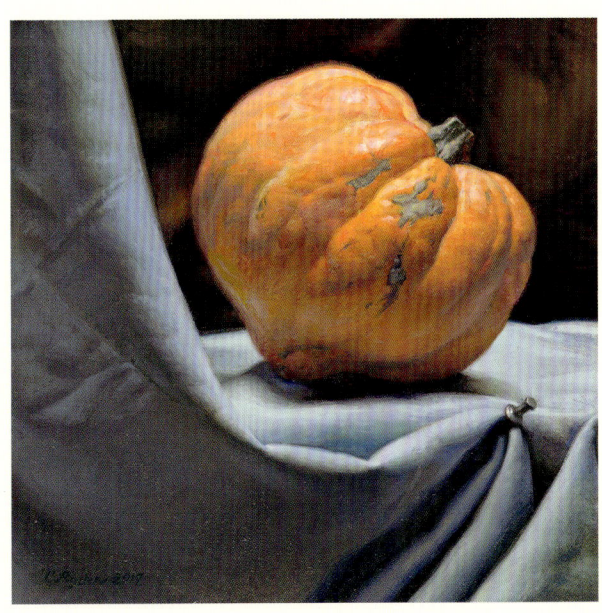

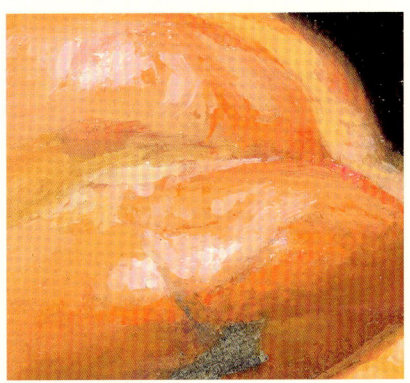

ABOVE: Celeste Ryder, *Swiftly Passing,* 2017, oil on panel, 8 × 8 inches (20.32 × 20.32 cm). Collection of Dr. Philip Walls of Lutherville, MD.

In the detail (right) of Celeste Ryder's painting *Swiftly Passing*, you can clearly see the inner and outer portions of the highlights.

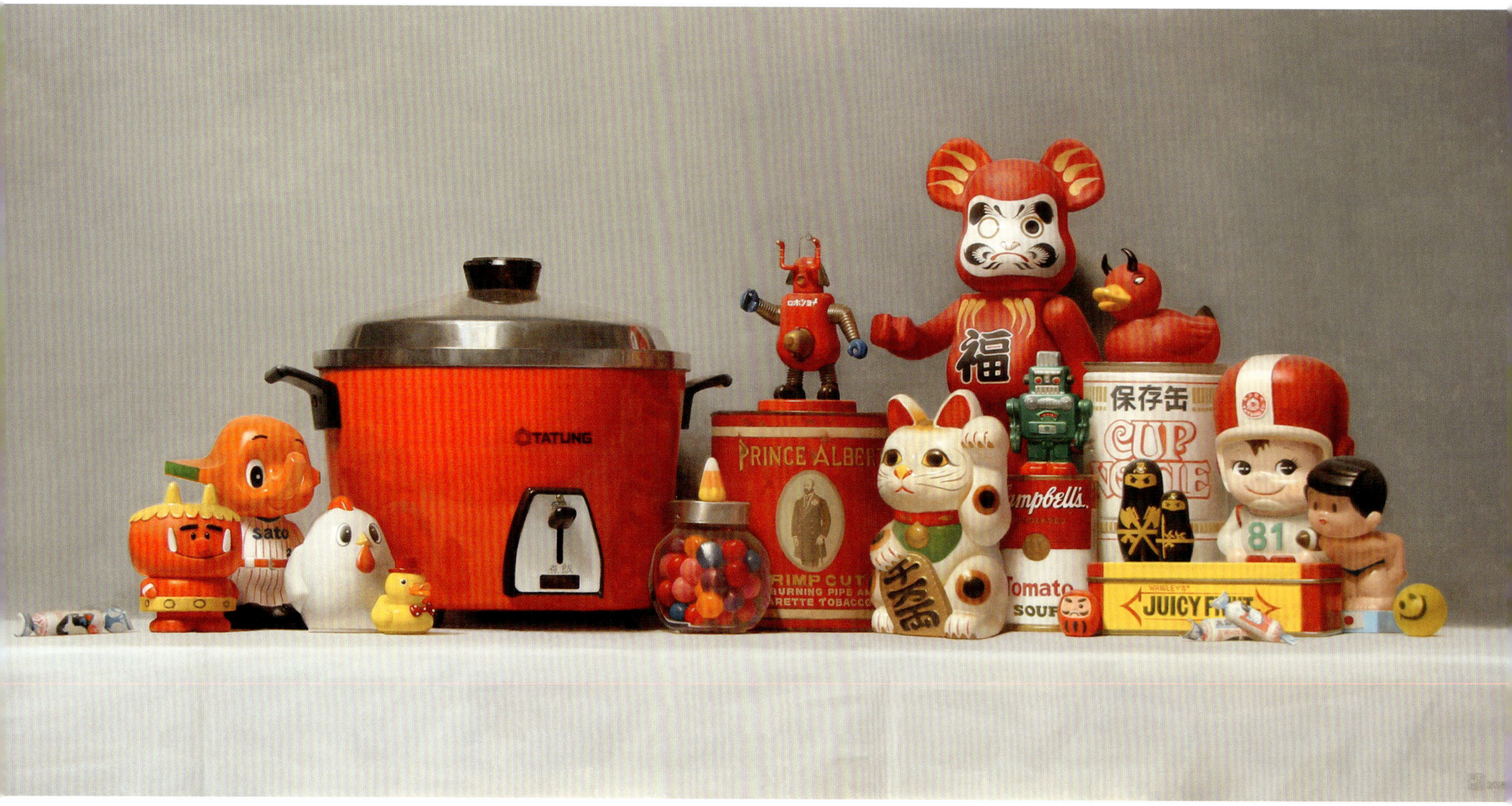

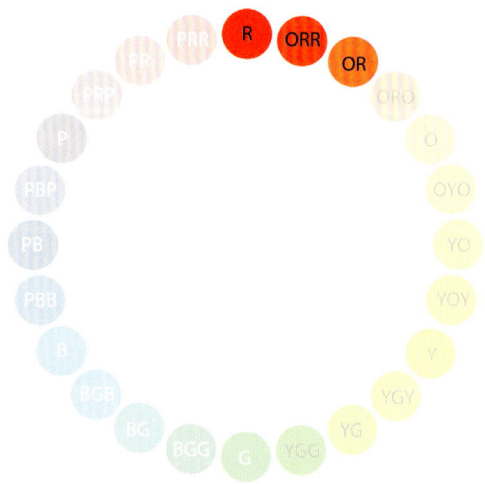

ANALOGOUS COLORS

Colors that are adjacent to one another on the color wheel are referred to as analogous colors. For instance, red, orange-red-red, and orange-red are next to each other and therefore analogous. Using analogous colors can add a cohesive look to a composition because they group as a color family.

TOP: Samuel Hung, *Family of Trinkets #3,* 2017, oil on panel, 22 ½ × 48 inches (57.15 × 121.92 cm). Courtesy of the artist.

Analogous colors—reds, oranges, and yellows—dominate and harmonize this composition by Samuel Hung.

Analogous colors are any sequence of colors adjacent to each other on the color wheel—in this case, red, orange-red-red, and orange-red.

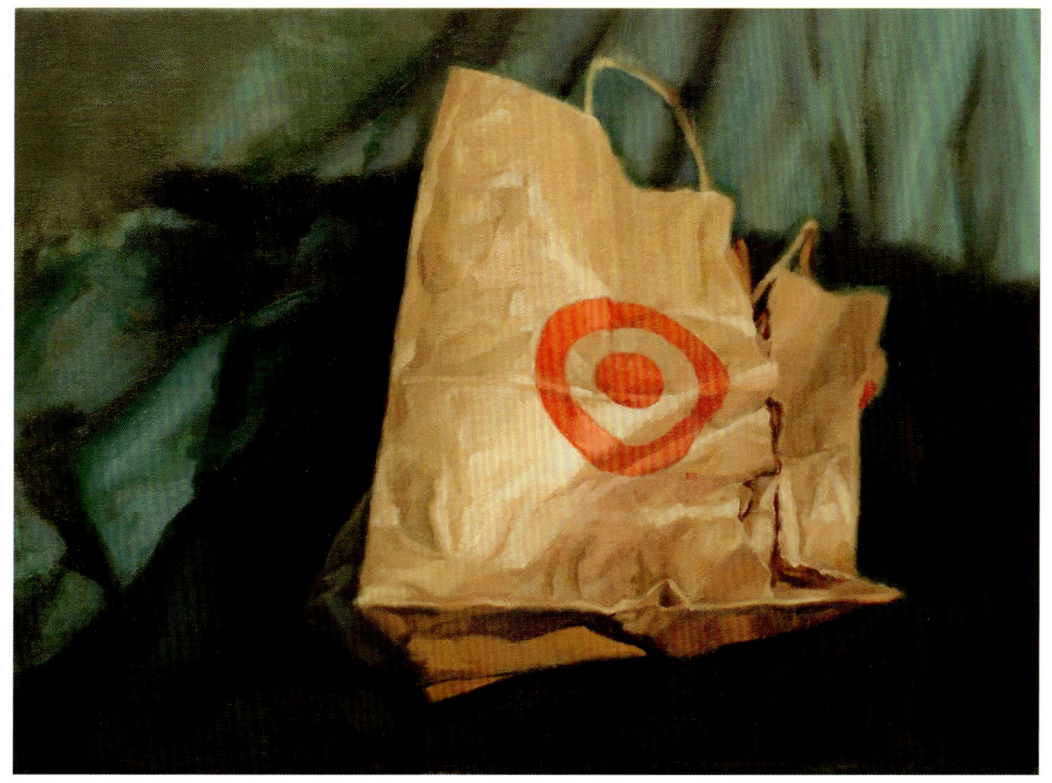

COLOR SCHEMES WITH COMPLEMENTARY COLORS

Color scheme is a term for the selection of colors an artist chooses for a painting. You can choose to use only a certain number of colors for any number of reasons, from enhancing a mood to creating an individual style. Using a color scheme can be a good way to balance a painting so one color does not become too dominant. One common color scheme involves the use of complementary colors—colors that are opposite one another on the color wheel. (You can also use the neighbor of a direct complement.)

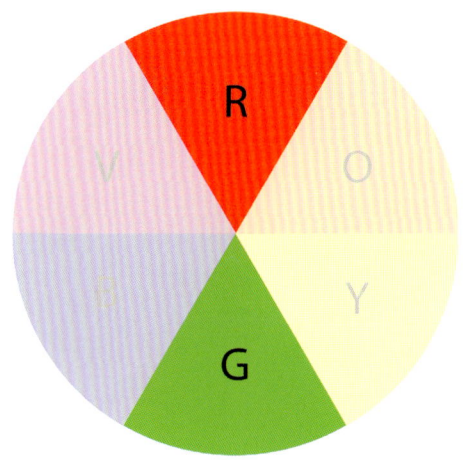

Red and green are complementary colors, meaning they are opposite each other on the color wheel.

ABOVE, LEFT: Kevin M. Wueste, *Paper Flowers 1,* 2016, oil on linen, 10 × 12 inches (25.4 × 30.48 cm). Courtesy of the artist.

In Kevin M. Wueste's *Paper Flowers 1,* the green of the background is offset by the complementary red of the Target bag's logo.

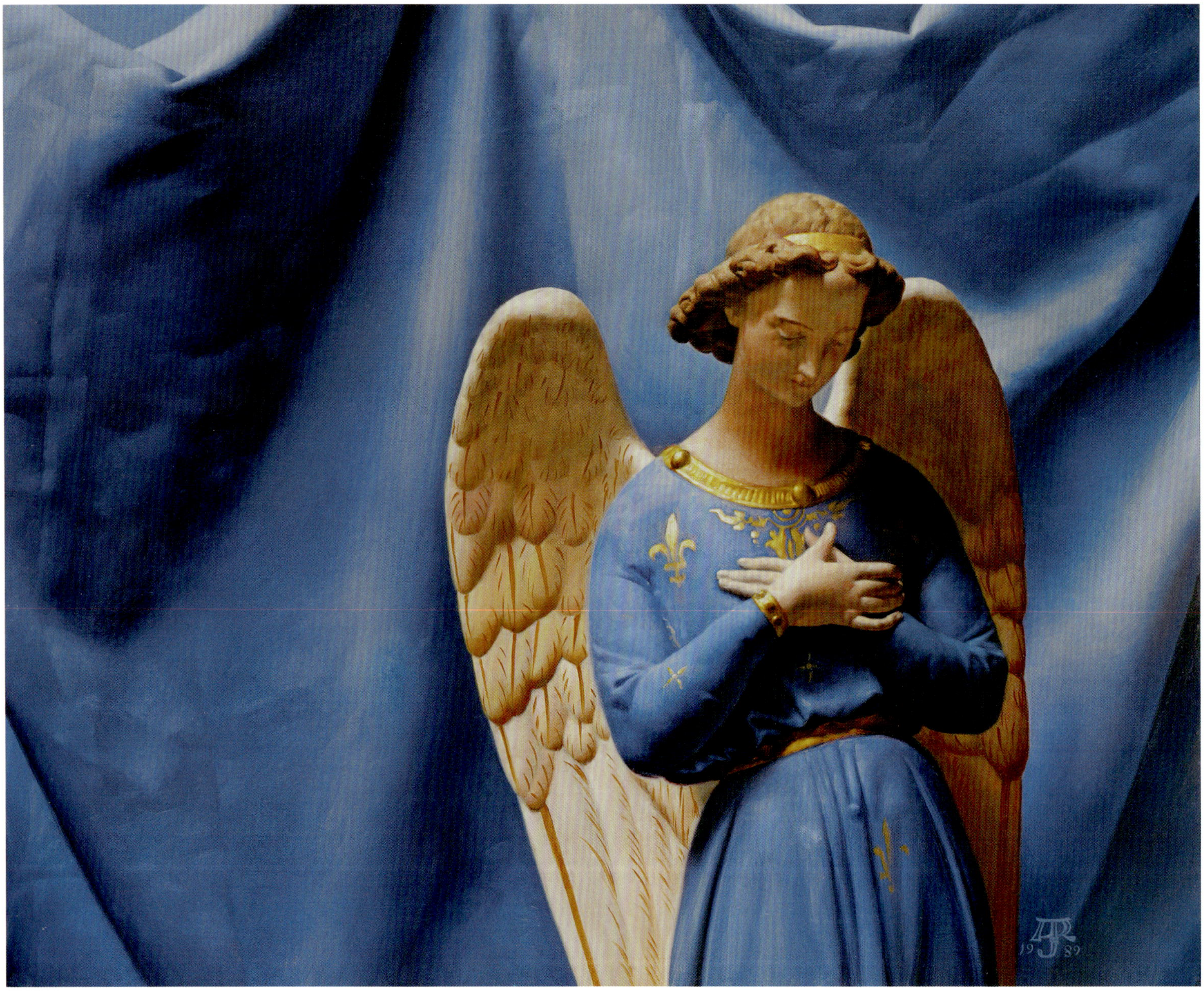

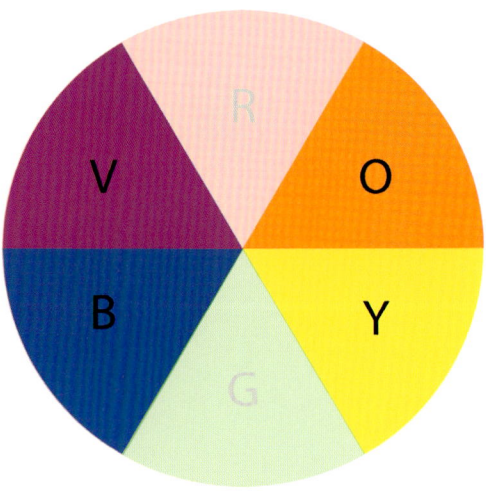

ABOVE: Anthony Ryder, *Blue Angel,* 1989, oil on linen, 17 × 20 inches (43.18 × 50.8 cm). Courtesy of the artist.

Anthony Ryder's *Blue Angel* contrasts a violet–blue color with an orange-yellow to create a complementary color scheme.

Violet and yellow are also complementary, as are blue and orange.

THE THREE DIMENSIONS OF COLOR

Over the centuries, lots of scientists and philosophers have weighed in on the topic of color, and color has been redefined many times along the way. Sir Isaac Newton's prism experiments of 1672 led to the understanding that the colors of the visible spectrum are the constituents of pure white light. Then, in the early nineteenth century, the work of German Romantic painter Philipp Otto Runge led to the insight that color can be better understood as a three-dimensional sphere than as a two-dimensional wheel.

Still later, in 1905, an American painter and art teacher named Albert Munsell devised a three-dimensional color system based on light rather than pigment. The Munsell Color System is widely used throughout the art world as the basis for defining colors. Gamblin Artists Colors developed a similar 3-D system, called the Multidimensional Approach to Color Mixing. I use a combination of these two systems when painting. (Gamblin's system is beautifully explained in a video on the Gamblin website; go to gamblincolors.com/navigating-color-space/.)

The three dimensions of color are hue, value, and chroma. Bringing them together forms a three-dimensional color space instead of a two-dimensional color wheel.

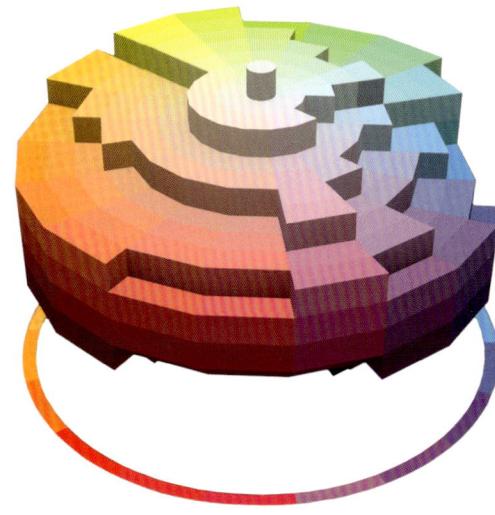

This 3-D model of color space, based on the Munsell Color System, shows the three dimensions of color: hues change as we circle around the model; values change as we go from top (lightest value) to bottom (darkest value); and chroma grows more intense as we proceed from the center to the periphery. Courtesy of Douglas Flynt.

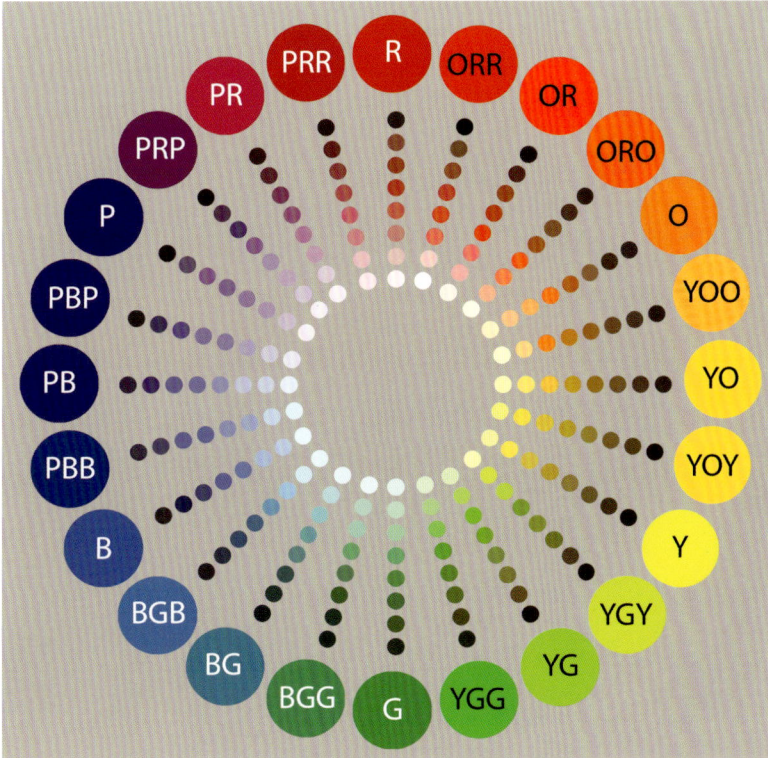

LEFT: Color values are plotted on this two-dimensional color wheel. For each hue, we see the range from the lightest value to the darkest.

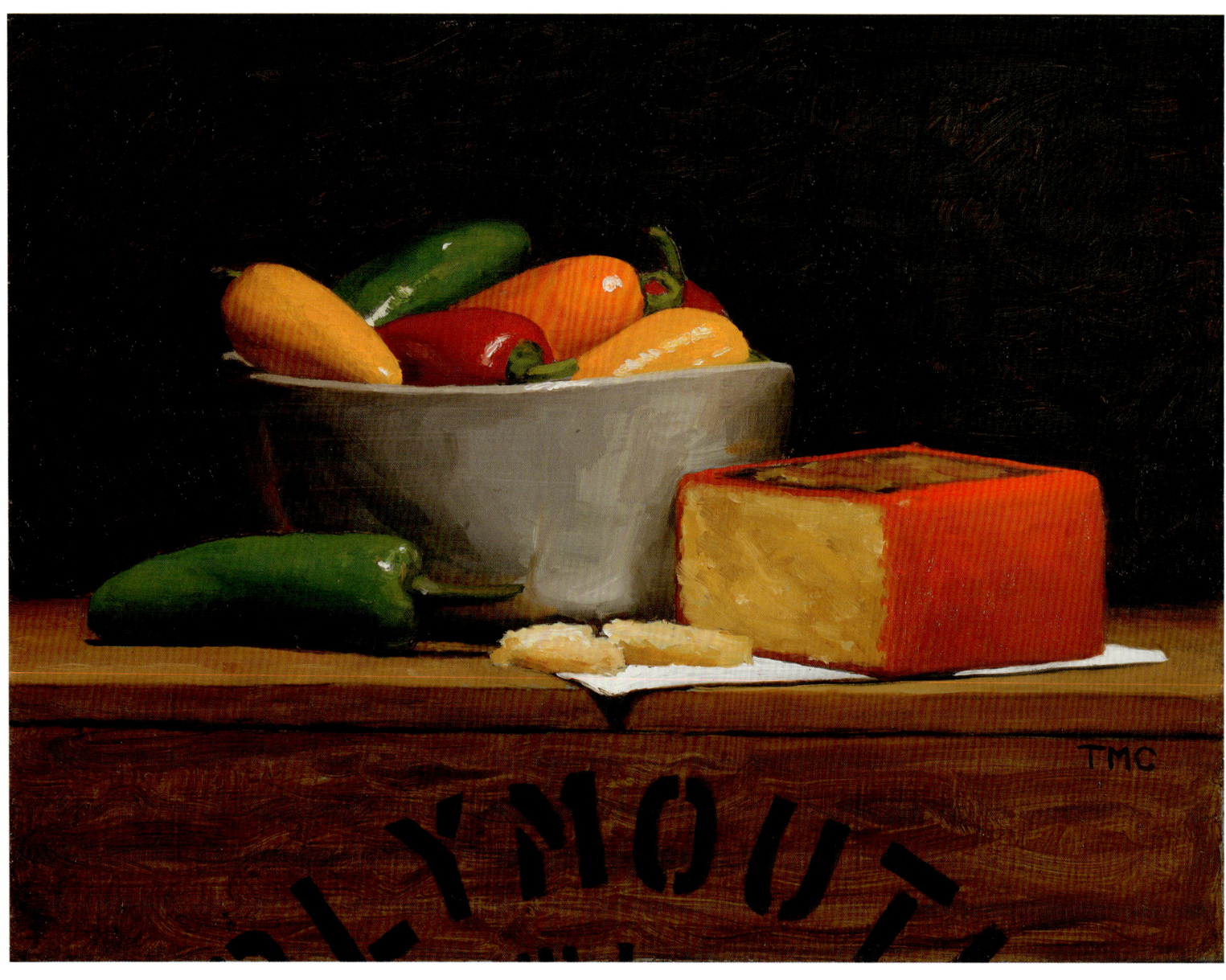

Hue

Something's *hue* is its basic color. The three primary and three secondary colors (red, yellow, blue, orange, green, violet) define the basic hues.

Value

Value is the relative lightness or darkness of anything we observe. Every color relates to a value, which you can easily see if you convert a color image into a black-and-white image. Mastering the relationship between color and value is an important key to building great paintings.

| 1 | 2 | 3 | 4 | 5 | 6 | 7 | 8 | 9 |

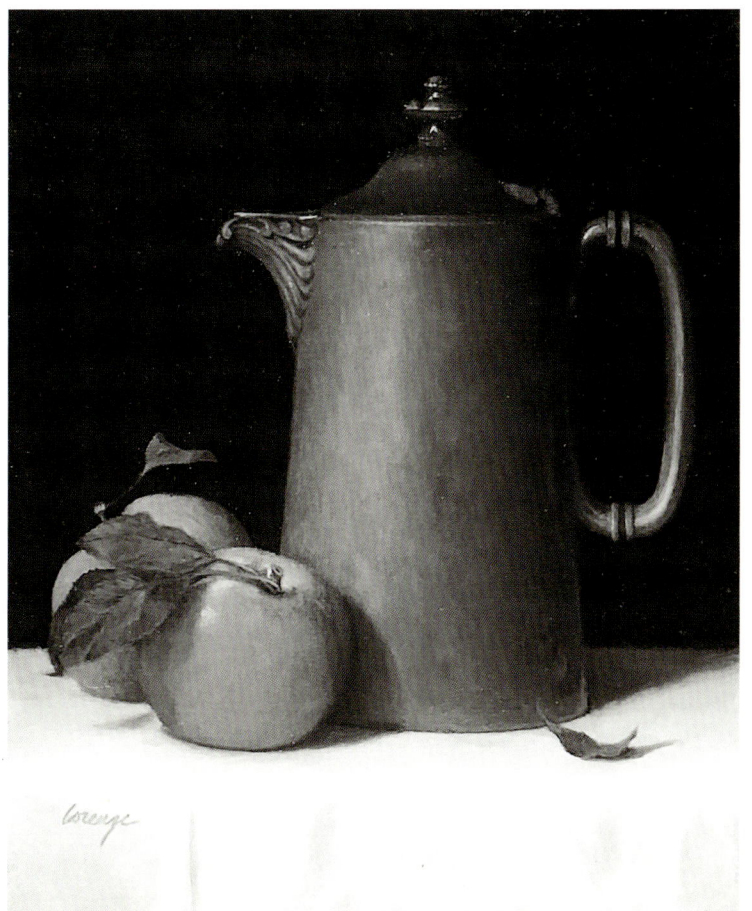
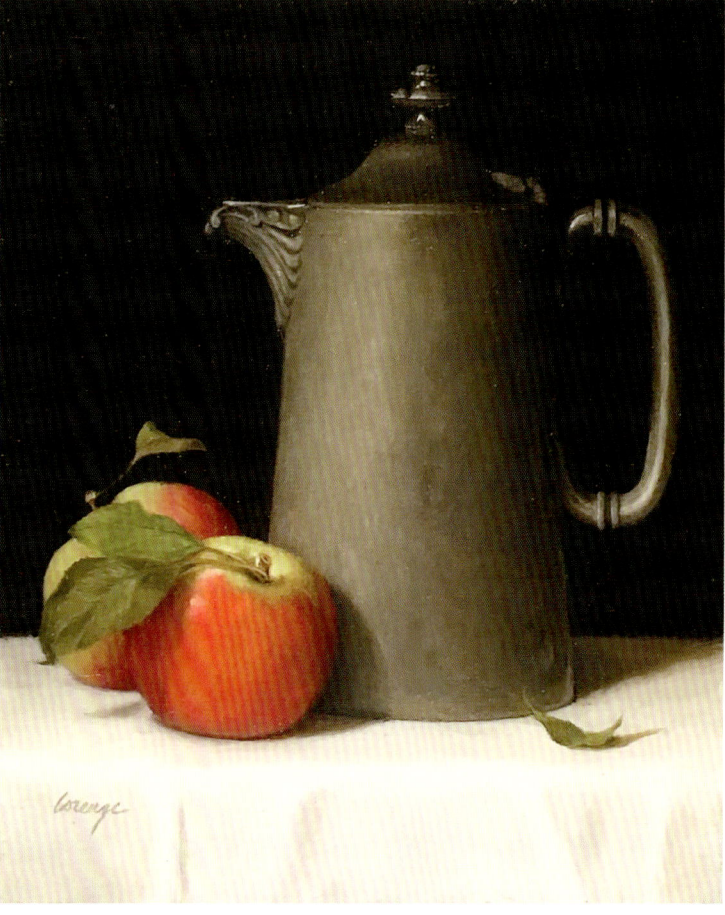

You can use a value scale to determine the value of a color. First, place a dab of the paint on the value that seems to most closely correspond to the paint color. Then place dabs of the same paint on the values to the left and right. Squint as you look at the scale. Whichever value the color disappears into is the value of the color. Once you have found the color's value, you may want to keep a record of it in your sketchbook to refer back to.

Converting a color image to black and white reveals the relative values of the colors.

BELOW: It is difficult to gauge the value of high chroma colors like cadmium orange. Here, I've placed dabs of cadmium orange (direct from the tube) on the middle ranges of the value scale. Converting the image to black and white reveals that the color has a value of about 5.

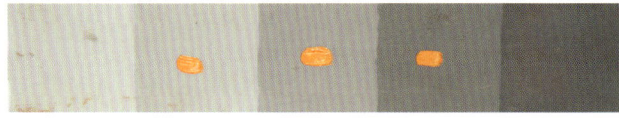
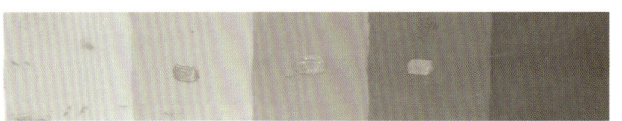
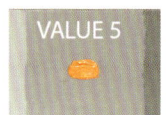

VALUE 5

Chroma

The term *chroma* refers to the intensity of a color. The center column in the chart at right shows a gray scale, which has no color. The spheres farthest from the gray scale have the greatest intensity of color, or the highest chroma. A color's chroma is usually judged in relation to the chroma of another color.

ABOVE: The lowest-chroma colors are closest to the gray scale; the highest-chroma colors are farthest away.

BELOW: Hovsep Pushman, *Twilight Tails, #407,* n.d., oil on canvas laid on board, 22 × 18 inches (55.9 × 45.7 cm). Photo courtesy of Heritage Auctions, HA.com.

Careful use of high-chroma colors can create drama in a painting. The color of this composition by Hovsep Pushman is mostly neutral, so the high-chroma details—the pink leaves, the figurine's blue robe, and the opalescent shimmer on the small pot's glaze—really stand out.

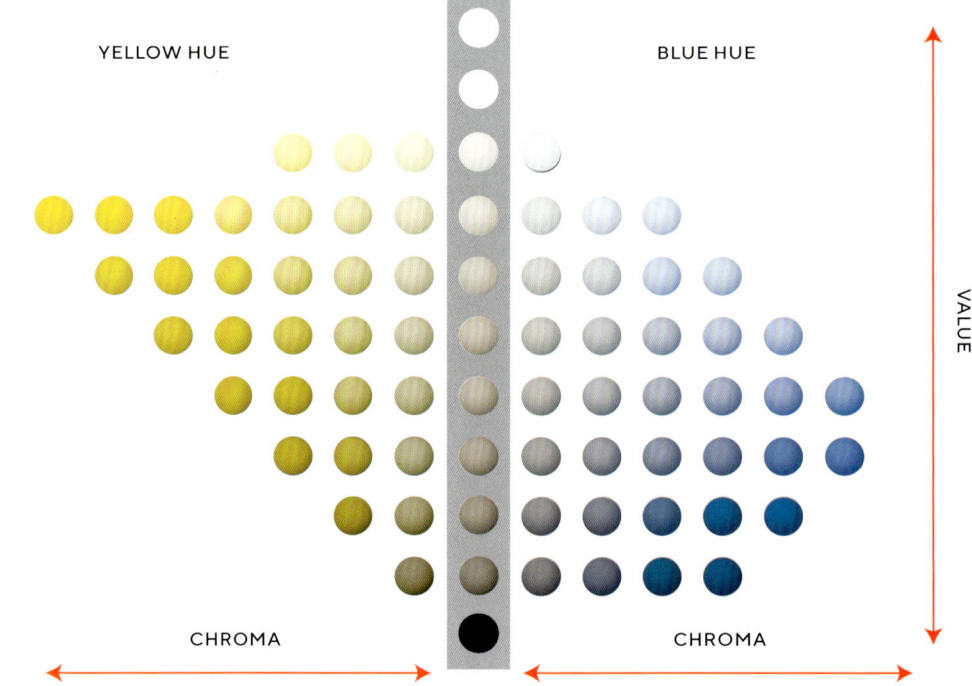

YELLOW HUE   BLUE HUE

VALUE

CHROMA   CHROMA

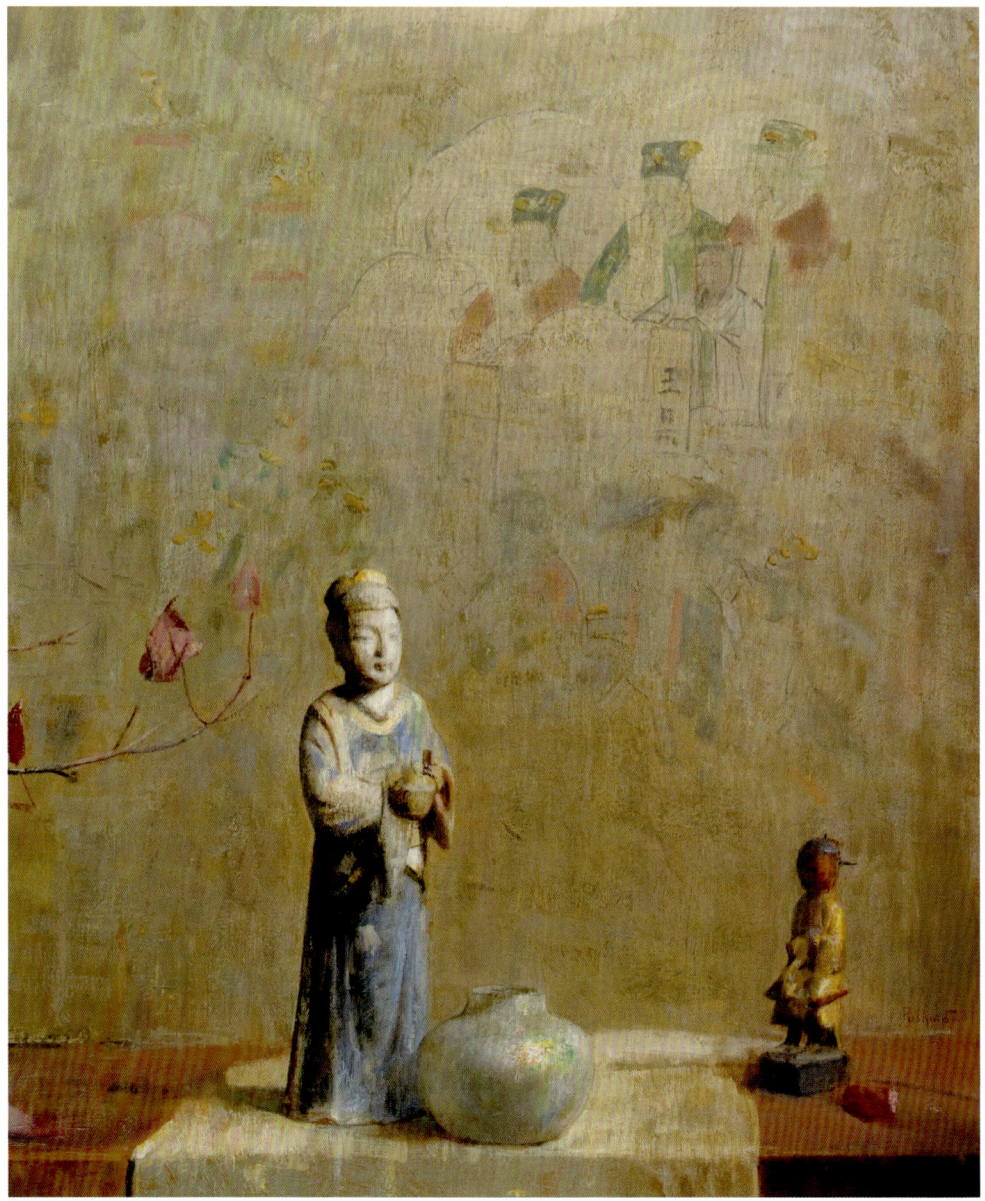

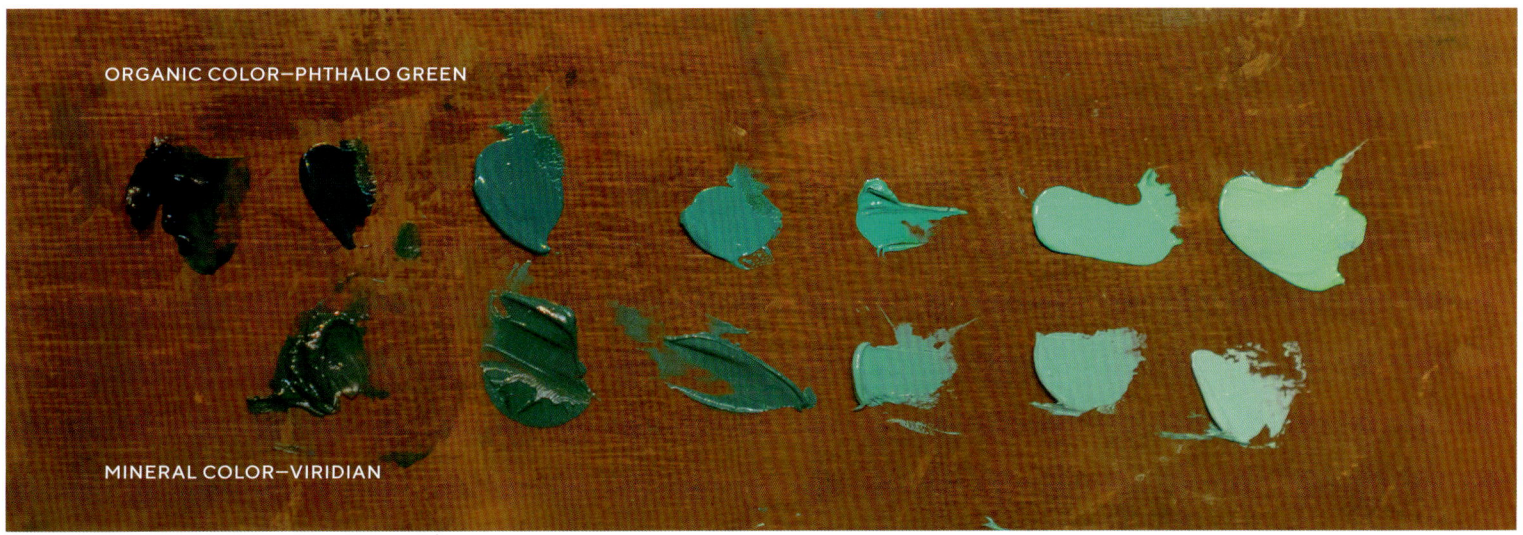

ORGANIC COLOR—PHTHALO GREEN

MINERAL COLOR—VIRIDIAN

WHITE AND BLACK AS COLORS

We generally think of white and black as having no color. But white and black pigments are, in fact, colors—very light and very dark colors, respectively.

White has the lightest value of any color on your palette. White paint belongs to one of the six hue families: specifically, it is a very low chroma yellow. There are four kinds of white paint that you will commonly come across: titanium white, flake white (also known as lead white), Cremnitz white, and zinc white. Each has its own characteristics. Titanium white—an opaque white that dries relatively fast and has really good tinting strength—is the most common and versatile of all the white paints. Flake white is fast drying but has a lower tinting strength than titanium; its consistency is stiff, which makes it great for impasto. Cremnitz white is a great alternative to flake white. I primarily use titanium white and flake white, and I recommend that you stay away from zinc white, because it dries to a brittle film that will cause your paint to become unstable over time.

Black has the darkest value on your palette, and that should guide your use of it. Reserve black for the darkest darks in your work, such as crevice shadows. Like white pigment, black pigment has a hue. If you add titanium white to Mars black, ivory black, or lamp black, you will see that each of these blacks is really a very deep violet-blue. Therefore, treat any of these blacks as a very dark violet-blue color and use it only when mixing the darkest cool colors.

You can mix your own black paints, for instance by combining very dark colors like alizarin crimson and ultramarine. By mixing your own, you can add a touch more color to your blacks.

ABOVE: Mineral colors like viridian lose chroma when they are mixed with white, whereas modern organic colors like phthalo green remain very high chroma even when mixed with white.

COLOR MIXING

Only rarely will a color right out of the tube be the exact color you want (although it can sometimes happen). You'll have to mix colors to get most of the colors you need. Color tends to be much more subtle than you might at first think. Generally, any color you see is a combination of at least two colors.

Plotting Tube Colors on the Color Wheel

When mixing colors, it's a good idea to know what you're starting out with. Plotting tube colors on a two-dimensional color wheel is a great way to see which hue each tube color is. Doing so creates a map that's similar to a subway map, enabling you to find the hue that will get you closest to your color destination.

Here we see where each tube color falls when plotted on a color wheel. In this scheme, lighter-value colors are closer to the center and darker-value colors are farther from the center. (This plotting does not take chroma into account.)

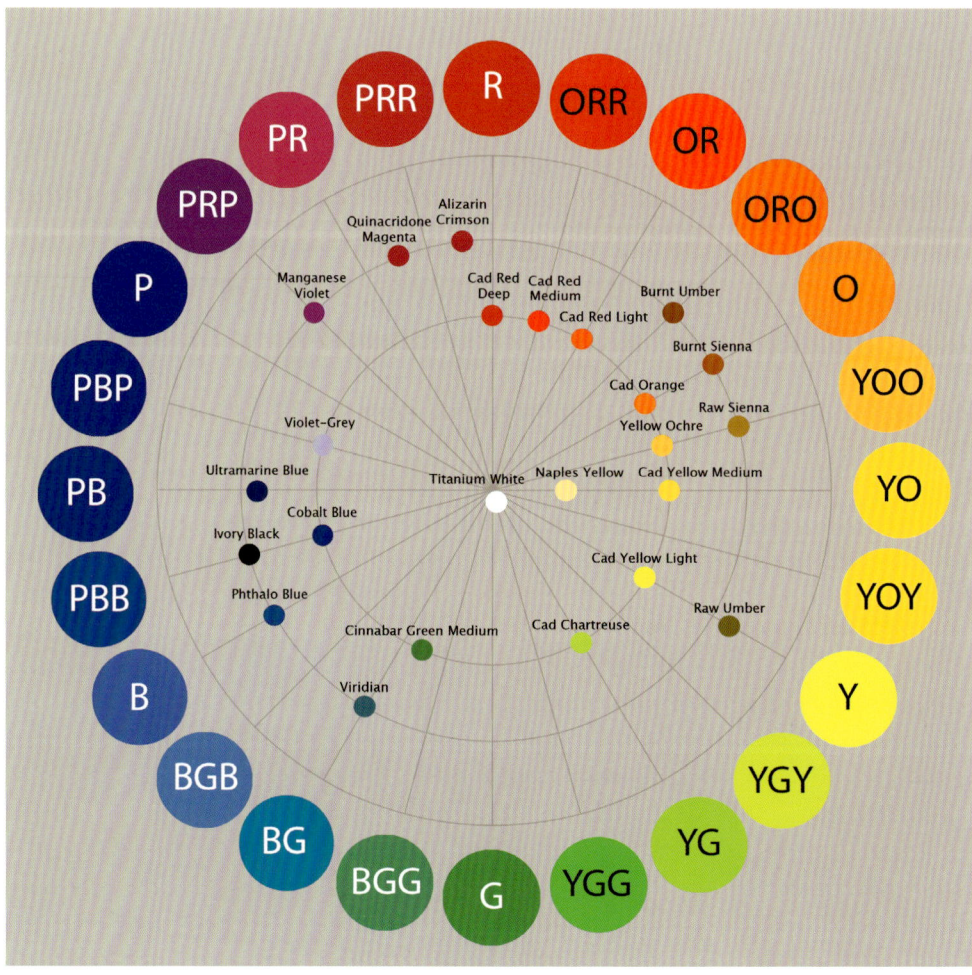

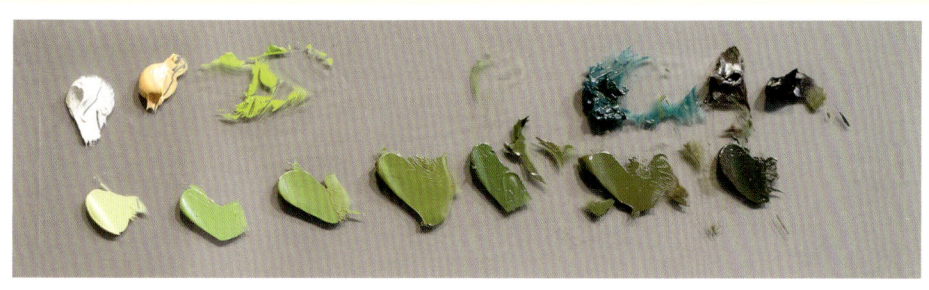

GLASS PALETTES

It's preferable to mix your colors on your palette, not on your painting surface. One of the best ways to do this is to mix with a palette knife on a glass palette. Placing a neutral gray paper beneath the palette, as shown, can help you see the hues clearly. (You might also place a value scale beneath the glass to help you gauge the values of the colors you're mixing.) Glass palettes have the additional advantage of being very easy to clean.

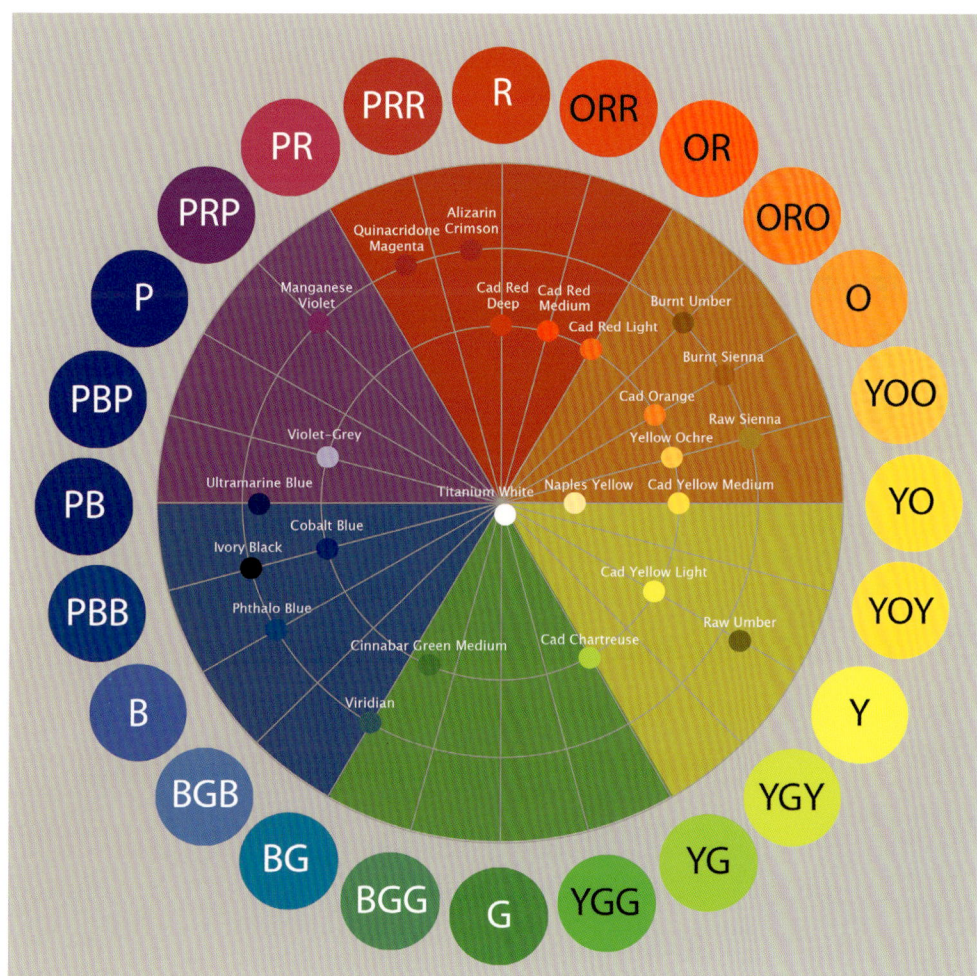

I highly recommend associating each color with the hue family it falls within. If you create such a color wheel with the tube colors you commonly use and keep it in your studio, you'll find that it's a fantastic help when you're having trouble mixing a color.

Finding the Local Color

When painting, it is important that you try to match colors to what you see and not to what you think you know. The term *local color* refers to the color that you actually perceive an object to be. If you were to paint a sphere cobalt blue, that would be the local color of the object. Local color can be seen most easily on matte surfaces as there is less glare from the light source affecting your perception.

Light temperature partly determines how you perceive an object's hue. The same green apple will not appear to have the same hue under a 3000 Kelvin light as under a 5500 Kelvin light. Here are photos of the same apple in three different lighting scenarios: neutral light, cool light, and warm light. Each looks to have a slightly different hue. Swatches of local color show the subtle shifts in hue.

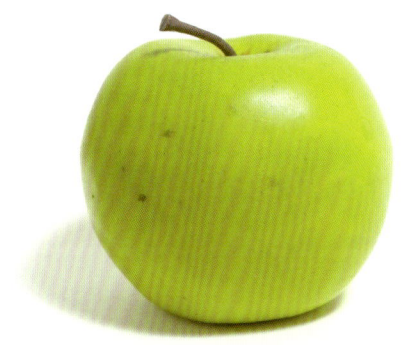 

Neutral light

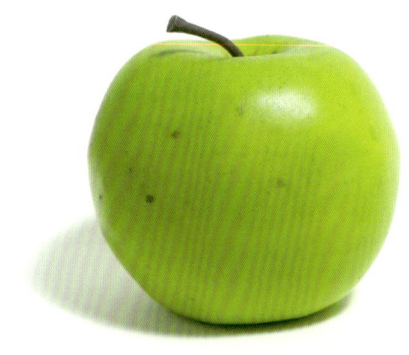 

Cool light

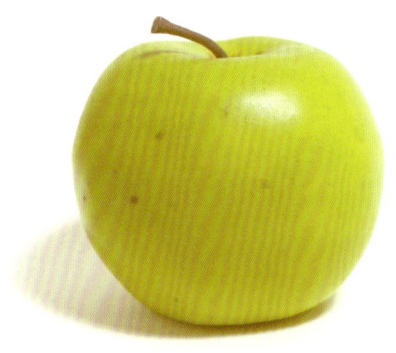 

Warm light

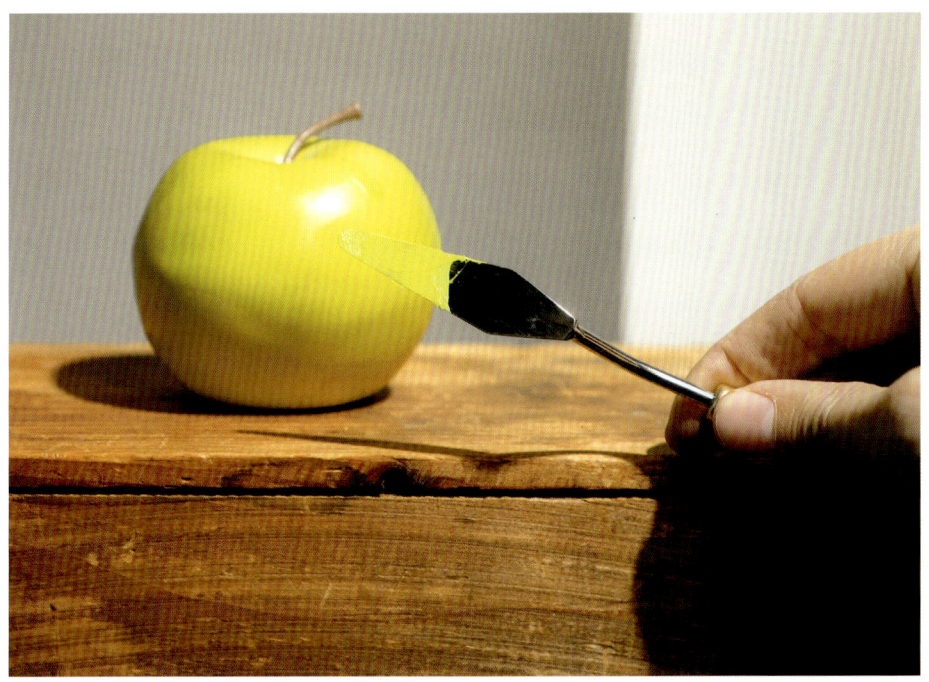

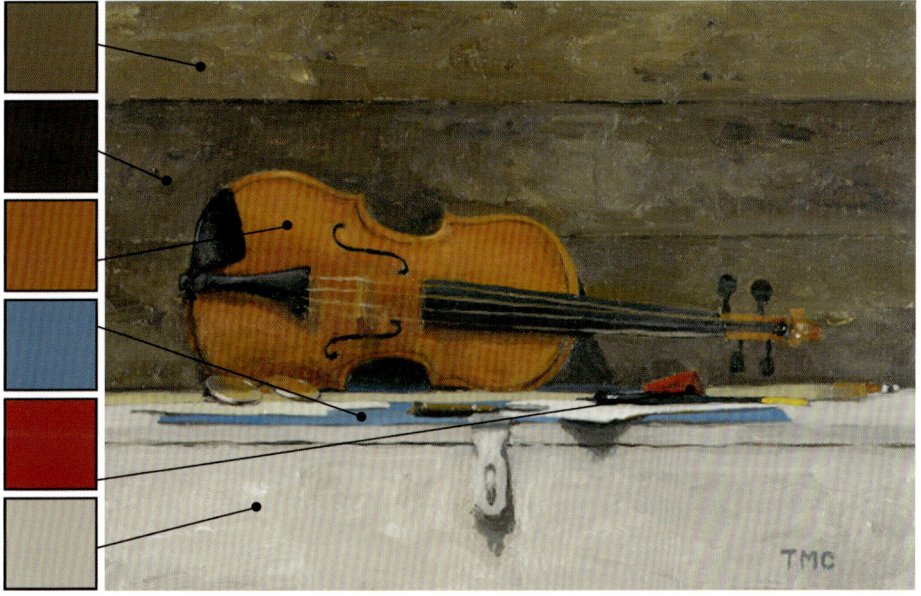

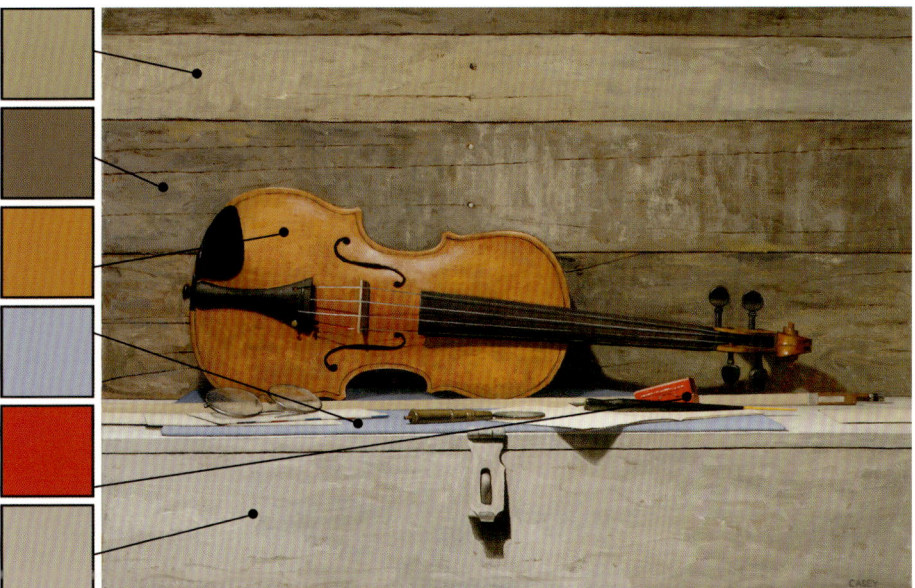

TOP: To determine whether a color you've mixed matches the local color you perceive, load some of the color onto a palette knife and hold it up to the object. Hold it as close as you can to the setup to ensure the hue isn't affected by light falloff, which may make your color matching inaccurate.

CENTER: Todd M. Casey, study for *Another Story*, 2015, oil on linen, 6 × 8 inches (15.24 × 20.32 cm). Courtesy of Rehs Contemporary Galleries, New York.

BOTTOM: Todd M. Casey, *Another Story*, 2015, oil on linen, 18 × 24 inches (45.72 × 60.96 cm). Courtesy of Rehs Contemporary Galleries, New York.

Different kinds of light shift the color and change the mood of a setup. At center is a poster study for my painting *Another Story*, done in cool light. The final painting, bottom, was done in a warmer light. The swatches show the subtle shifts of color in relation to the light.

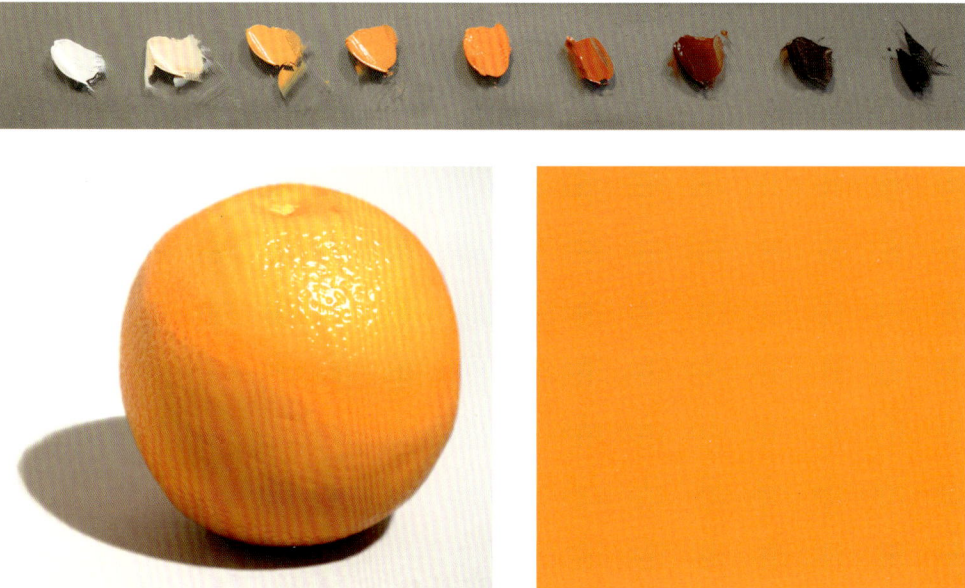

TOP: This color string for orange goes from lightest at left to darkest at right.

ABOVE: When mixing a string, start with the tube color that's closest to the object's local color. In the case of the orange at left, the closest tube color is cadmium orange, shown in the swatch at right.

Color Strings

When preparing to paint an object of one hue, you'll need to mix the full range of values for the hue that you observe. This light-to-dark series is referred to as a *color string*.

The biggest challenge when mixing a light-to-dark color string is to do so without changing the hue. That's because we rarely have perfect lighter or darker versions of a color. A common mistake is to use white to mix all the lighter values and black to mix all the dark values. This doesn't necessarily work because titanium white is a very low chroma yellow that will desaturate any color it is mixed with, and ivory black is a dark violet-blue that will shift any color it is mixed with toward violet-blue. Instead, you need to find lighter and darker colors that are close to the correct hue. This will ensure that the hue only changes the smallest amount. As you can see in the diagram at top left opposite, the colors on my palette that are in the closest proximity for my desired string are Naples yellow, yellow ochre, raw sienna, burnt sienna, and burnt umber. Burnt sienna is on the same trajectory, or hue angle, as cadmium orange according to my plotted colors (this may differ depending on the brand of paint). The rest of the colors are nearby, on either side of this trajectory.

When you mix a color that is *not* on the exact trajectory of your correct color, your color string is going to shift slightly toward the color to the left or right. (This is also called *hue drift*.) In the case shown in the diagrams, the hue will shift to the left if you mix orange with burnt umber but will shift to the right if you mix orange with

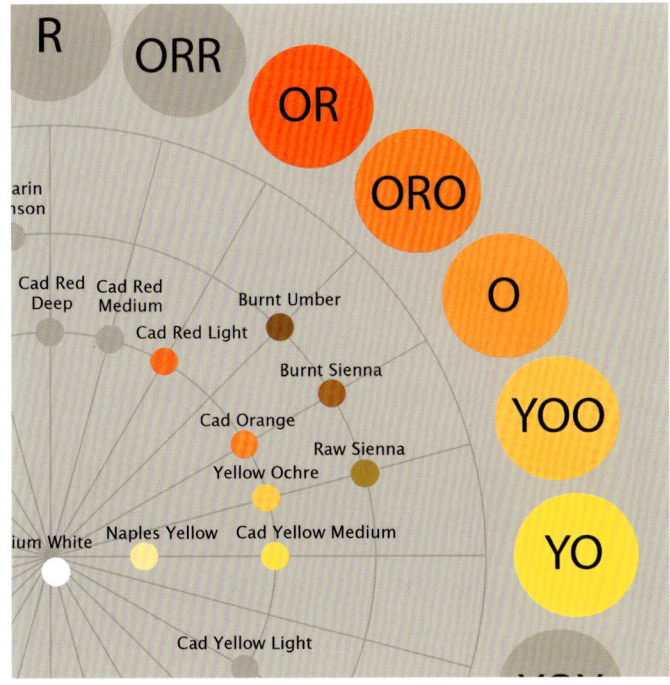

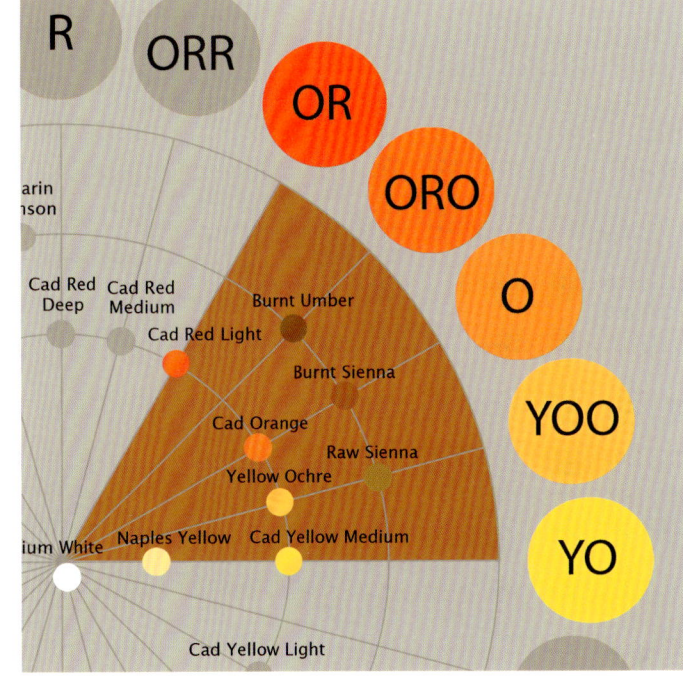

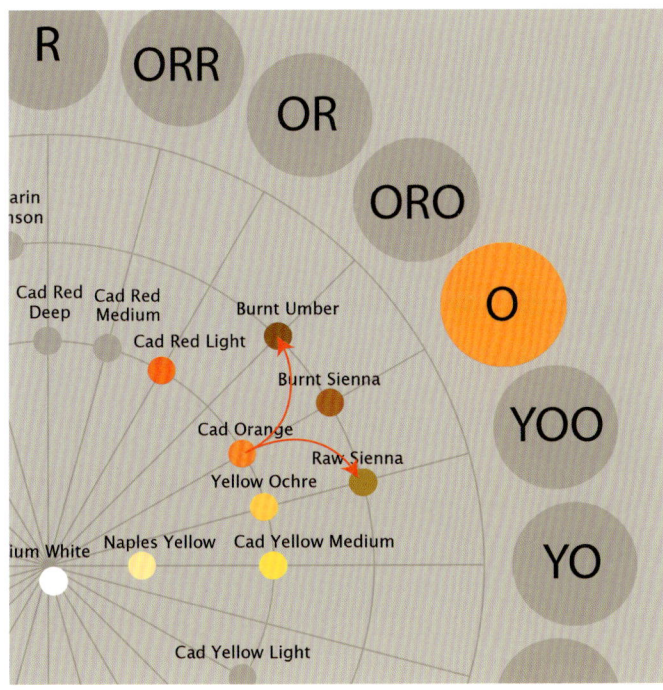

raw sienna. The trick is to make the value darker without shifting the hue too much. Sometimes this means that you have to go to the other side of the desired string hue to pull it back, much like a pendulum swinging.

Any time a color is mixed with another color, the resulting color will be toward the middle of those two colors. But almost any mixture of two colors will move through color space in an arc rather than a straight line. When I mix a color such as burnt umber with cadmium orange, for example, the hue may shift slightly from orange to orange-red-orange. There's almost always a slight shift in hue. You may have to live with these slight imperfections.

CLOCKWISE FROM TOP LEFT: Here you see all the colors that are closest to tube orange. These are the only colors that will be used to mix an orange (O) string.

Cadmium orange and burnt sienna are on the same trajectory, or hue angle, in this plotting of colors.

Hue will drift if you mix the basic hue—in this case, cadmium orange—with a color that's not on the same trajectory.

I like to think of color mixing as similar to math. For example, if a color has a value of 5 and I mix it with a color of value 8, I will most likely get a color whose value is mathematically in the middle—in this case, 6.5.

ABOVE, RIGHT: This wheel shows a light-to-dark mixture of each hue.

Mixing an Orange String

The goal when mixing a light-to-dark string is to achieve nine values that correspond to the values of the value scale. Start with the local color of the object, which is cadmium orange, a value 4. Then find the closest hue that is lower in value. Since there are no light orange hues, Naples yellow will have to do. For the lightest value, add white.

Now mix the darker colors. Mix cadmium orange and burnt sienna to match a value 5. Burnt sienna is a dark orange and by itself will be value 6. Then mix burnt sienna with burnt umber to achieve a value 7. Burnt umber out of the tube is value 8, and burnt umber and ivory black make the value 9 mixture.

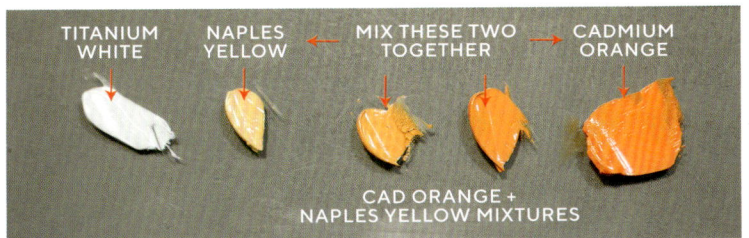

TITANIUM WHITE — NAPLES YELLOW ← MIX THESE TWO TOGETHER → CADMIUM ORANGE

CAD ORANGE +
NAPLES YELLOW MIXTURES

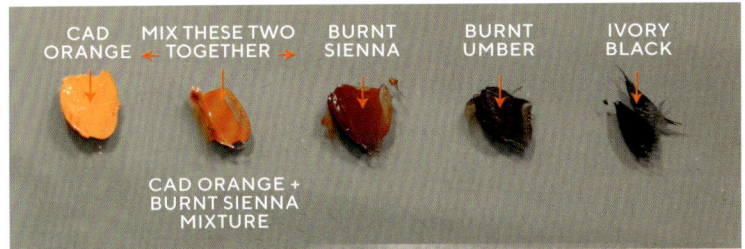

CAD ORANGE ← MIX THESE TWO TOGETHER → BURNT SIENNA — BURNT UMBER — IVORY BLACK

CAD ORANGE +
BURNT SIENNA
MIXTURE

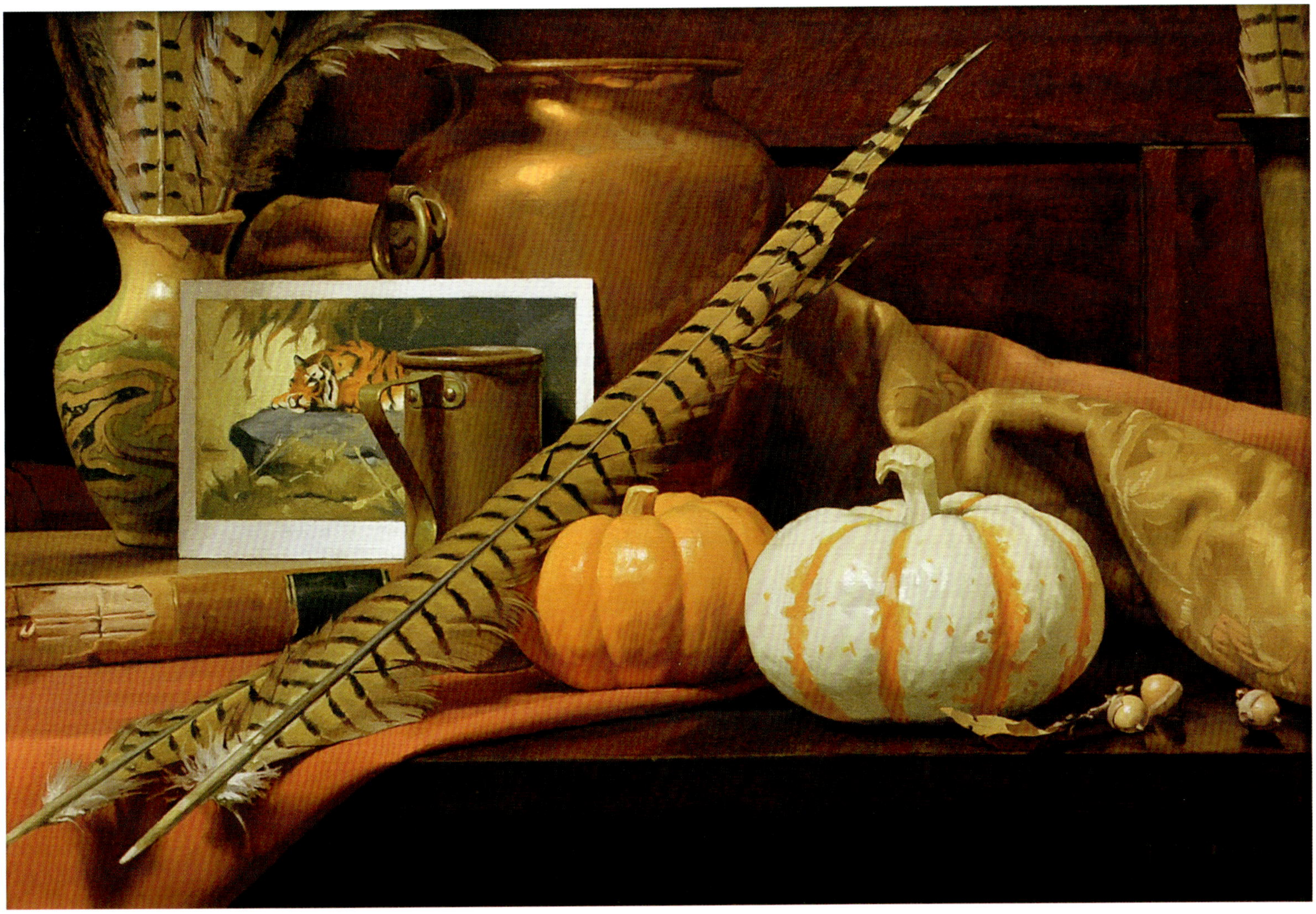

Sometimes I mix a half-step between 1 and 2 (1.5 value) using titanium white and a hint of Old Holland Naples Yellow Extra. I do this because value 1 is white out of the tube. A 1.5 value gives me a near-white with just a hint of the color present. Because no other color can achieve the value of black, I use black in the last two values, 8 and 9. It does shift the darkest orange hue through color space toward blue, but this is barely noticeable.

TOP: The lighter values in the orange string are made by mixing cadmium orange and Naples yellow; at the lightest end is titanium white from the tube. Burnt Sienna, burnt umber, and ivory black are used for the darker values in the string.

ABOVE: Douglas Flynt, *Two Tigers,* 2012, oil on linen, 10 × 14 inches (25.4 × 35.56 cm). Courtesy of the artist.

Douglas Flynt uses a predominantly warm orange-family color scheme in his painting *Two Tigers*.

STRINGS FOR OBJECTS WITH MULTIPLE HUE SHIFTS

Objects of "a single color" often have a bit of variation in hue—they're not just one straight line, light to dark, of one color. For instance, to paint the lime in the photo accurately, you'd have to mix strings that shift slightly so that you can capture the hue shifts that you see.

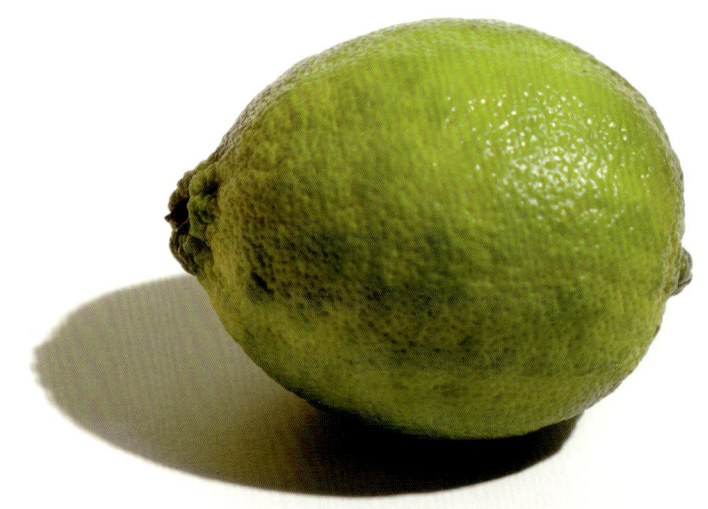

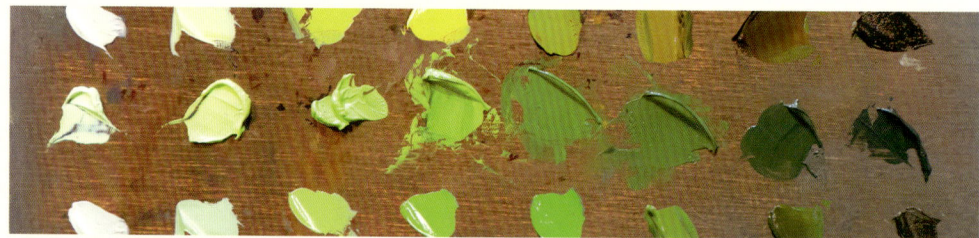

TOP AND CENTER: Capturing the shifting hues in this lime might require that you mix several slightly shifting strings of green.

RIGHT: Max Ginsburg, *Maxwell House Coffee*, 1976, oil on panel, 6 × 8 inches (15.24 × 20.32 cm). Courtesy of the artist.

There is quite a bit of variation in the green of the apple on the left in this painting by Max Ginsburg.

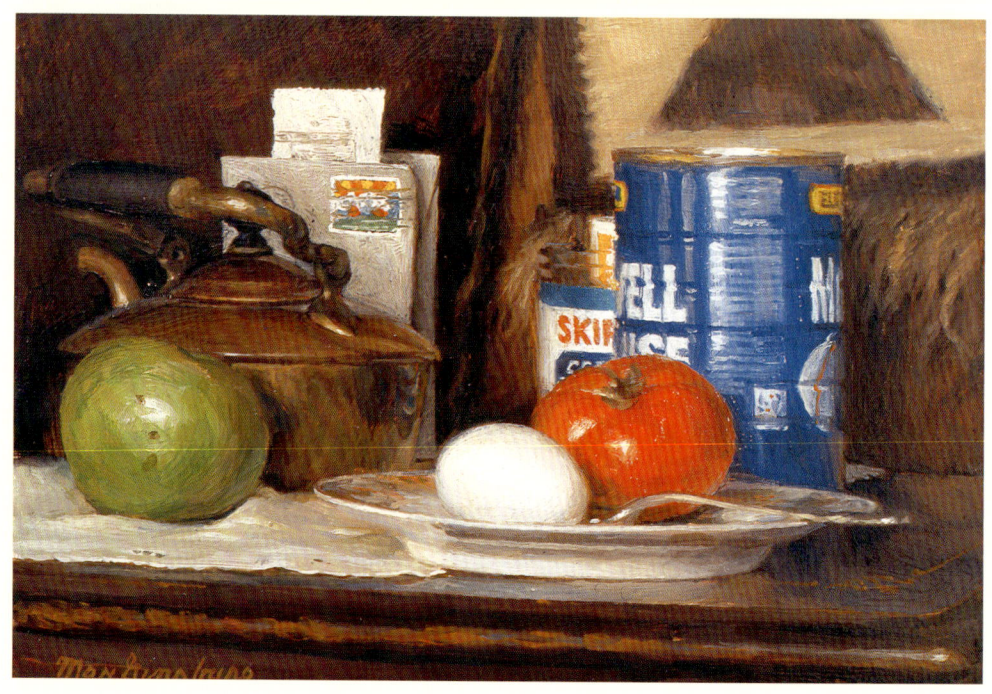

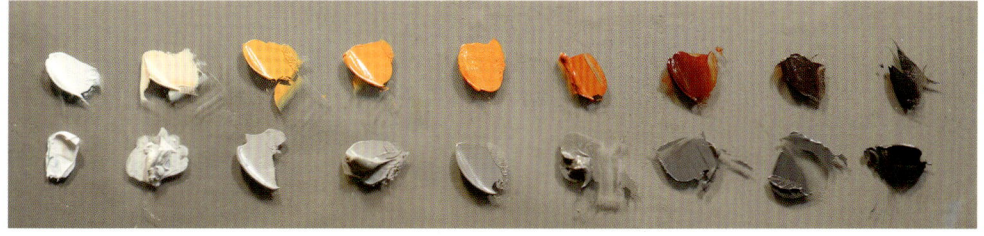

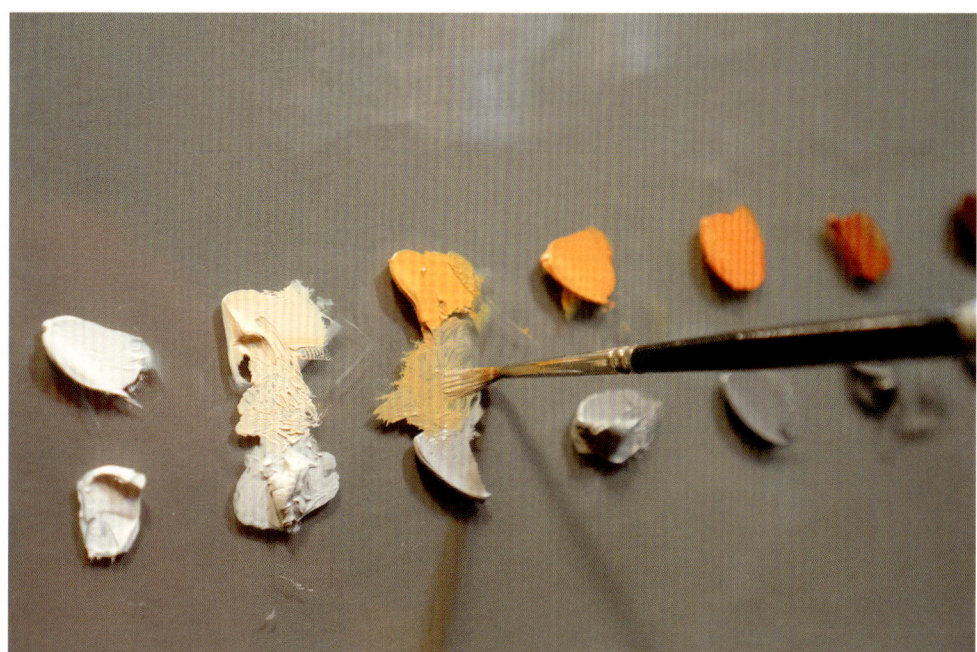

TIP

You don't always need so many colors to mix a light-to-dark string. For inorganic pigments like phthalo green, which are on the cool side of the color wheel, you can usually just use white and black to achieve a full color string.

Mixing a Color with a Neutral String

Mixing a color with a neutral string of paints is a great way to pull the chroma out of the color without changing the hue. (Sometimes the hue does change, but only very slightly.) By lining up a neutral string right next to a colored string, you can mix corresponding values to pull out the chroma. This is called *toning* a color.

A few manufacturers offer tubed neutral gray paints that are a great addition to a palette. Gamblin Artist's Oil Colors offers a Portland Grey Light, Portland Grey Medium, and Portland Grey Dark, which are values 2, 4, and 6, respectively. Once they are laid out on your palette you can mix them for the in-between values of 3 and 5. (Value 1 is simply titanium white. Values 7 and 8 are achieved by mixing black with value 6, and value 9 is simply ivory black.)

ABOVE: Here, an orange string is lined up above a neutral string so that their values correspond. When the two are mixed, they produce a semi-neutral string with a variety of muted orange colors.

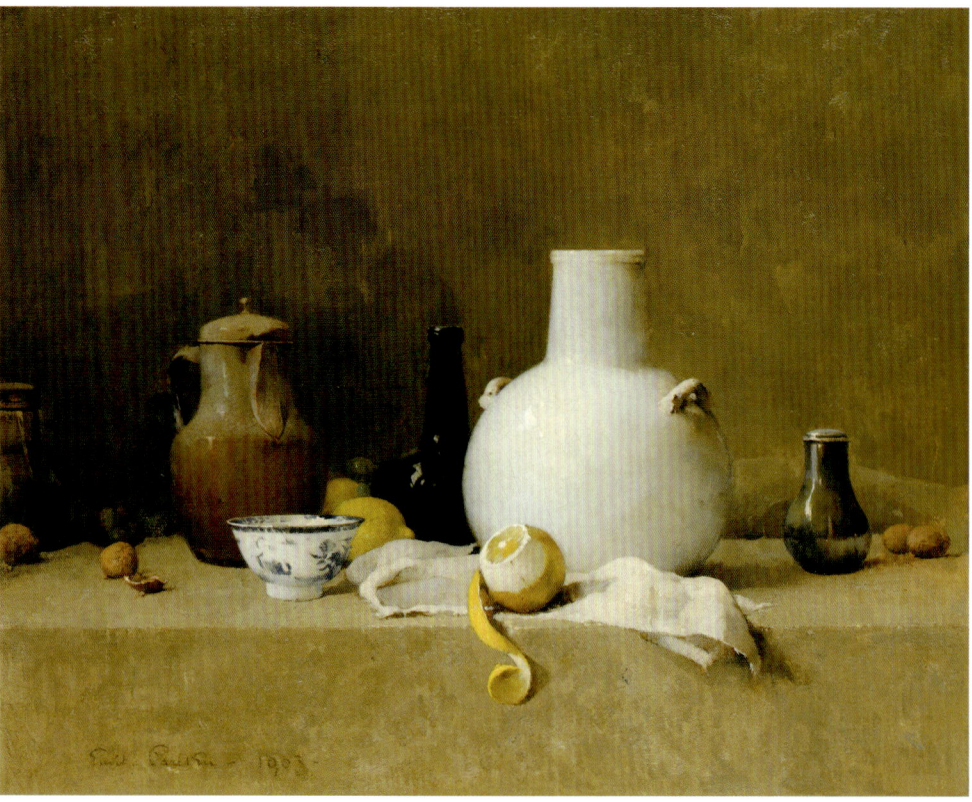

A subtle palette of grays can make for an intriguing painting, as this painting by Emil Carlsen shows.

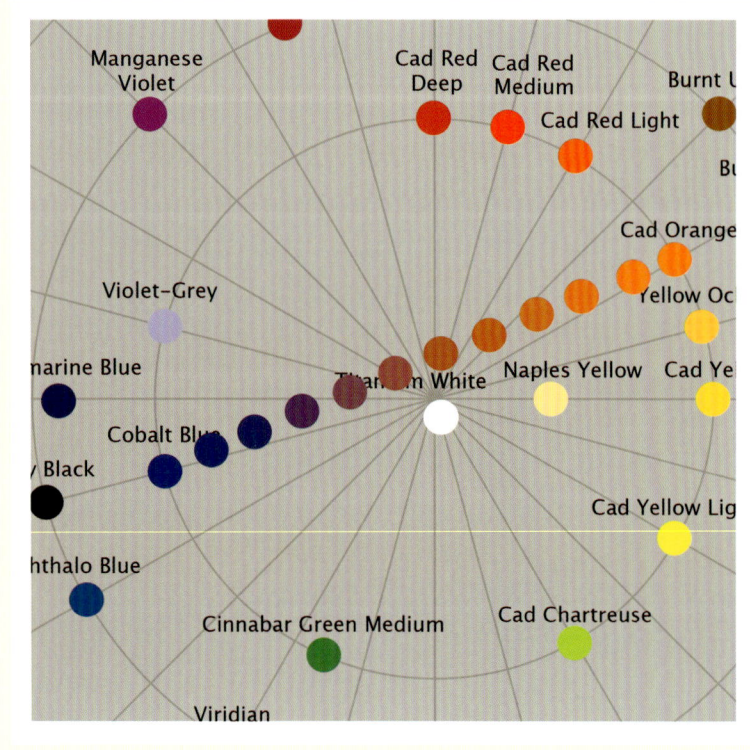

COMPLEMENTARY MUTES

There are several different ways to effectively achieve neutral mixtures. One way is to mix a color with its comple-ment (the color that lies directly across from it on the color wheel). The result is referred to as a complementary mute.

This kind of mixture, however, will almost never be perfectly neutral, because no pigment is actually the ex-act opposite of another pigment. In fact, mixing comple-mentary mutes can be fairly unpredictable. The closest you'll get to having a perfect neutral in the center of the string is with a mixture of alizarin crimson and viridian.

When you mix two complementary colors like the cadmium orange and cobalt blue shown here, you get a semineutral mixture but never a true neutral. Some artists choose to mix their neutrals this way, but it can be a bit unpredictable.

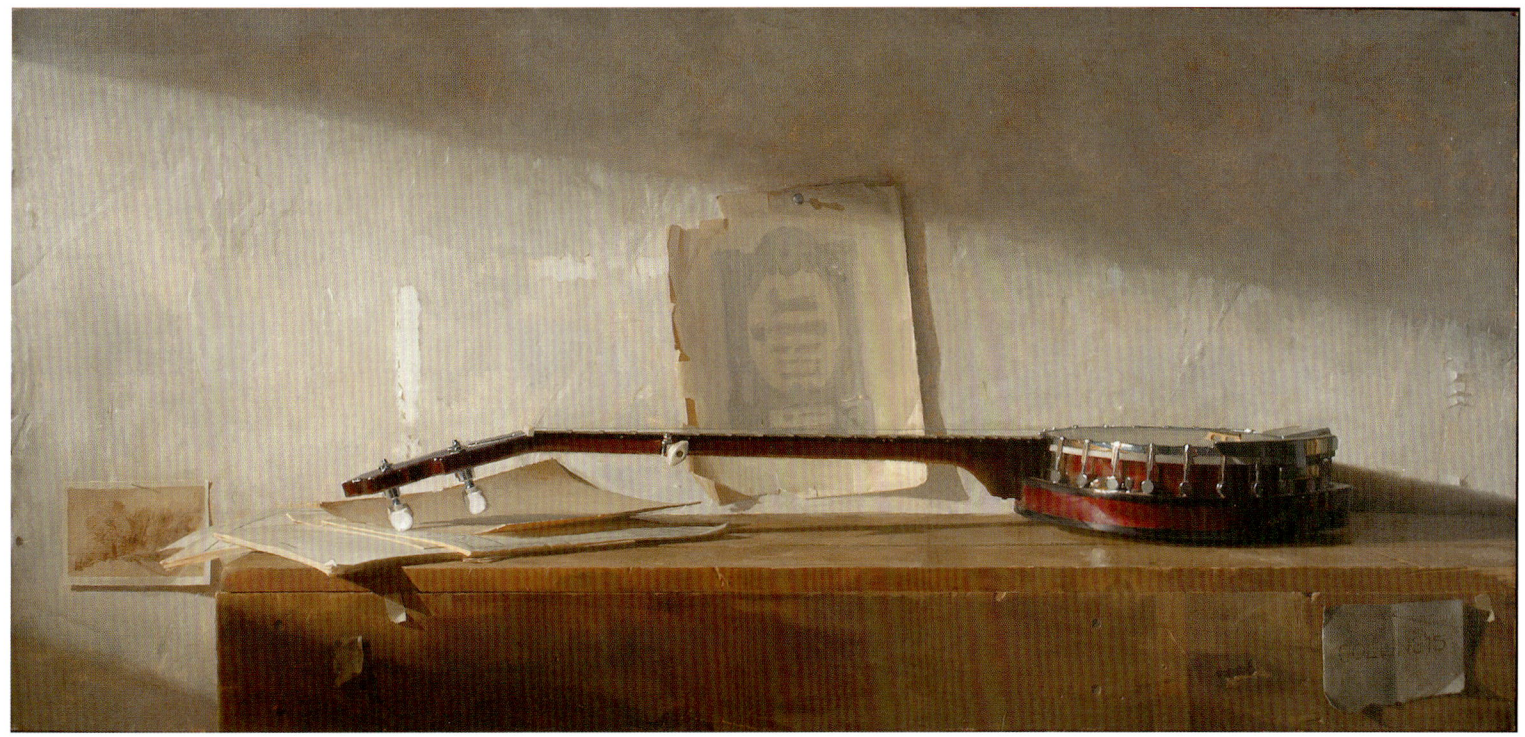

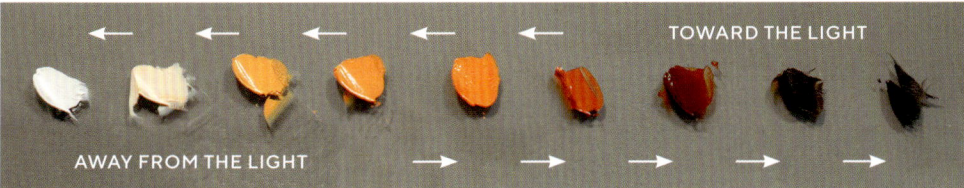

TOP: Jacob Collins, *Banjo*, 2015, oil on canvas, 26 × 54 inches (66.04 × 137.16 cm). Courtesy of Adelson Galleries.

Jacob Collins uses careful, subtle gray tones to accentuate the red banjo. A color string can be premixed, or mixed as the artist goes. Here, Collins mixes as he goes but still articulates his tonal progression in relation to the light source.

BOTTOM: Lighter values indicate that you are moving toward the light; darker values that you are moving away from the light.

Applying a Color String

Once you've mixed a color string on your palette, you can begin applying the paint to your canvas. Because you've worked out all the color information with the string, you can focus on articulating the object in relation to the light source. Applying color becomes an experience of constantly asking, "Am I moving toward or away from the light source?" This will determine which way you will move on the string—toward the lighter or the darker values.

Working without Color Strings

Mixing color strings is a great way to plan your painting. I find that I have great results when I paint with color strings, but at times I also try to paint without them. I identify the hue and get as close to it as I can, and then I look for the light and dark versions of that color, just as I would if I were premixing a string. Working without a premixed string feels a bit more organic, and I can be a bit looser with the color shifts.

I also enjoy the idea that I am not always going to have perfect color. It's more important that I go for a cohesive picture in which the form and values are expressed with close versions of the colors I see. If the color is slightly off, it's not usually a big deal.

THE PSYCHOLOGY OF COLOR

When a color dominates a painting, it may evoke an emotional response in the viewer—creating a mood and reaching the viewer on a deeper psychological level. Bold reds tend to evoke excitement, passion, danger, and warmth. (The advertising industry tends to use red a lot.) You should think long and hard when choosing a color that overpowers an image because of the potential psychological effect on the viewer.

ABOVE RIGHT: Each color can produce a range of emotional impacts on the viewer.

RIGHT: Carlo Russo, *Ignis Mare,* 2017, oil on linen, 21 × 24 inches (53.34 × 60.96 cm). Courtesy of the artist.

In *Ignis Mare*, artist Carlo Russo unified the image with red tones, giving the painting a nice warm feeling.

RED
Passion
Danger
Excitement
Stimulating

ORANGE
Warmth
Success
Impulse
Fun

YELLOW
Enthusiasm
Energy
Happy
Fun

BLACK
Power
Control
Authority
Luxury

GREEN
Safe
Environment
Wealth
Growth

BLUE
Open
Ambition
Dependable
Strength

PURPLE
Creative
Wise
Royalty
Fantasy

WHITE
Purity
Truth
Innocence
Clarity

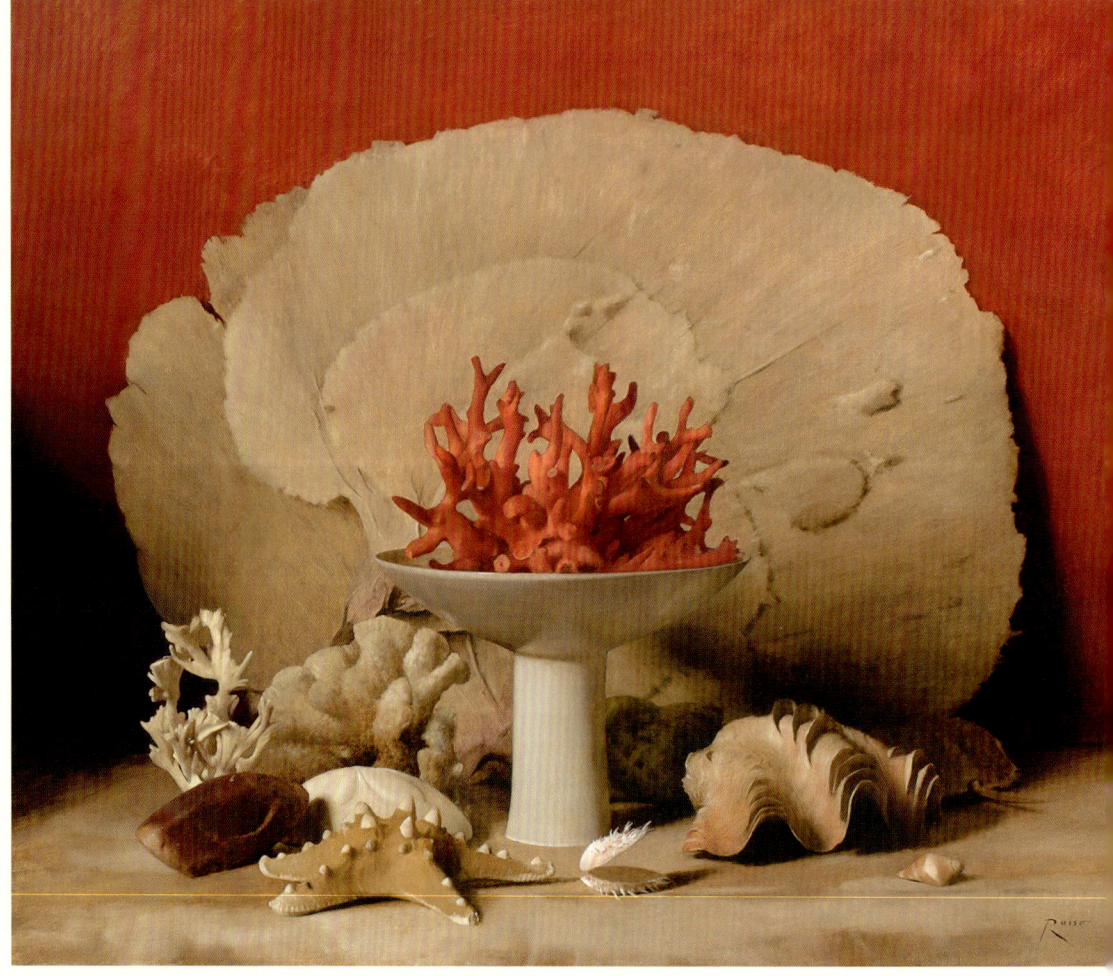

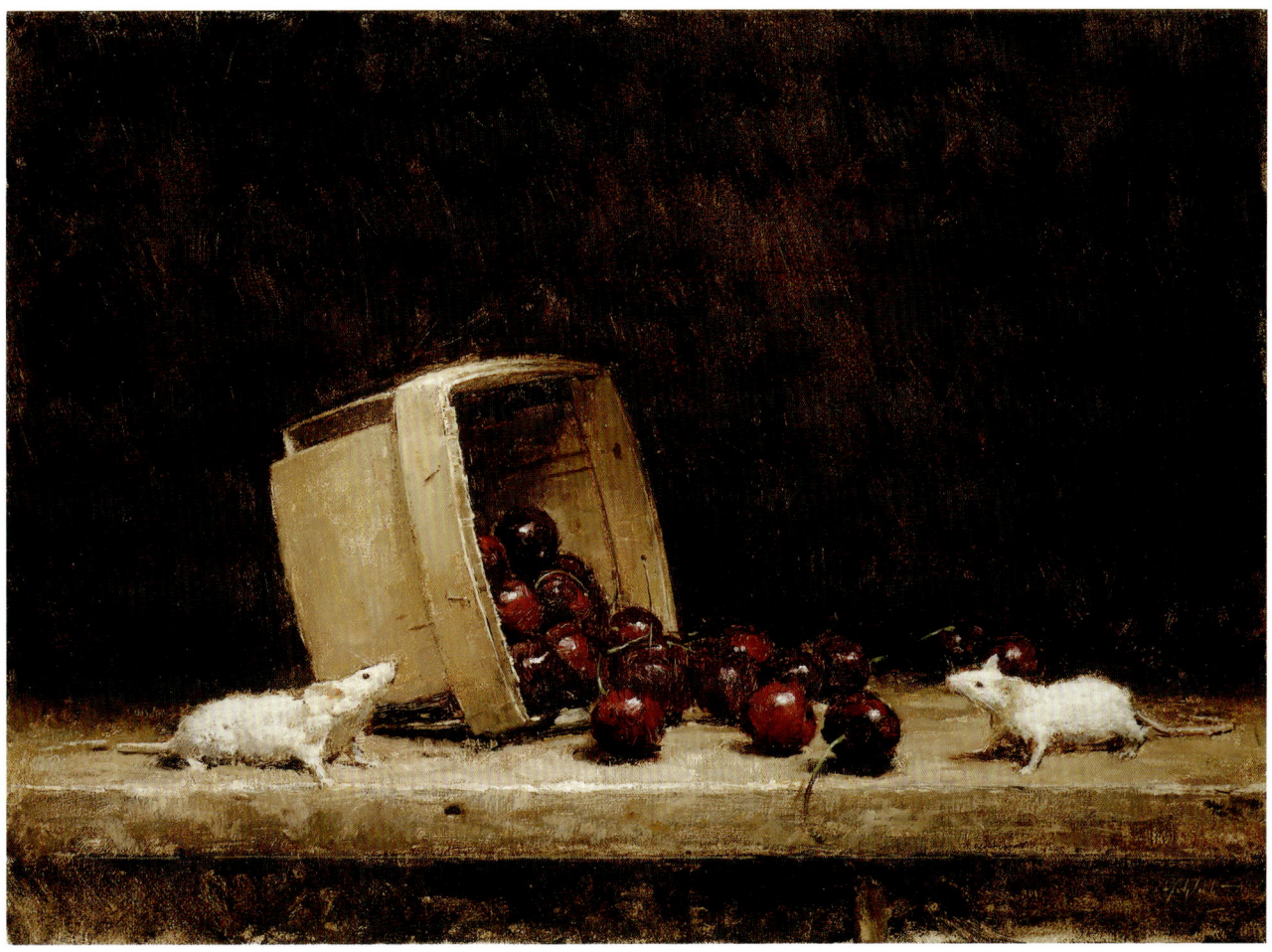

ABOVE: Travis Schlaht, *Mice and Cherries,* 2011, oil on linen, 12 × 16 inches (30.48 × 40.64 cm). Courtesy of the artist.

The use of black in the shadows under the mice and cherries really grounds the objects in this painting by Travis Schlaht. (The background is a combination of umbers and black.)

COLOR "RULES" THAT AREN'T TRUE

There are a number of "rules" about how color should be used that aren't true—or aren't always true. For instance, you might have heard that if you have warm light you should have cool shadow and vice versa. Yes, this is a common formula, but you shouldn't just follow formulas. Instead, you should observe what's in front of you. If an object is in warm light and does have a cool shadow, paint it that way, but if it doesn't, don't. Of course, you may make a stylistic choice to follow the so-called rule, but then you have to admit that you're taking the liberty *not* to paint what you see.

Another untrue "rule" is that you should never use black out of a tube—that you should mix your blacks yourself. The principle of mixing your own blacks originated with Impressionism. It relates more to painting out in nature, where there is a lot of color in shadows because of ambient light.

But there is nothing wrong with using black straight out of the tube. Artists like John Singer Sargent, James McNeill Whistler, and Winslow Homer used black quite often in their paintings. The most important thing about black is its value. It is all but impossible to mix a color with the same dark value as black. If you think of black as just its value, you'll use it in the correct places, like crevice shadows.

SETTING UP A PALETTE

You'll be making almost all your color decisions on your palette, so do your best to keep it clean and organized. Try not to grab paint with the brush right from the piles on your palette— you don't want to contaminate your pigments with a loaded brush. Instead, use a clean palette knife to pick up colors and place them in the mixing area.

My color palette takes cues from all the teachers I have studied with. Palettes are personal, so feel free to add or subtract any colors from what I offer. The colors I use are listed below. I've included *Colour Index* names (CINs) along with color names because colors from different manufacturers can be very different but will match more closely if they have the same CIN. (Note: Some of the colors have multiple CINs because they are mixtures of two or more pigments.) In a few cases, I specify a color from a particular manufacturer.

BELOW: This is my typical palette. All the colors are Gamblin Artist's Oil Colors except for cinnabar green medium (Rembrandt), violet-grey (Old Holland), and Naples yellow extra (Old Holland).

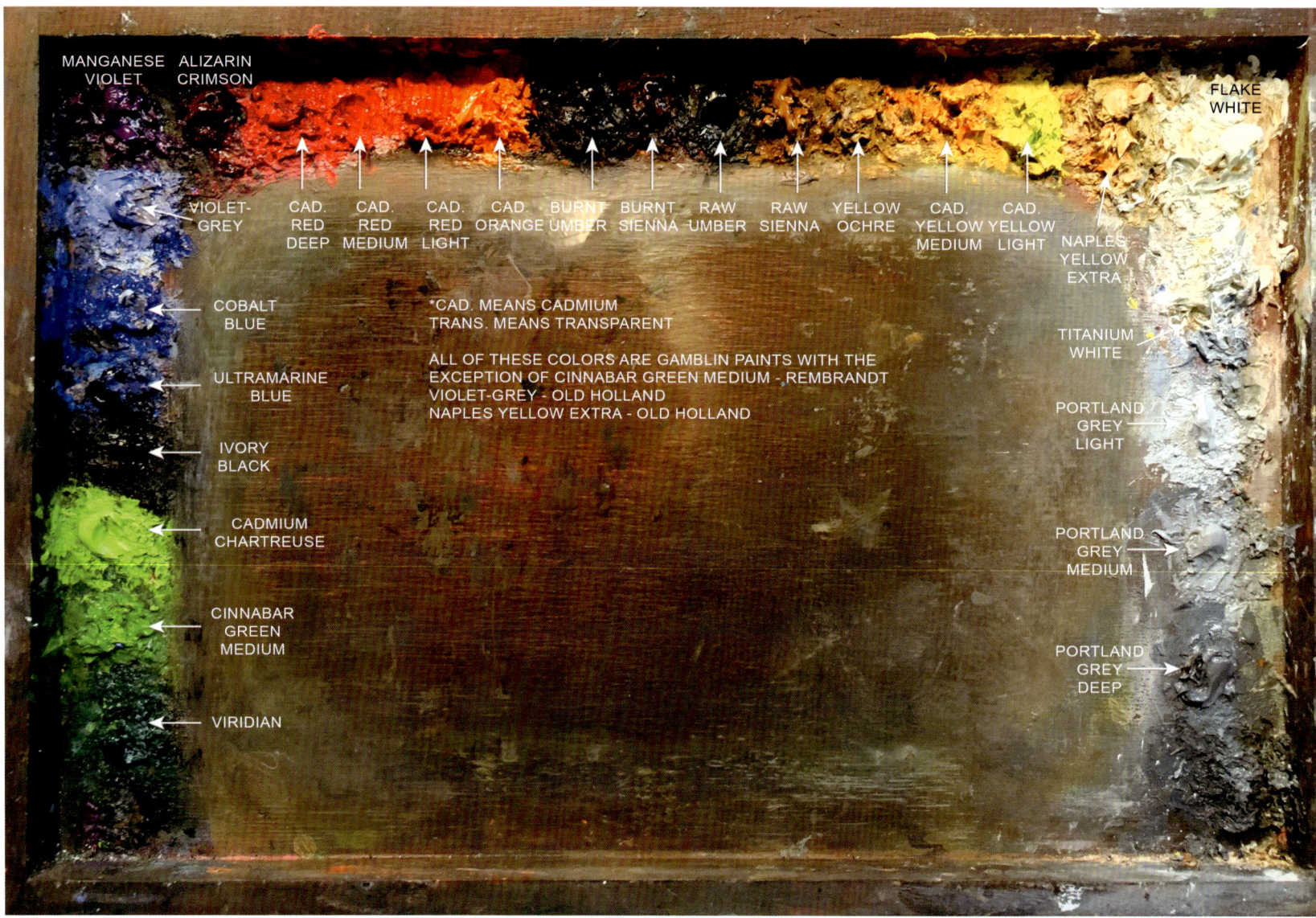

Yellows

Old Holland Naples Yellow Extra (PW 4, PW 6, PY 42)

cadmium yellow light (PY 35)

cadmium yellow medium (PY 37)

yellow ochre (PY 43)

raw sienna (PBr 7)

raw umber (PBr 7)

titanium white (PW 6)

Old Holland Flake White (PW 1, PW 4)

Orange

cadmium orange (PO 20)

Reds

cadmium red light (PR 108)

cadmium red medium (PR 108)

cadmium red deep (PR 108)

alizarin crimson (PR 83)

burnt umber (PBr 7)

transparent earth red (PR 101)

TIP

Storing colors you've premixed in plastic containers in the freezer can help slow down the oxidation process. If you mix a lot of a color for strings, you might think about buying empty paint tubes—available in most art supply stores—and tubing your mixed colors. This is a great way to extend the life of the paint.

Blues

Old Holland Violet-Grey (PW 6, PW 4, PG 18, PV 23, PB 29)

cobalt blue (PB 28)

ultramarine blue (PB 29)

ivory black (PBk 9)

Greens

cadmium chartreuse (PY 35, PG 18)

Rembrandt Cinnabar Green Medium (PY 154, PG 7, PY 42)

viridian (PG 18)

Violet

manganese violet (PV 16)

Grays

Gamblin Portland Grey Light (PW 6, PW 4, PBr 7, PBk 11)

Gamblin Portland Grey Medium (PW 6, PW 4, PBr 7, PBk 11)

Gamblin Portland Grey Deep (PW 6, PW 4, PBr 7, PBk 11)

What's great about this palette is I have a light, medium, and dark version of every color, all in close proximity to one another. This helps when form-painting, as we'll see in the next chapter.

MAKING COLOR DECISIONS

When trying to define the color of an object, start by asking these three questions: What hue is it? What is the color's value? And how chromatic/intense is the color? Answering these questions will get you closer to grabbing the correct color. Remember that the temperature of the light determines the way we observe color as well.

Beyond choosing the correct color for an object, there's the matter of deciding which colors to use, or emphasize, in a given painting. Color is tied to mood and emotions, so those need to be considered. If I want a dark and moody piece, I may go with a more traditional approach with a dark background. If I want a more contemporary approach, I may choose higher-chroma colors to dominate a painting. Once you learn all of the rules of color, you can also choose to "push," or exaggerate, the color or to use "broken color" (see page 283), as the Impressionists did. There are so many ways to work with color—and it's important to find the method that suits your temperament.

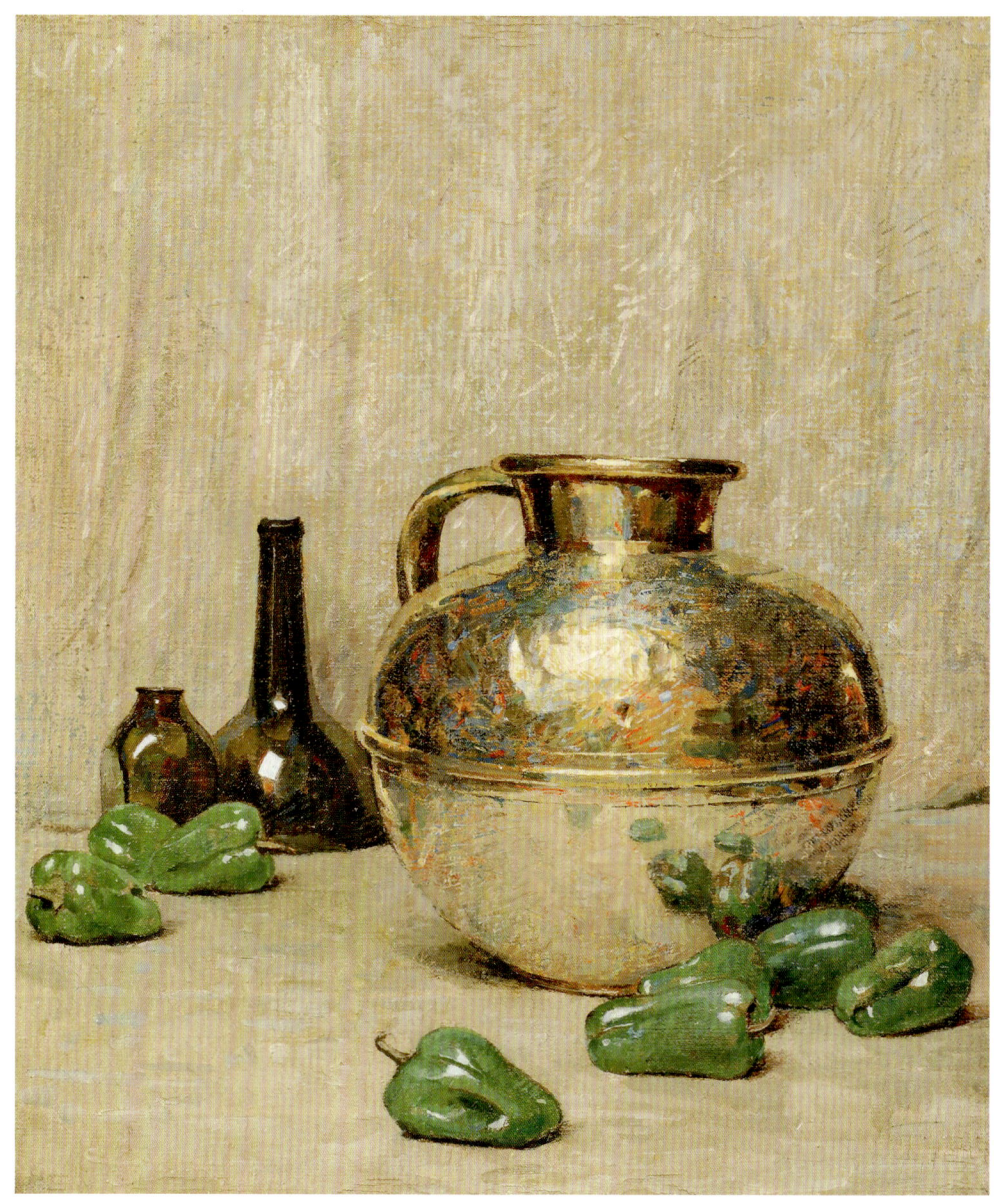

ABOVE: Dines Carlsen, *Still Life with Green Peppers,* 1931, oil on canvas, 24 × 20 inches (61 × 50.8 cm). Photo courtesy of Skinner, Inc., www. skinnerinc.com.

The colors that dominate a painting can affect how we feel about it. Here, Dines Carlsen's use of gold paint makes the image feel regal.

EXERCISE

DO A POSTER STUDY

A poster study is a small, preliminary, color version of a larger painting you plan to paint. Poster studies capture large shapes of color without going very far into the details. Doing a poster study is a fantastic way to work out your color, tonal, and compositional ideas before moving on to a larger final painting. The poster study is a very direct approach. Typically it is completed in one sitting—similar to an *alla prima* way of working.

For instructions on doing a poster study, see pages 292–296.

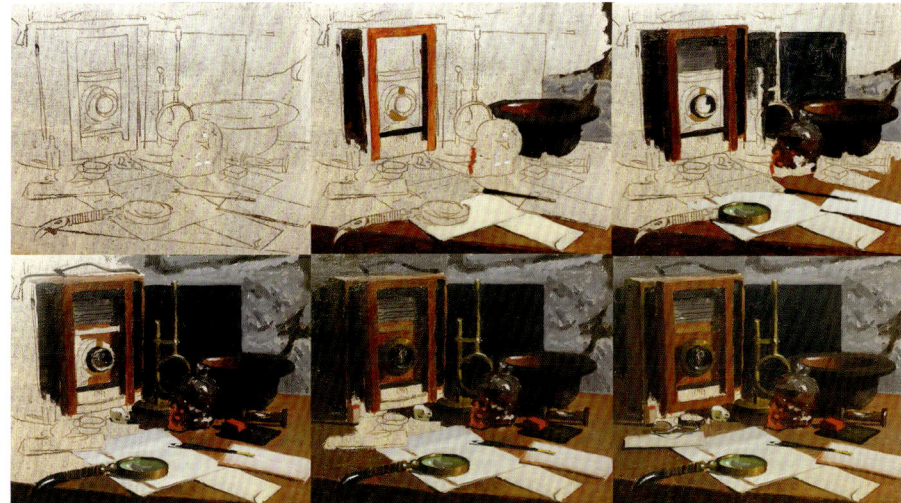

TOP: Stages of a poster study for my painting *Mr. Fixxer*.

BOTTOM: Todd M. Casey, poster study for *Mr. Fixxer,* 2018, oil on linen, 4 × 5 inches (10.16 × 12.7 cm).

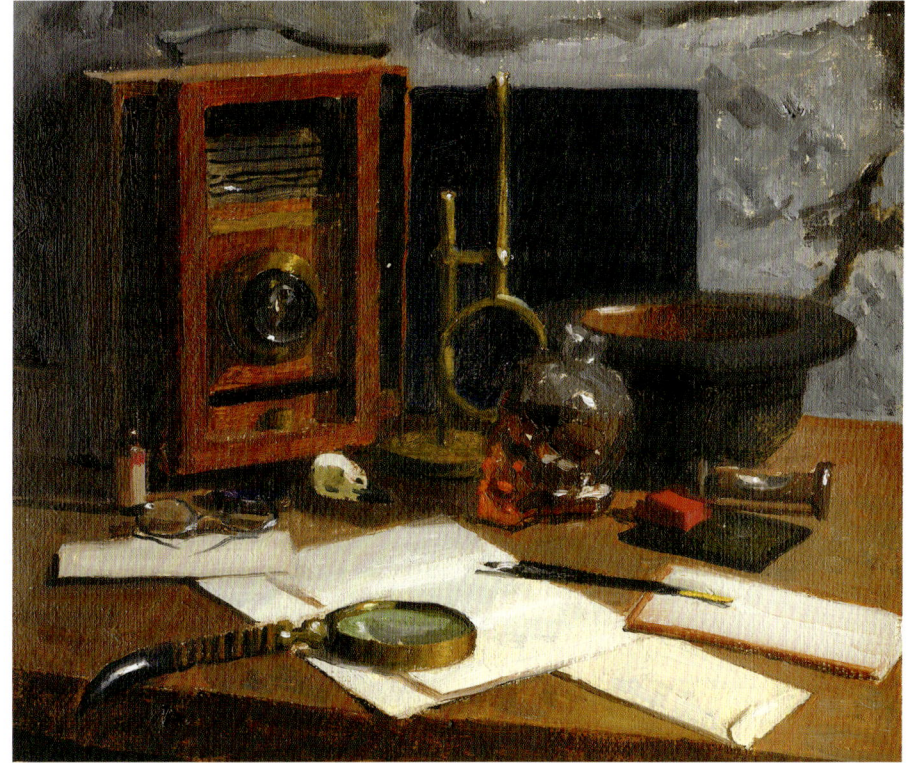

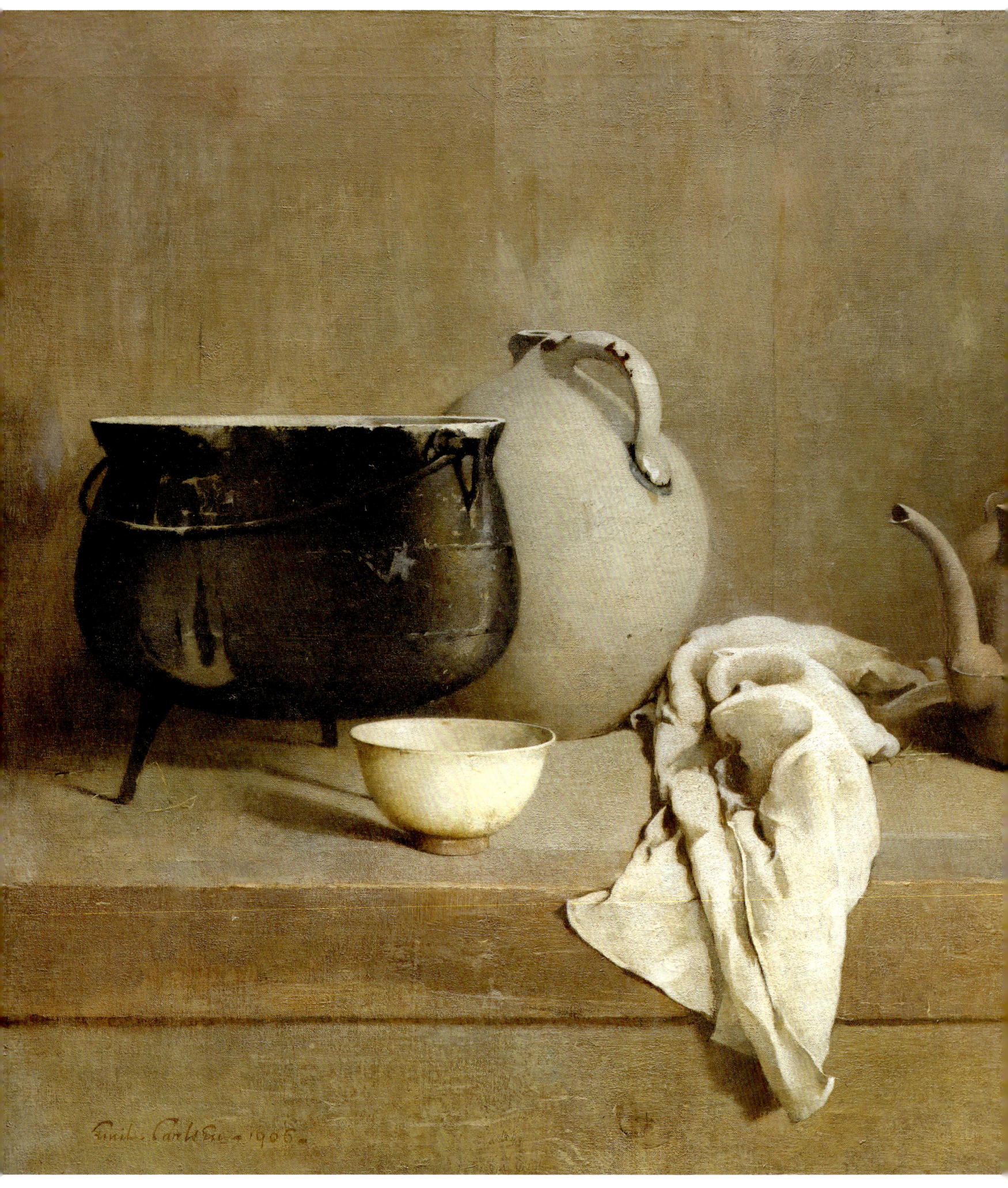

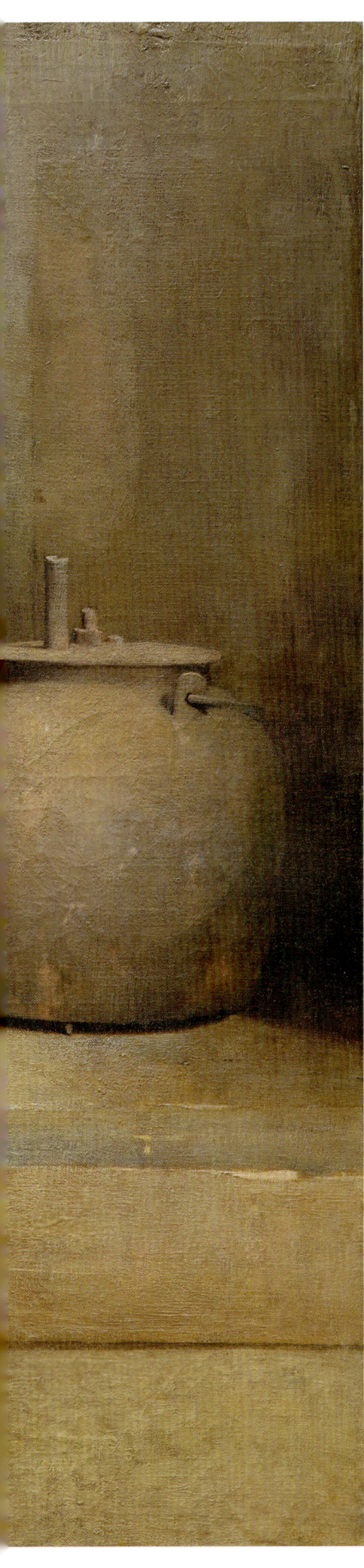

CHAPTER 7

MODELING FORMS: SCULPTING IN TWO DIMENSIONS

In building a statue, a sculptor doesn't keep adding clay to his subject. Actually, he keeps chiseling away at the nonessentials until the truth of his creation is revealed without obstruction.

BRUCE LEE

Representational painting is like a magical performance in which the artist fools the viewer's perception by creating a three-dimensional illusion on a two-dimensional surface. It's a lot like sculpting. In fact, in the academic tradition sculpture was intertwined with painting and the two were often taught together.

If you don't think like a sculptor, your paintings may appear flat. When painting, you've got to feel as if you're sculpting—pushing things back in space and pulling them forward into the light until they seem to be coming up off the surface.

LEFT: Emil Carlsen, *Study in Grey,* 1906, oil on canvas, 34 ¼ × 38 ⅜ inches (87 × 97.47 cm). Dallas Museum of Art, Munger Fund 1926.1.M.

MODELING FORM

Rendering the light and dark values of an observed object in an order that gives the appearance of volume is referred to as *modeling form*. In modeling form, we are combining all the concepts of light, drawing, value, and color to achieve form.

As I said in the previous chapter, every color relates to a value. It's often said that color gets all the attention but value does all the work. Indeed, accurate value structure and accurate drawing are the two most important aspects of a successful painting. If you nail these, you are well on your way to making a good painting. If your value structure works, you can get away with not having the color be super accurate.

PERCEPTION OF VALUE

In painting, we are always interpreting what we see and can never truly reproduce nature. For instance, our eyes can see many more variations in value than we could possibly reproduce with paint. This forces us to compress our range of values and to render form very subtly to overcome the limitations of our materials.

It's very hard for our brains to judge values accurately. In a sense, our brains just fail us. The images at bottom, below, provide an excellent example of this failure.

RIGHT: The range of values that can be achieved with pigments is narrower than the range of values we can observe in nature.

BOTTOM, LEFT TO RIGHT: The grid on the left shows gray squares in the light and shadow. Our eyes tell us that no value in the shadow is the same as any value in the light. But when we run a swatch of gray from square *B* up into square *A*, we can see that the gray square in the light has the same value as the white value in shadow.

We see value in the context of its surroundings. The gray square surrounded by black looks lighter than the gray square surrounded by white, but in fact both gray squares have the same value.

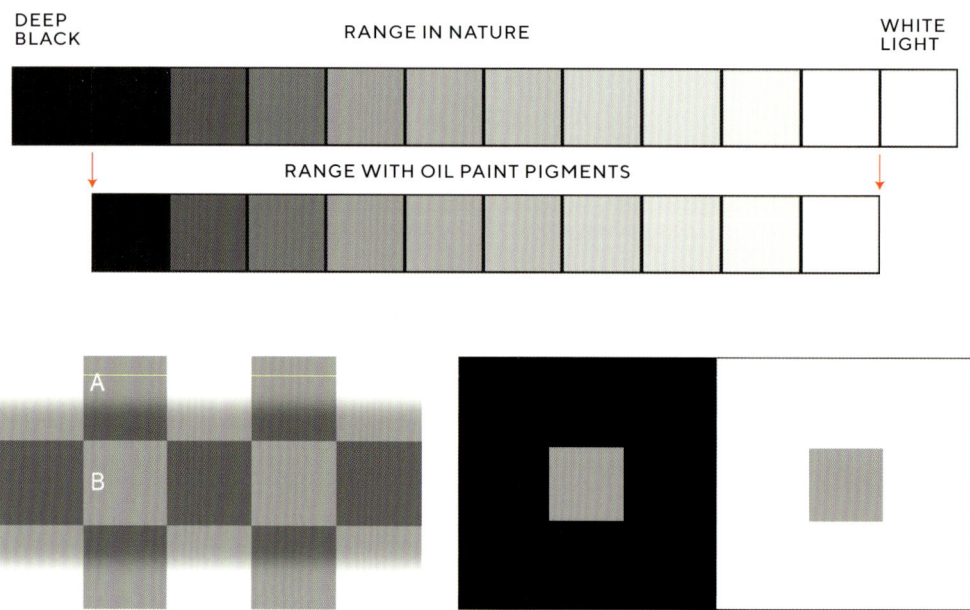

In psychology, this brain failure is known as the simultaneous contrast effect. Our brains don't gauge values accurately because what any value is surrounded by affects our perception greatly. For this reason, we have to be cautious when copying values optically. We must slowly grab bits of information to help us overcome these brain failures.

It's likewise very hard to judge the value of a color accurately; again, we're often misled by the context. The same color can appear to have different values (and also different hues) depending on what it is surrounded by.

RIGHT: Todd M. Casey, *Edison Stock Ticker*, 2017, oil on linen, 15 × 17 inches (38.1 × 43.18 cm). Private collection.

In this painting I used the same color—of the same value—on a portion of the ticker tape, a part of the book's spine, and the copper penny. But you'd never guess this just by looking at the painting. The square of color in the image at right reveals that the three apparently very different areas have the same value and hue.

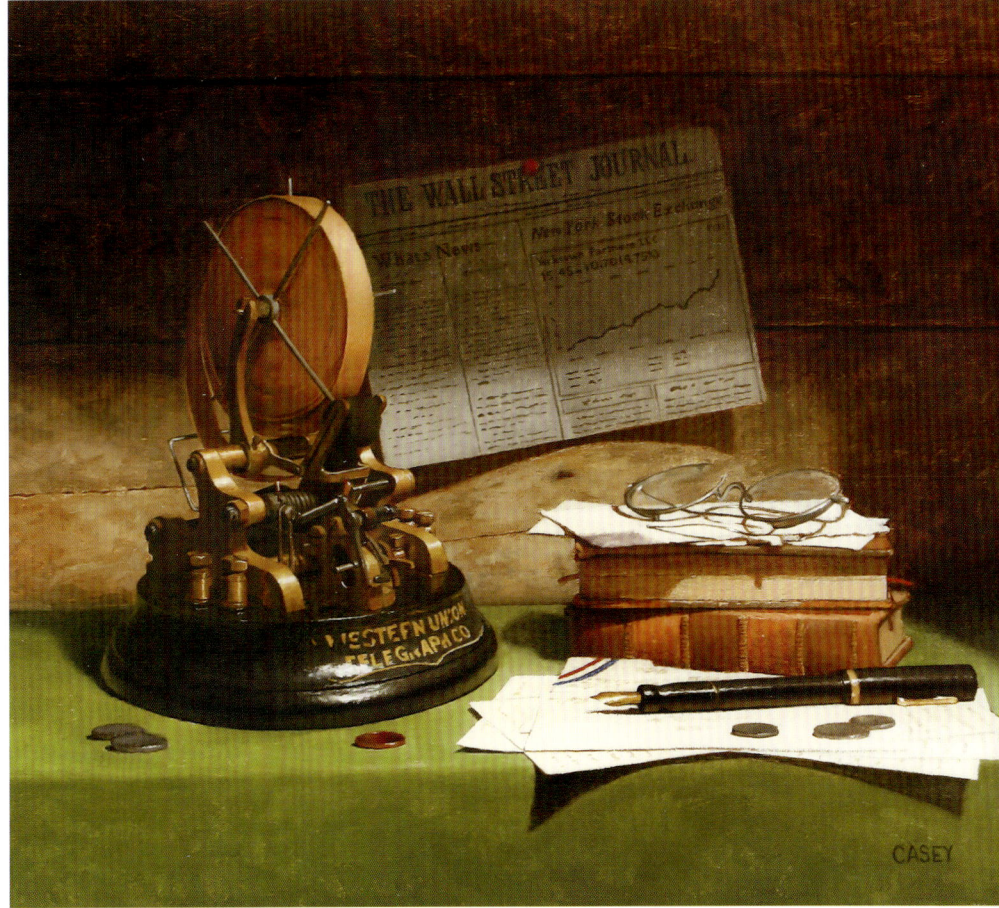

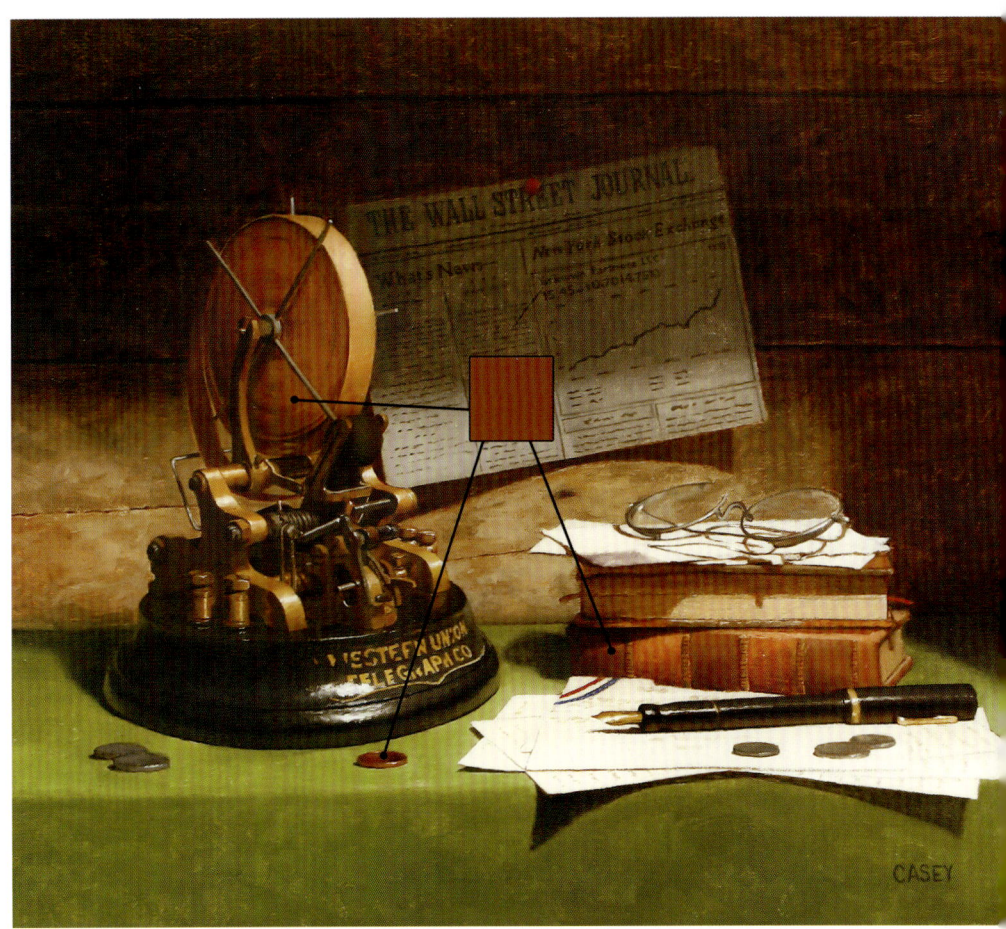

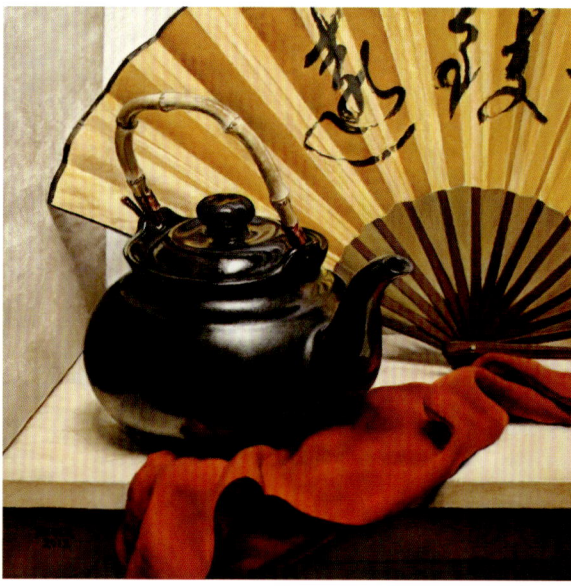
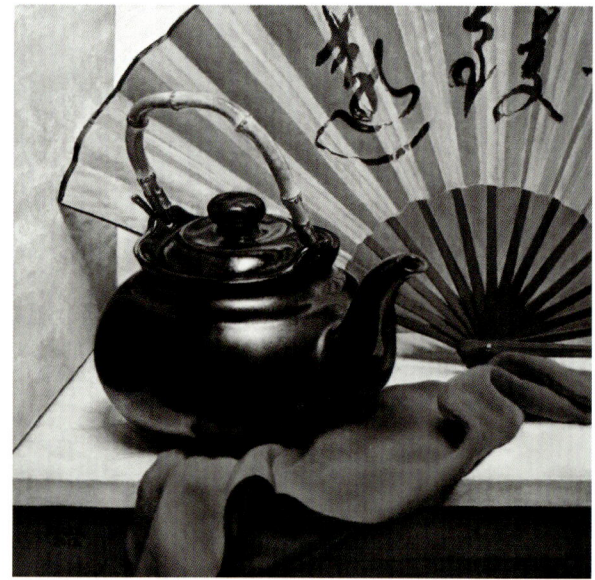

DETERMINING LOCAL VALUE

As I mentioned in the chapter on color, every color image has a value structure. To make a two-dimensional image appear three-dimensional, it is imperative to apply values correctly.

That said, it is very difficult to render an object in the *correct range* of values. For example, a specific, compressed value range would be required to accurately render each of the spheres shown in the image at left, below.

One way to determine the local value is to mix your best approximation of the value you think the object is. Then with a palette knife, hold a sample of the paint mixture to the setup to see if it matches the midtones.

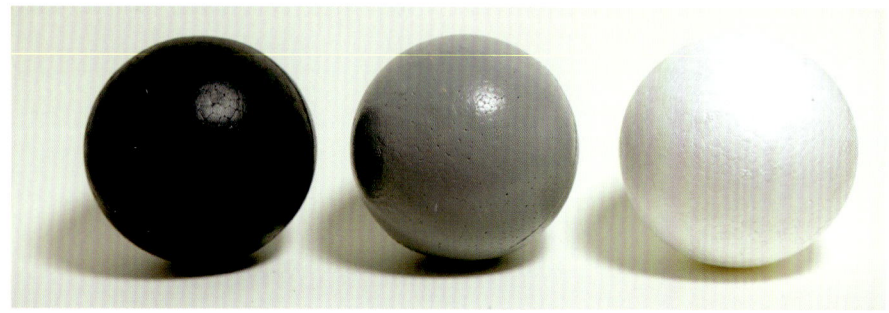

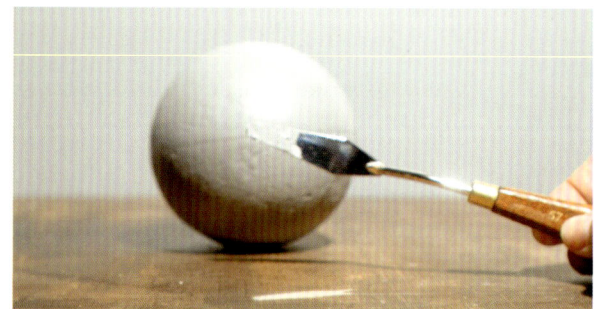

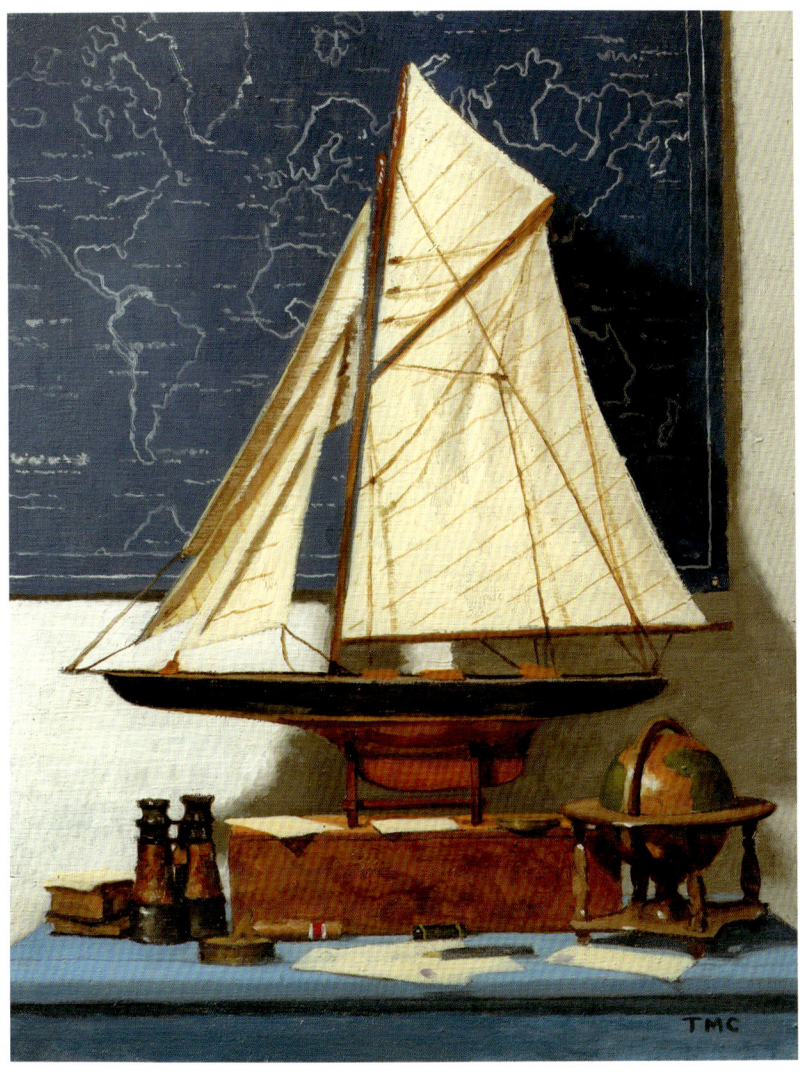
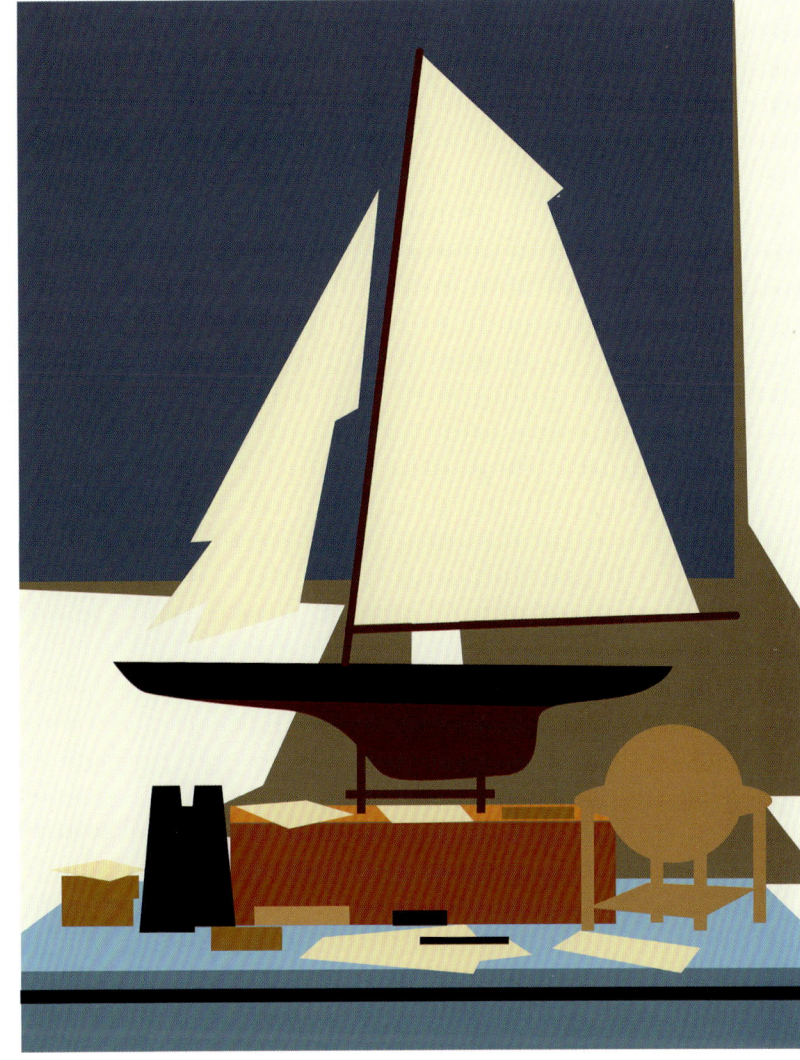

THE ILLUSION OF DEPTH

When we are painting forms we see, we are essentially describing the way the light is falling on the forms. When light strikes a surface to reveal the form it is hitting, it produces a perception of depth, and the painter's goal is to produce the illusion of that depth through value.

Even when light strikes a flat surface, there is a slow gradation of values known as light falloff. This is very important to recognize, because if one value covers too much of an area, it will appear flat—similar to a paper cutout.

In a controlled indoor environment such as your studio, dark values fall back in space and light values push forward. This helps you set up your value range. The

ABOVE: Todd M. Casey, *The World Traveler*, 2018, oil on panel, 8 × 6 inches (20.32 × 15.24 cm). Private collection.

On the left is my painting *The World Traveler*; on the right, an image of the painting with all indications of depth removed, so that everything appears as flat shapes. A painting starts to feel dimensional when small transitions of values are applied to each form, even areas that are virtually flat.

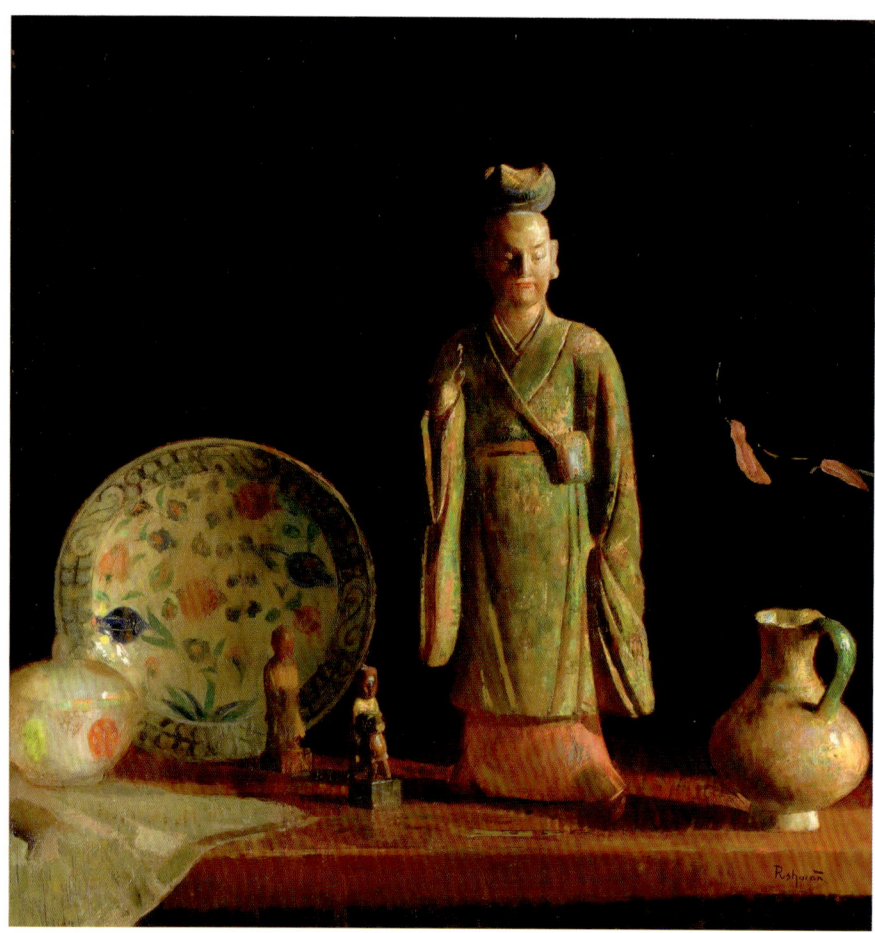
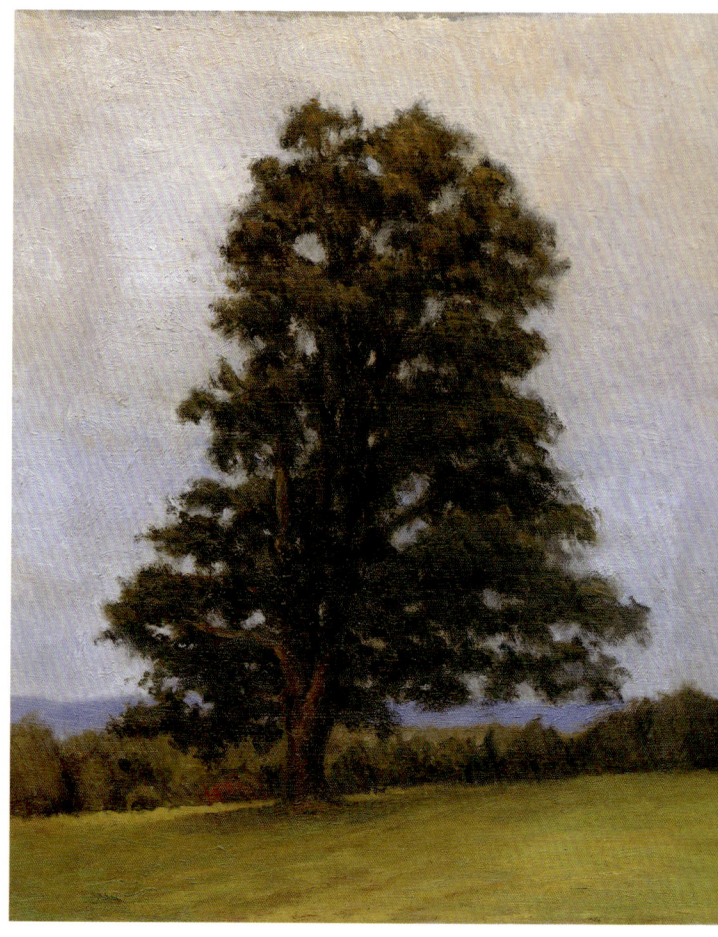

ABOVE, LEFT: Hovsep Pushman, *The Prince*, c. 1930, oil on board, 27 ½ × 25 ½ inches (69.9 × 64.8 cm). Photo courtesy of Heritage Auctions, HA.com.

ABOVE, RIGHT: Todd M. Casey, *Berman's Tree*, 2015, oil on panel, 10 × 8 inches (25.4 × 20.32 cm).

In the painting at the left, the darks recede and the lighter values come forward. It's just the opposite in most landscape painting. In outdoor scenes like the picture at right, objects get lighter as they move back in space.

opposite, however, is true outdoors in nature: things grow lighter as they move back in space. In an outdoor scene, higher-contrast areas appear closer to the viewer; lower contrast—due to moisture in the air—looks farther away. (This is what's known as atmospheric perspective.) You could have a studio setup in which the objects were backlit, making the background lighter than the foreground, but this sort of situation is very rare in still life painting.

ROUNDER VERSUS FLATTER FORMS

Rounder objects tend to have a faster rate of a value change. Flatter forms tend to roll very slowly and to change in value very gradually. This change in value on flatter forms is due to the light falloff, which should always be considered to add form to your painting. Sometimes it is quite noticeable, but at other times it is super subtle.

RIGHT: Todd M. Casey, *Blue Ballet,* 2015, oil on linen, 12 × 9 inches (30.48 × 22.86 cm). Courtesy of Rehs Contemporary Galleries, New York.

In this painting the roundness of the blue ballet squash is apparent. If the color and values are not applied in the correct range an object will appear flat.

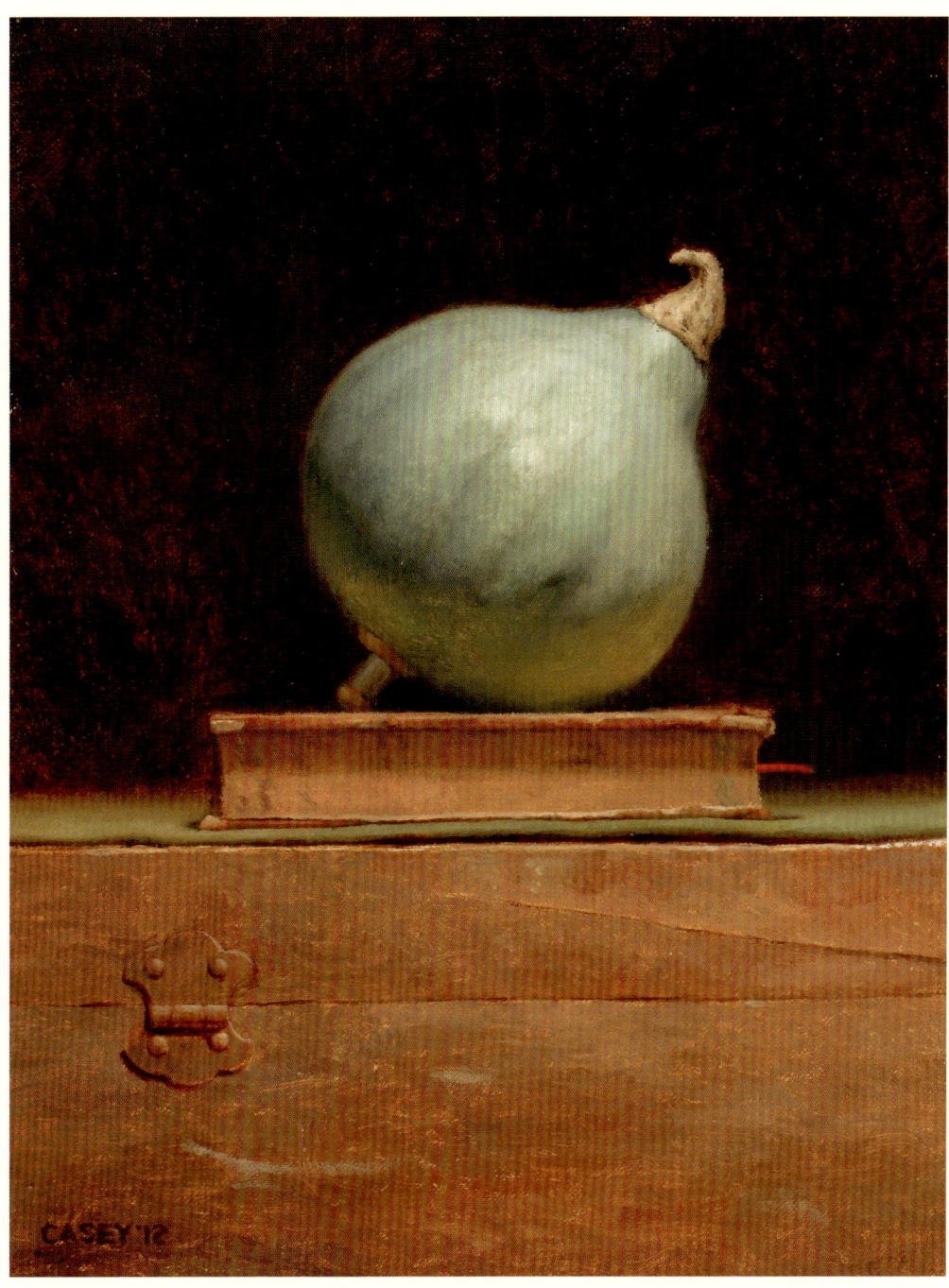

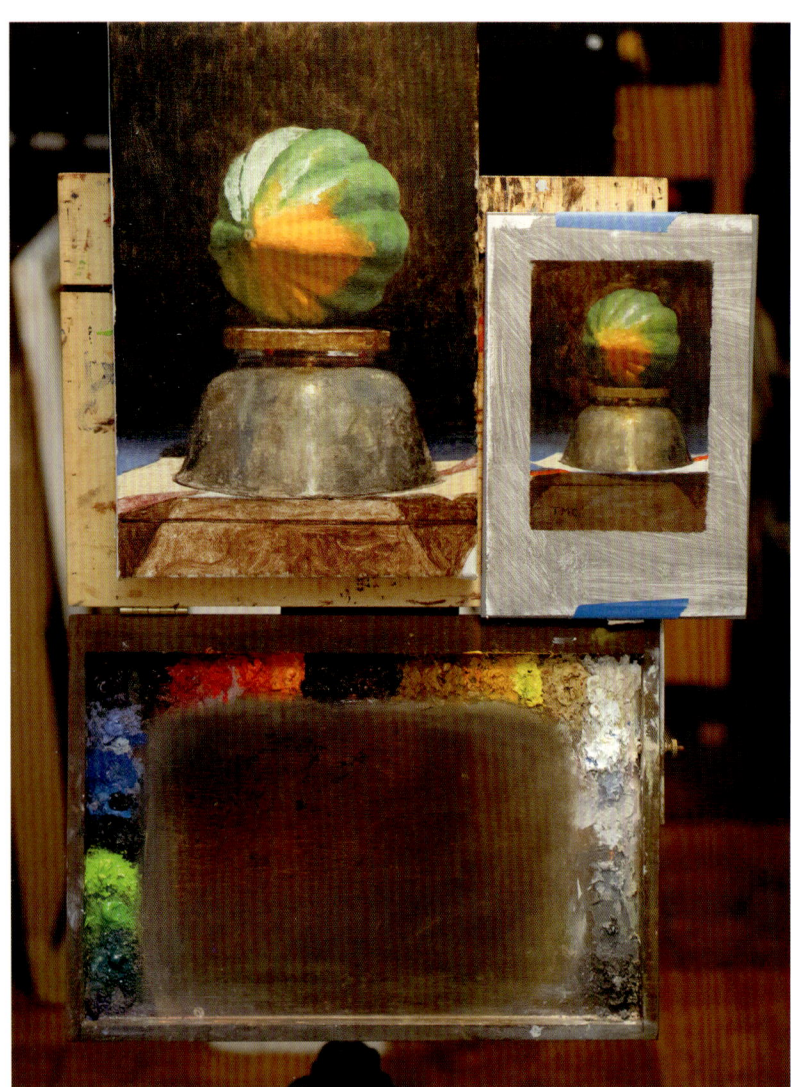

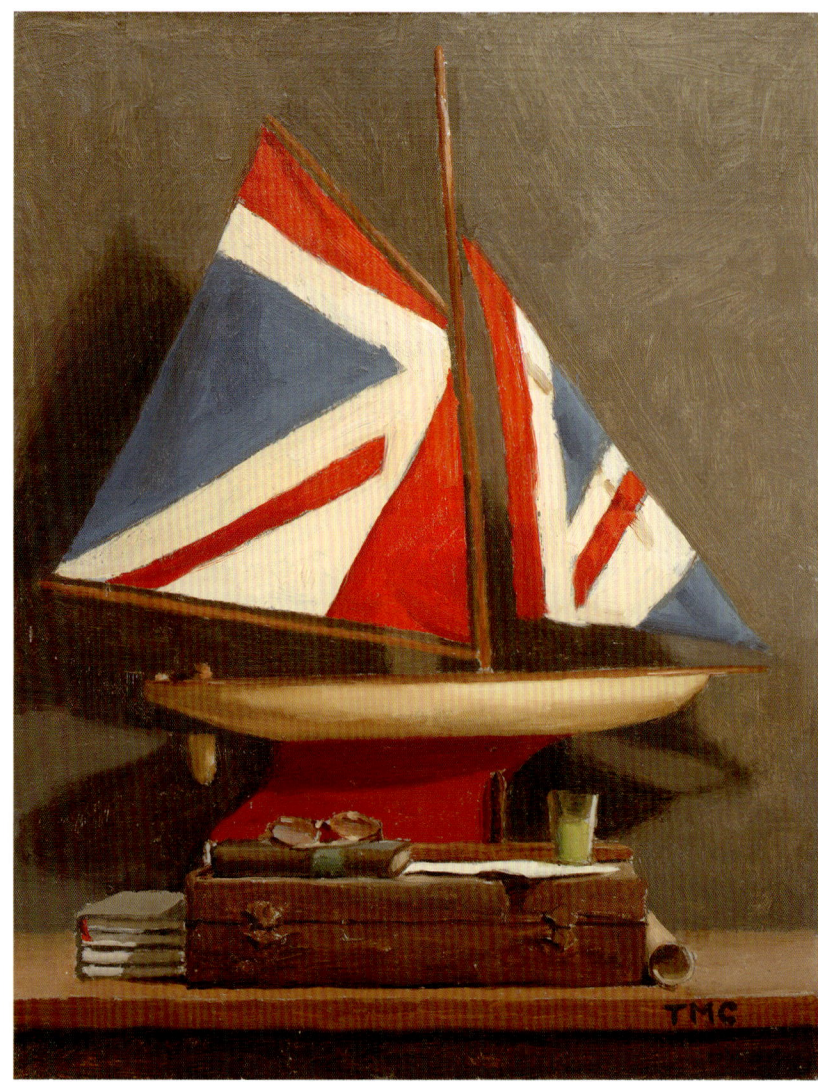

WORKING OPTICALLY: THE POSTER STUDY

Just as we work both optically and conceptually when drawing, we use the same two approaches when painting. The optical way of working is to paint what you see in front of you. It's a very two-dimensional way of thinking, in which you copy the information as you see it. Think of it as abstractly recording the two-dimensional shapes of light, shadow, and contour and also how the shapes interlock with one another. Essentially, it's copying what you see without thinking about what it is you are painting.

The poster study—the first step toward a final painting—is a purely optical experience. The aim is to observe how light falls on your setup and also work out your composition. Poster studies are small and slightly abstract—done with much less

TIP

While it is not imperative, I highly recommend that you tone your canvas rather than working on a white surface. It can be hard to gauge any values off a white surface, because every other color appears darker than the surface, which is the lightest color. (The same thing happens if you work on a black surface; every color you apply appears light in contrast.)

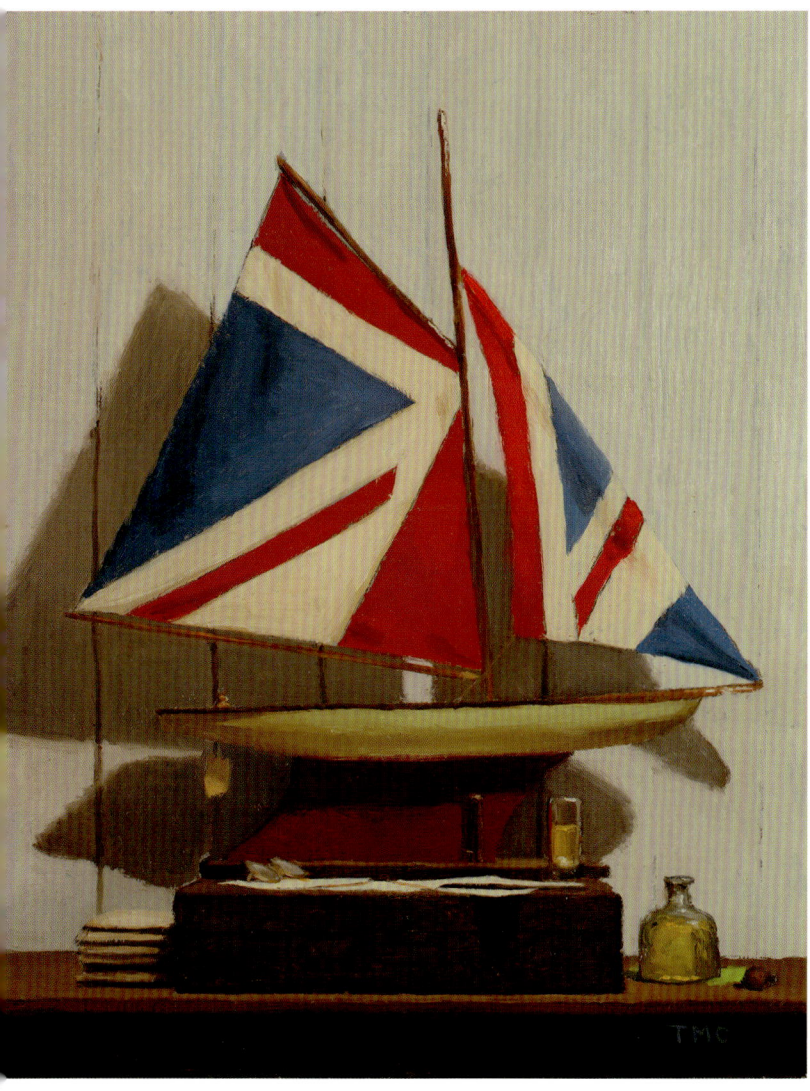
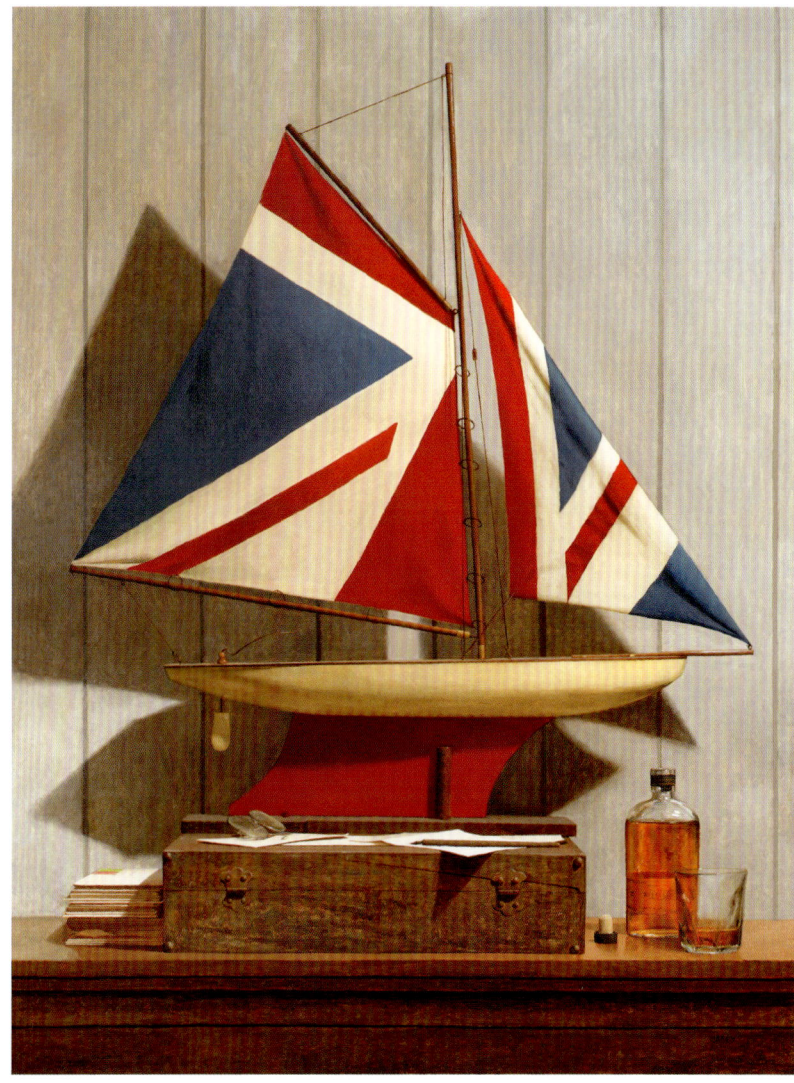

detail than the final painting. I like to think of them as the dress rehearsal before the big performance.

When working on a large painting, you can get wrapped up in the experience of modeling form with paint and can lose track of the big picture. The poster study is intended to provide you with a reference to keep you in check throughout the larger final painting. It helps you stay in the correct range of values so you don't make your tonal transitions progress too fast or too slow.

The first two values I locate on a poster study are the lightest light and the darkest dark (normally the highlight and the crevice shadow or a black object in shadow). The reason for this is that there is usually no guessing as to what each of these colors will be. They are the lightest and darkest pigments I have: black and white. Then, every other stroke of paint I put down will be darker than white and lighter than black.

OPPOSITE, LEFT: The poster study is meant to guide your work on the final painting. I usually hang it next to the final painting, so that I can refer to it as I work.

OPPOSITE, RIGHT, AND THIS PAGE: Todd M. Casey, two studies (each 8 × 6 inches) and final painting *The Great Escape,* 2015, oil on canvas, 48 × 36 inches (121.92 × 91.44 cm). All are in private collections.

I'll often do more than more than one poster study to work out a painting's composition and the narrative. These small paintings then guide the final painting, shown here above right.

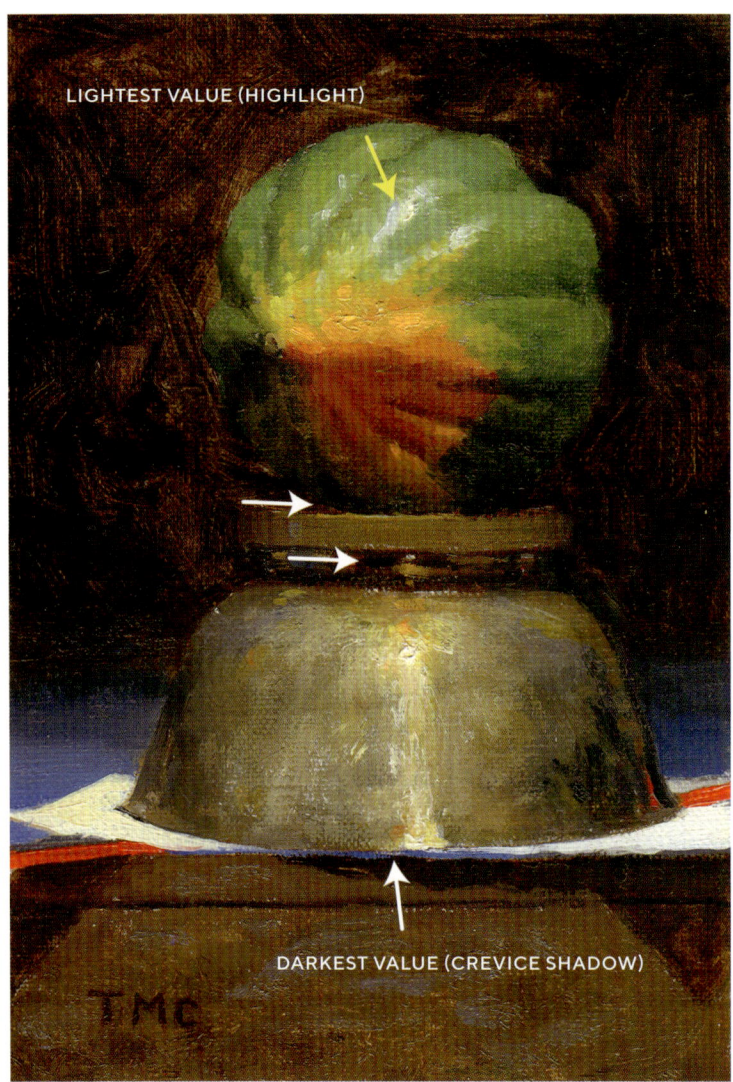

LIGHTEST VALUE (HIGHLIGHT)

DARKEST VALUE (CREVICE SHADOW)

TMC

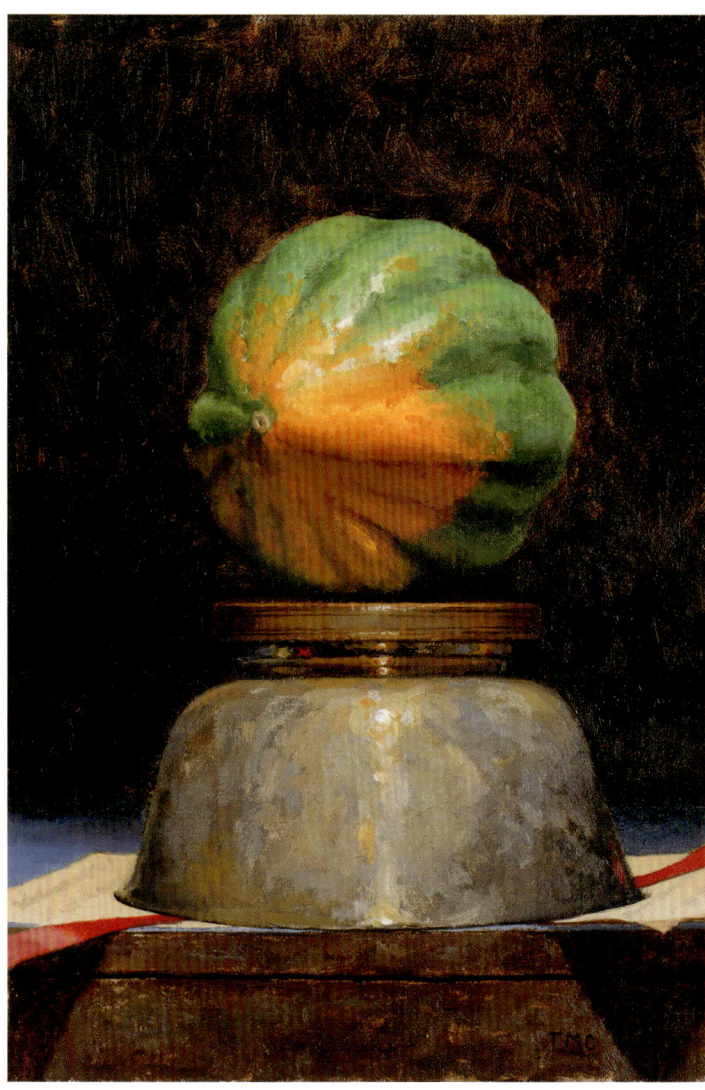

ABOVE, LEFT: Todd M. Casey, *Bowl with Acorn Squash*, 2019, oil on linen, 6 × 4 inches (15.24 × 10.16 cm). Courtesy of Rehs Contemporary Galleries, New York.

Finding the lightest value and the darkest value will set up your value range.

ABOVE, RIGHT: Todd M. Casey, *Silver Bowl with Acorn Squash*, 2019, oil on linen, 12 × 8 inches (30.48 × 20.32 cm). Courtesy of Rehs Contemporary Galleries, New York.

RIGHT: After you've laid in the lightest and darkest values, you must render the rest of the picture with the eight values in between.

Next, I render the form that has the largest range of value from dark to light. Most of the time this is a round object such as a fruit or vegetable. This lets me use the whole value scale and gives me a lot of information from which to gauge everything else. Each piece of information I add helps me get to the next stage, making the painting that much more accurate.

Finding three values that butt up against one another in a setup is a great way to figure out what those values are. This is called *triangulating values*, because you are deriving the information from three different values together.

SMALLER RANGE

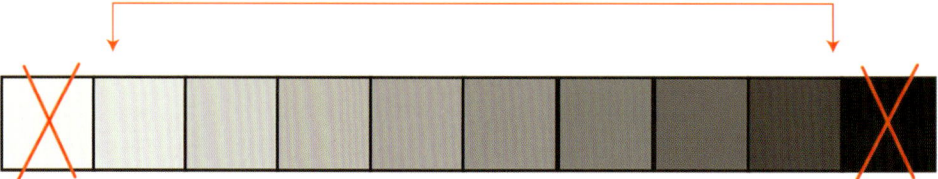

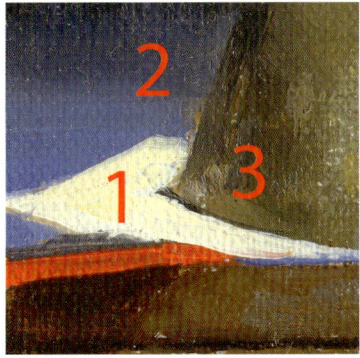
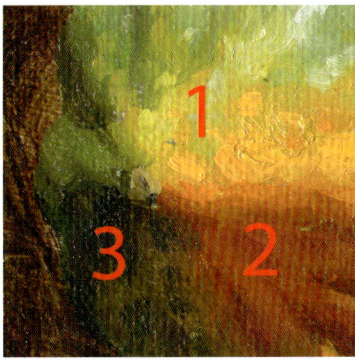
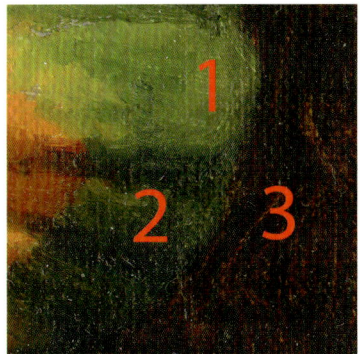
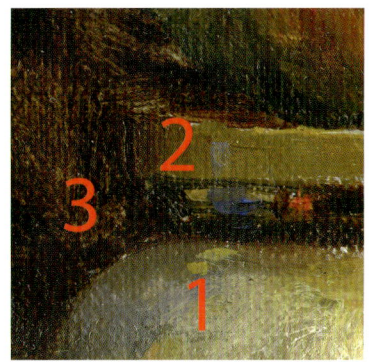

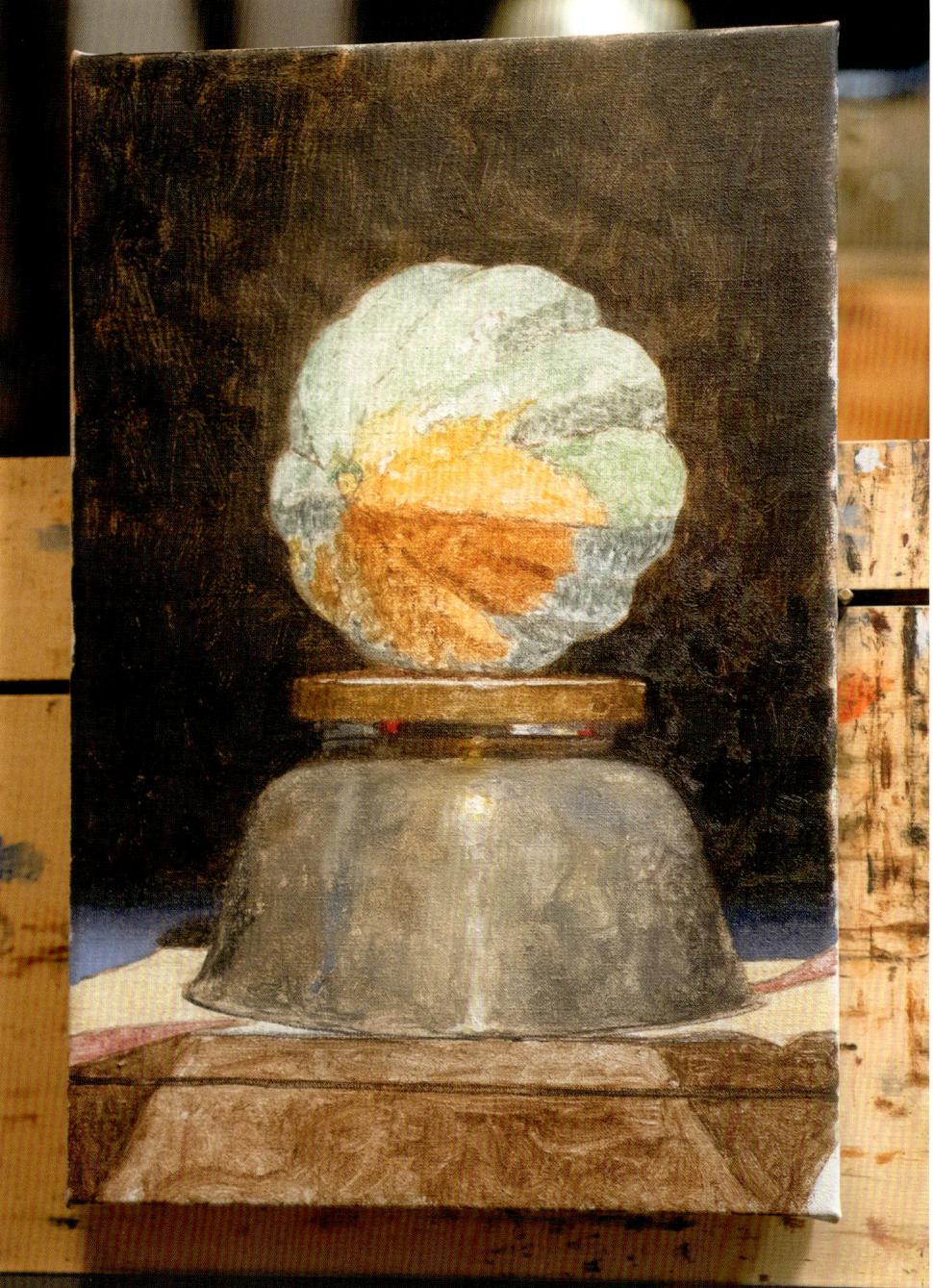

ABOVE: In each of these details from my painting *Bowl with Acorn Squash*, area 1 is lighter than area 2 and area 2 is lighter than area 3. When working on the painting, I triangulated adjacent values in each of these spots.

THE COLOR WASH-IN

Before I begin rendering forms, I like to start by laying down a thin layer of paint referred to as a wash-in. This is the first step in collecting color information and will help guide color decisions in every step after. Think of the wash-in as establishing the general color of each area.

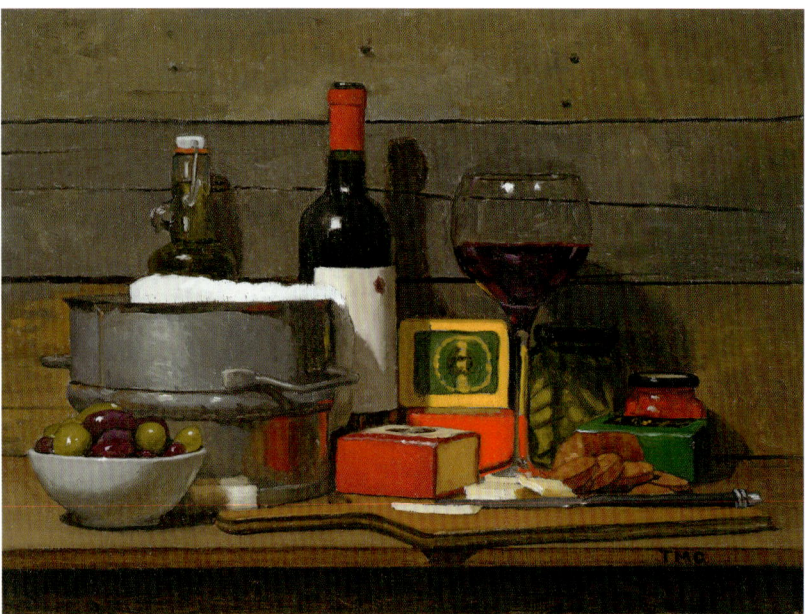

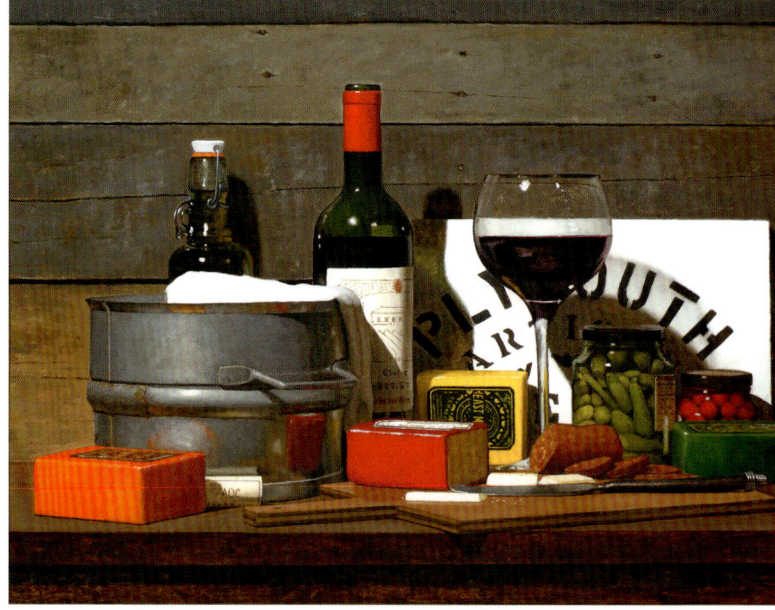

Here are two ways of working with the same setup: my study and the final painting of *Plymouth Cheese*. The study was done optically. The final painting—more refined, with subtler values—mixed the optical and the conceptual.

WORKING CONCEPTUALLY

The other way of working is the conceptual model, or the three-dimensional way of thinking. Working conceptually is about applying what you know about structure and perspective to your painting.

When you're working conceptually—as opposed to optically—you are not copying directly what you see in front of you. Instead, you're using your painterly tools—your knowledge of planes and your understanding of how to articulate light and model form—to describe light hitting forms. The goal is to achieve a tactile sensation of sculpting forms on a two-dimensional surface. Working conceptually also helps you navigate around some of the shortcomings of perception. For example, we can sometimes be misled by our eyes regarding what is in the light and what is in shadow. A conceptual model can help you identify the direction of a plane to determine whether it is in fact in light or shadow.

It's important to distinguish between the optical and conceptual modes, but it is most desirable to use both together, as they keep each other in check. The conceptual way of painting is a very sculptural approach and pushes depth in a painting. To heighten the illusion of depth, you can push it beyond what you actually observe. At a certain point, the painting has to function on its own, without the setup. So if you need to, feel free to push the illusion even further.

SIMPLIFYING INFORMATION

Just as you did when drawing, you want to imagine your objects as being composed of planes rather than curves when painting. Imagine drawing a grid of horizontal and vertical lines on a sphere, like latitude and longitude lines on a globe. If you think of each resulting square as a plane, the sphere resembles a disco ball. In 3-D modeling, this is referred to as a wireframe (or mesh). The wireframe allows you to simplify the information you see, treating it as a set of planes rather than curved surfaces. Flat planes make it easier to calculate the direction in which the plane is facing.

TIP

I highly recommend that you frequently get up and walk around your setup while painting. This will help you get a three-dimensional sense of the forms. When I was studying drawing and painting, we students would physically feel the forms we were depicting to understand the directions of the planes. I encourage you to do this, too. The tactile sensation really gives you a sculptural sense of the forms.

BELOW: To simplify a sphere, break down the curved surface into planes like those of a disco ball. Converting the curved surface to a set of planes makes it easy to tell where each portion of the sphere lies in relation to the light source.

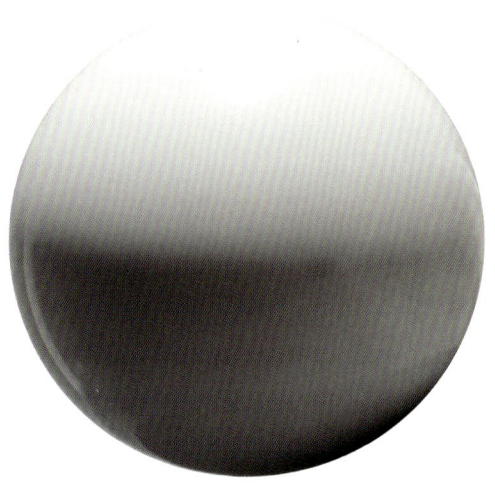
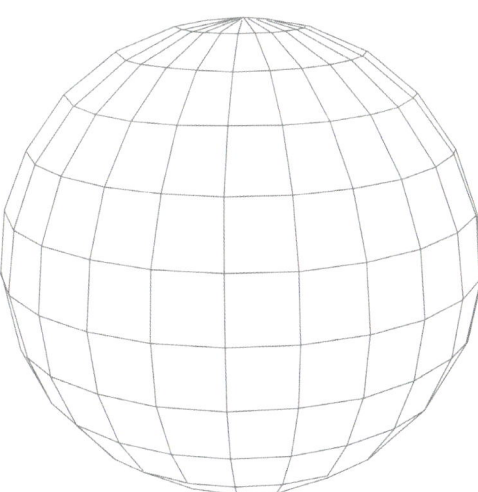
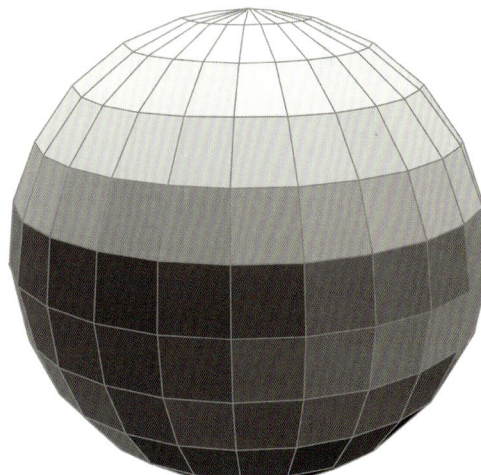

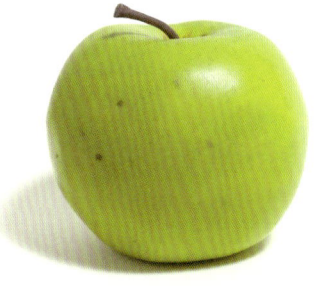

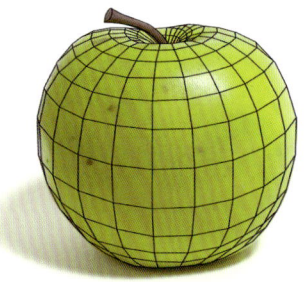

You can also break down more complex forms, like this apple, into planes to simplify what you see.

As with the sphere, you can break down more complex, real-life curved forms into a set of planes. As you look at the apple in the photo at left, you'll notice a distinct range of values going from light to dark. To approach a rendering of the apple, you should break down its curved surface into a set of flat planes and consider the geometry of the light in relation to each plane. The series of illustrations below demonstrate this process.

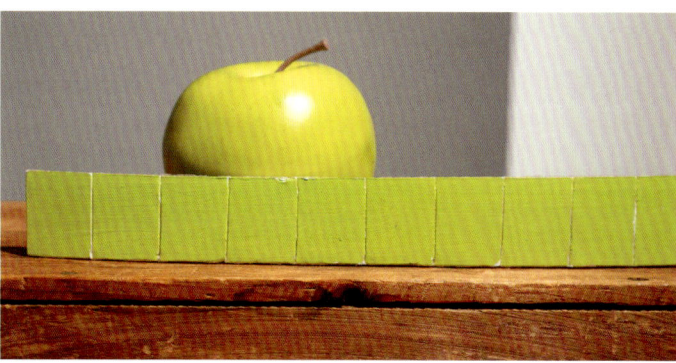

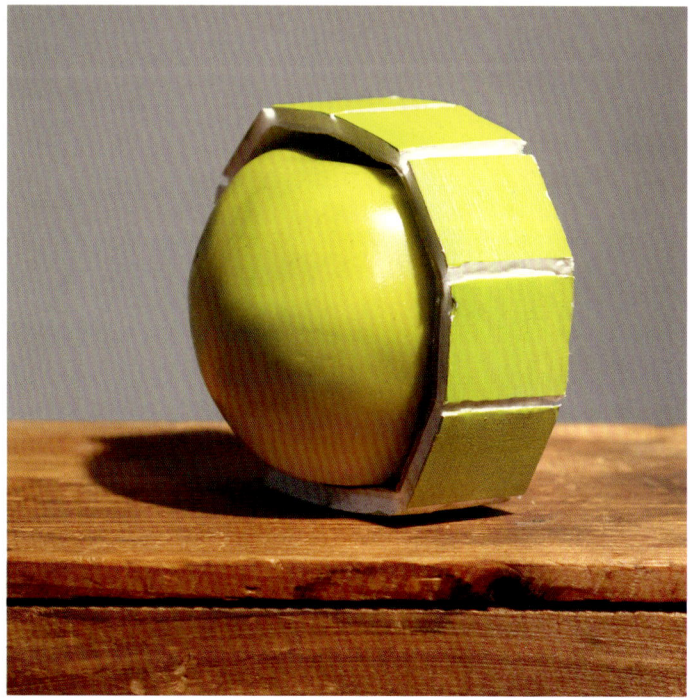

FAR LEFT: On this strip of foamcore with nine squares, I've painted the local color of the apple.

NEAR LEFT, TOP: As compared with the apple, the strip is flat and appears to have almost no form.

NEAR LEFT, BOTTOM: When the strip is wrapped around the apple, you see a gradation of values.

BELOW: This gradation of values resembles a value scale—but in green instead of gray.

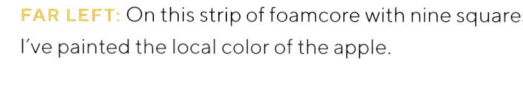

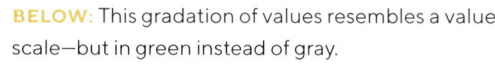

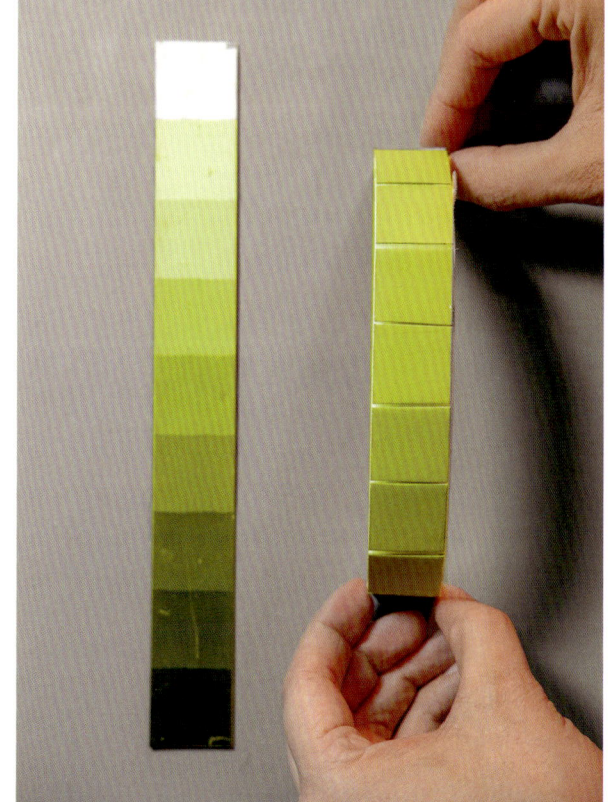

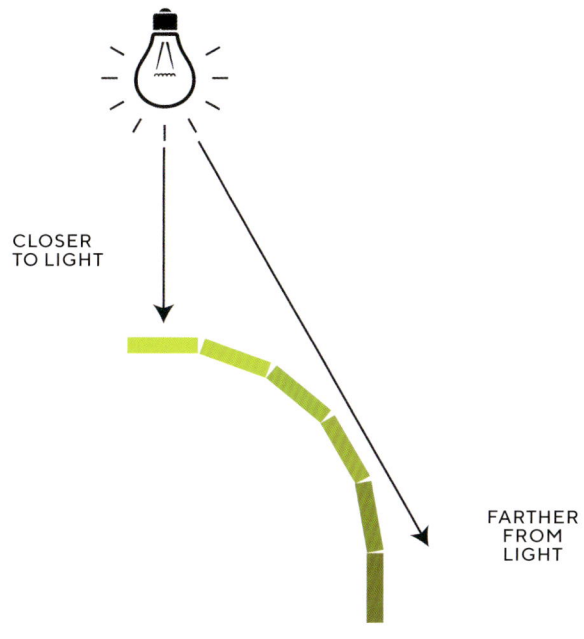

CLOSER
TO LIGHT

FARTHER
FROM
LIGHT

The light most facing plane is typically the lightest part of an object. As the plane begins to turn, it receives less light and darkens.

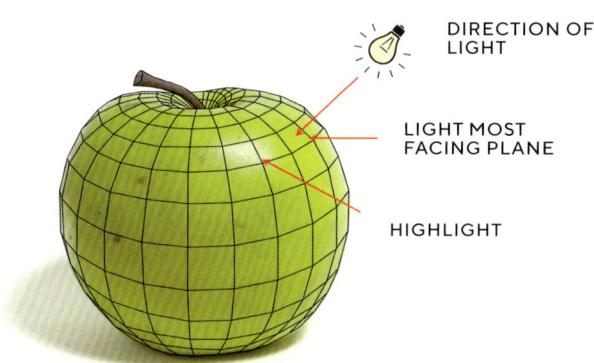

DIRECTION OF LIGHT

LIGHT MOST FACING PLANE

HIGHLIGHT

Finding the light most facing plane is the first step in articulating the direction of the light. The farther from the light a plane is, the darker it will appear.

PLANE ORIENTATION AFFECTING VALUE

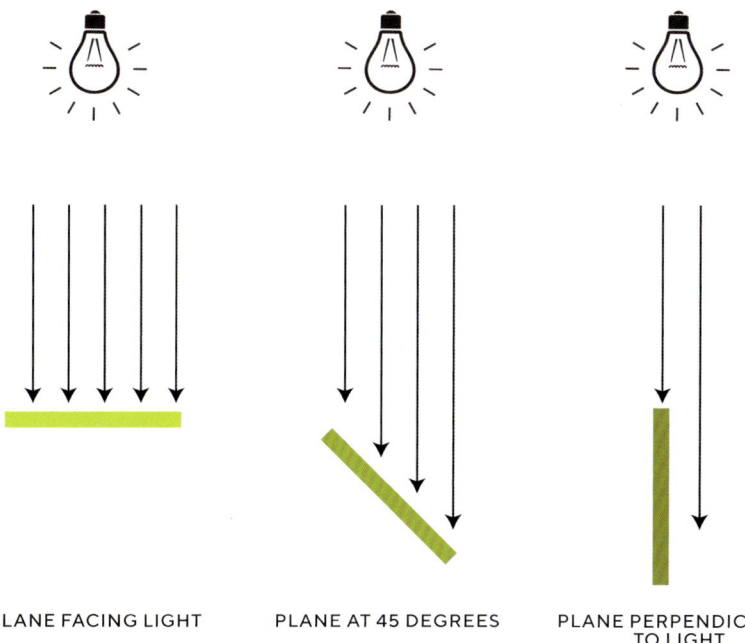

PLANE FACING LIGHT	PLANE AT 45 DEGREES	PLANE PERPENDICULAR TO LIGHT
IN FULL LIGHT	IN HALF LIGHT	IN SHADOW

When a plane faces the light, it receives more light waves/particles. As it begins to rotate away from the light, the plane grows darker and darker until it is facing away from the light source.

THE PROFILE OF AN OBJECT

Observing a form from different angles can help you understand what you're seeing—as if you were building a three-dimensional model of it in your mind. From each angle, the form will have a particular profile, and studying the profile will help you see which way each part of the form is facing. (On symmetrical objects, the profile is the same from every angle.)

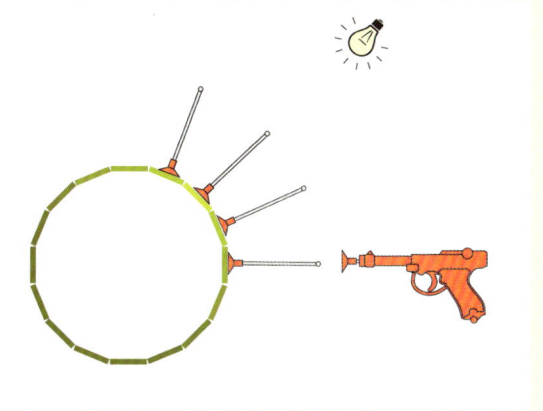

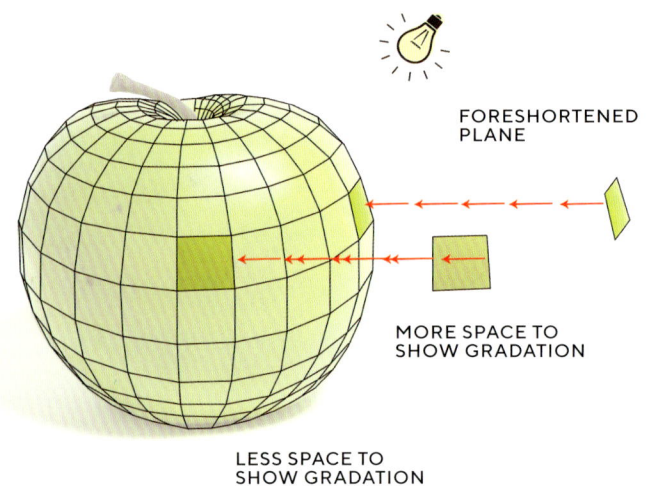

FORESHORTENED
PLANE

MORE SPACE TO
SHOW GRADATION

LESS SPACE TO
SHOW GRADATION

Each plane, no matter how big or small it appears, must show a value progression. When a plane is foreshortened there is a smaller area to show the transition of values, but it still has to be noted. If the plane is rendered as having just one value, it will appear flat.

FORESHORTENING OF PLANES

One the biggest challenges you face when modeling form is rendering a foreshortened plane. In addition to helping you observe value changes, a wireframe like the one covering the apple at left can also help you see how foreshortening is happening on any plane that is not directly facing you. You have to describe value changes on the foreshortened planes, as well, but you have a smaller space in which to do so.

APPLYING FORM TO A PAINTING

Now for the moment you've been waiting for: applying form to an actual painting. To do this, you'll combine the optical and the conceptual models and bring together all your knowledge of light, color, and value. In this demo, I will show how to paint one object—a lime—in a larger still life setup.

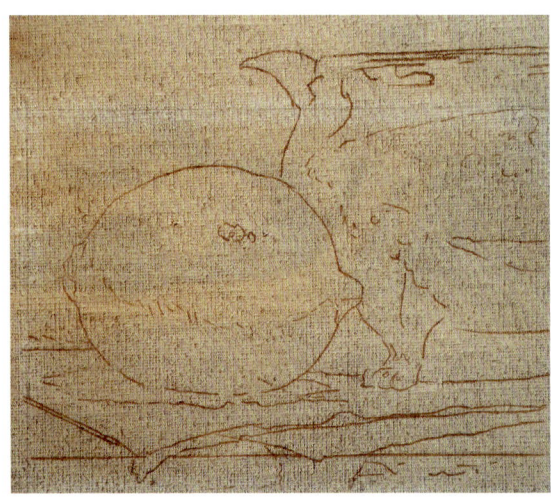

STEP 1: TRANSFER THE DRAWING

The first step is to transfer the drawing to the painting surface—in this case, linen that has been lightly toned with burnt umber. (See pages 187–188 for methods of transferring drawings.)

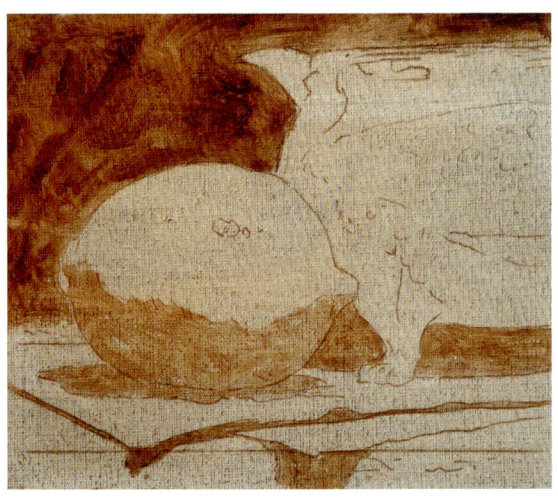

STEP 2: SEPARATE LIGHT FROM SHADOW

The next step is the underpainting, done with a color like burnt umber or raw umber. Just by separating light and shadow, you'll begin to give the image dimension. (See chapter 8 for a detailed discussion of underpainting.)

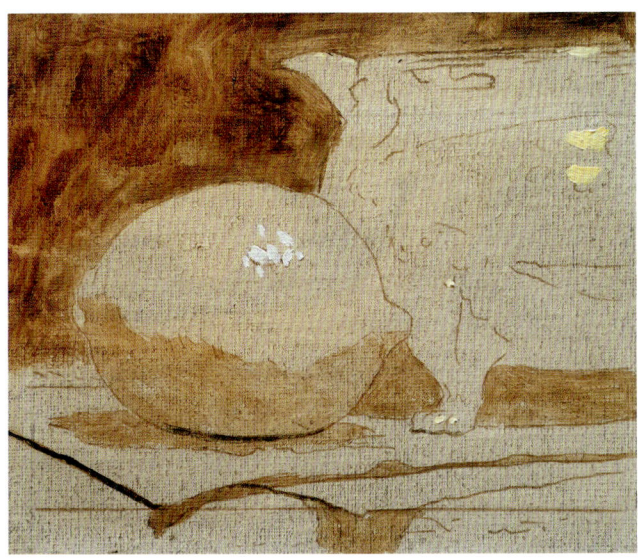

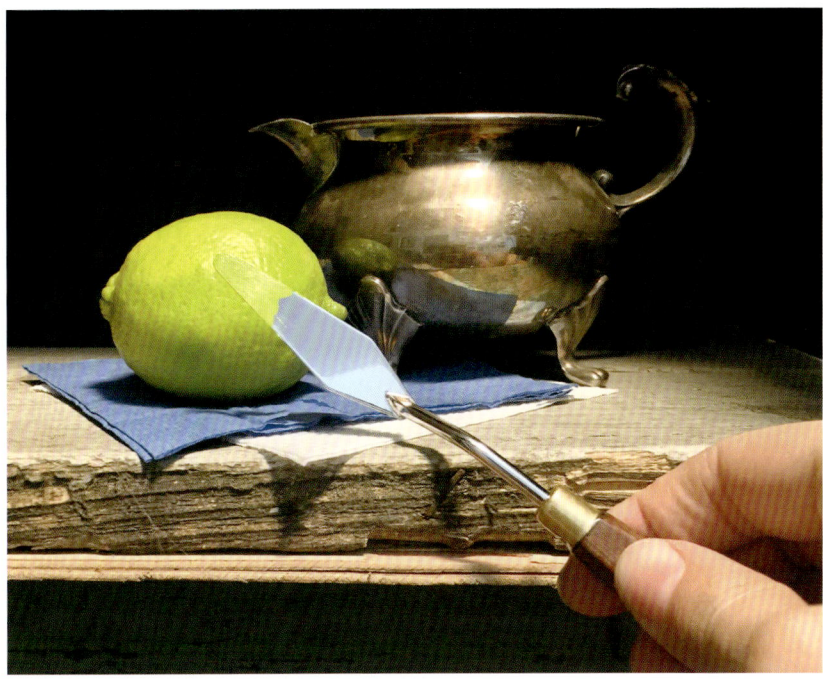

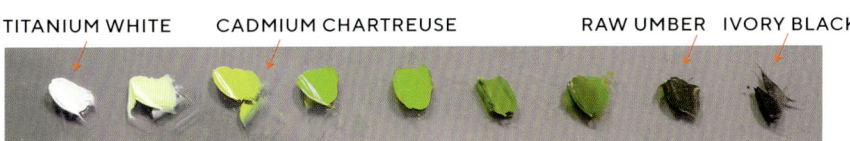

TITANIUM WHITE   **CADMIUM CHARTREUSE**   **RAW UMBER** **IVORY BLACK**

STEP 3: ESTABLISH THE LIGHTEST LIGHT AND DARKEST DARK

Next, establish the lightest light and the darkest dark values. On this lime, the lightest lights are the surface highlights. The darkest darks are the crevice shadows under the forms. By doing this, you're adding a bit more dimension—as in a heightened chalk drawing.

STEP 4: FIND THE LOCAL COLOR/VALUE AND MIX A LIGHT-TO-DARK STRING

Finding the local color of the lime is essential to mixing a light-to-dark string for that color. Mixing a color and then checking it by holding it up to the light part of the halftone will get you pretty close to the local color. Then, find lighter and darker versions of the color to mix a string. (See pages 216–223 on mixing color strings.)

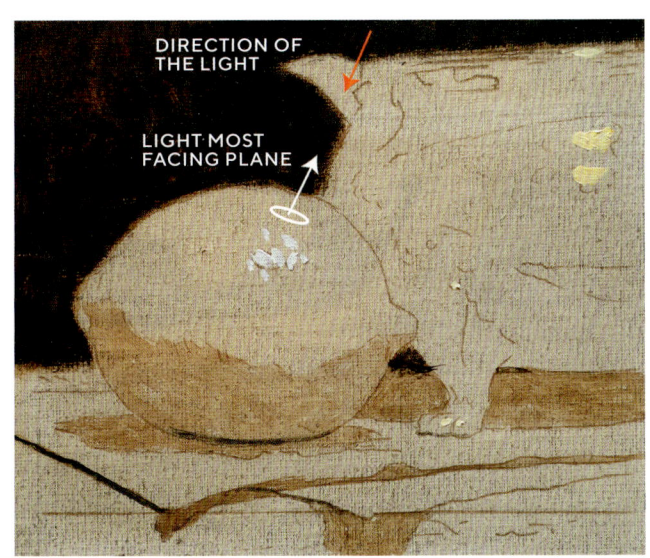

DIRECTION OF
THE LIGHT

LIGHT MOST
FACING PLANE

STEP 5: ESTABLISH THE DIRECTION OF THE LIGHT AND THE LIGHT MOST FACING PLANE

The first step in modeling form is to establish where the light is coming from. The direction of the light informs everything in a painting no matter how big or small the light source is. You may want to lightly draw an arrow at the top of your painting surface to indicate the light's direction. This will remind you to not fall into painting what you see but rather to paint with the light in mind. The light most facing plane should point to the light source. I often mark the light most facing plane, too.

When starting to render values, you must always find the light most facing plane. Finding this is like putting a stake in the ground to remind you of your lightest value.

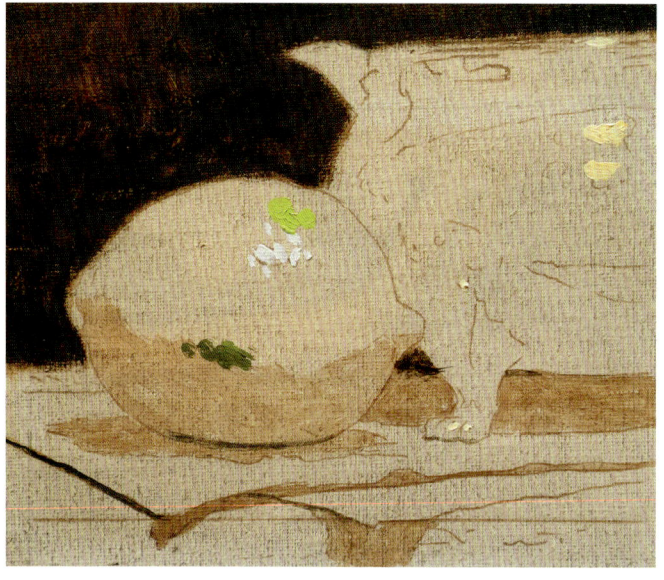
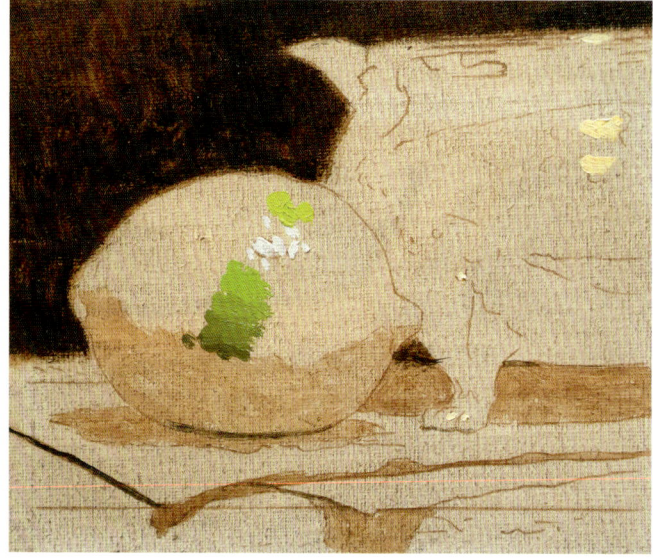

STEP 6: DEFINE THE TERMINATOR

I also stake out the terminator and then roll toward the light, painting all the transitional colors/values between it and the light most facing plane. Essentially, you are taking the colors from your color string and wrapping them onto the form in the correct order.

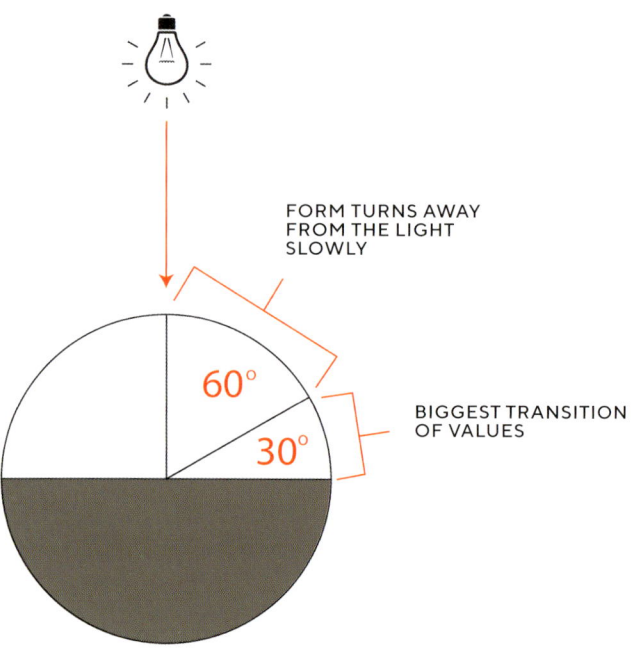

FORM TURNS AWAY
FROM THE LIGHT
SLOWLY

60°

30°

BIGGEST TRANSITION
OF VALUES

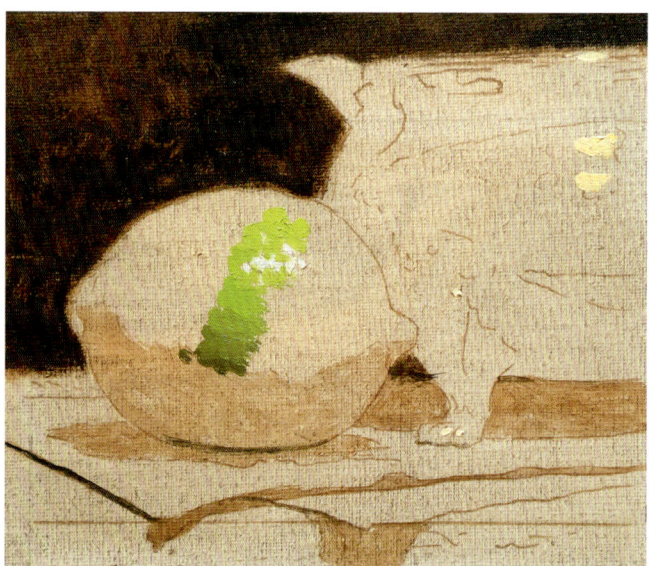

STEP 7: BEGIN ROLLING THE FORM

Now, roll the form toward the light source—applying the values from the terminator up to the light most facing plane. Remember that the biggest transition of values occurs right out of the shadow, in the area known as the halftone.

KEEP LIGHT AND SHADOW SEPARATE

On your palette, draw a line for the value of the terminator. This separates the light from the shadow on your value/color string. Don't let your darkest light (halftone) compete with your lightest dark (reflected light).

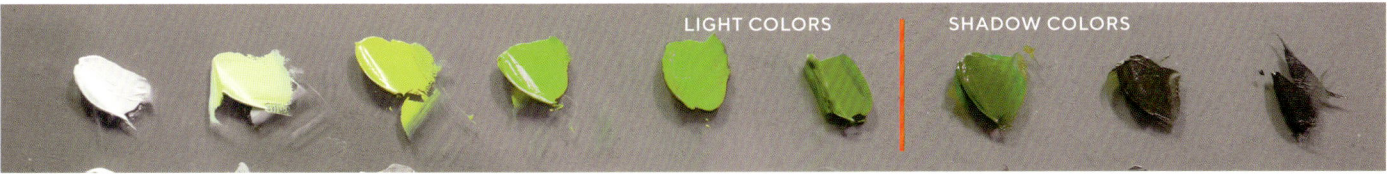

A line separates the light from the shadow on this color/value string. Don't cross the line over to the lights when painting the shadow and vice versa.

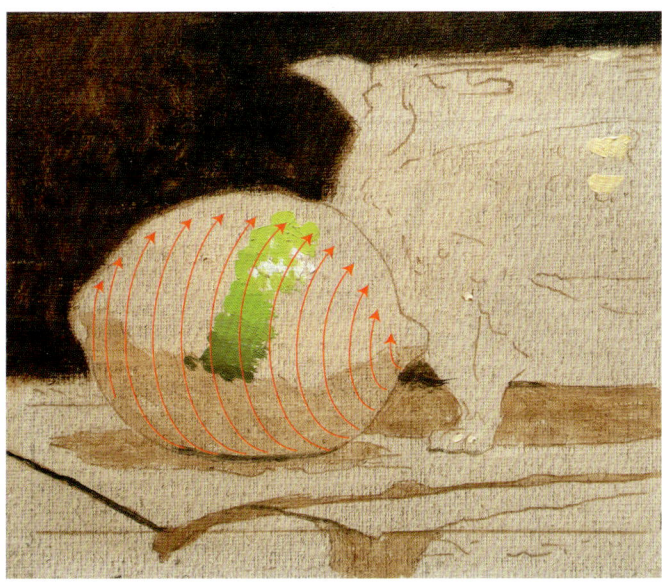

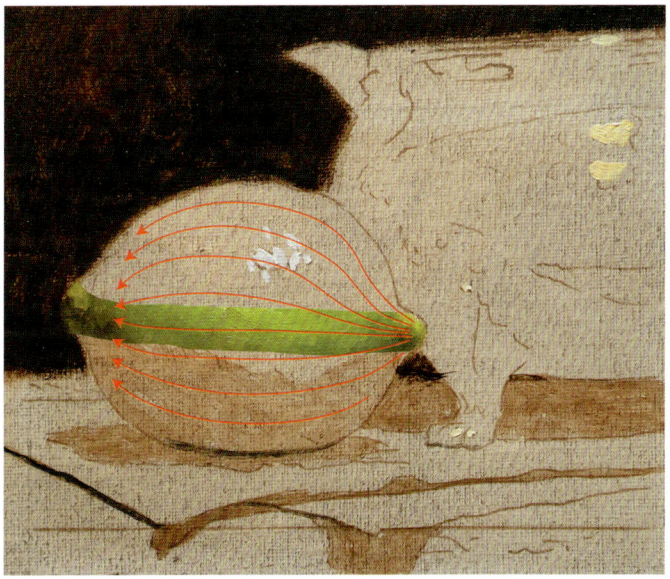

STEP 8: CONTINUE RENDERING THE FORM

As you continue to render the form, you can either follow the path of the light (as shown by the arrows in the image directly above) or you can render across the form (as shown in the image above right). I always roll forms from the shadow toward the light source (from dark to light), but you could choose to work in the opposite direction—light to dark—instead.

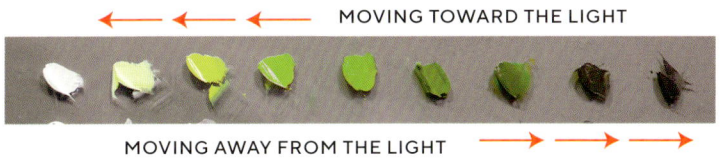

Rather than just copying values, I am always asking myself, Am I turning form toward the light or away from the light?

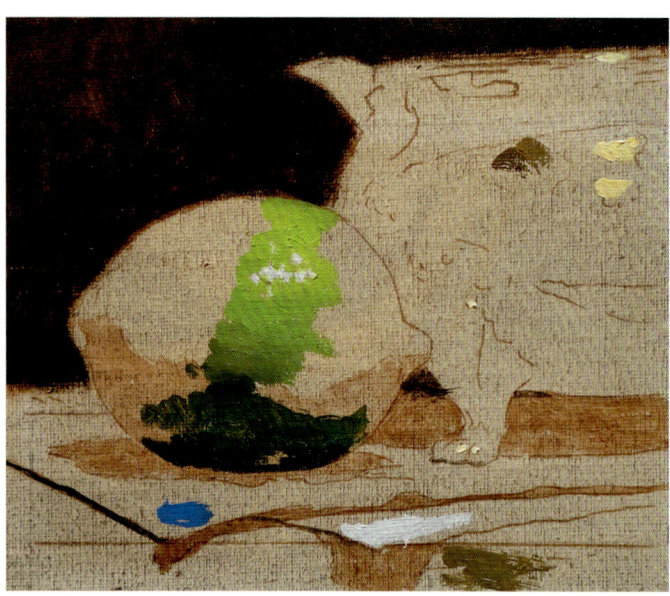 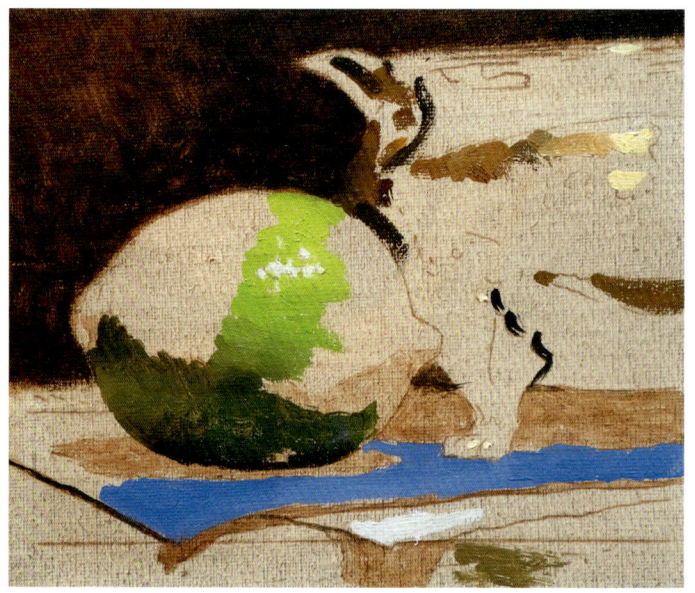

STEP 9: ADD SOME COLOR NOTES

Adding some color notes to surrounding objects is a great way to begin to see how the various colors of the composition will relate to each other.

Besides those color notes, though, do try to resist the urge to hop all around the painting adding color here and there. Instead, develop the painting so that it looks as if the painting is growing out of a center, as in the image above. Every area you paint should be connected to an area that has already been considered.

OPPOSITE: STEP 10 AND BEYOND: APPLY PAINT USING THE "TILING" METHOD

Opposite you see swatches of paint being applied in a tonal progression. Each brushstroke is either toward the light or away from the light. As you build color and value, use the "tiling" method of applying paint. In this method, all the mixing is done on the palette, not on the canvas. When you apply the paint, lay the swatches on as if you were placing separate tiles of paint on the canvas. It's important to make each tile of paint a tiny bit lighter or darker than the last bit of paint. This ensures that you are continuing to roll the forms in accordance with your conceptual knowledge of how light falls on forms. The photo at the bottom right, opposite, is the final painting.

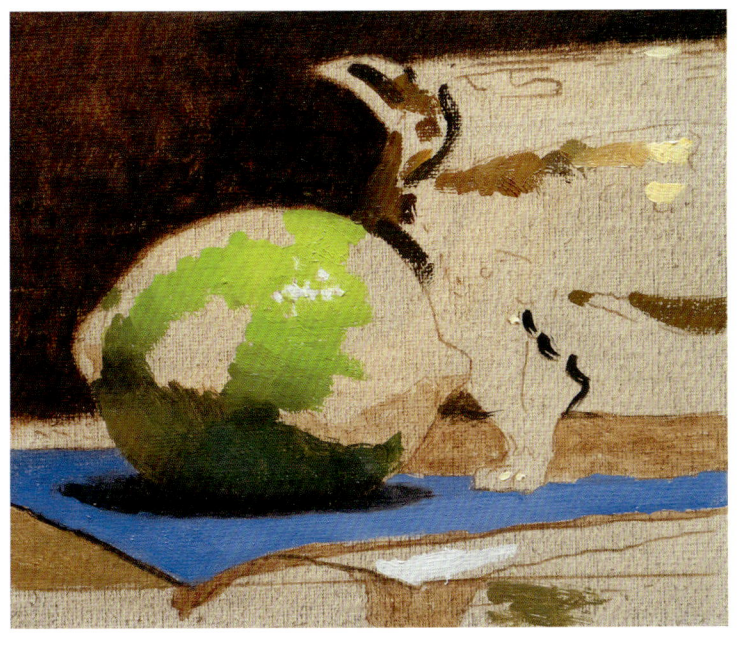 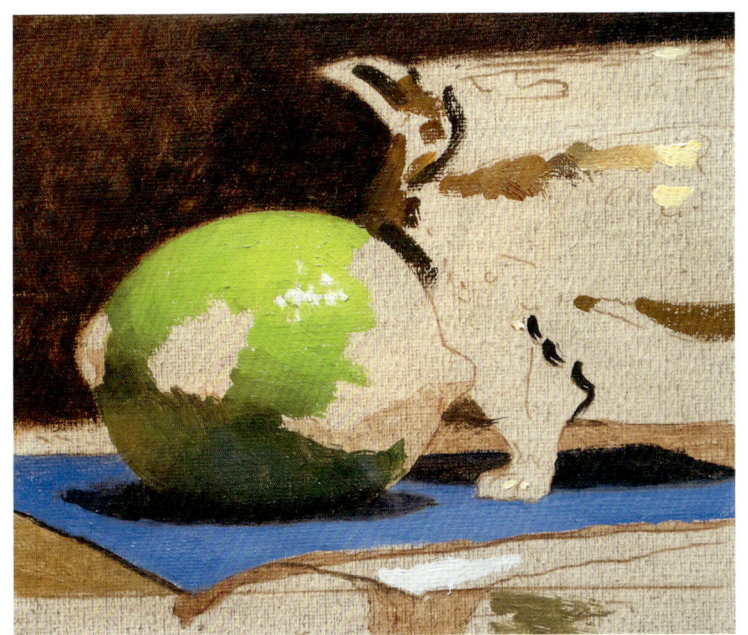

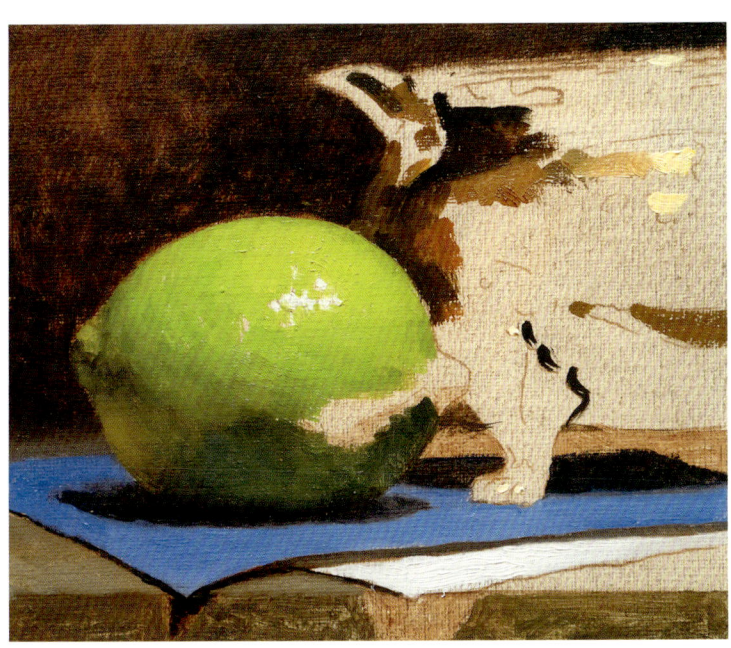 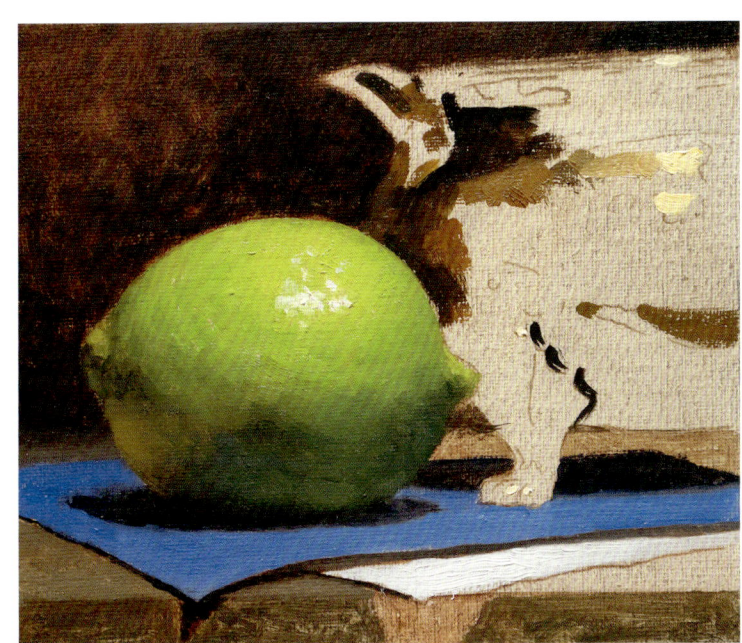

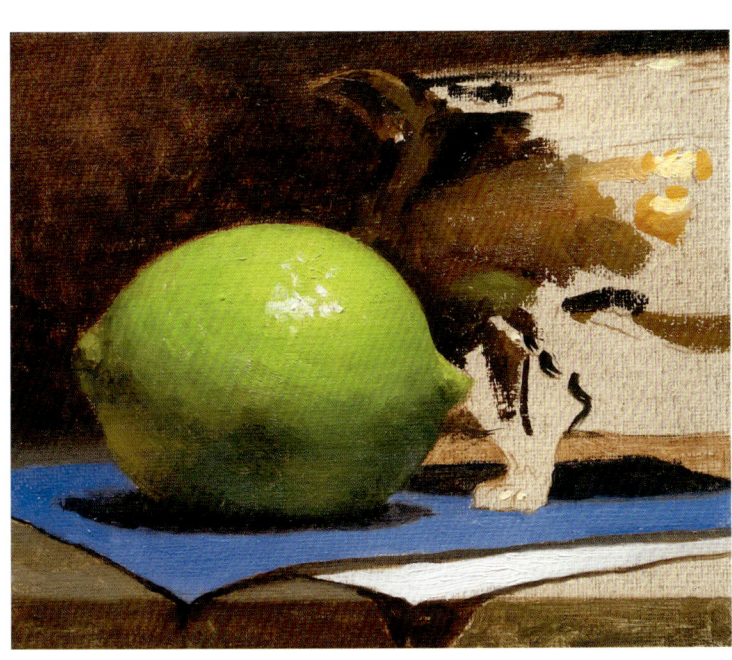 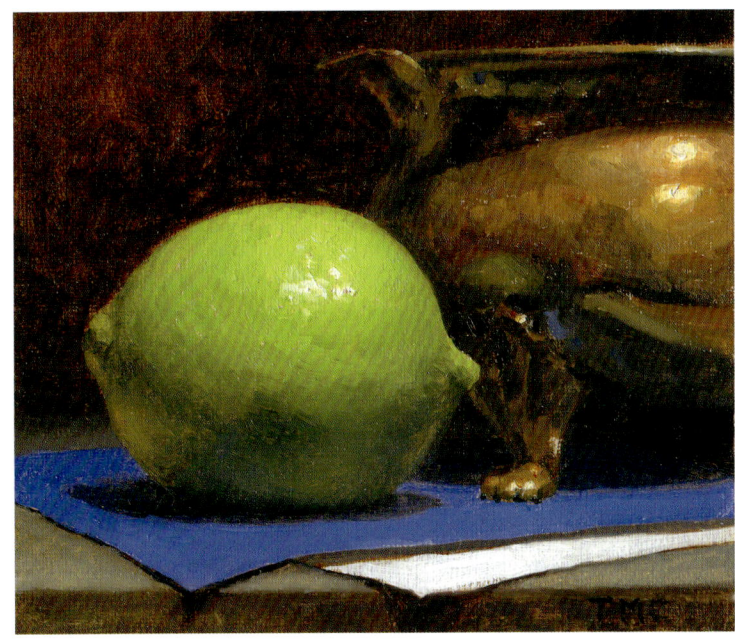

RENDERING SHADOWS

When working on shadows, try to use your peripheral vision to see the overall relationship among all the elements in the painting—to see the big picture rather than focusing on any individual object. You can do this by squinting or by standing far enough away to see the whole setup. The longer you stare at a shadowed area, the more you will see, and it's easy to observe too intensely and begin seeing all kinds of values in a shadow.

Shadows should be understated rather than overstated. The edges of objects in shadow should be soft so as not to draw attention to the shadows. Also, the shadows should not be flat—with just one value. There's still movement in values within them, even though the contrast is very low.

RIGHT In this close-up of the shadows in my painting *El Día de los Muertos*, you can see that the shadow is less interesting than the lights—which is as it should be.

OPPOSITE: Todd M. Casey, *El Día de los Muertos*, 2016, oil on panel, 8 × 10 inches (20.32 × 25.4 cm). Private collection.

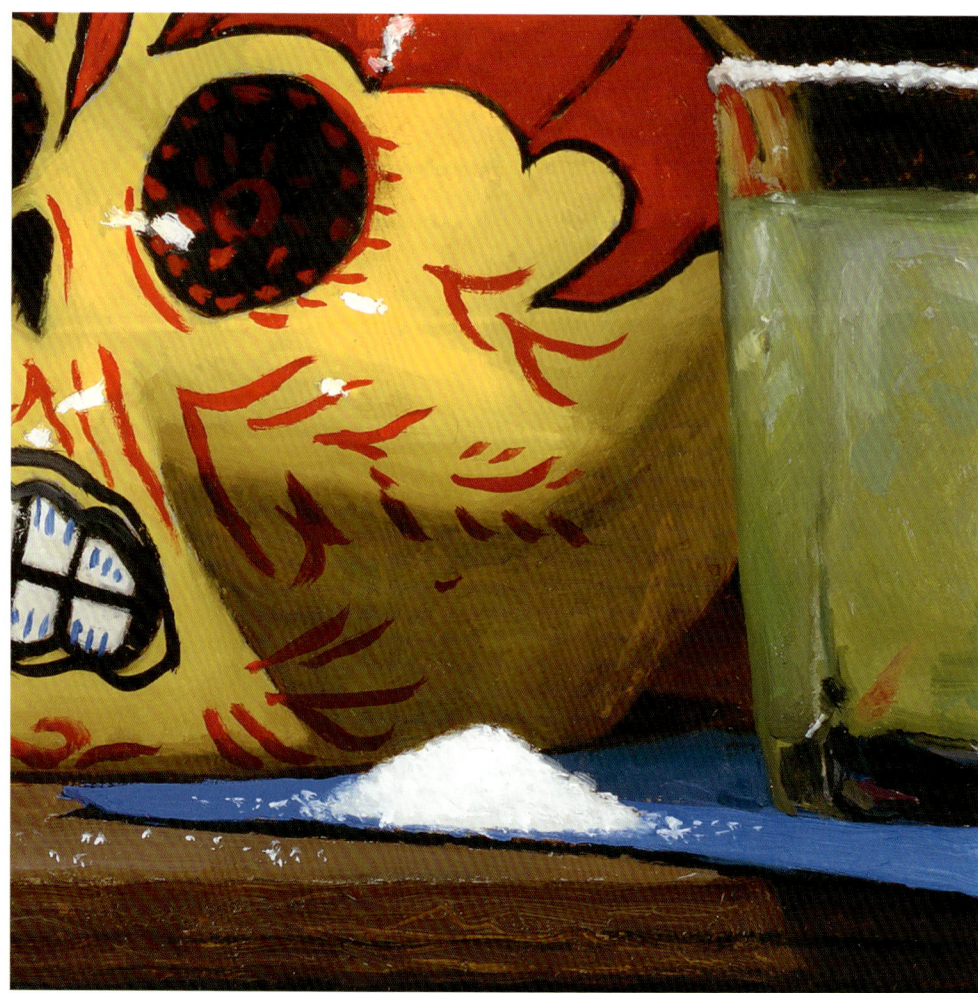

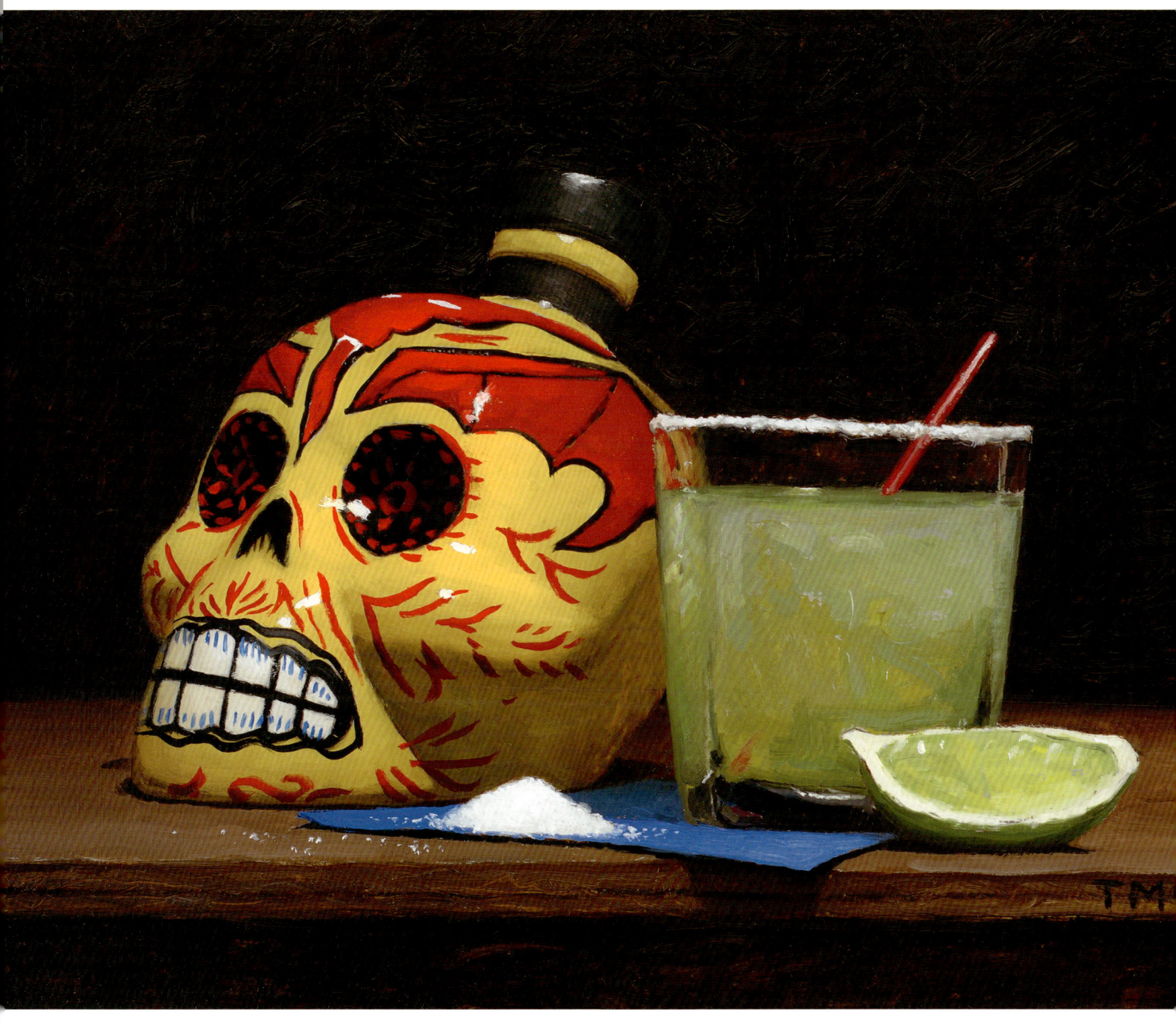

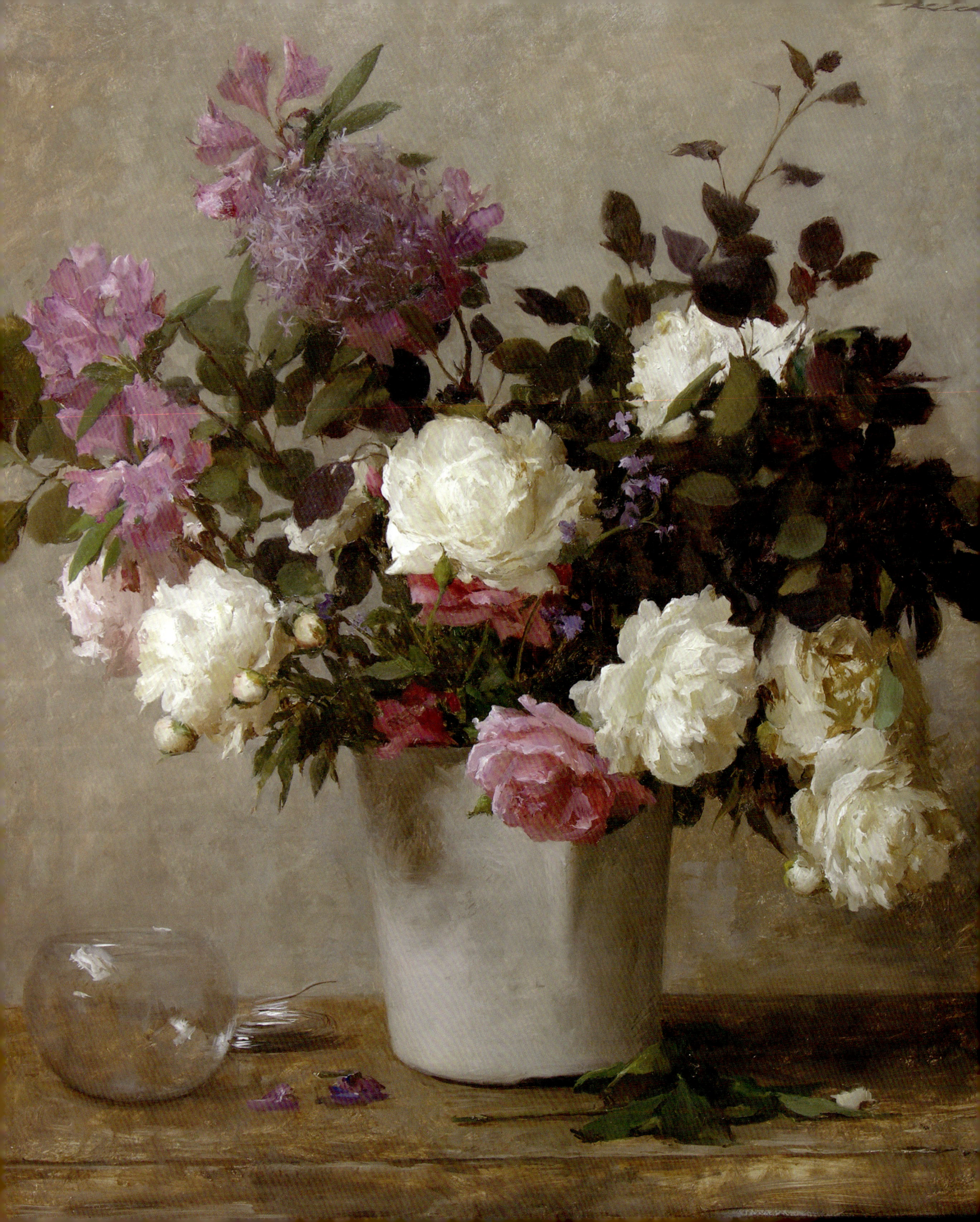

LOST EDGES AND HARD EDGES

Edges are fun to play around with. Having different kinds of edges in a painting can make the painting more interesting.

When two forms of similar value meet, you can "lose" an edge. A "lost edge" isn't really visible, but our brains tend to fill in the information. The opposite of a lost edge is a hard edge, in which two forms of contrasting values are placed next to one another.

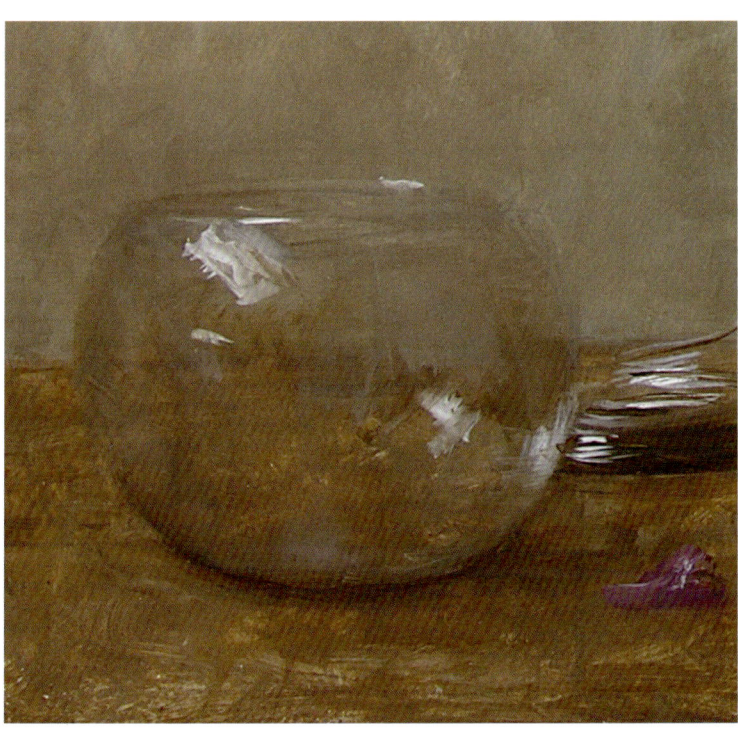

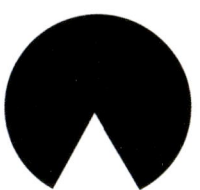

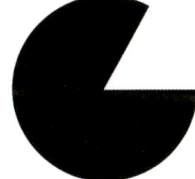

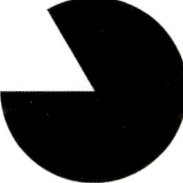

OPPOSITE: Michael Klein, *Garden Peonies,* 2016, oil on panel, 27 × 23 inches (68.58 × 58.42 cm). Courtesy of the artist.

ABOVE, LEFT: Losing an edge in a painting can add a bit of poetry, as in this detail of Michael Klein's painting *Garden Peonies.*

ABOVE, RIGHT: The lost edge is sometimes referred to as the "phantom edge phenomenon," in which we see a shape that is not actually there—as with the implied triangle in this image. When parts are left out of a shape, our brain automatically connects them.

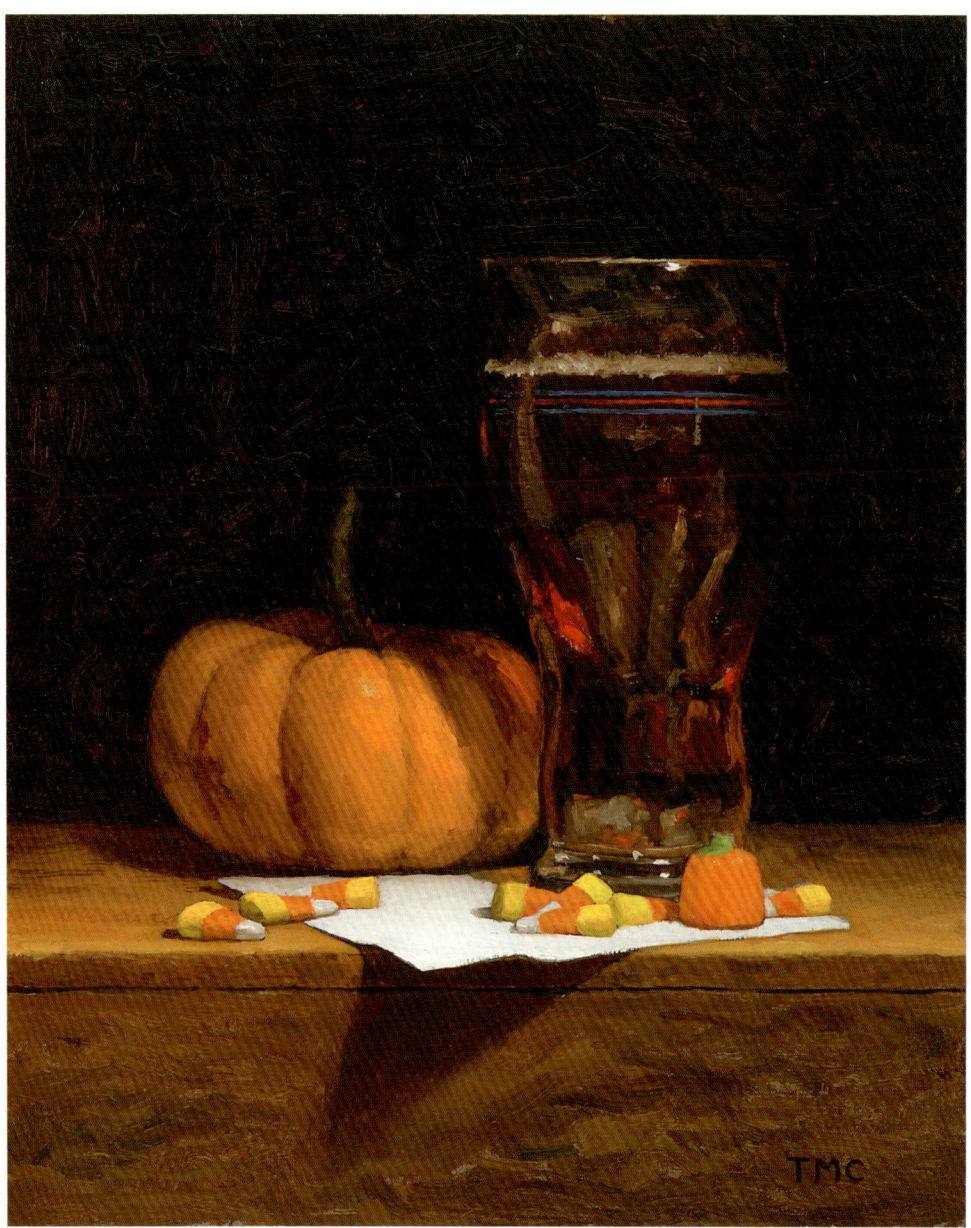

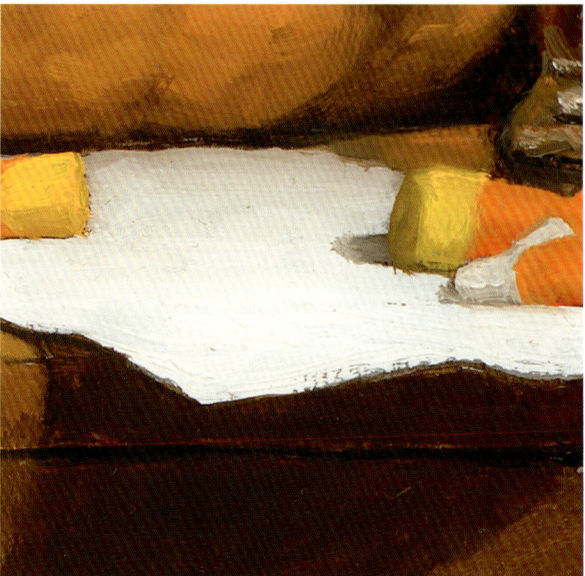

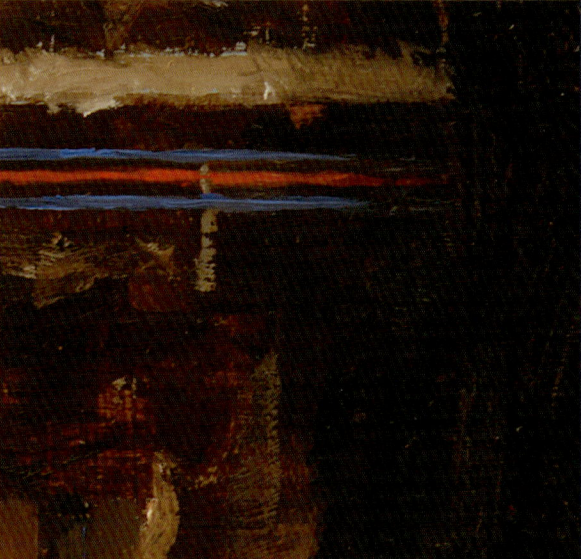

ABOVE, RIGHT: My painting *Octoberfest* has both hard and lost edges. The contrast of the white napkin against the cast shadow is a very definite hard edge. The edge of the beer glass, by contrast, disappears—lost against the background darkness. A variety of edges makes a painting more interesting.

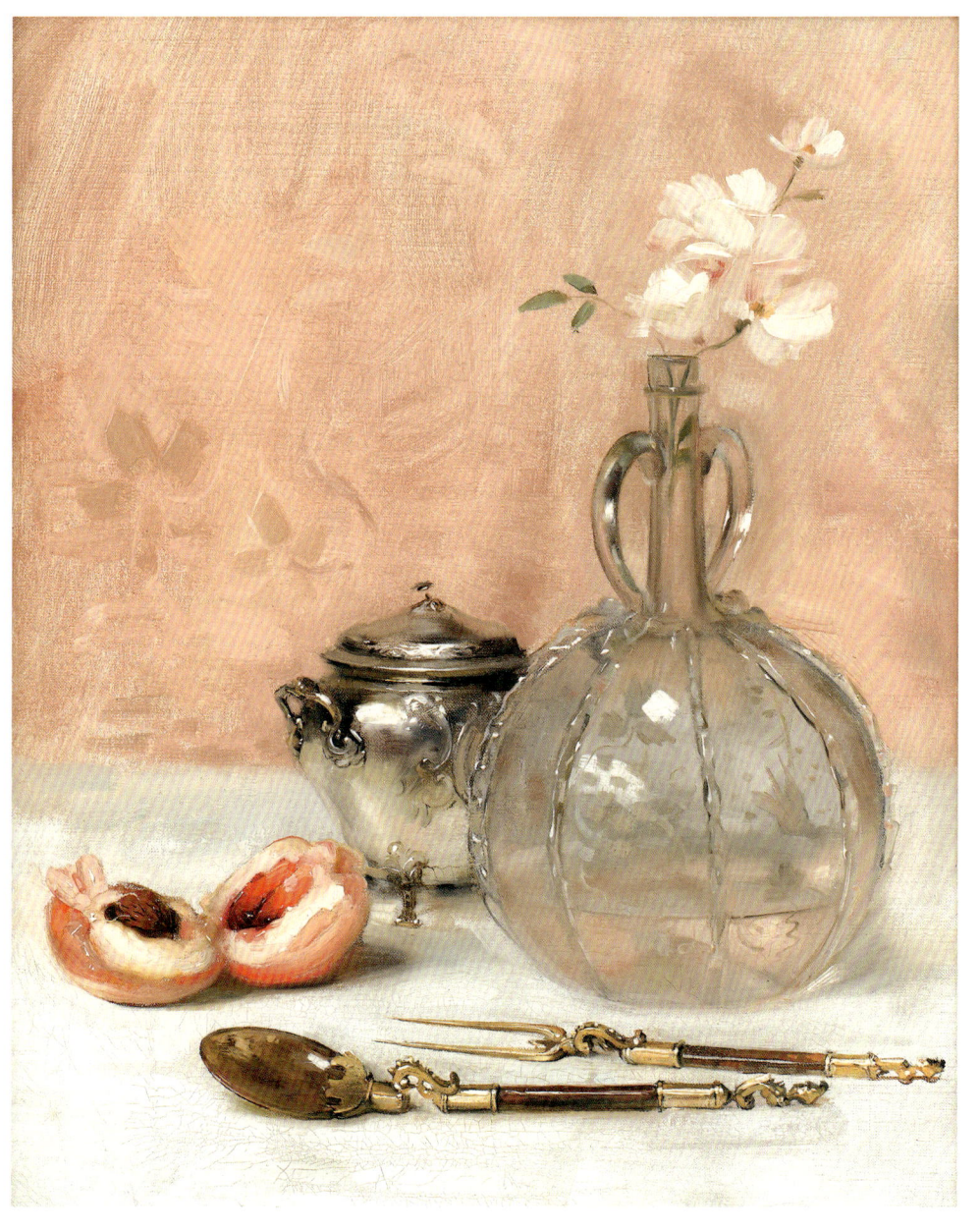

HIGH KEY VERSUS LOW KEY

Just as musicians can decide what key to set their music in, artists can decide to render an image in a high or a low key. *High key* means that the value structure of the image is predominantly light, and *low key* means that the painting's values are predominantly dark. Higher-key images tend to feel fresh and modern, while lower-key images tend to have a traditional, classic look.

LEFT: Joseph Bail (French, 1862–1921), *Still Life with a Decanter and Travel Fork and Spoon,* 1887, oil on canvas, 13 × 9 ½ inches (33 × 24.2 cm). Westimage/Art Digital Studio © Sotheby's 2019.

The range of value in this still life by Joseph Bail is predominantly light, so the painting is considered high key.

BELOW LEFT: Willem Claesz. Heda, *Still Life with Oysters, a Silver Tazza, and Glassware,* 1635, oil on wood, 19 ⅝ × 31 ¼ inches (49.8 × 80.6 cm). The Metropolitan Museum of Art, New York. From the collection of Rita and Frits Markus, bequest of Rita Markus, 2005.

This classic seventeenth-century Dutch still life is a low-key painting in which the dominant values are dark.

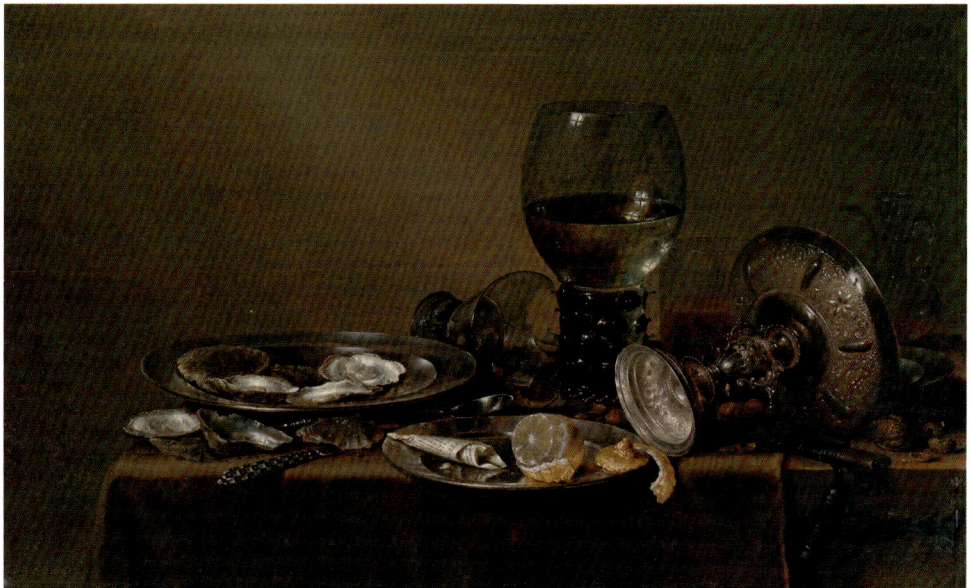

EXERCISES

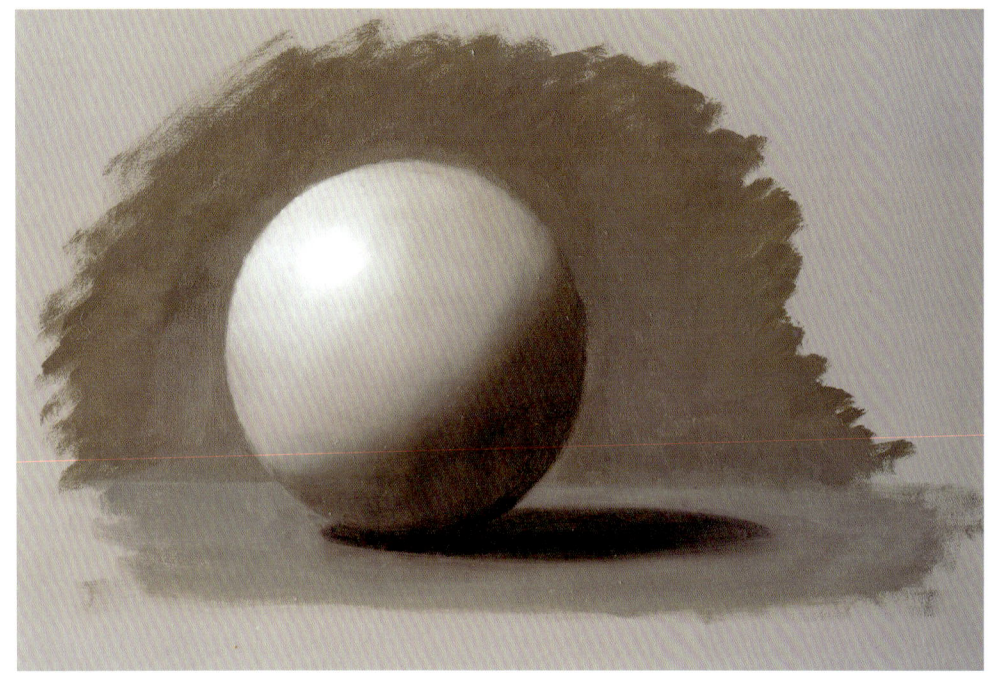

EXERCISE 1: RENDER A SPHERE

A great way to practice rendering form is to depict a sphere. As simple as this may seem, it is extremely difficult to do accurately. I recommend starting with a black-and-white sphere and then moving on to color spheres. If you can master a sphere, you can paint nearly anything.

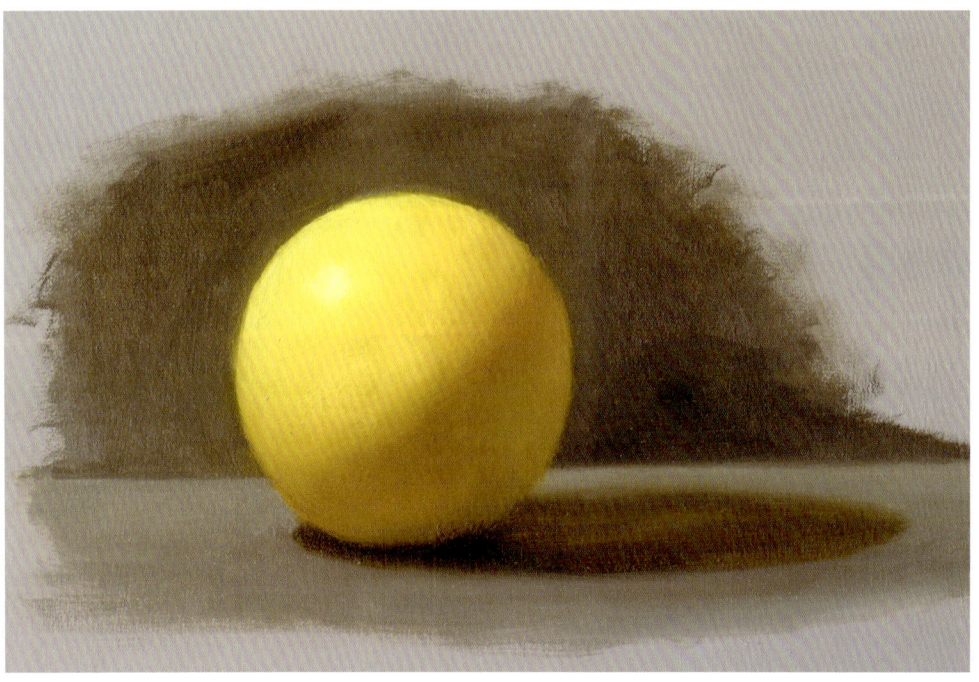

ABOVE, LEFT: Dorothy Lorenze, *Grey Sphere,* 2017, oil on panel, 9 × 12 inches (22.86 × 30.48 cm). Courtesy of the artist.

LEFT: Dorothy Lorenze, *Yellow Sphere,* 2017, oil on panel, 9 × 12 inches (22.86 × 30.48 cm). Courtesy of the artist.

EXERCISE 2: DO A CAST PAINTING

Painting monochromatic plaster casts is a great way to work on your values, since you're painting in just black, white, and shades of gray. Work on getting the form right, but try not to fix your mistakes as you go. Live with them, and then assess how "off" your image is once the painting is complete.

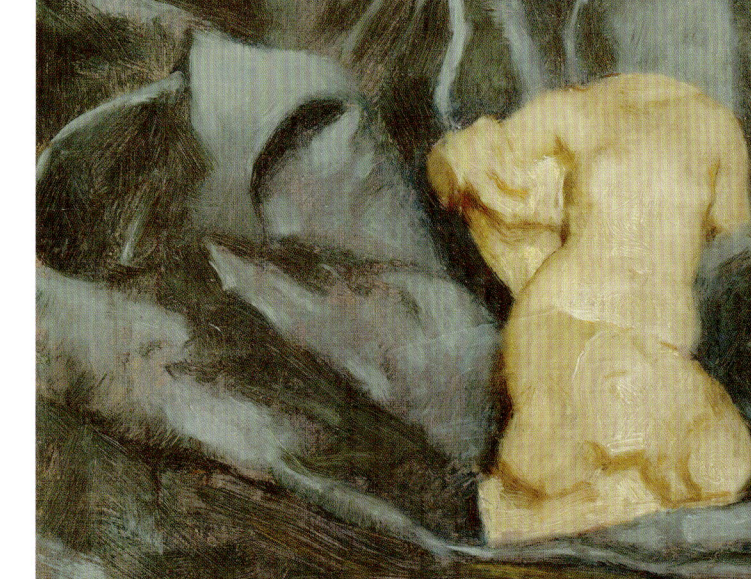

RIGHT: Dennis Miller Bunker (American, 1861–1890), *Marble Torso of a Woman,* about 1878, oil on canvas, 16 ¹⁵⁄₁₆ × 10 ⅝ inches (43 × 27 cm). Isabella Stewart Gardner Museum, Boston.

EXERCISES

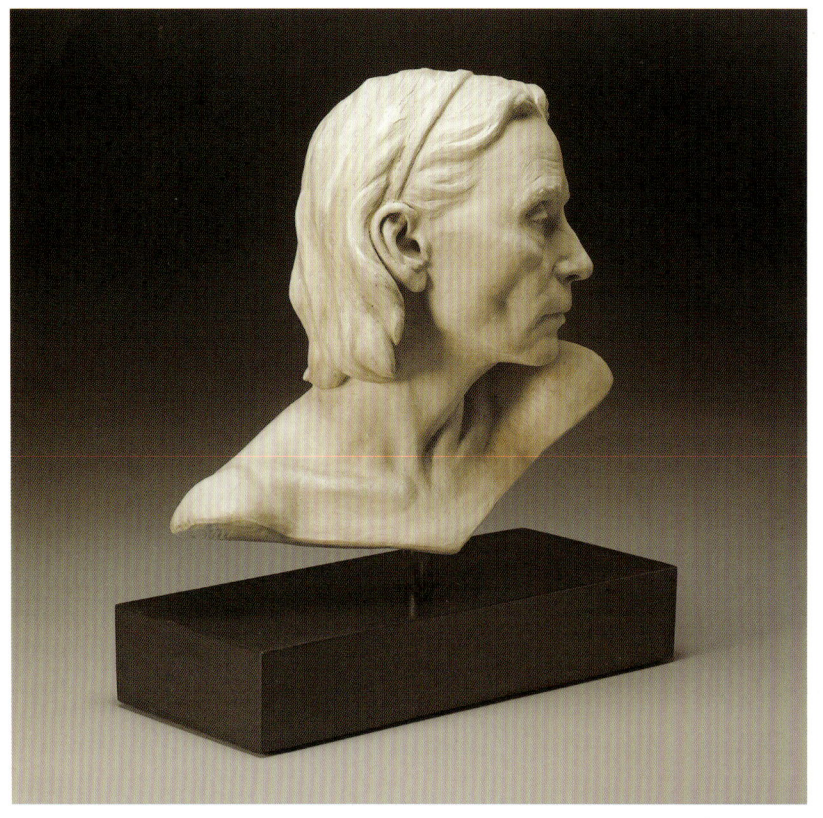

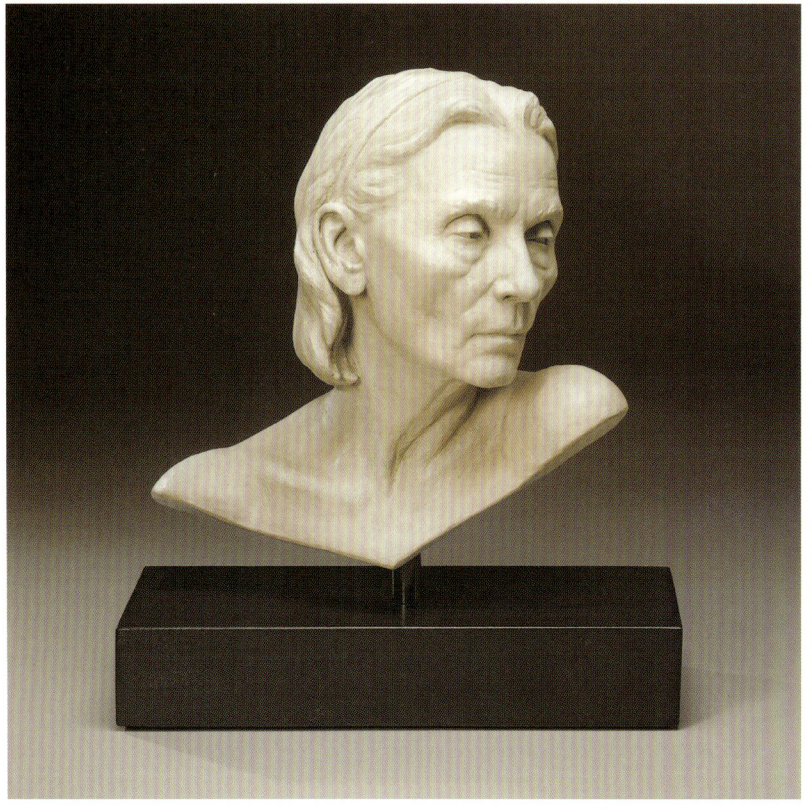

EXERCISE 3: TRY YOUR HAND AT SCULPTURE

Sculpting is a tremendous way to develop your understanding of three-dimensional form. When you sculpt forms, you begin to understand how they move and feel—and this will help you when you translate 3-D forms onto a 2-D surface. Sculpt anything you like—characters, portraits, figures—in any medium you choose. It will force you to think three-dimensionally.

Angela Cunningham, *Anna Nina* (four views), 2013, resin and wood, 17 × 11 × 7 inches (43.18 × 27.94 × 17.78 cm). Courtesy of the artist.

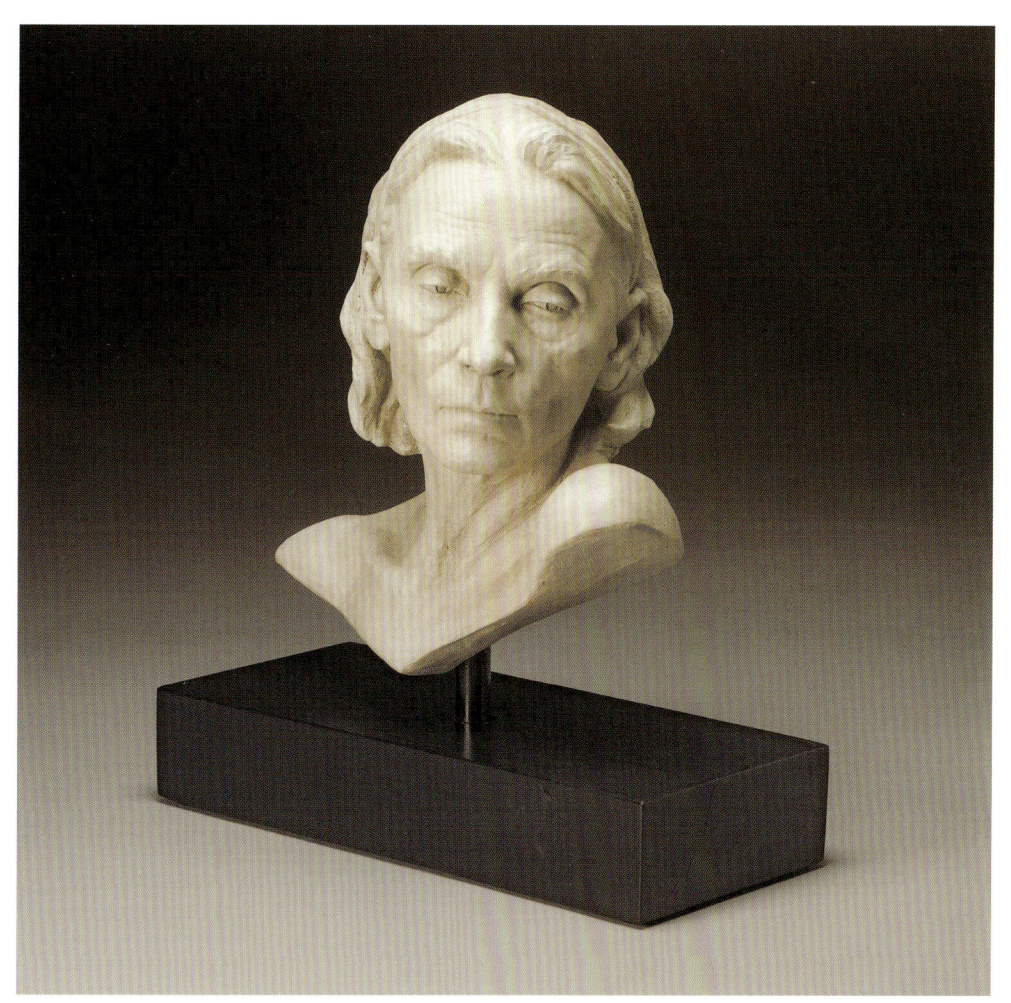

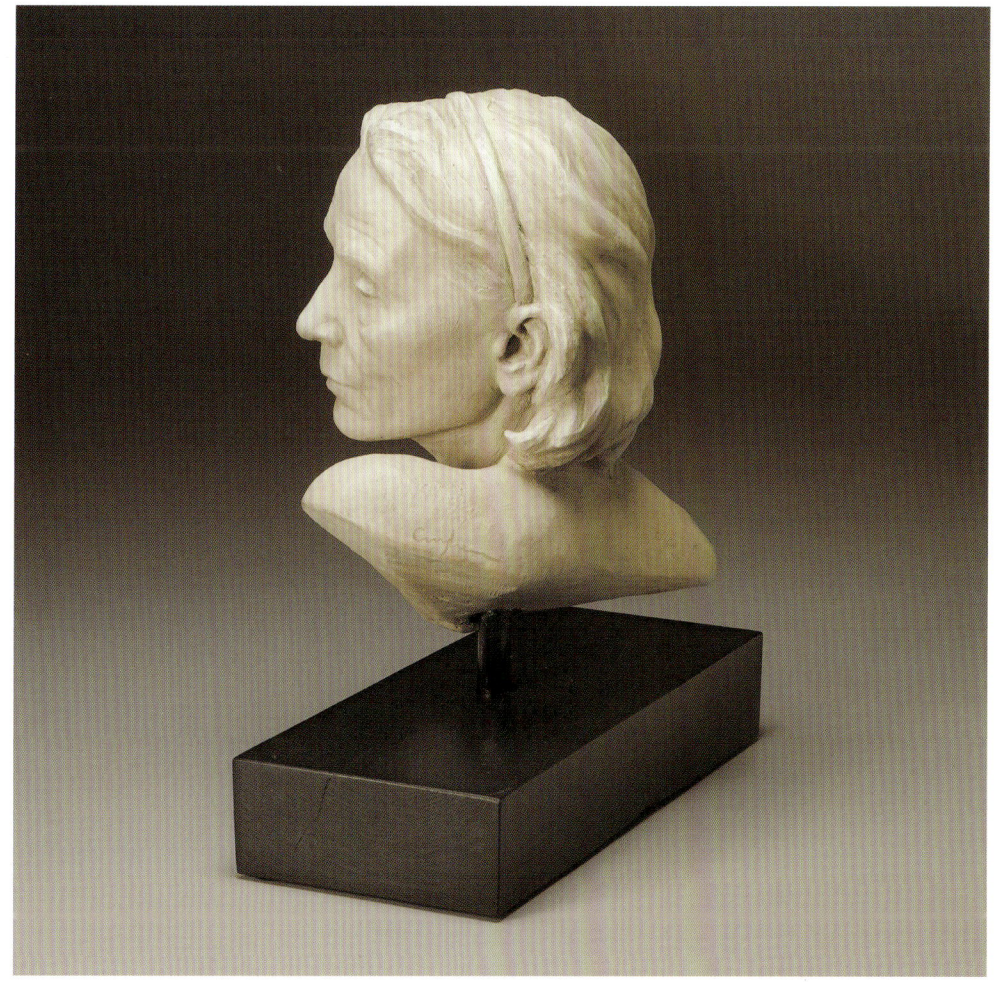

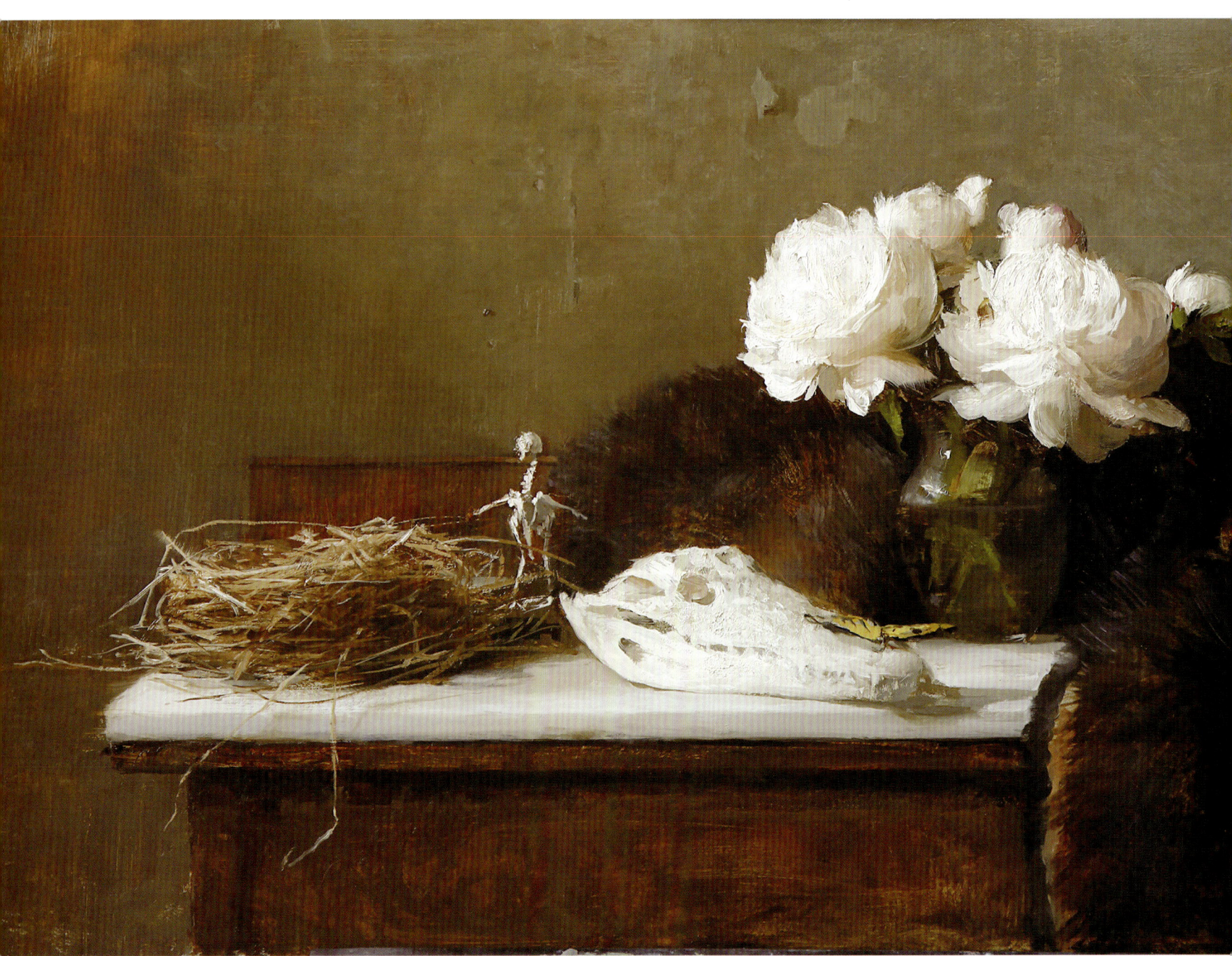

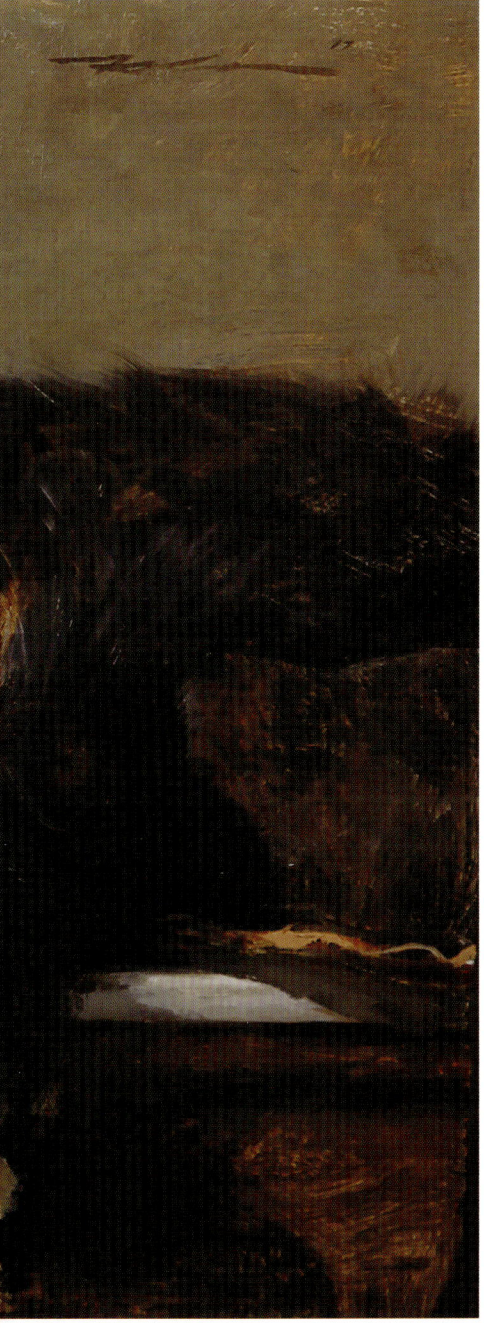

CHAPTER 8

APPLYING THE PAINT: GUIDELINES AND TECHNIQUES

Painting is easy when you don't know how,
but very difficult when you do.

EDGAR DEGAS

One of oil paint's greatest assets is its versatility. Each pigment has its own characteristics, and these differences can be used to achieve a variety of effects: transparency, opacity, luminosity, and textural variation.

There are many ways to build a painting—different strategies for applying paint that can lead to different stylistic effects. A few painters just lay down paint on a white canvas, but most don't. Depending on the desired result, they tone their canvas before beginning to paint, develop an underpainting, or employ specific methods of applying paint. There is no one way to paint. Each artist works differently, but there are a few basic rules. Let's look at one of those—the "fat over lean" rule—first.

LEFT: Michael Klein, *Suspended,* 2017, oil on panel, 18 × 30 inches (45.72 × 76.2 cm). Courtesy of the artist.

"FAT OVER LEAN"

At its most simple, oil paint is made up of a pigment and a binding agent, usually linseed oil. More oil can be added to paint out of a tube, in which case the oil is considered a medium.

Fat over lean means that the top layers of a painting should have a higher oil-to-pigment ratio than the lower layers of paint. To abide by the fat-over-lean rule, you'll use less oil during the early stages of a painting but more as the painting progresses and the layers of paint build. Layering your paint correctly is important for permanence. If paint is applied lean over fat, the top layer may dry before the bottom layer and cause the top layer to crack.

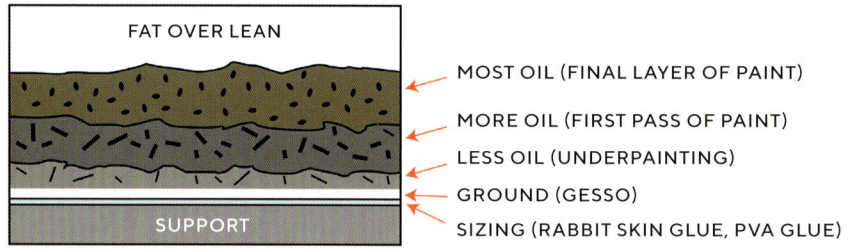

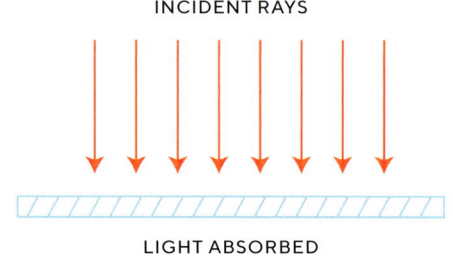

INCIDENT RAYS

LIGHT ABSORBED

Opaque paint

RIGHT: The first layers of a painting should be the sizing and a layer of gesso. Paint with less oil should then be applied for the initial underpainting, followed by paint with more and more oil as successive layers are applied.

OPACITY VERSUS TRANSPARENCY

When light strikes a surface painted with oil paint, it will either reflect off the surface (opaque paints) or absorb into the surface (transparent paints). Transparent paints are good for glazing, while opaque colors are better at covering other layers of paint. Pigments themselves are comparatively opaque or comparatively transparent, but the following factors also influence how opaque or transparent the painted surface will be:

* The size of the pigment particles and their dispersion in the binder
* The refraction index of the pigment (i.e., how much the direction of a light ray changes)
* The amount of medium added to the paint
* The thickness with which the paint is applied

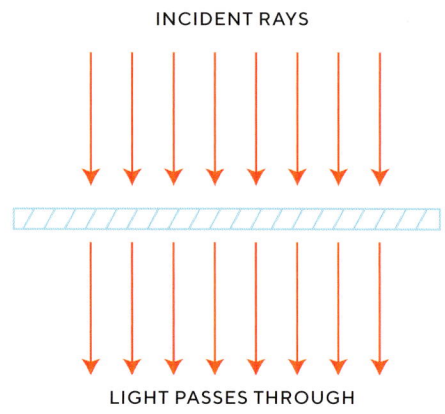

INCIDENT RAYS

LIGHT PASSES THROUGH

Transparent paint

TONING A CANVAS

The color of your canvas will affect every subsequent decision you make as you paint. Although some artists paint directly on white canvas, the traditional method is to add a tone to your canvas before starting. (Another term for toning a canvas is *imprimatura*, which means "first paint layer" in Italian.)

If you paint at all loosely or thinly, the tone of the canvas will work its way into the final painting, so it's really important to consider the color of the tone. Traditionally, tones were always a neutral or semineutral "dead" color like burnt umber or raw umber. A more modern way of working is to use a high-chroma color to tone your canvas. Unless you apply paint very thickly, the tone of the canvas will almost certainly shine through, and a high-chroma color like quinacridone magenta will likely affect all the colors applied on top of it.

To tone a canvas, mix mineral spirits (such as Gamsol) with oil paint at a ratio of 60/40 or 70/30 mineral spirits to paint. Rub this mixture into the canvas with a brush or rag. If you are using a brush, use a wide one (one or two inches) and don't apply the paint too thickly. In accordance with the fat-over-lean principle, this first layer should be thin.

TIP

You can choose *not* to tone your canvas. Depending on how loosely you apply your paint, this may mean that the white of the canvas will peek through your colors. If this is the effect you want, go for it!

BELOW, TOP ROW: Here are some of the traditional "dead colors" used to tone canvas. From left to right: burnt umber, raw umber, ivory black, and a neutral gray.

BELOW, BOTTOM ROW: You can also use higher-chroma colors as tones, though they are harder to cover up with paint. From left to right: sap green, burnt sienna, quinacridone magenta.

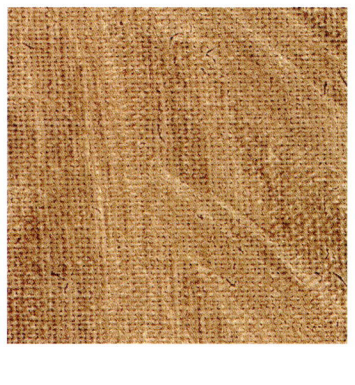
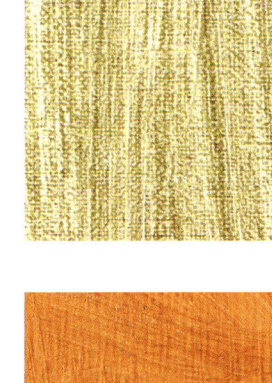

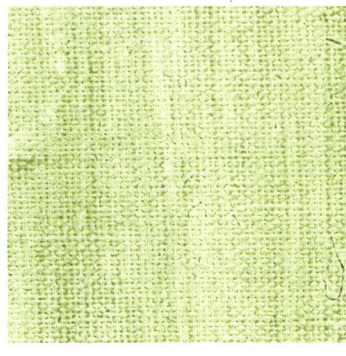
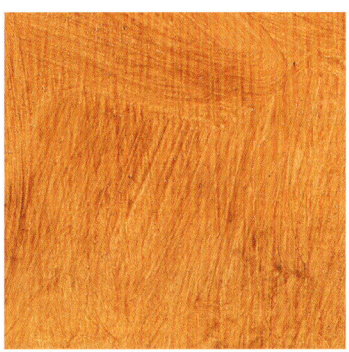
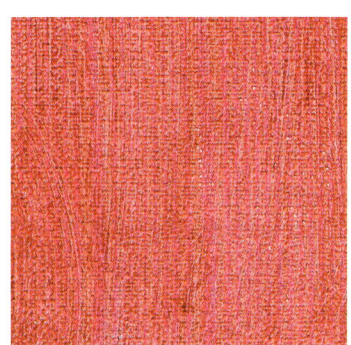

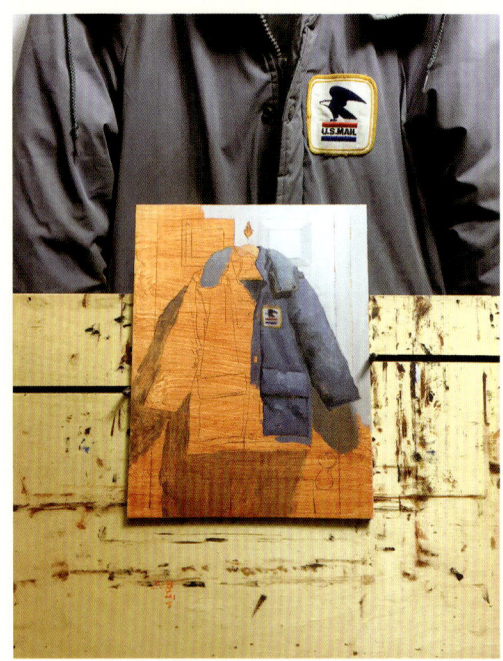
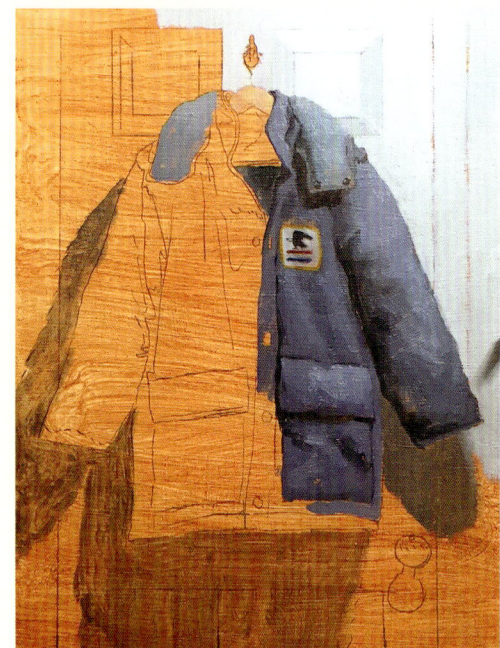
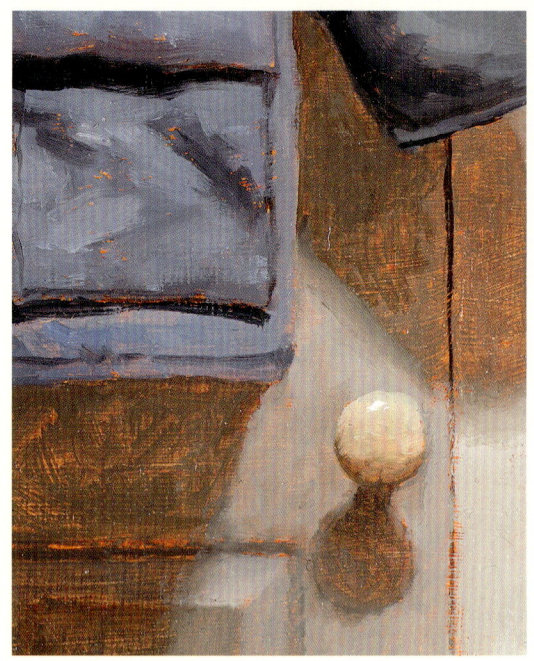

COOL VERSUS WARM UNDERTONES

I usually let some of the underpainting's color peek through my final paint layer. Burnt umber and raw umber are on the dull side, but burnt sienna is a great color for underpainting, as it will appear as a nice orange. If you are doing a very warm painting, you may want to use a cool underpainting (and vice versa). If the underpainting shines through the top layer of paint, the colors will appear to mix together when viewed from a distance.

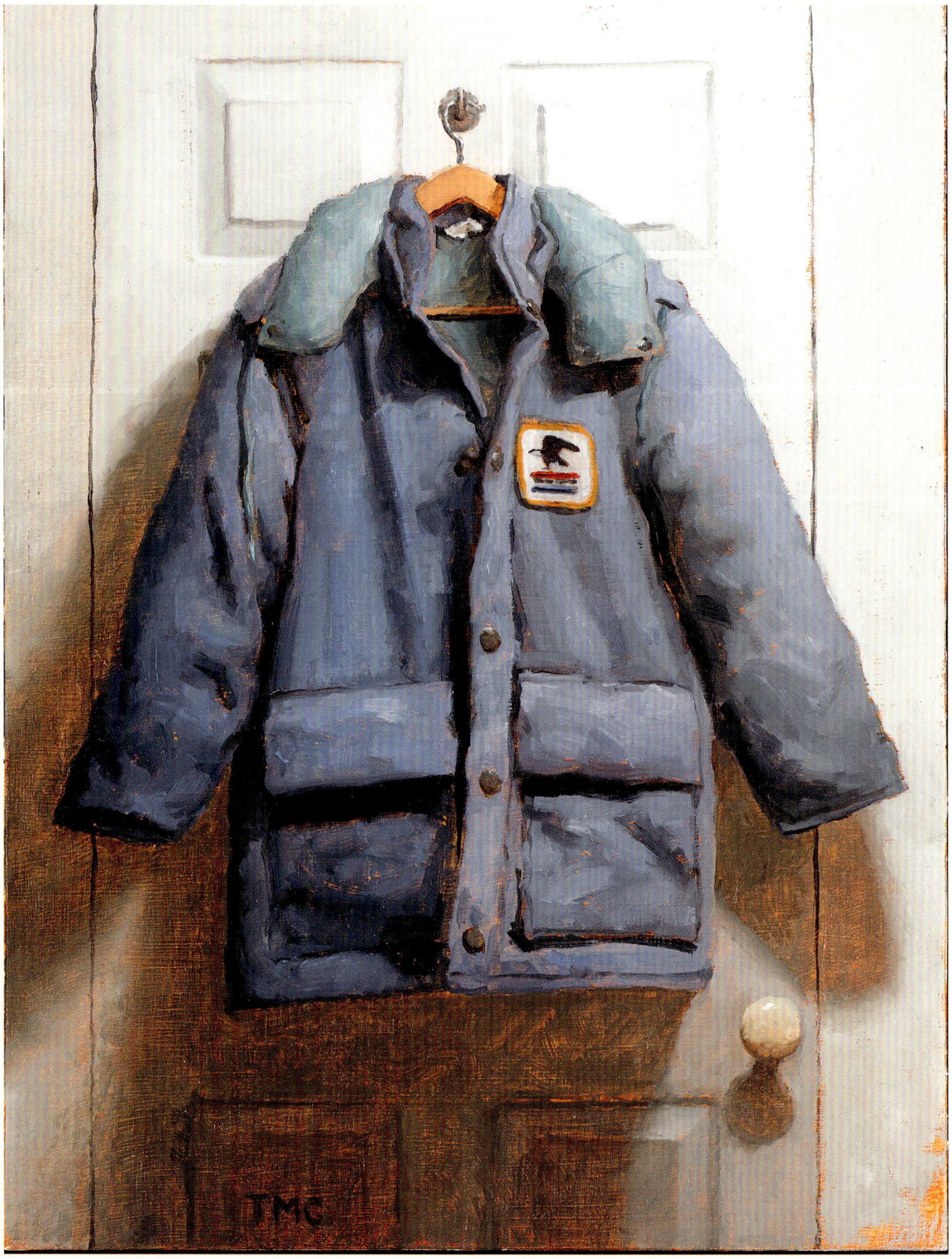

RIGHT: Todd M. Casey, *Dad's Uniform, Fall,* 2016, oil on panel, 8 × 6 inches (20.32 × 15.24 cm).

Knowing my painting *Dad's Uniform, Fall* would have a predominantly cool blue/purple color scheme, I chose a warm underpainting to complement the cool colors.

UNDERPAINTING

The underpainting is an integral part of traditional painting methods. An underpainting is used to work out the tonal relationships in a painting. It's a guide to the values of the layers of color that are applied afterward (the grisaille) or to both the values and the colors themselves (the wash-in).

The Grisaille—Open or Closed

Grisaille (pronounced grih-SIGH) is a French term for a monochromatic underpainting. Grisailles are traditionally done in the low-chroma earth colors burnt umber (which has a red/orange tinge) or raw umber (yellow/green), or in a true, middle-tone gray. A benefit of working with one of the earth colors is that they dry fast, usually within twenty-four hours of application.

In an *open grisaille*, the paint is diluted with solvent to achieve a value range that goes from dark to light. The darkest value is made with paint right out of the tube; each lighter value is created using a mineral spirit like Gamsol. This is the quicker type of underpainting. It doesn't produce a full range of values, but it comes very close.

BELOW, TOP: In an open grisaille, the lighter values are achieved by thinning the paint. In this value scale, burnt umber out of the tube is the darkest value (at right); each lighter value contains a greater proportion of solvent.

BELOW, BOTTOM LEFT: Artist Travis Seymour used burnt sienna for this open grisaille for his painting *Navel Oranges* (page 268).

BELOW, BOTTOM RIGHT: Seymour built up color over the underpainting.

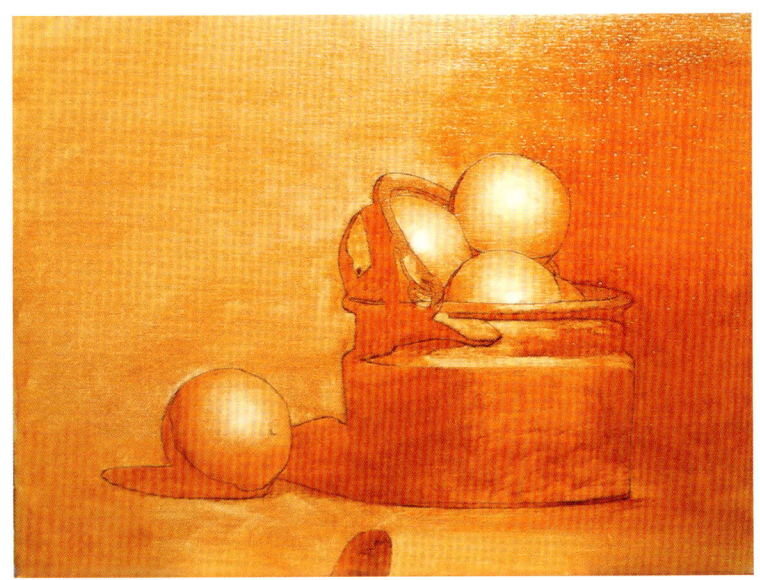

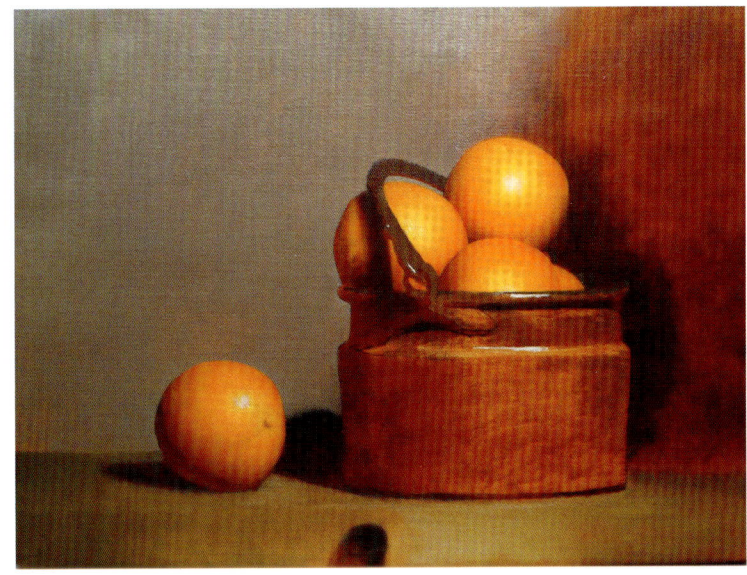

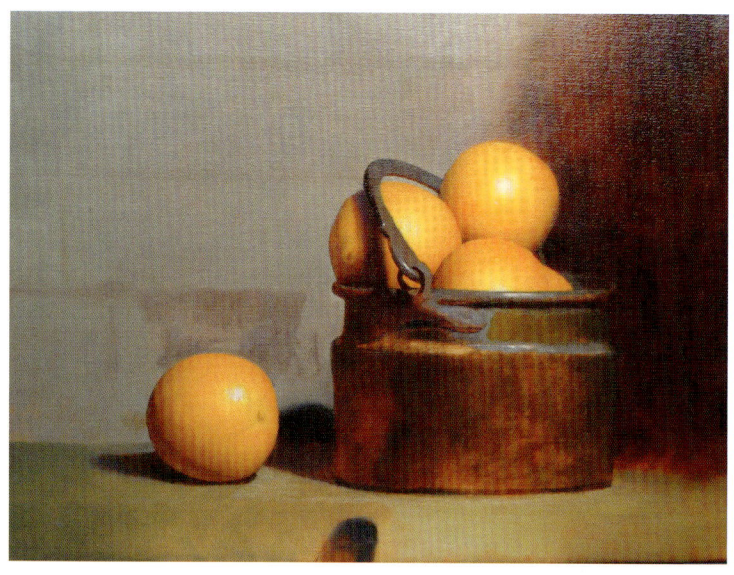

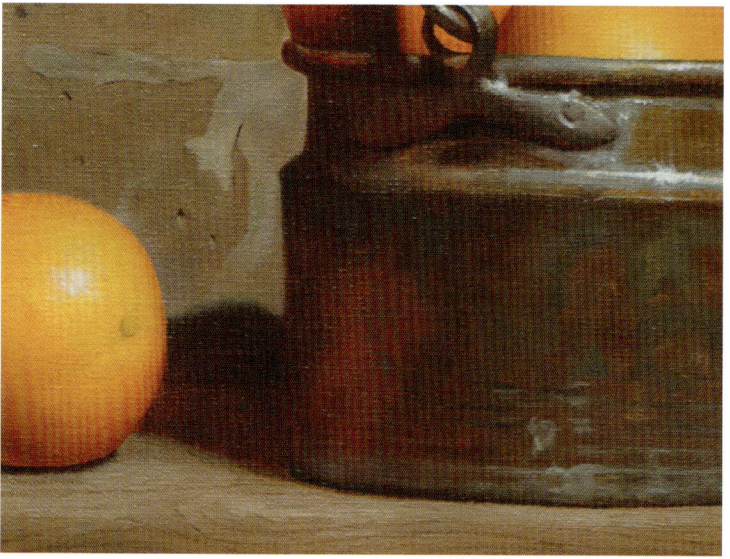

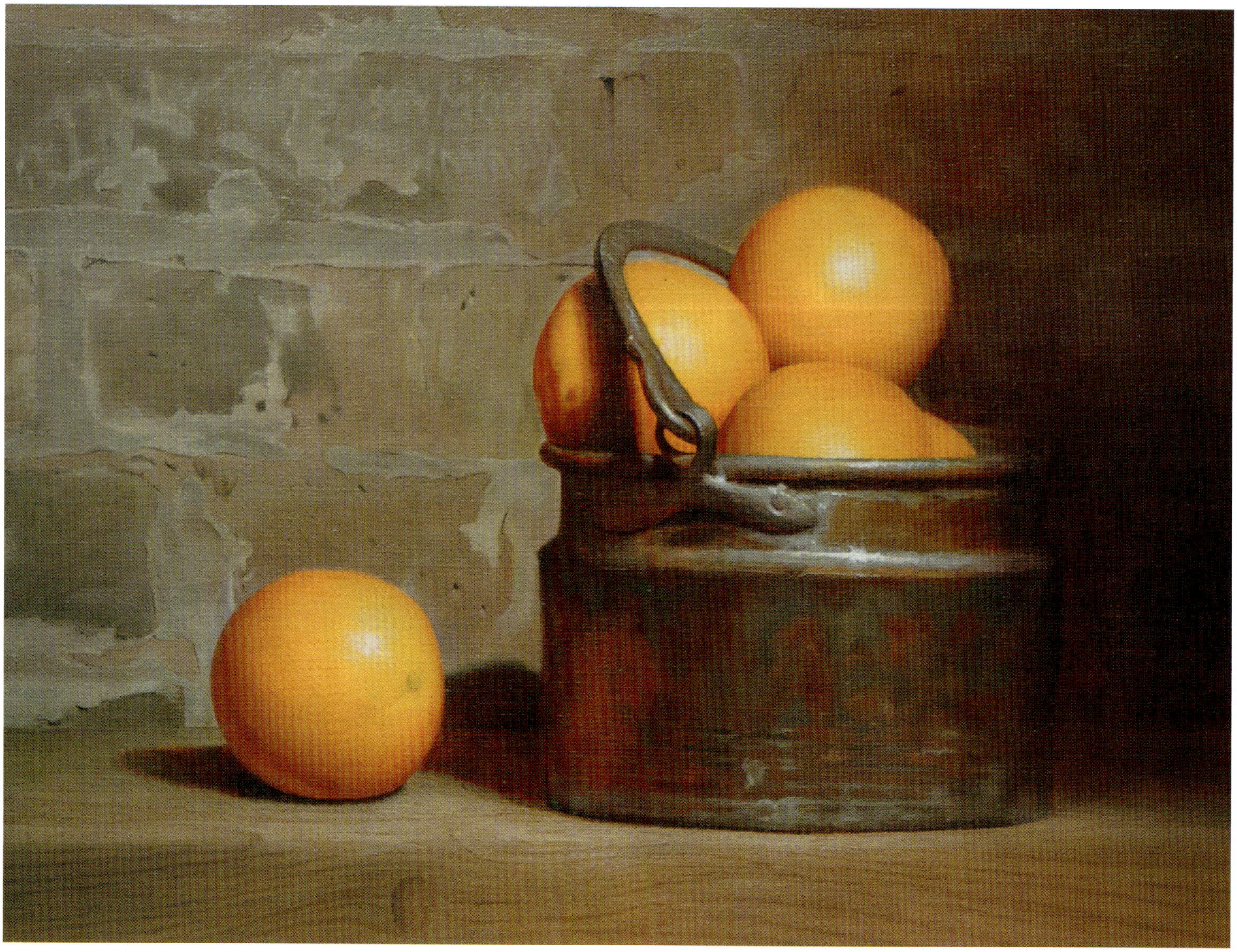

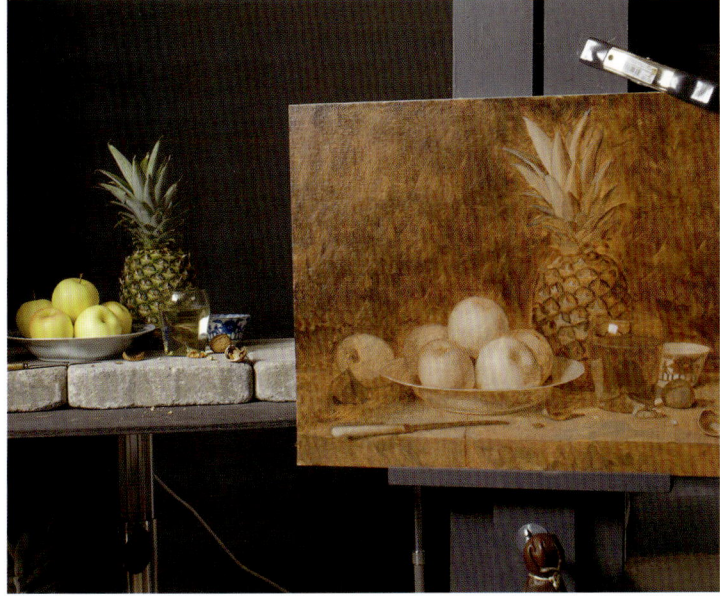

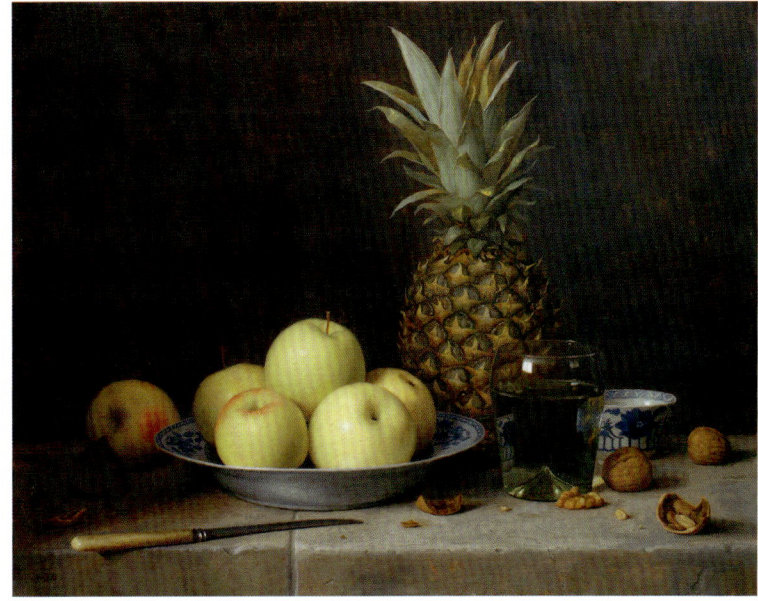

A *closed grisaille* is similar to an open grisaille but lets you achieve a full range of values. In a closed grisaille, white is mixed with the earth color to produce a full nine values from white to near-black. The paint is slightly thicker because it is not diluted with mineral spirits.

OPPOSITE, TOP LEFT: The burnt sienna of the underpainting brings warmth to the shadow at the right.

OPPOSITE, BOTTOM: Travis Seymour, *Navel Oranges,* 2016, oil on linen, 14 × 16 inches (35.56 × 40.64 cm). Courtesy of the artist.

As you can see in the detail at top right, opposite, the burnt sienna Seymour used for the underpainting affects the colors of the final painting.

TOP: A closed grisaille can achieve the full range of colors from white to near-black. The values of the underpainting will structure the values in each subsequent layer.

ABOVE, LEFT: Artist Justin Wood worked out a closed grisaille for his painting *Pineapple and Apples.* Notice how full the range of values is.

ABOVE, RIGHT: Justin Wood, *Pineapple and Apples,* 2018, oil on canvas, 16 × 20 inches (40.64 × 50.8 cm). Courtesy of the artist.

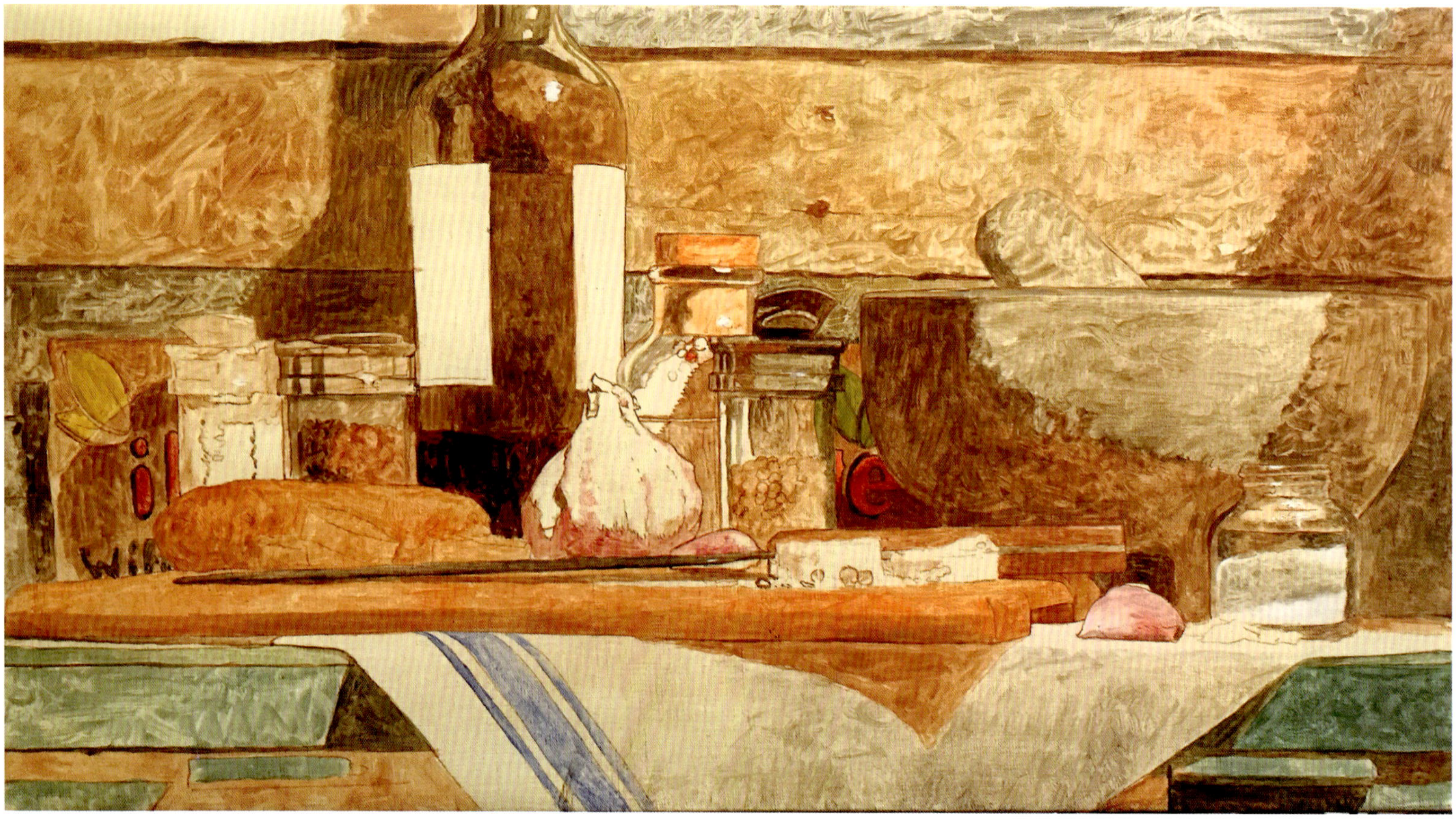

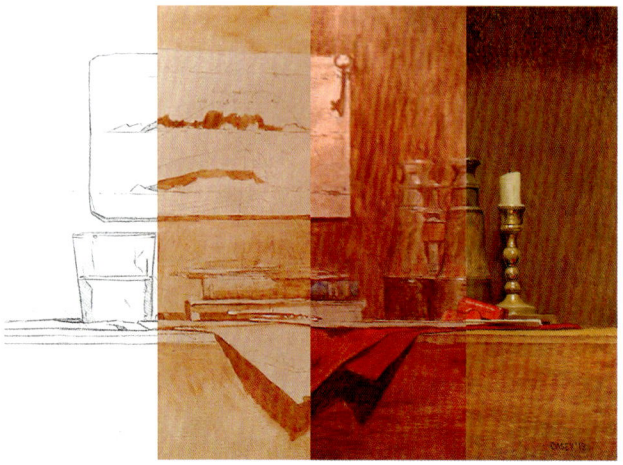

The wash-in for my painting *The Proper Beast* (page 111) looks like a textured watercolor.

Here is a composite of the stages that went into the creation of my painting *Shackleton's Dilemma*, opposite.

The Wash-In

A *wash-in* is a first pass of color applied to a painting surface that acts as an underpainting. The paint is diluted with mineral spirits so that the wash-in looks almost like a watercolor when completed. It provides a nice guide for the layers of paint applied thereafter.

INDIRECT VERSUS DIRECT PAINTING

Methods for applying paint to a surface fall into two general categories: *direct painting* and *indirect painting*. The indirect approach is the traditional way of working: the painting is built up in stages, starting with a preparatory drawing, then a toned canvas, and then an underpainting, over which layers of paint are added in succession using the underpainting as a guide. The indirect method requires a lot of patience, as each step is done in a separate session.

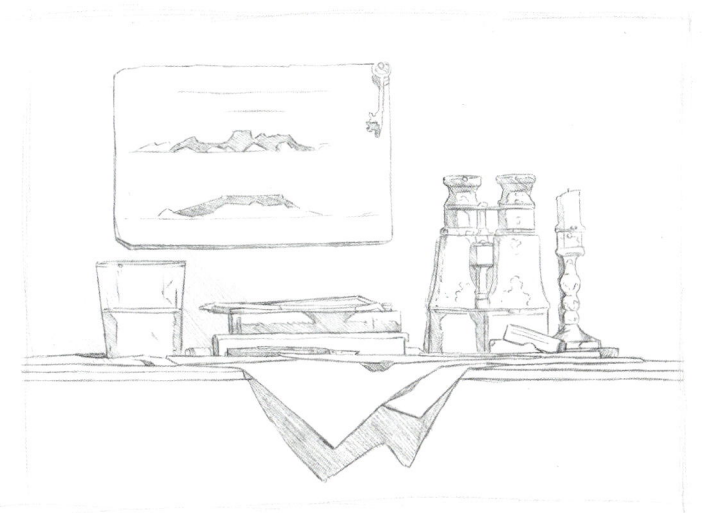

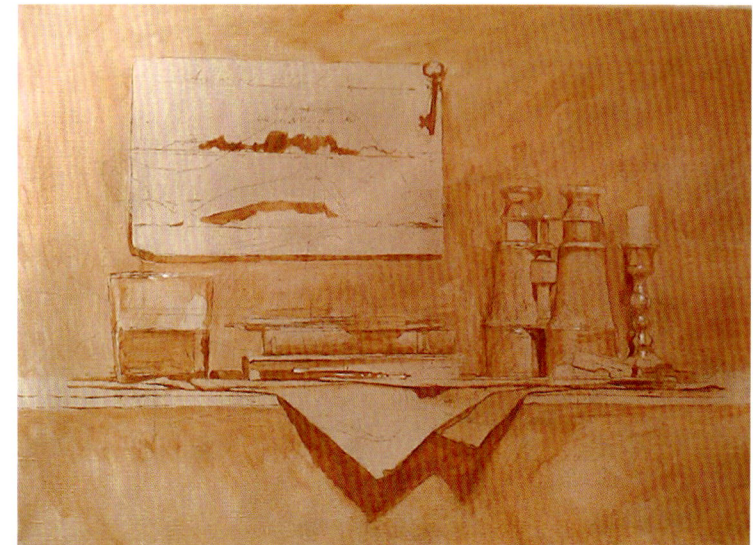

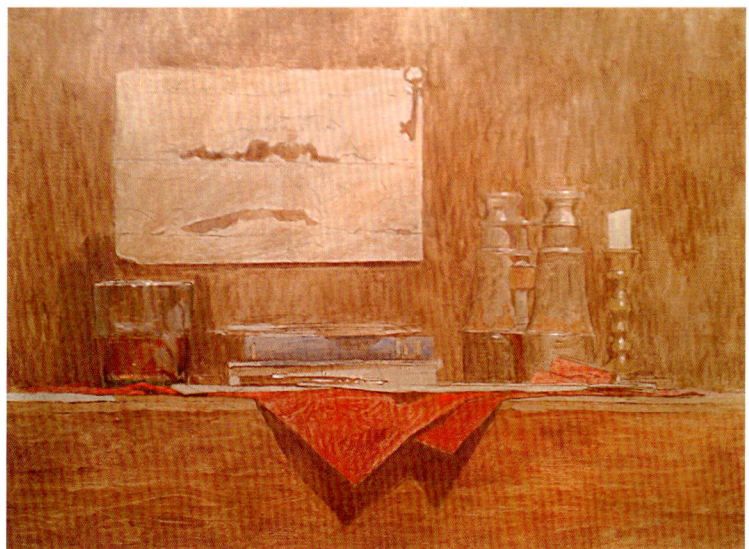

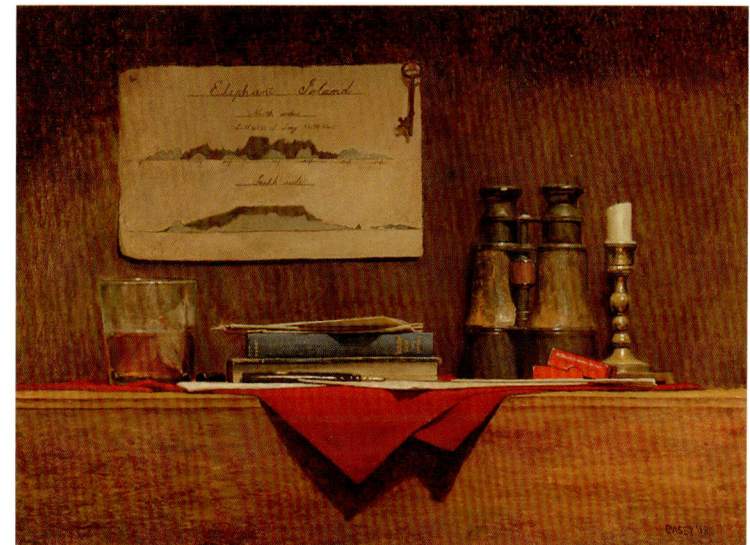

TOP LEFT: The indirect method begins with a preparatory drawing, which is then transferred to a toned painting surface.

TOP RIGHT: The painting itself begins with a grisaille underpainting.

ABOVE LEFT: A wash-in of color is added to the underpainting.

ABOVE RIGHT: Todd M. Casey, *Shackleton's Dilemma,* 2012, oil on linen, 18 × 24 inches (45.72 × 60.96 cm). Courtesy of Rehs Contemporary Galleries, New York.

The final painting is built up with layers of color.

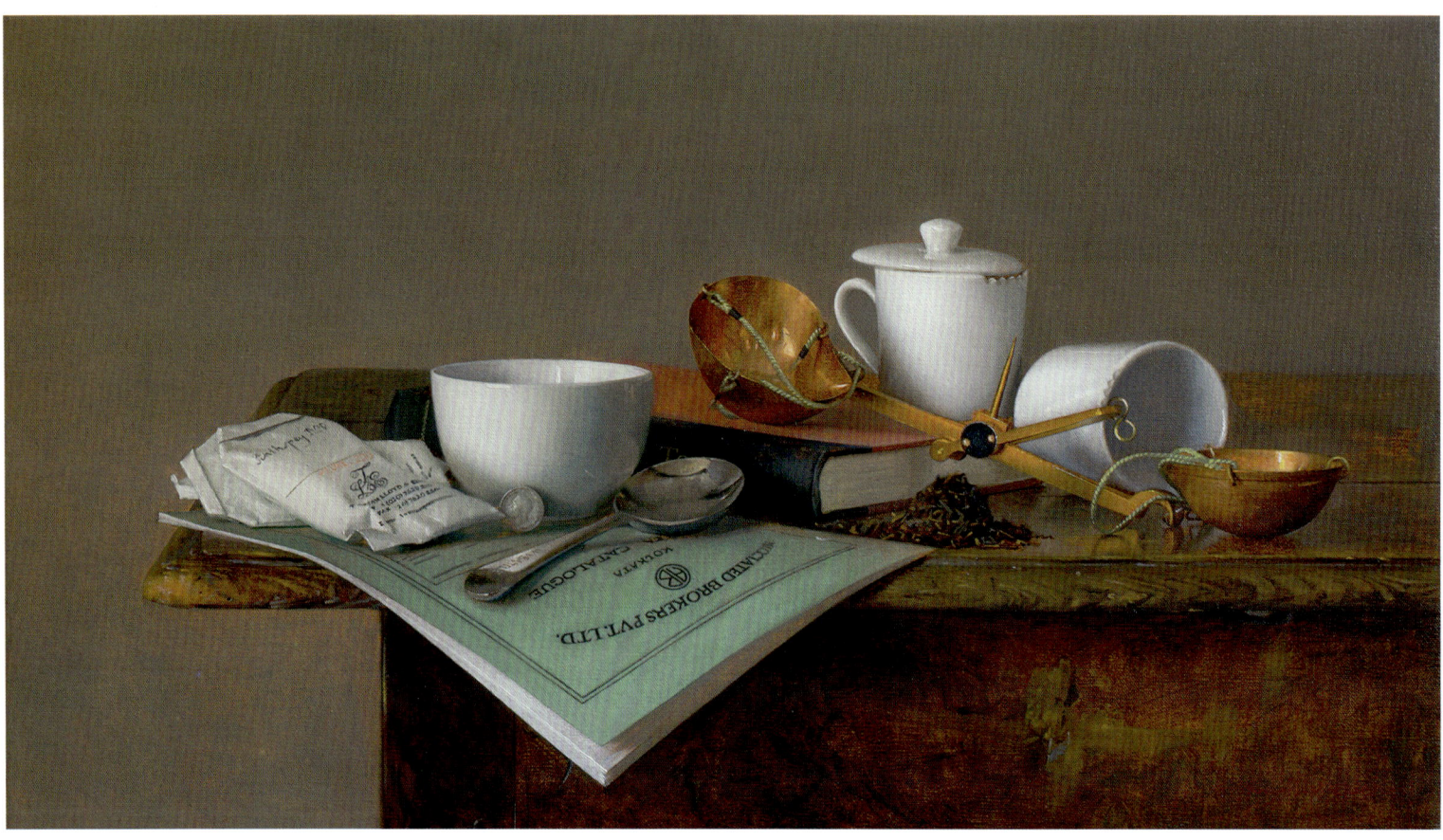

ABOVE: Nancy Fletcher, *The World of Tea,* 2016, oil on linen, 12 × 18 inches (30.48 × 45.72 cm). Courtesy of the artist.

Some contemporary artists still use traditional techniques of underpainting in their work, as is apparent in this painting by Nancy Fletcher.

OPPOSITE: Pieter Claesz., *Still Life with a Salt,* c. 1640–1645, oil on panel, 20 ¾ × 17 ¼ inches (52.8 × 44 cm). Photo courtesy of Rijksmuseum, Amsterdam. Bequeathed by Daniël Crena de Iongh, Wilton, Connecticut.

The Dutch were famous for using monochromatic underpaintings.

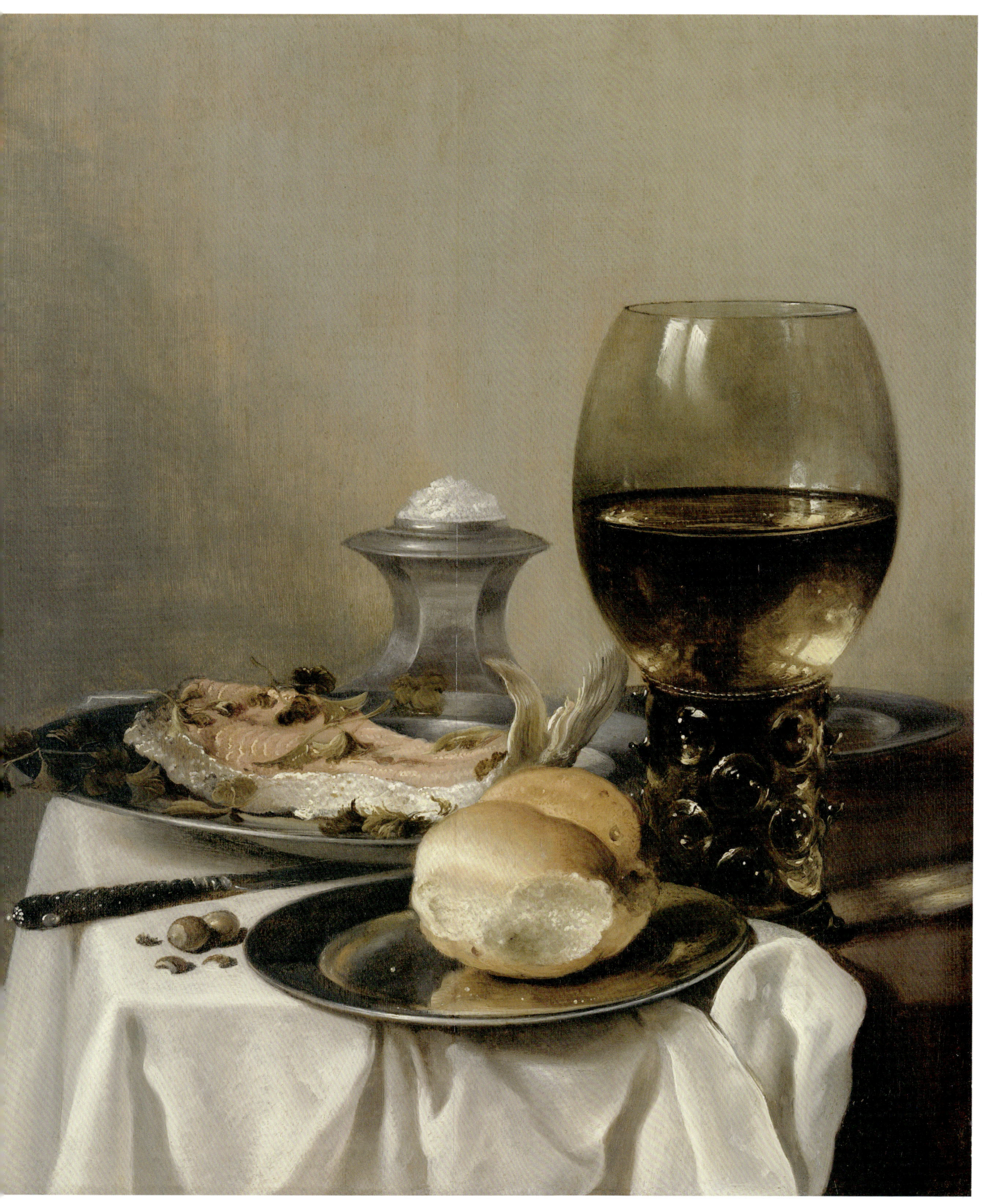

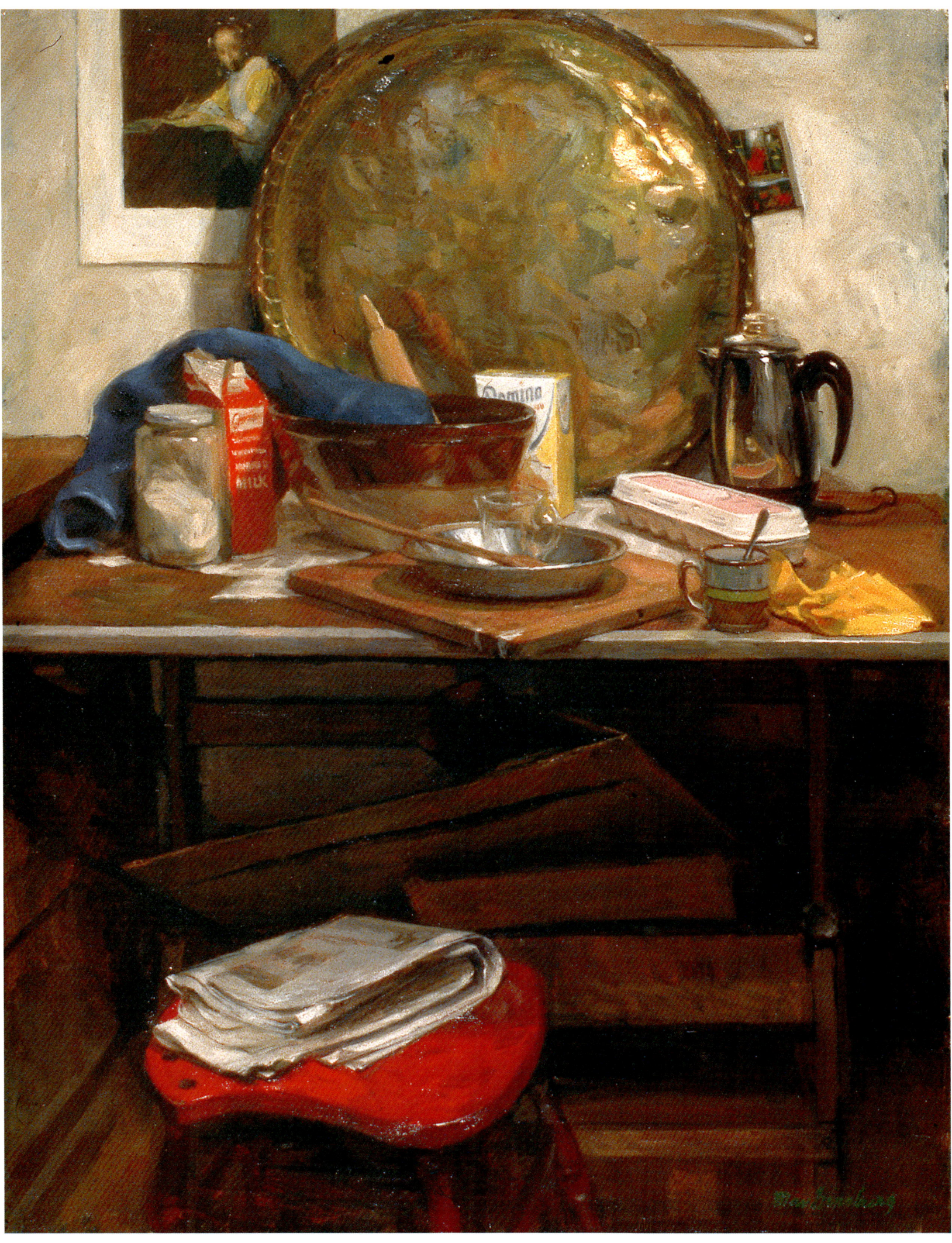

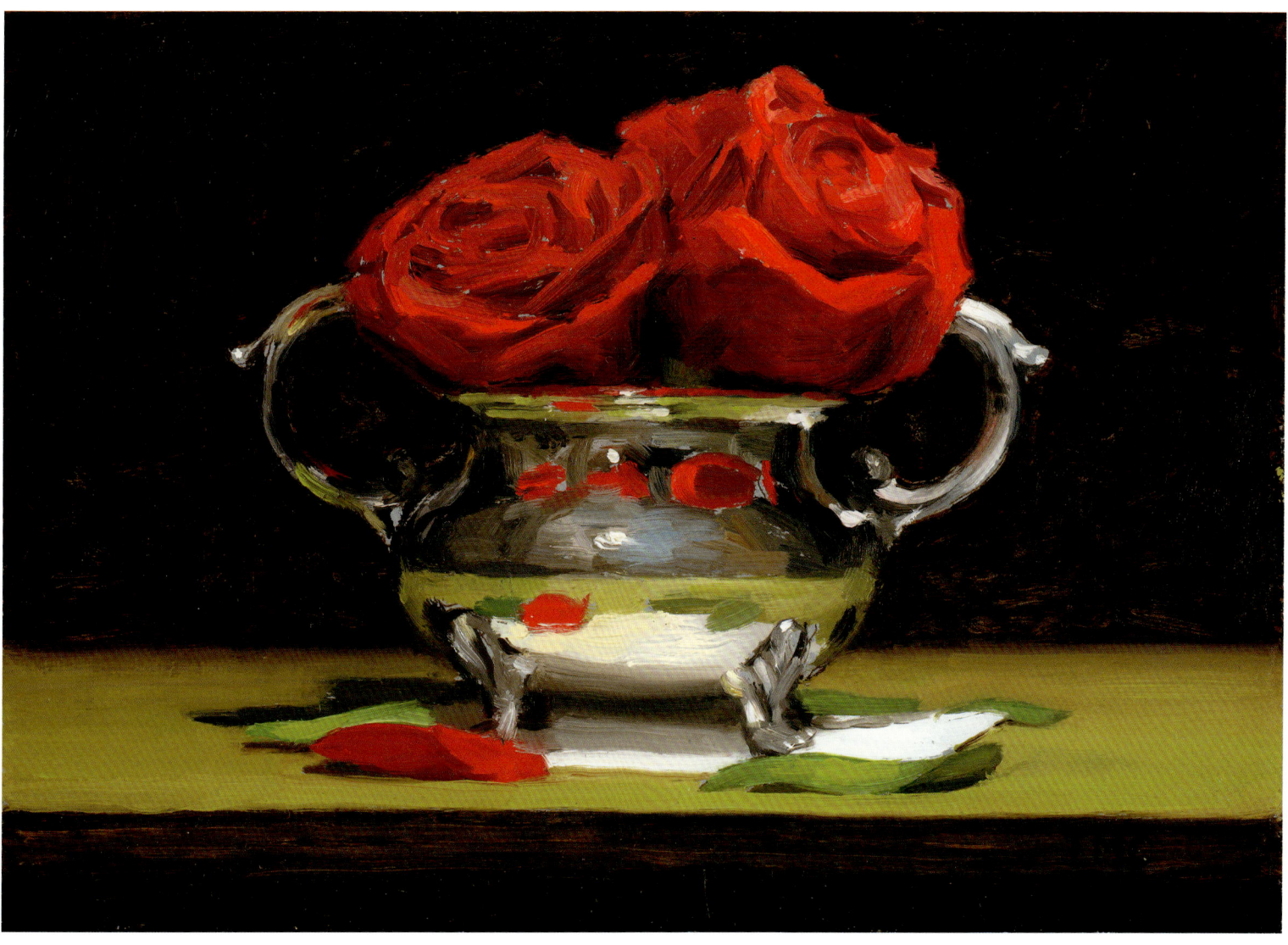

A direct approach, by contrast, means that you are working directly on the canvas, often without a preparatory drawing or underpainting. A common term for this is *alla prima*, which is an Italian phrase meaning "at the first try." Whereas in indirect painting you allow each layer to dry, at least somewhat, before applying the next, *alla prima* painting is a *wet-into-wet* technique.

A lot of the Impressionist painters adopted the *alla prima* approach. Their goal was to capture the light and its quickly changing effects, leading them to sometimes mix colors directly on the canvas. At the time, flat brushes had just become popular, so you see a lot of mark-making in Impressionist paintings.

One mistake that students commonly make with this technique is putting too much paint on the canvas and then trying to paint on top of it. The trouble is that they then have to add a lot more paint to cover the layer below. This can create quite a mess. To avoid this, consider washing in a quick underpainting or layer of color to map out your composition and drawing.

OPPOSITE: Max Ginsburg, *Studio Still Life*, 1978, oil on panel, 20 × 16 inches (50.8 × 40.64 cm). Courtesy of the artist.

Artists can work directly on the canvas without an underpainting or drawing, which is a bit harder to do. That was Max Ginsburg's technique in *Studio Still Life*.

ABOVE: Todd M. Casey, *Red Roses,* 2012, oil on panel, 6 × 8 inches (15.24 × 20.32 cm). Private collection.

I finished *Red Roses* in one three-to-four-hour sitting. This forced me to dive right into the painting, which is difficult because you must juggle drawing, color, values, and composition all at the same time.

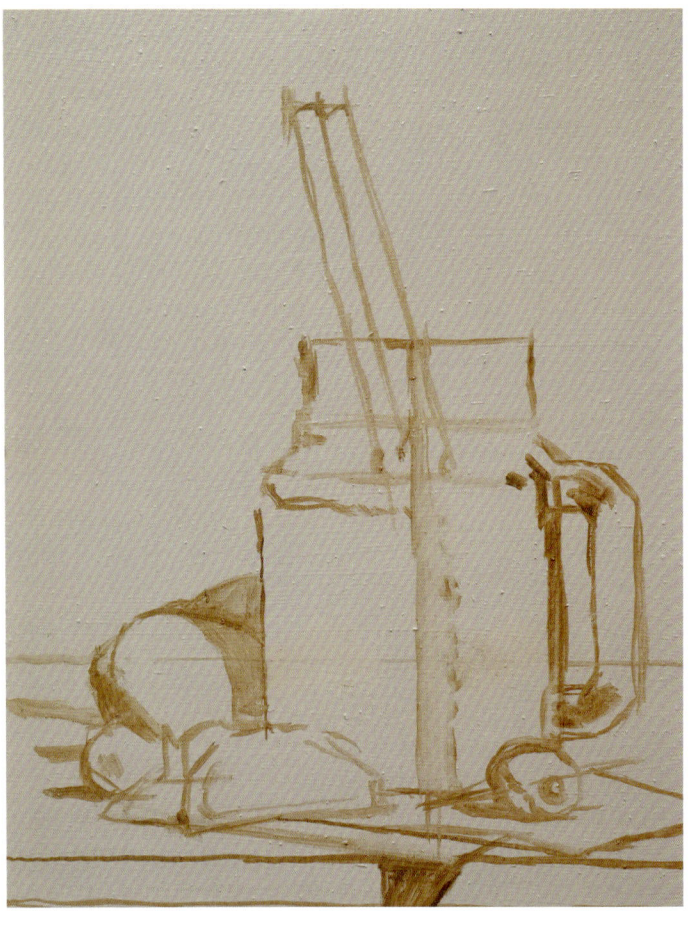

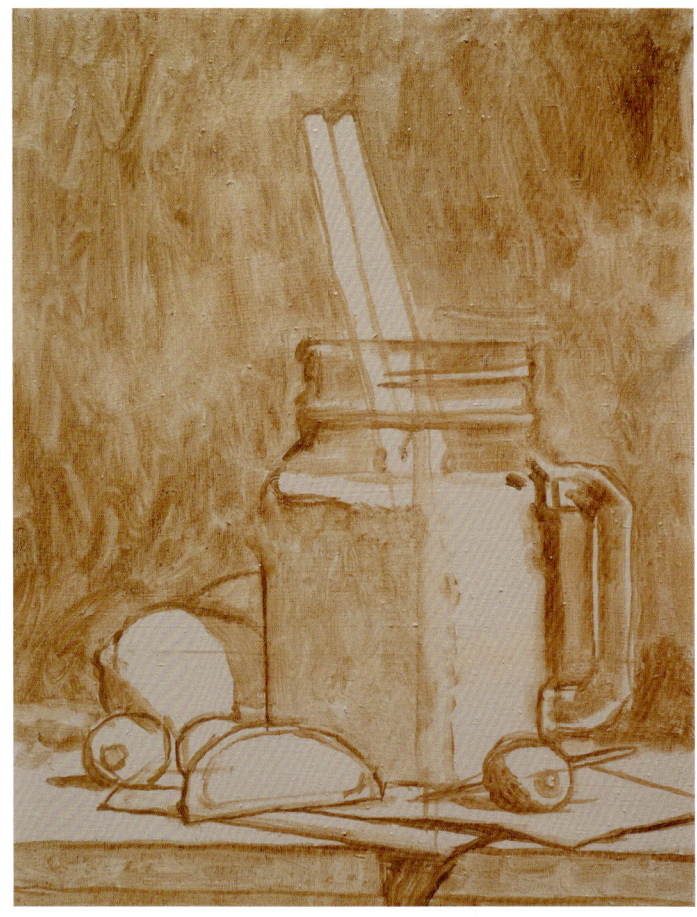

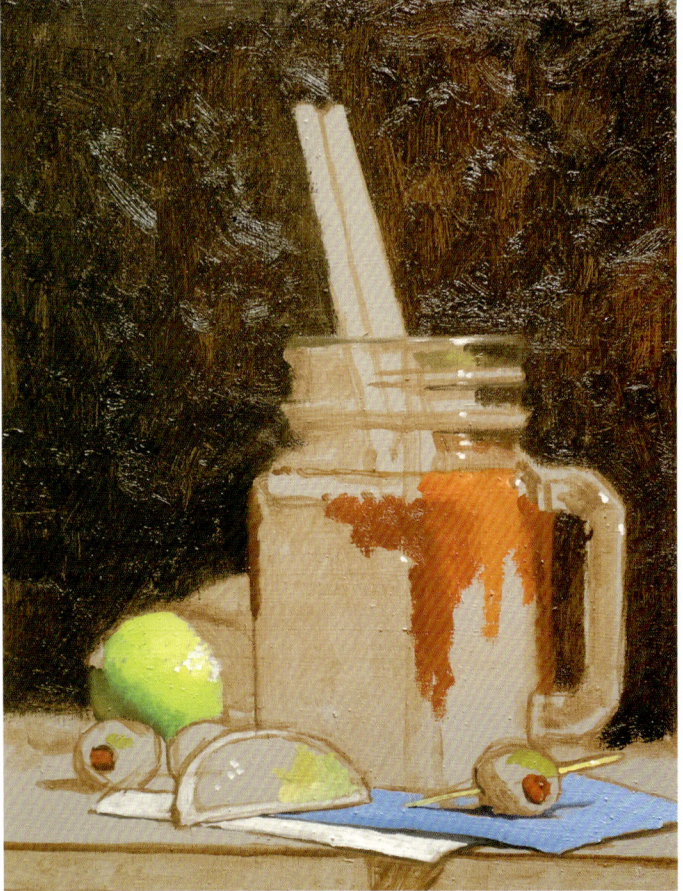

ABOVE LEFT: For my *alla prima* painting *Bloody Mary*, I first made a rough drawing directly on the canvas, using burnt umber with mineral spirits to keep it somewhat light. Keeping it light helps me see the composition without committing to the exact location of the information. After I commit, I make the contour and separation of light and shadow darker.

ABOVE RIGHT: I then did a quick open grisaille to establish some of the tonal relationships.

LEFT: This shows how *Bloody Mary* looked midway through, with some of the forms rendered.

OPPOSITE: Todd M. Casey, *Bloody Mary*, 2018, oil on panel, 9 × 6 inches (22.86 × 15.24 cm). Private collection.

This is the completed painting, with everything brought to a finished stage.

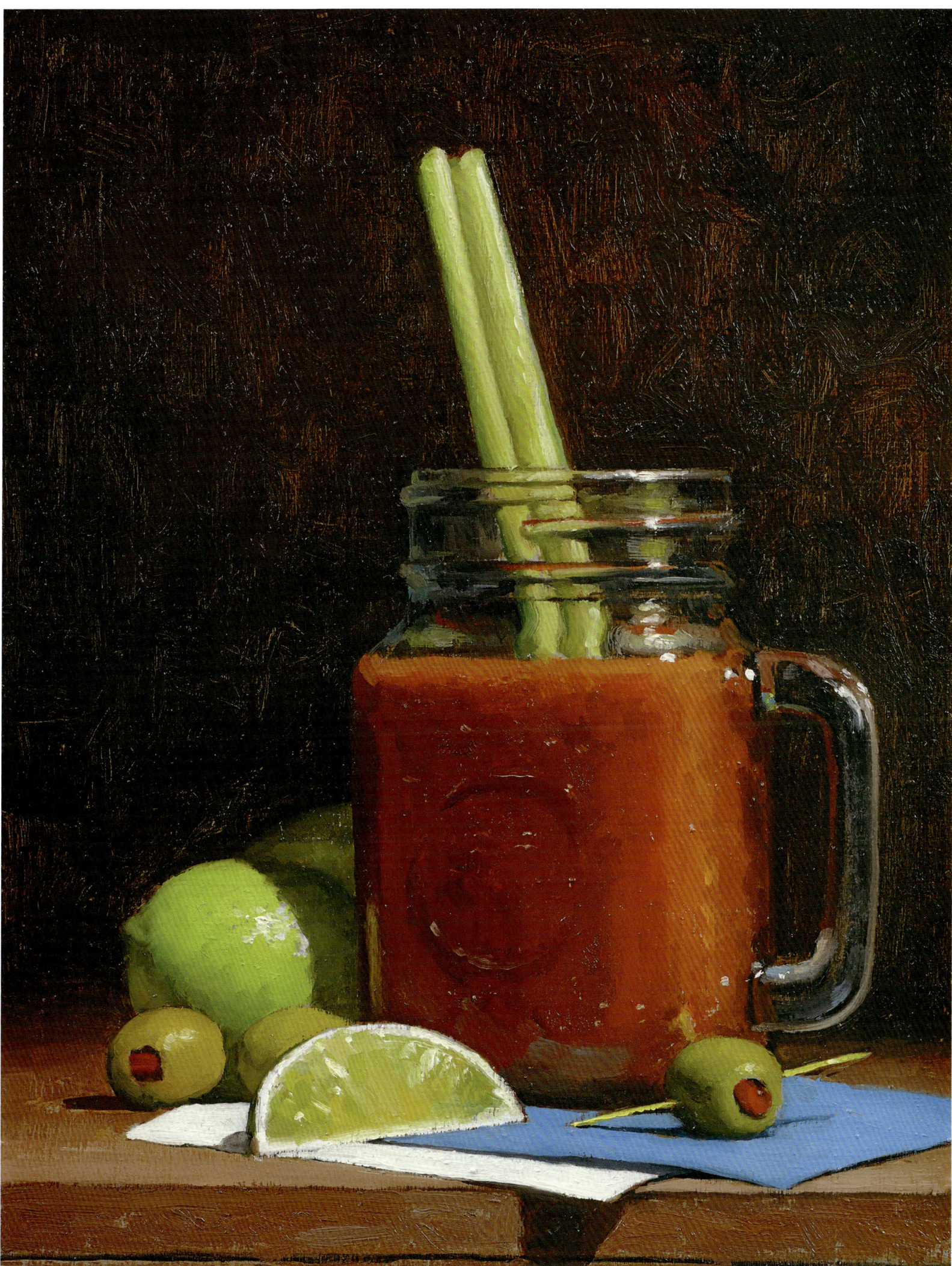

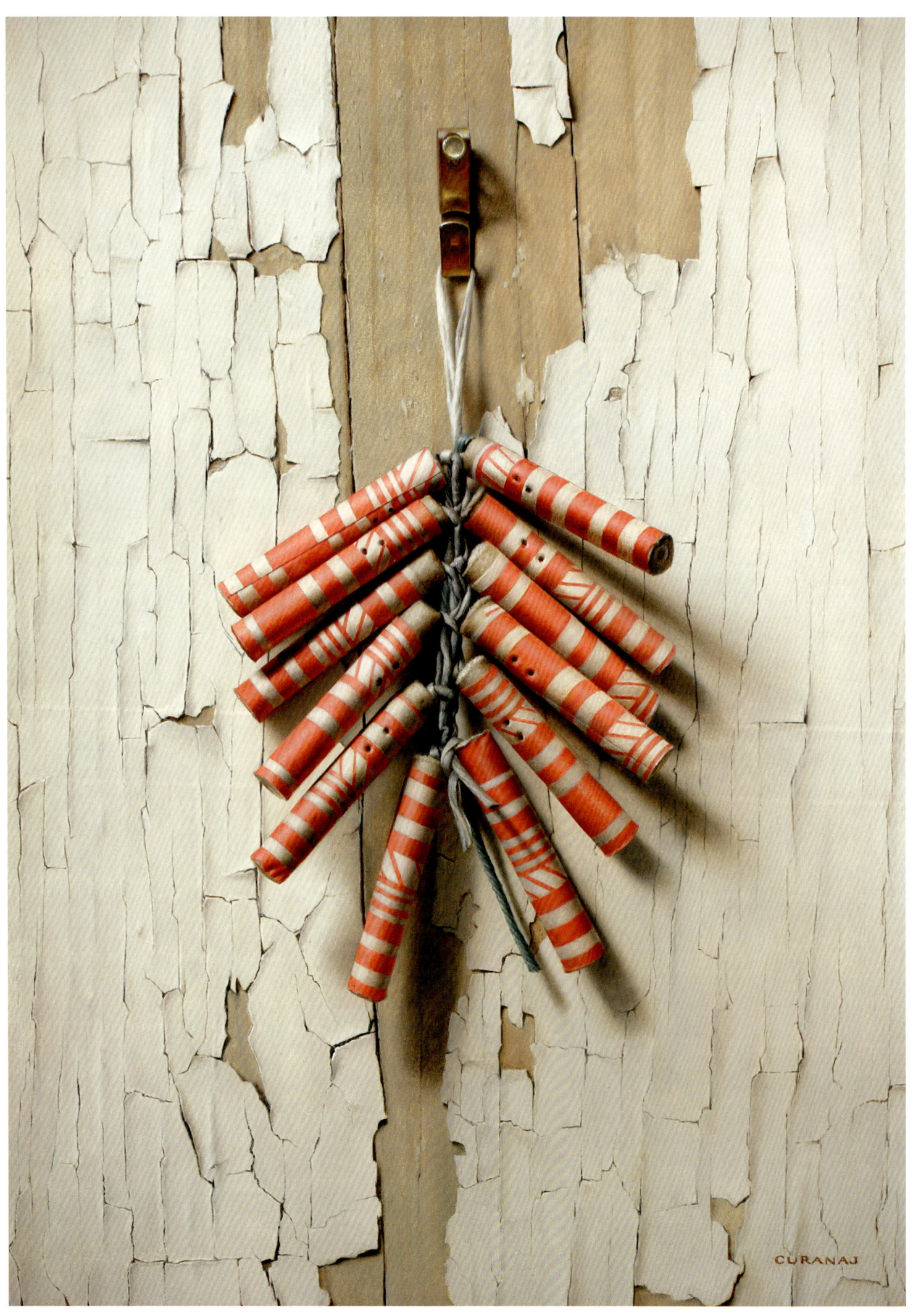

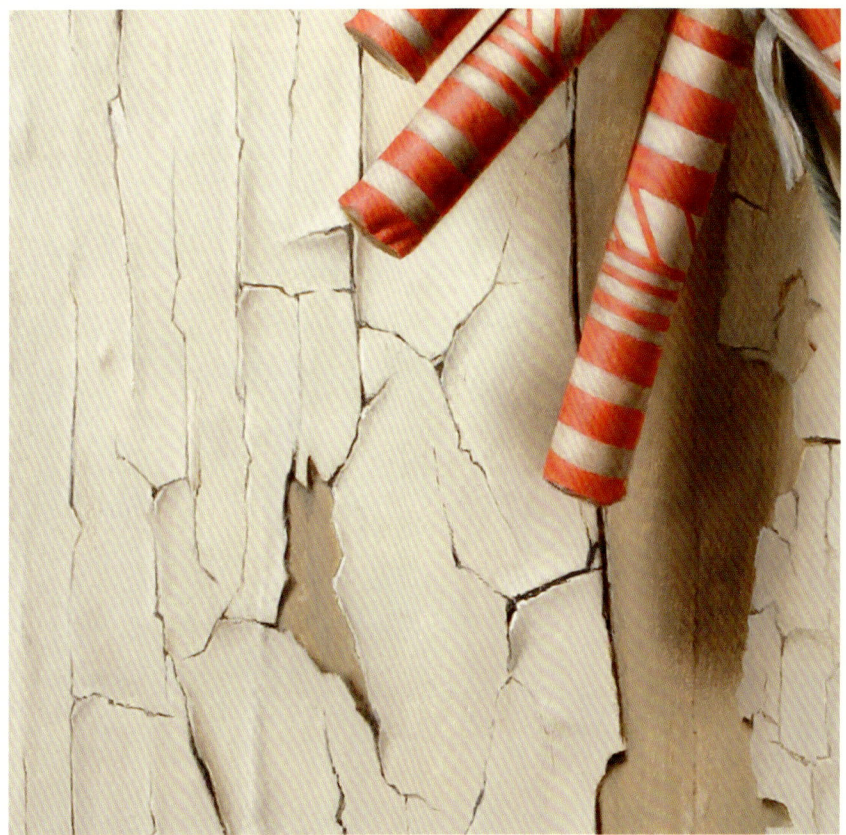

LEVEL OF FINISH

A painting is like visual poetry, but a poem can be very formal in terms of rhyme and meter or very informal, as in free verse. Similarly, you can do a painting that is so carefully developed that it has no visual brushstrokes—sometimes referred to as a "tight" painting—or you can choose to work much more freely, letting the brush-strokes remain visible.

OPPOSITE: Tony Curanaj, *Jumping Jack Flash,* 2015, oil on panel, 8 ½ × 6 inches (21.59 × 15.24 cm). Courtesy of the artist.

ABOVE: Tony Curanaj's trompe l'oeil *Jumping Jack Flash* is an example of a tight painting, in which no brushwork is visible.

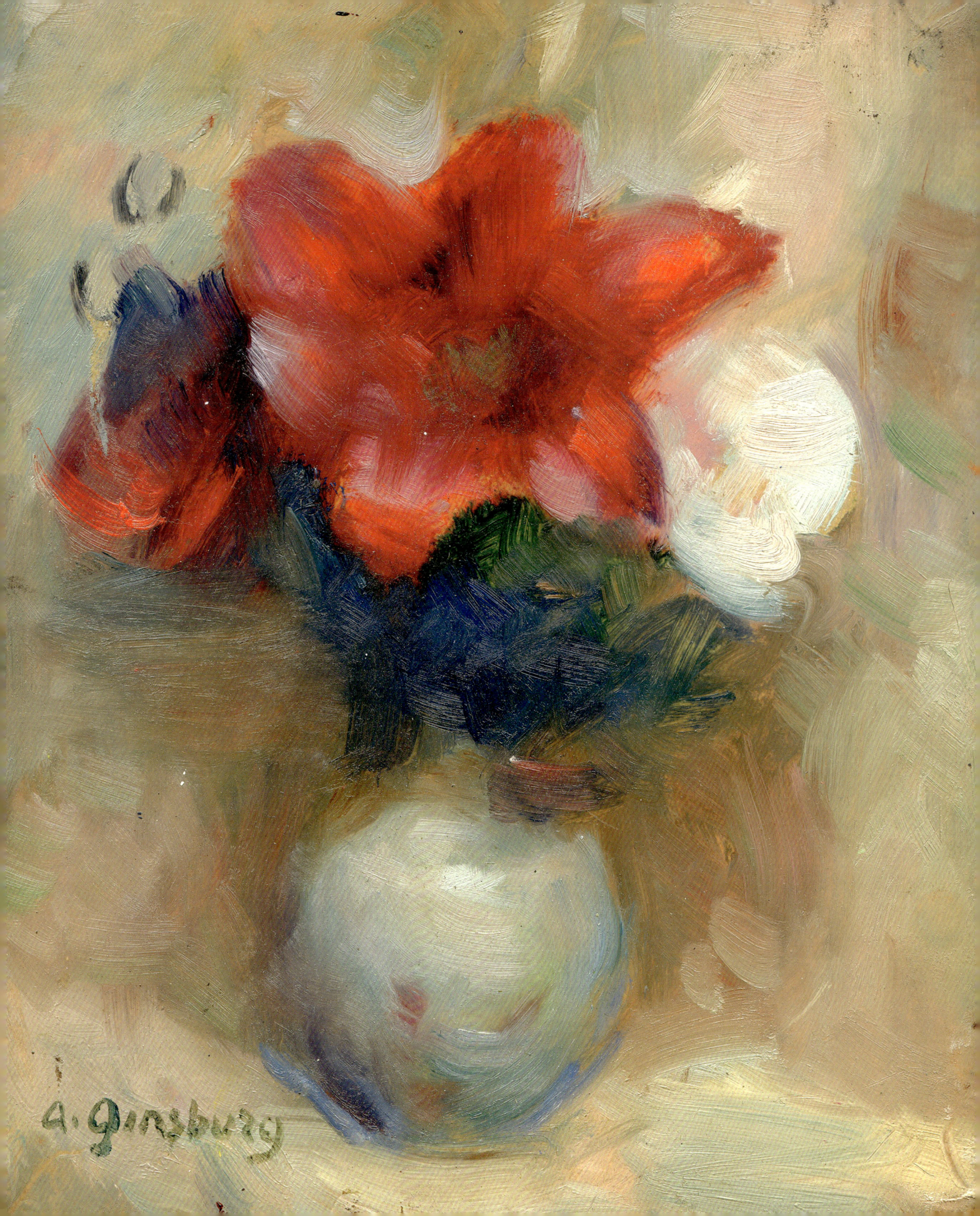

a. Ginsburg

MARK-MAKING AND BRUSH LANGUAGE

Different brushes leave different kinds of marks, depending on the type of hair, the shape, the amount of paint loaded onto the brush, the pressure applied, and the way the artist holds the brush. As an artist, you should make your own brush choices, so experiment and take note of the marks various brushes make.

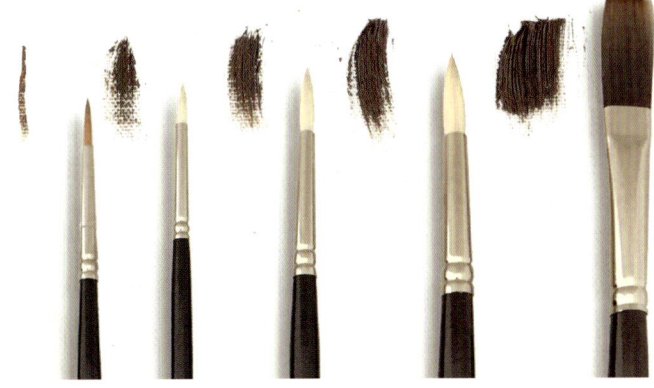

Having a variety of brushes provides many different options for mark-making.

Scumbling

Scumbling means to roughly apply a thin layer of paint to the painting surface or on top of another layer of paint. It only partially hides whatever is underneath, so patches of the canvas or underpainting show through. This allows for optical mixing, in which an underlayer and a layer above it create an affect you cannot get with just one layer of paint. Scumbling is often scrubbed in with a stiff bristle brush. It is sometimes referred to as dry brushing.

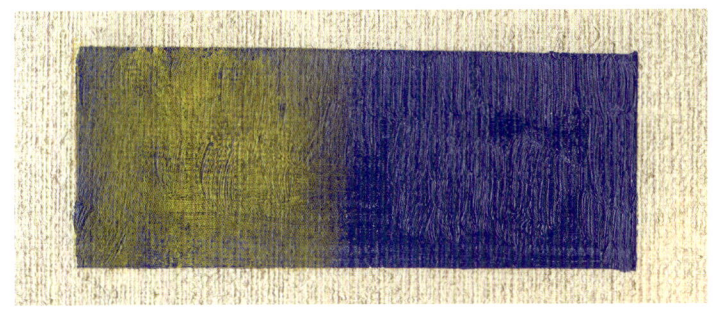

On the left cadmium yellow has been applied opaquely to linen. On the right, ultramarine mixed with Galkyd is glazed over the cadmium yellow.

Glazing

Glazing is applying a thin, translucent layer of color—usually suspended in a medium—atop another, dry layer of paint. Many mediums can be used for glazing; most are alkyd-based, which helps speed up the drying time. It's better to use relatively transparent paints (like alizarin crimson) for glazing.

Glazing produces an effect something like looking through stained glass. Before glazing, you must make sure that the area you want to glaze is absolutely dry. Glazing tends to be applied at the last stage of painting and can be a way of unifying an area—or the whole painting—with a color.

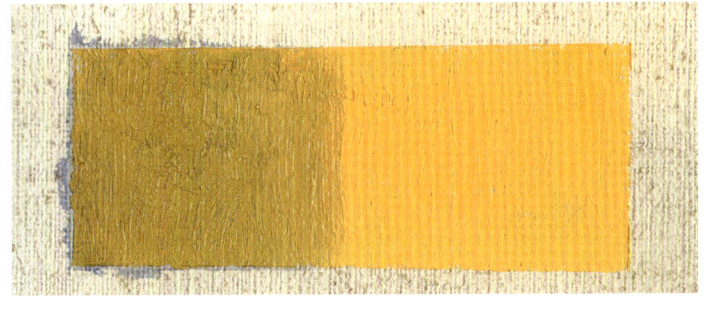

Here, cobalt blue was applied opaquely to linen. On the right, cadmium yellow is scumbled onto the blue underpainting.

OPPOSITE: Abraham Ginsburg (American, 1891–1963), *Flowers*, 1950, oil on panel, 10 × 8 inches (25.4 × 20.32 cm). Courtesy of Max Ginsburg.

This floral still life by Abraham Ginsburg illustrates a much looser, impressionistic approach to painting.

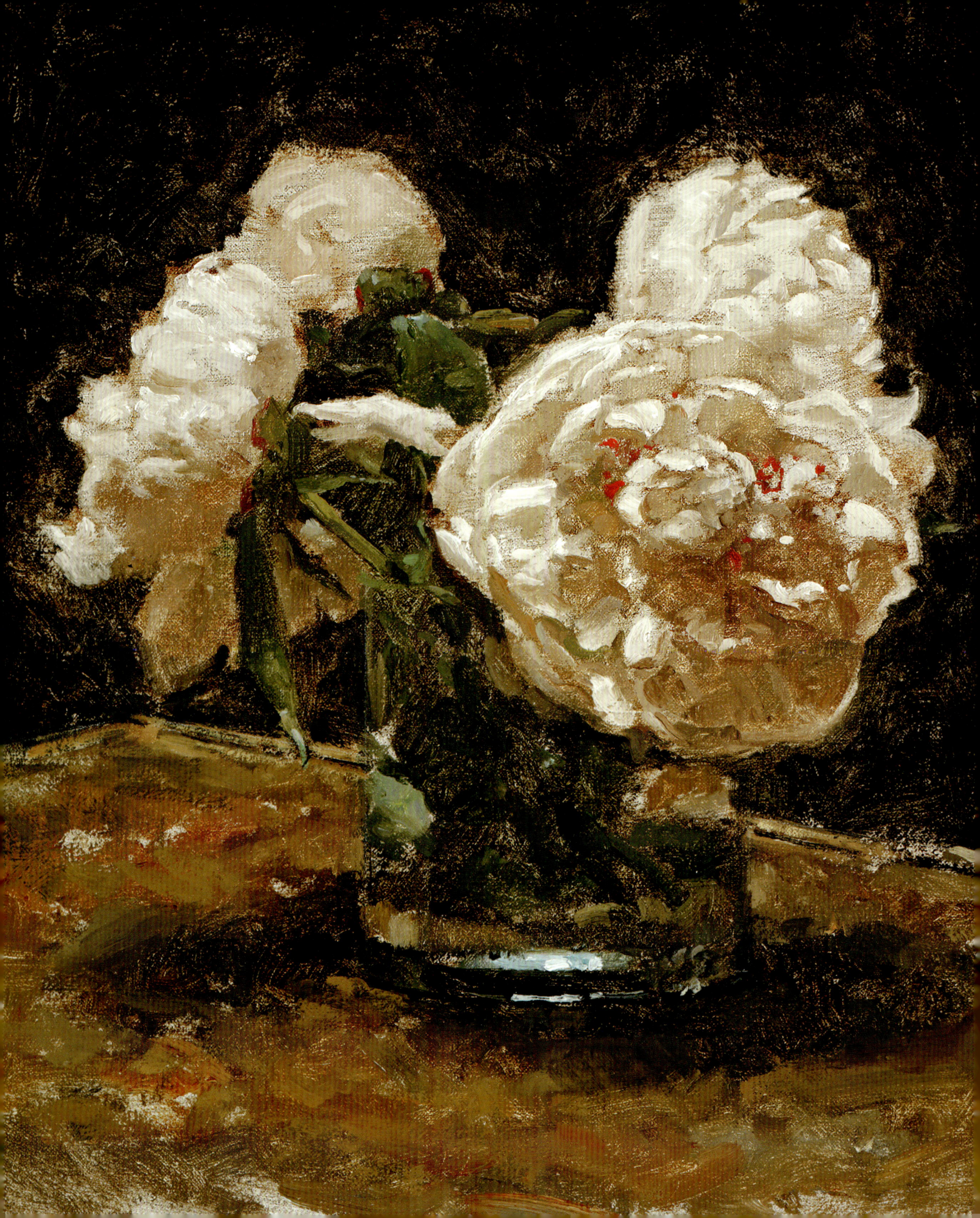

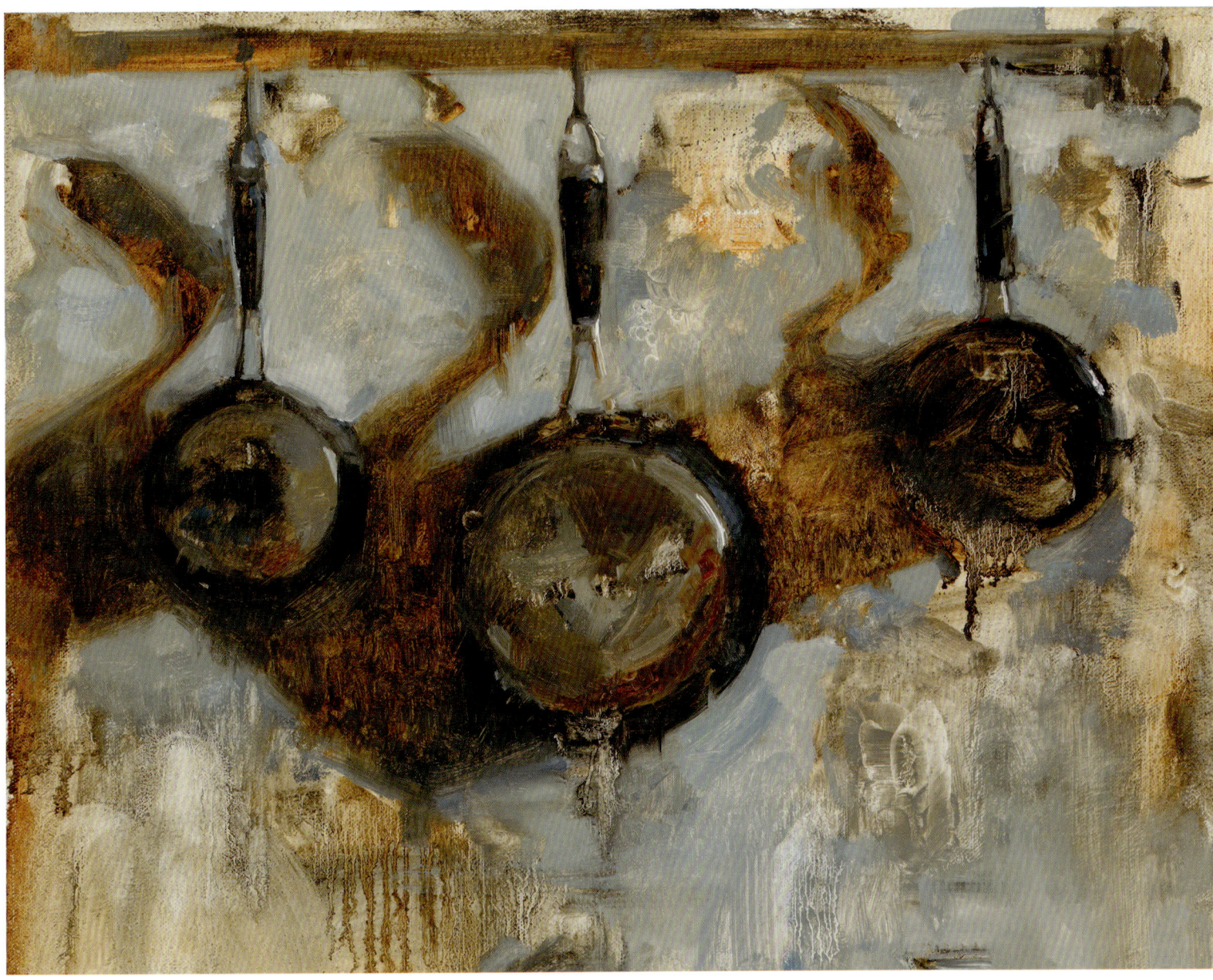

Broken Color

Broken color happens when areas of a lower layer of paint show through a layer on top. This can be done by adding medium to the upper layer of paint to make it more translucent or by leaving a bit of space between some brushstrokes. Broken color creates optical mixing—the viewer's eye blends the colors together. It also lets light transmit through layers to brighten up an area and add interest.

OPPOSITE: Travis Schlaht, *Peonies,* 2011, oil on linen, 15 × 14 inches (38.1 × 35.56 cm). Courtesy of the artist.

From a distance, the viewer's eye optically mixes broken colors together. As you move closer to Travis Schlaht's *Peonies,* you can see the areas of broken color more clearly.

ABOVE: Hyeseung Marriage-Song, *Shadows on a Wall,* 2018, oil on linen, 12 × 15 inches (30.48 × 38.1 cm). Courtesy of the artist.

Hyeseung Marriage-Song uses a very loose underpainting to provide a nice balance of texture in her painting *Shadows on a Wall.*

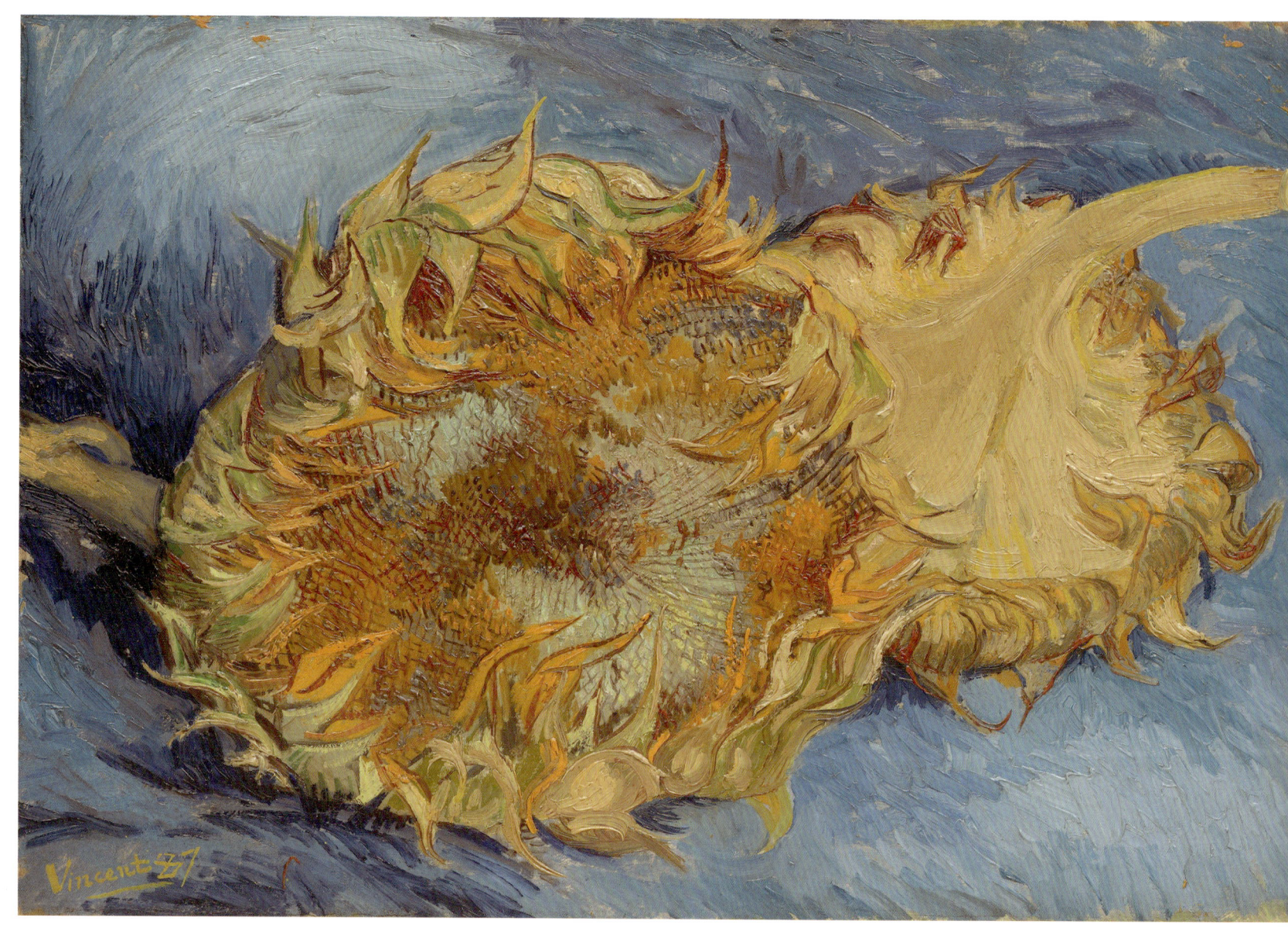

Impasto

Impasto involves applying paint very thickly with a brush or palette knife. When you view an impasto painting, the thickness is an important aspect of the visual experience, and the painting often looks luscious and juicy. Often artists use impasto to build up their lights more thickly than their shadows. Sometimes, impasto strokes are referred to as "bravura" because of their boldness.

ABOVE: Vincent van Gogh (Dutch, 1853–1890), *Sunflowers*, 1887, oil on canvas, 17 × 24 inches (43.2 × 61 cm). The Metropolitan Museum of Art, New York. Rogers Fund, 1949.

In *Sunflowers*, Vincent van Gogh used lots of paint in a thick, juicy, impasto application.

EXERCISE

PAINT THE SAME OBJECT USING DIFFERENT TOOLS

Do a few small paintings of the same object using just one brush or a knife for each painting. This will force you to exploit the full range of mark-making that can be achieved with each tool. Finding which tool makes marks you like is important. I tend to use a variety of brushes when I do a painting but use mostly flats and rounds in both synthetic and bristle hairs.

I painted this clementine using three different tools: a round brush (top), a flat brush (center), and a palette knife (bottom).

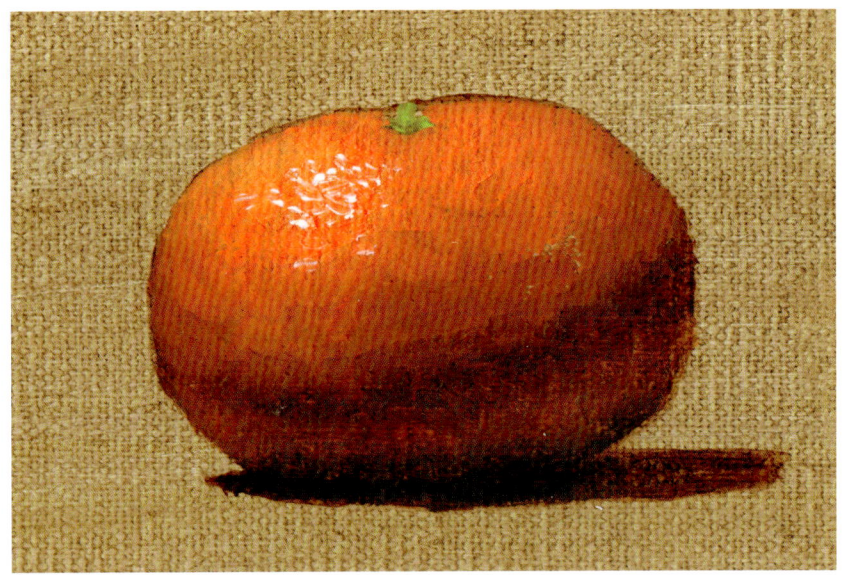

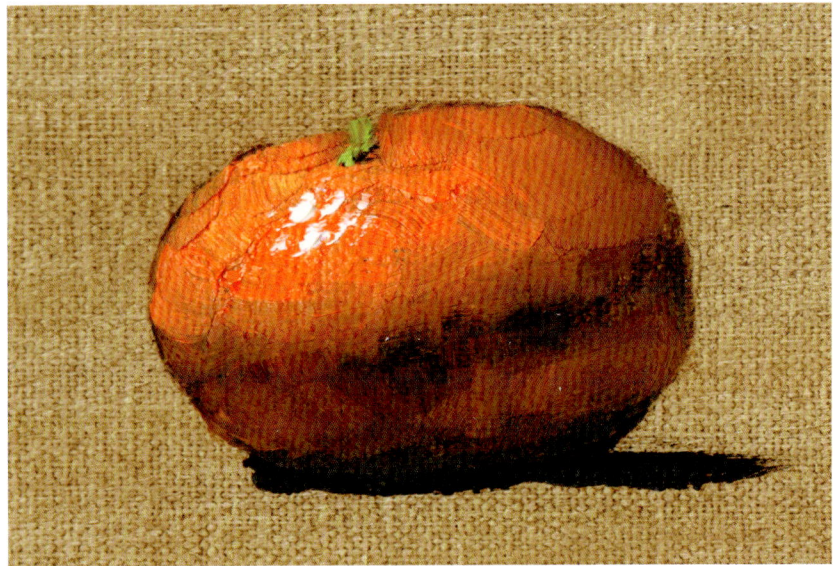

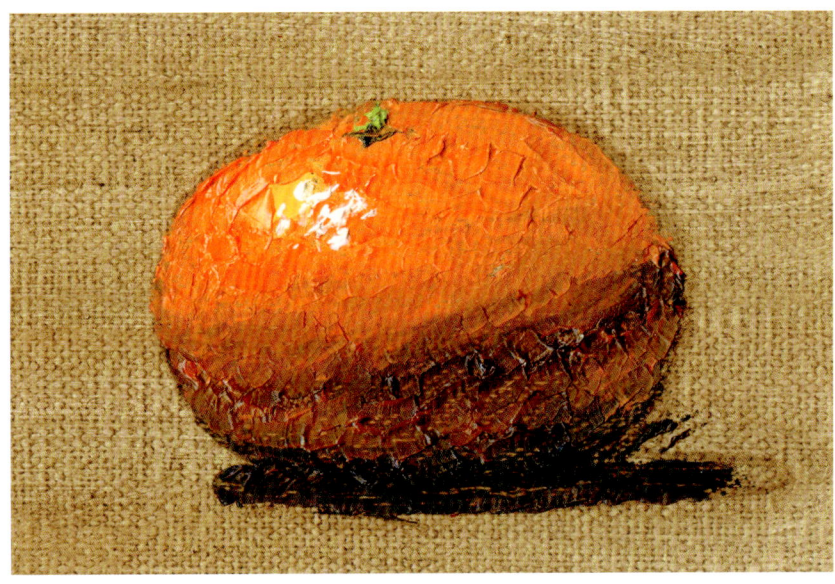

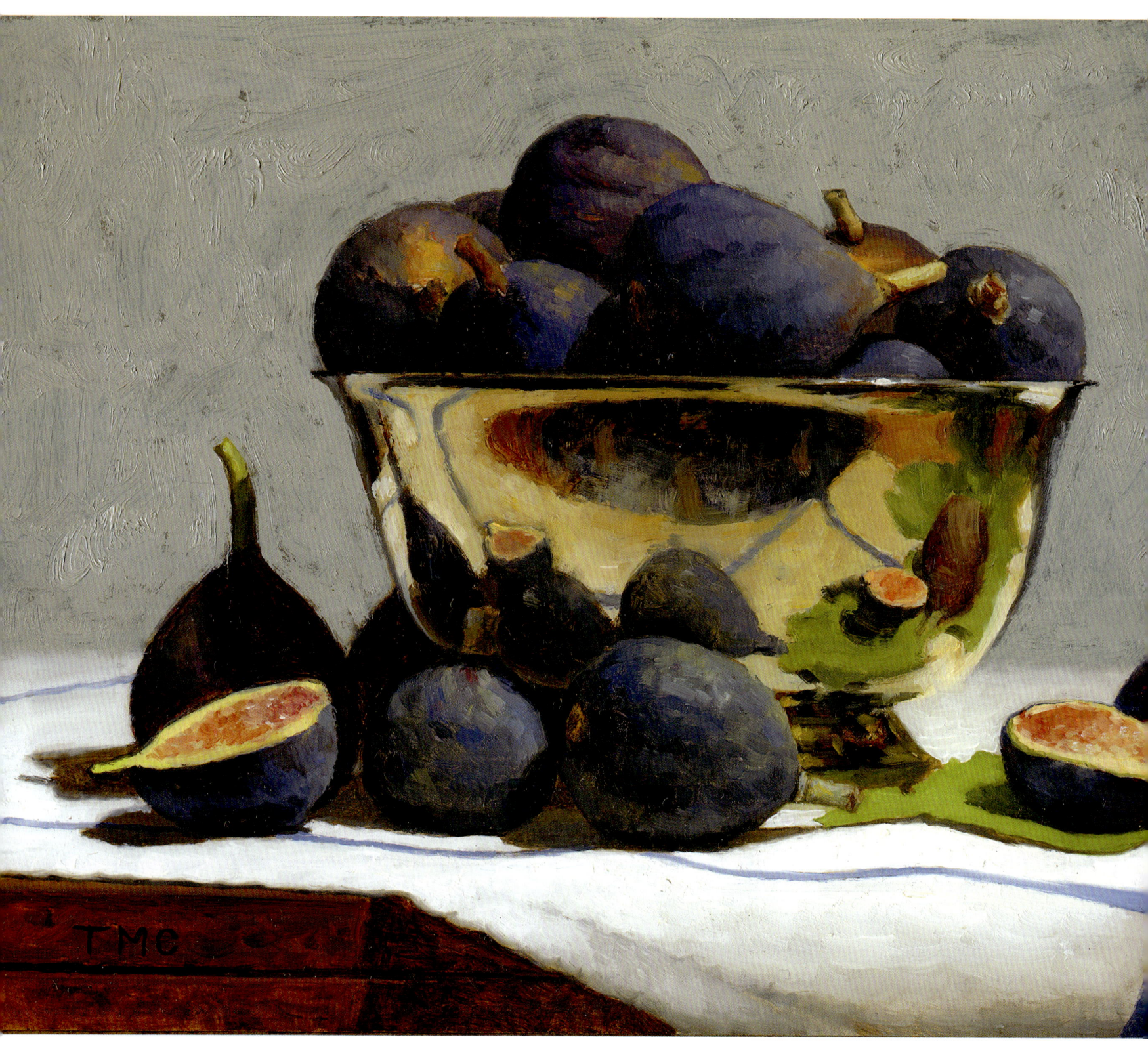

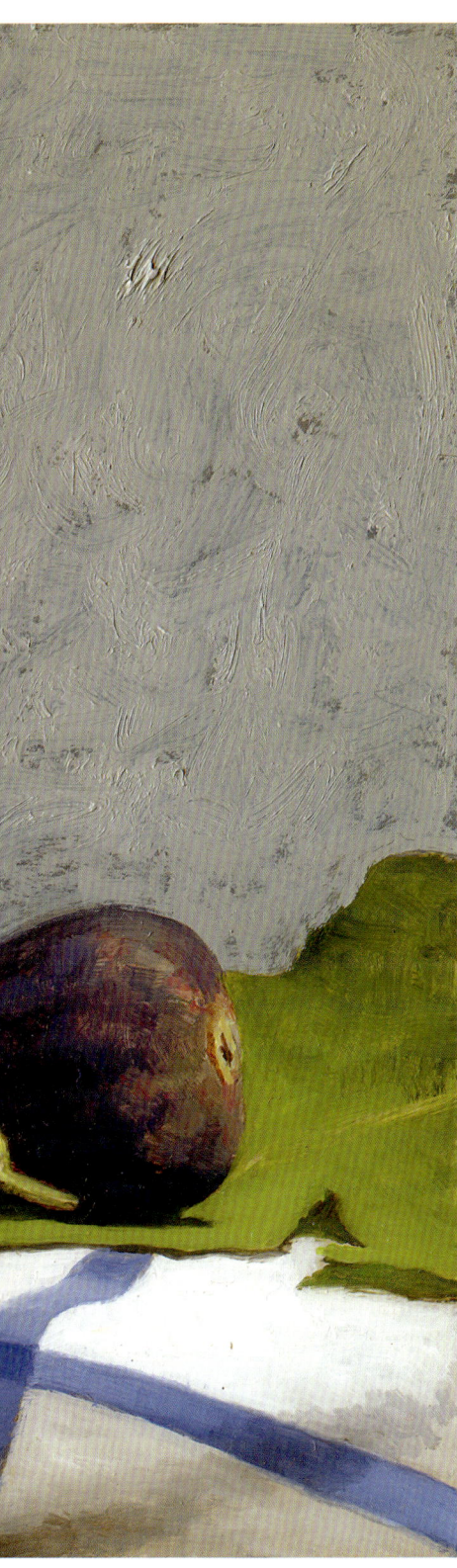

CHAPTER 9

PUTTING IT ALL TOGETHER: A STEP-BY-STEP GUIDE

Throw your heart into the picture and then jump in after it.

HOWARD PYLE

I n this final chapter I show you how a painting is made, from beginning to end, and explain all the steps and decisions made along the way. My painting *Silver Bowl with Figs* was done in three sittings over two days and took a total of about fifteen hours to complete, including arranging and lighting the setup, deciding on the composition, doing a poster study, executing the drawing, transferring the drawing to the panel, and then doing the final painting.

LEFT: Todd M. Casey, *Silver Bowl with Figs*, 2018, oil on panel, 6 × 9 inches (15.24 × 22.86 cm). Private collection.

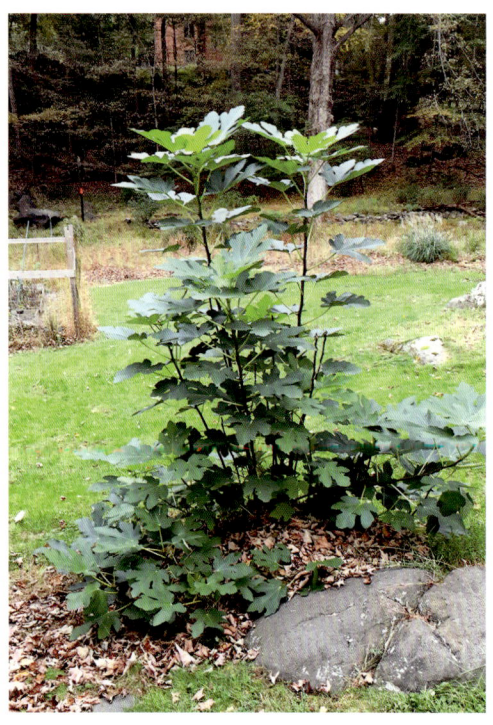

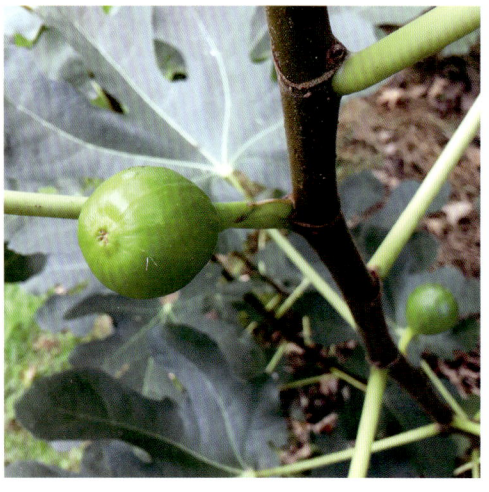

THE IDEA OR VISION

I chose to depict figs in a silver bowl because I wanted the challenges of painting a highly perishable subject and of painting reflections. But I also wanted to celebrate the first figs I ever grew!

The story behind this painting starts with my love for gardening. A few years ago, I wanted to add fig trees to my garden, so I bought three small fig saplings from a seed company in Petaluma, California. It takes an incredible amount of time and patience to raise a fig tree until it begins to fruit, usually about four years. I was a bit skeptical about whether my trees would ever fruit, but in 2018 they finally sprouted three little figs! As soon as I saw them, I knew I had to do a painting that had been in the back of my mind for years.

THE PROPS

The few figs I plucked from my trees weren't enough for the painting I envisioned, so I had to buy some more at the market. Besides the three figs from my own yellow long-neck trees, the fruits in the painting are black mission and brown turkey figs.

The silver bowl was lent to me by one of my students, who is constantly looking for good props. I had painted the bowl a few times and enjoyed it each time. It seemed like a good fit for my concept—that of offering fruit, as if someone had just picked some figs and filled a bowl with them for others to eat. Also, a mirrorlike object can add another dimension of depth to a painting, reflecting the environment outside the picture plane.

The white cloth with blue stripes has a nice "country" feeling to it, which felt appropriate with the setup. I live in an old farmhouse, so I was going for a country theme.

COMPOSING THE SETUP

Once the props were assembled, I placed everything in front of me. I began stacking the figs in the bowl so that when I sat back they would be visible at my eye level. After making a few adjustments, I sat down in my chair to analyze the setup.

The setup shown in the photo opposite looked pretty good because the repetition of shapes created unity throughout the design. I felt, though, that there was something missing, so I added a fake leaf that I keep around to see what a touch of green would do. It really balanced the design and increased the variety of color. At this point, the composition felt balanced. The fig at the right that's turned on its side and surrounded by the white cloth is the highest-contrast portion of the painting, making it the focal point.

PAINTING PERISHABLE OBJECTS

One of the first things I do when setting up a painting is to think about the order in which I'll render the objects. If the setup includes perishable objects, those must be painted first. I'm also aware that fruit can change color within just a few days. Therefore, time is of the essence.

If I cut into a fruit, the part exposed to the air becomes a priority, as it will rot very quickly. Freshly cut fruit may be juicy and show appealing drops of liquid on its surface, so it's important to observe those characteristics and take notes, especially when painting over multiple sessions.

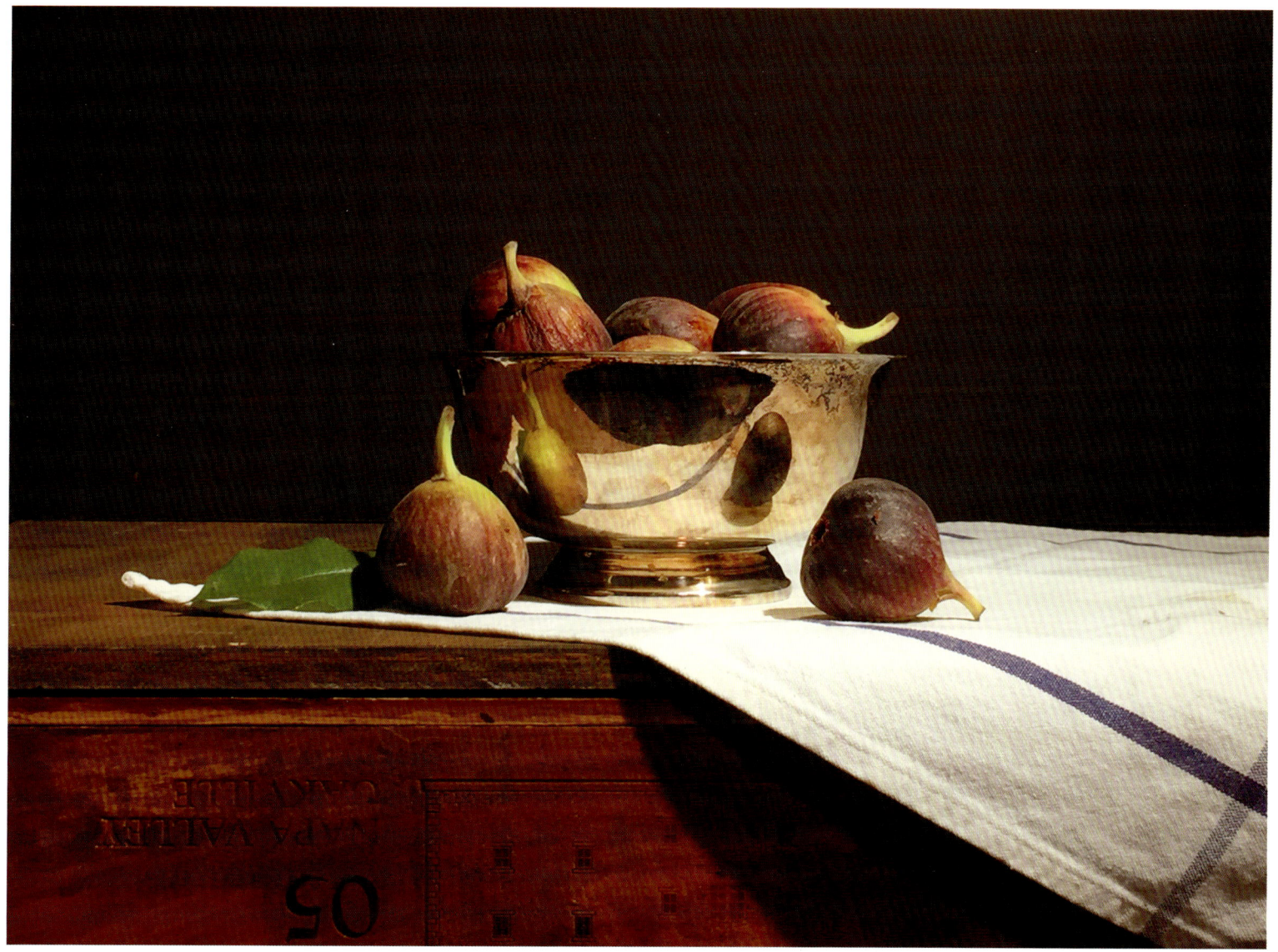

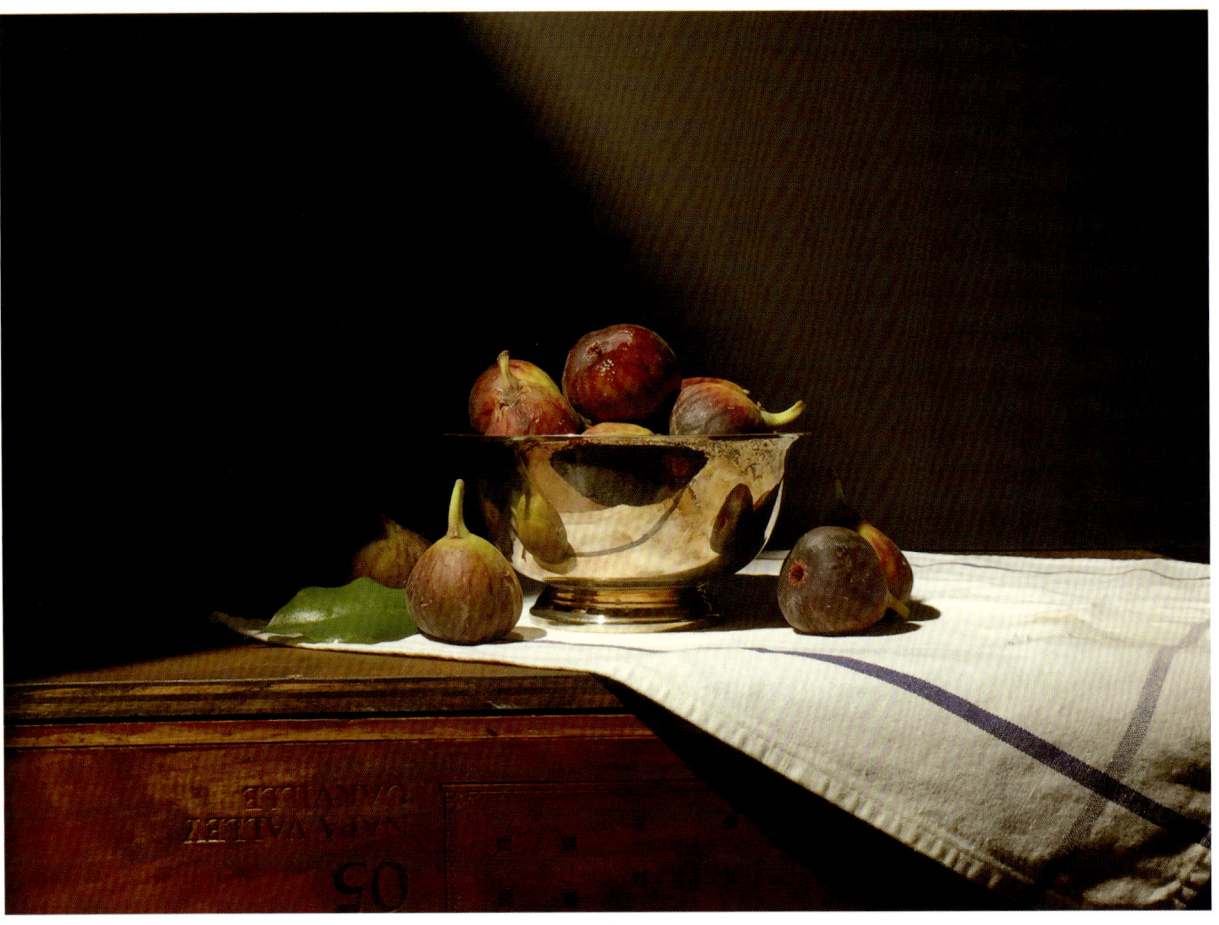

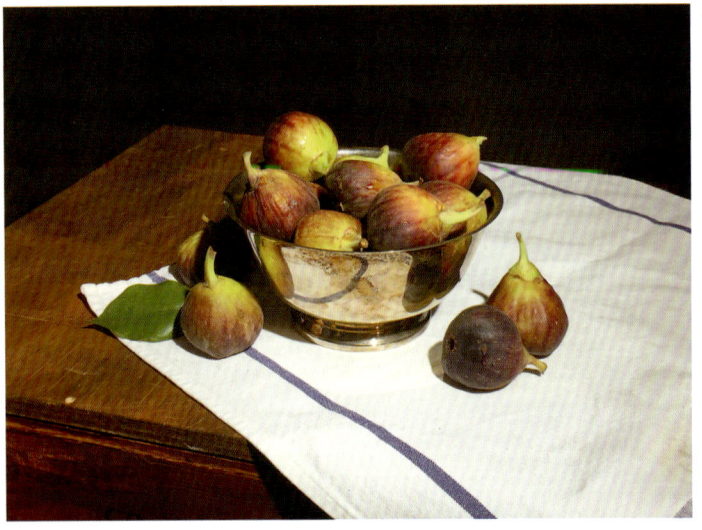

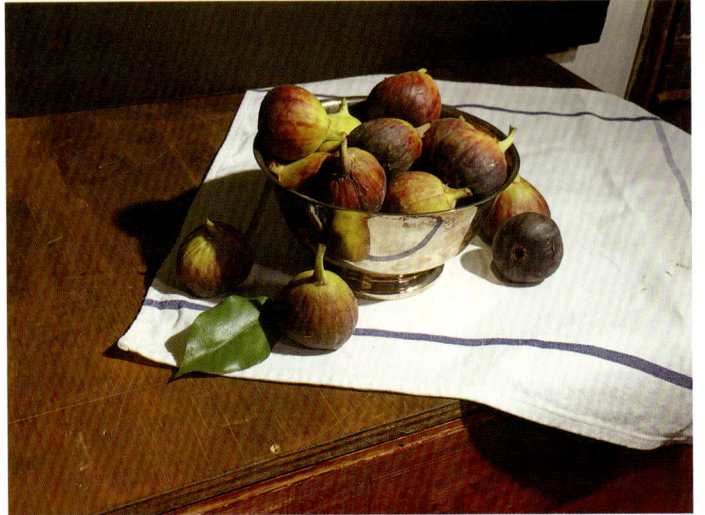

LIGHTING THE SETUP

Once a setup feels good, I try lighting it from different sides to consider all the possibilities. With this setup, I first tried lighting it from the top left, as shown above. This caused an unexpected cast shadow from my shadow box, creating a nice dark shape on the left side. But when I sat back and studied the effect, I felt it was perhaps too geometric and that it pulled the focus away from the setup, shifting it toward the dramatic lighting.

I also considered painting the setup from a couple of different angles, like those shown in the photos at left. But there was something about the front view that made me choose it over the other options. I somehow knew I was just meant to paint this from the front, at eye level.

I lit the setup with an 80-watt, 3000K halogen floodlamp.

CHOOSING A BACKGROUND COLOR

The background color affects a painting's overall look. For my figs painting, I wanted to see if I could get something that was between a classical and a contemporary look. As I've mentioned, traditional paintings tend to have dark backgrounds, while some contemporary paintings have lighter, more boldly colored backgrounds. I decided to try some colored backgrounds to see how this would affect the composition. I felt that the red background was too dominant. The moderately intense blue background worked better. The blue was analogous with the purple color of the figs and with the green leaf and also worked as a nice complement to the yellowish bowl.

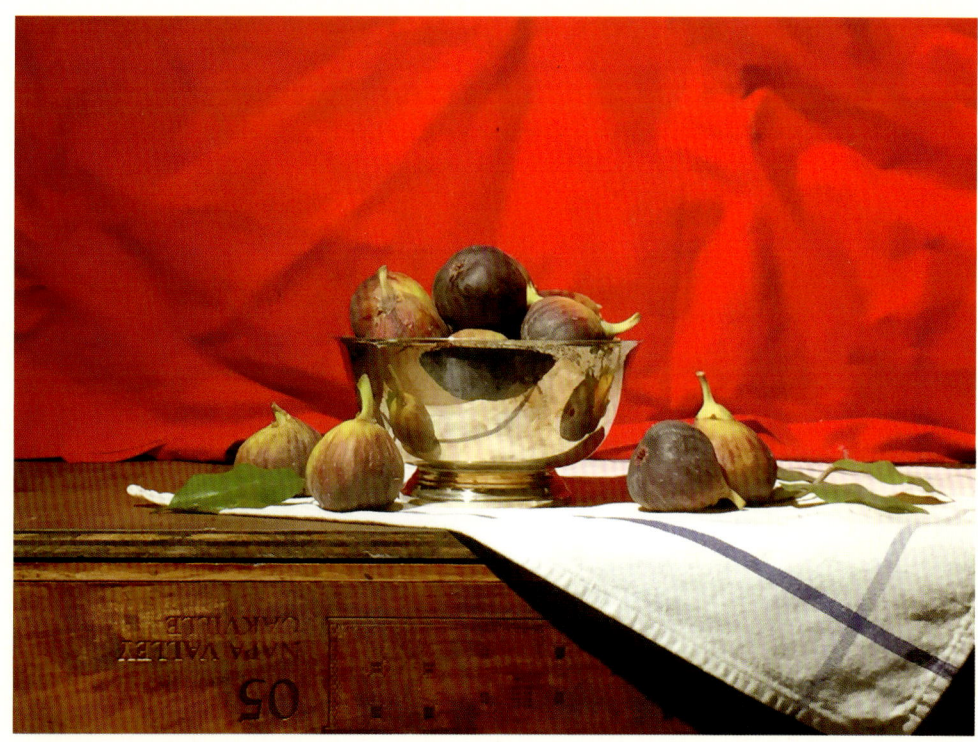

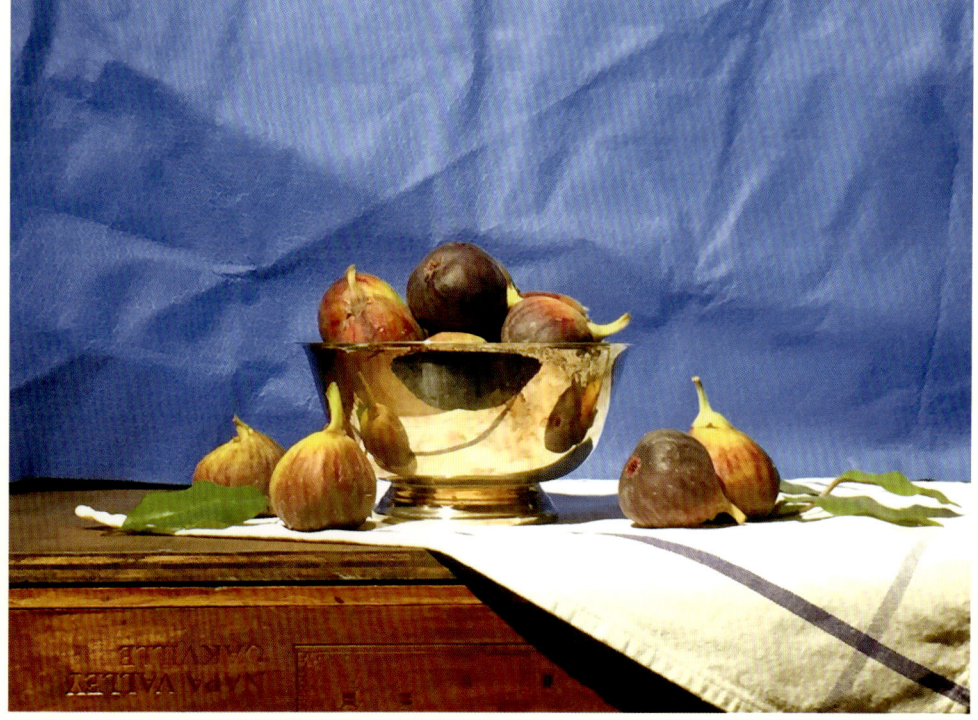

THE POSTER STUDY

Next, it was time to do a study so that I could spend some time observing the setup before making my final decisions on composition, lighting, and color choices. Poster studies help you work out an idea. You can do a poster study directly by drawing with your paint right onto your painting surface or indirectly by doing a drawing on paper and then transferring it to the canvas or panel. I find that doing a separate drawing first makes my poster studies a little more accurate than if I draw directly onto the canvas.

I apply color to a poster study in an optical manner. I try to see the big two-dimensional shapes of light and shadow and how they interlock with one another. I try *not to* render small transitions of value, because the poster study is only a guide for my larger painting. It's easy to get carried away when doing these small paintings, so try to resist the urge.

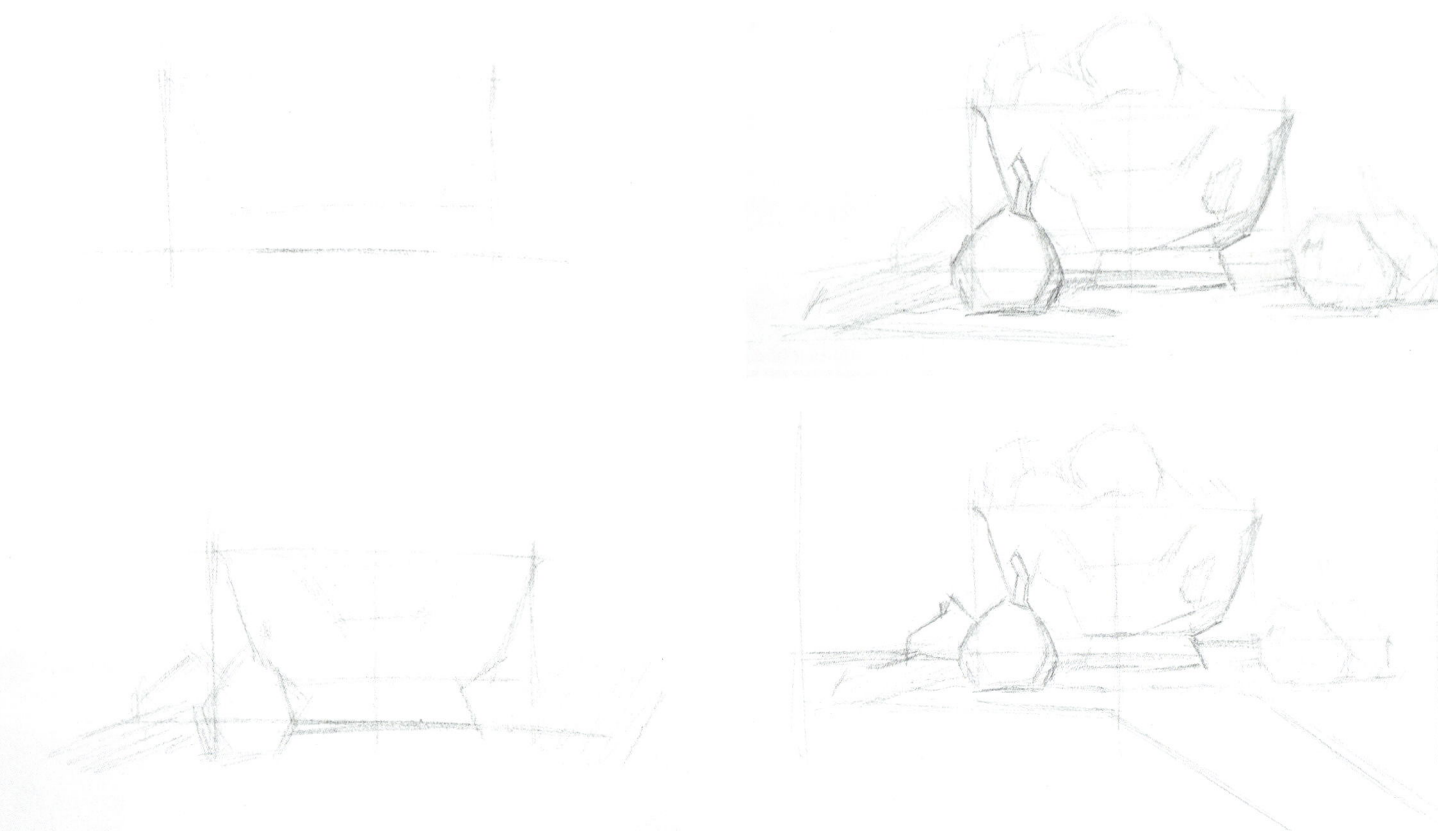

STEP 1

I start by drawing the bowl, as it is the largest shape I observe (top). Next, I mass in the smaller shapes and draw the envelope that contains the major shapes of the design (above).

STEP 2

Once the major shapes are worked out and the proportions feel accurate, I begin to refine the drawing, adding smaller elements and details (top). I further articulate some of the lines by darkening them (above).

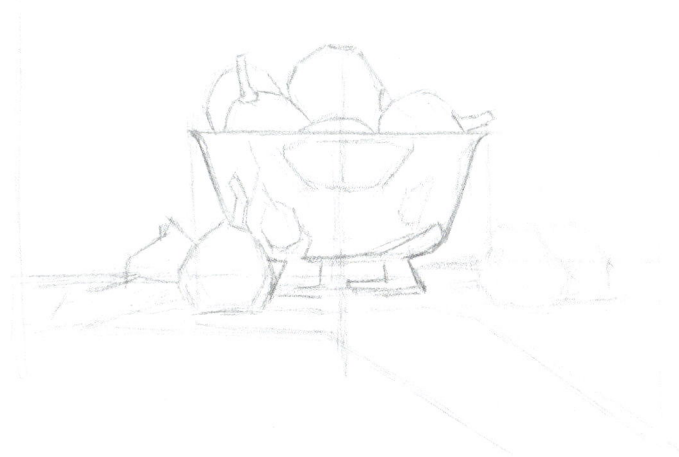

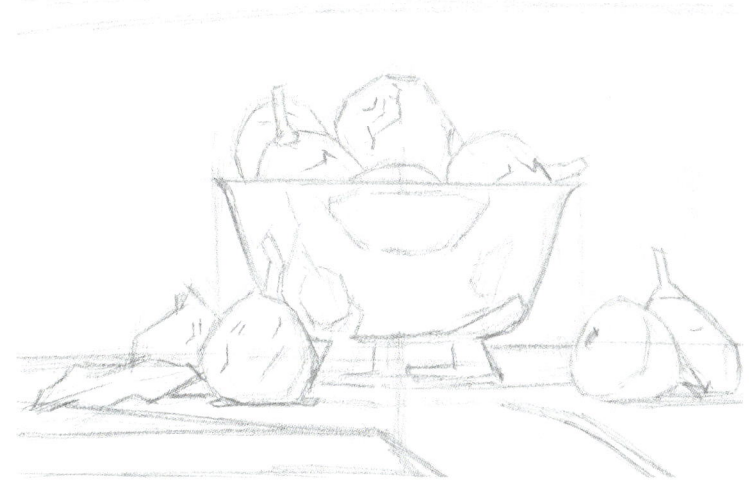

STEP 3

Once the drawing has been worked out (left), I decide how to crop the image for the painting. For this painting, I choose a landscape format. With the crop lines roughed in, I see that the size of the painting will be about 4 × 5 ½ inches.

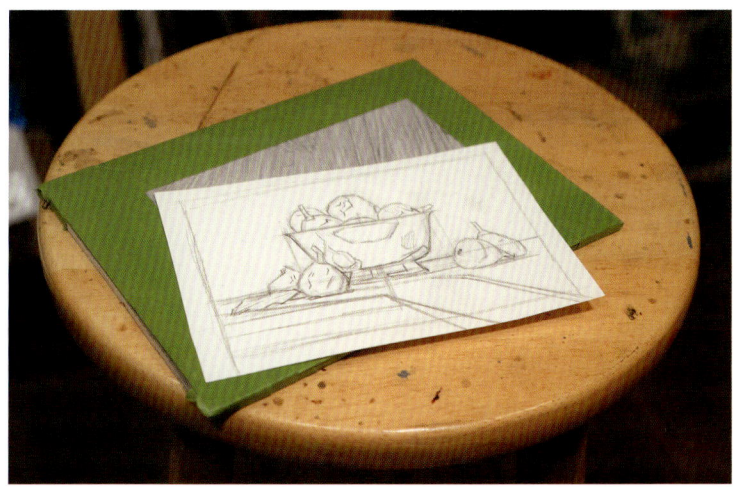

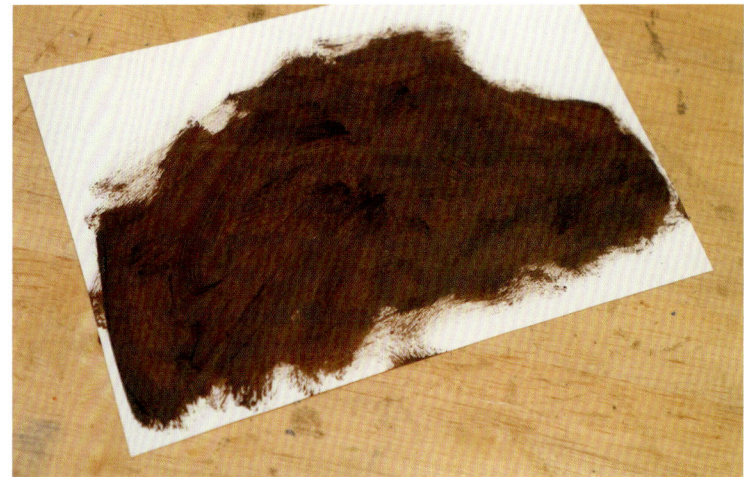

STEP 4

For the study, I choose a piece of linen with a gray tone scumbled on it. I tape the edges so that the study will have a nice clean edge.

STEP 5

Next, I mix some burnt umber with a little bit of Gamsol and scrub it onto the back of the drawing. I let the paint dry for a minute so the paper is not too wet. I'll use this to transfer the drawing—similar to a carbon transfer but using paint instead.

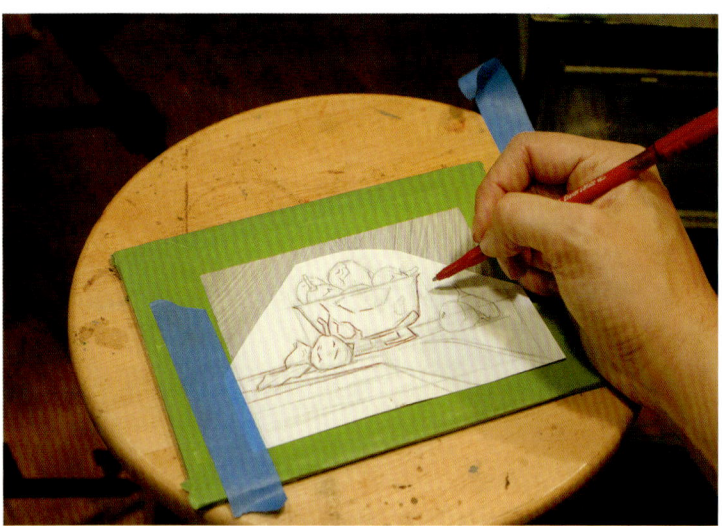

STEP 6

Now I tape the drawing to the board and trace the lines with a red pen. The red ink helps me see which lines I have gone over so I don't forget anything.

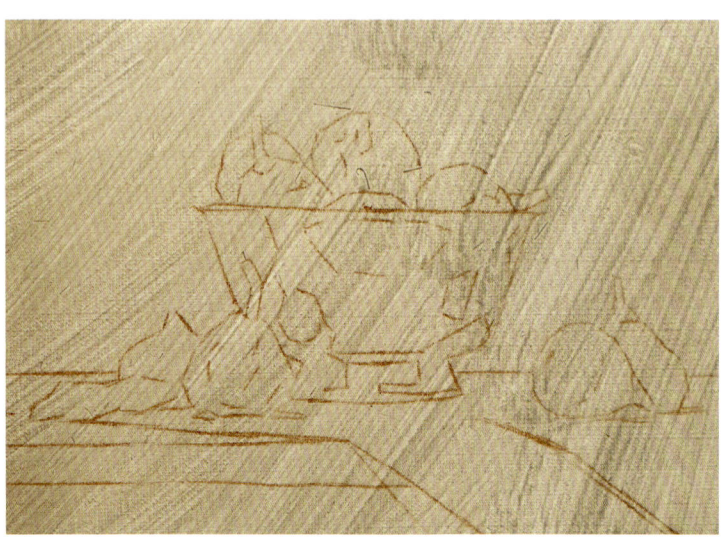 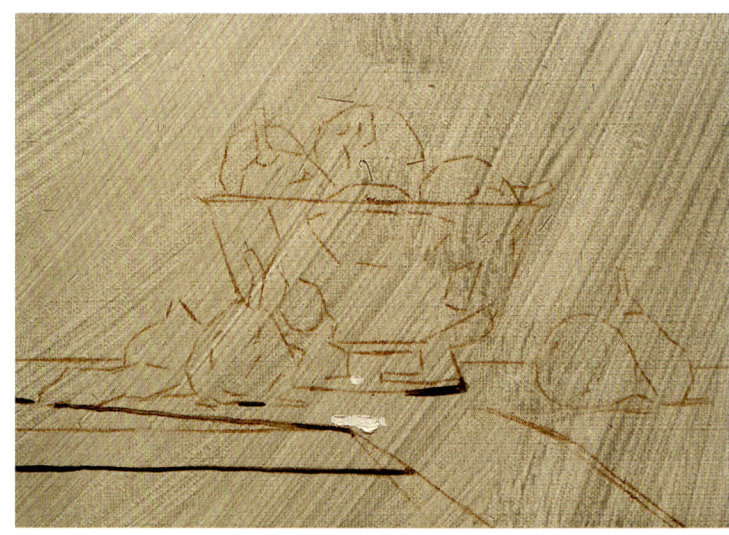

STEP 7

Once the transfer is complete, I have my drawing on the linen (left). I now approach the painting in a very optical way. I begin by establishing the lightest lights, which are the white cloth and the highlights, and the darkest darks, which are the crevice shadows (right).

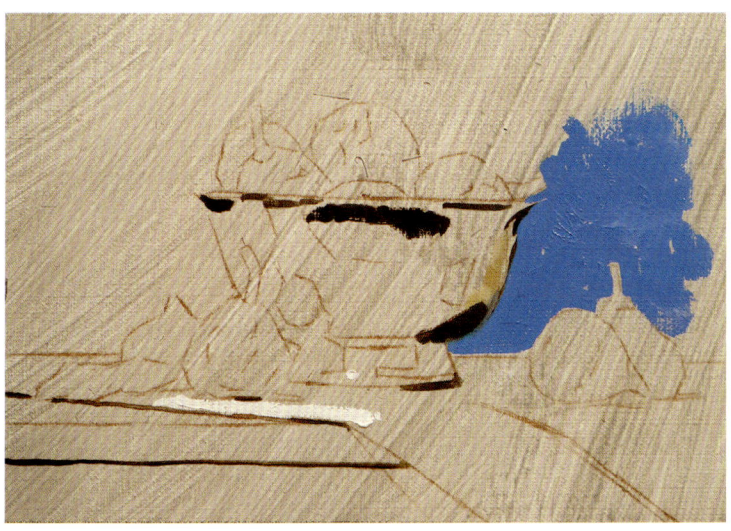 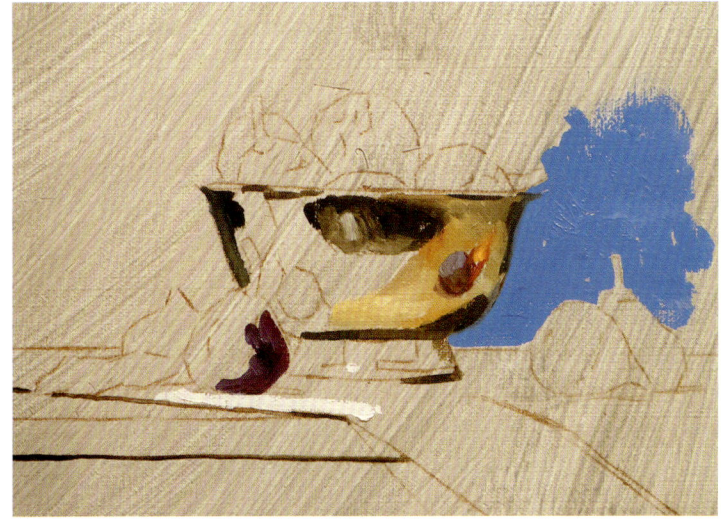

STEP 8

The blue in the setup is very dominant and will be the highest-intensity (highest-chroma) color in the painting. Establishing it at the beginning (left) will help me make other color decisions, since all the other colors will be less intense. I then go with a contrasting color like the yellow/gold of the bowl (right) to begin to establish the range of color in the study.

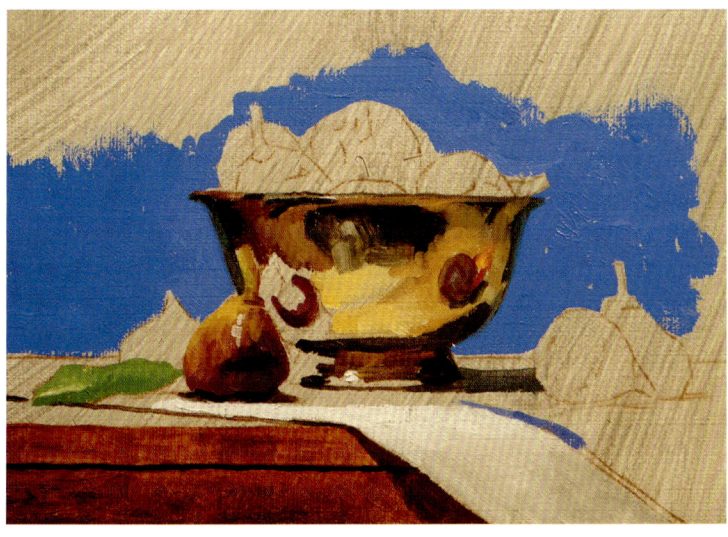 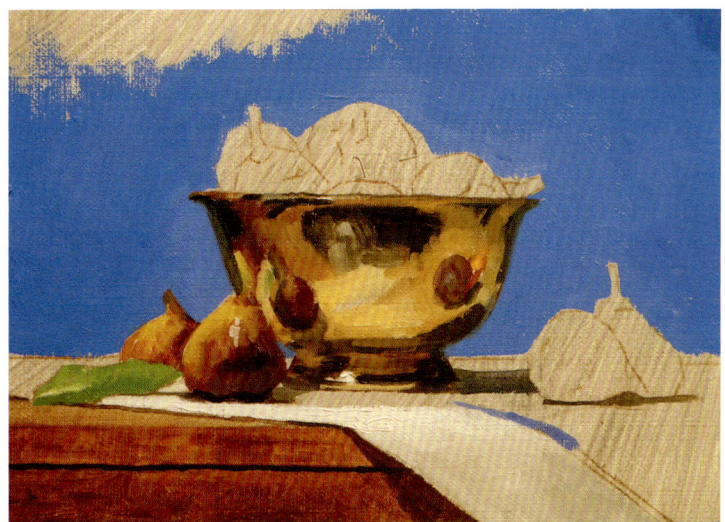

STEP 9

As colors are applied, the image emerges (left). At this stage I resist the urge to change anything, since making one change might cause me to change all of my decisions. Once I've completed the background and the bowl (right), I turn my attention to the figs inside the bowl. You may feel that you want to paint each object and all of its surroundings at the same time—but that's impossible! Each color and value is either right or wrong in relation to each other color and value.

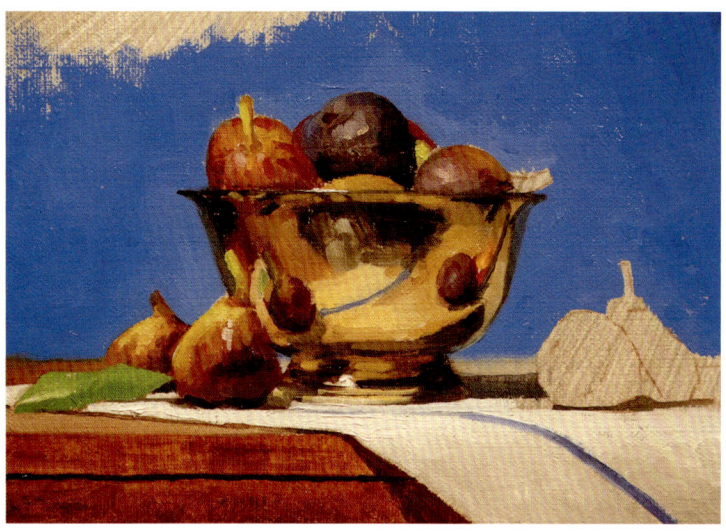
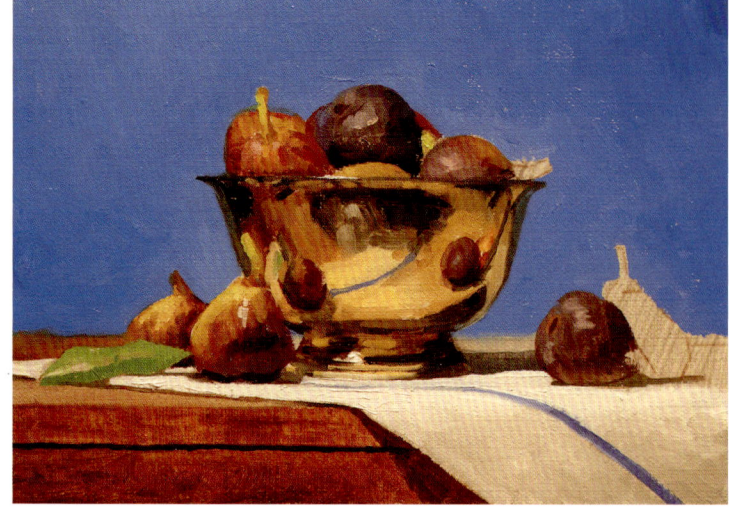

STEP 10

If the painting needs to be tweaked, I do it at the end. Often something will look off until the painting is completed and you have enough information to gauge the total effect.

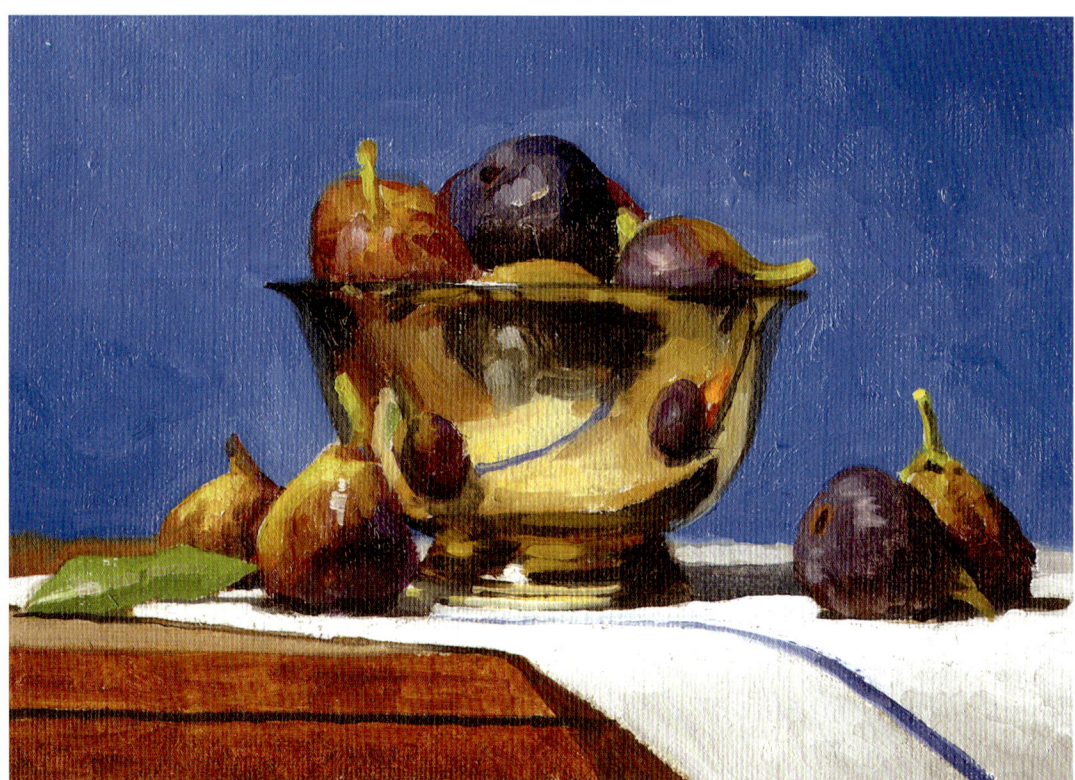

STEP 11

Here is the completed poster study, with its intense blue background. When I finished this particular study, I wasn't fully satisfied with it. It didn't give me enough information for a larger painting. I always strive to make my still life paintings believable and fully worked out, and while painting this study

I noticed that it's hard to see the difference between the two figs on the top left side of the bowl. I also didn't like the stand-in leaf: it doesn't look at all like a real fig leaf, which has a very different shape.

THE FINAL COMPOSITION

By this point, I've spent a lot of time with the setup, and I feel like I've had my "rehearsal" with it. So now I take all the mental notes I gathered from the study and refine the composition.

First, I decide to reject the blue background and to go with a light gray instead. The gray sits somewhere between the traditional and the contemporary, and this lighter background also contrasts with the figs, making them appear darker.

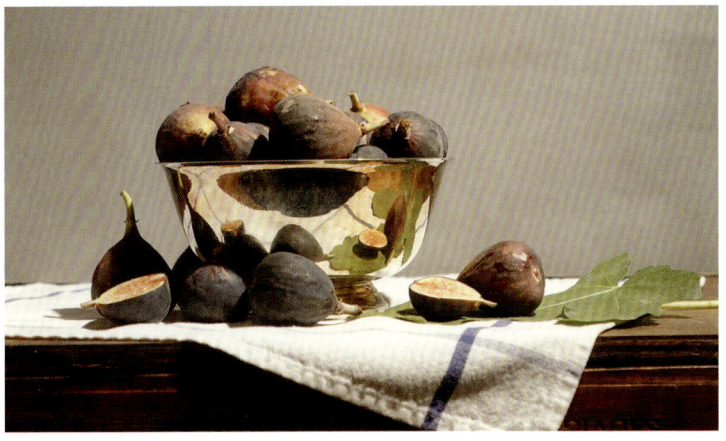

The figs are visually connected because they are all the same basic shape and their colors are analogous (close to each other on the color wheel). I decide to cut a few of the figs in half to imply that an action has just taken place. A small detail like this can often take the storytelling a little further than expected.

I place a white towel with a blue stripe below the bluish-purple figs, which helps lead the eye through the design. I know that I also want to include some green in this painting, as green signifies nature and the earth in the psychology of color. So I grab a real fig leaf from one of the trees in my yard to replace the fake leaf. I place it under the figs to break up the white space of the cloth. The leaf, its reflection in the bowl, and the stem of the upright fig at the left are all connected by their green color. The wood in the lower left corner also ties to the figs, with their analogous earth colors.

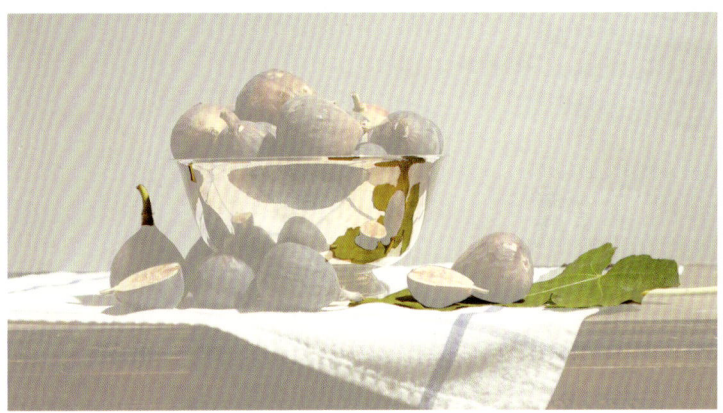

I choose to do a straight-on point of view so that the focus will be on the reflections in the bowl rather than the perspective. Most of the figs group together with the bowl on the left side of the painting, but there is a second, more isolated grouping off to the right. This gives room for the objects to breathe, but it also pulls the eye through the whole composition from left to right.

Now that the final composition is worked out, I begin the drawing that I will transfer to the painting surface.

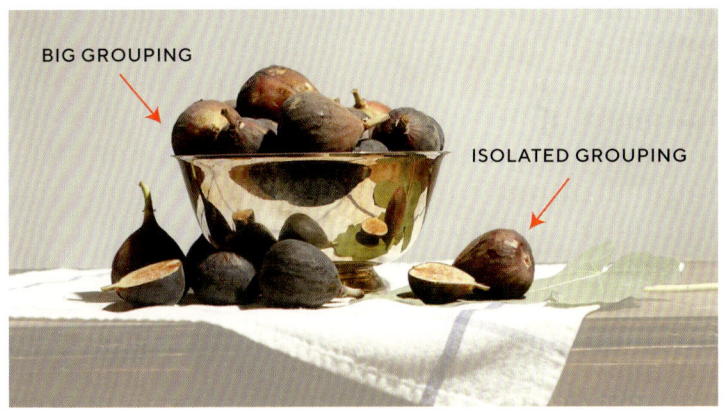

BIG GROUPING

ISOLATED GROUPING

THE FINAL DRAWING

Since I'm painting fresh fruit from life, I have to act quickly to get an accurate drawing. If this were a simpler setup, I would have done an *alla prima* drawing and painting (see page 275). But because of the setup's complexity, I choose to do a separate drawing that I will then transfer to canvas. A drawing for a painting like this can be executed in two to four hours' time. Here are the steps for the drawing:

STEP 1

I always draw before measuring, and I start by massing in the big shapes. This helps me see how the drawing will be laid out on the paper and is the first step in seeing how the shapes will relate to one another.

STEP 2

Next, I start to measure, looking for the height-to-width proportion of the center part of the drawing, the silver bowl. I also start to use tilts (see page 169) to find the envelope around the shapes. It's important to keep the lines big and light so that I can erase them if need be.

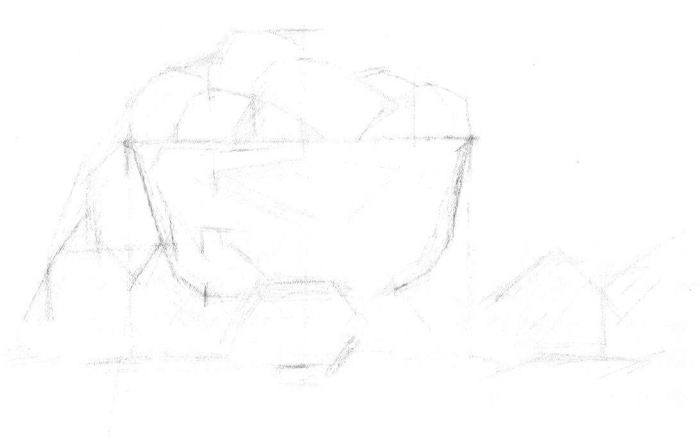
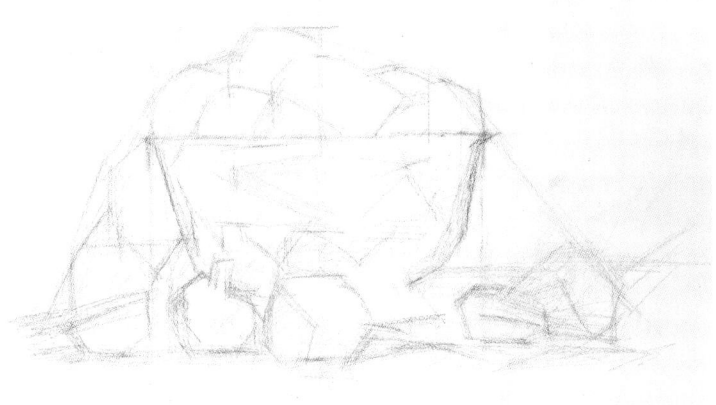

STEP 3

After establishing the envelope, I can start to break the shapes down a bit more. I look at the positive and negative spaces so that I can convey the information objectively. Slowly, the drawing's lines get darker as each shape is articulated.

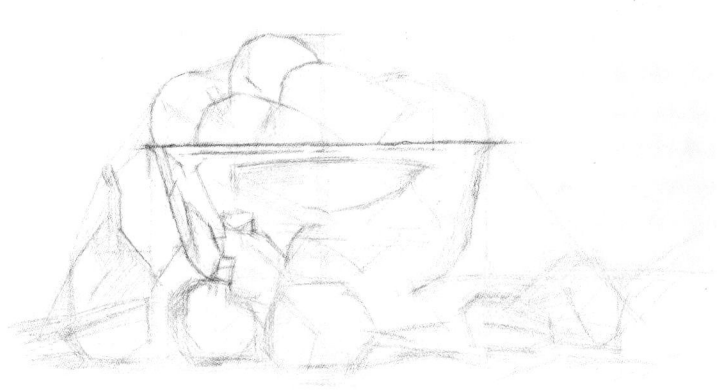
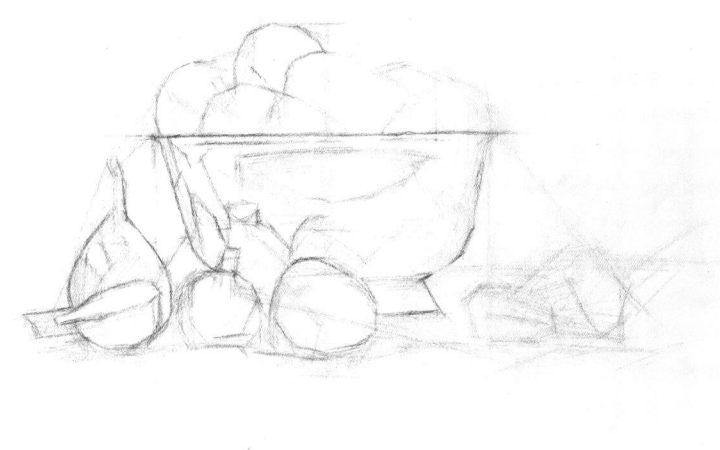

STEP 4

As all the shapes start to relate to one another, I slightly refine the bowl. Notice that I have drawn a line down the center so that I can measure from the inside out. I draw the figs on the bottom left darker.

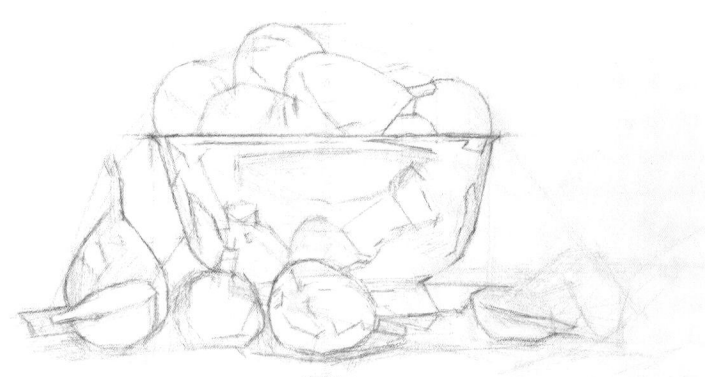
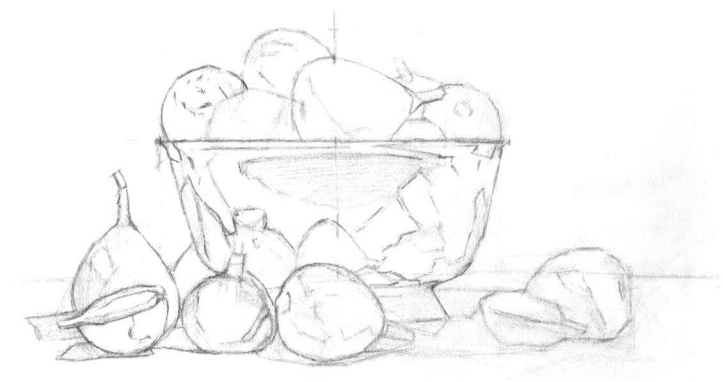

STEP 5

I slowly move from left to right to articulate each shape, defining its contour and its light and shadow. All the light and shadow shapes are constructed by considering them abstractly as pure shapes, not as identifiable objects.

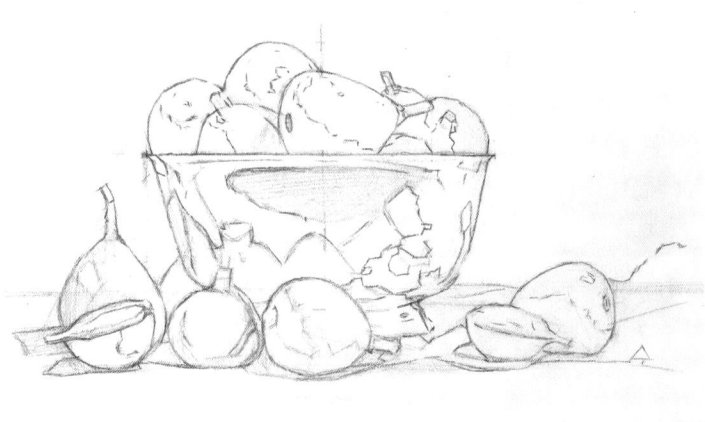
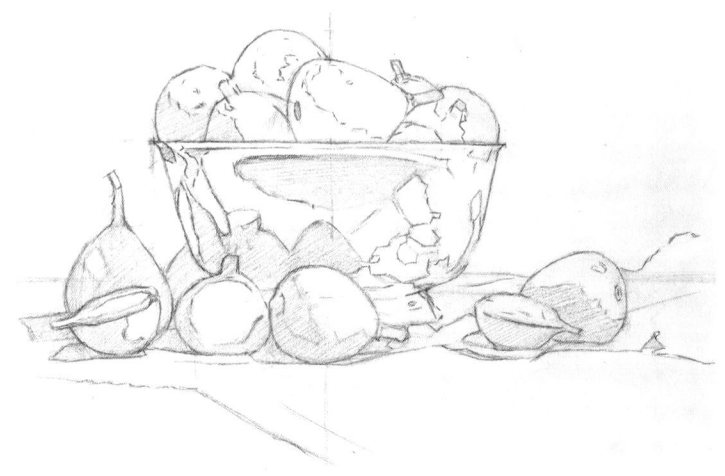

STEP 6

With each step I am refining the information, imposing a conceptual model on the drawing to help me think about how the light interacts with the figs' shapes.

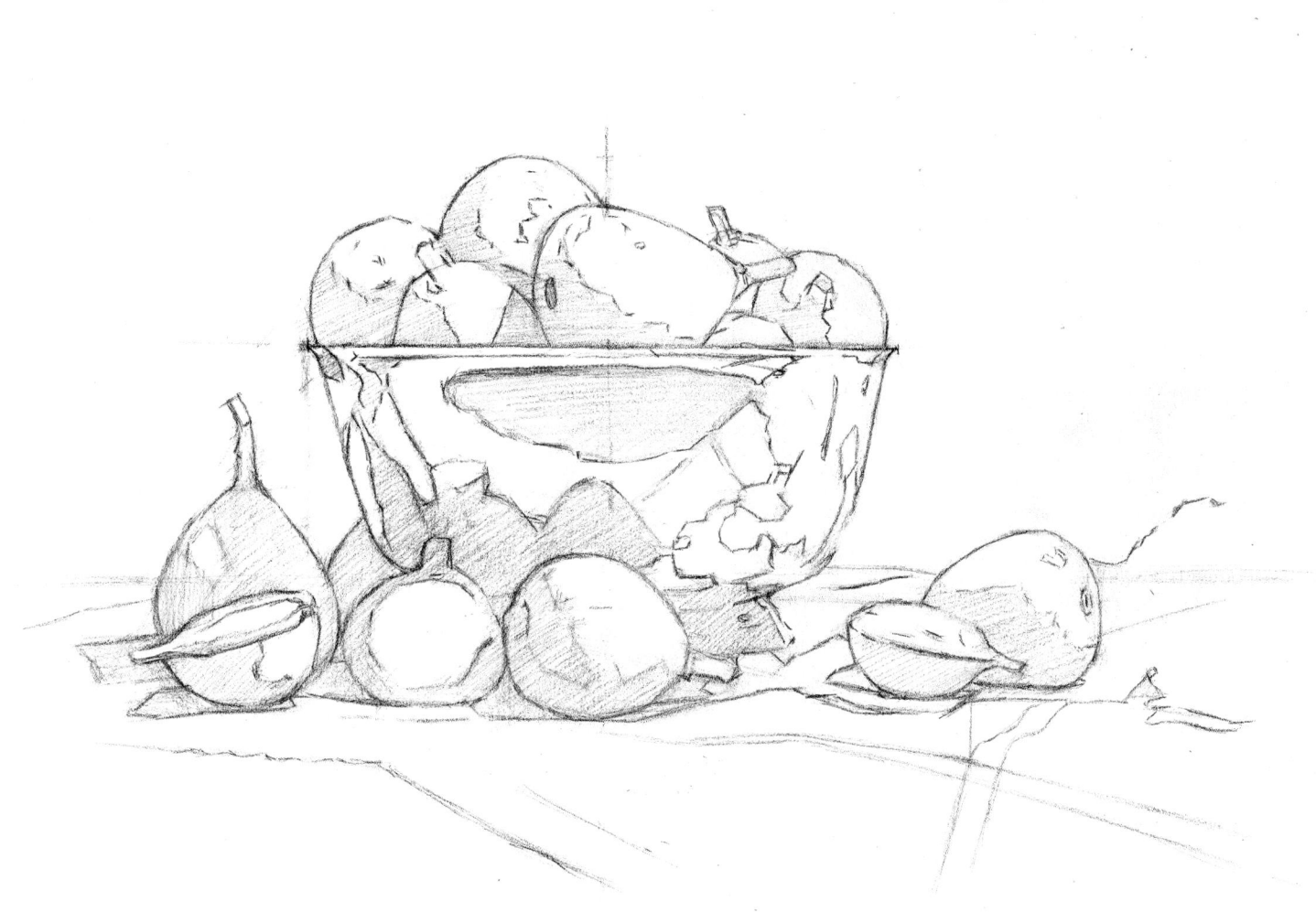

STEP 7

Here is the final 8 × 10-inch drawing. The proportions, perspective, and construction are all worked out. There's no need to add any rendering to this drawing because all of that will be done in paint. (I always draw on larger paper, scan it into my computer, and then decide on the size of the painting. When the drawing was cropped to my liking, it was 6 × 9 inches.)

TOOLS AND MATERIALS

For this painting, I used a warm-toned panel by Jack Richeson. I chose a 6 × 9-inch panel, which is good for still life painting, because the proportions have a cinematic feel. Panels like this are my favorite surfaces to paint on. Each surface you paint on will yield different results, so be consistent with your surfaces. If you switch back and forth between linen and panel, you may feel uneasy, because the paint application will vary.

The brushes I used for this painting were primarily Golden Taklon by Trekell Professional Art Supplies, with the addition of a few bristle brushes, also from Trekell. For oil paint colors, I used my full palette (see pages 226–227), and I used Gamsol as a solvent and paint thinner.

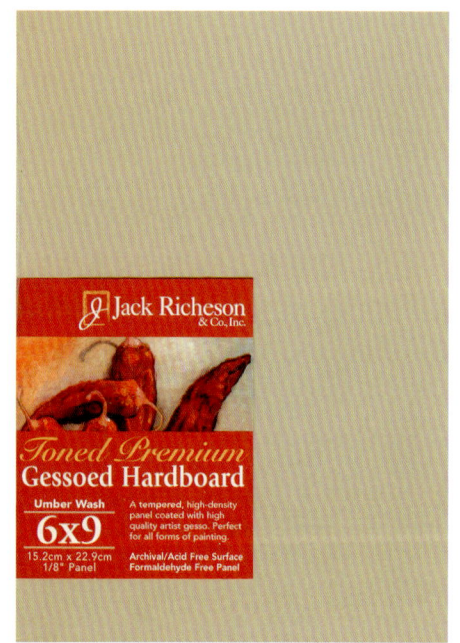 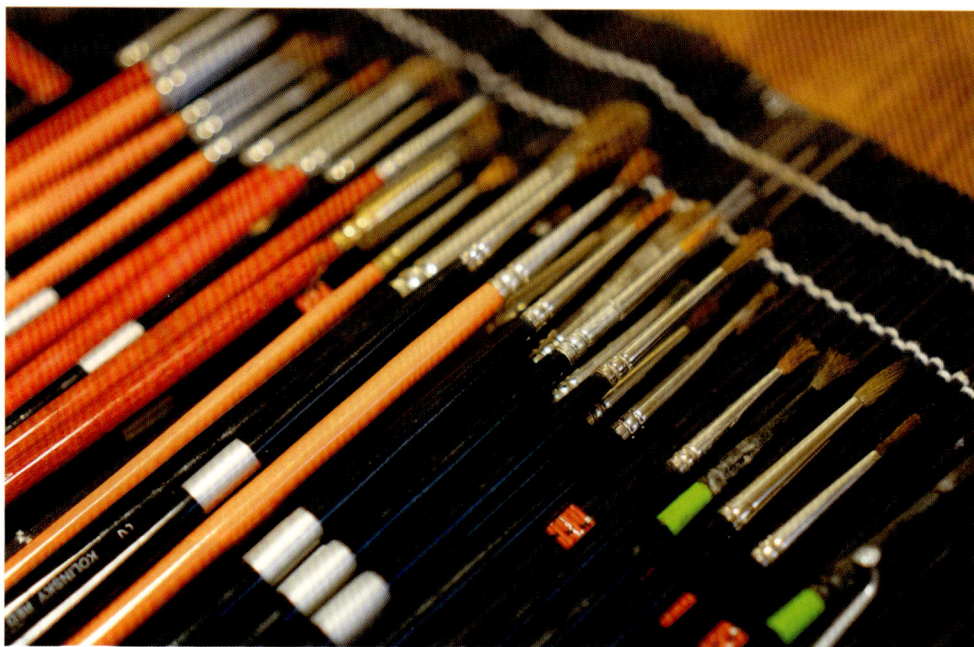

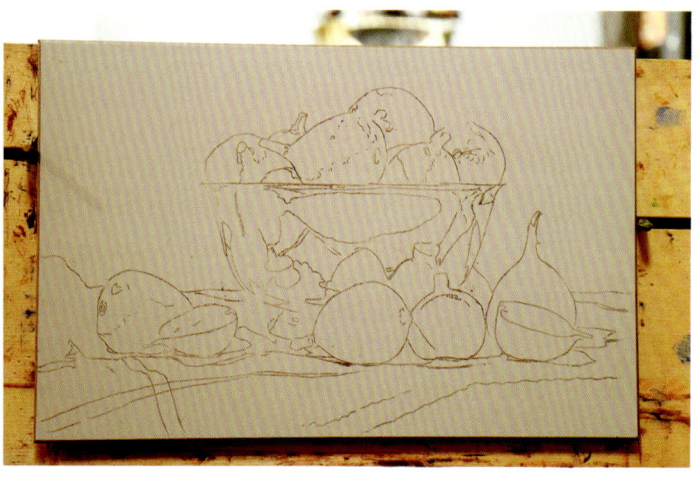

TRANSFERRING THE DRAWING

After finishing the drawing, I scan it and print it out at the size I want, then transfer it to a panel. I do this by mixing raw umber with a small amount of mineral spirits and then smearing the paint on the back of a copy of the drawing. Once the back of the paper is covered, I use a red ballpoint pen as a stylus to trace the drawing, transferring the lines onto the panel (see the transferring demo on pages 187–188). This gives me a nice line drawing, or cartoon, in oil paint to use as a guide.

THE WASH-IN

The first thing I do after transferring the drawing to the panel is a wash-in, using a synthetic-hair brush. (Synthetic-hair brushes are better for wash-ins than bristle or sable brushes.)

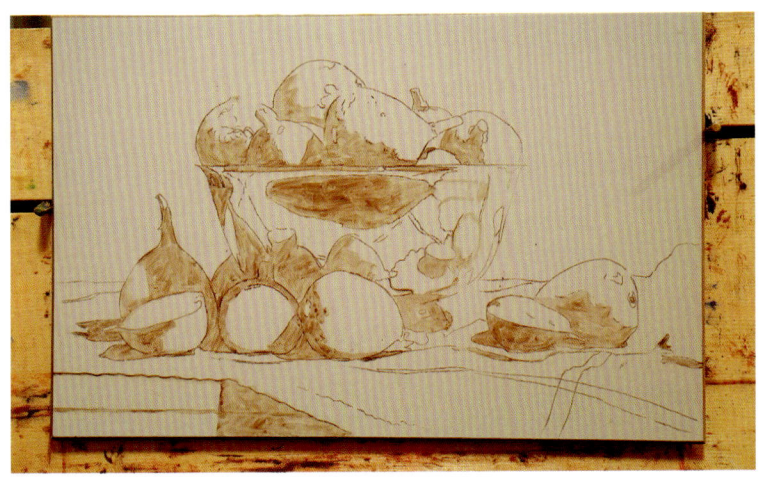

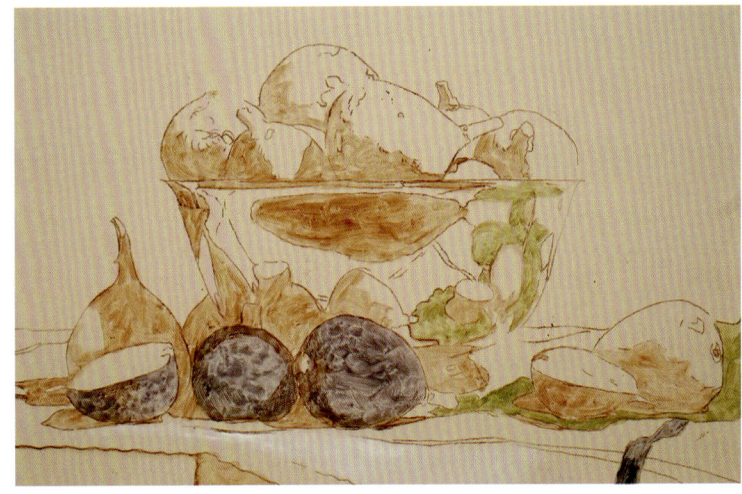

STEP 1

I first block in the shadows with some raw umber thinned with Gamsol. (Thinning the paints with Gamsol gives the wash-in a beautiful watercolor-like look.) Blocking in the shadows helps me clearly see the light and shadow separation (chiaroscuro) in the painting. I choose raw umber for washing in the darks because its dark yellow-green hue will lend a nice neutral, earthy color to the shadows. The great thing about earth colors is that they dry really fast, so I'll quickly be set up for the next step.

STEP 2

After blocking in the shadows, I begin to add color to the painting. I go form by form, articulating the light in relation to each object. Note: it's not necessary to nail the color at this point. Each hue applied subsequently will be a step closer to the actual color of the fig. When painting, you're collecting information—on hue, value structure, and chroma—piece by piece, so it's inevitable that some of this will not be perfect at first.

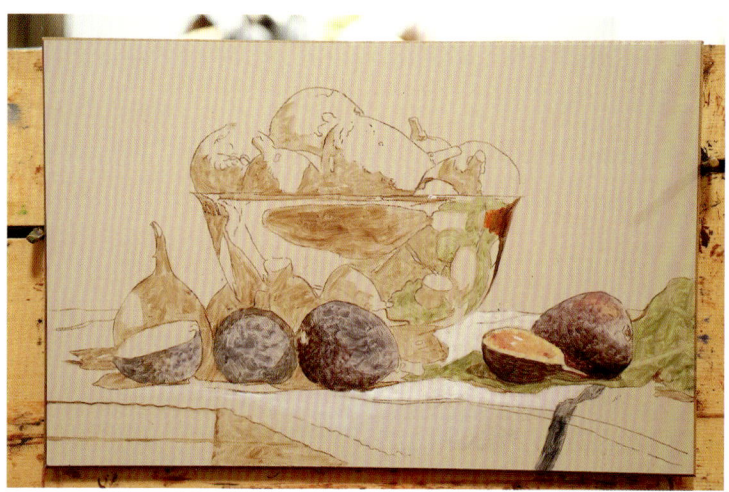

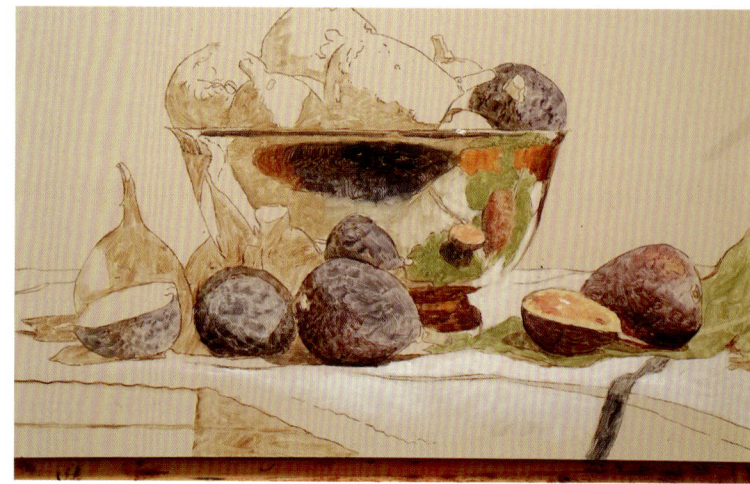

STEP 3

I put a white highlight on the rim of the bowl to remind myself that nothing can be lighter than this highlight. When starting a painting it's important to find the extremes of the value structure—the darkest darks and the lightest lights. Crevice shadows beneath objects tend to be the darkest and highlights tend to be the lightest.

STEP 4

As the forms start to take shape, I try not to hop from one place in the painting to another. Each form will be articulated in relation to an adjacent one that has already been washed in. Think of this as an ant crawling across a form: each form can only be reached by going over another form.

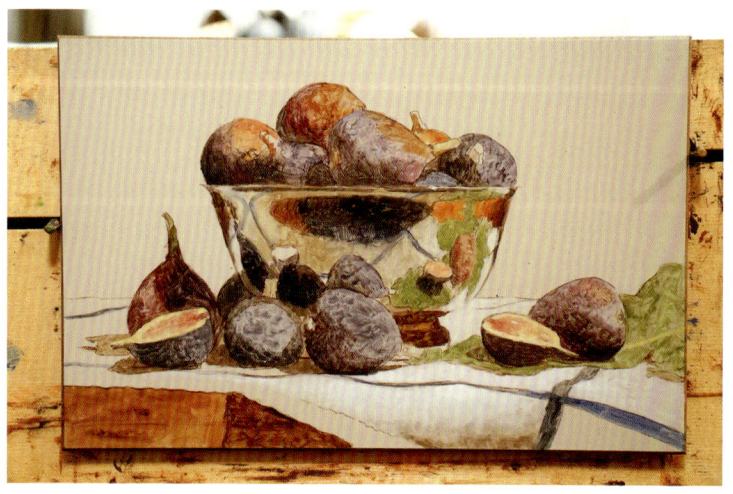

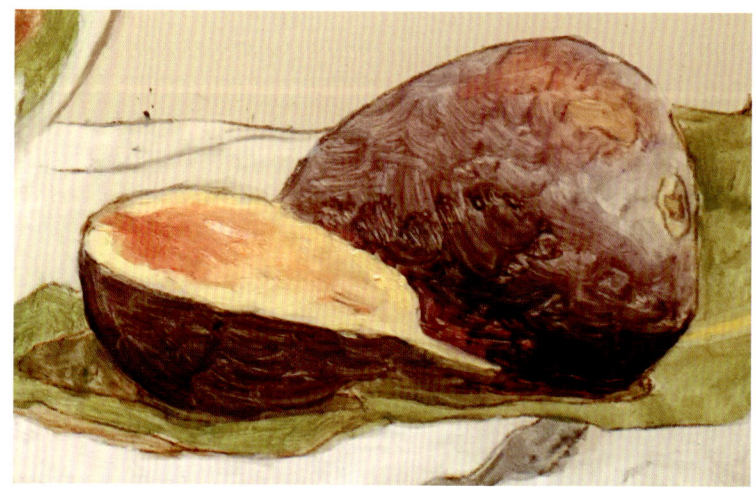

STEP 5

Here we see all the forms washed in with a pass of color, as well as a detail of some of the figs. Each color is close to where it should be, and I will use these colors to gauge the next pass of paint. It's easier to get a color correct when there is something to judge it against.

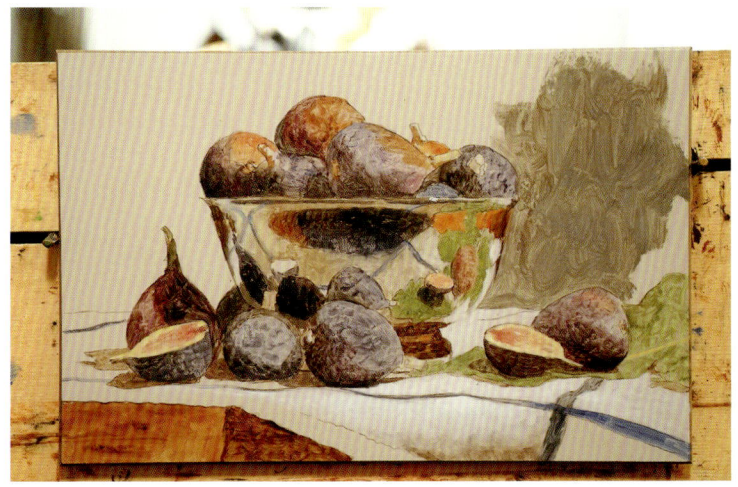

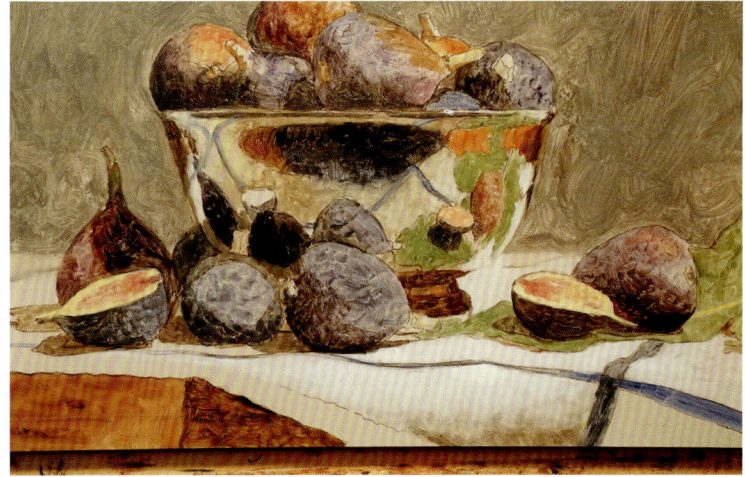

STEP 6

It is important to scumble in some background color at this stage, as this will affect all your decision-making moving for-ward. As Josef Albers noted in his book *Interaction of Color,* "In visual perception a color is almost never seen as it really is—as it physically is. This fact makes color the most relative medium in art."

TAKE A BREAK

After a completing a wash-in, I always take a break, which allows time for the paints to begin to dry and set up for the next pass of paint. It also gives me time to stop looking at the painting so that when I come back I can see it with fresh eyes. We can get oversaturated with looking at a setup, so time away is imperative.

Coming back to the work, I like to move my eyes from the painting to the setup back and forth repeatedly. If I notice anything off, I take note of it and make an adjustment. I also grab my mirror to take a look at the painting backwards, which helps me see things objectively.

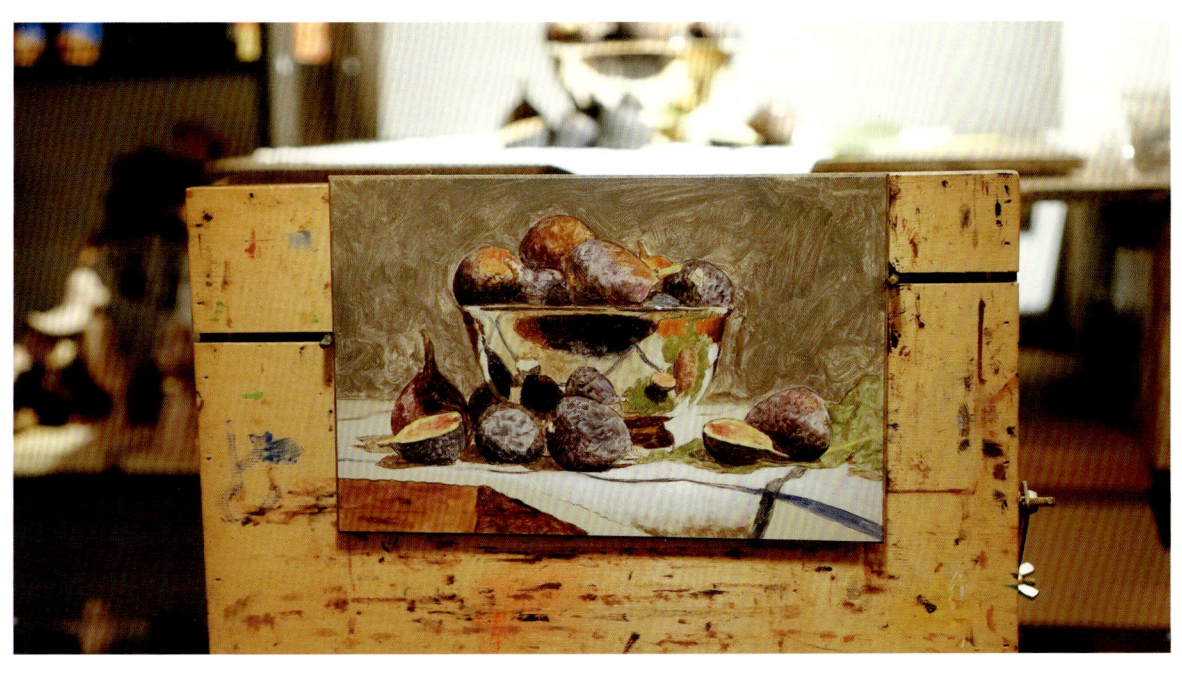

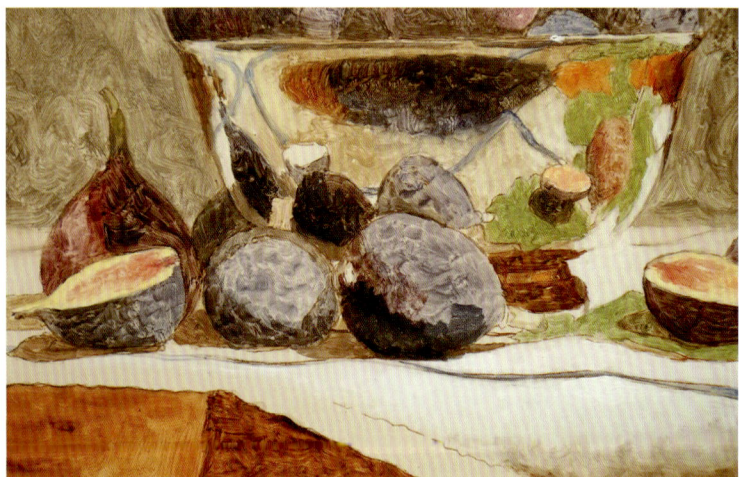

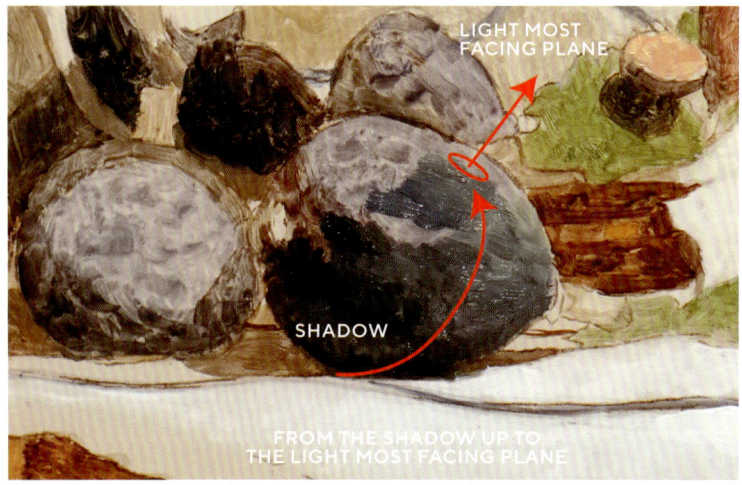

I always roll from the shadow up to the light most facing plane.

ROLLING THE FORM

Gauging everything against my initial color wash-in, I now apply a second pass of paint. I mostly use synthetic brushes—rounds, sizes 4 and 6—for this stage. Because the brushes are relatively small, I'm not putting too much paint on the surface, and parts of the underpainting can show through. This bit of broken color will give the viewer a nice sense of the complexity of layered paint in the finished work.

I try to visualize each form in relation to the light source, and I roll the forms one at a time, starting with a form on which it's easy to see light and shadow. Here that's the bluer fig near the center of the composition. Thinking about the proximity of each object to the light helps me decide how light or dark to render the object. Figs closer to the light will be a touch lighter, and those farther away will grow incrementally darker.

Notice that I roll from dark to light. To set up my range—to really get a sense of going up and down the value scale, with each piece of the form lighter or darker than the last—I can create a premixed string of color, laying out nine values on my palette that relate to all the colors on the fig. (I don't use the full value range on the fig, reserving my darkest darks and lightest lights.)

To determine my local color, I think about color space. Which color on my palette gets me closest to the color of the fig? My initial impression is that the fig is somewhere between purple and blue. The color that sits at purple-blue on my wheel is ultramarine. But when mixed to create lighter values, ultramarine will lose chroma, so I decide to mix it with cobalt blue. Cobalt blue is lighter and more chromatic, so it will yield lighter values that are more chromatic.

I now remember to think of color like a pendulum. I need to pull the blue toward purple-red. The color that will help me do this is alizarin crimson. Also, the skin of a fig isn't just one color, so I have to be ready to use analogous colors to help with the subtle shifts in hue.

With the observations I made on the color during the wash-in, I make a color string for the bluer figs. The local color is a mid-chroma purple-blue (cobalt blue, lamp black, and a touch of Old Holland Violet-Grey). To make the darker values, I add more lamp black. To mix the lighter values, I add Old Holland Naples Yellow Extra to the local color mixture. (Note: Naples yellow is a color that differs from manufacturer to manufacturer. I use Old Holland's Naples Yellow Extra, which is a mixture of titanium white, zinc white, and Mars orange. I would not use white for the lighter values here because it would make the color less chromatic. By finding a light color with more chroma, like Naples Yellow Extra, I keep a little more chroma in the mixture.)

Remember to identify a value for the terminator, and then draw a line to indicate that the dark values to the left of the line belong to the form's shadow and the light values to the right belong to the form's light. Don't cross this line when painting the shadow or the light.

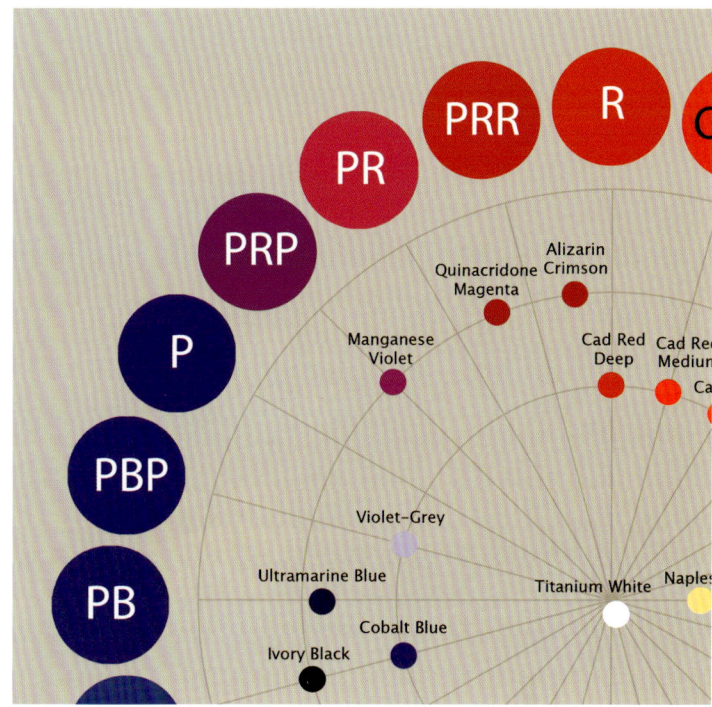

Alizarin crimson will pull the blue toward purple-red.

This color string for the bluer figs is based on a local color mixture (center square) of cobalt blue, Old Holland Violet-Grey, and lamp black. Lamp black is added to make the darker values to the left, and Old Holland Naples Yellow Extra is added to make the lighter values to the right.

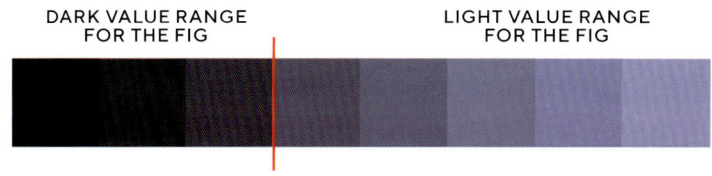

The red line separates the values of the shadow from the values of the light.

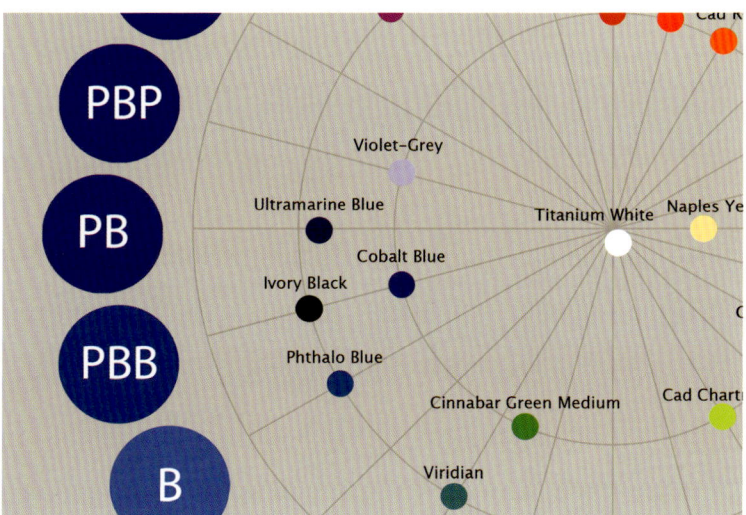

Ultramarine may be closer to the color of the fig, but it will lose chroma when lightened, so I decide to mix it with the higher-chroma cobalt blue.

STRING THEORY

Painting with strings is a great way to learn how to control color. Although I have moved away from premixing strings, I continue to think in terms of them when painting. I especially enjoy it if the color in a painting slightly vibrates on both sides of the actual hue, as this tends to bring objects to life.

The image at bottom right shows what the purple-blue string I mixed for the figs would look like if the hue were shifted slightly in opposite directions on the color wheel. Most mixtures are of more than two colors. Keep in mind that each color has its own properties and may be weaker or stronger than a color you are combining it with, so proportions always have to be adjusted.

ABOVE, RIGHT: Color mixtures are like a pendulum. Each color you add will shift a color in color space.

RIGHT: The color string in the center shifts toward blue in the string at the top and toward purple in the string at the bottom.

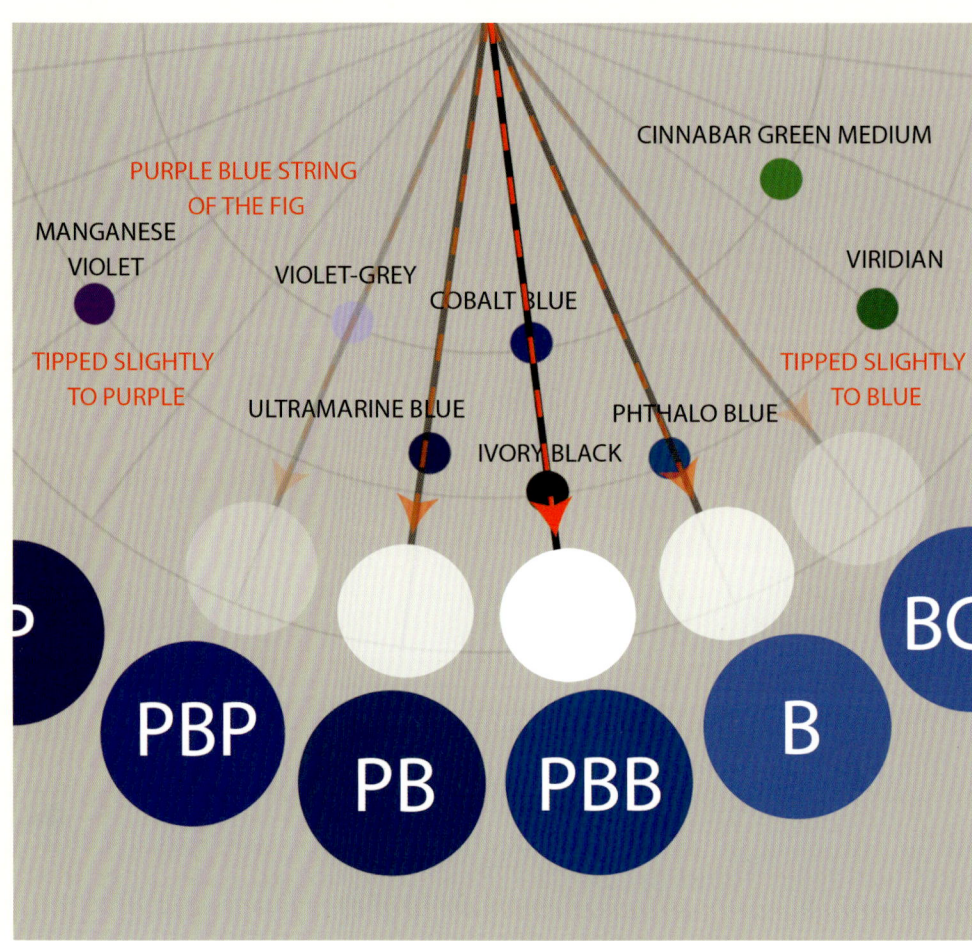

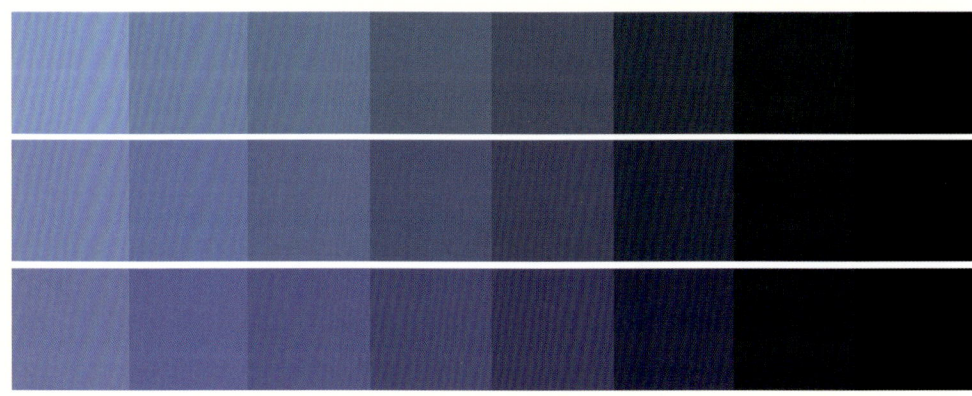

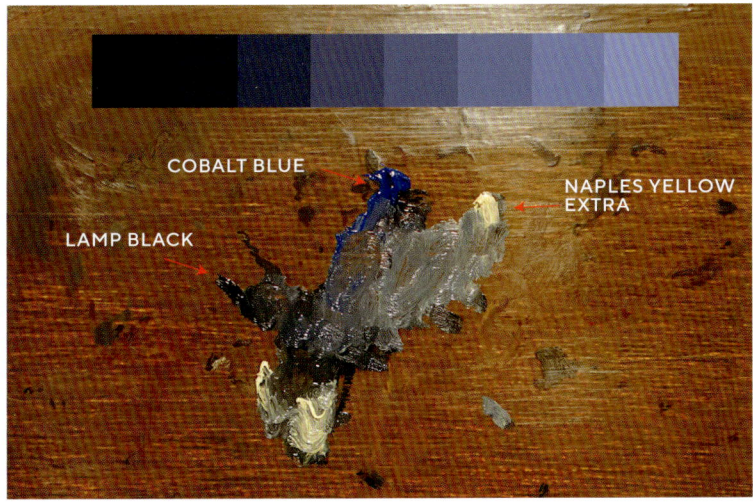

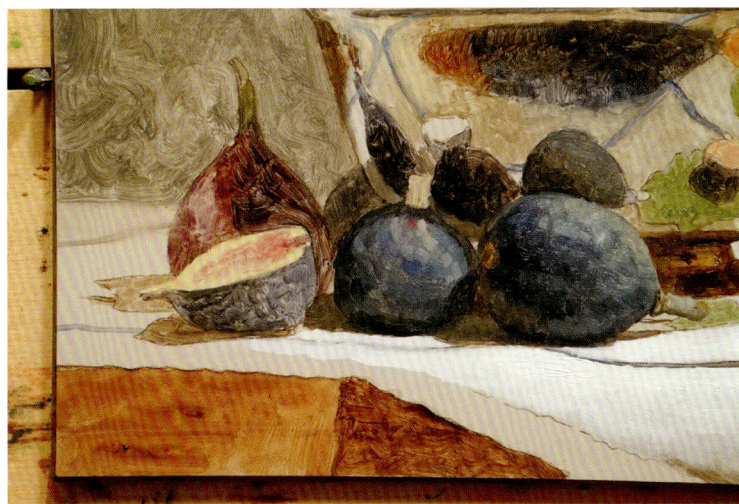

I now mix directly on my palette as I paint, but the principles I follow are the same as with a premixed string.

As I paint each form, I also try to paint the connecting forms and the cast shadows in relation to the light source.

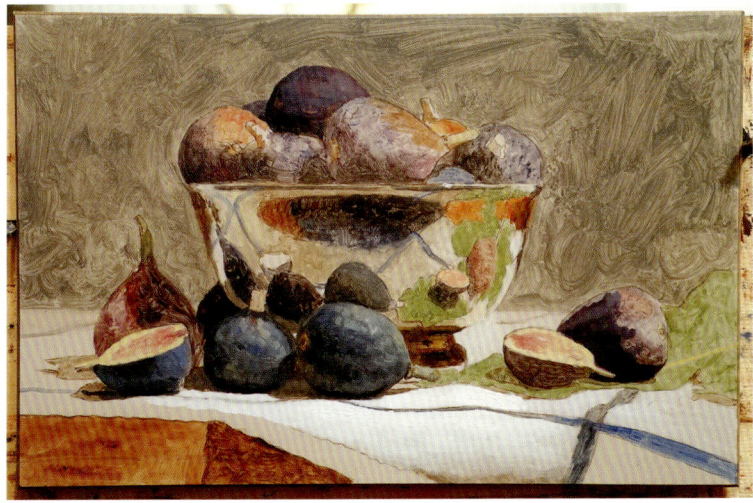

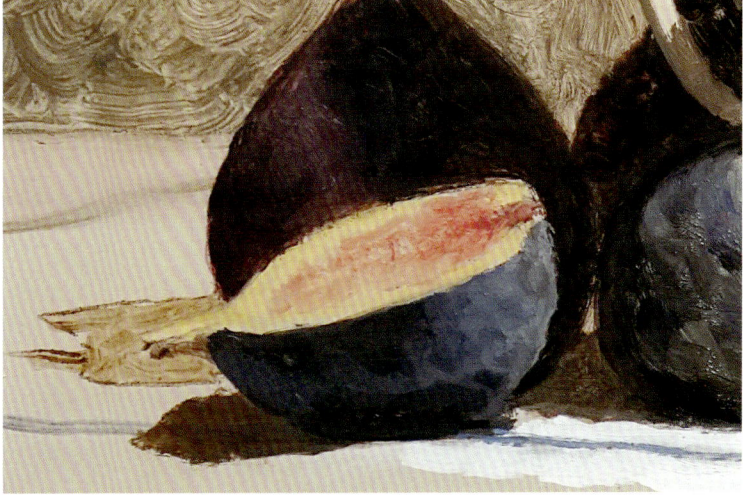

The figs in the bowl and those in the isolated grouping at the right are more purple in hue, so I add alizarin crimson to the blue string to capture their color.

I also have to keep in mind that all colors in the setup are affecting one another. For example, the white of the towel reflects up into the shadows of the figs, lightening them.

On my palette, I create little pools of the local color of the fig and from there mix lighter and darker values. This way of working is more organic than premixing nine pools of paint, but it's based on the same concepts.

I move from form to adjacent form, rendering each object in the same way, from dark to light. I also like to get some color notes on forms that are connected, so I add value and color to forms in the reflection on the bowl.

I keep working on the figs from the center leftward and then up into the figs in the bowl. I then move to the isolated grouping of figs on the right. Because there are two different varieties of figs in this painting, I start by painting the bluer figs because they are a more recognizable color. The figs in the bowl are a similar hue but are closer to purple. Therefore I grab some alizarin crimson to mix in with the blue string to tip it toward purple. I also add more colors to the reflections in the bowl.

WHEN PERISHABLE OBJECTS PERISH

Always tackle a perishable object first, as it will rot or wilt over time. Two days after I began working on this painting, the perishable things started to change. For example, the leaf had visibly wilted. Luckily, I was able to grab another leaf from the tree outside. I measured it to make sure it was the same size as the first one.

I also noticed that the figs had started to sprout mold. Actually, the figs had had some "blemishes" from the start—places where the fruits had been pierced or had already begun to rot. If these marks had added something to the painting, I would have painted them in, but I felt that idealizing the figs a bit would be more aesthetically pleasing, so I edited the blemishes out. I was able to do the same with the mold, but there may be cases where you have to replace a rotting fruit with a fresh one. If so, you may have to redraw the fruit. It is up to you to see if you can make it work or must get a new fruit.

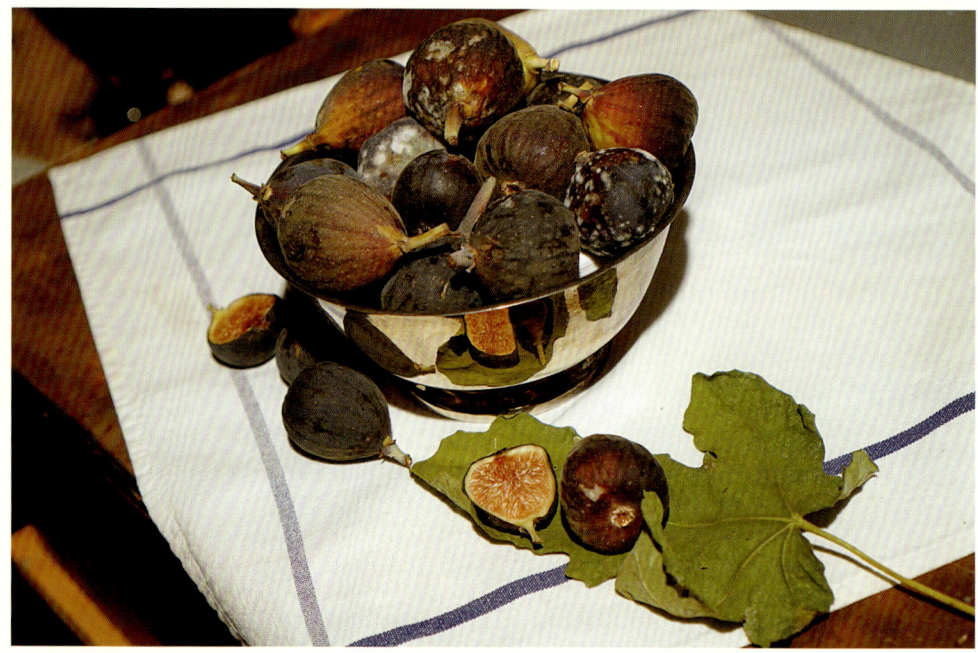

The leaf began to wilt and discolor.

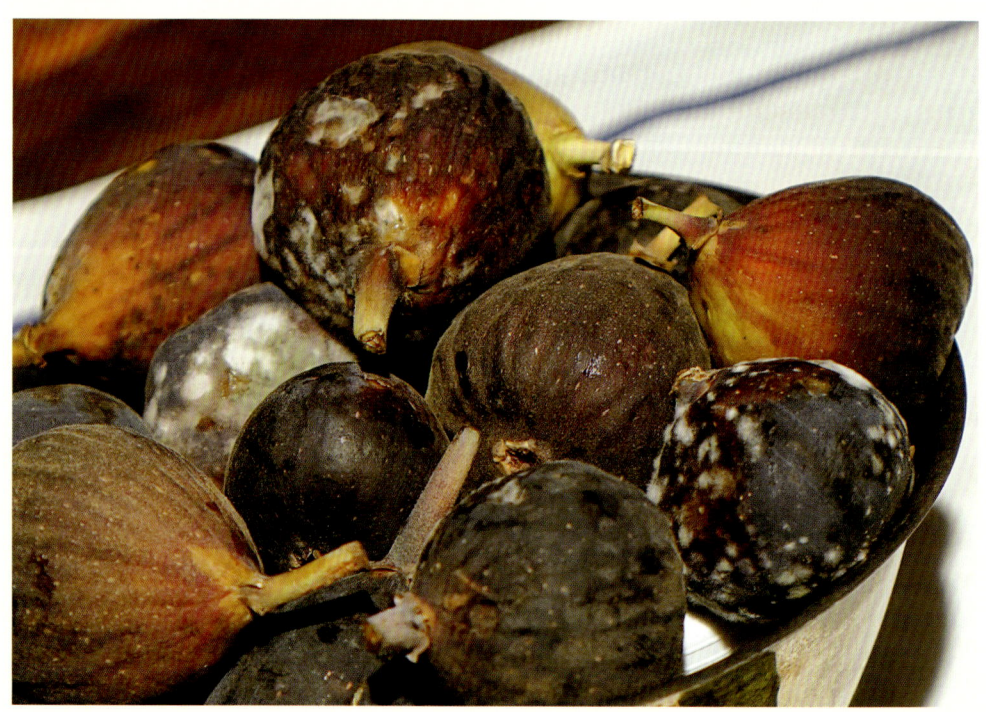

The figs grew moldy.

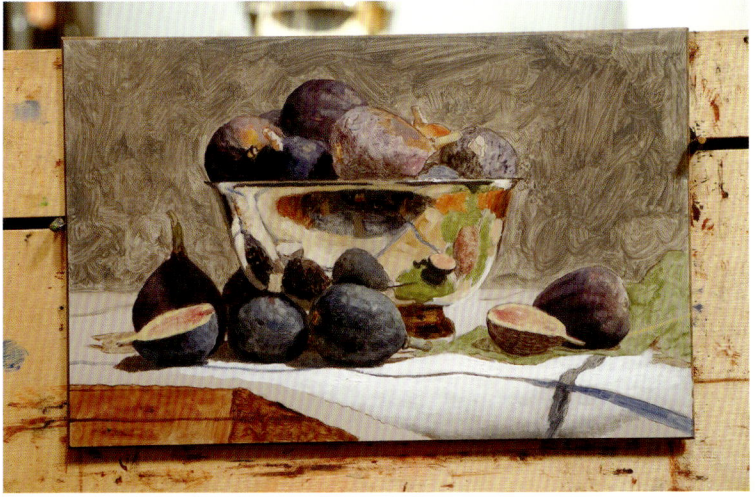

I hop around a bit to get different areas of the painting to come together.

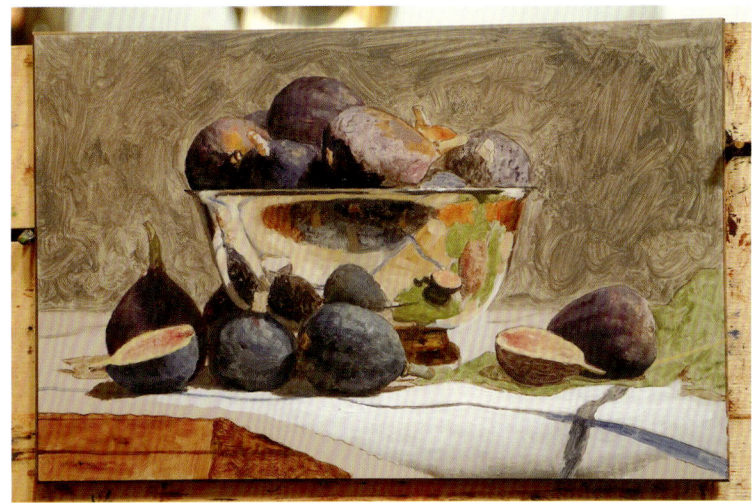

The lightest part of the shadow is darker than the darkest part of the light.

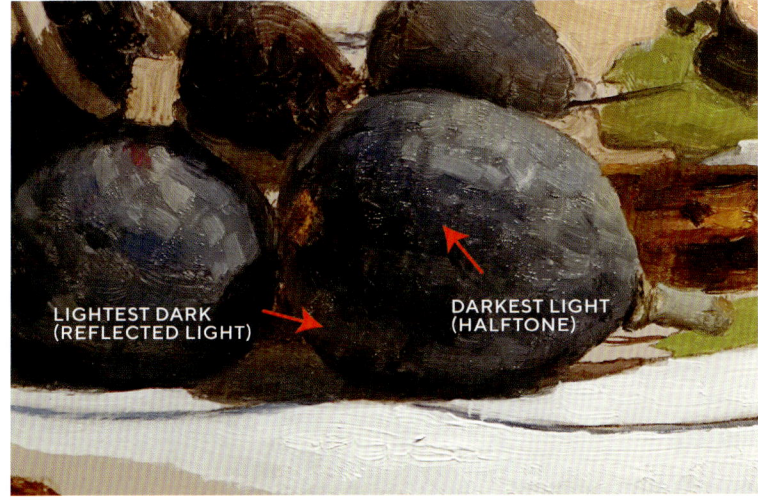

LIGHTEST DARK
(REFLECTED LIGHT)

DARKEST LIGHT
(HALFTONE)

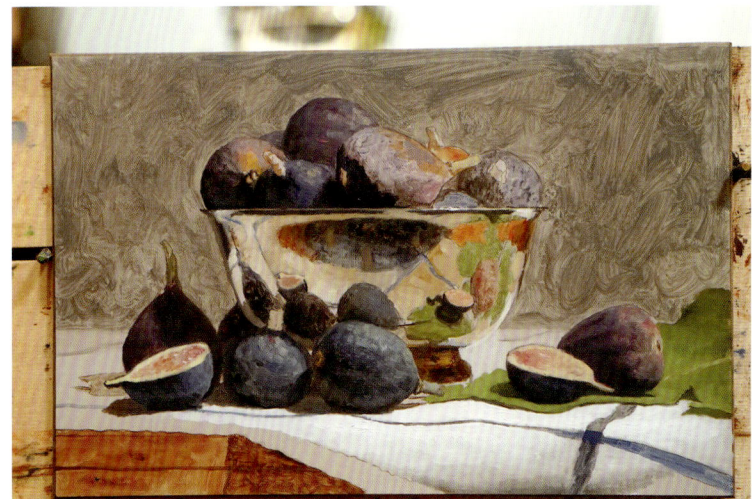

The green of the leaf balances the blue-violet of the figs.

I start applying white paint right out of the tube to the white cloth. Layering white paint over white paint gives me an opaque area, producing a nice variation between areas of the cloth that are thickly painted and those that are thinly painted. The range of values in the white cloth is very subtle, so getting as much range as I can is key. I find that layering white over white gives me surface texture variation as well as a slightly greater range of values.

At top right you can see how I render the shadows on the middle fig in front of the bowl. Reflected light is hard to get right, especially if the shadow is painted first. I like to do the reflected light last, so as not to over-render the shadow. As the great American illustrator Howard Pyle would tell his students, "Your darkest light should never compete with your lightest dark."

I now hop over to the right side of the painting to get the leaf correctly rendered, as this will bring nice variety to the piece.

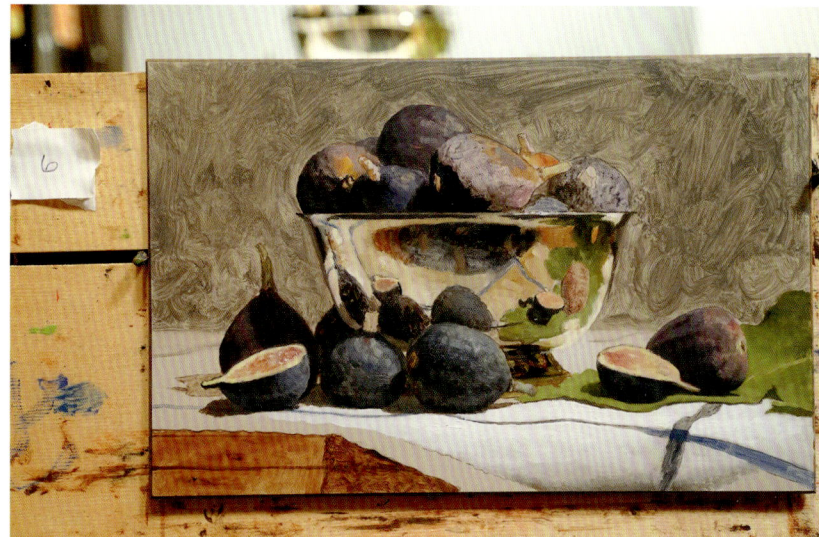

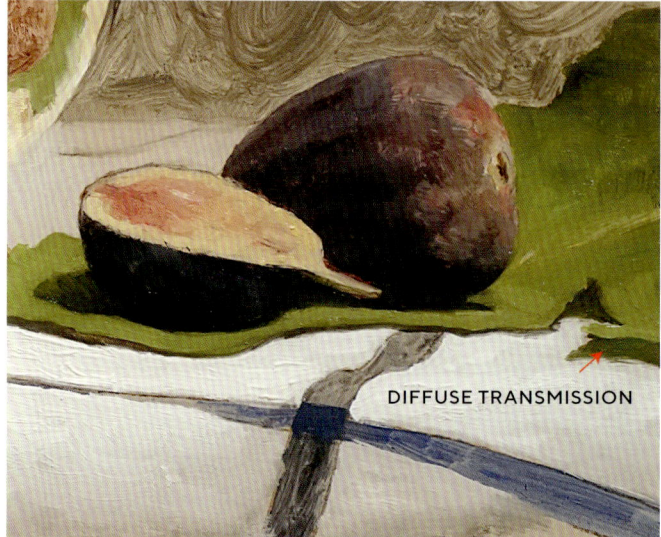

DIFFUSE TRANSMISSION

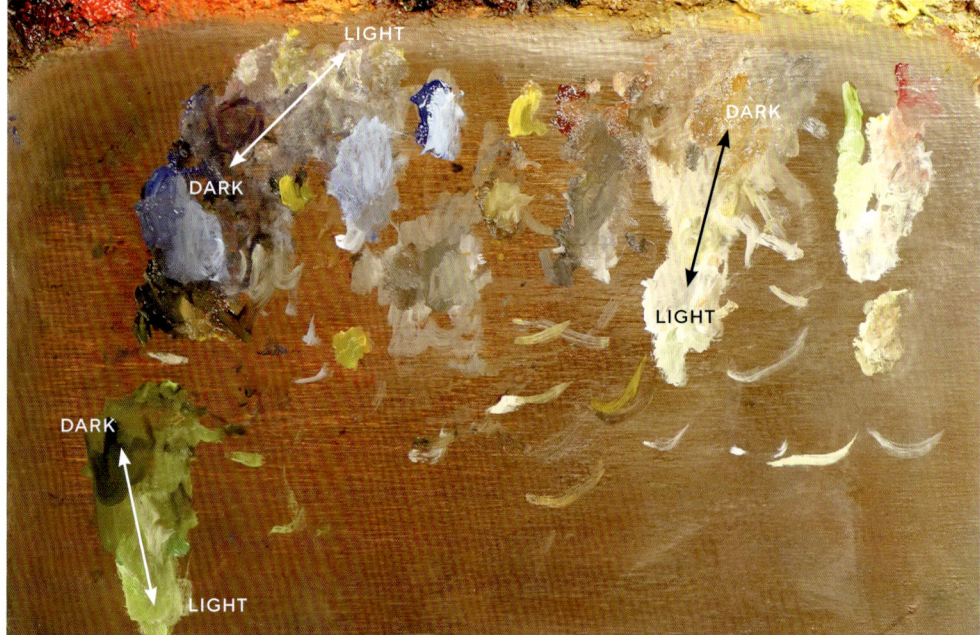

LIGHT

DARK

DARK

DARK

LIGHT

LIGHT

The green balances all the blue-purple. I then move into the reflection of the leaf on the bowl. Notice that I am hopping around. When painting conceptually, I don't hop around, because I want to get the form. But when painting optically, as now, I can hop around, as it will help me bring the picture together. Note, however, that I never add paint randomly.

I also paint the shadow cast by the leaf onto the white cloth. I notice that the color of the cast shadow is green, indicating that some light has passed through the leaf to affect the color of the cast shadow—a phenomenon called *diffuse transmission*.

I continue to create my mixtures of paint on my palette, above, rather than pre-mixing strings. This makes the small shifts that I'm painting feel more fluid, as I can pull a color into a pool of paint to tip it slightly one way or another.

THE BOWL— A CURVED MIRROR

The silver bowl is a curved mirror. It therefore has almost no observable form beyond what's conveyed by the distorted reflections on its surface and the light falloff that appears on the bowl, reflecting the environment.

A helpful way of thinking of the bowl's form is to conceptualize it as if it were matte. My crude sculpture at right, done with a kneaded eraser, shows me how the light is hitting the form—and that the bowl's underside is actually in shadow. I make note of this to ensure that this will come across even in the reflective surface.

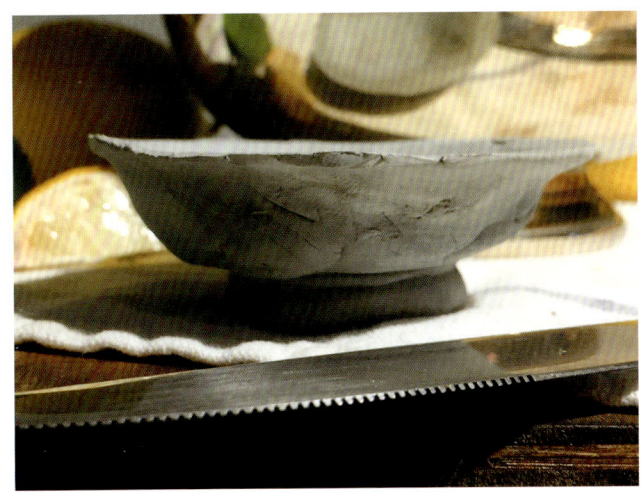

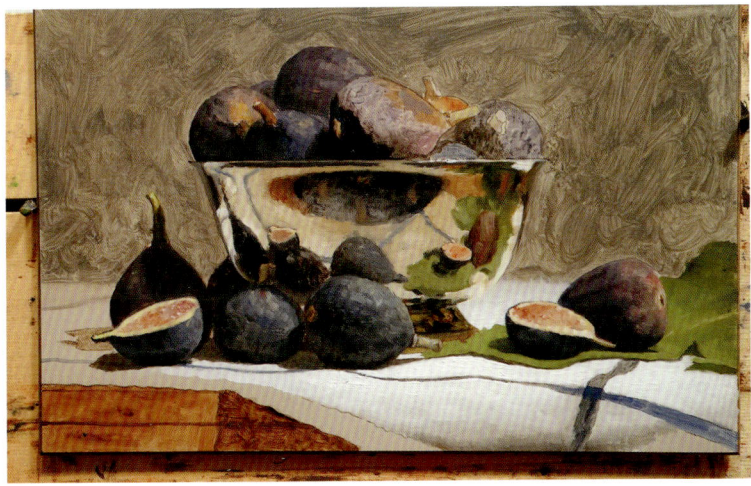

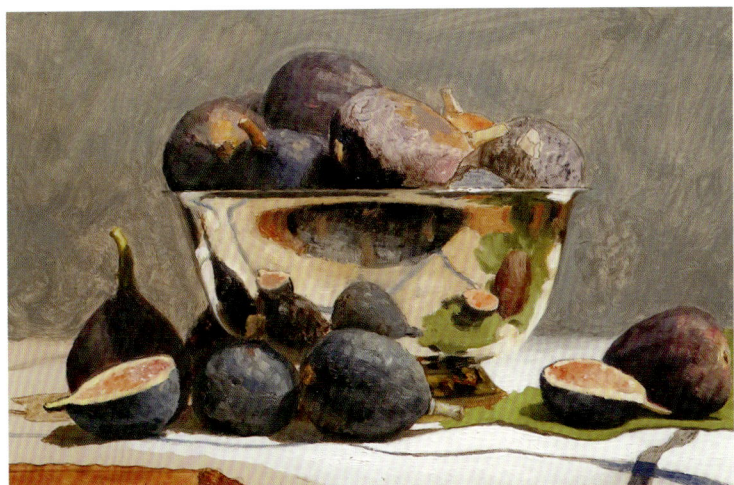

STEP 1

I add a second coat of paint to the background to bring the whole right side of the painting together. I'm always looking for lost edges, and this second coat of gray background paint helps me soften the edges of the bowl that disappear into the background. The same thing happens at the bottom right part of the bowl as it meets the white cloth.

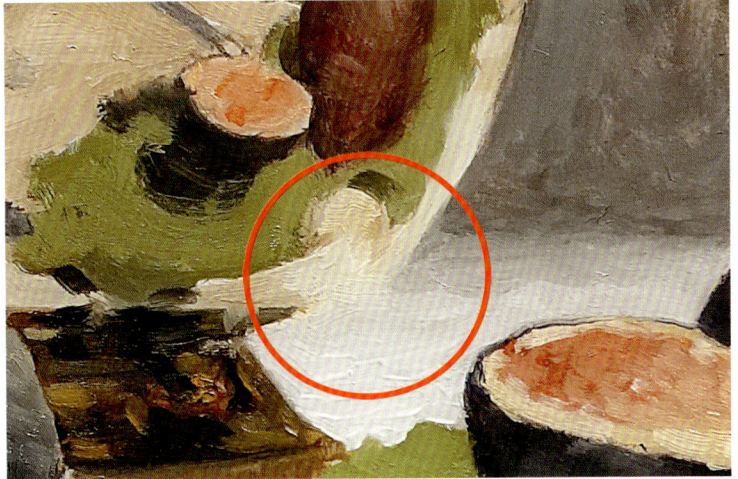

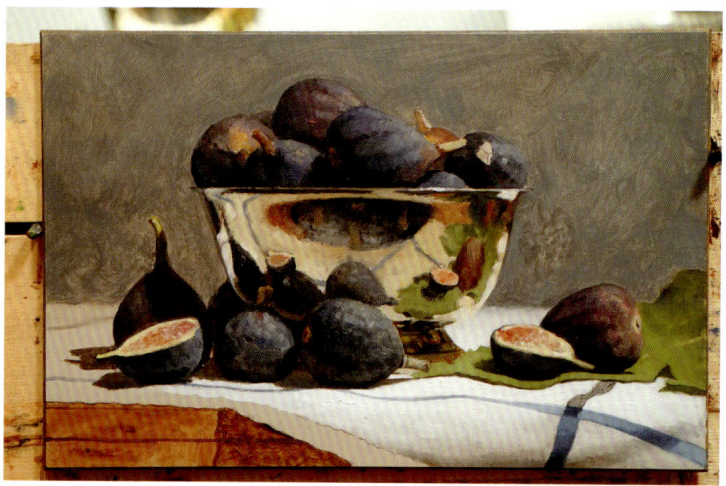

STEP 2

I now feel that there is enough information that I can begin rendering the rest of the figs inside the bowl.

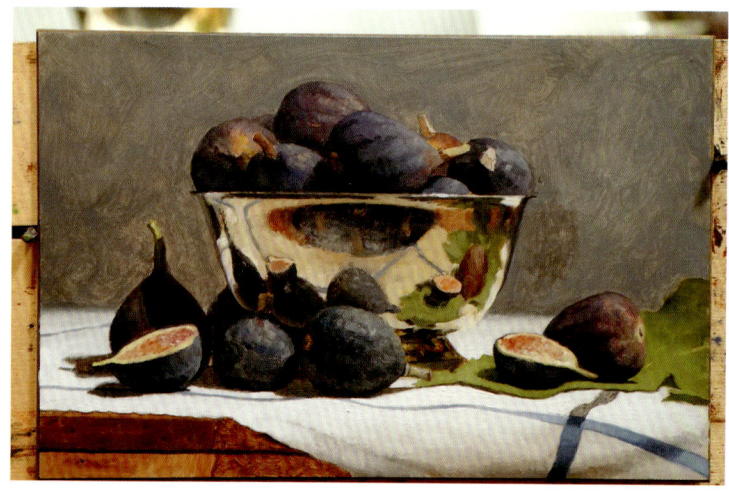

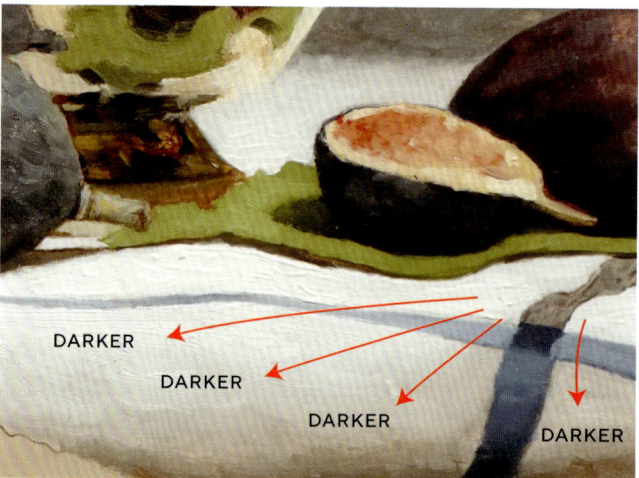

STEP 3

I continue painting the white cloth from the light, right side to the slightly darker left side and downward. I also put in the wood texture, which nicely balances the white cloth.

To create the illusion of the white cloth going back in space, I make it darker as it recedes. I also make the cloth darker as it falls over the edge in front. In both cases, the principle is that it grows darker as it moves away from the light.

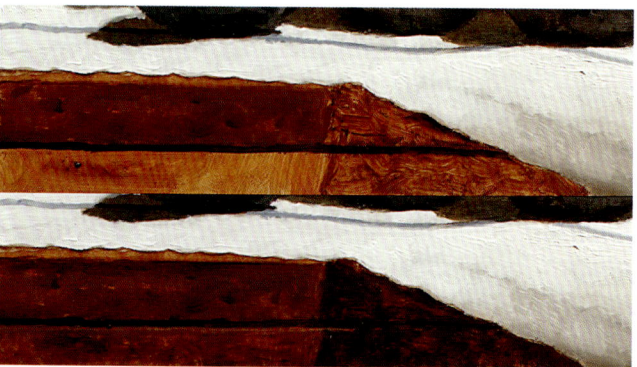

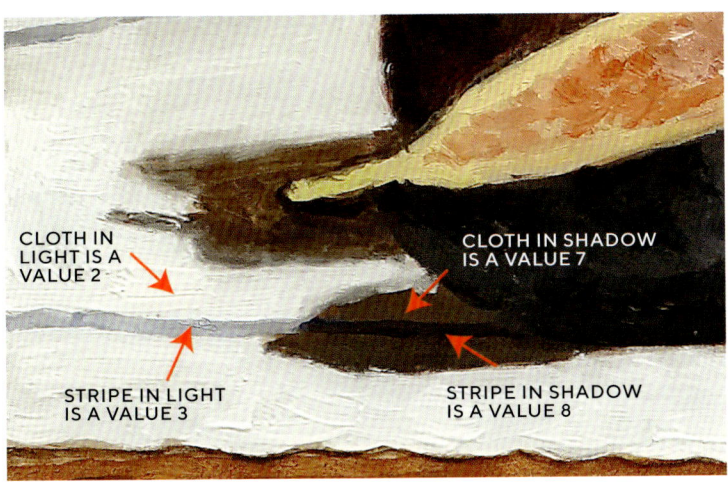

STEP 4

As I move leftward and paint the rest of the white cloth and stripe, I have to make sure that the one-value difference between the white cloth in light and in shadow is the same as between the stripe in light and in shadow. This gives a nice sense of light affecting the forms. The two areas will not relate to one another if they are too far apart in value.

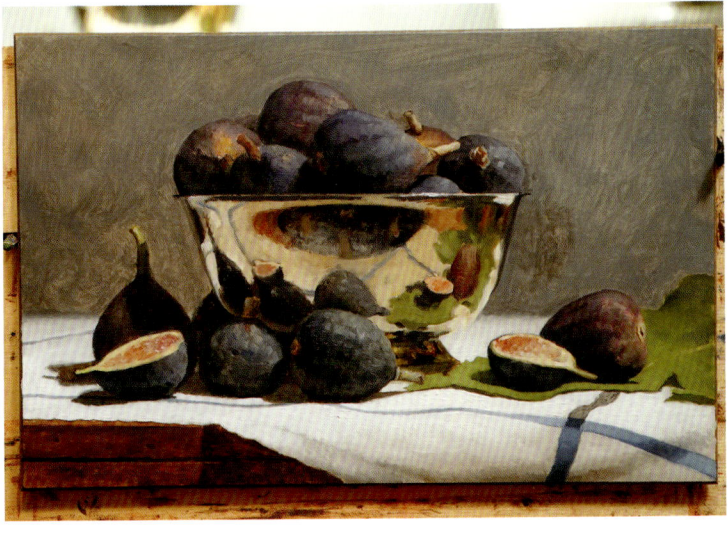

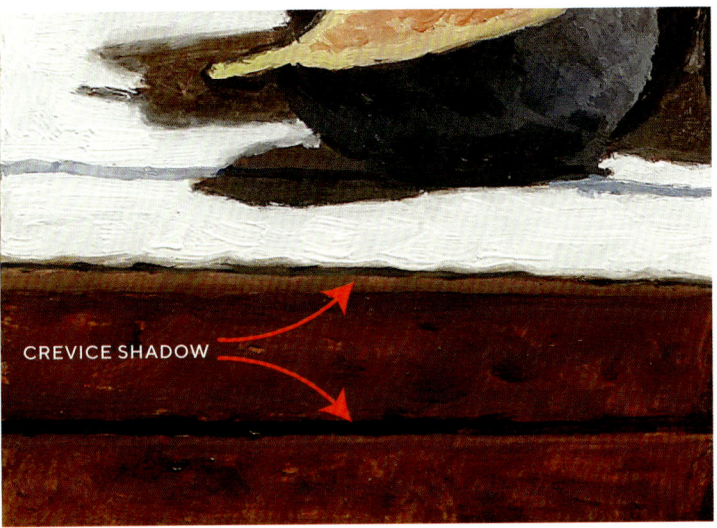

STEP 5

I now add smaller details, like the stems of the figs in the bowl.

STEP 6

I articulate the crevice shadow under the cloth, which gives depth to the cloth. I also paint the top plane of the wood to convey the sense that the plane is receiving raking light (as opposed to the plane of the box that is facing away from the light toward the viewer).

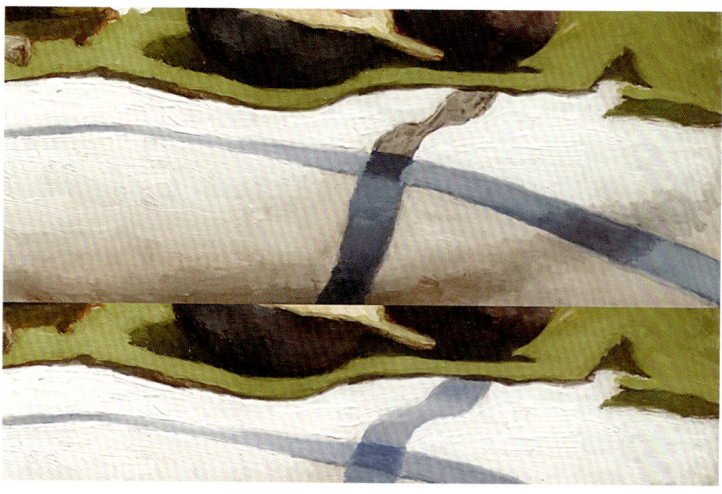

STEP 7

I now finish up smaller things, like the blue cross on the white fabric. The top part of the blue cross is in the light and therefore has to be lighter than the stripe closer to the bottom of the panel.

FINAL TWEAKS

After taking a break from looking at the painting, I came back with fresh eyes and made my last analysis. Being able to assess your painting is key to making good work. If something is not working, don't hold onto it.

The background of the painting felt a bit unfinished. Initially, I'd loved the look of the setup with a light background. So now I decided to make the background even lighter—but not so light that it would make the objects feel dark. I applied the gray background paint with a bristle brush, which forced me to use thicker paint. The thicker paint contrasted with the areas of thinner paint, nicely balancing the paint textures in the piece.

SURFACE TEXTURES

When there's a surface texture on an object in a painting—like a scrape, rust, or tarnish on the silver bowl—I add it to the painting last. I switch to a stiffer, bristle brush to apply the surface texture, and I make sure the paint beneath it has dried so that the brush rakes the surface.

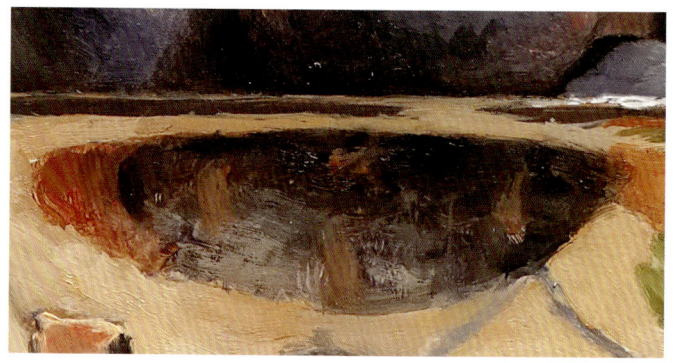

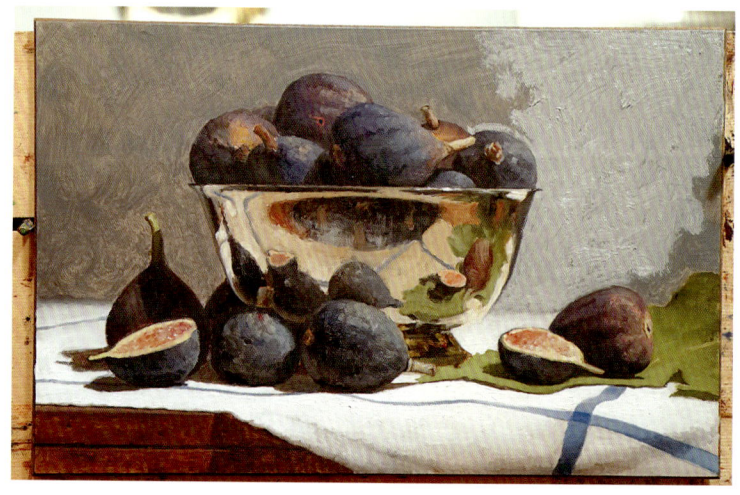

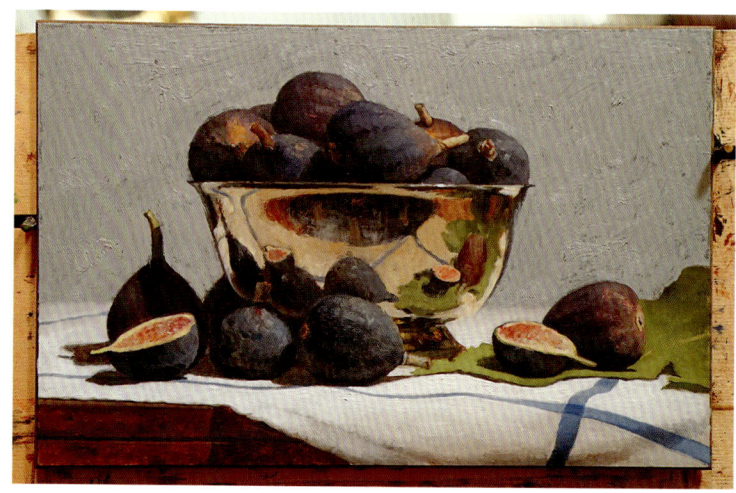

THE COMPLETED PAINTING

Here we have the final painting presented in a frame. A frame can make or break a painting, so choosing the right one is important. I often go with a dark frame with a gold lip—a very traditional frame. The gold really accentuates the painting. Stay away from cheap frames if you show professionally.

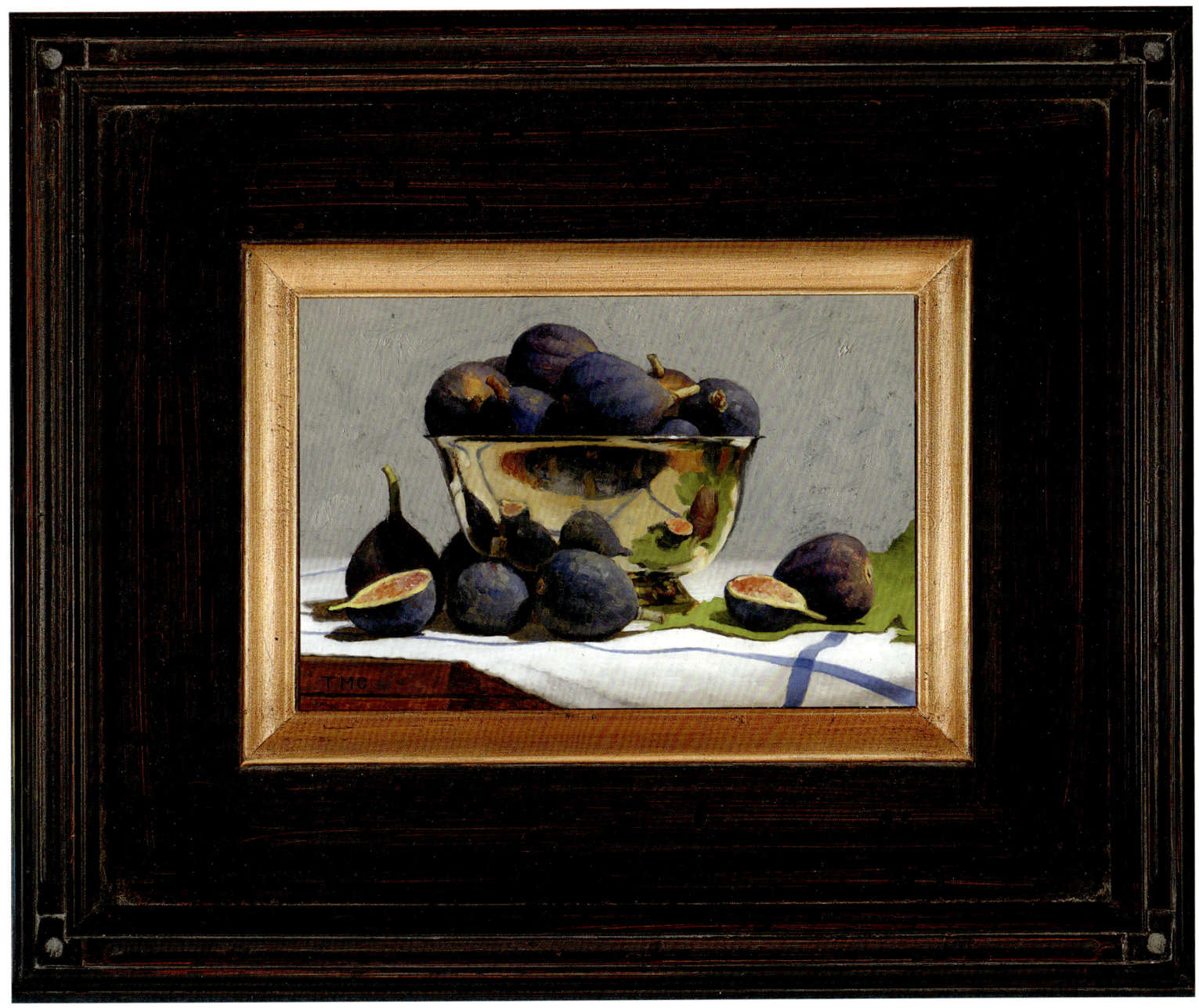

INDEX

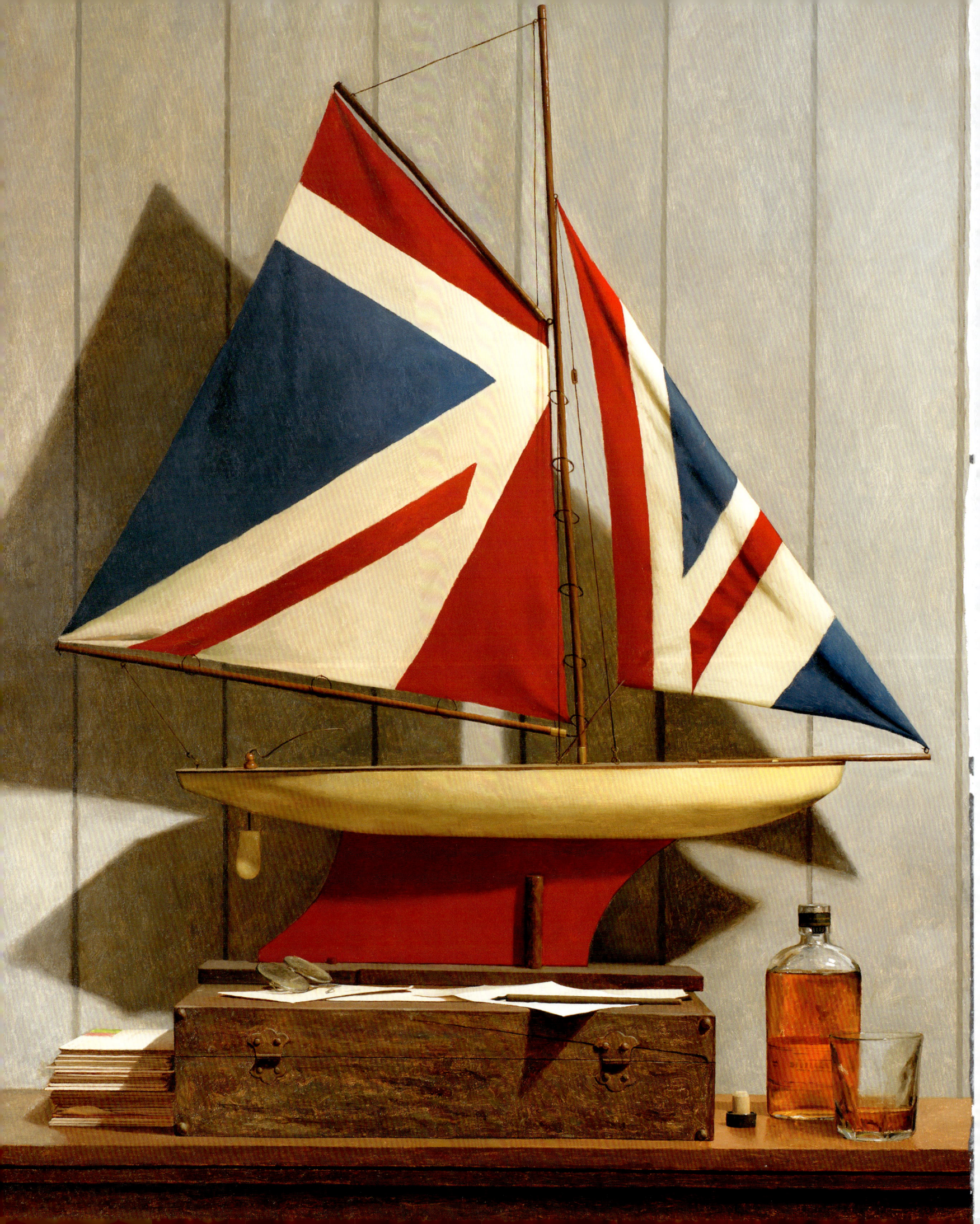

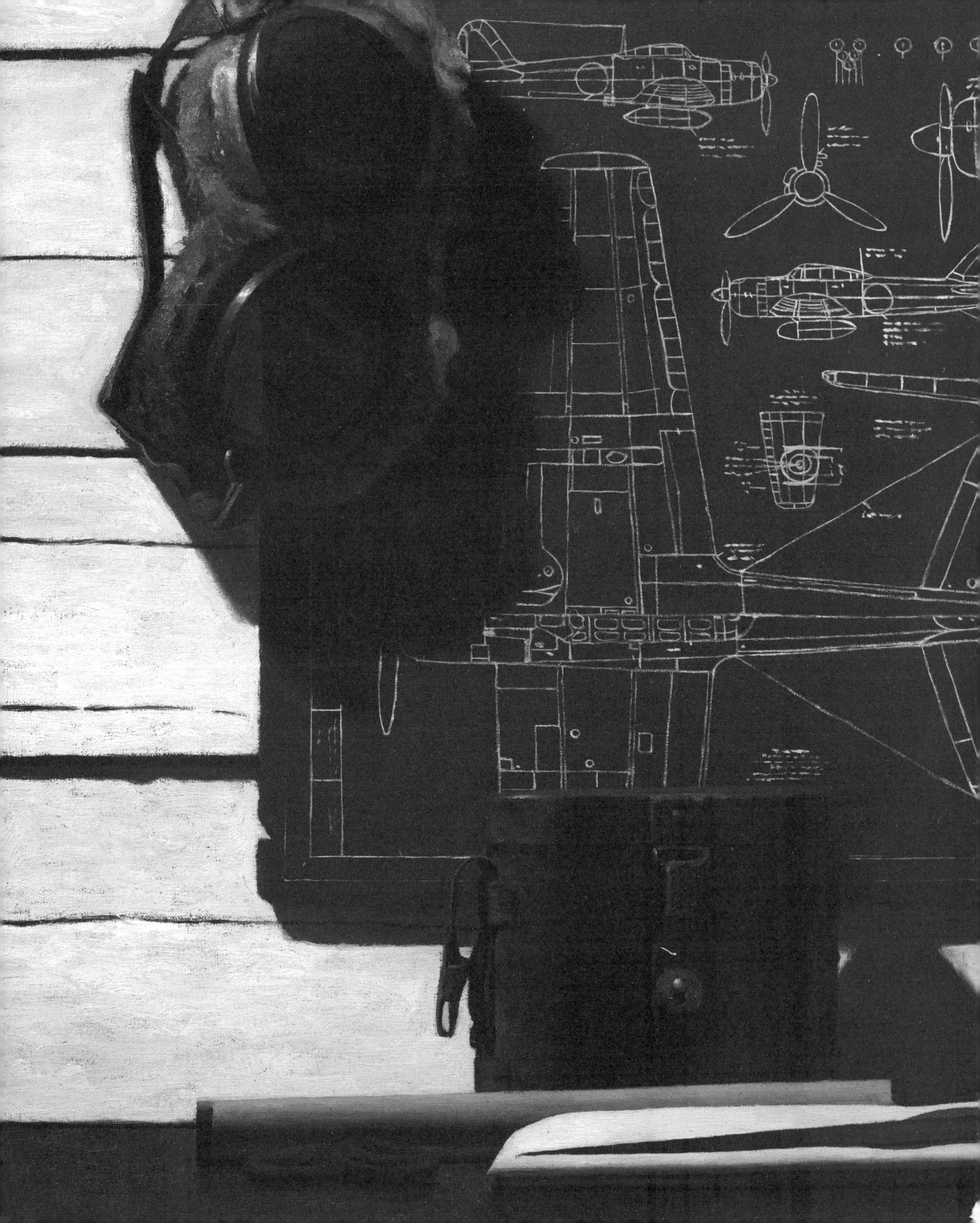